EXTENDING DOS

A Programmers's Guide to Protected-Mode DOS

Second Edition

Edited by Ray Duncan

Ray Duncan
Charles Petzold
Andrew Schulman
M. Steven Baker
Ross P. Nelson
Stephen R. Davis
Robert Moote

Addison-Wesley Publishing Company, Inc.
Reading, Massachusetts   Menlo Park , California   New York
Don Mills, Ontario   Wokingham, England   Amsterdam   Bonn
Sydney   Singapore   Tokyo   Madrid   San Juan
Paris   Seoul   Milan   Mexico City   Taipei

Library of Congress Cataloging-in-Publication Data

Extending DOS: a programmer's guide to protected-mode DOS / edited by
Ray Duncan . . . [et al.]—2nd ed.
p. cm.
Includes index.
ISBN 0-201-56798-9
1. Operating systems (Computers) 2. MS-DOS (Computer file) 3. PC
-DOS (Computer file) I. Duncan, Ray, 1952-
QA76.76.063E955 1991 91-41309
005.4'46—dc20 CIP

Managing Editor: Amorette Pedersen
Production Editor: Andrew Williams
Technical Consultant: Andrew Schulman
Cover design by: Copenhaver Cumpston
Illustrator: Darrell Judd
Set in 10.5-point Palatino by Benchmark Productions

3 4 5 6 7 -MA-97969594
Third printing, June 1994

Contents

Chapter 1

Programming the IBM PC

Ross Nelson

DOS Lives

The Intel 8086 architecture, the platform for the first version of DOS, was 13 years old when DOS 5.0 hit the streets in 1991. The hardware capabilities of personal computers have changed radically in those 13 years, yet there is very little difference between DOS 5.0 and its preceding versions, at least going back to version 2. Nevertheless, the enthusiastic response to DOS 5.0 has proven that the market for DOS and its applications is still vital. In spite of its deficits and many competitors, DOS lives.

But the late-night movie feel to the phrase "DOS Lives" is not inappropriate. Spare parts have been grafted on, features have been "borrowed" from other sources, and even external hardware has been used to prolong the viability of DOS. While Microsoft and IBM tinkered with Windows and OS/2, companies like Lotus, PharLap, and Quarterdeck were in the lab pushing the boundaries, extending DOS. Because these extensions were pioneered in various places at various times, there have been notable compatibility problems. In the first part of this chapter, I'll give you an overview of the extensions that have been developed (see Figure 1-1). In the second part, we'll look at the IBM PC architecture in detail and examine the technical considerations that drove these developments.

The driving force behind most of the extensions has been a hunger for memory. The design of the original IBM PC in allowed for 640KB of RAM in a fully configured system. This was a big leap over the 64KB typically available at the time, but it was merely a matter of time before the demand for software features outran the ability of the hardware to satisfy those demands.

The Quest for RAM

DOS is limited by the *real address mode* architecture of the 80x86 family of microprocessors. The 8086, which supported only real address mode (commonly called real mode), could address a maximum of 1MB of RAM. In addition, when IBM placed its software-compatible sibling, the 8088, into the first IBM PC, they reserved 384KB of the address space for controller hardware such as the video RAM and the BIOS (Basic Input/Output System) ROM, leaving 640KB for applications.

As users populated their systems with TSRs (Terminate-and-Stay-Resident-programs) and started filling their spreadsheets with vast quantities of data, the cry "More RAM" began to ring throughout the land. The first attempt to deal with the problem was the Expanded Memory Specification (EMS) board. This system used external hardware to bring 16KB chunks of memory into the address space (somewhere in the 384KB reserved area), up to four chunks at a time. The EMS system allowed for up to 8MB of additional memory. However, since the memory could be enabled and disabled only in 16KB chunks, EMS was primarily useful for storing data as opposed to storing program code. You couldn't really put a TSR in EMS memory, since you couldn't guarantee that the proper chunk would be available when the TSR was invoked. The other main drawback was that the application had to manage EMS memory. The program couldn't just allocate what memory it needed and use it, the way it could with the conventional 640KB of memory. Applications had to enable the right pages at the right times and disable unused pages. As annoying as this was, it did allow larger spreadsheets, and even TSR programs could be designed to use EMS memory in a limited manner.

Figure 1-1: The Intel 80x86 family tree.

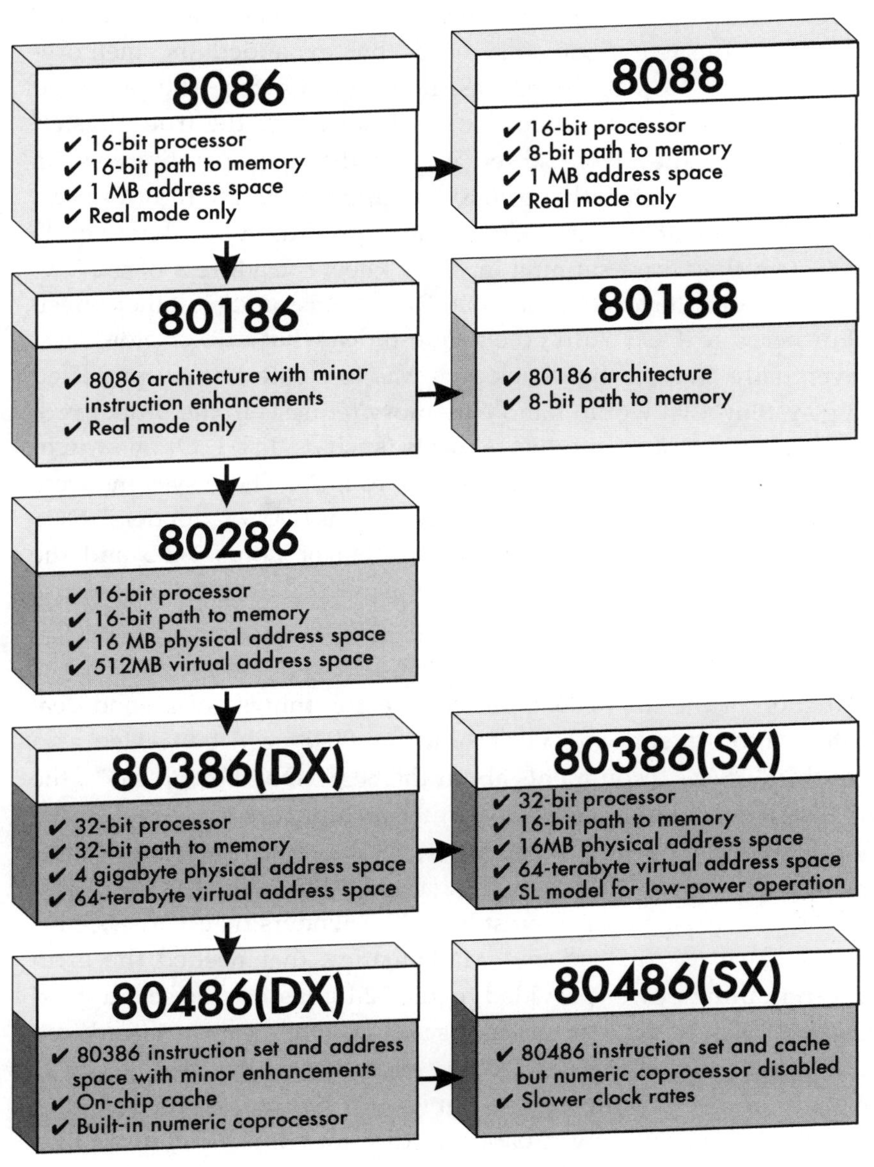

The Intel 80286

Meanwhile, Intel had introduced a new processor in the 80x86 line. The 80286, subsequently used in the PC/AT, offered a new processing mode called *protected virtual address mode* (protected mode, for short) that expanded the memory-addressing capabilities to 16 MB. There was, however, a catch. The protected mode environment assumed that applications did not know the true physical addresses of the memory they were stored in, and that the operating system would instead hand out *descriptors* that granted an application the right to use a block of memory. Unfortunately, most DOS applications did, in fact, know quite a bit about the system they were running in. They knew the address of the keyboard interrupt routine, or the location of video RAM, and countless other physical addresses. Furthermore, DOS hadn't the foggiest idea what a descriptor was.

The trick eventually adopted by developers was to create a small protected mode "operating system" that would handle memory requests in the proper protected mode manner, but deal with other requests (such as disk I/O) by switching back to real mode and passing the requests on to DOS. These systems were linked directly into the application and referred to as DOS extenders. DOS extenders were used in such products as Release 3.0 of Lotus 1-2-3 and the Informix SQL database.

The Intel 80386

With the introduction of the Intel 80386 microprocessor, things got a good deal more complicated. (From a software viewpoint, the 80486 can be treated as a faster variant of the 80386. All comments about the 80386 may be applied to the 80486 as well.) The extension of the 80x86 family architecture to 32-bits is discussed in more detail later, but this extension included 32-bit operations (addition, memory copy, etc.) and a 32-bit or 4 gigabyte address space. The 32-bit capabilities naturally increased user interest in DOS extenders that were 80386—specific. Programs, such as Autocad and Mathematica, that needed the extra throughput and computing power provided by the 32-bit instruction set adopted these extenders immediately. A more complex set of possibilities was introduced by the processor's *paging* capabilities and a new operating mode, the V86 or *virtual 8086 mode*. Both these capabilities are available only in protected mode.

Unfortunately, this array of new capabilities did not come without a price. Difficulties can arise when a program developed to make use of these advanced features is run at the same time as another program making a similar attempt. Since V86 mode is only available in protected mode, it implies that a small operating system running in protected mode must exist to control what's really going on. When you have more than one operating system that thinks it's "in control" (as operating systems tend to do), you tend to have a problem. Eventually, the Virtual Control Program Interface (VCPI, Chapter 8) and DOS Protected Mode Interface (DPMI, Chapter 9) were developed to arbitrate between such competing applications.

The problem that users currently face is that DOS extender-based applications and operating environments, such as Windows and DESQview, may or may not work together, depending on what standards they adhere to and when they were written. For example, Microsoft Windows 3.0, when running in "enhanced mode" on an 80386 or 80486, is DPMI-compatible. Thus, you can only run a DOS program that uses a 286 or 386 extender from inside Windows if the extender is DPMI-compliant. As a developer, you must be aware of the emerging standards and what programs your users will be running in conjunction with the applications you develop.

The IBM PC Architecture

When the IBM PC first appeared in 1981, it was available in two configurations: one was a "low-end" system with BASIC in ROM, 16KB of RAM, and a cassette port for external storage, and the other was a "high-end" system with a 5-1/4 inch floppy disk drive, 64K of RAM, and a disk operating system. Although the first IBM PC may not sound very impressive today, it set several important precedents at the time. It had an open architecture with an extensively documented expansion bus; it was built with off-the-shelf components and therefore could easily be cloned; and it was based on a 16-bit CPU, leapfrogging the other personal computers of the era, which were based on 8-bit microprocessors such as the 8080, Z80, and 6502.

The central processor chosen by IBM for its first PC was the Intel 8088, a slightly slower variant of the 8086. (As all the recent members of the processor family contain the numbers "86," we can reduce confusion by referring to both the 8088 and the 8086 by the designation 8086. The processors are fully software compatible.) The 8086 supported a physical address space of 1024KB, or 1 megabyte, but IBM's design restricted the operating system and application programs

Figure 1-2: The IBM PC address space.

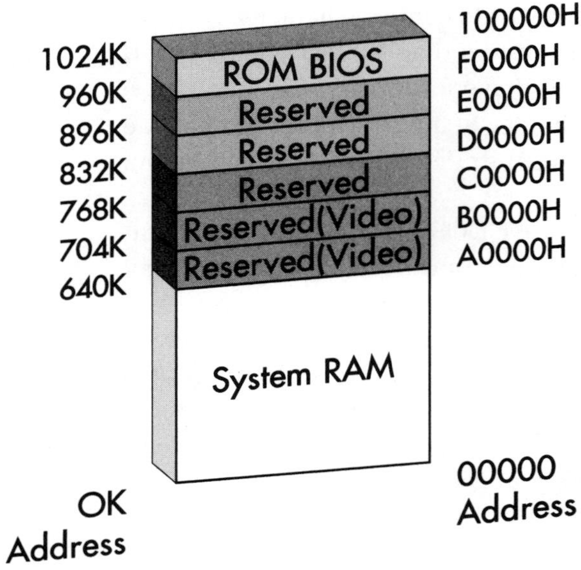

to the first 640KB of the address space, reserving the remaining 384KB for use by routines in read-only memory (ROM) and by hardware subsystems. Figure 1-2 shows how the address space was divided.

It cannot be said that the reserved portion of the address space was wasted. The top 64KB was used by the ROM BIOS (Basic Input/Output System), a set of routines that provided a standard software interface to essential PC components such as the video display, keyboard, and diskette controller. The ROM BIOS also contained test routines that checked out the PC's hardware when it was turned on or restarted, as well as a "bootstrap" program that initiated the loading of an operating system from a diskette. The PC's video adapters—the Monochrome Display Adapter (MDA) and Color/Graphics Adapter (CGA)—used the memory addresses 0B0000h to 0BFFFFh for RAM refresh buffers that controlled the appearance of the display.

As additional subsystems and adapters were introduced, they too were assigned ranges of memory addresses in the reserved 384KB area. For example, when the fixed disk controller was introduced in 1982, 16K was allocated for its on-board ROM containing the fixed disk firmware. The Enhanced Graphics Adapter (EGA), which arrived soon afterward, had 16KB of on-board ROM, too, and also used the memory addresses from 0A0000h to 0AFFFFh for its video refresh RAM in high-resolution graphics modes. By the time the PS/2 was announced in 1987, nearly every address in the upper 384KB had been spoken for, and the ROM BIOS itself had grown from 64KB to 128KB.

Although the ROM BIOS supplied a programmatic interface to the hardware, it provided no mechanisms for loading and executing programs, set no standards for disk formats, and had no ability to manage peripheral devices. Those duties fell to the operating system, and in fact, the original IBM PC was announced with no less than three different operating systems: Microsoft's MS-DOS, Digital Research's CP/M-86, and Softech's P-System. For various reasons, MS-DOS (marketed by IBM as PC-DOS, and usually referred to as DOS) rapidly became the operating system of choice, and the other two operating systems never achieved any significant base of users.

DOS proved to be another limiting factor in the evolution of personal computers, albeit in ways more subtle than the 640KB limit. Ironically, the earliest versions of MS-DOS were patterned closely after Digital Research's CP/M-80 operating system to aid developers in porting their applications from the 8-bit 8080- and Z80-based microcomputers that preceded the IBM PC; this resemblance underlies many problems that are still with us today. The first version of DOS, for example, had no programmatic interface for managing memory—when an application was loaded, it could use the entire address space in whatever manner it chose—and the performance of the video display drivers provided by DOS and the ROM BIOS was notoriously poor.

As a result, the halls of software development companies buzzed with PC "folklore" on how to do things faster or better—such as how to get DOS to use certain undocumented locations in memory, how to implement the fastest techniques for direct control of the video adapter, and how to push the serial communications controller beyond its documented capabilities. Many of the programs that exploited these non standard techniques became best-sellers, sometimes because their direct access to the hardware gave them a performance edge unequaled by their competitors. This, in turn, led others to use the same hardware-dependent techniques, all of which would later come back to haunt the manufacturers of PC software and hardware.

A New Family Member

Intel first began shipping its second generation 16-bit microprocessor, the 80286, in 1982. To those who were paying attention, the 80286 represented a significant advance in the capabilities of the microprocessor and pointed out the path that future generations would take. It extended the physical address space from 1 megabyte to 16 megabytes. It provided for the development of secure multitasking systems by including a mechanism with which one program could be prevented from corrupting the code or data of another. And it allowed applications to "overcommit" memory, running in a logical address space that was much larger than the physically available memory. It accomplished all of this through a mechanism called protected virtual address mode.

Before we discuss protected mode in more detail, however, we should quickly review memory addressing on the 8086.

8086 Memory Addressing

On the 8086, a memory address is made up of two parts: a segment and an offset. The 16-bit segment portion of the address, which is loaded into one of the 8086's four segment registers (CS, DS, ES, and SS), is simply multiplied by 16 by the hardware to specify the starting physical address of a block of memory. (To make the terminology even more confusing, such a block is also often referred to as a segment.) The offset, which is likewise a 16-bit value, determines which byte in a block of memory, or segment, is referenced: offset 0 refers to the first byte, offset 1 to the next, and so on. Since the offset can only take on values in the range 0000H through FFFFH, the largest chunk of memory that can be easily and continuously addressed is 64KB; although, since the values in segment registers correspond directly to memory addresses, a program can manipulate these values to use larger data structures.

The segment:offset nature of 8086 addressing is actually a remnant of an even earlier architecture. One of the goals of the Intel designers in creating the 8086 was a simple transition from the previous generation, the Intel 8080. On the 8080, all addresses were 16-bit values, stored either in a register or as a direct reference in an assembly language instruction. Division of the 8086's 1-megabyte address space into 64K segments allowed a straightforward emulation of the 8080's memory addressing. Programs could be ported directly from the 8080 to the 8086 by setting CS=DS=ES=SS, resulting in a single combined code and data segment and retaining the 16-bit, 64KB addressing model. New programs for the 8086 could use 32-bit addresses (both segment and offset) and access an entire megabyte.

The 8086's segmented architecture led to various styles of programming. If a program requires no more than 64KB of code and 64KB of data, it can load the segment registers once during its initialization and then ignore them. This style of application is called a small model program. The other extreme, called the large model, requires the programmer to deal with addresses as 32-bit quantities, loading a segment register with a new value for nearly every memory reference. Most 8086 high-level language compilers support both of these models. Many support other models as well; for example, using 32-bit addresses for code but only 16-bit references for data (medium model) or vice versa (compact model).

Protected Mode versus Real Mode

The 80286's protected mode derives its unique capabilities from a change in the way memory addresses are interpreted.

The 80286 CPU starts up in so-called real mode, which is basically an 8086 emulation mode; in this mode the 80286 forms addresses in exactly the same manner as an 8086. When the 80286 is switched into protected mode, however, it interprets the contents of a segment register in a radically different way. The value in a segment register is called a selector, and it is used by the CPU hardware as an index into a look-up table—called a descriptor table—which contains 24-bit physical base addresses for all the memory segments in the system.

Combination of a 24-bit base address from the look-up table with a 16-bit offset allows the CPU to address 16 megabytes of physical memory. Furthermore, because the same selector and offset (2CA7:0912, for example) may reference any one of many different physical addresses, depending on the base address in the look-up table, the protected-mode selector:offset pair is called a virtual address. The addressing methods used by the 8086 and by the 80286 in protected mode are contrasted in Figure 1-3.

To recapitulate, a program running on the 8086, or in real mode on the 80286 (or its successors), can read or write any desired memory location at any time, simply by loading an arbitrary value into a segment register. A real-mode operating system cannot monitor or restrict an application program's access to memory, shielding one application from another, because there is no hardware support for such restriction. A protected-mode application, however, can only "see" the memory addresses that the descriptor tables permit it to see. Control over the descriptor tables—and thus the correspondence between values in segment registers and physical memory addresses—is ordinarily reserved to an operating system.

The period immediately following the introduction of the 80286 represents one of the great missed opportunities of the computer industry. If IBM and

Figure 1-3: Addressing modes contrasted.

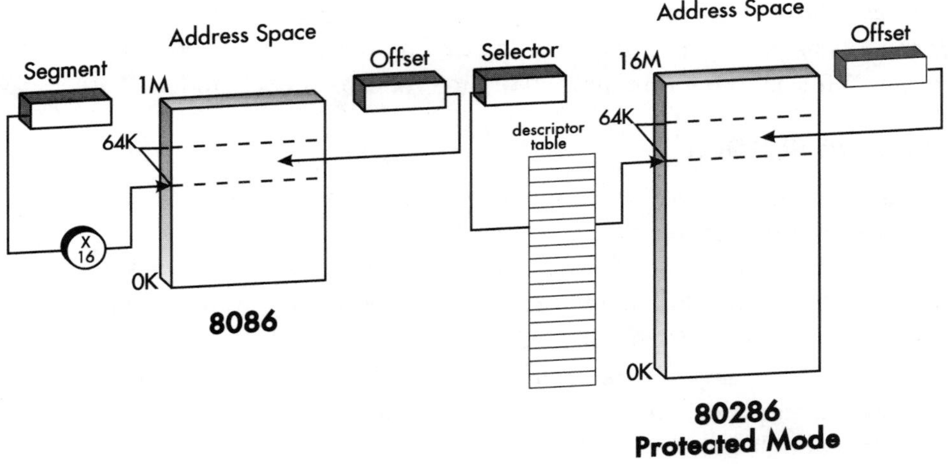

Microsoft had taken early notice of the 80286's characteristics to the extent of requiring adherence to DOS 2.0's memory management techniques, discouraging programmers from using hard-wired memory addresses and hardware I/O port addresses in their programs, and enhancing DOS and the ROM BIOS with some efficient and flexible video drivers, the transition between the 8086 and the protected-mode operation of the 80286 might have been relatively painless. Instead, direct hardware access techniques became even more entrenched in PC application software, and the design of DOS and the PC's hardware became a captive of the applications' behavior.

Solving Real Problems

Since protected mode didn't really become an issue for most programmers until several years after the PC/AT was introduced, other methods had to be used to squeeze programs into the limited memory supported by DOS. Among these were overlays, expanded memory (LIM EMS memory), and the limited use of extended memory by real-mode programs for storage of data.

Overlays

The first technique invented to deal with the problem of "too much program and not enough memory" is called overlaying. It predates the personal computer by many years and is best suited to applications that process data in orderly stages, or to those in which one of many different possible operations is selected early in the execution process.

An example of a program that might employ overlays is a compiler, which operates, let us say, in three stages or passes. The first pass reads in the source program, building the symbol table and checking for syntax errors. It creates a tokenized form of the source for use by the next pass. The second pass operates on the tokenized output of pass one, translating the high-level language to pseudo-assembler output. The third pass performs optimizations and converts the pseudo-assembler code to true object code.

Let us assume that the portion of our hypothetical compiler that performs I/O is used in all three passes, the symbol table functions are used in pass 1 and pass 2, the parser is only used in pass 1, the optimizer is only used in pass 3, and so on. To conserve memory, the parts of the compiler might be organized as shown in Figure 1-4. At any given time, only the code that is necessary for the

Figure 1-4: Overlaid processing.

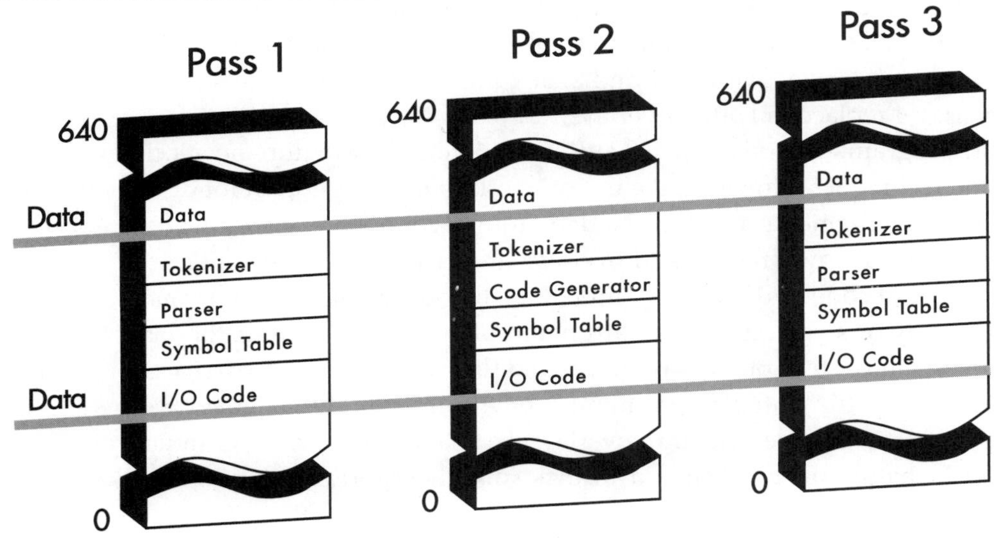

Figure 1-5: Hierarchal overlays.

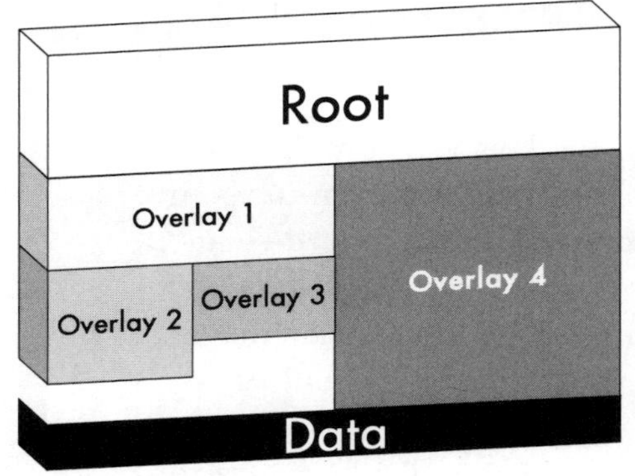

current phase of the compiler's execution is present in memory; the remainder is stored on disk until it is needed.

The portion of an overlaid program that is always resident is called the root. The portions that replace one another in memory as execution of the program progresses are called overlays. In the figure, the I/O code corresponds to the root; the other routines are the overlays. The code fragments that make up an overlay are grouped together and given an overlay name or number.

Overlays are typically built by a linker, which also generates or includes overlay manager code to manage the overlay loading process. The simplest linkers, such as Microsoft LINK, create a root area and a single level of overlays. More sophisticated linkers, such as Phoenix Technology's PLINK86 or Pocket Soft's .RTLINK, can create a hierarchical system of overlays, as shown in Figure 1-5. In this example, overlays 1 and 2, or 1 and 3, can be resident simultaneously. Overlay 4 replaces all other overlays.

Overlaid programs run on any DOS system and generally require no special programming techniques. However, the use of overlays has two important drawbacks: the overlay segments must be loaded from secondary storage on disk, which can be quite a slow process; and overlays are useful mainly for programs with a great deal of code and relatively little data, because most overlay managers cannot overlay or swap data. Programs manipulating large amounts of data, like spreadsheets, must find other ways to expand their effective memory space.

The rise of object-oriented programming environments has led to object-swapping systems which are similar to overlays, but have a much finer granularity. Individual objects can be swapped to disk (or other storage, such as EMS memory) on an object-by-object basis. Smalltalk and Borland's VROOM technology are examples of this type of system.

Expanded Memory

Lotus 1-2-3 is the archetypal spreadsheet, and it illustrates the needs of such programs for large amounts of fast storage. The basic concept of a spreadsheet is quite straightforward. The user is presented with a two-dimensional array of locations, or cells, each of which can contain either data or a formula to be evaluated. The more cells in use, the more memory is required.

By 1984, Lotus's customers were building spreadsheet models with thousands of cells and were running out of memory within the 640KB confines of DOS. Lotus needed a way to add more memory to the 8088. Since the data was accessed frequently, it was necessary to have rapid access, as close as possible to the speed of primary memory. Disk storage was out of the question. Eventually, Lotus worked together with Intel and Microsoft to devise a new species of fast storage: expanded memory.

Typically, when you add a memory board to a computer, the RAM addresses are fixed. For example, if you had two boards with 256KB RAM each, the first would most likely start at address 00000h and the second at address 040000h. In contrast, the memory on an expanded memory board has no fixed address. Instead, when an expanded memory board is installed, a page frame is chosen—a 64K block within the 384KB reserved area that doesn't conflict with other hardware, such as a video adapter or network card. Each 16KB chunk, or page, of expanded memory can then be dynamically assigned to an address within the page frame.

Lotus, Intel, and Microsoft also standardized a software interface for expanded memory boards and called it the Expanded Memory Specification, or EMS for short. The interface is typically implemented in a software module called an expanded memory manager, which is provided by the expanded memory board's manufacturer. The manager keeps track of which pages are in use, which may be used by a new application, and which pages are currently accessible. To make use of expanded memory, an application calls the manager to request the number of pages it needs to make its expanded memory pages available within the page frame as necessary, and finally to release its expanded memory pages before it terminates.

The primary advantage of expanded memory is that it works in any existing PC-compatible computer. An EMS-compatible memory board can be added to either an 8086- or 80286-based system. In newer machines with 80386 or 80486 microprocessors, no special expanded memory hardware is required; instead, software emulators use the hardware paging feature of these CPUs to implement the EMS standard. The main drawback to the use of expanded memory is that it requires special programming within the application; each page must be explicitly enabled by a call to the expanded memory manager when the data it contains is needed. Further discussion of expanded memory can be found in Chapter 2.

Extended Memory

The first IBM personal computer to incorporate the Intel 80286 CPU was the PC/AT, introduced in 1984. The PC/AT had a true 16-bit bus and the capacity to support the full 16 megabytes of RAM addressable by the 80286. The memory above the 1-megabyte boundary (called extended memory by IBM) could only be accessed by a program running in the 80286's protected mode. Realizing that a protected-mode operating system for the PC/AT might be a long time coming, IBM provided real-mode programs with limited access to the extra memory and protected mode in the form of several new ROM BIOS function calls.

The most important of the new ROM BIOS functions, Int 15h Function 87h, places the 80286 into protected mode, copies a block of data from an address anywhere in the 16-megabyte range to any other address, and returns to real mode. This simple function might have contended with EMS as a solution to the data storage problems of spreadsheets and similar programs, but there were a number of obstacles to its success. First, the function was not widely publicized when the PC/AT first appeared; most programmers had to stumble on it while reading the ROM BIOS program listings. The function was also significantly slower than expanded memory; an EMS driver can access a block of memory simply by enabling the required page, but the ROM BIOS function must change the CPU mode twice as well as copy the data back and forth.

The most significant weakness of ROM BIOS Int 15H Function 87H, however, is that it assumes a very simple operating model: one program "owns" all of extended memory. The EMS standard, by comparison, allows expanded memory to be shared between applications, TSRs, interrupt routines, and so on. In 1988, a standard called XMS (extended Memory Specification) was agreed upon to address ownership and allocation of extended memory blocks by multiple applications, in a manner similar to EMS. The details of programming under the XMS standard are covered in Chapter 3.

Although both EMS and XMS could satisfy a program's needs for large amounts of fast storage, neither proved to be without annoyances. An application has to specifically map or move data in and out of its conventional memory. A program has to deal somehow with data structures that don't fit into the maximum block that can be copied by a single call to Int 15H Function 87H, or into a single expanded memory page (or even the entire expanded memory page frame). Developers of large programs began to sigh longingly, "If we could run in protected mode, we could use all 16 megabytes as regular memory."

Using Protected Mode

The "protection" in protected mode is derived from an "operating system's-eye" view of the world. If you assume that microcomputers are just like mainframes and minicomputers, and as they get faster and more powerful people will want them to do anything a mainframe or mini can do, you must plan for multitasking.

If the computer is doing many things "simultaneously"—printing one document, editing another, and updating a database, for example—you don't want a bug in one program to affect any of the others. Protected mode isolates one program from another by not allowing direct access to any of the system resources. A level of indirection is imposed on all memory accesses, which can be validated by the operating system. We saw this in Figure 1-3: In protected mode, segment registers contain special values called selectors, which point to a system resource called a descriptor table. This table is interpreted by the CPU, but maintained by the operating system.

Under a true protected operating system, application programming is actually simplified. Selectors become just one less thing to worry about. No need to compute addresses or do segment arithmetic; the operating system doles out selectors at load time, or in response to memory allocation requests. Any attempt by an application to use an invalid or inappropriate selector results in a trap (software interrupt) that is serviced by the operating system. The operating system may handle the trap in a variety of ways, the most common being to terminate the offending program.

But the lack of a DOS-compatible operating system to manage the descriptor tables and other system resources tended to put a damper on the development of protected-mode PC software, no matter how desirable it appeared. For those who chose not to wait for a brand new operating system, protected mode created a bit of a mess. Their only option was to use a variation on the method IBM originally provided for memory transfers; that is, to run in protected mode part of the time, and in real mode part of the time. When the application was running and needed access to large amounts of memory, the processor would be in protected mode; when the application needed an operating system service (opening a file, for example), it would switch to real mode so that DOS could handle the request.

This simple-sounding solution is really quite a technical challenge, because it requires a far deeper understanding of protected mode than an application programmer would typically want or need under a true protected-mode operating system. To get a feel for the steps involved, we must examine protected mode in more detail.

Protected-Mode Details

The 80286 architecture assumes, as an underlying model, a group of cooperating tasks, supported by a reliable kernel operating system. To prevent intentional or inadvertent damage to one task by another, each task has a separate, local address space and access to the system's global address space. A privilege mechanism keeps operating system-level code and data secure from outside tampering.

As we have already seen, this entire system was made possible through one key architectural change in the transition between the 8086 and the 80286: the use of indirection in segment addressing. In the 8086, the contents of a segment register are simply multiplied by 16 to generate the base address of a memory segment. In the 80286's protected mode, the selectors found in segment registers are made up of three separate components, as shown in Figure 1-6.

The two low-order bits of the selector make up the Requested Privilege Level, or RPL. The 80286 supports four privilege levels, numbered from zero (most privileged) to three (least privileged). Applications almost universally run at the lowest privilege level, and all their selectors have an RPL of three. Bit 2 of the selector, the Table Indicator, or TI bit, indicates whether the specified segment comes from the local address space or the global address space. A value of 0 selects global addressing; a 1 selects local addressing. The 13 high-order bits act

Figure 1-6: A protected-mode selector.

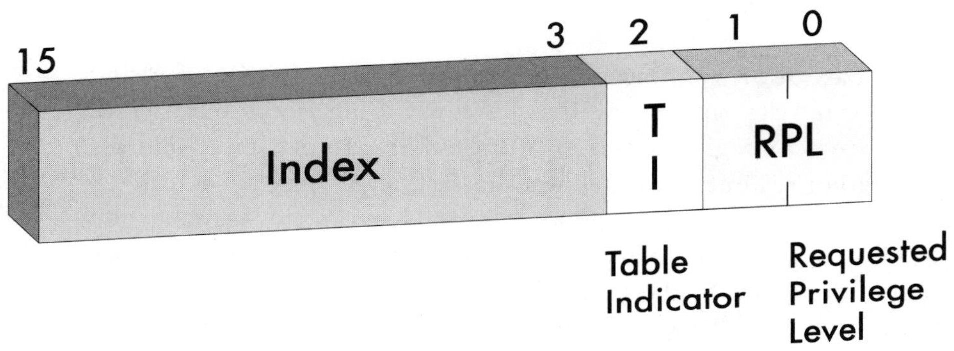

as an index into a descriptor table. The descriptor table—either a Global Descriptor Table (GDT) or a Local Descriptor Table (LDT), depending on the value of the TI bit—contains information about the segment, including the starting address.

Descriptors are at the heart of protected-mode operation because they fully describe and control all aspects of their corresponding memory blocks, or segments. Each descriptor contains a base (or starting) physical memory address for its segment, the length of the segment, the privilege level required to access the segment, and some bits that define usage attributes of the segment. A descriptor takes up 8 bytes. The C data structure used to access individual components of the descriptor is shown below:

```
#pragma  int16
typedef unsigned char byte;
typedef unsigned int word;
typedef unsigned long dword;
struct MEMSEG {
     word     limit;
     word     base_lo;
     struct {
     unsigned base_hi : 8;              // Note:  Ordering of bit fields is
     unsigned type : 4;                 // compiler dependent. Check your
     unsigned s : 1;                    // manual before using this struct.
     unsigned dpl : 2;
```

```
    unsigned present : 1;
             } ar;
    word     unused;
    };
end
```

Note that the base address found in a descriptor is 24 bits long, comprising the second word of the descriptor as well as the lower 8 bits of the third word; this allows a segment to begin anywhere in the 80286's 16-megabyte address space. The descriptor's limit field defines the last legal offset that can be addressed within the corresponding segment. In protected mode, segments are not always 64KB in size; the segment size is actually limit+1. If a program has only 20K of code, for example, the limit of the code segment descriptor is set accordingly; any attempt to branch beyond the bounds of the segment is automatically detected by the hardware and causes a special type of interrupt called a fault. Figure 1-7 shows the structure of an 80286 segment descriptor in a more diagrammatic fashion.

The access rights (AR) byte is located in the upper half of the third word of the descriptor. The fourth word is unused in the 80286 and must contain the value 0. The descriptor for a segment is accessed whenever a selector that points to it is loaded into a segment register, and the access rights byte is the first thing the processor examines. The bits in the AR byte are defined as follows:

- P—Present: This bit must be set to 1 to indicate that the data for this segment is actually present in memory. If P=0, a fault occurs when the selector is loaded.
- DPL—Descriptor Privilege Level: To access a segment, the privilege level of the executing program (called the Current Privilege Level, or CPL) must be equal to or more privileged than the DPL. If you try to access a descriptor that is more privileged than the executing code, protection faults will result.
- S—Segment: This bit is set to 1, indicating a memory segment. When S=0, the descriptor has a slightly different format and is used to define special system constructs.
- TYPE—Type: This field defines additional attributes of the segment. Bit 3 (mask 0x08) of this field is set to 1 if the segment is an executable segment. Any attempt to write to an executable segment causes a fault. For executable

segments, bit 2 (mask 0x04) is set to 1 to indicate a conforming segment (that is, a segment that changes privilege according to the privilege of the calling routine), and bit 1 (mask 0x02) is set to 1 if the segment may be read as data as well as executed as code. As you might expect, attempts to read non readable segments result in protection faults. If bit 3 is 0, the segment is a data segment. In this case, bit 2 is set to 1 to indicate an expand-down segment (a special segment type for stacks), and bit 1 is set to 1 to mark the segment as writable. If bit 1 is 0, the segment is read-only; this attribute is enforced via the protection mechanism as well. For both code and data segments, bit 0 (mask 0x01) of the TYPE field is 0 if the descriptor has never been accessed. The hardware sets bit 0 to 1 each time a selector pointing to the descriptor is loaded into a segment register.

Descriptors are grouped into tables, two of which are necessary for the system to operate correctly. The Global Descriptor Table (GDT) contains descriptors that are shared across the entire system and defines the global address space of the machine when it is in protected mode. The size and starting address of the GDT are defined by values in a special register, GDTR, which must be initialized before entering protected mode. Similarly, the IDTR contains the starting address and size of the Interrupt Descriptor Table (IDT). The IDT helps the system manage interrupts and is analogous to the set of interrupt vectors running from 0000:0000h to 0000:03FFh in real mode. In protected mode, however, the IDT is not restricted to starting at physical address 0, and it contains 8-byte descriptors rather than 4-byte pointers.

Figure 1-7: The 80286 segment descriptor.

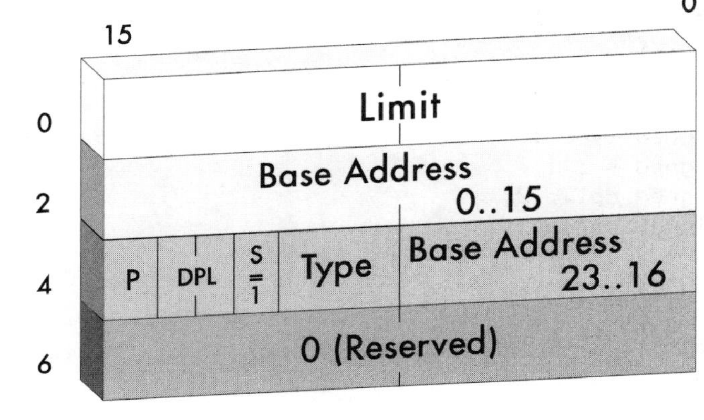

As described so far, the protected-mode

model is defined by the GDT and IDT, which contain descriptors that define code and data segments. These are not sufficient, however, to support two other 80286 features previously mentioned: multitasking and a local address space for use by each task. To see how these features are implemented, we must look at another class of descriptors called system descriptors. These descriptors are identified by a 0 in the S bit of the AR byte. The two possible formats are shown diagrammatically in Figure 1-8; the code structure is shown below.

```
#pragma  int16
typedef unsigned char byte;
typedef unsigned int word;
typedef unsigned long dword;
struct SYSSEG {
     word     limit;
     word     base_lo;

     struct {
     unsigned base_hi : 8;              // Note: Ordering of bit fields is
     unsigned type : 4;                 // compiler dependent. Check your
     unsigned s : 1;                    // manual before using this struct.
     unsigned dpl : 2;
     unsigned present : 1;
              } ar;
     word     unused;
     };

struct GATE {
     word     offset;
     word     select;
     struct {
     unsigned wc : 5;
     unsigned unused : 3;
     unsigned type : 4;
     unsigned s : 1;
     unsigned dpl : 2;
     unsigned present : 1;
              } ar;
     word     unused;
     };
```

The Present bit and DPL fields of system descriptors are used in the same manner as in segment descriptors. The TYPE field takes one of the values shown below and determines which of the two descriptor formats is being used.

- 0 Invalid descriptor
- 1 Task State Segment (TSS)
- 2 Local Descriptor Table (LDT)
- 3 Busy TSS
- 4 Call gate
- 5 Task gate
- 6 Interrupt gate
- 7 Trap gate

Descriptor types 1 through 3 have the format described by the SYSSEG structure in the C code above; types 4 through 7 use the GATE structure. A gate is a special kind of descriptor that allows transfer of control (via interrupt or subroutine call) between routines executing at different privilege levels. The SYSSEG descriptors look much like memory segments and, in fact, describe areas of

Figure 1-8: 80286 system descriptors.

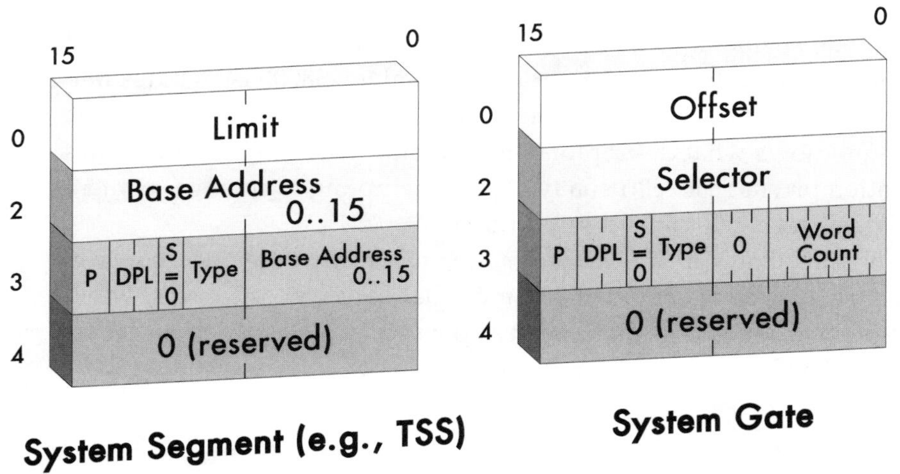

memory. Selectors pointing to these descriptors, however, cannot be loaded into segment registers. Editing the contents of a TSS or LDT requires creation of a data segment with the same base address and limit as the system segment. This technique is called aliasing.

The Local Descriptor Table (LDT) and Task State Segment (TSS) are critical to the implementation of multitasking and a local address space. The LDT descriptor points to a descriptor table that is used when the TI bit of a selector is 1, and the LDTR register always contains the selector of the currently active LDT. Each task has its own LDT, so that its private memory is "invisible" to all other tasks. The operating system changes the value in LDTR as it transfers control of the CPU from one task to another. The TSS contains a copy of all the general and segment registers for a given task. The operating system's dispatcher can switch tasks simply by branching to a TSS. All the registers and flags belonging to the current task are saved in its TSS, and the registers are loaded with the data saved in the new TSS.

A full description of the multitasking capabilities of 80286 protected mode is beyond the scope of this book; it is the addressing capabilities that concern us here. We now have enough information to create a picture of the structures that must be present in memory before protected-mode operation can continue.

Because protected-mode addressing is table-oriented, it is not possible for an application to "manufacture" segment addresses, as it can on the 8086. For example, the address of the video buffer for a color monitor begins at 0B8000h in most PCs. The real-mode segment value 0B800h points perfectly to the beginning of the buffer. In protected mode, however, the selector value 0B800h is an index into descriptor 1700h of the GDT with a Requested Privilege Level of 0. Only the operating system knows what descriptor is at that index, and any program running at application privilege level (usually 3) and attempting to access a segment at a higher privilege level will cause a protection fault.

Clearly, programs that run in protected mode must rely on the operating system to give them access to system memory and other hardware resources. "Well-behaved" real-mode applications that already do so will port easily to protected mode. In general, the things that must be avoided include:

- the use of constant or "hard-wired" segment or selector values
- segment or selector arithmetic, or use of segment registers for "scratch" storage
- access to memory not specifically allocated to the application by the operating system
- writing to code segments
- direct port I/O

Note that access to the I/O ports is restricted in protected mode as well. It's easy to see why, of course. If you assume a multitasking environment, it won't do to have more than one program attempting to control the same device. Requests for device input and output must be routed through the operating system, which can ensure sequential "ownership" of the device.

DOS Extenders

When a DOS-compatible protected-mode operating system failed to arrive in a timely fashion for the 80286, DOS extenders appeared instead. DOS extenders are something less than an operating system, but more than a subroutine library. Essentially, they act like an operating system when it comes to memory management features, hiding descriptor table management the way an operating system would, but they have no device handlers or file system. The DOS extender passes an application's requests for these features on to DOS.

The mechanism used to perform this digital legerdemain is called mode switching, and it is not something Intel had in mind when the 80286 was first created. The 80286, you may recall, was introduced in 1982, only one year after the IBM PC. Intel assumed that the advantages of protected mode were so apparent that everyone would convert, and real mode would become a distant memory. Besides, a transition mechanism between the two modes could jeopardize the security of protected-mode operation. Intel didn't realize that almost no one would pay any attention to protected mode until much later, when DOS applications dominated the marketplace.

As a result, the 80286 can only be returned to real mode by resetting the processor. Fortunately, the designers at IBM included a mechanism to perform this reset under software control when they created the PC/AT. They also included an option in the BIOS that allows you to resume program execution at a predetermined location after a reset, rather than always having to booting the operating system and start from scratch. The combination of these two capabilities allows an 80286 to run in protected mode, reset to real mode, run a specific routine, and reenter protected mode—or vice versa. One of the main functions of a DOS extender is to ensure that these mode transitions are properly managed.

If mode switches happened only at DOS system calls (Int 21h), the work of a DOS extender would be relatively straightforward; however, a number of the events in a PC are asynchronous or interrupt-driven. For example, when one of the keyboard's keys is pressed or released, the processor is signalled via an interrupt, and the interrupt handler routine for the keyboard is real-mode code located in the ROM BIOS. Similarly, DOS's date and time are updated by the real-mode interrupt handler for a timer-chip interrupt, which occurs 18.2 times per second.

The DOS extender must field all interrupts in protected mode, save the processor state, switch into real mode, reissue the interrupt so that it can be serviced by the appropriate interrupt handler, switch back to protected mode, and resume execution of the application. With these details taken care of, however, the application programmer is free to make use of the full protected-mode address space and other features of the 80286. Chapter 4 covers the popular DOS extenders for the 80286: 286/DOS-Extender, DOS/16M, and OS/286.

Intel's 32-bit Microprocessors

The lure of protected mode became even stronger in 1985, when Intel introduced its first 32-bit microprocessor, the 80386. The 80386 was followed in 1987 by the 80386SX, a 32-bit processor with a 16-bit hardware bus, and in 1989 by the 80486, a very fast processor with an on-chip cache and floating-point hardware. Intel also introduced a version of the 80486 without the floating-point hardware called the 80486SX. The suffix "DX" has come to be applied to the "standard" or full-featured version of an Intel CPU and "SX" to a reduced performance version. From a software point of view, the SX and DX versions of the 80386 and 80486 are virtually undistinguishable. The following description of the 80386, therefore, applies to all the 32-bit processor variants.

Like the 80286, the 80386 and 80486 support real-mode operation, for the sake of compatibility with DOS and its applications. They also support all the features of 16-bit protected mode on the 80286. But when an 80386 or 80486 is running in its preferred, native protected mode, it is a true 32-bit CPU with many new capabilities. All the registers and instructions (with the exception of segment registers and the instructions that manipulate them) are capable of dealing with data 32 bits at a time. Sixteen-bit operations are still supported, so the 32-bit registers have new names to distinguish them in instruction mnemonics. Table 1-1 lists the 16-bit general register names and their 32-bit counterparts.

Table 1-1: 16- and 32-bit general registers.

80286 General Registers	80386/80486 General Registers
AX, BX, CX, DX	EAX, EBX, ECX, EDX
SP, BP, DI, SI, IP	ESP, EBP, EDI, ESI, EIP

Even more important, addressing capabilities are extended too. Although selector values remain 16-bit, using the same GDT- and LDT-based descriptor table look-ups, the offset portion of an address is extended to 32-bits, allowing segment sizes of up to 4,096 megabytes, or 4 gigabytes. The "small" model of one code segment and one data segment now allows programs to use as much as 8 gigabytes of memory.

Intel achieved these extensions to the programming model without sacrificing 80286 compatibility by making use of the reserved field in the descriptor. Figure 1-9 shows the 80386/80486 descriptor format. (For ease of comparison, the descriptors are shown in 16-bit format. On the 80386 and 80486, however, only two 32-bit reads are required to load a descriptor, compared with the four 16-bit reads required on the 80286.)

Figure 1-9: 80386/80486 segment descriptor.

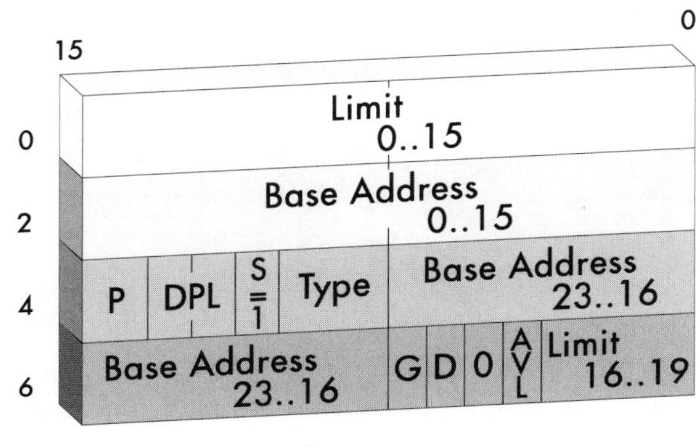

For memory-referencing descriptors, the base address portion has been extended from 24 bits to 32.

The limit field is now 20 bits rather than 16, and two bits named "G" and "D" have been added.

The G bit controls the granularity of the limit field. When G=0, the limit field has byte granularity, allowing a maximum segment size of 220, or 1 megabyte. When G=1, the limit field has 4KB or "page" granularity: each increment in the value of the limit increases the maximum segment size by 4,096 bytes. For instance, a page-granular segment with limit=3 contains 16KB of data.

The D bit determines the default operand and addressing modes. When D=0, segments behave as in 80286 protected mode, that is, instruction operands are 16 bits, and segment offsets may not exceed 0FFFFh. When D=1, the default operand size is 32 bits, and segment offsets may vary throughout the entire 4 gigabyte range, restricted, of course, by the descriptor's limit value.

The 80386 also introduced a significant change to the familiar 8086 instruction set. In the 8086 and 80286, registers can only be used as base or index registers for memory references in certain combinations, which are listed in Table 1-2. These restrictions apply in both real and protected modes.

Table 1-2: 8086/80286 addressing modes.

Operand	Description
DISP	16-bit displacement (offset)
[BX]+DISP	Base register + displacement
[BP]+DISP	Stack frame + displacement
[SI]+DISP	Source index + displacement
[DI]+DISP	Destination index + displacement
[BX]+[SI]+DISP	Base + index + displacement
[BX]+[DI]+DISP	Base + index + displacement
[BP]+[SI]+DISP	Stack frame + index + displacement
[BP]+[DI]+DISP	Stack frame + index + displacement

As you can see, the registers AX, CX, DX, and SP cannot be used in 8086 or 80286 address computations. In contrast, on the 80386 and 80486, register addressing is fully generalized, and any of the eight general registers, EAX, EBX, ECX, EDX, EBP, ESP, ESI, and EDI, may be used. The three fundamental forms of 32-bit addressing are shown in Table 1-3.

Table 1-3: 32-bit addressing modes.

Operand	Description
DISP	Displacement alone (32-bits)
[REG]+DISP	Base register + displacement
[REG]+[REG*SCALE]+DISP	Base register + scaled index register + displacement

The first two addressing modes are simply generalized forms of the original 8086 displacement and base-plus-displacement addressing modes. The third form is like 8086 base-plus-index addressing, except that the index register is automatically multiplied by a scale value of 1, 2, 4, or 8. To illustrate, consider the C language code fragment below and the assembler code that a compiler might generate.

```
/* C language */
int i;
long sum, vector[400];
   ...
sum += vector[i]

; 8086/80286 assembler
I         DW    ?
SUM       DD    ?
VECTOR    DD    400 * (?)
    ...
          MOV    SI, I               ; get index
          SHL    SI, 2               ; scale for long integers
          MOV    AX, VECTOR[SI]      ; fetch array value
          MOV    DX, VECTOR[SI]+2
          ADD    SUM, AX             ; compute sum
          ADC    SUM+2, DX

; 80386/80486 assembler
I         DD    ?
SUM       DD    ?
VECTOR    DD    400 * (?)
    ...
          MOV    EAX, I              ; get index
          MOV    EAX, VECTOR[EAX*4]; fetch indexed array value
          ADD    SUM, EAX            ; compute sum
```

The 8086 or 80286 version uses three registers and includes a separate operation to adjust the index for the operand size. The 80386 or 80486 version requires only one register and performs the index scaling on the fly.

If you are willing to limit your market to customers who have 32-bit machines, there are DOS extenders that allow you to create applications that fully exploit the 32-bit registers, enhanced instruction set, and enormous address space of the processor. Chapters 5 and 8 contain a discussion of these products. As time goes on, taking this step becomes less and less of a limiting factor.

Earlier in the chapter, we introduced paging, a hardware address mapping feature introduced in the 80386. Recall that in protected mode on the 80286 a selector:offset pair is converted to a physical address by fetching the base address from the descriptor table and adding the offset. On the 80386, the base address and offset are combined to form a 32-bit linear address, which can then be passed through the CPU's paging mechanism to yield the final, physical address. In effect, paging allows each 4KB block of RAM to have its own virtual address. Figure 1-10 illustrates a simplified version of what happens on the 80386 when paging is enabled.

The designers of the 80386 added paging to support the needs of high-performance, virtual-memory operating systems. But paging can also be put to use serving DOS applications by emulating EMS hardware with extended memory. Since the 80386's paging operates on 4KB boundaries, four 80386 pages can be used to simulate one EMS page. By manipulating the page tables, an EMS emulator can, in effect, create an EMS page frame—responding to an application's EMS mapping requests by page-table mapping linear addresses within the page frame onto physical addresses above the 1-megabyte boundary.

One 80386 = Many DOS Machines

One of the most interesting features of the 80386 is its virtual 8086 mode. As we saw earlier in the chapter, the model underlying protected mode is one of multiple tasks sharing the resources of the processor. The state of each task, that is, the contents of its CPU flags and registers, is stored in the TSS for a suspended task, and in the actual machine registers when the task is running. On the 80386, a bit named "VM" was added to the flags register. When VM=1 in an executing task, the task is executing in V86 mode, and the GDT and LDT are not used. Instead, the selector values are multiplied by 16 (as in real mode) to generate a linear

Figure 1-10: Virtual address translation through paging.

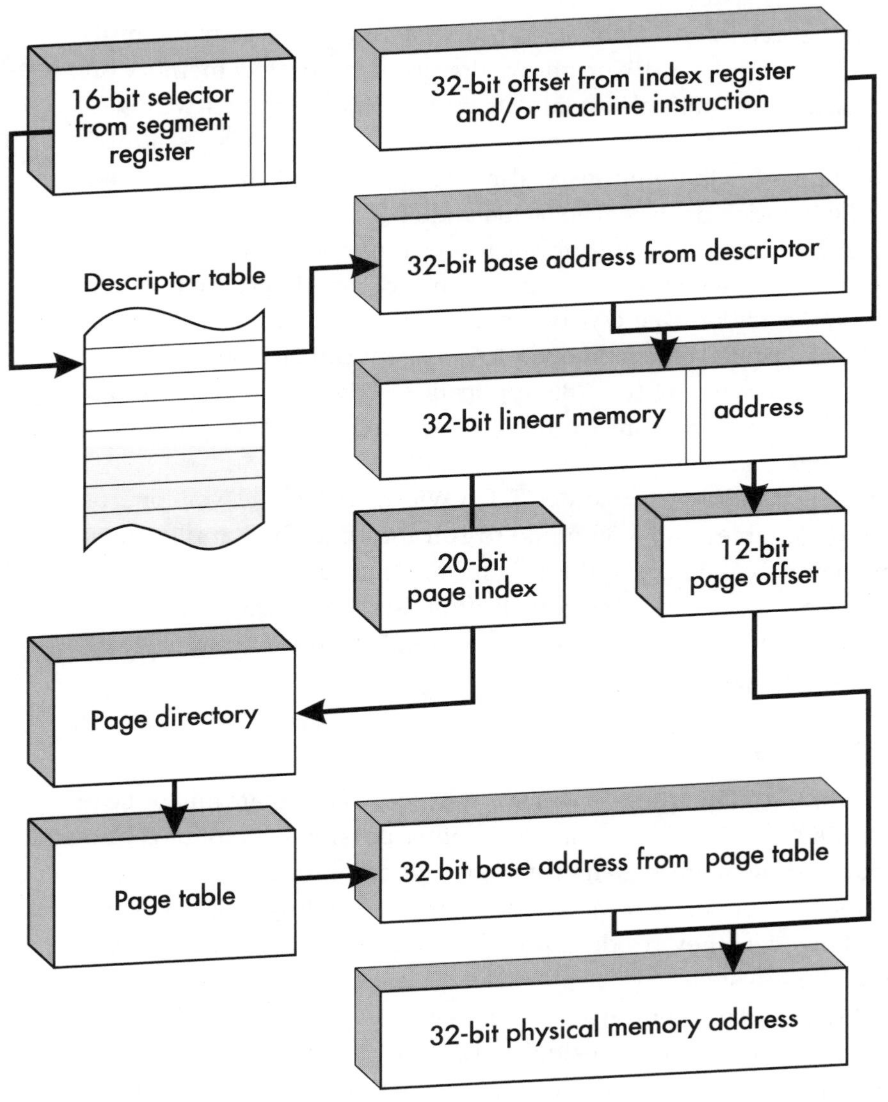

address, which is still subject to translation via the paging mechanism. Consequently, it is possible to run more than one real-mode program at a time in separate "V86 machines" each program under the illusion that it is running in the fixed, 1-megabyte address space of the 8086.

Paging also helps solve the problem of sharing system resources among multiple tasks. Because the paging hardware allows the system to protect memory on a page-by-page basis, an operating system can trap a V86 program's writes to screen memory, possibly redirecting (remapping) the output to a "shadow" buffer. This makes it possible to "window" real-mode applications that do not use the DOS or ROM BIOS video drivers. The 80386 and 80486 also allow an operating system to selectively intercept a V86 application's I/O port reads and writes. The operating system can then let the I/O operation proceed, divert the I/O to a different port, or even carry out the I/O on behalf of the application. Interrupts that are serviced by the protected-mode operating system can also be "reflected" into a V86 machine for service by the V86 application. This global ability of an operating system or control program to monitor and control a V86 program's I/O and memory access is known as device virtualization.

OS/2 version 2.0, Windows version 3, DESQView, and some versions of UNIX exploit the page tables and V86 mode to run multiple DOS applications concurrently. The major weaknesses in this scheme are that each DOS program is confined within its V86 machine to the 640KB limit, and the DOS programs—which have not been written with multitasking in mind—can't communicate or cooperate effectively with each other.

Operating Environments

We have seen some of the techniques by which a developer can create an application that surpasses DOS-imposed boundaries. Another possibility is to make use of the features provided by operating environments. Operating environments are similar to DOS extenders, but appear more like separate operating systems. They are not complete, however; they reside "on top" of DOS and make use of DOS services and the DOS file system.

Two of the most popular operating environments are DESQview and Windows. These programs are covered extensively in Chapters 6 and 7. They embody two very different philosophies and place very different requirements on the developer.

DESQview, from Quarterdeck, is the simpler of the two environments. Its primary advantage to the end user is multitasking. Developers get a larger task space for their applications than would be available under DOS. DESQview makes more memory available by managing EMS memory in a very efficient manner. DESQview runs well on any computer with EMS hardware, or on an 80386- or 80486-based system using V86 mode and paging. Very little extra work is required to make an application DESQview-compatible.

Windows, on the other hand, imposes a radically different "world view" on an application. Standard DOS programs are essentially incompatible with Windows, although they can still be run, either by switching to real mode or as a V86 task. In general, though, applications must be completely redesigned to use the features Windows provides. In return, Windows offers a great deal to the end user: a uniform graphical interface, multitasking with transparent swapping of applications to expanded memory, "cut and paste" of text and graphics between applications, and more. But these features come at a price. Users will want an 80286 or later processor in their machine and a high-resolution monitor.

Developers pay a price as well; application development time is far longer under Windows than under DOS, and there is a steep learning curve. Applications developed under Windows do, however, have some advantages that DOS programs do not, and device independence is one of the most important. Applications developed for DOS have to deal with display and printer hardware on their own. Software developers must be aware of the popular monitors and printers, and write the appropriate support code for their applications. Windows applications, on the other hand, will work unchanged on any hardware supported by Windows device drivers.

What About OS/2?

The first version of OS/2, the protected-mode operating system co-developed by IBM and Microsoft for the 80286, arrived in 1987 after many delays. The early releases suffered from bugs and performance problems, but by V1.3, OS/2 was generally accepted as a useful, stable system. OS/2's road to acceptance has been long and arduous and is not assured even yet. Acceptance would have been difficult to achieve even if the only obstacle had been the lack of applications written for the system, but there were additional problems as well. A shortage of RAM chips in 1987-1988 made conversion to OS/2 prohibitively costly. The arrival of

OS/2's graphical user interface, Presentation Manager, was delayed until late 1988. And not until the Release 2.0 at the end of 1990 could OS/2 take advantage of the 32-bit addressing, paging, and V86 mode capabilities available in the 80386 and 80486.

At this time, OS/2's role is more clearly defined, even if its future is still hazy. Presentation Manager has been stabilized, a new file system called HPFS offers much better disk performance than DOS, and key applications have become readily available. Release 2.0, with its 32-bit support, is likely to become the "standard version," with the 80286 market left to DOS and Windows. Unfortunately, the IBM/Microsoft alliance is not what it once was. When IBM and Microsoft were both preaching the same message regarding the future operating system for the IBM PC family, it appeared that OS/2's success was only a matter of time. The two behemoths of the industry now preach different gospels, and it is unclear which will prevail. As a result, growth in the installed base of OS/2 continues to be painfully slow. If you choose to develop for OS/2, you should view it as a strategic investment of time and effort that is not likely to pay off for several years if at all, unless your market is tightly bound to IBM strategic policies.

Choosing Your Market

Although part of DOS's popularity stems from sheer inertia, market dynamics plays a part as well. In 1984, 8086/8088-based machines numbered just under three million and accounted for 99 percent of the PC-compatible market, with 1 percent of the market owned by the 80286-based AT and its clones. Three years later, the 80286 machines had garnered 29 percent of the market with over four and a quarter million units, and the 80386-based computers were just trickling in at 2 percent market share and 300,000 machines sold. By 1993, it is projected that 32-bit machines will account for over two-thirds of new machine sales and nearly 15 million in unit sales.

New computers that are 8086-class machines now account for a tiny share of the market, but the number of 8086-class PCs is still large, due to the popularity of low-end laptops and the installed base of existing machines. None of these machines, however, will ever run a protected-mode application or address of more than 1 MB of memory (aside from EMS), and some developers, notably Borland and Fox, are quick to point out how efficient their programs are in this relatively constrained environment. Even if you choose to develop for the growing population of 80286/386/486 machines, you may still find it advantageous to support the DOS market. Although the future may belong to Windows or OS/2, DOS is still the operating system of choice today.

For those who plan to continue serving the DOS market, the rest of this book describes a number of specific tools available to help you push beyond the historical limits of DOS. Table 1-4, below, outlines the options available to you, along with their advantages and disadvantages.

Table 1-4: Current options for extending or replacing DOS.

Method	Advantages	Disadvantages
Overlay	Works on any PC.	Does not support "large data" applications well. Not very fast.
EMS	Works on any PC. No special hardware on 386/486 PCs.	Cost of memory board on 8086 and 286 PCs. Requires special programming.
XMS	No special hardware required. Access to "unused" extended memory.	Requires 80286 or later CPU. Requires special programming.
286 DOS Extender	All protected-mode features available. Transparent access >640K.	May not be compatible with Windows or OS/2. Requires 286 or later CPU.
386 DOS Extender	32-bit math and addressing. Transparent access >640K.	May not be compatible with Windows or OS/2. Requires 386 or later CPU.
DESQview	Multitasking and other features without special programming.	Not compatible with OS/2. Requires EMS (or 386/486 emulation) for best performance.
Windows	Graphical user interface. Device independence. Rapidly expanding user base.	Steep learning curve. Non-preemptive multitasking. Requires 80286 or later CPU.
OS/2	Transparent access >640K. Multitasking, graphical user interface, and networking.	Current user base very small. Steep learning curve. Requires at least 3 megabytes RAM.

Method	Advantages	Disadvantages
UNIX	Well known/liked in academic and workstation markets. Multitasking and networking. Applications portable to other UNIX systems.	Small, specialized user base. Higher hardware and software costs. Little or no binary compatibility.

Chapter 2

Expanded Memory and the EMS

Ray Duncan

Expanded memory is essentially bank-switched memory—fast storage, which can be larger than the CPU's normal address space, and which is subdivided into smaller chunks (called *pages*) that can be independently mapped in or out of the CPU's address space on demand. As a simple approximation, you can think of bank-switched memory as a deck of cards, where different information can be stored on each of the cards, but only the information on the card that is currently at the top of the deck can be read or changed.

Bank-switched memory is not exactly a new concept. It was used extensively on Apple II and S-100 bus computers to overcome the 64KB address limitations of their CPUs, and in the earliest days of the IBM PC, bank-switched memory boards called JRAMs were sold in truckloads by a company named Tall Tree Systems. But the particular type of bank-switched memory known as *expanded memory* has been enormously successful because its sponsors defined it as a software interface rather than in hardware.

The origins of the Lotus/Intel/Microsoft (LIM) Expanded Memory Specification (EMS) have already become somewhat apocryphal. The first EMS, developed jointly by Intel and Lotus, was announced and distributed to software developers at the Atlanta Spring Comdex in 1985. For some unknown reason this document was given the version number 3.0. Microsoft, which was looking for a way to relieve Windows' hunger for memory, quickly bought into the EMS concept. After some minor changes, a new specification—version 3.2—was released as a joint effort of Intel, Lotus, and Microsoft in September of the same year.

EMS didn't become an industry standard without a few squeaks of dissent, however. The ink was hardly dry on the EMS before some of the LIM axis' competitors proposed an alternative standard called the AST/Quadram/Ashton-Tate Enhanced Expanded Memory Specification (AQA EEMS). The EEMS was a proper superset of the original EMS, but expanded, with more flexible mapping functions for use in multitasking environments such as DESQview. Fortunately for software and memory board designers everywhere—who already had enough things to worry about—the good sense of the marketplace prevailed, and the AQA EEMS quickly faded into obscurity.

EMS version 3.2 was completely stable for about two years, and by the end of that period it had gained remarkably broad support among both software and hardware manufacturers. Scores of memory expansion boards appeared on the market that could be configured as expanded memory, while the ability to exploit expanded memory turned up in every class of software from spreadsheets to network drivers to pop-up notepads. And, of course, expanded memory became the natural ally of every vendor of a RAMdisk, disk cache, or print spooler. The programmers responsible for maintaining MS-DOS itself, on the other hand, were much slower to take advantage of expanded memory. MS-DOS 4.0, released in 1988, was the first version that recognized expanded memory at all, and it used that memory only for certain private tables and buffers.

In October, 1987, Lotus, Intel, and Microsoft released version 4.0 of the EMS. Version 4.0 supports four times as much expanded memory as version 3.2, as well as many additional function calls for use by multitasking operating systems. In particular, EMS 4.0 allows an operating system to run multiple applications at the same conventional memory addresses by paging the applications in and out of expanded memory. Some of the characteristics of the three versions of EMS are compared in Table 2-1.

As the second edition of this book goes to press in 1991, it is becoming evident that EMS is stagnant technology with a rapidly declining relevance to programmers. The focus for new application development is definitely on the direct use of extended, rather than expanded, memory using the XMS, VCPI, and DPMI interfaces discussed in Chapters 3, 8, and 9. This trend is driven by the steady shift of new machine sales toward 386 and 486-based PCs and the rapid migration of the installed base to DOS 5.0 and Windows 3.0. Many of the more important Windows applications only run in protected mode, where expanded memory is irrelevant (because the EMS interface is a real-mode interface), and many traditional DOS character-oriented applications are now being sold in protected-mode DOS extender-based versions as well.

However, the EMS interface is deeply entrenched—much like the IBM ROM BIOS Int 10H interface for video output—and it will be with us for a long time to come. Furthermore, EMS will likely remain the only standardized interface to large fast storage on extremely low-end 8086- or 8088-based "pocket" or "palmtop" computers. So a thorough understanding of the EMS interface is a vital component in your programming bag of tricks, even if EMS-awareness is no longer an indispensable feature in shrink-wrapped commercial applications.

Table 2-1: Comparison of the various EMS versions. The number of function calls shown here includes all distinct subfunctions defined in the EMS.

EMS Version	Release Date	Memory Supported	Function Calls	Page Size	Page Mapping
3.0	April '85	8 megabytes	14	16KB	above 640KB
3.2	September '85	8 megabytes	18	16KB	above 640KB
4.0	October '87	32 megabytes	58	any size	anywhere

Components of Expanded Memory

It is important not to confuse expanded memory and *extended memory*. Both are frequently available on the same machine; in fact, many memory boards can be set up to provide either expanded memory or extended memory or a mixture of both. But extended memory can only be accessed in the protected mode of the 80286, 386, and 486 processors, whereas expanded memory can be accessed in real mode and therefore can be installed and used on 8086/88-based machines such as the original PC and PC/XT. If you skipped Chapter 1, it may be helpful to go back and review the material in that chapter now, before reading on.

When you install expanded memory in your computer, you are really installing a closely integrated hardware/software subsystem (we'll ignore EMS emulators and simulators for the moment). In most cases, the hardware portion is a plug-in board that has some of the elements of an ordinary memory board and some of an "adapter" for a peripheral device: it has memory chips, to be sure, but it also has I/O ports, which must be written by the CPU to make portions of that memory addressable. On some of the more recent, highly integrated PCs and portables, the logic to control expanded memory is located right on the system board and can be configured with the ROM BIOS SETUP utility.

The software component of an expanded memory subsystem is called the Expanded Memory Manager (EMM). It is installed when the system is booted, with a DEVICE= directive in the CONFIG.SYS file, just like a device driver. In fact, an EMM has several of the attributes of a real character device driver: it has a device driver *header*, a routine that can handle a subset of the requests that the DOS kernel likes to make on device drivers, and it has a *logical device name*. This device name is always EMMXXXX0, regardless of who manufactured the expanded memory board or wrote the EMM.

But the device driver aspects of an EMM are really tangential. The EMM's main jobs are to control the expanded memory hardware, to administer expanded memory as a system resource that may be used by many different programs at once, and to service the function calls defined in the EMS. Programs request these expanded memory functions from the EMM directly, via a software interrupt that MS-DOS considers "reserved;" the MS-DOS kernel does not participate in expanded memory management at all.

A summary of the complete EMS interface can be found in Appendix A at the end of the book. The summary may appear bewildering at first, but for purposes of a typical application program, you can ignore all but the rather small subset of EMS functions that are listed in Table 2-2. This subset is straightforward to use and reasonably symmetric. For example, the EMS function number is always placed in register AH, logical page numbers typically go in register BX, expanded memory handles in register DX, and so on. Control is transferred from the application program to the EMM by executing a software Int 67H. All EMS functions indicate success by returning zero in register AH, or failure by returning an error code in AH with the most significant bit set (see Table 2-4 at the end of the chapter).

Table 2-2: Summary of the EMS functions most commonly used in application programs.

Expanded Memory Function	Call With	Returns
Get Status	AH = 40H	AH = status
Get Page Frame Address	AH = 41H	AH = status BX = page frame segment
Get Number of Expanded Memory Pages	AH = 42H	AH = status BX = available pages DX = total pages
Allocate Pages	AH = 43H BX = number of pages	AH = status DX = EMM handle
Map Expanded Memory Page	AH = 44H AL = physical page BX = logical page DX = EMM handle	AH = status
Release Pages	AH = 45H DX = EMM handle	AH = status
Get EMM Version	AH = 46H	AH = status AL = version

In short, the general form of an assembly language EMM function call is:

```
mov     ah,function     ; AH = EMS function number
.                       ; load other registers
.                       ; with function-specific
.                       ; values or addresses
int     67h             ; transfer to EMM
or      ah,ah           ; test EMS function status
jnz     error           ; jump, error detected
```

If you prefer to program in C, you can easily request EMS services without resorting to assembly language by means of the int86() or int86x() functions. The framework for such calls is:

```
#include <dos.h>

union REGS regs;
```

```
regs.h.ah = function;         // AH = EMS function number
.                             // load other registers
.                             // with function-specific
.                             // values or addresses
int86(0x67, &regs, &regs);    // transfer to EMM
if(regs.h.ah)                 // test EMS function status
    error();                  // execute if error detected
```

The remainder of the examples in this chapter are provided in assembly language, but you should find it quite straightforward to convert these to the equivalent C code, using the example above as a model.

Obtaining Access to Expanded Memory

When you want to use expanded memory in one of your programs, the first step is to establish whether the EMM is present or not. You can do this by one of two methods: the *open file* method or the *interrupt vector* method.

The "open file" method is so called because it is based on using MS-DOS Int 21H Function 3DH to open the EMM by its logical name—just as though it were a character device or a file. Assuming that the open operation is successful, your program must then make sure that it didn't open a real file with the same name by accident. This unlikely possibility can be ruled out by calling the Int 21H Function 44H (IOCTL) subfunctions 0 (get device information) and 7 (get output status). Finally, the program should close the EMM with Int 21H Function 3EH to avoid the needless expenditure of a handle—you can't do anything else with the handle anyway. The procedure for testing for the presence of the Expanded Memory Manager using the DOS open and IOCTL functions is illustrated below:

```
emmname db      'EMMXXXX0',0    ; guaranteed device name for
                                ; Expanded Memory Manager
        .
        .
        .
                                ; attempt to "open" EMM...
        mov     dx,seg emmname  ; DS:DX = address of EMM
        mov     ds,dx           ; logical device name
        mov     dx,offset emmname
        mov     ax,3d00h        ; fxn. 3DH = open
        int     21h             ; transfer to MS-DOS
        jc      error           ; jump if open failed
```

```
                                ; open succeeded, make sure
                                ; it was not a file...
        mov     bx,ax           ; BX = handle from open
        mov     ax,4400h        ; fxn. 44H subfun. 00H =
                                ; IOCTL get device info.
        int     21h             ; transfer to MS-DOS
        jc      error           ; jump if IOCTL call failed

        and     dx,80h          ; bit 7=1 if char. device
        jz      error           ; jump if it was a file
                                ; EMM is present, make sure
                                ; it is available...
                                ; (BX still contains handle)
        mov     ax,4407h        ; fxn. 44H subf. 07H =
                                ; IOCTL get output status
        int     21h             ; transfer to MS-DOS
        jc      error           ; jump if IOCTL call failed
        or      al,al           ; test device status
        jz      error           ; if AL=0 EMM not available
                                ; now close handle ...
                                ; (BX still contains handle)
        mov     ah,3eh          ; fxn. 3EH = close
        int     21h             ; transfer to MS-DOS
        jc      error           ; jump if close failed
        .
        .
        .
```

The interrupt vector method relies on the fact that an EMM, if it is installed, will necessarily have captured the vector for Int 67H, by placing the address of its EMS function call entry point in the vector. An application program testing for the presence of an EMM can simply fetch the contents of the vector, then determine whether the segment portion of the vector points to a device driver header that contains the logical device name EMMXXXX0. Example code for testing for the presence of the Expanded Memory Manager by inspection of the EMM's interrupt vector and device driver header can be found below:

```
emmint  equ     67h             ; Expanded Memory Manager
                                ; software interrupt

emmname db      'EMMXXXX0'      ; guaranteed device name for
                                ; Expanded Memory Manager
```

```
        .
        .
        .
        xor     bx,bx               ; first fetch segment from
        mov     es,bx               ; EMM interrupt vector
        mov     es,es:[(emmint*4)+2]

                                    ; assume ES:0000 points
                                    ; to base of the EMM...
        mov     di,10               ; ES:DI = address of name
                                    ; field in driver header
        mov     si,seg emmname      ; DS:SI = EMM driver name
        mov     ds,si
        mov     si,offset emmname
        mov     cx,8                ; length of name field
        cld
        repz    cmpsb               ; compare names...
        jnz     error               ; jump if driver absent
        .
        .
        .
```

Which method you choose for detecting the presence of the EMM depends on the type of program you are writing. For conventional application programs, the open file method is preferred, because it is "well-behaved"—it relies only on standard MS-DOS function calls, and is thus least likely to run into conflicts with TSRs, device drivers, interrupt handlers, or multitasking program managers. The interrupt vector method is considered "ill-behaved" because it involves inspection of memory not owned by the program. But when you are designing a device driver that uses expanded memory, you must employ the interrupt vector method, for reasons that will be explained later in the chapter.

Once your program has established that an EMM is present, it should call the EMM's "get status" function (Int 67H Function 40H) to make sure the expanded memory hardware is present and functional. After all, the fact that the EMM itself is installed doesn't guarantee that the associated hardware is also installed (although most EMMs do abort their own installation if the hardware is missing). It is also appropriate for your program to call the "get EMM version" function (Int 67H Function 46H) at this point, to make sure that all of the EMS functions that it intends to use are actually supported by the resident EMM.

Next, your program should call the "get number of pages" function (Int 67H Function 42H) to determine how much expanded memory is available. This function returns both the total number of physically installed pages, and the number of pages that have not already been allocated to other programs. In most cases the two numbers will be the same, unless your program is running under a multitasking program manager alongside other applications that use expanded memory, or unless TSRs or device drivers that use expanded memory have been previously loaded.

If the number of free expanded memory pages is less than your program needs or expects, it must decide whether to continue execution in a "degraded" fashion or simply display an advisory message and terminate. If there are sufficient pages available, however, the program can proceed to call the "allocate EMS pages" function (Int 67H Function 43H) for the necessary amount of expanded memory. The EMM's allocation function returns an "EMS handle"—a 16-bit value that symbolizes the program's expanded memory pages, and must be used in all subsequent references to those pages. This handle is exactly analogous to the file or device handles you are already accustomed to from your previous MS-DOS programming experience.

The last step in obtaining expanded memory resources is to call the EMS "get page frame address" function (Int 67H Function 41H). This function returns the segment, or paragraph, address of the base of the EMM's page frame—the area used by the EMM to map logical expanded memory pages into conventional memory. The page frame address never changes after the system is booted, so you only need to request it once, during your program's initialization code.

A typical sequence of testing EMM status, allocating some EMS pages, and fetching the page frame address is demonstrated below:

```
pneeded equ     4                   ; number of EMS pages needed

pframe  dw      0                   ; page frame address
tpages  dw      0                   ; total EMS pages
apages  dw      0                   ; available EMS pages
handle  dw      0                   ; handle for allocated pages
        .
        .
        .
        mov     ah,40h              ; get EMS system status
        int     67h                 ; transfer to EMM
        or      ah,ah               ; check for EMM error
```

```
jnz     error           ; jump, error occurred

mov     ah,46h          ; check EMM version
int     67h             ; transfer to EMM
or      ah,ah           ; check for EMM error
jnz     error           ; jump, error occurred
cmp     al,32h          ; make sure EMS 3.2+
jb      error           ; jump if EMS 3.0

mov     ah,42h          ; get number of EMS pages
int     67h             ; transfer to EMM
or      ah,ah           ; check for EMM error
jnz     error           ; jump, error occurred
mov     tpages,dx       ; save total EMS pages
mov     apages,bx       ; save available EMS pages
cmp     bx,pneeded      ; enough pages available?
jb      error           ; jump, too few pages

mov     ah,43h          ; allocate EMS pages
mov     bx,pneeded      ; number of pages needed
int     67h             ; transfer to EMM
or      ah,ah           ; check for EMM error
jnz     error           ; jump, pages not allocated
mov     handle,dx       ; got pages, save handle

mov     ah,41h          ; get page frame address
int     67h             ; transfer to EMM
or      ah,ah           ; check for EMM error
jnz     error           ; jump, error occurred
mov     pframe,bx       ; save segment of page frame
.
.
.
```

Using Expanded Memory

The logical EMS pages owned by a program and associated with a particular EMS handle are numbered *0* through *n-1*, where *n* is the total number of pages originally allocated to that handle. In EMS 3.0 and 3.2, the pages are always 16KB in length. EMS 4.0 allows pages of other sizes to be allocated and used, but it is best to avoid use of "nonstandard" page sizes so that your program will be compatible with the broadest possible range of EMS hardware and software.

A program gains access to the contents of one of its expanded memory pages by calling the "map EMS page" function (Int 67H Function 44H). The EMM accomplishes the mapping by writing commands to the I/O ports on the expanded memory board; logic on the board then ties the memory chips that hold the data for that logical page to the address and data lines of the system bus, so that the logical page becomes visible in the CPU's normal address space.

In EMS 3.0 and 3.2, a mapped page is always made available in the EMM's page frame, which is in turn located at unused addresses above the 640KB boundary. The page frame is 64KB long, and is divided into four 16KB physical pages numbered 0 through 3; thus, a maximum of four different logical pages can be simultaneously accessible. This mapping process is diagrammed in Figure 2-1.

Figure 2-1: Diagram of the relationship between expanded memory and conventional memory.

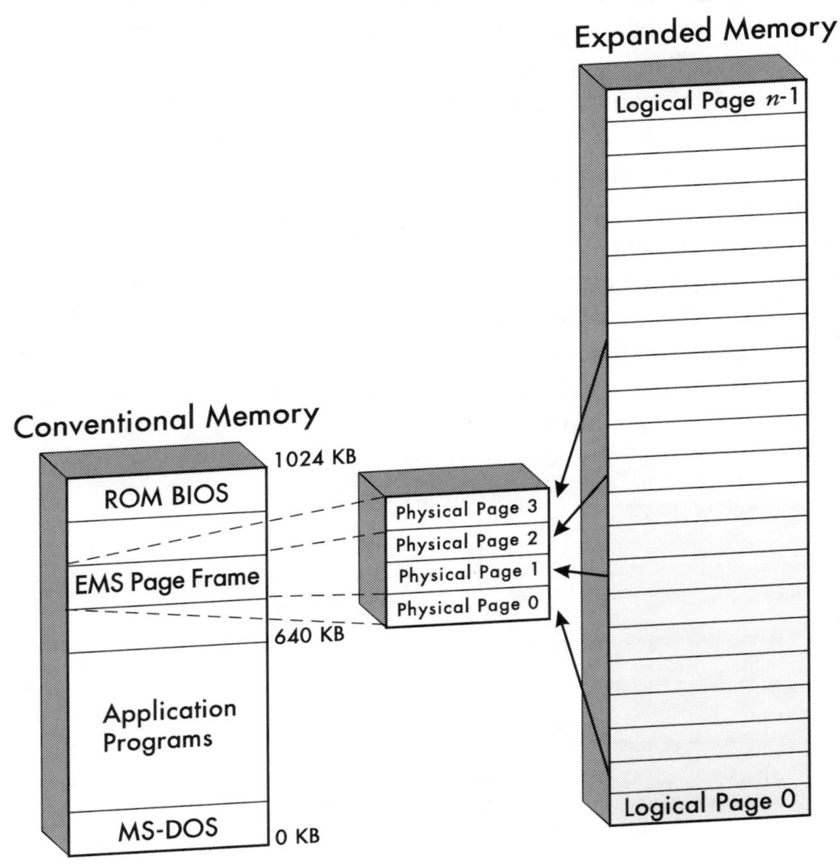

In EMS 4.0, an EMS 3.x-compatible page frame is supported for compatibility reasons, but the page frame may be larger than 64KB, and there may also be multiple page frames. EMS 4.0 also allows pages to be mapped below the 640KB boundary on demand, if the proper hardware support is present. But it's best to avoid these paging capabilities that are unique to EMS 4.0 in ordinary application programs, because most of them are designed for use by operating systems. For example, Windows 3.0, when running in real mode with "large frame EMS" enabled, can use the enhanced EMS 4.0 calls to "swap" applications in and out of conventional memory on each context switch (see Chapter 6).

Once a logical page has been mapped to a physical page, it can be inspected and modified with the usual CPU memory instructions. When dealing with the standard EMS 3.x page frame and page sizes, address calculations are straightforward. A far pointer to a mapped page, which is composed of a segment and offset, is built up as follows. The page frame base address returned by Int 67H Function 41H is already in a form that can be loaded directly into a segment register. The offset portion of the far pointer is obtained by multiplying the physical page number (0-3) by 16,384 (4000H), and adding a logical page displacement in the range 0-16,383 (0-3FFFH).

For example, if the address returned by the "get page frame address" function is D000H, and logical page 1 for a particular EMM handle has been mapped to physical page 3, then the data in that logical page can be accessed at physical memory addresses D000:C000H through D000H:FFFFH. The process of mapping a logical page to a physical page, calculating the memory address of the page, and writing data to it, is demonstrated below:

```
pagelen equ     4000h               ; standard EMS page size

pframe  dw      0                   ; page frame address
logpage dw      1                   ; logical page number
phypage dw      3                   ; physical page number
handle  dw      0                   ; handle for EMS pages

        .
        .
        .
        mov     ah,44h              ; map EMS page
        mov     bx,logpage          ; logical page 1
                                    ; physical page 3
        mov     al, byte ptr phypage
```

```
mov     dx,handle       ; EMS handle
int     67h             ; transfer to EMM
or      ah,ah           ; check for EMM error
jnz     error           ; jump, error occurred
                        ; form far pointer to page
mov     es,pframe       ; ES = page frame segment
mov     ax,pagelen      ; calculate offset of
mul     phypage         ; physical page in frame
mov     di,ax           ; let ES:DI = page address

xor     ax,ax           ; now zero out the
mov     cx,pagelen      ; mapped page
rep stosb
```

This code fragment assumes the page frame address was fetched with a call to Int 67H Function 41H earlier in the program's execution, and that a valid EMS handle was previously obtained with a call to Int 67H Function 43H.

In programs that take advantage of EMS 4.0's ability to support more than four physical pages or more than one page frame, it may be preferable to use a lookup technique to translate physical page numbers to far pointers. Your program can call EMS Int 67H Function 58H Subfunction 00H to get a list of the physical page numbers and their physical memory addresses.

It is often helpful to think of the expanded memory owned by a program as a sort of virtual file with a length of n*16,384 bytes (where n is the number of allocated EMS pages). To access a particular piece of data in the file, the program first performs a "seek" operation to the nearest sector boundary: it divides the byte offset of the data within the virtual file by 16,384 to find the logical page number, and maps that logical page to a physical page. The remainder, when the byte offset is divided by 16,384, is the offset of the data within the logical page, which can be combined with the page frame base address and the offset of the physical page within the page frame to form a far pointer in the manner described.

When your program is finished using expanded memory, it must be sure to deallocate its EMS handle and logical pages by calling the "release EMS handle" function (Int 67H Function 45H) before terminating. If it fails to do so, the expanded memory owned by the program will be lost and unavailable for use by other programs until the system is restarted. MS-DOS cannot clean up a program's expanded memory resources automatically at termination because MS-DOS does not participate in the expanded memory management in the first

Figure 2-2: General procedure for expanded memory usage by an application program.

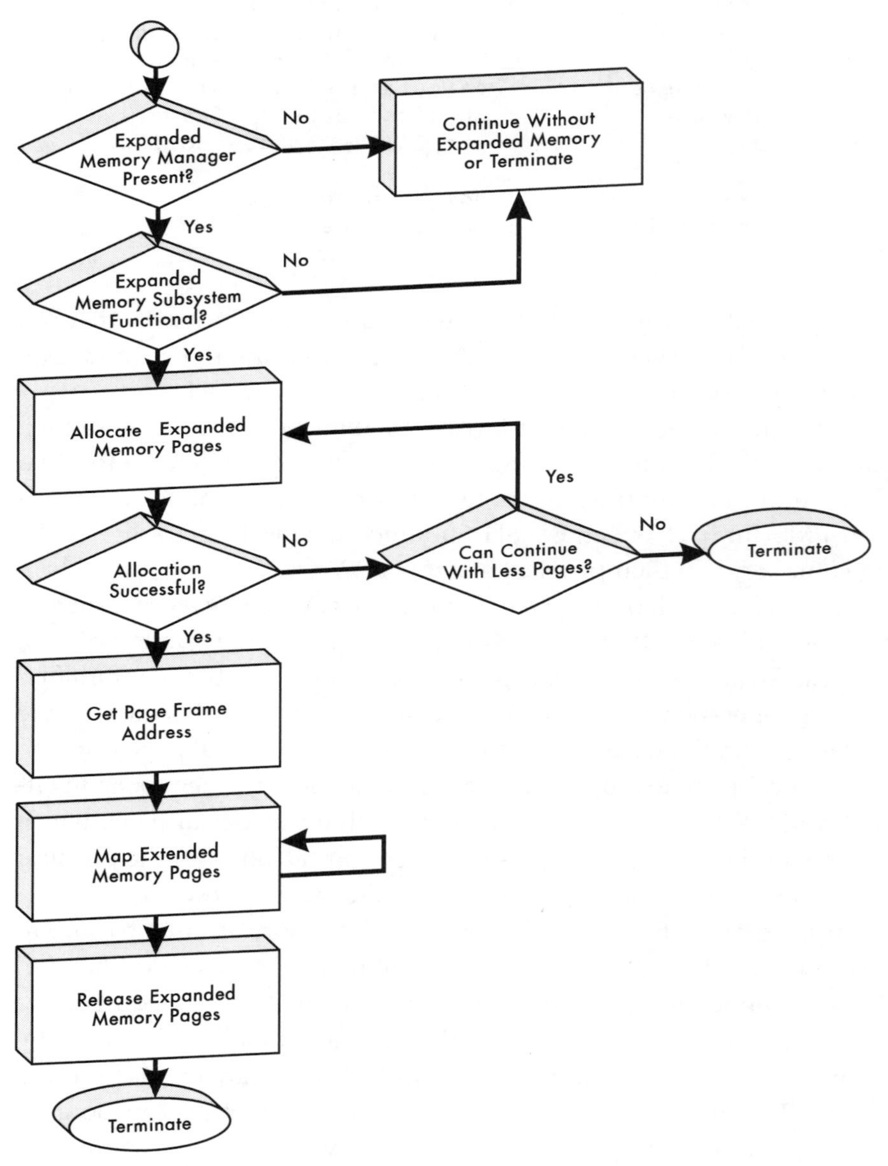

place. For the same reason, programs using EMS should contain their own critical error and Control-C handlers, so they cannot be terminated unexpectedly.

A sketch of the entire process of using expanded memory in an application is shown in Figure 2-2.

EMS Pitfalls for Drivers and TSRs

Using expanded memory in a device driver or TSR utility is somewhat more problematic than in a normal application program. You must concern yourself not only with the logic of your own program, but with protecting yourself against every possible use (and misuse) of expanded memory by other active programs, whether they be drivers, TSRs, or applications.

When a driver or TSR gets control, the state of the system is, by nature, sensitive and unpredictable. In the first place, the driver or TSR was undoubtedly called as the direct or indirect result of the user's interaction with an application program, and that application may well be using expanded memory too. It is crucial that any use of expanded memory by the foreground application not be disturbed. Therefore, it is vitally important that the driver or TSR save the expanded memory mapping context (the association of specific logical expanded memory pages with physical locations in the CPU's address space) at entry, and restore that same context before it exits.

In each successive revision of the EMS, new functions have been defined for saving and restoring the expanded memory subsystem state (summarized in Table 2-3). In EMS version 3.0, Functions 47H and 48H provided all-or-nothing capability on a per-handle basis. If the driver or TSR owned only one expanded memory handle, then it could save only one mapping context at a time. In EMS version 3.2, Function 4EH (which actually consists of four distinct subfunctions) was added, allowing a program to selectively save and restore as many mapping contexts as it had memory to put them in. This made things a lot easier for multitasking program managers, since it allowed them to associate a mapping context with each active application.

In EMS version 4.0, the number of expanded memory pages that can be simultaneously mapped into conventional memory is much larger, and the overhead of saving and restoring the complete mapping state has grown proportionately. Consequently, Function 4FH was added to manipulate partial mapping contexts. Version 4.0 also defines a host of other new functions directly or indirectly related to page mapping, ranging from mapping of multiple pages with one call (optionally followed by a jump or call to code within the pages) to support for multiple sets of hardware mapping registers. These functions are intended primarily for use by operating systems, so we won't discuss them further here.

Table 2-3: Summary of the EMS functions related to saving and restoring the expanded memory mapping context.

Expanded Memory Function	Call With	Returns	EMS Version
Save Page Map	AH = 47H DX = EMM handle	AH = status	3.0
Restore Page Map	AH = 48H DX = EMM handle	AH = status	3.0
Save Page Map	AH = 4EH AL = 00H ES:DI = buffer	AH = status	3.2
Restore Page Map	AH = 4EH AL = 01H DS:SI = buffer	AH = status	3.2
Save and Restore Page Map	AH = 4EH AL = 02H DS:SI = restore buffer ES:DI = save buffer	AH = status	3.2
Get Size of Page Map Information	AH = 4EH AL = 03H	AH = status AL = size (bytes)	3.2
Save Partial Page Map	AH = 4FH AL = 00H DS:SI = map list ES:DI = buffer	AH = status	4.0
Restore Partial Page Map	AH = 4FH AL = 01H DS:SI = buffer	AH = status	4.0
Get Size of Partial Page Map Information	AH = 4FH AL = 02H BX = number of pages	AH = status AL = size (bytes)	4.0

When you are writing a device driver or TSR, you must also concern yourself with a difficult issue that doesn't arise in normal MS-DOS application programming: the lack of availability of MS-DOS services after your program is originally installed. A device driver is allowed to use a limited number of MS-DOS Int 21H functions *during* installation, but none at all thereafter. As for TSRs, they are typically activated during a hardware interrupt (such as the reception of a keystroke), and since the state of MS-DOS at the time of the interrupt cannot be known in advance, they must rely on undocumented flags and structures to determine whether MS-DOS function calls can be made safely. This all implies that your driver or TSR should perform all the status checks it can, and acquire all the expanded memory resources it expects to ever need, at the time it gets loaded—because interaction with the user at any later point (even to display an error message) will be much more difficult.

One last potential problem we should mention is that the amount of stack space available at the time your TSR or driver is invoked is indeterminate. MS-DOS itself uses three different stacks, depending on the type of function call in progress; applications customarily have their own stacks, whose depth is totally at the discretion of the developer; interrupt handlers often switch to their own stacks; and last but not least, the amount of stack space required by EMS functions may vary from one Expanded Memory Manager (EMM) to another as well as from version to version. The safest strategy is for your driver or TSR to always switch to its own generously sized stack, before using any EMS functions.

EMS Emulators

From the very beginning, the Expanded Memory Specification was formulated strictly as a software interface, without hardware dependence of any kind (other than the assumption that the software is running on an Intel 80x86 CPU). We'll never know whether this was just a happy accident or a stroke of genius on the part of the original Lotus/Intel/Microsoft designers, but the payoff is the same in any event: the nature of the Expanded Memory Specification allows expanded memory functionality to be provided on systems that do not contain any expanded memory hardware at all. Programs that provide expanded memory services in the absence of expanded memory hardware are called expanded memory emulators or *simulators*, and they fall into three classes: disk-based EMS emulators, 286 extended memory-based EMS emulators, and 386/486-specific memory managers that export the EMS interface.

Disk-based EMS emulators, such as Turbo EMS or Above Disk, support the EMS Int 67H interface, but store the data in allocated EMS pages in a swap file on disk. When an application requests an EMS page to be mapped into the page frame, the emulator reads the EMS page's data in from the swap file and makes it available in RAM. Disk-based EMS emulators will run on any type of PC, from the original 8088-based model on up, but have two severe disadvantages: they are very slow compared to true EMS based on bank-switched memory, and the page frame is almost always located low in conventional memory rather than above the 640K boundary. The unusual location of the page frame causes trouble for some application programs that are not completely well-behaved in their use of EMS services.

80286 extended memory-based EMS emulators are similar to disk-based EMS emulators, in that they typically create a page frame in conventional memory below the 640KB boundary. However, these emulators are significantly faster than disk-based emulators because they store the data in the simulated EMS pages in extended memory rather than on disk, using ROM BIOS Int 15H Function 87H to move the data between extended memory and the page frame when a mapping is requested by an application program. On older PC/ATs and clones, such an extended memory-based EMS emulator may allow you to gain the benefits of EMS without purchasing any additional hardware. However, better performance will be obtained by reconfiguring the system's extended memory as expanded memory when the hardware allows it, or by purchasing and plugging in a new board that can supply true expanded memory.

A 386/486-based memory manager such as Qualitas's 386-to-the-Max, Quarterdeck's QEMM, or DOS 5.0's EMM 386, implements EMS emulation by taking on the role of a little operating system. The memory manager itself runs in the 386/486's 32-bit protected mode, and MS-DOS and its application programs run under the memory manager's supervision in Virtual 86 Mode. This arrangement gives the memory manager complete control over the address space seen by MS-DOS and other real-mode programs; it can use the 386/486 page tables to make any 4KB physical memory page appear at any address within the Virtual 86 Machine. For example, EMM 386 can remap extended memory into the "holes" between video adapters and the ROM BIOS, so that device drivers and TSRs can be loaded above the 640KB boundary.

Use of Virtual 86 Mode also allows a 386/486-based memory manager to intercept software interrupts, which puts it into a position to simulate EMS memory without the real-mode application's knowledge or cooperation. The memory manager uses extended memory for storage of EMS pages, and simply uses the 386/486 page tables to map the simulated EMS pages on demand into a simulated EMS page frame within the Virtual 86 Machine. The speed of EMS emulation by 386/486-based memory managers is uniformly excellent, because page table manipulation and mode switching on 80386/486 CPUs is very fast. Some memory managers provide additional capabilities as well: 386-to-the-Max actually exports three out of four of the important software interfaces for memory management: EMS, XMS (Chapter 3), and the VCPI (Chapter 8), while DOS 5.0 with Windows 3.0 exports all four (including DPMI), and on a 386/486 can also set up multiple Virtual 86 Machines and perform true preemptive multitasking of MS-DOS applications.

Programming Example: The EMSDISK.SYS Driver

In order to provide a practical example of expanded memory usage by an application program, TSR, or device driver, I've included the source code for a simple EMS-aware RAMdisk (virtual disk) called EMSDISK.ASM. EMSDISK demonstrates the procedure for testing for the existence and functionality of expanded memory that must be used by a driver or TSR. It contains examples of expanded memory allocation, mapping, and the saving and restoring of mapping contexts.

For maximum portability, EMSDISK does not attempt to take advantage of the features of EMS version 4.0; it only relies on functions that are available in EMS version 3.2. Furthermore, EMSDISK.SYS is a simple program as device drivers go; it contains only the essential routines (initialization, build BPB, media check, read, and write) that allow MS-DOS to recognize it as a valid block device.

You may find it helpful to consult a general text on MS-DOS (such as my own book *Advanced MS-DOS Programming,* 2nd Edition) for further information about device driver structure and components.

To assemble and link the file EMSDISK.ASM into the executable device driver EMSDISK.SYS, enter the following commands:

```
MASM EMSDISK;
LINK EMSDISK;
EXE2BIN EMSDISK.EXE EMSDISK.SYS
DEL EMSDISK.EXE
```

(The Linker will display the message *Warning: No Stack Segment*. This warning can be ignored.) To install EMSDISK, add the line:

```
DEVICE=EMSDISK.SYS  nnnK
```

to your CONFIG.SYS file and reboot the system. Make sure that the DEVICE= line for EMSDISK.SYS follows the DEVICE= line that loads your expanded memory manager (such as EMM.SYS for Intel Above Boards). The logical drive identifier that will be assigned to EMSDISK depends on the number of block devices that are already present in the system at the time EMSDISK is loaded.

The parameter nnnK on the DEVICE= directive is the desired size of the RAMdisk in kilobytes. If this parameter is missing, or is larger than the amount of free expanded memory, EMSDISK will use all of the expanded memory that is available. For example, if fixed disk drive C: is currently the last drive in your system, you could create a 1-megabyte virtual disk drive D: by adding the following line to CONFIG.SYS:

```
DEVICE=EMSDISK.SYS 1024K
```

When EMSDISK is loaded, it will display a sign-on message and, under DOS 3.0 or later, its drive identifier. If EMSDISK can't find a previously loaded expanded memory manager, or is unable to allocate or initialize its expanded memory pages, it will abort its own installation with an error message.

EMS Example Program

```
; EMSDISK.ASM --- Expanded Memory RAMdisk
; Copyright (C) 1991 Ray Duncan
;
; To build:     MASM EMSDISK;
;               LINK EMSDISK;
;               EXE2BIN EMSDISK.EXE EMSDISK.SYS
;               DEL EMSDISK.EXE
```

```
;
; To install:   copy EMSDISK.SYS to the root directory of your
;               boot disk, then add the line
;
;                       DEVICE=EMSDISK.SYS nnnK
;
;               to the CONFIG.SYS file.  This line must follow
;               the DEVICE= line that loads the Expanded Memory
;               Manager.  The parameter nnn is the desired
;               RAMdisk size in KB.  If nnn is missing or zero,
;               all available expanded memory is used.
;
_TEXT   segment public 'CODE'

        assume  cs:_TEXT,ds:_TEXT,es:_TEXT

        org     0

maxcmd  equu    24                      ; maximum driver command code

cr      equ     0dh                     ; ASCII carriage return
lf      equ     0ah                     ; ASCII line feed
blank   equ     020h                    ; ASCII space code
tab     equ     09h                     ; ASCII tab character
eom     equ     '$'                     ; end of message signal

emm_int equ     67h                     ; EMM software interrupt

psize   equ     16384                   ; bytes per EMS page
ssize   equ     512                     ; bytes per sector
dsize   equ     256                     ; entries in root directory

spp     equ     psize/ssize             ; sectors per page

request struc                           ; request packet template
rlength db      ?                       ; length of request packet
unit    db      ?                       ; unit number
command db      ?                       ; driver command code
status  dw      ?                       ; driver status word
reserve db      8 dup (?)               ; reserved area
media   db      ?                       ; media descriptor byte
address dd      ?                       ; memory address for transfer
count   dw      ?                       ; byte/sector count
sector  dw      ?                       ; starting sector number
request ends                            ; end request packet template
```

```
                                        ; device driver header
header  dd      -1                      ; link to next driver in chain
        dw      0                       ; driver attribute word
        dw      strat                   ; "Strategy" entry point
        dw      intr                    ; "Interrupt" entry point
        db      1                       ; number of units, this device
        db      7 dup (0)               ; reserved area

rqptr   dd      ?                       ; address of request packet

savesp  dw      0                       ; save MS-DOS kernel's SS:SP
savess  dw      0

availp  dw      0                       ; logical EMS pages available
totalp  dw      0                       ; total EMS pages in system
ownedp  dw      0                       ; RAMdisk size in EMS pages
pframe  dw      0                       ; segment address of page frame
handle  dw      0                       ; expanded memory handle
dosver  db      0                       ; MS-DOS major version no.

xfrsec  dw      0                       ; current sector for transfer
xfrcnt  dw      0                       ; sectors already transferred
xfrreq  dw      0                       ; number of sectors requested
xfraddr dd      0                       ; working address for transfer

array   dw      bpb                     ; BPB pointer array

bootrec equ     $                       ; EMSDISK boot record
        jmp     $                       ; phony JMP instruction

        nop
        db      'IBM  3.3'              ; OEM identity field
                                        ; BIOS Parameter Block (BPB)
bpb     dw      ssize                   ; 0   bytes per sector
        db      0                       ; 2   sectors per cluster
        dw      1                       ; 3   reserved sectors
        db      1                       ; 5   number of FATs
        dw      dsize                   ; 6   root directory entries
        dw      0                       ; 8   total sectors
        db      0f8h                    ; 0AH media descriptor
        dw      0                       ; 0BH sectors per FAT
br_len  equ     $-bootrec               ; length of boot record

        even                            ; force word alignment
        dw      128 dup (0)
stk     equ     $                       ; local stack for device driver
```

```
;
; Driver 'strategy' routine; called by MS-DOS kernel with
; ES:BX pointing to driver request packet.
;
strat   proc    far

        mov     word ptr cs:rqptr,bx    ; save address of request packet
        mov     word ptr cs:rqptr+2,es
        ret                             ; back to MS-DOS kernel

strat   endp

;
; Driver 'interrupt' routine, called by MS-DOS kernel immediately
; after call to 'strategy' routine to process I/O request.
;
intr    proc    far

        push    ax                      ; save general registers
        push    bx
        push    cx
        push    dx
        push    ds
        push    es
        push    di
        push    si
        push    bp
        mov     ax,cs                   ; make local data addressable
        mov     ds,ax
        mov     savess,ss               ; save DOS's stack pointers
        mov     savesp,sp
        mov     ss,ax                   ; set SS:SP to point to
        mov     sp,offset stk           ; driver's local stack

        les     di,rqptr                ; let ES:DI = request packet
        mov     bl,es:[di.command]      ; get BX = command code
        xor     bh,bh
        cmp     bx,maxcmd               ; make sure it's legal
        jle     intr1                   ; jump, function code is ok
        mov     ax,8003h                ; set Error bit and code
        jmp     intr3                   ; for "unknown command"

intr1:  or      bx,bx                   ; is it init call? (function 0)
        jz      intr2                   ; yes, skip save of context
        mov     ah,47h                  ; fxn 47h = save page mapping
```

```
        mov     dx,handle               ; EMM handle for this driver
        int     emm_int                 ; transfer to EMM
        or      ah,ah                   ; jump if EMM error while
        jnz     intr5                   ; saving page mapping context

intr2:  shl     bx,1                    ; form index to dispatch table
        call    word ptr [bx+dispch]    ; branch to command code routine
                                        ; should return AX = status
        les     di,rqptr                ; restore ES:DI = request packet

intr3:  or      ax,0100h                ; merge Done bit into status,
        mov     es:[di.status],ax       ; store into request packet
        mov     bl,es:[di.command]      ; was this initialization call?
        or      bl,bl
        jz      intr4                   ; yes, skip restore of context

        mov     ah,48h                  ; fxn 48h = restore page mapping
        mov     dx,handle               ; EMM handle for this driver
        int     emm_int                 ; transfer to EMM
        or      ah,ah                   ; jump if EMM error while
        jnz     intr5                   ; restoring page mapping

intr4:  mov     ss,savess               ; central exit point
        mov     sp,savesp               ; restore DOS kernel's stack
        pop     bp                      ; restore general registers
        pop     si
        pop     di
        pop     es
        pop     ds
        pop     dx
        pop     cx
        pop     bx
        pop     ax
        ret                             ; back to MS-DOS kernel
intr5:                                  ; catastrophic errors come here
        les     di,rqptr                ; ES:DI = addr of request packet
        mov     es:[di.status],810ch    ; set Error bit, Done bit, and
        jmp     intr4                   ; error code for general failure

intr    endp

;
; Dispatch table for device driver command codes
;
dispch  dw      init                    ;  0 = initialize driver
        dw      medchk                  ;  1 = media check on block device
```

```
        dw      bldbpb                  ;  2 = build BIOS parameter block
        dw      error                   ;  3 = I/O control read
        dw      read                    ;  4 = read from device
        dw      error                   ;  5 = non-destructive read
        dw      error                   ;  6 = return current input status
        dw      error                   ;  7 = flush device input buffers
        dw      write                   ;  8 = write to device
        dw      write                   ;  9 = write with verify
        dw      error                   ; 10 = return current output status
        dw      error                   ; 11 = flush output buffers
        dw      error                   ; 12 = I/O control write
        dw      error                   ; 13 = device open        (DOS 3.0+)
        dw      error                   ; 14 = device close       (DOS 3.0+)
        dw      error                   ; 15 = removeable media   (DOS 3.0+)
        dw      error                   ; 16 = output until busy  (DOS 3.0+)
        dw      error                   ; 17 = not used
        dw      error                   ; 18 = not used
        dw      error                   ; 19 = generic IOCTL      (DOS 3.2+)
        dw      error                   ; 20 = not used
        dw      error                   ; 21 = not used
        dw      error                   ; 22 = not used
        dw      error                   ; 23 = get logical device (DOS 3.2+)
        dw      error                   ; 24 = set logical device (DOS 3.2+)


;
; Media Check routine (command code 1).  Returns code indicating
; whether medium has been changed since last access.
;
medchk  proc    near

        mov     byte ptr es:[di+14],1   ; set "media not changed" code
        xor     ax,ax                   ; return success status
        ret

medchk  endp

;
; Build BPB routine (command code 2).  Returns pointer to valid
; BIOS Parameter Block for logical drive.
;
bldbpb  proc    near

        mov     word ptr es:[di+20],cs  ; put BPB address in packet
        mov     word ptr es:[di+18],offset bpb
        xor     ax,ax                   ; return success status
```

```
        ret

bldbpb  endp

;
; Read routine (command code 4).  Transfers logical sector(s)
; from RAMdisk storage to specified address.
;
read    proc    near

        call    setup                   ; set up transfer variables

read1:  mov     ax,xfrcnt               ; done with all sectors yet?
        cmp     ax,xfrreq
        je      read2                   ; jump if transfer completed
        mov     ax,xfrsec               ; get next sector number
        call    mapsec                  ; and map it
        jc      read4                   ; jump if mapping error
        les     di,xfraddr              ; ES:DI = requestor's buffer
        mov     si,ax                   ; DS:SI = RAMdisk address
        mov     ds,pframe
        mov     cx,ssize/2              ; transfer logical sector from
        cld                             ; RAMdisk to requestor
        rep movsw
        push    cs                      ; restore local addressing
        pop     ds
        inc     xfrsec                  ; advance sector number
        add     word ptr xfraddr,ssize  ; advance transfer address
        inc     xfrcnt                  ; count sectors transferred
        jmp     read1                   ; go do another sector

read2:                                  ; all sectors successfully
        xor     ax,ax                   ; transferred, return ok status

read3:  les     di,rqptr                ; get address of request packet
        mov     bx,xfrcnt               ; poke in actual transfer count
        mov     es:[di.count],bx        ; (in case an error aborted
        ret                             ; the transfer early)

read4:  mov     ax,800bh                ; come here if mapping error,
        jmp     read3                   ; return read fault error code

read    endp

;
; Write (command code 8) and Write with Verify (command code 9)
```

```
; routine.  Transfers logical sector(s) from specified address
; to RAMdisk storage.
;
write   proc    near

        call    setup                   ; set up transfer variables

write1: mov     ax,xfrcnt               ; done with all sectors yet?
        cmp     ax,xfrreq
        je      write2                  ; jump if transfer completed
        mov     ax,xfrsec               ; get next sector number
        call    mapsec                  ; and map it
        jc      write4                  ; jump if mapping error
        mov     di,ax                   ; ES:DI = RAMdisk address
        mov     es,pframe
        lds     si,xfraddr              ; DS:SI = requestor's buffer
        mov     cx,ssize/2              ; transfer logical sector from
        cld                             ; requestor to RAMdisk
        rep movsw
        push    cs                      ; restore local addressing
        pop     ds
        inc     xfrsec                  ; advance sector number
        add     word ptr xfraddr,ssize  ; advance transfer address
        inc     xfrcnt                  ; count sectors transferred
        jmp     write1                  ; go do another sector

write2:                                 ; all sectors successfully
        xor     ax,ax                   ; transferred, return ok status

write3: les     di,rqptr                ; get address of request packet,
        mov     bx,xfrcnt               ; poke in actual transfer count
        mov     es:[di.count],bx        ; (in case an error aborted
        ret                             ; the transfer early)

write4: mov     ax,800ah                ; mapping error detected,
        jmp     write3                  ; return write fault error code

write   endp

;
; Dummy routine for command codes not supported by this driver.
;
error   proc    near

        mov     ax,8103h                ; return error code 3
        ret                             ; indicating 'unknown command'
```

```
error   endp

;
; Map into memory a logical "disk" sector from the EMS
; pages allocated to the RAMdisk.
;
; Call with:    AX     = logical sector number
;
; Returns:      CY     = clear if no error
;               AX     = offset within EMS page frame
;               AX,CX,DX destroyed
;
;               CY     = set if EMM mapping error
;               AX,CX,DX destroyed
;
mapsec  proc    near

        mov     dx,0                    ; divide sector no. by sectors
        mov     cx,spp                  ; per page, to get EMS page number
        div     cx                      ; now AX=EMS page,DX=rel. sector
        push    dx                      ; save sector within page
        mov     bx,ax                   ; BX <- EMS page number
        mov     ax,4400h                ; fxn 4400h = map phys. page 0
        mov     dx,handle               ; EMM handle for this driver
        int     emm_int                 ; transfer to EMM
        or      ah,ah                   ; test for EMM error
        jnz     maps1                   ; jump, EMM error detected
        pop     ax                      ; get relative sector in page
        mov     cx,ssize                ; relative sector * size =
        mul     cx                      ; offset into EMS logical page
        clc                             ; return CY=clear for no error
        ret                             ; back to caller

maps1:  add     sp,2                    ; EMM mapping error detected
        stc                             ; clear stack and return CY=set
        ret                             ; to indicate error

mapsec  endp

;
; Set up to perform Read or Write subfunction by copying
; requestor's buffer address, starting sector, and sector
; count out of request packet into local variables.
;
setup   proc    near
```

```
        push    es                      ; save request packet address
        push    di
        mov     ax,es:[di.sector]       ; initialize starting sector
        mov     xfrsec,ax
        mov     ax,es:[di.count]        ; initialize sectors requested
        mov     xfrreq,ax
        les     di,es:[di.address]      ; initialize requestor's
        mov     word ptr xfraddr,di     ; buffer address
        mov     word ptr xfraddr+2,es
        mov     xfrcnt,0                ; initialize transfer count
        pop     di                      ; restore request packet address
        pop     es
        ret

setup   endp

;
; Initialization routine, called at driver load time.  Returns
; address of 'init' label to MS-DOS as start of free memory, so
; that memory occupied by 'init' and its subroutines is reclaimed.
;
init    proc    near

init1:  mov     ax,3000h                ; fxn 30h = get DOS version
        int     21h                     ; transfer to MS-DOS
        mov     dosver,al               ; save major version number

init2:  xor     ax,ax                   ; check if EMM driver present
        mov     es,ax                   ; if EMM is present, address in
        mov     bx,emm_int*4            ; vector points to EMM driver.
        mov     es,es:[bx+2]            ; now ES:0000 = EMM header
        mov     di,10                   ; ES:DI = addr of device name
        mov     si,offset emm_name      ; DS:SI = name to match
        mov     cx,8                    ; length of device name
        cld
        repz cmpsb                      ; compare EMM name
        jz      init3                   ; jump if name matched
        mov     dx,offset msg1          ; if name didn't match,
        jmp     abort                   ; driver is absent, exit

init3:  mov     ah,40h                  ; fxn 40h = get EMM status
        int     emm_int                 ; transfer to EMM
        or      ah,ah                   ; check for EMM error
        jz      init4                   ; jump, driver is OK
        mov     dx,offset msg2          ; EMM is non-functional,
```

```
        jmp     abort                   ; error message and exit

init4:  mov     ah,46h                  ; fxn 46h = get EMM version
        int     emm_int                 ; transfer to EMM
        or      ah,ah                   ; check for EMM error
        jz      init5                   ; jump, no error
init45: mov     dx,offset msg3          ; error occurred, display
        jmp     abort                   ; error message and exit

init5:  cmp     al,030h                 ; must be version 3.0+
        jae     init6                   ; jump if version is OK
        mov     dx,offset msg6
        jmp     abort                   ; wrong EMM version, exit

init6:  mov     ah,41h                  ; fxn 41h = get page frame
        int     emm_int                 ; transfer to EMM
        or      ah,ah                   ; check for EMM error
        jnz     init45                  ; error occurred, exit
        mov     pframe,bx               ; save page frame segment

        mov     ah,42h                  ; fxn 42h = get no. of pages
        int     emm_int                 ; transfer to EMM
        or      ah,ah                   ; check for EMM error
        jnz     init45                  ; error occurred, exit
        mov     totalp,dx               ; save total EMS pages
        mov     availp,bx               ; save available EMS pages
        mov     ownedp,bx               ; default allocated=available
        or      bx,bx                   ; any pages available?
        jnz     init7                   ; yes, proceed
        mov     dx,offset msg4          ; no pages left, exit
        jmp     abort

init7:                                  ; get KB from DEVICE= line
        les     di,rqptr                ; ES:DI = request packet
        lds     si,es:[di+18]           ; DS:SI = CONFIG.SYS text

init71: lodsb                           ; scan for end of driver name
        cmp     al,blank
        ja      init71                  ; loop while within name
        dec     si                      ; point to delimiter and
        call    atoi                    ; convert KB size parameter
        push    cs                      ; make our data addressable
        pop     ds
        or      ax,ax                   ; size parameter missing?
        jz      init74                  ; yes, use available pages
        mov     dx,ax                   ; save copy of KB
```

```
        mov     cx,4                        ; divide KB by 16 to get
        shr     ax,cl                       ; requested EMS pages
        and     dx,0fh                      ; round up needed?
        jz      init73                      ; jump if multiple of 16 KB
        inc     ax                          ; round up to next page

init73: cmp     ax,availp                   ; requested > available?
        ja      init74                      ; yes, use available
        mov     ownedp,ax                   ; no, save requested pages

init74: mov     ah,43h                      ; fxn 43h = allocate pages
        mov     bx,ownedp                   ; no. of pages to request
        int     emm_int                     ; transfer to EMM
        or      ah,ah                       ; check for EMM error
        jz      init8                       ; jump if allocation OK
        mov     dx,offset msg5              ; allocation failed, display
        jmp     abort                       ; error message and exit

init8:  mov     handle,dx                   ; save EMM handle for pages
        call    makebpb                     ; set up BIOS Parameter Block
        call    format                      ; format the RAMdisk
        jnc     init9                       ; jump if format was OK
        mov     dx,offset msg7              ; error during formatting,
        jmp     abort                       ; display error and exit

init9:  call    signon                      ; display driver sign-on message
        les     di,cs:rqptr                 ; restore ES:DI=request packet
        mov     word ptr es:[di.address],offset init    ; set address of
        mov     word ptr es:[di.address+2],cs           ; end of driver
        mov     byte ptr es:[di+13],1   ; driver has 1 logical unit
        mov     word ptr es:[di+20],cs  ; address of BPB array
        mov     word ptr es:[di+18],offset array
        xor     ax,ax                       ; return success status
        ret

;
; EMM initialization failed, display error message and abort
; installation of the EMSDISK device driver.
;
abort:  push    dx                          ; save error message address
        mov     ah,9                        ; fxn 9 = display string
        mov     dx,offset ermsg             ; address of error heading
        int     21h                         ; transfer to MS-DOS
        mov     ah,9                        ; fxn 9 = display string
        pop     dx                          ; address of error description
        int     21h                         ; transfer to MS-DOS
```

```
        les     di,cs:rqptr             ; restore ES:DI=request packet
        mov     word ptr es:[di.address],0      ; set break address
        mov     word ptr es:[di.address+2],cs   ; to start of driver
        mov     byte ptr es:[di+13],0   ; set logical units = 0
        xor     ax,ax                   ; but return success status
        ret

init    endp

;
; Set up total sectors, sectors per cluster, and sectors per FAT
; fields of BIOS Parameter Block according to size of RAMdisk.
;
makebpb proc    near

        mov     ax,ownedp               ; calc RAMdisk total sectors,
        mov     cx,spp                  ; update BIOS parameter block
        mul     cx
        mov     bpb+8,ax

        mov     cx,2                    ; calc sectors per cluster
makeb1: mov     ax,bpb+8                ; try this cluster size...
        mov     dx,0                    ; divide total sectors by
        div     cx                      ; sectors per cluster.
        cmp     ax,4086                 ; resulting clusters < 4087?
        jna     makeb2                  ; yes, use it
        shl     cx,1                    ; no, sec/cluster*2
        jmp     makeb1                  ; try again

makeb2: mov     byte ptr bpb+2,cl       ; sectors per cluster into BPB
        mov     dx,ax                   ; now AX = total clusters
        add     ax,ax                   ; clusters*1.5 = bytes in FAT
        add     ax,dx
        shr     ax,1
        mov     dx,0                    ; bytes in FAT/ bytes/sector
        mov     cx,ssize                ; = number of FAT sectors
        div     cx
        or      dx,dx                   ; any remainder?
        jz      makeb3                  ; no,jump
        inc     ax                      ; round up to next sector

makeb3: mov     bpb+0bh,ax              ; FAT sectors into BPB
        ret                             ; done with BPB now

makebpb endp
```

```
;
; Format RAMdisk.  First write zeros into all sectors of reserved
; area, FAT, and root directory.  Then copy phony boot record to
; boot sector, initialize medium ID byte at beginning of FAT, and
; place phony volume label in first sector of root directory.
; Returns Carry = clear if successful, Carry = set if failed.
;
format  proc    near

        mov     bx,0                    ; first clear RAMdisk area
fmt1:   cmp     bx,ownedp               ; done with all EMS pages?
        je      fmt2                    ; yes, jump
        push    bx                      ; save current page number
        mov     ax,4400h                ; fxn 4400h = map phys. page 0
        mov     dx,handle               ; EMM handle for this driver
        int     emm_int                 ; transfer to EMM
        pop     bx                      ; restore page number
        or      ah,ah                   ; if bad mapping give up
        jnz     fmt9                    ; (should never happen)
        mov     es,pframe               ; set ES:DI = EMS page
        xor     di,di
        mov     cx,psize/2              ; page length in words
        xor     ax,ax                   ; fill page with zeros
        cld
        rep stosw
        inc     bx                      ; increment page and loop
        jmp     fmt1

fmt2:                                   ; copy phony boot sector
        mov     ax,0                    ; map in logical sector 0
        call    mapsec
        jc      fmt9                    ; jump if mapping error
        mov     di,ax                   ; ES:DI = sector 0
        mov     es,pframe
        mov     si,offset bootrec       ; DS:SI = boot record
        mov     cx,br_len               ; CX = length to copy
        rep movsb                       ; transfer boot sector data
        mov     ax,1                    ; map in logical sector 1
        call    mapsec                  ; (first sector of FAT)
        jc      fmt9                    ; jump if mapping error
        mov     di,ax                   ; ES:DI = sector 1
        mov     es,pframe
        mov     al,byte ptr [bpb+0ah]   ; put media descriptor byte
        mov     es:[di],al              ; into FAT byte 0, force
        mov     word ptr es:[di+1],-1   ; bytes 1-2 to FFH
        mov     al,byte ptr [bpb+5]     ; first directory sector =
```

```
        xor     ah,ah                   ; no. of FATS * length of FAT
        mul     word ptr [bpb+0bh]      ; plus reserved sectors
        add     ax,word ptr [bpb+3]
        call    mapsec                  ; map in directory sector
        jc      fmt9                    ; jump if mapping error
        mov     di,ax                   ; copy volume label to
        mov     es,pframe               ; first sector of directory
        mov     si,offset volname
        mov     cx,vn_len
        rep movsb
        clc                             ; return CY = clear,
        ret                             ; format was successful

fmt9:   stc                             ; return CY = set,
        ret                             ; error during format

format  endp

;
; Display sign-on message, logical volume (if DOS 3.0 or later),
; amounts of installed, available, and allocated expanded memory.
;
signon  proc    near

        les     di,rqptr                ; ES:DI = request packet
        mov     al,es:[di+22]           ; get drive code from header,
        add     al,'A'                  ; convert it to ASCII, and
        mov     dcode,al                ; store into sign-on message

        mov     ax,totalp               ; format KB of EM installed
        mov     dx,16
        mul     dx                      ; pages * 16 = KB
        mov     cx,10
        mov     si,offset kbins
        call    itoa                    ; convert KB to ASCII

        mov     ax,availp               ; format KB of EM available
        mov     dx,16
        mul     dx                      ; pages * 16 = KB
        mov     cx,10
        mov     si,offset kbavail
        call    itoa                    ; convert KB to ASCII

        mov     ax,ownedp               ; format KB assigned to RAMdisk
        mov     dx,16
        mul     dx                      ; pages * 16 = KB
```

```
        mov     cx,10
        mov     si,offset kbasn
        call    itoa                    ; convert KB to ASCII

        mov     ah,9                    ; fxn 9 = display string
        mov     dx,offset ident         ; address of program name
        int     21h                     ; transfer to MS-DOS

        mov     dx,offset dos2m         ; check DOS version, if
        cmp     dosver,2                ; DOS 2 can't know drive
        je      sign1
        mov     dx,offset dos3m         ; if DOS 3 can display drive

sign1:  mov     ah,9                    ; display KB of EMS memory
        int     21h                     ; installed, available, assigned
        ret                             ; back to caller

signon  endp

;
; Convert ASCII string to 16-bit binary integer.  Overflow
; is ignored.  Conversion terminates on first illegal character.
;
; Call with:    DS:SI = address of string
;               where 'string' is in the form
;               [whitespace][sign][digits]
;
; Returns:      AX    = result
;               DS:SI = address+1 of terminator
;
atoi    proc    near                    ; ASCII to 16-bit integer

        push    bx                      ; save registers
        push    cx
        push    dx
        xor     bx,bx                   ; initialize forming answer
        xor     cx,cx                   ; initialize sign flag

atoi1:  lodsb                           ; scan off whitespace
        cmp     al,blank                ; ignore leading blanks
        je      atoi1
        cmp     al,tab                  ; ignore leading tabs
        je      atoi1

        cmp     al,'+'                  ; proceed if + sign
        je      atoi2
```

```
        cmp     al,'-'                  ; is it - sign?
        jne     atoi3                   ; no, test if numeric
        dec     cx                      ; was - sign, set flag

atoi2:  lodsb                           ; get next character

atoi3:  cmp     al,'0'                  ; is character valid?
        jb      atoi4                   ; jump if not '0' to '9'
        cmp     al,'9'
        ja      atoi4                   ; jump if not '0' to '9'
        and     ax,0fh                  ; isolate lower four bits
        xchg    bx,ax                   ; multiply answer x 10
        mov     dx,10
        mul     dx
        add     bx,ax                   ; add this digit
        jmp     atoi2                   ; convert next digit

atoi4:  mov     ax,bx                   ; result into AX
        jcxz    atoi5                   ; jump if sign flag clear
        neg     ax                      ; make result negative

atoi5:  pop     dx                      ; restore registers
        pop     cx
        pop     bx
        ret                             ; back to caller

atoi    endp

;
; Convert 16-bit binary integer to ASCII string.
;
; Call with:    AX    = 16-bit integer
;               DS:SI = buffer to receive string,
;                       must be at least 6 bytes long
;               CX    = radix
;
; Returns:      DS:SI = address of converted string
;               AX    = length of string
;
itoa    proc    near                    ; convert binary int to ASCII

        add     si,6                    ; advance to end of buffer
        push    si                      ; and save that address
        or      ax,ax                   ; test sign of 16-bit value,
        pushf                           ; and save sign on stack
        jns     itoa1                   ; jump if value was positive
```

```
        neg     ax                      ; find absolute value

itoa1:  cwd                             ; divide value by radix to
        div     cx                      ; extract next digit
        add     dl,'0'                  ; convert remainder to ASCII
        cmp     dl,'9'                  ; in case converting to hex
        jle     itoa2                   ; jump if in range 0-9
        add     dl,'A'-'9'-1            ; correct digit if in range A-F

itoa2:  dec     si                      ; back up through buffer
        mov     [si],dl                 ; store this character
        or      ax,ax                   ; value now zero?
        jnz     itoa1                   ; no, convert another digit
        popf                            ; original value negative?
        jns     itoa3                   ; no, jump
        dec     si                      ; yes,store sign into output
        mov     byte ptr [si],'-'

itoa3:  pop     ax                      ; calculate length of string
        sub     ax,si
        ret                             ; return to caller

itoa    endp

;
; Miscellaneous data and text strings used only during
; initialization, discarded afterwards to save memory.
;
ident   db      cr,lf,lf
        db      'EMSDISK Expanded Memory RAMdisk 1.1'
        db      cr,lf
        db      'Copyright (C) 1991 Ray Duncan'
        db      cr,lf,lf,eom
dos3m   db      'RAMdisk will be drive '
dcode   db      'X.'
        db      cr,lf,lf
dos2m   label   byte
kbins   db      '       KB expanded memory installed.'
        db      cr,lf
kbavail db      '       KB expanded memory available.'
        db      cr,lf
kbasn   db      '       KB assigned to RAMdisk.'
        db      cr,lf,lf,eom

emm_name db     'EMMXXXX0',0            ; logical device name for
                                        ; expanded memory manager
```

```
ermsg   db      cr,lf
        db      'EMSDISK installation error:'
        db      cr,lf,eom

msg1    db      'expanded memory manager not found.'
        db      cr,lf,eom

msg2    db      'expanded memory not functional.'
        db      cr,lf,eom

msg3    db      'expanded memory manager error.'
        db      cr,lf,eom

msg4    db      'no expanded memory pages available.'
        db      cr,lf,eom

msg5    db      'expanded memory allocation failed.'
        db      cr,lf,eom

msg6    db      'wrong expanded memory manager version.'
        db      cr,lf,eom

msg7    db      'unable to format RAMdisk.'
        db      cr,lf,eom

volname db      'EMSDISK    '           ; phony volume label
        db      08h                     ; volume label attribute byte
        db      10 dup (0)              ; reserved
        dw      0                       ; time = 00:00:00
        dw      1641h                   ; date = February 1, 1991
        db      6 dup (0)
vn_len  equ     $-volname

_TEXT   ends

        end
```

Table 2-4: Expanded Memory Manager standardized error codes.
The error codes 90H and above are only supported in EMS version 4.0.

Error Code	Meaning
80H	Internal error in expanded memory manager software (may indicate corrupted memory image of driver)
81H	Malfunction in expanded memory hardware
82H	Memory manager busy
83H	Invalid handle
84H	Function not defined
85H	Handles exhausted
86H	Error in save or restore of mapping context
87H	Allocation request specified more pages than are physically available in system; no pages were allocated
88H	Allocation request specified more pages than are currently available; no pages were allocated
89H	Zero pages cannot be allocated
8AH	Requested logical page is outside range of pages owned by handle
8BH	Illegal physical page number in mapping request
8CH	Page mapping hardware-state save area is full
8DH	Mapping context save failed; save area already contains context associated with specified handle
8EH	Mapping context restore failed; save area does not contain context for specified handle
8FH	Subfunction parameter not defined
90H	Attribute type not defined
91H	Feature not supported
92H	Source and destination memory regions have same handle and overlap; requested move was performed, but part of the source region was overwritten
93H	Specified length for source or destination memory region is longer than actual allocated length
94H	Conventional memory region and expanded memory region overlap
95H	Specified offset is outside logical page
96H	Region length exceeds 1 megabyte
97H	Source and destination memory regions have same handle and overlap; exchange cannot be performed
98H	Memory source and destination types are undefined
99H	Error code currently unused

Error Code	Meaning
9AH	Alternate map or DMA register sets are supported, but specified alternate register set is not supported
9BH	Alternate map or DMA register sets are supported, but all alternate register sets are currently allocated
9CH	ternate map or DMA register sets are not supported, and specified alternate register set is not zero
9DH	Alternate map or DMA register sets are supported, but the alternate register set specified is not defined or not allocated
9EH	Dedicated DMA channels not supported
9FH	Dedicated DMA channels are supported, but specified DMA channel is not supported
A0H	No handle found for specified name
A1H	Handle with same name already exists
A3H	Invalid pointer passed to function, or contents of source array corrupted
A4H	Access to function denied by operating system

Chapter 3

Extended Memory and the XMS

Ray Duncan

Extended memory is the term for RAM storage at addresses above the 1-megabyte boundary on 80286-, 80386-, and 80486-based PCs. This distinguishes such memory from *conventional memory*, which is at addresses below 1 megabyte, or *expanded memory*, which is essentially bank-switched memory divided into pages that can be mapped into the conventional memory address space (expanded memory is discussed in Chapter 2). A sketch of the relationship between conventional memory and extended memory is shown in Figure 3-1.

If you own an IBM PC/AT, PS/2, or a 286-, 386-, or 486-based clone of any brand, you probably have at least a small amount of extended memory in your system. These days, such machines typically arrive with 1 megabyte or more of RAM installed on the motherboard, of which 512KB or 640KB starts at address 0, and the remainder begins at 1 megabyte. In addition, if you have purchased an add-in memory board for an AT-class machine, that board can probably be configured either as extended memory, expanded memory, or a combination of both.

Thus, extended memory is a readily available resource, and protected-mode operating systems such as OS/2 and UNIX can effectively use all the extended memory you can plug into your machine for execution of programs and storage of data. MS-DOS and its client programs, on the other hand, can gain access to this memory only with great difficulty. Why? The reason is neither complicated nor obscure. It is because MS-DOS runs on 80286/386/486 CPUs in real mode—a sort of 8086/88 emulation mode—which has important implications for the way addresses are generated.

Figure 3-1: Relationships between conventional and extended memory.

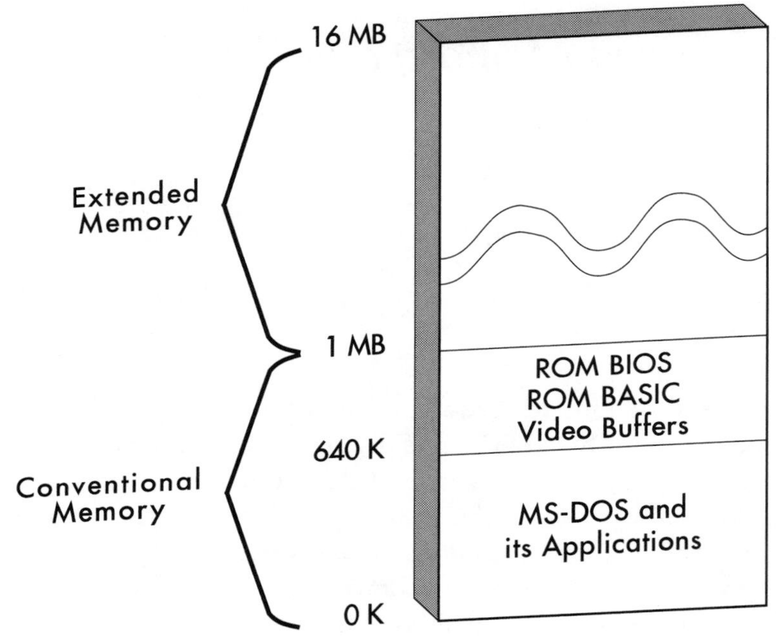

Programmers think in terms of segments, selectors, and offsets, but the CPU views memory as a simple, linearly addressed array of bytes. In real mode, the CPU selects a particular memory location by shifting the contents of a segment register left four bits and adding it to a 16-bit offset, forming a 20-bit physical address. But extended memory lies (by definition) above the 1-megabyte boundary (100000H), so all physical addresses that correspond to extended memory have at least 21 significant bits. In other words, real-mode programs can't "see" extended memory because they simply can't generate the appropriate addresses.

There are ways around this seemingly impenetrable addressing barrier, however, as we all know from our own daily experience. We've all got RAMdisks, disk caches, print spoolers, and TSRs that ostensibly run in real mode but are able to exploit extended memory when it is present. The eXtended Memory Specification (XMS), which was released in 1988 as a collaborative effort of Microsoft, Intel, Lotus, and AAST Research, was designed to bring all such programs into harmony: it defines a software interface for extended memory access comparable to the role of the LIM EMS for expanded memory.

Unfortunately, it will not suffice to simply describe the XMS and move on to other topics, as we could safely do for EMS in Chapter 2. By the time the XMS appeared, 80286-based PCs had been on the market for four years, and other methods of extended memory management had already evolved and were in common use. As matters stand today, there are no less than 6 different software interfaces for access to or management of extended memory that a programmer must be aware of:

- The ROM BIOS extended memory access function (Int 15H Function 87H)
- The VDISK or bottom-up allocation method
- The Int 15H or top-down allocation method
- The XMS software interface
- The VCPI software interface (discussed in Chapter 8)
- The DPMI software interface (discussed in Chapter 9)

This is an intimidating list, but things are not as bad as they look. The success of DOS 5.0 and Windows 3.0, both of which rely on the XMS interface, is forcing developers of memory managers, DOS extenders, and other extended-memory-aware programs to move rapidly toward XMS compatibility. And the VCPI and DPMI interfaces are ordinarily not relevant to a program unless it is going to run in protected mode at least part of the time. But it is not yet possible to simply write your program under the assumption that the XMS interface is always going to be available, so we will spend some time discussing extended memory addressing, the ROM BIOS, VDISK, and Int 15H before we talk about XMS.

Reaching Extended Memory in Real Mode

The first thing to understand about using extended memory is that there is no free lunch: a program *does* (with two bizarre exceptions, to be explained later in this chapter) need to be running in protected mode in order to read and write memory locations above the 1-megabyte boundary. And moving safely from real mode to protected mode and back again is a non-trivial chore.

The first step, getting into protected mode from real mode, is not all that difficult. Simply set the PE (protect enable) bit in the CPU's machine status word (known as MSW on the 80286, CR0 on the 80386 and 80486). Unless the other required housekeeping has been done, though, your program will just crash immediately. As we saw in Chapter 1, certain data structures and CPU registers must be initialized for protected-mode execution that have no meaning in real mode. For example, your program must set up a global descriptor table (GDT) that controls protected-mode memory mapping, segment types, and access rights; load the address of the table into the CPU's GDT pointer register; and finally, load all segment registers with valid selectors that refer to the GDT.

Assuming that your program manages to enter protected mode properly, and read or write the data in extended memory that it is interested in, it must then return to real mode to continue its main line of execution. After all, your program needs to be able to invoke MS-DOS to read or write files and interact with the user, but MS-DOS will be quite confused if your program calls it in protected mode.

Faced with this challenge, your first inclination might be to haul down your handy *Intel 80286 Programmer's Reference* and look up the machine instruction that switches the CPU from protected mode to real mode. Surprisingly enough, there is no such instruction. When the 80286 was designed, the Intel engineers never dreamed that somebody would ever want to make a transition from the clearly superior protected mode back to dull old real mode! Luckily, there is an escape hatch, however undesirable it may sound: if the CPU is halted and restarted, it restarts in real mode.

On 80286-based PC/AT class machines, the actual technique used by the ROM BIOS (and hence by VDISK and most other extended-memory-aware programs) to return to real mode is as follows: a "magic" value is stored into a reserved memory location, the contents of the stack and general registers are saved in other reserved memory locations, a special command is sent to the keyboard controller, and the CPU is halted. The keyboard controller, in its own good time, recognizes the command and responds with a signal that resets the CPU.

After the reset by the keyboard controller, the CPU begins execution at FFFF:0000H, as usual, and enters the ROM BIOS Power-Up-Self-Test (POST) sequence. The POST checks for the "magic" value that was saved in RAM earlier, recognizes that the machine is waking up from an intentional halt, restores the stack and registers, and returns control to the previously executing program rather than continuing with the ROM bootstrap. The turnaround time on this process can be on the order of several milliseconds, and it has been aptly characterized by Microsoft's Gordon Letwin as "turning off the car to change gears."

Things aren't quite so bad on 80286-based PS/2 or 80386/486-based machines. 80286-based PS/2s have special hardware support that allows a faster reset cycle (though the CPU still needs to be halted to accomplish it). 80386/486-based machines, on the other hand, can accomplish the switch back to real mode by simply clearing the PE bit in CR0, and don't need to halt the CPU at all. This is because by the time the 80386 was being designed, it was becoming obvious that MS-DOS and the programs that run under it weren't going to disappear.

The ROM BIOS Extended Memory Functions

Luckily, even from the earliest days of the PC/AT, MS-DOS programmers who wish to use extended memory for data storage have never needed to worry too much about the details of protected-mode programming and mode transitions. The PC/AT ROM BIOS provides two functions that give access to extended memory in a hardware-independent manner: Int 15H Function 87H, which copies a block of data from any location in conventional or extended memory to any other location, and Int 15H Function 88H, which returns the amount of extended memory installed in the system. The parameters and results of these two functions are outlined below:

Int 15H Function 88H—Get Extended Memory Size

Call with:

```
AH   = 88H
```

Returns:

```
AX   = amount of extended memory (in KB)
```

Int 15H Function 87H—Move Extended Memory Block

Call with:

```
AH              = 87H
CX              = number of words to move
ES:SI           = segment:offset of global descriptor table
```

Returns:

If function successful

```
Carry flag      = clear
AH              = 00H
```

If function unsuccessful

```
Carry flag      = set
AH              = status
                  01H     if RAM parity error
                  02H     if exception interrupt error
                  03H     if gate address line 20 failed
```

When Int 15H Function 87 is called, registers ES:SI point to a partially filled-in global descriptor table (GDT), with room for six descriptors (see Figure 3-2). The first descriptor is a dummy and corresponds to a null selector in the range 0000-0003H. Null selectors get special treatment from the hardware in protected mode; they are safe values that you can always load into a segment register as long as you don't try to address anything with them.

Table 3-1: The portions of the global descriptor table for Int 15H Function 87H that must be initialized by the calling program.

Byte(s)	Contents
00H-0FH	reserved (should be 0)
10H-11H	segment length in bytes (2*CX-1 or greater)
12H-14H	24-bit linear source address
15H	access rights byte (always 93H)
16H-17H	reserved (should be 0)
18H-19H	segment length in bytes (2*CX-1 or greater)
1AH-1CH	24-bit linear destination address
1DH	access rights byte (always 93H)
1EH-2FH	reserved (should be 0)

Figure 3-2: The descriptor table used by ROM BIOS Int 15H Function 87H.

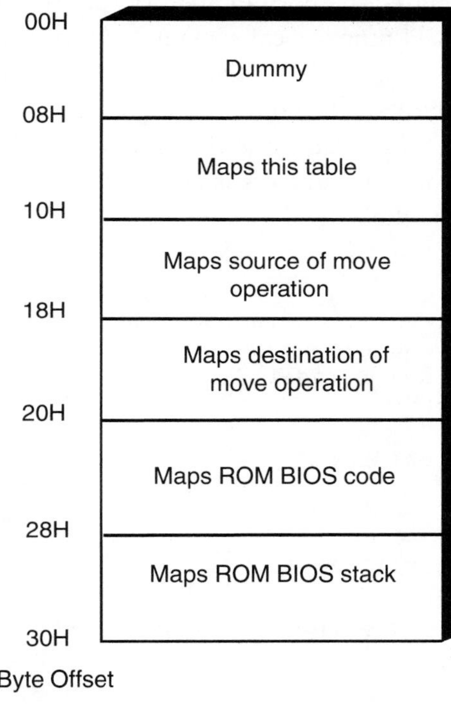

Two of the descriptors supply the source and destination addresses of the memory block that the program is asking the ROM BIOS to move on its behalf. The descriptors must be initialized with base addresses, an appropriate length, and an "access rights" byte of 93H. The remaining three descriptors are used by the ROM BIOS to provide addressability to its own code, data, and stack while it is executing in protected mode. The calling program initializes these to zero, and the ROM BIOS takes care of the remaining necessary initialization of the table before it switches the CPU into protected mode.

The most important thing you need to notice about the descriptor table is that the addresses you place in it are 24-bit linear byte addresses—numbers from 000000H to FFFFFFFH—rather than the more familiar segment:offset pairs. As we have already said, to convert the latter into the former, you merely shift the segment left 4 bits and then add the offset. The three bytes of a linear address are stored in their natural order, with the least significant byte at the lowest address.

The easiest way to cope with extended memory in an application program is to encapsulate the Int 15H Function 87H function calls inside MASM subroutines with more sensible parameters. The source file EXTMEM.ASM, shown below, contains two such routines for use with small model C programs: GETXM and PUTXM. These procedures are called with source and destination addresses and a length in bytes. The conventional memory address is assumed to be a normal far pointer (segment and offset), while the extended memory address is a linear, physical address.

```
; EXTMEM.ASM --- Routines to transfer data between
;                conventional and extended memory.
;                For use with small model C programs.
; Copyright (C) 1989 Ray Duncan
;
; Assemble with: MASM /Zi /Mx EXTMEM;

DGROUP  group   _DATA

_DATA   segment word public 'DATA'

gdt     db      30h dup (0)     ; global descriptor table

_DATA   ends


_TEXT   segment word public 'CODE'

        assume  cs:_TEXT,ds:DGROUP

args    equ     [bp+4]          ; offset of arguments, small model
source  equ     word ptr args
dest    equ     word ptr source+4
len     equ     word ptr dest+4

;
; GETXM copies data from extended memory to conventional memory.
;
; status = getxm(unsigned long source, void far *dest, unsigned len)
;
; Status is zero if move successful, nonzero if move failed:
; 1 = parity error, 2 = exception interrupt error, 3 = gate A20 failed
```

```
;
        public  _getxm
_getxm  proc    near

        push    bp              ; set up stack frame
        mov     bp,sp
        push    si              ; protect register variables
        push    di

                                ; DS: SI points to GDT
        mov     si,offset DGROUP:gdt

                                ; store access rights bytes
        mov     byte ptr [si+15h],93h
        mov     byte ptr [si+1dh],93h

        mov     ax,source       ; store source address
        mov     [si+12h],ax     ; into descriptor
        mov     ax,source+2
        mov     [si+14h],al

        mov     ax,dest+2       ; destination segment * 16
        mov     dx,16
        mul     dx
        add     ax,dest         ; + offset -> linear address
        adc     dx,0
        mov     [si+1ah],ax     ; store destination address
        mov     [si+1ch],dl     ; into descriptor

        mov     cx,len          ; store length into source
        mov     [si+10h],cx     ; and destination descriptors
        mov     [si+18h],cx

        shr     cx,1            ; convert length to words
        mov     ah,87h          ; Int 15H Fxn 87h = block move
        int     15h             ; transfer to ROM BIOS

        mov     al,ah           ; form status in AX
        cbw

        pop     di              ; restore registers
        pop     si
        pop     bp
        ret                     ; back to caller

_getxm  endp
```

```
;
; PUTXM copies data from conventional memory to extended memory.
;
; status = putxm(void far *source, unsigned long dest, unsigned len)
;
; Status is zero if move successful, nonzero if move failed:
; 1 = parity error, 2 = exception interrupt error, 3 = gate A20 failed
;
        public  _putxm
_putxm  proc    near

        push    bp                  ; set up stack frame
        mov     bp,sp
        push    si                  ; protect register variables
        push    di

                                    ; DS: SI points to GDT
        mov     si,offset DGROUP:gdt

                                    ; store access rights bytes
        mov     byte ptr [si+15h],93h
        mov     byte ptr [si+1dh],93h

        mov     ax,dest             ; store destination address
        mov     [si+1ah],ax         ; into descriptor
        mov     ax,dest+2
        mov     [si+1ch],al

        mov     ax,source+2         ; source segment * 16
        mov     dx,16
        mul     dx
        add     ax,source           ; + offset -> linear address
        adc     dx,0
        mov     [si+12h],ax         ; store source address
        mov     [si+14h],dl         ; into descriptor

        mov     cx,len              ; store length into source
        mov     [si+10h],cx         ; and destination descriptors
        mov     [si+18h],cx

        shr     cx,1                ; convert length to words
        mov     ah,87h              ; Int 15H Fxn 87h = block move
        int     15h                 ; transfer to ROM BIOS

        mov     al,ah               ; form status in AX
```

```
        cbw

        pop     di              ; restore registers
        pop     si
        pop     bp
        ret                     ; back to caller

_putxm  endp

_TEXT   ends

        end
```

GETXM and PUTXM do all the necessary housekeeping required by the ROM BIOS, converting addresses as necessary and placing the addresses, lengths, and access right bytes into the descriptor table. Both routines return a false flag if the move was successful, or a true flag if it failed. In the latter case, the value of the flag is 1 if there was a memory parity error, 2 if an interrupt exception occurred, or 3 if extended memory could not be accessed due to a problem with the A20 address line.

Primitive Extended Memory Management

You've probably noticed the major flaw in the extended memory functions supported by the ROM BIOS: while they let you access any location in extended memory quite freely, they do not make any attempt to arbitrate between two or more programs or drivers that are using extended memory at the same time. For example, if both an application program and a RAMdisk use the ROM BIOS functions to put data in the same area of extended memory, no error is returned to either program, but the data of one or both programs may be destroyed.

Since neither IBM nor Microsoft came up with any standard scheme for the cooperative use of extended memory by DOS programs during the first few years of the PC/AT's existence, third-party software developers were left to their own devices. Eventually, almost all of them settled on one of two methods for extended memory management, which we may call the "VDISK method" and the "Int 15H method." Nearly all DOS Extenders still use one of these two methods if they find themselves running in an environment where XMS, VCPI, and DPMI are not present.

VDISK.SYS is a fairly conventional RAMdisk installable device driver that IBM has been supplying with PC-DOS since version 3.0. From the beginning, VDISK was capable of using either conventional or extended memory to create a virtual disk drive and, in the most recent versions, can make use of expanded memory as well. The source code for VDISK has always been included in the PC-DOS retail package, so it has (for better or worse) become a model for the implementation of many other companies' RAMdisks.

When VDISK is loaded, it allocates extended memory to itself from the 1-megabyte boundary, upwards, and saves information about the amount of extended memory it is using in two places: in a data structure located in conventional memory and found via the Int 19H vector, and in a data structure located in extended memory at the 1-megabyte boundary. If additional copies of VDISK are loaded (to create additional logical RAMdisk drives), they look at each of these areas to determine the amount and location of extended memory still available, then update them to reflect any additional extended memory they have reserved for their own use.

Applications which adopt the VDISK method of extended memory management merely need to inspect and update the Int 19H and extended memory indicators in the same manner as VDISK itself. Unfortunately, in actual practice, some applications update only the Int 19H area and some update only the extended memory area. This means that if you adopt the VDISK technique in your own applications, you must program very defensively and check both areas. If the two indicators differ, you must assume that the lesser amount of extended memory is available, then update both allocation signatures to be correct and consistent for any programs that are loaded after yours.

The Int 15H method of extended memory management is much less complicated. The application calls Int 15H Function 88H first to find out how much extended memory is available, then "hooks" the Int 15H vector to intercept calls by other programs. When the program sees a subsequent call to Int 15H Function 88H, it returns a reduced value that reflects the amount of extended memory it is using (passing all other Int 15H calls onward to the original owner of the interrupt vector). In this way, the program can deceive subsequently loaded applications into believing that the extended memory it is using does not exist.

In summary, the VDISK method allows extended memory to be allocated upward from the 1-megabyte boundary, and the Int 15H method allows extended memory to be allocated downward from the top. Both management methods are in common use, so you must take both into account in your own programs if you intend to use extended memory in the absence of an XMS-compatible memory manager.

The VDISK Indicators

Now we can examine the specific details of how the VDISK memory management approach works.

VDISK takes over the Int 19H vector, which normally contains the address of the ROM BIOS routine to reboot the system, and points it to an Int 19H handler within itself. This new handler does nothing more than transfer control to the original handler, so its presence does not affect the system's operation at all. However, a program can fetch the segment portion of the Int 19H vector, assume that it points to the beginning of a VDISK driver if one is loaded, and use it to determine whether a VDISK driver is, in fact, present. If a VDISK driver is loaded, its name and the address of the first free (unallocated) extended memory can be found at fixed offsets from its base.

The exact memory addresses to be inspected can be extracted from the VDISK.LST file that is included on the IBM PC-DOS distribution disks. As an example, suppose we placed the line:

```
DEVICE=VDISK.SYS /E
```

in the CONFIG.SYS file for a PC-DOS 3.3 system and rebooted. (The /E switch directs VDISK to use extended memory.) During system initialization VDISK would display a message advising that it had created a 64KB RAMdisk (the default size) on logical drive F. We then inspect the Int 19H vector, and find that it contains the address 1BF3:008EH. Figure 3-3 contains a hex dump of addresses 1BF3:0000H through 1BF3:003FH—the first 64 bytes of the VDISK driver.

Bytes 00H through 11H are the VDISK device driver header, which contains information about the driver's entry points, capabilities, and other information of interest to the MS-DOS kernel. In this example, bytes 12H through 2BH are the initial portion of a volume label that VDISK places in the root directory of its RAMDISK. As you can see, the label contains the string "VDISK," and the PC-DOS version number. Finally, bytes 2CH through 2EH contain the linear address

Figure 3-3: The first 64 bytes of the VDISK device driver for PC-DOS 3.3.

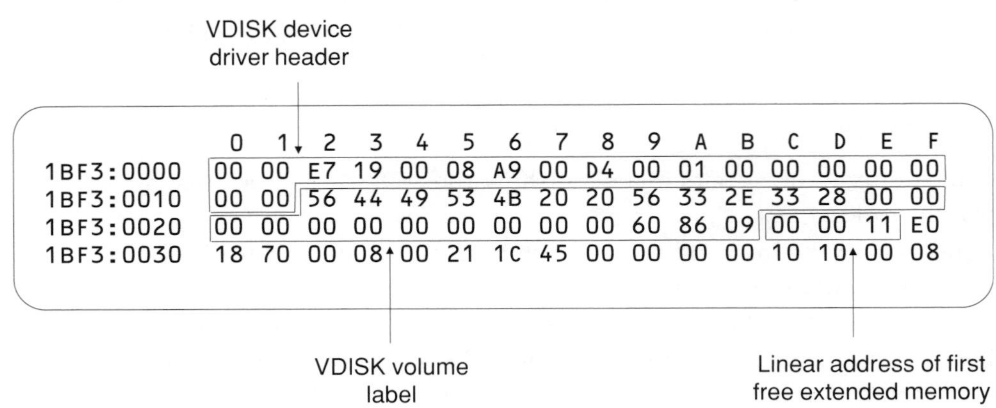

of the first free byte of extended memory: 110000H in this example (1MB + 64KB, since VDISK is using the 64KB starting at 1 megabyte).

Now let's take a look at the VDISK allocation information stored in extended memory. Figure 3-4 contains a hex dump of addresses 100000H through 10003FH, in other words, the first 64 bytes at the 1-megabyte boundary. This memory is part of the first logical sector of VDISK's RAMdisk storage, so VDISK makes it look like the boot sector of a normal MS-DOS block device. Offsets 00H-02H contain zero to show that the disk is not bootable, bytes 03H-0AH are the "OEM identity field" and contain the string "VDISK3.3," and bytes 0BH-1DH are the "BIOS Parameter Block" (BPB) from which MS-DOS can calculate the locations of the FAT, root directory, and so on.

The two bytes at offset 01EH and 1FH are the ones we are particularly interested in here. By studying the source code for VDISK, we find that these two bytes are treated as a WORD field, and contain the address of the first free extended memory in kilobytes. In this particular case, the word contains 0440H (1088), which is again 1MB (1024KB) + 64KB.

The responsibilities of a program that wants to use the VDISK method for extended memory management are now more clear. It must first find the total amount of extended memory available by calling Int 15H Function 88H (this protects it against programs that use the Int 15H management method). It must then inspect the Int 19H vector to determine whether the vector points to the base of a previously loaded VDISK driver.

If a VDISK driver is already resident, the new program must inspect the fields within the driver itself and the boot block at the 1-megabyte boundary to determine the starting address of available extended memory, using the higher of the two if they are inconsistent. It must then decide how much memory to reserve for itself, and update the two fields just mentioned to reflect that amount of allocated extended memory.

Figure 3-4: The first 64 bytes of extended memory when VDISK is loaded.

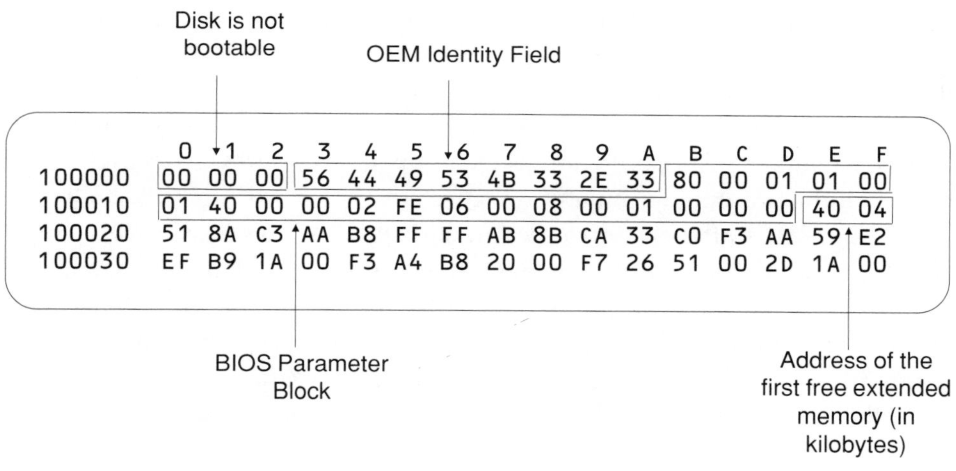

If no VDISK driver is present in the system, the program can take the easy way out and hook the Int 15H vector to use the Int 15H method of memory management. Alternatively, it can pretend that it is a VDISK, pointing the Int 19H vector to something that appears to be a VDISK driver header, and creating a phony boot block at 1 megabyte. In either case, the program must also install its own Control-C (Int 23H) and critical-error (Int 24H) handlers so that it cannot be terminated unexpectedly.

Regardless of the allocation method used, the program must be careful to exit gracefully, so that it removes all evidence of its presence, and any extended memory it used is not orphaned. If the Int 15H vector was captured, the vector must be restored to point to the previous owner; if the VDISK indicators were modified, they must be returned to their proper state to "release" the memory. This can be quite tricky if another driver or TSR has allocated some extended memory to itself after the application program in question.

The eXtended Memory Specification (XMS)

The VDISK and Int 15H management methods described have serious weaknesses. First, neither method is immune to non-cooperating applications that simply switch into protected mode, find the size of extended memory by reading and writing it directly, and then use it all without regard to other, previously loaded programs. Second, neither management technique is dynamic; both allocate memory in a first-in-last-out manner. If a program terminates out of order, that program's extended memory is not available for use by other programs until all the extended memory that was allocated afterward by other applications is also released. Finally, MS-DOS does not participate in the expanded memory management, so it cannot "clean up" a program's expanded memory resources if the program terminates unexpectedly.

During 1988 (four years after the introduction of the PC/AT), two long overdue proposals for a more sophisticated, cooperative use of extended memory under DOS appeared. One of the proposals, the Virtual Control Program Interface, is applicable only to 80386/486-based systems, and is discussed in more detail in Chapter 8. The other is the eXtended Memory Specification (XMS), which was a collaborative effort of Microsoft, Intel, AST Research, and Lotus Corp.

The XMS defines a software interface for 80286-, 80386-, and 80486-based PCs that allows real-mode application programs to use extended memory, as well as certain areas of conventional memory not ordinarily managed by MS-DOS, in a cooperative and hardware-independent manner. The XMS defines functions calls that allocate, resize, and release memory blocks of three basic types:

- upper memory blocks (UMBs) at addresses between 640KB and 1024KB (1MB)
- the so-called "high memory area" (HMA) at addresses between 1024KB and 1088KB (more about this later)
- extended memory blocks (EMBs) from addresses above 1088KB.

The XMS also provides hardware-independent control over the CPU's address line A20, which must be enabled to read or write extended memory. A summary of the XMS functions can be found in Table 3-2, and a complete description of the XMS programming interface can be found in Appendix B.

We will not mention UMBs further in this chapter, for two reasons. First, they lie below the 1 MB boundary and thus can be accessed with ordinary real-mode addressing techniques. Second, DOS 5.0 grabs all UMBs during its initialization and makes them available to applications via its normal "allocate memory block" function (Int 21H Function 48H). Thus, in a DOS 5 system, attempts by an application to allocate UMBs via the XMS interface will always fail.

Table 3-2: Summary of functions defined by the Microsoft/Intel/Lotus/AST eXtended Memory Specification (XMS).

Function	Description
Driver information	
00H	Get XMS version
High memory area management	
01H	Allocate high memory area
02H	Free high memory area
A20 line management	
03H	Global enable A20 line
04H	Global disable A20 line
05H	Local enable A20 line
06H	Local disable A20 line
07H	Query A20 line state
Extended memory block (EMB) management	
08H	Query free extended memory
09H	Allocate extended memory block
0AH	Free extended memory block
0BH	Move extended memory block
0CH	Lock extended memory block
0DH	Unlock extended memory block
0EH	Get handle information
0FH	Resize extended memory block

Upper memory block (UMB) management

10H	Allocate upper memory block
11H	Free upper memory block

Using XMS Support

An installable device driver that implements the XMS is called an eXtended Memory Manager (XMM). The prototype XMM provided by Microsoft, named HIMEM.SYS, is installed by adding a DEVICE= line to the CONFIG.SYS file, and rebooting the system. The current version of HIMEM.SYS accepts seven optional switches on the DEVICE= line that loads the driver:

- /hmamin=*n* — specifies the minimum number of kilobytes in the high memory area (HMA) that a program may use (0-63, default = 0).
- /numhandles=*n* — sets the maximum number of XMS handles that may be active at any one time (0-128, default = 32).
- /int15=xxxx — allocates xxxx kilobytes of extended memory for programs that use the Int 15H or top-down method for allocation of extended memory.
- /machine:xxxx — selects a special machine-specific A20 handler (default=1, for IBM PC/AT).
- /a20control:on | off — determines whether HIMEM.SYS will take control of the A20 line if A20 is already on when HIMEM.SYS is loaded.
- /shadowram:on | off — specifies whether HIMEM.SYS will switch off "shadow RAM" and add that RAM to its memory pool.
- /cpuclock:on | off — determines whether HIMEM.SYS will affect the clock speed of the computer; selecting /cpuclock:on will slow down HIMEM.SYS but improve accuracy of the system clock.

A program can determine whether any XMM is available by setting AX to 4300H and executing an Int 2FH. If the driver is present, the value 80H is returned in AL; if the driver is absent, AL is returned unchanged or with some other value. For example:

```
        mov   ax,4300h          ; 4300H = get install status
        int   2fh               ; call driver
        cmp   al,80h            ; status = installed?
        je    present           ; yes, driver is present
        jmp   absent            ; no, driver is absent
```

This differs from the convention used by the MS-DOS extensions PRINT, SHARE, ASSIGN, and APPEND, which are also accessed via Int 2FH (using other values in AH, of course). These return AL = FFH if they are already installed.

After a program has established that the XMS driver is available, it obtains the entry point of the driver by executing Int 2FH with AX = 4310H. The entry point is returned in registers ES:BX and must be saved in a variable:

```
xmsaddr dd    ?                 ; receives entry point
        .
        .
        .
                                ; get address of XMS
                                ; driver entry point...
        mov   ax,4310h          ; func. 43H subf. 10H
        int   2fh               ; invoke driver
        mov   word ptr xmsaddr,bx
                                ; save far pointer
        mov   word ptr xmsaddr+2,es
                                ; to entry point...
```

Once the entry point is in hand, the program enters the driver by a far call, without further resort to Int 2FH. A particular XMS function is selected by the value in AH; other parameters are passed in registers. At least 256 bytes of stack space should be available when your program requests an XMS function. The general form of the call is:

```
xmsaddr dd    ?                 ; receives entry point
        .
        .
        .
                                ; request XMS function...
        mov   ah,function       ; AH = function number
```

```
        .                       ; load other registers with
        .                       ; function-specific values
        call [xmsaddr]          ; indirect far call to driver
```

Most XMS functions return a status in register AX: 0001H if the function succeeded, or 0000H if the function failed. In the latter case, an error code is also returned in register BL with the high bit set (see Table 3-5 at the end of the chapter). Other results are also passed back in registers.

A typical program's use of an XMM to manage extended memory is shown in the following list:

1. Establish presence of the XMM using Int 2FH. If the XMM is not present, the program must determine whether it can continue without extended memory, or attempt to allocate extended memory using the VDISK or Int 15H methods described earlier in this chapter.
2. Allocate one or more extended memory blocks with XMS Function 09H. The XMM returns a handle for each allocated block. (An extended memory block handle, like a file handle, is an arbitrary number, and its value has no direct relationship to the memory block's location).
3. Copy data between conventional memory and extended memory using XMS Function 0BH. This function requires a parameter block that specifies the source and destination addresses in terms of a handle and a 32-bit offset. If a handle is nonzero, it refers to an allocated extended memory block, and the offset is from the base of that block. If the handle is zero, then conventional memory is being addressed, and the 32-bit offset position contains a far pointer in standard Intel format.
4. Before terminating, the program releases its extended memory block handle(s) with XMS Function 0AH, so that the corresponding memory can be reused by other programs.

A code skeleton for the complete process of detecting the XMS driver, obtaining its entry point, allocating extended memory, and releasing extended memory is listed below:

```
resize equ      64                      ; KB extended memory to allocate
        .
        .
```

```
        .
xmm     dd      0                         ; far pointer to XMM entry point
total   dw      0                         ; total KB ext. memory avail.
largest dw      0                         ; size of largest block in KB
handle  dw      0                         ; extended memory block handle

movpars equ     $                         ; XMS Function 0BH param block
movelen dd      0                         ; length to move in bytes
shandle dw      0                         ; source handle
soffset dd      0                         ; source offset or far pointer
dhandle dw      0                         ; destination handle
doffset dd      0                         ; dest. offset or far pointer

mybuf   db      256 dup (?)               ; contains data to be moved to
                                          ; extended memory block
bufsize equ     $-mybuf                   ; length of data to be moved

        .
        .
        .
        mov     ax,4300h                  ; check if XMM present
        int     2fh                       ; using multiplex interrupt
        cmp     al,80h                    ; status = installed?
        jne     error                     ; no, proceed

        mov     ax,4310h                  ; XMM available, request
        int     2fh                       ; entry point via multiplex
        mov     word ptr xmm,bx           ; interrupt and save it
        mov     word ptr xmm+2,es

        mov     ah,8                      ; get available extended memory
        call    xmm                       ; transfer to XMM
        mov     total,dx                  ; save total KB available
        mov     largest,ax                ; save largest free block
        cmp     dx,reqsize                ; enough memory?
        jb      error                     ; insufficient memory, jump

        mov     ah,9                      ; function 9 = allocate block
        mov     dx,reqsize                ; DX = block size desired in KB
        call    xmm                       ; transfer to XMM driver
        or      ax,ax                     ; allocation successful?
        jz      error                     ; jump if allocation failed
        mov     handle,dx                 ; save extended memory handle

                                          ; set up param block for move
```

```
                                        ; from 'mybuf' to ext. memory
        mov     shandle,0               ; zero out source handle
        mov     word ptr soffset,offset mybuf   ; source address in
        mov     word ptr soffset+2,seg mybuf    ; conventional memory
        mov     ax,handle               ; destination handle for
        mov     dhandle,ax              ; extended memory block
        mov     word ptr doffset,0      ; destination 32-bit offset
        mov     word ptr doffset+2,0    ; within extended memory block
        mov     word ptr movelen,bufsize; length of data to move
        mov     word ptr movelen+2,0

        mov     ah,0bh                  ; function 0BH = move data
        mov     si,offset movpars       ; DS:SI = param block address
        call    xmm                     ; transfer to XMM driver
        or      ax,ax                   ; any error?
        jz      error                   ; jump if error occurred

        mov     ah,0ah                  ; function 0AH = release block
        mov     dx,handle               ; DX = extended memory handle
        call    xmm                     ; transfer to XMM driver
        or      ax,ax                   ; any error?
        jz      error                   ; jump if error occurred
```

As an alternative to using XMS Function 0BH, the program can "lock" its extended memory block with XMS Function 0CH, obtaining the current physical base address of the block. The program can then use Int 15H Function 87H to move data in or out of extended memory. When the program is finished with an access to extended memory, it unlocks its block again with XMS Function 0DH, allowing the XMM to move the allocated block around in order to coalesce free blocks and satisfy other allocation requests.

Programming Example: The XMSDISK.SYS Driver

In order to demonstrate extended memory and XMS interface programming in more detail, I've included the source code for a simple XMS-aware RAMdisk (virtual disk) called XMSDISK.ASM. XMSDISK contains examples of extended memory allocation and access via the XMS interface, and is highly parallel to the EMSDISK program we already saw in Chapter 2. In order to keep the code as easy to understand as possible, I have made no attempt to optimize XMSDISK for maximum performance (e.g. by performing multisector transfers).

To assemble and link the file XMSDISK.ASM into the executable device driver XMSDISK.SYS, enter the following commands:

```
MASM XMSDISK;
LINK XMSDISK;
EXE2BIN XMSDISK.EXE XMSDISK.SYS
DEL XMSDISK.EXE
```

The Linker will display a warning message about a missing stack segment and possibly (depending on which version of the Linker you are using) a missing start address. Both of these warnings can be ignored.

To install XMSDISK, copy XMSDISK.SYS to the root directory of your boot drive, add the line:

```
DEVICE = XMSDISK.SYS  nnnK
```

to your CONFIG.SYS file, and reboot the system. Make sure that the DEVICE=XMSDISK.SYS line follows the DEVICE= line that loads your XMS-compatible memory manager (HIMEM.SYS, 386MAX.SYS, etc.). The parameter nnnK in the DEVICE=XMSDISK.SYS line is the desired size of the RAMdisk in KB. If this parameter is missing, or is larger than the amount of extended memory not already allocated by other programs, XMSDISK will use all available extended memory by default.

When XMSDISK is loaded, it will display a sign-on message, the amount of extended memory available and the amount used for the RAMdisk, and the RAMdisk drive identifier. The logical drive identifier that is assigned to XMSDISK depends on the number of block devices that are already present in the system when XMSDISK is loaded. If XMSDISK can't find an XMS-compatible memory manager, it will abort its own installation with an error message.

For example, if your system includes floppy drives A: and B: and fixed disk drive C:, has at least 1 MB of free extended memory, and an XMS-compatible memory manager is present, the following line in CONFIG.SYS will create a 1 MB RAMdisk as drive D:

```
DEVICE = XMSDISK.SYS 1024K
```

XMS Example Program

```
; XMSDISK.ASM --- XMS-aware RAMdisk device driver
; Copyright (C) 1991 Ray Duncan
;
```

```
;To build:     MASM XMSDISK;
;               LINK XMSDISK;
;               EXE2BIN XMSDISK.EXE XMSDISK.SYS
;               DEL XMSDISK.EXE
;
; To install:   copy XMSDISK.SYS to the boot disk, add
;
;                       DEVICE=XMSDISK.SYS  nnnK
;
;               to the CONFIG.SYS file.  This must follow
;               the DEVICE= line that loads the XMM (usually
;               HIMEM.SYS).  The parameter nnn is the desired
;               RAMdisk size in KB.  If nnn is missing or zero,
;               all available extended memory is used.
;
_TEXT   segment public 'CODE'

        assume  cs:_TEXT,ds:_TEXT,es:NOTHING

        org     0

maxcmd  equ     24                      ; maximum driver command code

cr      equ     0dh                     ; ASCII carriage return
lf      equ     0ah                     ; ASCII line feed
blank   equ     020h                    ; ASCII space code
tab     equ     09h                     ; ASCII tab code
eom     equ     '$'                     ; end of message indicator

secsize equ     512                     ; bytes per sector (IBM standard)
dirsize equ     256                     ; entries in root directory


request struc                           ; request packet template
len     db      ?                       ; length of request packet
unit    db      ?                       ; unit number for this request
command db      ?                       ; request packet's command code
status  dw      ?                       ; status returned by driver
       db      8 dup (?)                ; reserved area
media   db      ?                       ; media descriptor byte
address dd      ?                       ; memory address for transfer
count   dw      ?                       ; byte/sector count value
sector  dw      ?                       ; starting sector value
request ends                            ; end request packet template
```

```
header equ      $                       ; device driver header
        dd      -1                      ; link to next driver
        dw      0                       ; device attribute word
        dw      strat                   ; "Strategy" entry point
        dw      intr                    ; "Interrupt" entry point
        db      1                       ; number of units, this device
        db      7 dup (0)               ; reserved (block drivers)

rqptr   dd      ?                       ; address of request packet

savesp  dw      0                       ; save MS-DOS kernel SS:SP
savess  dw      0

xmm     dd      0                       ; address of XMM entry point
handle  dw      0                       ; handle for extended memory block
total   dw      0                       ; total extended mem available (KB)
largest dw      0                       ; largest free block available (KB)
alloc   dw      0                       ; extended memory allocated (KB)
clust   dw      0                       ; total clusters in RAMdisk

xfersec dw      0                       ; current sector for transfer
xfercnt dw      0                       ; sectors successfully transferred
xferreq dw      0                       ; number of sectors requested

array   dw      bpb                     ; array of pointers to BPBs
                                        ; for each logical unit

movpars equ     $                       ; XMS Func. 0BH parameter block
movelen dd      0                       ; length to move in bytes
shandle dw      0                       ; handle for source block
soffset dd      0                       ; source offset or far pointer
dhandle dw      0                       ; handle for destination block
doffset dd      0                       ; destination offset or far pointer

bootrec equ     $                       ; XMSDISK boot record
        jmp     $                       ; phony JMP instruction
        nop
        db      'IBM  3.3'              ; OEM identity field
                                        ; BIOS Parameter Block (BPB)
bpb     dw      secsize                 ; 0   bytes per sector
        db      2                       ; 2   sectors per cluster
```

```
        dw      1                             ; 3   reserved sectors
        db      1                             ; 5   number of FATs
        dw      dirsize                       ; 6   root directory entries
        dw      0                             ; 8   total sectors
        db      0f8h                          ; 0AH medium descriptor byte
        dw      0                             ; 0BH sectors per FAT
bootrec_len equ $-bootrec                     ; length of boot record

        even                                  ; force word alignment
        dw      128 dup (0)
stk     equ     $                             ; local stack for driver

;
; Driver 'strategy' routine; called by MS-DOS kernel with
; ES:BX pointing to driver request packet.
;
strat   proc    far                           ; driver 'strategy' routine

        mov     word ptr cs:rqptr,bx          ; save request packet address
        mov     word ptr cs:rqptr+2,es
        ret                                   ; back to MS-DOS kernel

strat   endp

;
; Driver 'interrupt' routine, called by MS-DOS kernel immediately
; after call to 'strategy' routine to process I/O request.
;
intr    proc    far

        push    ax                            ; save all registers
        push    bx
        push    cx
        push    dx
        push    ds
        push    es
        push    di
        push    si
        push    bp

        mov     ax,cs                         ; make local data addressable
        mov     ds,ax
        mov     savess,ss                     ; save DOS kernel's stack
        mov     savesp,sp
        mov     ss,ax                         ; set SS:SP to point to
        mov     sp,offset stk                 ; driver's local stack
```

```
        les     di,rqptr                ; ES:DI = request packet
        mov     bl,es:[di.command]      ; get BX = command code
        xor     bh,bh
        cmp     bx,maxcmd               ; make sure it's legal
        jle     intr1                   ; jump, function code is ok
        mov     ax,8003h                ; return 'unknown command' error
        jmp     intr2

intr1:  shl     bx,1                    ; branch to command code routine
        call    word ptr [bx+dispch]    ; must return AX = status
        les     di,rqptr                ; ES:DI = request packet again

intr2:  or      ax,0100h                ; merge 'done' bit into status
        mov     es:[di.status],ax       ; store into request packet

        mov     ss,savess               ; restore DOS kernel's stack
        mov     sp,savesp

        pop     bp                      ; restore general registers
        pop     si
        pop     di
        pop     es
        pop     ds
        pop     dx
        pop     cx
        pop     bx
        pop     ax
        ret                             ; back to kernel

intr    endp

;
; Dispatch table for device driver command codes
;
dispch  dw      init                    ;  0 = initialize driver
        dw      medchk                  ;  1 = media check on block device
        dw      bldbpb                  ;  2 = build BIOS parameter block
        dw      error                   ;  3 = I/O control read
        dw      read                    ;  4 = read from device
        dw      error                   ;  5 = non-destructive read
        dw      error                   ;  6 = return current input status
```

```
        dw      error                   ;  7 = flush device input buffers
        dw      write                   ;  8 = write to device
        dw      write                   ;  9 = write with verify
        dw      error                   ; 10 = return current output status
        dw      error                   ; 11 = flush output buffers
        dw      error                   ; 12 = I/O control write
        dw      error                   ; 13 = device open       (DOS 3.0+)
        dw      error                   ; 14 = device close      (DOS 3.0+)
        dw      error                   ; 15 = removeable media  (DOS 3.0+)
        dw      error                   ; 16 = output until busy (DOS 3.0+)
        dw      error                   ; 17 = not used
        dw      error                   ; 18 = not used
        dw      error                   ; 19 = generic IOCTL    (DOS 3.2+)
        dw      error                   ; 20 = not used
        dw      error                   ; 21 = not used
        dw      error                   ; 22 = not used
        dw      error                   ; 23 = get logical device(DOS 3.2+)
        dw      error                   ; 24 = set logical device(DOS 3.2+)

;
; Media Check routine (command code 1).  Returns code indicating
; whether medium has been changed since last access.
;
medchk  proc    near

        mov     byte ptr es:[di+14],1; return "not changed" code
        xor     ax,ax                   ; return success status
        ret

medchk  endp

;
; Build BPB routine (command code 2).  Returns pointer to valid
; BIOS Parameter Block for logical drive.
;
bldbpb  proc    near

        mov     word ptr es:[di+20],cs ; put BPB address in packet
        mov     word ptr es:[di+18],offset bpb
        xor     ax,ax                    ; return success status
        ret

bldbpb  endp
```

```
;
; Read routine (command code 4).  Transfers logical sector(s)
; from RAMdisk storage to specified address.
;
read    proc    near

        mov     ax,es:[di.sector]       ; ES:DI = request packet
        mov     xfersec,ax              ; save starting sector number
        mov     ax,es:[di.count]
        mov     xferreq,ax              ; save sectors requested
        mov     xfercnt,0               ; init sectors transferred count
        mov     ax,word ptr es:[di.address]
        mov     word ptr doffset,ax     ; requestor's buffer address
        mov     ax,word ptr es:[di.address+2]
        mov     word ptr doffset+2,ax
        mov     ax,handle               ; source handle = extended
        mov     shandle,ax              ; memory block handle
        mov     dhandle,0               ; destination handle = 0
        mov     word ptr movelen,secsize; logical sector length

read1:  mov     ax,xfercnt              ; done with all sectors yet?
        cmp     ax,xferreq
        je      read2                   ; jump if transfer completed

        mov     ax,xfersec              ; source offset =
        mul     bpb                     ; sector no. * bytes/sector
        mov     word ptr soffset,ax
        mov     word ptr soffset+2,dx

        mov     ah,0bh                  ; move this sector from
        mov     si,offset movpars       ; extended memory to requestor
        call    xmm
        or      ax,ax                   ; any error?
        jz      read4                   ; yes, abort transfer

        inc     xfersec                 ; advance sector and address
        add     word ptr doffset+2,(secsize/16)
        inc     xfercnt                 ; count sectors transferred
        jmp     read1
```

```
read2:                                  ; all sectors transferred,
        xor     ax,ax                   ; return success status

read3:  les     di,rqptr                ; get address of request packet
        mov     bx,xfercnt              ; return sectors transferred count
        mov     es:[di.count],bx
        ret

read4:  mov     ax,800bh                ; XMM error, return 'read fault'
        jmp     read3

read    endp

;
; Write (command code 8) and Write with Verify (command code 9)
; routine.  Transfers logical sector(s) from specified address
; to RAMdisk storage.
;
write   proc    near

        mov     ax,es:[di.sector]       ; ES:DI = request packet
        mov     xfersec,ax              ; save starting sector number
        mov     ax,es:[di.count]
        mov     xferreq,ax              ; save sectors requested
        mov     xfercnt,0               ; init sectors transferred count
        mov     ax,word ptr es:[di.address]
        mov     word ptr soffset,ax     ; requestor's buffer address
        mov     ax,word ptr es:[di.address+2]
        mov     word ptr soffset+2,ax
        mov     ax,handle               ; destination handle = extended
        mov     dhandle,ax              ;                     memory handle
        mov     shandle,0               ; zero out source handle
        mov     word ptr movelen,secsize; logical sector length

write1: mov     ax,xfercnt              ; done with all sectors yet?
        cmp     ax,xferreq
        je      write2                  ; jump if transfer completed

        mov     ax,xfersec              ; destination offset =
        mul     bpb                     ; sector no. * bytes/sector
        mov     word ptr doffset,ax
        mov     word ptr doffset+2,dx
```

```
        mov     ah,0bh                  ; move this sector from
        mov     si,offset movpars       ; requestor to extended memory
        call    xmm
        or      ax,ax                   ; any error?
        jz      write4                  ; yes, abort transfer

        inc     xfersec                 ; advance sector and address
        add     word ptr soffset+2,(secsize/16)
        inc     xfercnt                 ; count sectors transferred
        jmp     write1

write2:                                 ; all sectors successfully
        xor     ax,ax                   ; transferred, return ok status

write3:
        les     di,rqptr                ; get address of request packet
        mov     bx,xfercnt              ; return actual transfer count
        mov     es:[di.count],bx
        ret

write4: mov     ax,800ah                ; XMM error, return 'write fault'
        jmp     write3

write   endp

;
; Dummy routine for unsupported driver command codes
;
error   proc    near

        mov     ax,8103h                ; return 'unknown command' error
        ret

error   endp

;
; Initialization routine, called at driver load time.  Returns
; address of 'init' label to MS-DOS as start of free memory, so
; that memory occupied by 'init' and its subroutines is reclaimed.
;
init    proc    near                    ; command code 0 = initialize

        mov     ax,4300h                ; check if XMM present
        int     2fh
        cmp     al,80h                  ; status = installed?
```

```
        je      init1                   ; yes, proceed
        mov     dx,offset msg1          ; no, display error message
        jmp     init8                   ; and abort installation

init1:  mov     ax,4310h                ; XMM available, request entry
        int     2fh                     ; point and save it
        mov     word ptr xmm,bx
        mov     word ptr xmm+2,es

        mov     ah,8                    ; get available extended memory
        call    xmm                     ; transfer to XMM
        mov     total,dx                ; save total KB available
        mov     largest,ax              ; save largest free block
        cmp     largest,64              ; at least 64 KB available?
        jae     init2                   ; yes, proceed
        mov     dx,offset msg2          ; no, display error message
        jmp     init8                   ; and abort installation

init2:  les     di,rqptr                ; ES:DI = request packet
        lds     si,es:[di+18]           ; point to CONFIG.SYS line

init3:  lodsb                           ; scan for end of driver name
        cmp     al,blank
        ja      init3                   ; loop while within name
        dec     si                      ; point to delimiter and
        call    atoi                    ; convert size parameter
        push    cs                      ; make our data addressable
        pop     ds
        or      ax,ax                   ; size parameter missing?
        jz      init4                   ; yes, use all extended memory
        cmp     ax,largest              ; requested  available?
        jna     init5                   ; no, jump

init4:  mov     ax,largest              ; use all of available memory

init5:  mov     alloc,ax                ; save requested size
        mov     dx,ax                   ; DX = RAMdisk size in KB
        mov     ah,9                    ; XMS function 9 = allocate
        call    xmm                     ; transfer to XMM
        or      ax,ax                   ; allocation successful?
        jnz     init6                   ; yes, proceed
        mov     dx,offset msg3          ; no, display error message
        jmp     init8                   ; and abort installation

init6:  mov     handle,dx               ; save extended memory handle
        call    makebpb                 ; set up Bios Parameter Block
```

```
        call    format                  ; format the RAMdisk
        jnc     init7                   ; jump if no error during format
        mov     dx,offset msg4          ; formatting error, exit
        jmp     init8

init7:  les     di,rqptr                ; ES:DI = request packet
        mov     al,es:[di+22]           ; get drive code from header,
        add     al,'A'                  ; convert to ASCII for output
        mov     ident1,al
        mov     ax,total                ; convert KB available to ASCII
        mov     si,offset ident2
        mov     cx,10
        call    itoa
        mov     ax,largest              ; convert KB largest free block
        mov     si,offset ident3
        call    itoa
        mov     ax,alloc                ; convert KB allocated to ASCII
        mov     si,offset ident4
        call    itoa

        mov     dx,offset ident         ; display sign-on message
        mov     ah,9                    ; function 9 = display string
        int     21h                     ; transfer to MS-DOS

                                        ; set top of driver address
        mov     word ptr es:[di.address],offset init
        mov     word ptr es:[di.address+2],cs
        mov     byte ptr es:[di+13],1   ; indicate 1 logical unit
        mov     word ptr es:[di+20],cs  ; return address of BPB array
        mov     word ptr es:[di+18],offset array
        jmp     init9

init8:                                  ; XMSDISK initialization failed
        push    dx                      ; save specific error message
        mov     dx,offset errmsg        ; display error heading
        mov     ah,9                    ; function 9 = display string
        int     21h                     ; transfer to MS-DOS
        pop     dx                      ; display error description
        mov     ah,9                    ; function 9 = display string
        int     21h                     ; transfer to MS-DOS

        les     di,cs:rqptr             ; ES:DI=request packet
        mov     word ptr es:[di.address],0  ; driver end = start
        mov     word ptr es:[di.address+2],cs
        mov     byte ptr es:[di+13],0   ; set logical units = 0
```

```
init9:  xor     ax,ax                   ; return success status
        ret

init    endp

;
; Set up total sectors and sectors per FAT fields of BIOS Parameter
; Block according to size of RAMdisk.  Calculate and save total
; clusters (indicates whether 12-bit or 16-bit FAT will be used).
;
makebpb proc    near

        mov     ax,alloc                ; get size of allocated block
        mov     dx,1024                 ; convert KB to bytes
        mul     dx                      ; divided by bytes/sector
        div     word ptr bpb            ; gives AX = total sectors
        mov     bpb+8,ax                ; update BPB with total sectors
        xor     dx,dx                   ; sectors / (sectors/cluster)
        xor     ch,ch                   ; = total clusters
        mov     cl,byte ptr bpb+2
        div     cx
        mov     clust,ax                ; save total clusters
        cmp     ax,4086                 ; clusters  4087?
        jna     makeb1                  ; yes, jump
        shl     ax,1                    ; no, assume 16-bit FAT
        jmp     makeb2                  ; clusters * 2 = bytes/FAT

makeb1: mov     dx,ax                   ; if clusters  4087, 12-bit FAT
        add     ax,ax                   ; clusters * 1.5 = bytes/FAT
        add     ax,dx
        shr     ax,1
        jnc     makeb2
        inc     ax                      ; round bytes up if necessary

makeb2: xor     dx,dx                   ; (bytes/FAT) / (bytes/sec)
        div     word ptr bpb            ; = sectors/FAT
        or      dx,dx                   ; any remainder?
        jz      makeb3                  ; no,jump
        inc     ax                      ; round up to next sector

makeb3: mov     bpb+0bh,ax              ; update FAT size in BPB
        ret

makebpb endp

;
```

```
; Format RAMdisk.  First write zeros into all sectors of reserved
; area, FAT, and root directory.  Then copy phony boot record to
; boot sector, initialize medium ID byte at beginning of FAT, and
; place phony volume label in first sector of root directory.
;
format  proc    near

        push    ds                      ; initialize sector buffer
        pop     es                      ; to zeros so we can clear
        mov     di,offset secbuf        ; out reserved area, FAT,
        mov     cx,secsize              ; and root directory
        xor     al,al
        rep stosb

        mov     ax,bpb+6                ; no. of directory entries
        mov     cx,32                   ; * (32 bytes/entry)
        mul     cx                      ; = bytes in root directory
        div     bpb                     ; / (bytes/sector)
        or      dx,dx                   ; = sectors in root directory
        jz      fmt1
        inc     ax                      ; round up any partial sector

fmt1:   add     ax,bpb+3                ; + reserved sectors
        add     ax,bpb+0bh              ; + sectors in FAT
        mov     xferreq,ax              ; = total sectors to clear
        mov     xfercnt,0               ; initialize sector counter

                                        ; set up move parameter block
        mov     word ptr movelen,secsize; length to move
        mov     shandle,0               ; source handle and address
        mov     word ptr soffset,offset secbuf
        mov     word ptr soffset+2,cs
        mov     ax,handle               ; destination extended memory
        mov     dhandle,ax              ; block handle
        mov     word ptr doffset,0      ; initial destination offset
        mov     word ptr doffset+2,0

fmt2:   mov     ah,0bh                  ; write this sector
        mov     si,offset movpars       ; DS:SI = parameter block
        call    xmm                     ; transfer to XMM
        or      ax,ax                   ; test move status
        jnz     fmt3
        jmp     fmt5                    ; abort if move failed

fmt3:   add     word ptr doffset,secsize; increment destination address
        adc     word ptr doffset+2,0
```

```
        mov     ax,xfercnt              ; count sectors initialized
        inc     ax
        mov     xfercnt,ax
        cmp     ax,xferreq              ; done yet?
        jne     fmt2                    ; not done, write another

        mov     ax,bpb+3                ; calculate offset of first
        mul     bpb                     ; FAT sector in RAMdisk buffer
        mov     word ptr doffset,ax     ; set destination address
        mov     word ptr doffset+2,dx

        mov     al,byte ptr bpb+0ah     ; set up medium ID byte
        mov     secbuf,al               ; in first FAT sector
        mov     word ptr secbuf+1,-1    ; assume 12-bit FAT
        cmp     clust,4086              ; more than 4086 clusters?
        jna     fmt4                    ; no, jump
        mov     secbuf+3,0ffh           ; yes, use 16-bit FAT

fmt4:   mov     ah,0bh                  ; write first FAT sector
        mov     si,offset movpars
        call    xmm
        or      ax,ax                   ; test move status
        jz      fmt5                    ; abort if move failed

        mov     word ptr doffset,0      ; offset of logical sector 0
        mov     word ptr doffset+2,0
        mov     word ptr soffset,offset bootrec
        mov     word ptr movelen,bootrec_len
        mov     ah,0bh                  ; copy phony boot record
        mov     si,offset movpars       ; to logical sector 0
        call    xmm
        or      ax,ax                   ; test move status
        jz      fmt5                    ; abort if move failed

        mov     ax,bpb+0bh              ; calculate offset of first
        add     ax,bpb+3                ; root directory sector
        mul     bpb                     ; in RAMdisk buffer
        mov     word ptr doffset,ax
        mov     word ptr doffset+2,dx
        mov     word ptr soffset,offset volname
        mov     word ptr movelen,volname_len
        mov     ah,0bh                  ; copy phony volume label
        mov     si,offset movpars       ; to first directory sector
        call    xmm
        or      ax,ax                   ; test move status
        jz      fmt5                    ; abort if move failed
```

```
        clc                             ; successful format,
        ret                             ; return CY = clear

fmt5:   stc                             ; format failed,
        ret                             ; return CY = set

format  endp

;
; Convert ASCII string to 16-bit binary integer.  Overflow
; is ignored.  Conversion terminates on first illegal character.
;
; Call with:    DS:SI = address of string
;               where 'string' is in the form
;               [whitespace][sign][digits]
;
; Returns:      AX    = result
;               DS:SI = address+1 of terminator
;
atoi    proc    near                    ; ASCII to 16-bit integer

        push    bx                      ; save registers
        push    cx
        push    dx
        xor     bx,bx                   ; initialize forming answer
        xor     cx,cx                   ; initialize sign flag

atoi1:  lodsb                           ; scan off whitespace
        cmp     al,blank                ; ignore leading blanks
        je      atoi1
        cmp     al,tab                  ; ignore leading tabs
        je      atoi1

        cmp     al,'+'                  ; proceed if + sign
        je      atoi2
        cmp     al,'-'                  ; is it - sign?
        jne     atoi3                   ; no, test if numeric
        dec     cx                      ; was - sign, set flag

atoi2:  lodsb                           ; get next character

atoi3:  cmp     al,'0'                  ; is character valid?
        jb      atoi4                   ; jump if not '0' to '9'
        cmp     al,'9'
        ja      atoi4                   ; jump if not '0' to '9'
```

```
        and     ax,0fh                      ; isolate lower four bits
        xchg    bx,ax                       ; multiply answer x 10
        mov     dx,10
        mul     dx
        add     bx,ax                       ; add this digit
        jmp     atoi2                       ; convert next digit

atoi4:  mov     ax,bx                       ; result into AX
        jcxz    atoi5                       ; jump if sign flag clear
        neg     ax                          ; make result negative

atoi5:  pop     dx                          ; restore registers
        pop     cx
        pop     bx
        ret                                 ; back to caller

atoi    endp

;
; Convert 16-bit binary integer to ASCII string.
;
; Call with:    AX    = 16-bit integer
;               DS:SI = buffer to receive string,
;                       must be at least 6 bytes long
;               CX    = radix
;
; Returns:      DS:SI = address of converted string
;               AX    = length of string
;
itoa    proc    near                        ; convert binary int to ASCII

        add     si,6                        ; advance to end of buffer
        push    si                          ; and save that address
        or      ax,ax                       ; test sign of 16-bit value,
        pushf                               ; and save sign on stack
        jns     itoa1                       ; jump if value was positive
        neg     ax                          ; find absolute value

itoa1:  cwd                                 ; divide value by radix to
        div     cx                          ; extract next digit
        add     dl,'0'                      ; convert remainder to ASCII
        cmp     dl,'9'                      ; in case converting to hex
        jle     itoa2                       ; jump if in range 0-9
        add     dl,'A'-'9'-1                ; correct digit if in range A-F

itoa2:  dec     si                          ; back up through buffer
```

```
        mov     [si],dl                 ; store this character
        or      ax,ax                   ; value now zero?
        jnz     itoa1                   ; no, convert another digit
        popf                            ; original value negative?
        jns     itoa3                   ; no, jump
        dec     si                      ; yes,store sign into output
        mov     byte ptr [si],'-'

itoa3:  pop     ax                      ; calculate length of string
        sub     ax,si
        ret                             ; return to caller

itoa    endp

;
; Miscellaneous data used during initialization, then discarded.
;
ident   db      cr,lf,lf                ; sign-on message
        db      'XMSDISK Extended Memory RAMdisk'
        db      cr,lf
        db      'Copyright (C) 1991 Ray Duncan'
        db      cr,lf,lf
        db      'XMSDISK will be drive '
ident1  db      'X:',cr,lf
        db      'Extended memory available:'
ident2  db      '       KB',cr,lf
        db      'Largest free memory block:'
ident3  db      '       KB',cr,lf
        db      'Extended memory allocated:'
ident4  db      '       KB',cr,lf,lf,eom

errmsg  db      cr,lf
        db      'XMSDISK installation error:'
        db      cr,lf,eom

msg1    db      'Extended Memory Manager not found.'
        db      cr,lf,eom

msg2    db      'Insufficient extended memory available.'
        db      cr,lf,eom

msg3    db      'Extended memory allocation failed.'
        db      cr,lf,eom

msg4    db      'Unable to format RAMdisk.'
        db      cr,lf,eom
```

```
volname db      'XMSDISK    '               ; phony volume label
        db      08h                         ; volume label attribute byte
        db      10 dup (0)
        dw      0                           ; time = 00:00:00
        dw      1641h                       ; date = February 1, 1991
        db      6 dup (0)
volname_len equ $-volname

secbuf  db      secsize dup (?)             ; sector buffer for format

_TEXT   ends

        end
```

The High Memory Area

If you follow the trade press, you may remember a certain amount of publicity and claims of increased performance surrounding the release of Microsoft Windows version 2.1, which was concurrently—by a strange coincidence—renamed Windows/286. In its press releases, Microsoft stated that it had "found" an extra 64KB of memory to put Windows kernel code in, and this allowed Windows to run much faster because it drastically reduced the amount of segment swapping. This mysterious 64KB of memory, which Microsoft dubbed the "high memory area" (HMA), is actually the first 64KB of extended memory, less 16 bytes. But how was it possible for Windows/286, a real-mode program, to execute code out of extended memory?

The answer is clever, yet extremely simple. Recall the scheme by which physical addresses are generated in real mode: the contents of a segment register are shifted left four bits and added to a 16-bit offset. On an 8086/88 machine, if the result overflows the 20-bit addresses supported by the CPU, the address simply wraps; i.e., the upper bits are discarded. For example, an 8086/88 will interpret the address FFFF:FFFFH as 0000:FFEFH. Of course, 80286- and 80386/486-based PCs can support larger physical addresses (24 bits and 32 bits respectively), but this is ordinarily not apparent when MS-DOS is running, because these machines have special hardware to disable the most significant address lines in real mode, making them behave more like a classic 8086/88-based PC.

Now imagine the consequences if your program is running on an 80286-based PC and you enable the A20 line to allow the generation of 21-bit physical addresses, and then place the value FFFFH in one of the segment registers. When

FFFFH is shifted left four bits and added to a 16-bit offset, the result is in the range FFFF0H-10FFEFH. In other words, enabling the A20 line allows the first 65,520 bytes of extended memory to be addressed *without leaving real mode.*

The XMS specification bears on the discovery of the HMA in two ways. First, it provides a hardware-independent method of enabling or disabling the A20 line. This eliminates the need for programs to write directly to the ports that control the A20 line (possibly interfering with each other, especially in the case of interrupt handlers), and ensures that the toggling of the A20 line is always done in the most efficient way. Second, it arbitrates the use of the high memory area between competing programs.

The management of the high memory area is not very complex, since the HMA is so small, and it is always allocated as a unit. A device driver or TSR program that uses the HMA should store as much of its code there as possible, since the remainder will simply be lost for use by other programs. If the driver or TSR cannot exploit nearly all of the HMA, it should leave it available for use by subsequently loaded programs. The user can enforce such good behavior with the /HMAMIN switch, which causes allocation requests for the HMA to fail if they are smaller than the specified value.

Device drivers and TSRs must not leave the A20 line permanently turned on. Although it might seem difficult to believe, some applications rely on the wrapping of memory addresses at the 1-megabyte boundary, and will overwrite the HMA instead if the A20 line is left enabled. Similarly, interrupt vectors must not point directly into the HMA, since the A20 line will not necessarily be enabled at the time that the interrupt is received, so the code that comprises the interrupt handler might not be visible. If the HMA is still available when a normal application runs, the application is free to use as much or as little of the HMA as it wishes, with the following restrictions:

- Far pointers to data located in the HMA cannot be passed to MS-DOS since MS-DOS normalizes pointers in a manner that invalidates HMA addresses.
- Disk I/O directly into the HMA by any method is not recommended. The behavior of some clone disk controllers—when handed addresses that fall within the HMA—may vary.

Since the advent of DOS 5.0, the existence of the HMA has become nearly a moot issue for developers. DOS 5.0 is able to put its kernel in the HMA at boot time, and nearly every user takes advantage of this capability in order to maximize the amount of free conventional memory. Thus, it is rare indeed for an ordinary application to find the HMA available on a DOS 5 system. However, if an application is lucky enough to allocate the HMA for its own use, it must be sure to release the HMA before terminating. Otherwise, the HMA will remain allocated and unavailable to other programs until the system is restarted.

LOADALL: The Back Door to Extended Memory

There are two methods by which programs can obtain access to data in extended memory while the CPU is in real mode. The first of these methods, which relies on placing the special value FFFFH in a segment register along with manipulation of the bus's A20 address line, has already been described in the section on the *High Memory Area*. Unfortunately, this technique only provides access to the first 65,520 bytes of extended memory. The second method, which employs the 80286's undocumented LOADALL instruction, can be used to reach *any* location in extended memory.

To understand how LOADALL can provide this magical capability, we must first recall how the Intel CPUs generate physical memory addresses. In real mode, the contents of a segment register is shifted left by four bits (i.e., multiplied by 16) and added to a 16-bit offset to form a 20-bit physical address. In protected mode, an additional layer of address indirection is added. The upper 13 bits of the segment register are used as an index into a *descriptor table*—a special data structure that is manipulated by the operating system and interpreted by the hardware—and a 24-bit physical memory address is generated by combining a base address from a descriptor with a 16-bit offset.

Fortunately, while the explanation in the preceding paragraph is correct and useful in the abstract, it is not a *complete* description of how the CPU produces physical memory addresses. Imagine the penalty in CPU cycles and execution time if the CPU actually had to perform a 4-bit shift on the contents of a segment register each time a program referenced memory in real mode! Worse yet, try to envision the cost in CPU cycles and bus traffic if the CPU had to fetch a 24-bit physical address from a descriptor each time a program accessed memory in protected mode! By looking in the Intel manuals, however, we can see that the cost of a memory reference in protected mode is usually the same as in real mode (unless a segment register is also being loaded, as in the case of "far" JMPs and CALLs), which is a clue that something else must be going on.

This something else turns out to involve the existence of a set of *shadow registers* on the CPU chip called *descriptor caches*—one for each segment register. Whenever a segment register is loaded with a POP or MOV instruction, the CPU calculates (in real mode) or fetches (in protected mode) the true physical base address and length of the designated memory segment, and caches these values in the associated shadow register. Subsequently, each time the segment register is referenced by an instruction that accesses memory, the CPU simply adds the base address from the descriptor cache to the offset specified in the instruction to quickly form the final physical memory address.

The essential action of the LOADALL instruction is to initialize the contents of every CPU register and flag including the descriptor caches we have just been discussing from a 102-byte table stored in a specific format at physical memory address 00800H (see Tables 3-3 and 3-4). It seems that the original intent of the LOADALL instruction was only to aid in CPU testing, which is why it was never included in any Intel manuals. But since LOADALL allows arbitrary physical base addresses to be forced into the shadow registers, it can also be exploited by a real-mode application program to read or write memory locations that would not otherwise be addressable.

The LOADALL instruction is not supported by the Microsoft Macro Assembler, but you can include its op-code (0FH 05H) in your programs with DB statements. LOADALL must be used with great caution though. If an interrupt occurs after you execute LOADALL, but before you complete the access to extended memory, the interrupt handler may load the segment register and thus change the contents of the associated descriptor cache, and your extended memory read or write will go astray. Therefore, interrupts must be blocked throughout the execution of code that relies on LOADALL. Furthermore, the 102 bytes starting at address 00800H lie within memory controlled by MS-DOS, so you must carefully save and restore this area.

Assuming LOADALL is used cautiously, can it be used safely? That is, can we expect a program containing the LOADALL instruction to run correctly and reliably on a range of DOS versions, PC clone brands, and hardware configurations? The answer, at least on 80286-based PCs, seems to be a qualified *yes.*

Microsoft uses LOADALL in the RAMDRIVE.SYS virtual disk driver supplied with Windows and the OEM versions of MS-DOS, and also uses it in the DOS compatibility environment of OS/2, so we can predict (given Microsoft's close relationship with Intel) that LOADALL isn't likely to vanish from future steppings of Intel's 80286 chips. For the same reason, the 80286 CPUs from second sources such as AMD and Harris will be obligated to support LOADALL indefinitely.

On 80386- or 80486-based PCs, the answer is not so clear-cut. The Intel 80386 and 80486 CPUs do not support the 80286's LOADALL op-code (although they may have different, undocumented LOADALLs of their own), so execution of the 80286 LOADALL triggers an *invalid op-code* exception. In order for programs containing LOADALL to run properly, the ROM BIOS must field the exception, examine the instruction that caused the interrupt, and emulate the action of LOADALL if necessary.

Table 3-3: The data structure used by the undocumented 80286 LOADALL instruction. This structure must always be located at physical memory address 00800H, and is used to initialize all CPU registers and flags.

Memory Access	CPU Register
0800-0805H	none
0806-0807H	MSW (Machine Status Word)
0808-0815H	none
0816-0817H	TR Register (Task Register)
0818-0819H	CPU Flags Word
081A-081BH	IP Register (Instruction Pointer)
081C-081DH	LDTR Register (Local Descriptor Table Register)
081E-081FH	DS Register
0820-0821H	SS Register
0822-0823H	CS Register
0824-0825H	ES Register
0826-0827H	DI Register
0828-0829H	SI Register
082A-082BH	BP Register
082C-082DH	SP Register
082E-082FH	BX Register
0830-0831H	DX Register

Memory Access	CPU Register
0832-0833H	CX Register
0834-0835H	AX Register
0836-083BH	ES Descriptor Cache
083C-0841H	CS Descriptor Cache
0842-0847H	SS Descriptor Cache
0848-084DH	DS Descriptor Cache
084E-0853H	GDTR (Global Descriptor Table Register) Cache
0854-0859H	LDTR (Local Descriptor Table Register) Cache
085A-085FH	IDTR (Interrupt Descriptor Table Register) Cache
0860-0865H	TSS (Task State Segment) Descriptor Cache

*See Table 3-4 for the format of the fields for the descriptor cache, GDTR cache, LDTR cache, and IDTR cache.

Table 3-4: The format of the 6-byte fields in the LOADALL data structure which are used to load the CS, DS, ES, and SS descriptor caches, GDTR cache, LDTR cache, and IDTR cache.

Offset	Contents
0-2	24-bit segment base address, with least significant byte at lowest address, and most significant byte at highest address
3	Access rights byte for CS, DS, ES, and SS descriptor caches; 0 for GDTR, LDTR, and IDTR caches
4-5	16-bit segment size

Table 3-5: XMS error codes.

Value	Meaning
80H	Function not implemented
81H	VDISK device driver was detected
82H	A20 error occurred
8EH	General driver error
8FH	Unrecoverable driver error
90H	High memory area does not exist
91H	High memory area already in use
92H	DX is less than /HMAMIN= parameter
93H	High memory area not allocated
94H	A20 line still enabled

Value	Meaning
A0H	All extended memory is allocated
A1H	Extended memory handles exhausted
A2H	Invalid handle
A3H	Invalid source handle
A4H	Invalid source offset
A5H	Invalid destination handle
A6H	Invalid destination offset
A7H	Invalid length
A8H	Invalid overlap in move request
A9H	Parity error detected
AAH	Block is not locked
ABH	Block is locked
ACH	Lock count overflowed
ADH	Lock failed
B0H	Smaller UMB is available
B1H	No UMBs are available
B2H	Invalid UMB segment number

Chapter 4

16-bit Protected-Mode DOS Extenders

Andrew Schulman

MS-DOS is an operating system imprisoned by the 1-megabyte limits of Intel 80x86 real mode, yet it can be made to run protected-mode programs that break through these confines. Software that runs protected-mode programs under MS-DOS is called a *DOS extender.* A protected-mode program that runs under DOS is called a "DOS-extended" application.

The primary benefit to protected mode is that applications can *directly* access more memory. While the EMS and XMS specifications discussed in Chapters 2 and 3 also provide DOS applications with more than 640KB bytes of memory, they do so *indirectly*. For example, memory allocated via EMS or XMS cannot be directly passed to a C run-time library function. Instead, an EMS logical page must first be mapped to a physical page, and an XMS block must first be copied to conventional memory. In protected-mode DOS, by contrast, any difference between conventional and extended memory simply disappears.

As discussed in Chapter 1, there are two main forms of protected mode: 16-bit and 32-bit. This chapter shows how 16-bit protected-mode applications can be run under real-mode MS-DOS; the next chapter shows how the same thing can be done with 32-bit protected-mode applications.

There are two primary reasons to use 16-bit rather than 32-bit protected mode: first, you can continue using the same software development tools (such as 16-bit Microsoft C and Borland C++) that you currently use to produce real-mode programs, and second, the resulting 16-bit protected-mode programs can run on 80286 machines as well as on 80386 and 80486 machines. In contrast, with 32-bit protected-mode DOS extenders, you must switch to new 32-bit development tools (such as a 32-bit C compiler like Watcom C/386 or MetaWare High C), and the resulting programs cannot run on 80286 machines. On the other hand, as the next chapter shows, there are many benefits to 32-bit protected mode.

This chapter focuses almost exclusively on one 16-bit protected-mode DOS extender—286 | DOS Extender from Phar Lap Software (Cambridge, Massachusetts). Other 16-bit DOS extenders include DOS/16M from Rational Systems (Natick, Massachusetts) and OS/286 or EDU-16 from Ergo Computing (Peabody, Massachusetts). No explanation has ever been found for the high concentration of DOS extender vendors in the Boston area! A programming project in Appendix E uses Rational Systems' protected-mode C interpreter, Instant-C, which incorporates a run-time version of DOS/16M.

It should be noted that, after writing the version of this chapter for the first edition of *Extending DOS*, which focused on DOS/16M, the author went on to join Phar Lap Software and was active in the design, implementation, and documentation of 286 | DOS-Extender. In fact, several aspects of 286 | DOS-Extender were designed to make producing DOS-extended applications much easier than was possible at the time of the first edition of *Extending DOS*.

If a DOS extender is anything that runs protected-mode programs under MS-DOS, then Microsoft Windows 3.x is obviously a 16-bit DOS extender, because Windows programs (with the annoying but unimportant exception of Windows 3.0 Real mode) now run in protected mode. However, Windows differs from the normal model of a DOS extender, because, far from attempting to provide transparent access to extended memory, the Windows application program interface (API), as seen in Chapter 6, seems more like the interface to an entirely new operating system than a protected-mode extension to DOS.

In any event, the contrast between Windows on the one hand and the Massachusetts-born-and-bred DOS extenders on the other does bring out one of the major design goals of products like 286 | DOS-Extender: *transparency*. As much as possible, a DOS extender should do the right thing without forcing the programmer to rewrite code. When porting a C program to protected mode, for instance, the programmer should be able to continue using the entire C run-time library, including printf() and malloc(). Similarly, as much DOS-specific code as possible (INT 21h calls, for example) should continue working in protected mode, only better.

Since the primary benefit of a DOS extender is access to multimegabytes of memory, large programs have the most to gain from using a DOS extender. (Although programs with a small amount of code but large data requirements clearly also benefit.) Such large programs are frequently written in C, so this chapter contains a number of sample programs in C.

On the other hand, when porting to protected mode, the few thorny areas tend to be confined to a small part of the program written in assembly language (or in highly machine-specific C), so we will use examples in assembler (or C with inline assembly language) as well.

Isn't the 286 Outdated?

Because 16-bit protected mode was first introduced on the 80286, the DOS extenders to be discussed in this chapter are sometimes called "286-based" DOS extenders. In fact, the main product to be discussed here is called 286|DOS-Extender. This is quite confusing, because 16-bit DOS extenders also run on 80386 and 80486 machines. On the other hand, they will not run on 8086 or 8088 hardware, because those microprocessors do not support protected mode. Thus, the 286 designation merely indicates that the 80286 is the lowest possible, least powerful, microprocessor on which this software will run. Nonetheless, the question remains: why would someone with an 80386 or 80486 would want to develop 80286-style software?

The reason is simple: right now, if you are developing software for real-mode MS-DOS—even if every user of the software proceeds to then run it on a 80286, 80386, or even 80486—you are, in fact, producing *8088*-based software. Real-mode software is still 8088 software, no matter how fast or expensive the machine it runs on. Thus, while 286-based protected-mode software may not sound "cutting edge," it is way ahead of where much PC software is today. Without some form of protected-mode operating environment, such as Windows or a DOS extender, even the hottest 80486 can only be used as a fast 8088.

By using a 16-bit protected-mode DOS extender like 286 | DOS-Extender, you will cut yourself off from customers with XTs, but not from customers with 286-based notebook and laptop computers, nor from the vast quantities of ATs used in business. And while you don't get the wonderful benefits of 32-bit protected mode, you do, on the other hand, get to continue using your present development tools, which is not possible if you make the leap to 32-bit protected mode. Using a 16-bit protected-mode DOS extender is, in other words, a *compromise*.

In fact, with DOS extenders, compromise is the name of the game. By making a compromise between the desire to break the 640KB DOS barrier on the one hand, and the desire to stay plugged into the vast DOS marketplace on the other, with a DOS extender you, in many ways, combine the best of both worlds. You have continued access to MS-DOS (INT 21h) and BIOS services, with the ability to develop multimegabyte programs and use the native protection capabilities of the Intel microprocessors, which lie fallow in real mode.

Without protected mode, the new machines are all dressed up with nowhere to go. But without MS-DOS, there is practically no market for your software. A DOS extender neatly solves this dilemma by creating the illusion that MS-DOS is a protected-mode operating system. This is quite a useful illusion.

DOS: The Outer Limits

To demonstrate how programming for a 16-bit DOS extender differs from "normal" DOS programming, it is useful to construct a program that manipulates a large amount of data. One of the touted benefits of DOS extenders is that they break the 640KB barrier, so we need to see how difficult it is to get at this extra memory, and what special steps (if any) are involved.

With just a few lines of C code, the following small program, BIG.C, will let us explore some of the outer limits of DOS. Using absolutely normal C constructs, the program attempts to use 1 megabyte of memory, by trying to create a 512x512 two-dimensional array of longs:

```
/* BIG.C */

#include <stdlib.h>
#include <stdio.h>

#define SIZE    512
```

```
static long array[SIZE][SIZE];

main()
{
    int i, j;

    printf("Using %lu-byte array\n",
        (long) SIZE * SIZE * sizeof(long));

    for (i=0; i<SIZE; i++)
    {
        for (j=0; j<SIZE; j++)
            array[i][j] = (long) i * j;
        printf("%d\r", i);
    }

    printf("done\n");
    return 0;
}
```

BIG.C can be compiled in "large" model, using either Microsoft C:

```
C:\DOSX>cl -AL big.c
```

or Borland C++ (which also compiles C programs):

```
C:\DOSX>bcc -ml big.c
```

The first thing that happens when we try to compile, link, and run this straightforward program under MS-DOS is that the compiler complains about the size of the array. For example, with Microsoft C:

```
big.c (21) : error C2125 : 'array': allocation exceeds 64K
```

Oh, right! Already we've run into one of the fundamental limitations of 16-bit code: memory segments cannot be greater than 64KB in size. Because 2^16 is 64KB, there is an inseparable linkage between 16-bit code and 64KB maximum segment size. Sixteen-bit protected mode is *not* going to solve this for us either. (But, 32-bit protected mode solves this problem in a flash, and in fact, this is a major reason to move to 32-bit protected mode.)

Fortunately, there is an easy workaround: the huge keyword, supported by nearly all C compilers for the PC. Simply by tacking the word "huge" onto our array declaration, the compiler automatically generates code to support "huge" (that is, greater than 64KB byte) data objects, by allocating and managing multiple 64KB segments to hold them. This slows down the code somewhat, but it will let us get on with our example. If you are familiar with how slow "huge" pointer arithmetic can be, don't worry. We're just using one in BIG.C because it makes a good example; protected-mode DOS extenders don't in any way require "huge" pointers. For the sake of this example, then, we need to change the line:

```
static long array[SIZE][SIZE];
```

so that it now reads:

```
static long huge array[SIZE][SIZE];
```

With this change in place, we can recompile with Microsoft C, and see what happens. This time, the error message goes away and CL proceeds to run the Microsoft linker. LINK grinds away for a seeming eternity, tells us that it has created a temporary file, and finally emits BIG.EXE. Despite the fact that our array is initialized entirely to zeros and could therefore be packed in some way, BIG.EXE ends up 1,055,321 bytes large.

Anyhow, we've got our executable file. Now, we proceed to run it from the DOS prompt ...

```
C:\DOSX>big
```

... and the machine hangs, or the program displays black and white smiley faces (ASCII codes 1 and 2), or the program returns us to the DOS prompt without having done anything (and the machine then hangs in the middle of the next program we try to run)! What a mess!

Perhaps things will go better with Borland C++. After rebooting (or, if running under Windows 3 Enhanced mode, at least throwing away the DOS box and getting a new one), we try bcc -ml big.c . BCC compiles the program and proceeds to run Borland's Turbo linker, TLINK. Here, finally, we get some reasonable results:

```
Fatal: Relocation item exceeds 1Meg DOS limit.
```

This seems definitive. Our straightforward C program can't be run under MS-DOS.

Protected-Mode MS-DOS

Or can it?

Let's return to Microsoft C and compile with an additional command-line switch-Lp, which the Microsoft documentation says "causes the linker to create a protected-mode executable file":

```
C:\DOSX>cl -AL -Lp big.c
```

Since this switch just affects the linker, we don't even really need to recompile; we can use the existing BIG.OBJ:

```
C:\DOSX>cl -AL -Lp big.obj
```

Microsoft C and the linker grind away for a much shorter time now and produce a much smaller 6,827-byte BIG.EXE. (Your mileage may vary slightly.) It seems that when linking for protected mode, the Microsoft linker is far more intelligent about packing down static zero-initialized data. But how do we know the array is really there? Let's run Microsoft's useful EXEHDR utility (which comes with Microsoft C) and see what it can tell us about this protected-mode executable we apparently created:

```
C:\DOSX>exehdr big.exe
Microsoft (R) EXE File Header Utility  Version 2.01
Copyright (C) Microsoft Corp 1985-1990.  All rights reserved.

Module:                     big
Description:                big.exe
Data:                       NONSHARED
Initial CS:IP:              seg   1 offset 00d6
Initial SS:SP:              seg  19 offset 0000
Extra stack allocation:     0a00 bytes
DGROUP:                     seg  19
```

```
no. type address  file  mem   flags
  1 CODE 00000200 01362 01362
  2 DATA 00000000 00000 10000
  3 DATA 00000000 00000 10000
  4 DATA 00000000 00000 10000
  5 DATA 00000000 00000 10000
  6 DATA 00000000 00000 10000
  7 DATA 00000000 00000 10000
  8 DATA 00000000 00000 10000
  9 DATA 00000000 00000 10000
 10 DATA 00000000 00000 10000
 11 DATA 00000000 00000 10000
 12 DATA 00000000 00000 10000
 13 DATA 00000000 00000 10000
 14 DATA 00000000 00000 10000
 15 DATA 00000000 00000 10000
 16 DATA 00000000 00000 10000
 17 DATA 00000000 00000 10000
 18 DATA 00000000 00000 00200
 19 DATA 00001600 00491 004a0
```

Let's see, sixteen segments at 10000h bytes apiece. Yep, our 1-megabyte array is there alright. Now, let's run this baby under MS-DOS and break the 640KB barrier:

```
C:\DOSX>big
This program cannot be run in DOS mode.
```

Aargh! MS-DOS doesn't know how to run one of these protected-mode executables, even though it was generated by Microsoft's own linker!

This is where the DOS extender comes in. With Phar Lap's 286|DOS-Extender Software Development Kit (SDK), this program, produced with the Microsoft C -Lp switch, *can* be run "in DOS mode":

```
C:\DOSX>run286 big
Using 1048576-byte array
done
```

Simply by sticking "RUN286" before the name of the protected-mode program on the DOS command line, we formed a bridge between MS-DOS and the wide open spaces of protected mode.

With Borland C++, the process of producing a protected-mode DOS application is even easier, because the 286 | DOS-Extender SDK comes with a "driver" for Borland C++ called BCC286. The BCC286 driven runs BCC and TLINK, passing in all the appropriate command line options, startup code, libraries and gizmos so that, at the other end, a protected-mode executable pops out, which is ready to run from the DOS command line without your even having to explicitly type "RUN286." (RUN286.EXE still must be somewhere on the path, however, as must another file, DOSCALLS.DLL, which we'll explain later.):

```
C:\DOSX>bcc286 big.c

C:\DOSX>big
Using 1048576-byte array
done
```

Naturally, these protected-mode DOS programs are not limited to 1 megabyte of memory. The true limit for 16-bit protected mode is more like 16 megabytes (hence, the name DOS/16M, which Rational Systems uses for its DOS extender).

For example, if you have over 4 megabytes of memory on your machine, you could #define SIZE in BIG.C to 1024 and recompile to create a 1024x1024 array of longs under MS-DOS:

```
C:\DOSX>run286 big
Using 4194304-byte array
done
```

To run this program, you might not even need that much physical memory. If you are running in a DOS box under Windows 3 Enhanced mode, which provides virtual memory to protected-mode DOS applications, you may be able to create a 4-megabyte array, without having 4 megabytes of memory. BIG.EXE can access this virtual memory without any changes to the source code, and without recompiling or relinking. Virtual memory is a good example of transparency. Note too that Phar Lap's 286 | DOS-Extender, like all good DOS extenders, supports every conceivable memory-management compatibility specification, including the DOS Protected-Mode Interface (DPMI), which is why a protected-mode application such as BIG.EXE can run in a DOS box under Windows in the first place.

No More Overlays

Very large arrays such as we just used in BIG.EXE arise frequently in math and FORTRAN programs, but this may not be exactly what you have in mind when you think of a "large" DOS application.

Perhaps your DOS application simply has a lot of *code*, in the same way that BIG.EXE has a lot of data. In that case, you may currently be using *overlays*. These work okay for a while, but a program (like one well-known DOS word-processing program) can become so heavily overlaid with great features (i.e., more code) that it stutters when a user presses the page-down key.

That is usually a good time to consider using a DOS extender. In the same way that DOS extenders can load a program under MS-DOS with a megabyte or more of data, so too can they load a program with a megabyte or more of code. The editor has forbid me to include my favorite 100,000-line program in the pages of this book, however, so I won't be able to show an example. In any case, getting rid of overlays, loading awesome amounts of code under DOS, is another good reason to use a protected-mode DOS extender.

One important point to consider, though, is that something similar to an overlay may still be useful, even under the wide open skies of protected mode. Let's say your program requires 8 megabytes of memory. (This is not a joke, by the way; at least one major mathematics program—oink! oink!—uses that much memory.) Do you want to require your users to have at least 8 megabytes of extended memory?

Perhaps so, but another alternative is to use the protected-mode equivalent of overlays: dynamic link libraries (DLLs). As we will see later, 286 | DOS-Extender makes these available under MS-DOS. For now, the point is simply that gaining a multimegabyte address space under DOS does not tear down all barriers; you still must consider how much memory your end users can reasonably be expected to have. One of the problems with a DOS extender is that by providing, say, a five-fold expansion of your program's address space it can encourage companies to keep around bloated code that, in a more restrictive environment, would have to be trimmed down, rewritten, or perhaps just plain thrown away.

Big Malloc

So far, we have seen that protected-mode DOS extenders allow you to load huge arrays and large amounts of code under DOS. And we have noted that a DLL can be used as a sort of protected-mode overlay for those times when you need to load an 8-megabyte program on a machine with "only" 4 megabytes of memory. (Of course, virtual memory serves the same purpose.)

Another typical way that programs use memory, though, is *dynamically*, via a function such as malloc() in C, or, by going straight to DOS, via the Allocate Memory Block call (INT 21h AH=48h). A program may need only a small amount of memory in which to load, but then may run into roadblocks in real-mode MS-DOS, depending on the size of the documents or spreadsheets or databases that a user tries to read in or create.

We can simulate this situation with another small program, LIST.C, which creates a linked list as large as available memory. By running the program first in real mode and then in protected mode, we will get a sense of how dynamic memory allocation works:

```
/* LIST.C */

#include <stdlib.h>
#include <stdio.h>
#ifdef __BORLANDC__
#include <alloc.h>
#else
#include <malloc.h>
#endif
#include <time.h>

typedef struct node {
    struct node *next;
    unsigned long num;
    char *data;
    } NODE;

main(int argc, char *argv[])
{
    NODE *p, *q;
    time_t t1, t2;
    unsigned long nodes = 0;
    unsigned nodesize = (argc > 1) ? atoi(argv[1]) : 128;
```

```
    time(&t1);

    /* allocate linked list that consumes all available memory */
    for (q = NULL; ; q->next = p)
    {
        p = q;

        if ((q = malloc(sizeof(NODE))) == NULL)
            break;
        if ((q->data = malloc(nodesize)) == NULL)
        {
            free(q);
            break;
        }

        memset(q->data, 0, nodesize); /* touch every byte */
        *(q->data) = 'x';
        q->data[nodesize-1] = 'y';    /* show q can be dereferenced */

        q->num = nodes++;
        if ((nodes % 1000) == 0)      /* display odometer */
            printf("%lu nodes, %lu seconds, %luK bytes\r",
                nodes, time(&t2) - t1,
                nodes * (nodesize + sizeof(NODE)) >> 10L);
    }

    /* memory exhausted: display results */
    printf("%lu nodes, %lu seconds, %luK bytes\n",
        nodes, time(&t2) - t1,
        nodes * (nodesize + sizeof(NODE)) >> 10L);

    /* in reverse order, deallocate the nodes */
    for ( ; p != NULL; p = q)
    {
        q = p->next;
        if (p->num != --nodes)
            printf("list corrupt: nodes=%lu num=%lu\n", nodes, p->num);
        free(p->data);
        free(p);
    }

    /* zero nodes remaining indicates success */
    return nodes;
}
```

When we compile for real-mode DOS with large-model Microsoft C and run the resulting program on an 80386 with 2 megabytes of memory, the results are pretty much what we would expect from real mode:

```
C:\DOSX>cl -AL list.c

C:\DOSX>list
3359 nodes, 2 seconds, 459K bytes
```

That there are 2 megabytes of memory in the machine is irrelevant to this program; the program is running in real mode, so it doesn't see the extra memory. LIST could allocate additional memory if run on a machine with a good memory manager such as EMM386, QEMM, or 386MAX, but at the absolute very best it would get only 1 megabyte in real mode.

If we now take the same LIST.OBJ file produced above, relink it for protected mode, and run under 286 | DOS-Extender, the results make a lot more sense:

```
C:\DOSX>cl -AL -Lp list.obj

C:\DOSX>run286 list
10885 nodes, 28 seconds, 1488K bytes
```

We allocated a linked list that is over three times larger than in real mode, on the exact same hardware, with the same calls to malloc(), and with the same source code. In fact, we just relinked without recompiling, which indicates how similar 16-bit real-mode and 16-bit protected-mode code are. This underscores the fact that a DOS extender is meant to work with your existing setup, only better. It aims to be an unobtrusive improvement.

On the other hand, we can also see that, while the protected-mode linked list is three times larger, it also took *fourteen* times as long to allocate! If we examine the "history" displayed by LIST, we can see that this additional time occurred almost entirely toward the very end, when the C heap manager was trying to find the last few drops of available memory:

```
1000 nodes, 0 seconds, 136k bytes
2000 nodes, 1 seconds, 273k bytes
3000 nodes, 1 seconds, 410k bytes
4000 nodes, 2 seconds, 546k bytes
```

```
5000 nodes, 3 seconds, 683k bytes
6000 nodes, 3 seconds, 820k bytes
7000 nodes, 4 seconds, 957k bytes
8000 nodes, 5 seconds, 1093k bytes
9000 nodes, 7 seconds, 1230k bytes
10000 nodes, 11 seconds, 1367k bytes
10885 nodes, 28 seconds, 1488k bytes
```

However, this unfortunate thrashing at the bitter end (for the final 885 nodes, the program allocated only 7KB bytes per second!) has to do with the compiler's run-time library, not with the DOS extender. Many compilers have C heap managers that were written under the assumption that they would never have to manage more than 640KB bytes of memory. These heap managers can behave badly when suddenly confronted with large numbers of memory blocks that have to be managed.

To see that this is not an inevitable part of working with a DOS extender, we can create a protected-mode version of LIST.C using Borland C++ instead of Microsoft C. Here, the performance is sane:

```
C:\DOSX>bcc286 list.c

C:\DOSX>list
9720 nodes, 3 seconds, 1328K bytes
```

It should be noted again that all these tests were run on a machine with "only" 2 megabytes of physical memory. On a machine with more memory, naturally the protected-mode version of LIST would allocate a correspondingly larger linked list. In contrast, no matter how much memory we added to a machine, and now matter how well we fine-tuned DOS with LOADHIGH and DEVICEHIGH statements, the real-mode version would, of course, always be stuck at some size less than 1 megabyte.

With the same .OBJ as in real mode, it's obvious that no additional code has been written to access extended memory. Contrast this to DOS extensions such as EMS or XMS, which also provide access to more memory, but do so *indirectly*. As explained in Chapters 2 and 3, to allocate expanded memory with EMS or extended memory with XMS, you need to make separate calls to these memory managers. In real mode, for example, the C malloc() function cannot allocate immediately dereferenceable memory from EMS or XMS. Running in protected mode under a DOS extender, the distinctions between various sources of expanded and extended memory are all managed by the DOS extender, which provides your application with a single "pool" of memory.

And allocation is only the beginning. When *using* memory in a high-level language, you would like to employ a simple pointer dereference. But EMS requires that you map the logical page to a physical page, and XMS requires that you copy from extended to conventional memory before you can access memory allocated using these specifications.

In contrast, LIST.C freely uses expressions such as p->num, *(q->data), and q->data[nodesize-1], without knowing whether a given node happens to be located in extended or conventional memory. With a DOS extender, this distinction nearly disappears: it's all just memory.

So far, we've made major strides with zero changes to our source code. However, slightly different coding of LIST.C could have produced incompatibilities with protected mode. For example, LIST.C uses the ANSI C time() function to calculate how long memory allocations take in protected versus real mode. If, rather than call time(), we had instead peeked at low-memory BIOS location 46Ch, we would most likely (depending on how we formed the pointer) have generated a protection violation under a DOS extender. Later on, we will see why this is so, and will see how to safely peek directly at absolute physical locations in protected-mode.

Protected-mode

It should be noted that 16-bit DOS extenders are not limited to programs written in C. For example, Phar Lap's 286 | DOS-Extender also supports C++, FORTRAN, FORTH, and other languages.

C++ programs, for instance, can just as easily run under protected-mode DOS. The C++ new operator in protected-mode DOS works in exactly the same way as the C malloc() function: instead of halting at somewhere around 640KB, operator new can be used to allocate multimegabytes of memory. Other C++ constructs, such as the iostream input and output operators and static constructors and destructors, work just the way one would expect from having used C++ in real-mode DOS.

The next sample program, NEW286.CPP, dynamically allocates memory allocation like the LIST sample program, but uses a number of C++ features. The

C++ set_new_handler() function is particularly useful here, because it lets NEW286 install a handle that will automatically be called when operator new fails. This considerably simplifies the program's main loop, as shown here:

```
// NEW286.CPP

#include <stdlib.h>
#include <iostream.h>
#include <new.h>

class msg {
public:
   msg()  { cout << "hello from " << __FILE__ << "\n" ; }
   ~msg() { cout << "bye\n" ; }

static msg banner;  // test C++ static constructors, destructors

static unsigned long bytes = 0;
static unsigned long allocs = 0;
static unsigned blk_size = 10240;

void new_fail(void)     // called when new fails
{
   if (blk_size)
      blk_size >>= 1;  // try to allocate a smaller block
   else
   {  // memory exhausted
      cout << "Allocated " << bytes << " bytes\n" ;
      exit(1);
   }
}

main()
{
   char *p;

   set_new_handler(new_fail);    // install handler

   for (;;)
   {
      p = new char[blk_size];    // allocate memory
      memset(p, 0, blk_size);    // touch every byte
      *p = 'x';                  // do something, anything with
      p[blk_size-1] = 'y';       //    the allocated memory
```

```
        bytes += blk_size;
        allocs++;
        if ((allocs % 25) == 0)    // odometer
           cout << "Allocated " << bytes << " bytes\n" ;
    }
    /*NOTREACHED*/
}
```

It's not even worth showing the real-mode version this time, since by now it's pretty obvious how it will behave. To compile this C++ program for protected-mode DOS, you would use BCC286 (Microsoft C does not at this time support C++ programs):

```
C:\DOSX>bcc286 new286.cpp
```

Because 286 | DOS-Extender is compatible with the DPMI specification, this protected-mode C++ program can access virtual memory when running under Windows 3.x Enhanced mode. On a 4 MB machine, for example, about 8 MB of memory can be allocated via operator new:

```
C:\DOSX>new286
hello from new286.cpp
Allocated 8294400 bytes
bye
```

Creating the Illusion

It was noted earlier that a DOS extender creates the illusion that MS-DOS is a protected-mode operating system. We've just seen that, indeed, normal-looking C and C++ programs, started from the DOS command line, can access multi-megabytes of memory.

But *where* is the illusion being maintained? Does 286 | DOS-Extender replace your compiler, your linker, the run-time library, or DOS itself?

None of the above, really:

- Unlike a 32-bit DOS extender which, as noted earlier, requires that you switch to all new and exciting development tools, a 16-bit DOS extender can work with your existing compiler, because 16-bit protected-mode code is identical to "clean" 16-bit real-mode code; that is, to real-mode code that doesn't violate any of the rules of protected mode. The difference is almost entirely in how the processor uses segment registers to form addresses (see Chapter 1).

- Although other DOS extenders do require "postprocessing" of a linker's output, 286 | DOS-Extender works with standard, out-of-the-box linkers from Microsoft C (5.1 and higher) and Borland C++ (2.0 and higher), or with third-party linkers such as Optlink from SLR Systems. The only requirement is that the linker be capable of producing the same "segmented" executable file format as used by Windows and OS/2. This does rule out older linkers such as the "overlay" linkers once included with DOS.
- Although all DOS extenders *do* come with replacement routines for the run-time library, this is merely to make the library "clean" for protected mode, and not to provide the DOS extender's basic functionality. For example, while a DOS extender may supply a replacement version of the malloc() function, this isn't really where the DOS extender lives, as it were.
- As the name implies, a DOS extender does not replace DOS, but instead extends it. We saw earlier that RUN286.EXE runs straight from the DOS command line. Thus, when a protected-mode program runs under RUN286, DOS is still present and available. For example, all file I/O is done through DOS. The DOS extender does not know how to do file I/O, nor should it.

So where then *does* the DOS extender do its work? We can find out by using yet another memory-hungry program—DOSMEM.C. This program uses C only as a way to display its results. It allocates memory, not via a C run-time library function, but directly from MS-DOS, using inline assembly language to call the DOS Allocate Memory function (INT 21h AH=48h). To understand DOSMEM.C, you should recall that the DOS memory-allocation function has the following parameters and return value:

```
INT 21h Function 48h
Allocate Memory
Call with:
   AH = 48h
   BX = number of 16-byte paragraphs of memory
Returns:
   If successful:
```

```
      Carry flag = clear
      AX = initial segment of allocated block
   If failed:
      Carry flag = set
      AX = error code (8 = insufficient memory)
      BX = number of 16-byte paragraphs in largest available block
```

Because this function expects, in the 16-bit BX register, a count not of bytes but of 16-byte paragraphs, more than 64KB bytes can be requested at a time. This is the basis for allocating "huge" (greater than 64KB byte) memory blocks under MS-DOS. In fact, up to FFFFh paragraphs (1 megabyte) can be requested. However, real-mode DOS programmers know that a request for FFFFh paragraphs of memory can *never* succeed, so this function is often used to determine how much memory is available. If the program asks for FFFFh paragraphs, DOS fails the request and returns in the BX register the number of paragraphs that actually *are* available.

With that preface, here is DOSMEM.C:

```
/* DOSMEM.C */

#include <stdlib.h>
#include <stdio.h>
#include <dos.h>

main()
{
   unsigned segment, avail;
   char far *fp;
   _asm mov ah, 48h
   _asm mov bx, 0FFFFh
   _asm int 21h
   _asm jc error
   _asm mov segment, ax
   fp = MK_FP(segment, 0);
   *fp = 'x';  /* make sure it's genuine memory */
   printf("Allocated FFFFh paragraphs: %Fp\n", fp);
   return 0;
error:
   _asm mov avail, bx
   printf("Only %04X paragraphs available\n", avail);
   return 1;
}
```

When DOSMEM is compiled and linked for real mode, the request for FFFFh paragraphs inevitably fails, and the program displays the (much smaller) number of paragraphs actually available. For example:

```
C:\DOSX>cl dosmem.c

C:\DOSX>dosmem
Only 72F7 paragraphs available
```

This is such a standard part of DOS programming that you often lose sight of its absurdity. If there are 2 megabytes of memory in a machine, why should a request for 1 megabyte inevitably fail? And yet, anything else would strike the seasoned DOS programmer as strange.

By now, you will probably not be too surprised to hear that, running in protected mode under a DOS extender, a request for FFFFh paragraphs can easily *succeed*. In fact, you might say that this sort of strangely reasonable behavior is precisely the reason to use a DOS extender:

```
C:\DOSX>cl -Lp dosmem.c

C:\DOSX>run286 dosmem
Allocated FFFFh paragraphs: 0235:0000
```

But even if the success of a request for FFFFh paragraphs is no longer surprising, there is one aspect to DOSMEM.C that is new: we have allocated this memory with a direct low-level DOS call, rather than with a C or C++ construct. This shows that the DOS extender does its work, not through the compiler or run-time library, but much lower, *at the INT 21h level*. This is where the illusion of protected-mode DOS is created.

INT 21h is the software interrupt that programs use to procure services from MS-DOS. Files are opened, for example, by setting the processor's AH register to the value 3Dh, putting other parameters (such as a pointer to the name of the file to be opened) in other registers, and then generating a software interrupt 21h. Similarly, we just saw that memory is allocated with INT 21h AH=48h. These requests are normally serviced by MS-DOS because DOS installs a handler for INT 21h, but any program can handle an interrupt.

A DOS extender "hooks," that is, installs a handler for, INT 21h *in protected mode*. This means that any time a protected-mode application generates an INT 21h—(either through a direct INT 21h call or because it has made a run-time library call such as printf() or malloc() which in turn has made an INT 21h call) it is caught by the DOS extender. This in fact is a good definition: a DOS extender is a piece of software that provides INT 21h services in protected mode. A protected-mode program can make INT 21h calls, pass in protected-mode pointers, and get back protected-mode values. To the program, it looks, sounds, and smells as if it's running under a protected-mode version of MS-DOS.

What do we mean by protected-mode pointers? In the output of RUN286 DOSMEM above, note that the program not only indicated that it allocated a memory block of FFFFh paragraphs, but also displayed the far pointer to this block: 0235:0000.

This address looks a little strange, because paragraph 0235h seems to be too low in memory. However, in protected mode, the address 0235:0000 has nothing whatever to do with absolute memory location 02350h. Instead, 0235h is a protected-mode selector that is essentially an index into a table of segment descriptors used by the chip. As explained in Chapter 1, these descriptors in turn contain the base address, size, and protection "access rights" of the corresponding segment. Thus, memory management in protected mode is somewhat indirect, but all the indirection is managed entirely by the chip, "inside" an instruction (such as MOV AX, ES:[BX] or LDS SI, DWORD PTR [BP+6]) that involves segment registers.

A protected-mode program running under MS-DOS freely uses such protected-mode pointers whenever it (or the run-time library functions it uses) makes DOS calls for example, to perform file I/O. Even the tiny strings in the DOSMEM example are located in extended memory; ultimately, this involves an INT 21h call (using a protected-mode pointer) to write one of these strings to stdout.

It was noted earlier that a DOS extender does not, and should not, know how to do file I/O. But MS-DOS does not know how to handle data located in extended memory (above 1 megabyte), nor can it handle protected-mode pointers! So, how can INT 21h file I/O services be made available in protected mode, work with data in extended memory, and manipulate protected-mode pointers?

Quite simply, the DOS extender provides a *translation layer* for any INT 21h requests that it does not itself completely service. Whenever your protected mode program issues an INT 21h, the DOS extender catches it (because it installed an INT 21h handler), checks the function request in the AH register, and acts either as a replacement for, or as a front-end to, real-mode MS-DOS. The DOS extender can service the request itself (in the case of memory allocating or starting another protected-mode program, for example); or it can translate the request into real-mode terms (by copying data from extended memory into a conventional-memory *transfer buffer*, for example), switch the machine back into real mode, resignal the INT 21h, translate any return value into protected-mode terms, and switch the machine back into protected mode. This process is known as *reflecting* the interrupt and occurs "inside" the INT instruction without your program's knowledge. Incidentally, this is the same mechanism that protected-mode Windows uses when Windows programs need to perform file I/O.

It's important to note that actual translation is only required for INT 21h calls that involve segment registers (notably DS and ES). As noted earlier, the difference between real mode and 16-bit protected mode involves the interpretation of the segment registers. Any of the many INT 21h calls that don't involve segment registers (and, therefore, far pointers to data buffers) can be handled simply by reissuing the interrupt in real mode (that is switching to real mode, generating the interrupts, and switching back to protect mode).

By providing protected-mode surrogates for INT 21h calls, the DOS extender allows your program to think it is running under a protected-mode version of DOS. The program can call INT 21h in protected mode without worrying about the fact that its file I/O buffers are probably located in extended memory. The DOS extender's INT 21h handler invisibly takes care of all the details of transferring data between conventional memory (where real-mode DOS can get at it) and extended memory (where your protected-mode program probably allocated it). It also converts between real-mode pointers (which are all DOS understands) and protected-mode pointers (which are all your program understands).

What is the performance penalty for all this? It is hardly noticeable, except for programs that make enormous numbers of DOS calls. But programmers who are concerned with getting good performance shouldn't make lots of DOS calls anyway! For example, a program that does many reads of a small number of bytes, seeking on disk, will behave badly under a DOS extender, because the processor is being switched between real and protected mode for each DOS call. But such a program ought to be modified, even for real mode, so that it instead does a smaller number of larger reads, seeking for data in memory instead of on disk.

To summarize, a DOS extender allows MS-DOS to be called from protected mode by installing a protected mode INT 21h handler, which does roughly the following:

- puts the CPU into real mode
- performs various protected- to real-mode translations
- invokes the old real-mode INT 21h
- performs real- to protected-mode translations
- returns to protected mode

Real-mode MS-DOS thinks it is talking to a typical real-mode program, and your protected-mode program thinks MS-DOS knows how to handle its requests. The DOS extender sits in the middle, talking out of both sides of its mouth.

INT 21h Isn't Enough

To create a useful environment for PC software, however, it is not sufficient for a DOS extender merely to provide INT 21h services in protected mode. Many programs bypass DOS for everything except file I/O, memory allocation, and EXECing other programs. Since one of the goals of a DOS extender is make as much existing code as possible work without alteration, in protected mode, a realistic DOS extender must support a lot more than INT 21h.

Just as with protected-mode INT 21h, a DOS extender provides protected-modes BIOS services such as the keyboard (INT 16h) and video (INT 10h). For example, when running in protected mode under a DOS extender, the following code is perfectly fine:

```
#include <dos.h>

#define GET_VIDEO_MODE   0x0F

int video_mode(void)
{
   union REGS r;
```

```
    r.h.ah = GET_VIDEO_MODE;
    int86(0x10, &r, &r);
    return r.h.al;
}
```

The equivalent code would work equally well in inline assembler, or in a separate .ASM module, or using Borland register pseudovariables:

```
int video_mode(void) //inline assembler
{
    _asm mov ah, GET_VIDEO_MODE
    _asm int 10h
    _asm xor ah,ah
    /* two-byte quantity returned in AX */
}

int video_mode(void) //Borland C++ register psevdovariables
{
    _AH = GET_VIDEO_MODE;
    geninterrupt(0x10);
    return _AL;
}
```

Thus, the DOS extender also creates the illusion of protected-mode ROM BIOS services.

But even this is insufficient. There will always be *some* interrupt-based service that a DOS extender doesn't provide in protected mode, perhaps because it is too new, or because the DOS extender vendor wasn't aware of it, or didn't realize its importance, or was afraid of it, or whatever.

What happens when a program that has been ported to protected mode, using a DOS extender, needs to use an interrupt or function that the DOS extender *doesn't* provide in protected mode? As noted earlier, one of the key aims of a DOS extender is *transparency*; we've seen what a good job a DOS extender does in providing this transparency for protected mode DOS calls. What happens when, for one reason or another, transparency is not possible?

For example, 286 | DOS-Extender for one reason or another happens not to provide BIOS disk services (INT 13h) in protected mode. Consequently, functions such as _bios_disk() in Microsoft C and biosdisk() in Borland C++ are not supported. Does this mean that 286 | DOS-Extender programs can't make INT 13h calls?

Not at all. What it does mean is that INT 13h is only available in real mode. Since the DOS extender sits on top of an existing DOS/BIOS configuration, rather than replacing it, DOS and BIOS, plus any TSRs or device drivers you loaded, are still and available. The question then is really to what extent the DOS extender provides services for accessing all this real-mode code and data from a protected-mode program.

286 I DOS-Extender provides an extensive set of functions called the Phar Lap Application Program Interface (PHAPI), which will be discussed in detail later in this chapter. One of the PHAPI functions, DosRealIntr(), generates real-mode software interrupts from a protected-mode program. Another function, DosAllocRealSeg(), allocates a buffer in conventional memory and returns both a real-mode and a protected-mode address for it. A protected-mode program can peek and poke the buffer with the protected-mode pointer while passing the equivalent real-mode pointer to any real-mode code that needs it.

Other DOS extenders provide similar functionality. This emphasis on mixing real and protected mode is one of the features that distinguishes a DOS extender from both the OS/2 and Windows APIs. In designing both APIs, Microsoft has failed to provide adequate facilities for mixing modes, assuming that, since protected mode is so vastly superior to real mode, real mode would simply go away. The long-time DOS extender vendors are under no such illusion. Even while large numbers of applications are being ported to protected mode, the fact remains that massive numbers of PC device drivers, networks, TSRs, libraries, and so on, remain in real mode and realistically will for years. A DOS extender thus must make it easy for protected-mode programs to use this vast library of PC real-mode software.

On the other hand, it does look as though the DOS extender has here failed to provide transparency. Instead of simply generating an INT 13h AH=2 to read a sector, for example, a protected-mode program now has to call Dos-AllocRealSeg() to allocate a conventional-memory buffer, and then use DosRealIntr() to generate a real-mode INT 13h, passing in a real-mode pointer to our buffer. This is not a lot of work, but it's hardly transparent.

Here too DOS extenders provide a solution: just as the DOS extender itself hooks interrupts in protected mode, to give your program the illusion of a protected-mode DOS or protected-mode BIOS, any decent DOS extender will provide services so that you too can hook protected-mode interrupts. In

286\DOS-Extender, for instance, the PHAPI provides functions such as DosSetProtVec().

A program could use DosSetProtVec() to install its own INT 13h handler, for example. This protected-mode INT 13h handler would provide other parts of the program with the ability to simply issue INT 13h BIOS disk calls in protected mode. The handler would do all the work of calling DosRealIntr() and DosAllocRealSeg(); the rest of the program would be provided with transparent access. Even the _bios_disk() and biosdisk() functions from Microsoft C and Borland C++ would instantly start working in protected mode.

Speaking of interrupts, it probably ought to be stated quite simply that *interrupt handling is the key aspect of a DOS extender*, not only because this is how DOS programs expect to access operating-system services, but also because robust commercial applications rely heavily on proper support for Ctrl-C (INT 23h), Ctrl-Break (INT 1Bh), and Critical Error (INT 24h). Furthermore, a DOS extender must handle (and additionally provide services so that your application can handle) external hardware interrupts such as the timer tick (INT 8), keyboard (INT 9), and COM1 (INT 0Ch). Both real- and protected-mode handlers are required for these external interrupts because they arrive asynchronously without regard to whether the processor is in real mode or in protected mode.

Thus, a DOS extender is a bundle of interrupt handlers: protected-mode handlers for software interrupts issued by your application, plus real- and protected-mode handlers for external hardware interrupts.

The RUN286 Loader

But there's more to a DOS extender than simply providing interrupt handlers. In particular, how did the program get running in protected mode in the first place? Real-mode MS-DOS, in particular the DOS EXEC function (INT 21h AH=4Bh), does not know how to load and run protected-mode programs. We've seen that RUN286.EXE can run protected-mode programs from the DOS command line, but what does RUN286 actually do?

RUN286 is a *loader*. Just as the DOS EXEC function knows how to load and run real-mode DOS .EXE and .COM files, RUN286 contains code that knows how to load protected-mode executable files.

A protected-mode loader such as RUN286 is itself essentially a *real-mode* program. It can be run directly from the DOS command line and starts off running in real mode. The loader constructs several Intel-defined data structures required for protected mode—a global descriptor table (GDT), local descriptor table (LDT), and interrupt descriptor table (IDT). It then switches the machine into protected mode and loads your program. In setting up the IDT, the loader has also installed its protected-mode INT 21h handler. Whenever your program makes a DOS call, the DOS extender handles it as described earlier. When your program exits by calling the DOS termination function (INT 21h AH=4Ch), the DOS extender puts the computer back into real mode and exits back to DOS.

The preceding paragraph contains several oversimplifications, which will be cleared up later in this chapter. For now, however, the basic picture is accurate enough: a DOS extender is a mode-switcher, a loader, and a set of interrupt handlers.

A DOS extender can build the protected-mode descriptor tables when it starts up in real mode. In fact, the GDT *must* be built in real mode, which is why 286, 386, and 486 machines boot up in real mode, even though their "native" mode is protected. (Without a protected-mode environment such as a DOS extender, of course, such machines never *leave* real mode to fulfill their true destiny.) The GDT register (GDTR) and IDT register (IDTR) are each loaded with 6 bytes containing the size and base address of the corresponding table, and the LDT register (LDTR) is loaded with a selector to the LDT. For example:

```
ldgt fword ptr gdt_desc     ; load GDT
lidt fword ptr idt_desc     ; load IDT
lldt ax                     ; load LDT
```

Once there is a GDT, the computer can be put into protected mode by setting the bottom bit of the machine status word (MSW), using the following instructions (the jmp clears the instruction pipeline):

```
smsw ax                    ; store MSW
or al, 1                   ; set protect-enable (PE) bit
lmsw ax                    ; load MSW
jmp $+2                    ; clear pipeline
```

It is important to emphasize that we are talking here about what a DOS extender does, *not* what you have to do. Your DOS-extended application does not start running until the machine is already in protected mode with the descriptor tables set up and the DOS extender's interrupt handlers in place.

That's the point we have reached in this grossly oversimplified (as we will see below in the "Compatibility" section) mini-tour of DOS extender initialization. The machine is now in protected mode, and the DOS extender can load your protected-mode program.

This brings up another interesting question: what type of executable file format does a DOS extender load? The answer to this question is entirely up to the DOS extender. Until recently, all DOS extenders loaded files with a .EXP (protected-mode executable) extension, but each extender had its own format. This meant that special purpose tools were need to create and debug such ad hoc executables.

This is no longer necessary because Microsoft has defined a standard for 16-bit protected-mode executables: the segmented executable file format, used by Windows and OS/2 1.x. What makes this format important is not that it is technically any better or worse than the various DOS extender .EXP formats. Its importance is simply that almost all important development tools for the PC now understand this format. For example, the Microsoft C -Lp switch produces such files and so do newer versions of Borland TLINK.

Thus, the two most important development tools for the PC—Microsoft C and Borland C++—can *today* produce protected-mode executables. By themselves, these executables will not run under character-mode MS-DOS, but are instead intended for environments such as Windows and OS/2. But, considering the enormous number of copies sold of these two compilers, the proper role for a DOS extender today is to do whatever it takes to get these protected-mode executables running under DOS. If the Microsoft -Lp switch produces OS/2 executables, for example, then a DOS extender should load OS/2 executables under DOS. Q.E.D.

This is exactly what 286|DOS-Extender does. Rather than define yet another .EXP format, Phar Lap instead chose to support the output of the Microsoft -Lp switch. Every box of Microsoft C comes with a perfectly adequate protected-mode run-time library, startup code, linker, and debugger. These happen to be for OS/2 development, so 286|DOS-Extender loads 16-bit character-mode OS/2 executables under MS-DOS, including the OS/2 version of the compiler and protected-mode CodeView (CVP). OS/2 itself, of course, plays no part at all and is not required for developing or running protected-mode DOS applications.

With Borland C++, 286 | DOS-Extender employs some of the Borland Windows development tools, making them serve double duty for protected-mode DOS development. In addition to linking protected-mode DOS executables with TLINK, we will see later that 286 | DOS-Extender also uses Turbo Debugger for Windows (TDW), running it outside Windows or in a DOS box inside Windows as a debugger for protected-mode DOS programs.

Using the segmented-executable file format explains why we were earlier able to use Microsoft's EXEHDR utility to snoop on the contents of a 286 | DOS-Extender program. We also could have used Borland's TDUMP utility. For more information on the segmented executable file format, see Charles Petzold's article "Segmented (New) .EXE File Header Format," in Ray Duncan (ed.), *The MS-DOS Encyclopedia*, Redmond WA: Microsoft Press, 1988, pp. 1487—1497.

In addition to getting an instant supply of protected-mode compilers, libraries, linkers, and debuggers, there's another benefit to supporting the same executable file format as Windows and OS/2: *dynamic linking*. 286 | DOS-Extender consists not only of RUN286.EXE, but also of several dynamic link libraries (DLLs) for providing different plug-in APIs under MS-DOS. For example, DOSCALLS.DLL, VIOCALLS.DLL, KBDCALLS.DLL, and MOUCALLS.DLL support a large subset of the OS/2 API under DOS.

This is why the Microsoft C -Lp switch can be used so seamlessly to produce 286 | DOS-Extender applications: Microsoft thinks it is emitting an OS/2 executable, and the executable thinks it is running under OS/2, but it's not. At the same time, the program can freely make INT 21h or BIOS calls, access the hardware with IN and OUT instructions, call real-mode code, and do all sort of things that wouldn't be possible under OS/2. Essentially, one gets the benefits of OS/2 without all the DOS incompatibilities that perhaps caused OS/2 to do so poorly in the marketplace to begin with.

An additional benefit to loading OS/2-style and Windows-style executables under DOS is that their file format includes a so-called "real-mode stub." This is the portion of the executable that runs under real-mode MS-DOS. Typically, the stub is nothing more than a tiny DOS program that prints a message such as "This program cannot be run in DOS mode" or "This program requires Microsoft Windows."

However, any arbitrary real-mode program can be used as for the stub. Such a stub could even launch a DOS extender and then reinvoke the protected-mode component of the executable. This is exactly how the protected-mode executables generated by BCC286 run under real-mode DOS, rendering the DOS extender invisible.

This is also how 286 | DOS-Extender applications are prepared for end users. Like most DOS extenders, 286 | DOS-Extender requires a run-time license agreement before applications can be distributed to end users, because you are distributing not only your DOS-extended application but the DOS extender itself. The Phar Lap Run Time Kit (RTK) comes with a utility, BIND286, which can embed a complete copy of the DOS extender as the real-mode stub of your protected-mode executable.

Compatibility

So far, writing a DOS extender sounds like it would be fairly simple: you dig out the Intel documentation, set up some descriptor tables, code up some interrupt handlers, switch into protected mode, load a program, jump to its CS:IP entry point, and handle its software interrupts. When done, you switch back to real mode and exit to DOS.

This is all well and good, but what if the DOS extender is not started under plain-vanilla MS-DOS? What if a user wants to a run a DOS-extended application under Windows Enhanced mode, or on a machine running a 386-based expanded memory manager such as EMM386, QEMM, or 386MAX? What if the user has DOS 5 with the XMS memory manager HIMEM.SYS installed? What if VDISK or another disk cache is running, already using some extended memory?

There are many different solutions available to the memory-management problems of DOS, described elsewhere in this book, and a user may be employing several of them. A DOS extender, therefore, needs to be a "team player" rather than a star. A user shouldn't have to edit CONFIG.SYS and reboot, or even get out of Windows, to use your DOS-extended application; similarly you shouldn't have to edit CONFIG.SYS and reboot to develop the program.

Thus, there is another aspect to a DOS extender—compatibility—which tends to undermine some of what was said before about how a DOS extender sets up descriptor tables, switches into protected mode, and so on. In addition, the earlier discussion of DOS extender initialization didn't take on the question of how extended memory is allocated, but it implied that the DOS extender just *uses* it, (probably with the INT 15h calls described in Chapter 2 of this book in the section on "The ROM BIOS Extended Memory Functions").

That's fine if the DOS extender is starting on a "raw," plain-vanilla DOS machine, with no memory-management or multitasking software in use. But fewer and fewer machines today fit that category. At the very least, it seems likely that either HIMEM.SYS or an expanded memory manager will be present when a DOS extender starts. If a DOS extender simply came along and tried to set up its own descriptor tables, grab extended memory, and switch into protected mode, the result would be a mess. At the very best, the DOS extender would see that it couldn't initialize, and the user would be unable to run his/her program without removing the other software. This would be unacceptable.

What is required, then, is some sort of standard that a DOS extender can use to cooperate with memory managers and multitaskers. The two key standards, discussed elsewhere in this book, are the Virtual Control Program Interface (VCPI) and the DOS Protected Mode Interface (DPMI). Such standards are mostly of concern to DOS extenders themselves, not to DOS-extended applications. For developers and users of DOS-extended applications, all that should matter is whether a given DOS extender supports these standards.

What does it mean for a DOS extender to "support" a standard such as VCPI or DPMI?

- At startup, a DOS extender must find out if DPMI is available, using the INT 2Fh AX=1687h call described in Chapter 9. If DPMI is available, the DOS extender must use the appropriate DPMI services rather than use its own code for setting up descriptor tables, switching into protected mode, and so on. For example, instead of executing the series of instructions shown earlier for setting the PE bit in the MSW, the DOS extender would call the DPMI "real to protected mode switch entry point." The DOS extender would similarly use DPMI services for allocating memory, installing interrupt handlers, working with descriptors, and so on.

  Phar Lap's 286 | DOS-Extender consists internally of two components known to its creators as Mr. Ed and Wilbur. Mr. Ed contains all the code that would be used if DPMI is *not* present, and Mr. Ed presents Wilbur with a DPMI-like interface. Thus, Wilbur remains unchanged regardless of whether DPMI is present, and the Mr. Ed code is not loaded if DPMI is present.

- If DPMI is not present, the DOS extender must then see if VCPI is present, using the INT 67h AX=DE00h call described in Chapter 8. If VCPI (and, in most cases, DPMI) is present, the machine is not even in real mode, but in virtual-8086 (V86) mode. Because virtual-8086 mode is a sort of 1-megabyte protected mode, setting the PE bit would not put the machine into protected mode for the simple reason that the PE bit is *already* set. That is, when a user has a program such as EMM386, QEMM, or 386MAX installed, the machine is effectively *already in* protected mode! Here, then, the DOS extender would use the VCPI mode-toggling function, INT 67h AX=DE0Ch, to switch between V86 and protected mode. The DOS extender would similarly use VCPI services for allocating memory.
- If neither DPMI nor VCPI are present, the DOS extender must call INT 2Fh AX=4300h to see if an XMS memory manager, such as HIMEM.SYS, is present. As explained in Chapter 3, XMS provides functions for allocating extended memory (referred to as EMBs) and managing the processor's A20 line. A DOS extender running alongside an XMS driver must use the XMS driver's services rather than its own code for these things. XMS does not, however, provide mode-switching functions, so the DOS extender uses its own code for such functions.
- Finally, if there is a program installed that uses the VDISK or INT 15h methods to manage extended memory, the DOS extender plays by the VDISK or INT 15h rules, such as they are.

The end result of all this checking and use of other programs' services is that DOS-extended applications can run in a wide variety of configurations. If a DOS extender supports DPMI, applications that use this DOS extender can run under Windows 3.0 Enhanced mode (see Figure 4-1) or even under OS/2 2.0; if a DOS extender supports VCPI, applications that use this DOS extender can run alongside an expanded-memory manager such as EMM386, QEMM, or 386MAX. It is important to emphasize that all the code needed to work with these different standards is contained inside the DOS extender, not inside the DOS-extended applications. The DOS extender, as always, presents its applications with a clean, uncluttered view of protected-mode MS-DOS.

Figure 4-1: Two copies of a protected-mode DOS application running under Microsoft Windows Enhanced mode.

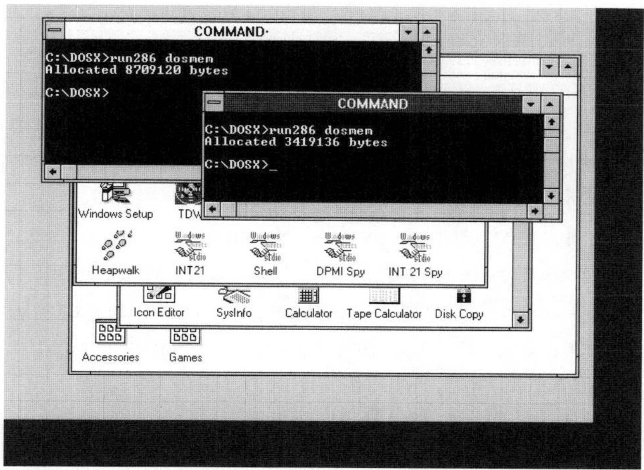

Debugging with CVP and TDW under DOS

We now have a protected-mode program that can be run straight from the DOS command line, which is compatible with the widest possible variety of DOS memory-management software.

Now, how do we *debug* one of these things?

In the rush to get protected-mode programs running under DOS, the question of debugger support is, unfortunately, sometimes overlooked. But this question really is quite important if a DOS extender is to truly provide applications with an environment that, aside from the presence of multimegabytes of memory, looks completely "normal."

Obviously, we can't use a real-mode debugger with our protected-mode program, so we'll need a protected-mode debugger. What is a protected-mode debugger, though? For example, Borland C++ comes with TD286, where the debugger itself runs in protected mode to leave more conventional memory free for the application being debugged. However, to paraphrase Charlie the Tuna, we're not looking for debuggers that run in protected mode; we're looking for debuggers that can run protected-mode programs.

Because most DOS extenders have their own proprietary executable file format, a debugger must understand this format. The responsibility for creating debuggers then usually rests on the shoulders of the company that makes the DOS extender. In some cases, such as Rational Systems' "D" source-level debugger (discussed in the first edition of *Extending DOS*), the results are excellent. In other cases, DOS extenders fail to provide any sort of source-level debugging at all, forcing developers to debug their protected-mode application in assembly language with some sort of SYMDEB clone.

Even when a company does have the expertise to build its own great protected-mode DOS source-level debugger, it isn't always what a developer wants. Frequently, users of Microsoft C or Borland C++ want to continue running the same debugger for protected-mode DOS that they ran in real mode. In Microsoft C, this means CodeView (CV), and in Borland C++, it is Turbo Debugger (TD).

Because Microsoft and Borland *already make* versions of their debuggers that can load and run protected-mode programs, the solution seems obvious: the DOS extender should use these for debugging. But protected-mode CodeView (CVP) is actually an OS/2 program, and Turbo Debugger for Windows (TDW) is a Windows program.

This is where the greatest benefit comes from using the standard, segmented-executable file format. 286 | DOS-Extender, because it uses the same format used by Windows and OS/2, can load both CVP and TDW under character-mode DOS, running them as debuggers for protected-mode DOS applications. Because CVP is a multithreaded application, 286 | DOS-Extender must supply DLLs that support, under DOS, OS/2 functions such as DosCreateThread(), DosEnterCritSec(), and DosSemWait(). Naturally, 286 | DOS-Extender must also supply an MS-DOS version of the OS/2 debugging function DosPTrace(), on which CVP is based.

Similarly, to support TDW, 286 | DOS-Extender must supply protected-mode DOS versions of the Windows DLLs (KERNEL.DLL, USER.DLL, WINDEBUG.DLL, and WIN87EM.DLL) that supply functions used by TDW such as WinExec(), GlobalAlloc(), and the undocumented WinDebug() and SetEventHook() calls.

Having made the typical engineer's mistake of putting the cart before the horse, by describing how 286 | DOS-Extender is able to run CVP and TDW under DOS—before explaining how a developer *uses* them—it is now time to describe how to use these debuggers with 286 | DOS-Extender. To prepare a protected-mode DOS application for source-level debugging, you use exactly the same command-line switches as when you prepare to debug a real-mode application. To debug, you simply start the debugger under 286 | DOS-Extender. For example, with Microsoft C, you compile with the bizarrely non-mnemonic -Zi switch:

```
C:\DOSX>cl -Lp -AL -Zi list.c

C:\DOSX>run286 \c600\binp\cvp list
```

Likewise, with Borland C++, you use the -v switch:

```
C:\DOSX>bcc286 -v new286.cpp

C:\DOSX>run286 \borlandc\bin\tdw new286
```

In addition, because many people find Turbo Debugger vastly superior to CodeView, yet want to use the Microsoft C optimizing compiler, they can use Borland's TDCONVRT program to convert protected-mode Microsoft C programs for use with TDW:

```
C:\DOSX>cl -Lp -AL -Zi list.c

C:\DOSX>\borlandc\bin\tdconvrt -c list.c

C:\DOSX>run286 \borlandc\bin\tdw list
```

As the screen shots in Figures 4-2 and 4-3 show, these versions of CodeView and Turbo Debugger look exactly like the versions a Microsoft C or Borland C++ user would be accustomed to from real mode.

One difference between protected-mode and real-mode debugging is that if a protected-mode program contains a bug that violates the rules of protected mode, the debugger catches the protection violation, displays a message, and lands you right on the offending line of code. If the bug is nested deeply inside many function calls, you can generally use the debugger's stack walkback to see how your program got there.

One serious problem with using CVP and TDW for protected-mode DOS debugging, however, is that neither debugger knows about mixing real-and protected-mode code, installing mixed-mode interrupt handlers, or any of the other groovy low-level capabilities that are typically provided by a DOS extender, but which were left out of the OS/2 and Windows APIs. Likewise, neither debugger provides access to the protected-mode descriptor tables, which you occasionally want when debugging protected-mode DOS programs.

Figure 4-2: Debugging a protected-mode DOS application with Microsoft Code View (CVP).

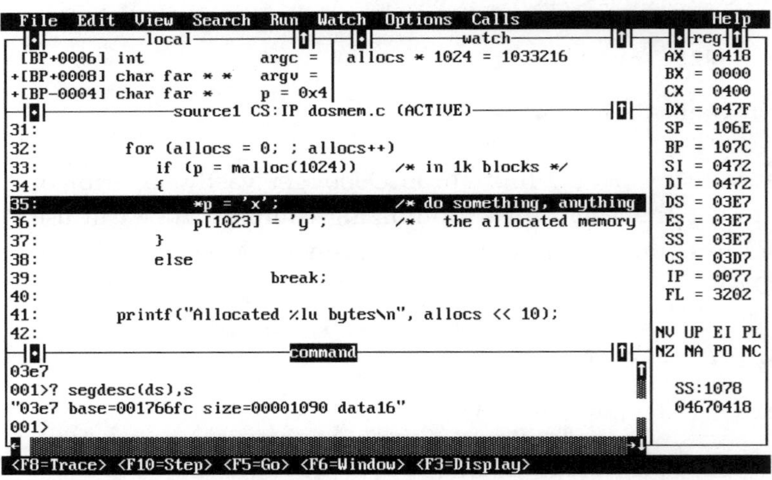

Fortunately, the debuggers can themselves be extended in various ways. For example, CodeView has a feature that makes the debugger moderately extensible. As noted in the *Microsoft C Advanced Programming Techniques* manual, any C function in your program can be called from the CVP Command window (the > prompt) or the Watch window (accessed with the Watch Add... menu), using the following syntax:

```
? function(args)
```

Figure 4-3: Debugging a protected-mode DOS application, written in C++, with Turbo Debugger (TDW).

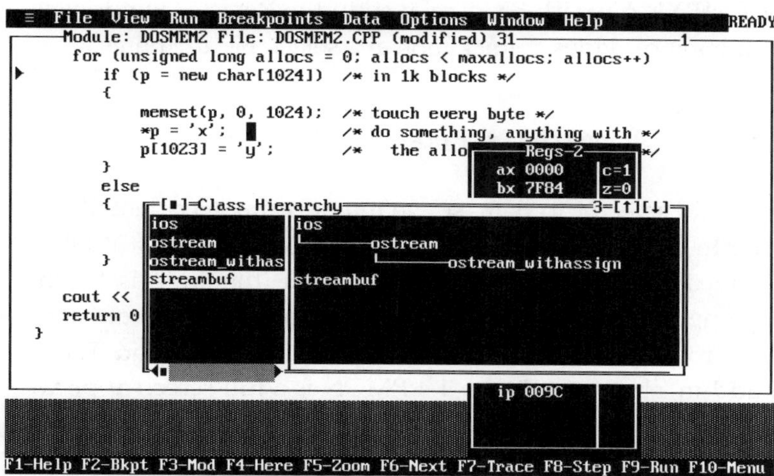

The function does not even have to be called by your program to be available for evaluation. Since any function can be evaluated, you can simply include a debugging .OBJ in your executable and call the functions from CVP. The 286 | DOS-Extender SDK includes a small file, D.C, which can be used to enhance debugging with functions such as:

```
typedef unsigned short SEL;
typedef unsigned long ULONG;
void far *protvec(int intno);   // return protected-mode interrupt vector
void far *realvec(int intno);   // return real-mode interrupt vector
char far *segdesc(SEL sel);     // return string representation of descriptor
SEL maprealseg(unsigned mpara, ULONG size);  // access real-mode memory
unsigned loadmod(char far *modname);  // load a DLL
void far *procaddr(unsigned modhand, char far *funcname); // link to a function
```

For example, in the case of a protection violation, you most want to know whether a selector is, valid and, if it is, how big its corresponding segment is, and whether the segment is code or data. By finding this out, you can tell if your code violated protection with a completely bogus pointer, or because the offset was off-by-one, or because you are accidentally trying to overwrite code, or whatever.

Let us pretend a program has GP faulted, and CVP has placed the cursor on the line of code MOV ES:[BX], AX with BX displayed in the Register window as 1400h. The segdesc() function provides a quick look at a selector's attributes:

```
? segdesc(es),s
"0397 base=0017C97A size=00001400 data16"
```

Clearly, ES holds a valid selector to data, so we're not trying (accidentally or intentionally) to overwrite code. However, we are trying to write into a WORD PTR (2 bytes) at offset 1400h, and the last valid BYTE offset (the limit) is 1400h. Thus, the code is off-by-one, trying to write a WORD when only a BYTE remains.

286 | DOS-Extender provides an even better way to extend CVP and TDW: the PMON debugger add-in, shown in Figure 4-4 PMON is a full-screen application, which can be used with CVP and TDW to provide the following functions not present in CVP or TDW but useful during debugging:

- Display the LDT
- Display the GDT
- Display interrupt vectors
- Display exception vectors
- Get the address of a DLL function
- Translate an address to the name of a DLL function

After starting PMON and the debugger with a "command line from hell" such as:

```
C:\DOSX>run286 \run286\bin\pmon \c600\binp\cvp list
```

you can, at any time, switch from CVP to PMON by hitting the hot key CTRL-ALT-BACKSPACE. Interestingly, this "hot key" is not unique to PMON. 286 | DOS-Extender supports "sessions" or "screen groups" (a concept borrowed from OS/2) in which multiple programs can run, each in its own screen group. The hot key CTRL-ALT-BACKSPACE switches between sessions.

Figure 4-4: The Global Description Table (GDT) window in Phar Lap's protected-mode monitor (PMON) debugger.

```
PMON: Protected Mode Monitor 1.3   Copyright (C) 1991 Phar Lap Software, Inc.

GDT Sel #0000 - Not Present
GDT Sel #0008 - CODE Base=00042290 Limit=0FFFF DPL=0 U16 Byte ER NC ACC
GDT Sel #0010 - DATA Base=00045340 Limit=0FFFF DPL=0 U16 Byte RW EU ACC
GDT Sel #0018 - DATA Base=00047960 Limit=0FFFF DPL=0 U16 Byte RW EU
GDT Sel #0020 - LDT Base=00110000 Limit=00FFF
GDT Sel #0028 - DATA Base=00110000 Limit=00FFF DPL=0 U16 Byte RW EU ACC
GDT Sel #0030 - DATA Base=000453E6 Limit=007FF DPL=0 U16 Byte RW EU
GDT Sel #0038 - DATA Base=00045C16 Limit=00187 DPL=0 U16 Byte RW EU
GDT Sel #0040 - DATA Base=00000400 Limit=0FFFF DPL=3 U16 Byte RW EU
GDT Sel #0048 - DATA Base=00000000 Limit=0FFFF DPL=0 U16 Byte RW EU
GDT Sel #0050 - 286TSS Base=00045BEA Limit=0002B DPL=0 BUSY
GDT Sel #0058 - DATA Base=00045BEA Limit=0002B DPL=0 U16 Byte RW EU
GDT Sel #0060 - DATA Base=0009EEF0 Limit=0FFFF DPL=0 U16 Byte RW EU ACC
GDT Sel #0068 - DATA Base=0009F1F0 Limit=0FFFF DPL=0 U16 Byte RW EU ACC
GDT Sel #0070 - DATA Base=0009F4F0 Limit=0FFFF DPL=0 U16 Byte RW EU
GDT Sel #0078 - DATA Base=0009F7F0 Limit=0FFFF DPL=0 U16 Byte RW EU
GDT Sel #0080 - DATA Base=00000000 Limit=0FFFF DPL=0 U16 Byte RW EU
```

Isn't There Any Work Involved?

At this point, it should be clear that most real-mode DOS code will work, *as is*, under a 16-bit DOS extender. In the case of 286 | DOS-Extender, all you need to do is add the -Lp switch to your Microsoft C command lines, or use BCC286 instead of BCC in your Borland C++ makefiles, and you're on your way.

The best way to port a DOS program to a 16-bit DOS extender is (in the words of a well-known footwear advertisement) to "just do it." Construct a new batch file or makefile, recompile or relink your program, and *see if it runs*.

At this point, the typical software engineer wants to know, "Where's the work?"

The likelihood is that such a simply ported program will actually run for a while, but will eventually break one of protected mode's rules and terminate with a protection violation or *GP fault*, similar to an "unexpected application error" (UAE) in Windows. We saw what this looks like when running CVP or TDW. Here's what a GP fault looks like in 286 | DOS-Extender, when not running a debugger:

```
C:\DOSX>run286 phoobar
Fatal error 286.3330: General protection fault detected.
PID=0001  TID=0001  SID=0001  ERRORCODE=0000
AX=0000  BX=0000  CX=0400  DX=0000  SI=0384  DI=0384  BP=0E8C
CS:IP=022F:00BC   DS=024F  ES=0000  SS:SP=024F:0E82   FLAGS=3206
```

The message "General protection fault detected" is an indication that your program has, in some way, violated the rules of protected mode. This does not necessarily mean a bug in your program, but it does point to something that will have to be changed to work in protected mode. The CPU signals a GP fault when your program tries to violate protection. (This is why it's called protected mode!) Thus, protected mode is a superb environment for software development: the hardware will help you find bugs and trouble spots.

It is, however, important to understand what types of errors protection mode *won't* catch. All protection in 16-bit protected mode is essentially at a *segment* level, so the processor won't catch any misuse of memory *within* a segment. For example, the C malloc() function suballocates multiple blocks of memory out of a single segment; if your code oversteps the bounds of one malloc block into another, the processor cannot view this as an error. Furthermore, the processor does not know about such C constructs as the const keyword.

The rules of 16-bit protected mode, then, protect segments (32-bit protected mode does have page-level protection, with finer granularity). These rules prevent writing into code segments, executing data segments (Don't worry—we'll see how to execute data in a few minutes!), reading or writing past the end of a segment (that is, the example we used earlier in the discussion of debugging), or using a segment that doesn't belong to you. More specifically, the rules are

- Don't peek or poke memory not owned by your program.
  Example: *((unsigned long far *) 0x46C)
- Don't turn absolute memory addresses into segment:offset addresses.
  Example: *((unsigned char far *) 0xB8000000L)
- Don't execute data, or modify code.
  Example: See the source code for most compilers' implementations of the int86x() function.
- Don't move data into code segments.
  Example: MOV CS:foo, AX

- Don't misuse segment registers.
  Example: Using ES as a scratchpad register.
- Don't perform real-mode address arithmetic
  Example: Pointer normalization.
- Don't peek or poke past the end of a segment.
  Example: *((int *) 0xFFFF)
- Don't write into read-only segments, and don't read execute-only segments.
- Don't dereference NULL pointers.
  Example: *((int far *) 0L)
- Don't dereference bogus pointers.
  Example: *((int far *) MK_FP(rand(), rand()))

In general, there are three circumstances in which programs might violate one or more of these rules:

- The program contains an outright bug that somehow went undetected in real mode.
  Example: dereferencing a bogus pointer to yield a value that is never used, or that is a "don't care" item. In protected mode, the simple act of dereferencing a bogus pointer, even if the resulting value doesn't matter, causes a GP fault.
- The program implicitly relies on an aspect of real mode that is not present in protected mode.
  Example: accessing well-known memory locations, such as the BIOS data area or video display memory, by turning the memory location (such as 46Ch) into a segment:offset far pointer (such as 0040:006CH).) In protected mode, there is no equivalence between absolute memory locations and segment:offset pointers. To access memory locations outside your program, you must first "map" them into your program's address space. This is described in more detail below.
- The program uses services that the DOS extender does not transparently provide in protected mode.
  Example: Calling undocumented DOS functions. While all DOS extenders provide INT 21h in protected mode (as noted earlier, that's essentially the

definition of a DOS extender), few of them support undocumented DOS functions (such as INT 21h AH=52h) in protected mode. Calling unsupported functions from protected mode generally won't immediately cause a GP fault, but the call will return incorrect results that will eventually cause a GP fault. To call such functions from a DOS extender, you must drop down into real mode to generate a *real-mode* interrupt. This is also described in more detail below.

In the remainder of this chapter, we will examine the code changes that might be required or desirable when porting real-mode DOS code to a DOS extender (code ported from non-Intel architectures will, somewhat ironically, probably require even fewer changes). The key areas of change are:

- Outright bugs: fix them!
- Executing data or self-modifying code: eliminate, or use aliases.
- Address arithmetic: eliminate or use "huge" arithmetic.
- Peeking/poke real-mode addresses: first map them in.
- Calling unsupported interrupts or functions: call them from real mode.
- File I/O performance problems: do disk reads and writes in larger blocks
- Handling Ctrl-C, Ctrl-Break, Critical Error interrupts: pass them up to protected mode.
- Dealing with GP faults: use exception handling.

Bugs!

There is an almost magical quality to real mode: since practically nothing is illegal, almost any operation does *something*, and consequently, many things work even though they ought not to. Take the following program as an example:

```
/* BAD.C */

main()
{
   int far *fp;
   *fp = 666;
}
```

In real mode, this program executes without complaint:

```
C:\TEST>cl bad.c

C:\TEST>bad
```

The problem, of course, is that BAD never initializes the far pointer fp; we have no idea where it's pointing! The equivalent assembly-language code looks like this:

```
        ; space reserved for fp at [bp-4]
        ;    but not initialized
0019    les bx, dword ptr [bp-4]
001C    mov word ptr es:[bx], 666
```

In real mode, this code pokes the beastly value 666 into a *random* location in memory. This program might run one million times before causing a problem, and the problem might manifest itself hours after BAD itself has been run.

When BAD is relinked for protected mode, the results are quite different:

```
C:\TEST>cl -Lp bad.c

C:\TEST>run286 bad
Fatal error 286.3330: General protection fault detected.
PID=0001  TID=0001  SID=0001  ERRORCODE=0018
AX=0004  BX=0BDE  CX=0019  DX=008B  SI=00DA  DI=00DA  BP=0BE2
CS:IP=0205:0019   DS=020D  ES=020D  SS:SP=020D:0BDE   FLAGS=0206
```

Here, the attempt to load a bogus value into the ES register causes an immediate GP fault, because in protected mode, you are not allowed to load random values into segment registers. Quite simply, fewer operations are legal; you can do *less* in protected mode than you can in real mode. This is a case where limitations and restrictions are good; they help by hindering.

Of course, no one would write a BAD program. But it's quite likely that any sizeable program developed for the PC in real mode, and never ported to protected mode or to a machine with a non-Intel processor, will contain code like this. For example, Borland's venerable TCALC demonstration spreadsheet program, included with Turbo C/C++ and with Borland C++, contains, in TCUTIL.C, the following function:

```
void updateoflags(int col, int row, int display)
/* Starting in col, moves back to the last TEXT cell
   and updates all flags */
{
   while ((cell[col][row] == NULL) && (col-- > 0));
   if ((cell[col][row] != NULL) &&
       (cell[col][row]->attrib == TEXT) &&
       (col >= 0))
         setoflags(col, row, display);
}
```

Notice the order in which the tests are performed: the test of whether a column number is valid (col >= 0) comes *after* col has already been used as an array index. In real mode, if col <= 0, this picks up garbage from memory (and then does nothing with it). In protected mode, attempting to access the cell array with an invalid index can cause a GP fault, which seems preferable to the free-and-easy methods of real mode. The code should be changed so that it tests for (col >= 0) *first*.

This is one type of change you might need to make to your code before it will run under a protected-mode DOS extender. The GP fault mechanism will gladly locate all such spots in your program. (This is how the bug in TCALC was found.)

Real-Mode Practices

DOS software often implicitly relies on two aspects of real mode: the ability to write data in a code segment, and the ability for address offsets to "roll over" into address segments. Both practices are illegal in protected mode. However, because both practices are sometimes used for good reason, DOS extenders do provide equivalent functionality in a way that does not violate protection.

Impure Code

Protected mode forbids writing into a code segment. Normally, this is a wonderful feature, because it prevents overwriting-code bugs. Furthermore, making sure that a code segment contains only executable code (pure code) allows it to be shared by tasks in a multitasking environment and to be discarded rather than swapped in a virtual-memory environment.

But what if a program *deliberately* stores data in a code segment?

It seems that almost any .ASM file you pick up will contain at least one instance of this. Using a CS: override in the *source* for an MOV does *not* cause a GP fault, because reading from a code segment is permissible (unless someone has deliberately turned on the execute-only, no-read bit in the segment's descriptor):

```
mov ax, cs:request
```

However, using a CS: override in the *destination* for an MOV—that is, *writing* into a code segment—definitely does cause a GP fault:

```
mov cs:request, ax
```

Unfortunately, the use of CS as a storage area is not always so explicit. For example, assembly-language code that uses the SEGMENT and ASSUME directives can easily construct "impure code" without using an explicit CS: override. This is particularly common in code that was once destined to be used in a .COM file:

```
_TEXT   segment public 'CODE'
        assume CS:_TEXT, DS:_TEXT
;; ...
        mov request, ax
```

Code that uses the newer Microsoft assembler (MASM) directives such as DOSSEG and .CODE is less likely to contain impure code, but it's still possible:

```
;       impure.asm
        .286
        dosseg
        .model large
        .code
request dw ?
start:
        mov request, 1234h
        end start
```

Fortunately, MASM has an option to check for impure code. If you put the .286 or .286p directive at the top of a source file, and use the option -p when you assemble, MASM locates all lines containing an impure memory reference:

```
C:\DOSX>masm -p impure;
impure.ASM (8) : warning A4100: Impure memory reference.
```

Borland's Turbo Assembler (TASM) provides the same feature, with the warning message *CS override in protected mode.*

Having located all such places in your code, you next have to ask why data is being stored in a code segment. Often, it's simply unnecessary (probably a relic of code that used the .COM format) and can easily be fixed. The previous example could be rewritten so that it works in both protected and real mode, simply by putting the data where it belongs in the data segment:

```
        .286
        dosseg
        .model large
        .data
request dw ?
        .code
start:
        mov request, 1234h
        end start
```

Sometimes, however, it really does make sense to keep data in a code segment. For example, an interrupt service routine (ISR) frequently is written with at least one variable accessible from CS, since that is the only segment register whose value is known when the ISR is invoked.

This is not an issue for ISRs written in C, because the compiler's _interrupt keyword takes care of loading DS (DGROUP) on entry to the ISR. Any C function with the _interrupt or _loadds keyword receives a prolog like the following:

```
push ds
mov ax, DGROUP
mov ds, ax
```

From this point on, the code in the interrupt handler can address anything in the program's DGROUP, even though at entry to the handler only CS:IP is known. Assembly-language programs that use DOSSEG ordering (highly recommended when running under 286 | DOS-Extender) can use this same technique, and thereby keep data out of their code segments.

However, if you *still* want to store data in CS—to write (horrors!) self-modifying code, for example—this too is possible in protected mode. You can continue to read data out of the code segment with a CS: override, but to write data into the code segment, you will need to create an "alias" selector. Likewise, in protected mode, you can also (horrors!) execute data by creating a code alias for a data segment.

Perhaps you are familiar with *aliases* from Windows programming or from OS/2: the idea is that multiple protected-mode selectors can share the same base address and limit (size), but have different "access rights." The same segment of memory can be viewed by one selector as code and by another as data.

In Windows 3 (which, remember, is really just a protected-mode DOS extender with a pretty user interface and a difficult API), protected-mode programs can use the AllocDStoCSAlias() function for executing data; this function accepts a data selector and returns a code alias that can be used to execute code in a data segment (that is, executable data). There is also an undocumented Windows function, AllocCStoDSAlias(), that performs the opposite transformation, allowing code segments to be read and written (that is, self-modifying code). But this is usually undesirable because Windows code segments should be discardable and shareable, which self-modified code segments obviously are not.

In OS/2, the function DosCreateCSAlias() is used to allocate executable aliases for data segments. Interestingly, this same function is provided by 286 | DOS-Extender as part of the Phar Lap API (PHAPI). As noted earlier in this chapter, 286 | DOS-Extender provides, under MS-DOS, a subset of the OS/2 API. Normally, you don't need to use these functions, because equivalent functionality is provided by the INT 21h interface. However, there is obviously no INT 21h function for managing code/data aliases. The PHAPI (whose name is a weak pun on Microsoft's ill-fated FAPI, or Family API) includes those OS/2 functions, such as DosCreateCSAlias(), that a DOS developer might need, plus numerous additional functions for mixing real- and protected-mode code, generating real-mode interrupts, accessing real-mode memory, handling interrupts and exceptions, and the like.

The following is a rather contrived example of how a real-mode program with executable data would be modified for protected mode:

```
/* CODEDATA.C */
#ifdef DOSX286
```

```
#include <phapi.h>
#endif

typedef unsigned char BYTE;

BYTE data[] = {
/*  op    ?l    ?h   */
    0xb8, 0x00, 0x00,          /* MOV AX, 0 */
    0xbb, 0x00, 0x00,          /* MOV BX, 0 */
    0xb9, 0x00, 0x00,          /* MOV CX, 0 */
    0xba, 0x00, 0x00,          /* MOV DX, 0 */
    0xcd, 0x00,                /* INT 00 */
    0xcb,                      /* RETF */
    } ;

void (far *code)(void);

void put(char *s)
{
    enum {
        AL=1, AH=2, BL=4, BH=5, CL=7, CH=8, DL=10, DH=11, INTNO=13
        } offsets;

    while (*s)
    {
        data[AH] = 2;              /* AH=2h */
        data[INTNO] = 0x21;        /* INT 21h */
        data[DL] = *s;             /* DL=char */
        (*code)();
        s++;

        if (! *s) break;
        data[AH] = 0x0E;           /* AH=0Eh */
        data[AL] = *s;             /* AL=char */
        data[BH] = 0;              /* BH=page */
        data[INTNO] = 0x10;        /* INT 10h */
        (*code)();
        s++;
    }
}

main()
{
#ifdef DOSX286
    void far *fp;
```

```
    USHORT ret;
    SEL cs;

    fp = (void far *) data;
    if (ret = DosCreateCSAlias(SELECTOROF(fp), &cs))
        return ret;
    code = MAKEP(cs, OFFSETOF(fp));
    put("This is a test of executable data\r\n");
    DosFreeSeg(cs);
#else
    code = (void (far *)()) data;
    put("This is a test of executable data\r\n");
#endif
    return 0;
}
```

In this program, the data[] array holds Intel instructions, represented as an array of bytes. The put() function modifies the instructions by poking values into the data[] array; it uses the (*code)() function pointer to execute these instructions. In real mode, data[] and (*code)() hold the same value. In protected mode, of course, trying to execute data would cause an immediate GP fault, so the program calls DosCreateCSAlias()—data[] and (*code)() still correspond to the same piece of memory, but they hold different (aliased) values.

Note that this program creates an alias only once, and then uses it for the duration of the program. This use of an alias is typical for protected-mode, and, in fact, is somewhat typical of PHAPI functions in general: they tend to be used at program startup and termination.

Address Arithmetic

Our second aberrant (and abhorrent) real-mode practice, address arithmetic, is based on the assumption that address offsets can be "rolled over" into address segments. As an example, take the real-mode pointer 1234:5678. Because of the way real-mode addressing works (see Chapter 1), this pointer actually refers to the linear address (1234h*10h)+5678h = 179B8h:

```
12340
 5678
179B8
```

Now, this same linear address 179B8h is also representable in real mode by *other* segment:offset pairs—most obviously 179B:0008h.

This concerns us here because some programs like to keep their far pointers "normalized," that is, with an offset that is always less than 10h. This is not possible in protected mode; the xxxx and yyyy portions of an xxxx:yyyy far pointer are discrete units that can't be combined. Fortunately, as you will see below, in protected mode there is *no need* to normalize pointers in the first place.

On the other hand, certain forms of 16-bit protected mode address manipulation *are* the same in real mode; should you need it, there is even a kind of protected-mode address arithmetic, using the "huge shift" and "huge increment" that we will discuss below.

First, the useful FP_SEG(), FP_OFF(), and MK_FP() macros still work in 16-bit protected mode (the 32-bit protected mode versions are completely different):

```
typedef unsigned short WORD;
typedef unsigned long DWORD;
typedef void far *FP;
#ifdef LVALUE
#define FP_SEG(fp)        (*((WORD *) &(fp)+1))
#define FP_OFF(fp)        (*((WORD *) &(fp)))
#else
#define FP_SEG(fp)        ((WORD)((DWORD)(fp) >> 16))
#define FP_OFF(fp)        ((WORD)(fp))
#endif
#define MK_FP(s, o)     ((FP)(((DWORD)(s) << 16) \ (o)))
```

For example:

```
extern char far *foo;
WORD sel = FP_SEG(foo);
```

or:

```
extern WORD _psp;
struct PSP far *psp_ptr = MK_FP(_psp, 0);
```

Here, however, the similarity between real mode and 16-bit protected mode ends. For example, the following, which uses the "LVALUE" form of the macros, makes no sense in protected mode:

```
FP_SEG(foo)++;
```

In real mode, adding 1 to a segment value describes a location one paragraph (16 bytes) higher in memory, and is equivalent to adding 10h (16 bytes) to the pointer offset. In protected mode, as we noted, there is no carry from the offset into the selector. While adding 1 to a selector is permissible (the preceding code does *not* cause a GP fault), *dereferencing* (i.e., trying to use) the resulting pointer definitely does not produce the expected results and usually will cause a GP fault.

Code written for real mode sometimes relies on the ability to convert between a segment:offset pointer and its underlying absolute address:

```
#define PTRTOABS(fp)          (DWORD) ((FP_SEG(fp) << 4) + FP_OFF(fp))
#define ABSTOPTR(abs)         (MK_FP((DWORD) (abs) >> 4, (abs) & 0x0F))
```

Because many segment:offset combinations point to the same absolute address in real mode, the pointers must be "normalized" reliably; compare two real-mode pointers for equality:

```
#define NORMALIZE(fp)        (ABSTOPTR(PTRTOABS(fp)))
#define CMP_PTR(fp1,fp2)     (NORMALIZE(fp1) == NORMALIZE(fp2))
```

But, this doesn't make any sense in protected mode. Instead, you can think of protected-mode pointers as already "normalized." To compare two pointers for equality, just compare them:

```
#define CMP_PTR(fp1,fp2) ((fp1) == (fp2))
```

To see if one pointer is located within the same segment as another pointer, real-mode code generally manipulates their underlying absolute addresses. But since the underlying absolute address is of almost no concern to us in protected mode, and since the only meaningful item you can look at is the selector value itself, this comparison becomes:

```
#define SAME_SEG(fp1,fp2)     (FP_SEG(fp1) == FP_SEG(fp2))
```

In short, certain operations that are required in real mode, because of the way addressing works, simply become unnecessary in protected mode.

There is still a problem, however. While 16-bit far pointers can only address 16 bits at a time, the MS-DOS memory-allocation function (INT 21h AH=48h) can allocate blocks of memory larger than 64KB. We saw earlier that this function is passed the number of 16-byte *paragraphs* to be allocated, and returns the initial segment of the entire block. The block is composed of multiple contiguous segments. The problem is, in a block of memory greater than 64KB bytes in length, how do you jump from one segment or selector to the next?

If you use your compiler's "huge" pointers, the segment arithmetic is taken care of for you; this carries over into protected mode. Code that relies entirely on the compiler's huge arithmetic will port to protected mode without incident. However, for various reasons, some programs do their own huge arithmetic. In general, throwing out the "home style" address arithmetic and using the compiler's huge pointers instead will fix the problem. But, for those protected-mode programs that need to do their own address arithmetic, there is a relatively simple solution: the "huge shift" and the "huge increment."

The huge increment is the number that must be used to get from one segment to the next in a huge block; the huge shift is simply the value by which 1 is shifted to get the increment:

```
hincr = 1 << hshift;

char far *big;
FP_SEG(big) += hincr;
```

Note that real mode *implicitly* has a huge shift and huge increment; you simply don't think about them. To get from one 64KB block to the next in real mode, you add 1000h to the segment:

```
#define hshift  12
#define hincr   1000h
```

Huge allocations in protected mode consist of multiple contiguous selectors. However, because of the way protected-mode selectors look (Chapter 1 explains how the bottom three bits of a selector are used), "contiguous" selectors are in fact a minimum of *eight* (1 << 3) apart; that is, the next selector in a Local Descriptor

Table (LDT) after 03B7h, for example, would be 03BFh. Thus, 3 is the *minimum* possible value for the protected-mode huge shift, and 8 is the minimum possible value for the huge increment. In any case, the particular value doesn't matter because any given protected-mode environment lets you query these two values.

The Windows kernel provides two dynamically linked variables, __ahshift and __ahincr (not documented in the Windows *Programmer's Reference*, but described briefly in Chapter 16 of the Windows *Guide to Programming*), that can be used to perform protected mode segment arithmetic. In 286 | DOS-Extender, as in OS/2, two functions are supplied: DosGetHugeShift() and DosGetHugeIncr(). For example:

```
#include <phapi.h>
// ...
unsigned short hincr;
DosGetHugeIncr(&hincr);
// ...
FP_SEG(fp) += hincr;
```

Whether you let a compiler do huge arithmetic for you, or do it yourself, note that it is the selector that increments; offsets remain unchanged. This means that protected-mode huge arithmetic can be somewhat faster than real-mode huge arithmetic. In Borland C++, for example, protected-mode code *must* use the -h option for "fast" huge arithmetic, because the default, (slower) method normalizes pointers and is, therefore, incompatible with protected mode. The downside is that any given element in a protected-mode huge array cannot straddle segments; keeping the element size at a power of two guarantees this.

Limits to Transparency

Our next class of changes possibly required for protected mode involves interrupts, functions, and absolute memory locations that a given DOS extender may not support in protected mode. While it is the job of a DOS extender to make protected mode look as much like the real-mode DOS environment as possible (with the exception, of course, of its limited address space!), there will always be some piece of functionality that a given DOS extender does not provide in protected mode. Quite simply, there are limits to transparency. Possible problem areas are:

- Using unsupported absolute memory locations
  Example: *((unsigned short far *) MK_FP(0xb800, 0))
- Using unsupported software interrupts
  Example: INT 5Ch (NetBIOS)
- Using undocumented DOS calls
  Example: INT 21h AH=52h (Get List of Lists)
- Taking over interrupts
  Examples: Ctrl-C (INT 23h), Ctrl-Break (INT 1Bh), Critical Error (INT 24h)

Don't be alarmed by this list. *Unsupported* simply means that the DOS extender doesn't provide *transparent* access. You can still do all this in a protected-mode DOS program, but you do have to take some extra steps. If the DOS extender provides an adequate API for accessing real-mode interrupts, functions, and memory locations from protected mode, however, this ends up not being terribly important. On the other hand, if the DOS extender does not provide such an API, then it can be a terrible hassle, as numerous Windows programmers will testify. Accessing real-mode code or data from a Windows program usually requires going directly to low-level DPMI INT 31h services, or using undocumented Windows functions. It is vital that a DOS extender provide a good API for accessing real-mode code and data.

Peeks and Pokes, Direct Screen Writes

Because of the poor performance of both the MS-DOS and the BIOS output functions, many PC programs produce screen output by writing directly to video memory at an address such as B800:0000h, EGA/VGA graphics are implemented, in part, by directly writing to graphics-mode memory at A000:0000h.

As you would expect by now, protected-mode code cannot directly bang on a protected-mode address such as B800:0000h and expect output to appear on the screen. More likely, a GP fault message will appear.

For example, the program, VIDTEST.C, displays the string "hello world!" 30,000 times in a random x,y location on the screen, in a random screen attribute. We will see how to port this program to protected mode, using the example of 286 | DOS-Extender:

```
/* VIDTEST.C */

#include <stdlib.h>
#include <stdio.h>
#include <time.h>
#include <dos.h>

#define SET_VIDEO_MODE      0x00
#define SCROLL_UP           0x06
#define GET_VIDEO_MODE      0x0F
#define NORMAL              (1+2+4)
#define REVERSE             (16+32+64)
#define TEXTBW80            2
#define TEXTC80             3
#define TEXTMONO            7

static unsigned char far *vid_mem;

/* turn (x,y) into offset from beginning of vid */
#define SCR(y,x)        (((y) * 160) + ((x) << 1))

#define MAKEWORD(l, h) |
    (((unsigned short) (l)) | ((unsigned short) (h)) << 8)

int video_mode(void)
{
    _asm mov ah, GET_VIDEO_MODE
    _asm int 10h        ; mode returned in AL
    _asm xor ah, ah     ; zero AH, to return value in AX
}

void set_mode(unsigned char mode)
{
    _asm mov ah, SET_VIDEO_MODE
    _asm mov al, mode
    _asm int 10h
}

void clear(int y1, int x1, int y2, int x2, int attr)
{
    _asm mov ax, (SCROLL_UP << 8)
    _asm mov bh, attr
    _asm mov ch, y1
    _asm mov cl, x1
    _asm mov dh, y2
    _asm mov dl, x2
    _asm int 10h
}
```

```
void cls(void)
{
    clear(0, 0, 24, 79, NORMAL);
}

unsigned get_vid_mem(void)
{
    int vmode = video_mode();
    unsigned short vid_seg;

    if (vmode == TEXTMONO)
        vid_seg = 0xB000;
    else if ((vmode == TEXTBW80) || (vmode == TEXTC80))
        vid_seg = 0xB800;
    else
        return 0;

    return vid_seg;
}

/* write a string p at (x,y), with attributes */
void wrt_str(int y, int x, int attr, unsigned char *p)
{
    unsigned short far *v = vid_mem + SCR(y, x);
    int ok = 80 - x;
    while (ok && *p)
    {
        *v++ = MAKEWORD(*p++, attr);
        ok--;
    }
}

main()
{
    int i;
    time_t t1, t2;

    time(&t1);
    FP_SEG(vid_mem) = get_vid_mem();
    FP_OFF(vid_mem) = 0;
    cls();
    for (i=30000; i--; )
        wrt_str(rand() % 25, rand() % 80, rand() % 0xFF,
            "hello world!");
    time(&t2);
```

```
    cls();
    printf("%lu seconds\n", t2 - t1);
    return 0;
}
```

This program GP faults in protected mode the first time it tries to load the video segment (either B800h or B000h) into a segment register. This occurs the first time the function wrt_str() is called, in this line of code:

```
*v++ = MAKEWORD(*p++, attr);
```

So that this program will run in protected mode, we need a protected-mode selector *whose base address* is either B8000h or B0000h. In some cases, protected-mode environments come with selectors predefined, which "map" these and other well-known absolute memory locations. For example, Windows provides two variables, __B800H and __B000H, which can be used to do direct screen writes; these variables are used by those Windows programs, such as CVW (CodeView for Windows) and TDW (Turbo Debugger for Windows), which do direct screen writes. Needless to say, the value of __B800H is *not* B800h; instead, it is some selector whose base address is B8000h.

Even if such a predefined selector is not available, most protected-mode environments make it easy for you to create one. In 286 | DOS-Extender, you would use the PHAPI function DosMapRealSeg(), which takes a real-mode paragraph address (such as B800h) and a length (which can be greater than 64KB) and gives back a protected-mode selector that maps that address. For example, we can create variables with the same names that Windows uses:

```
unsigned short __B800H, __B000H;
DosMapRealSeg(0xB000, 10000L, &__B000H);
DosMapRealSeg(0xB800, 10000L, &__B800H);
```

Armed with DosMapRealSeg(), it is trivial to fix VIDTEST.C (or any other full-screen DOS application) so that it runs in protected mode. Only one change, to the get_vid_mem() function, is required:

```
#ifdef DOSX286
#include <phapi.h>
```

```
unsigned get_vid_mem(void)
{
    int vmode = video_mode();
    unsigned short vid_seg;
    unsigned short sel;

    if (vmode == TEXTMONO)
        vid_seg = 0xB000;
    else if ((vmode == TEXTBW80) || (vmode == TEXTC80))
        vid_seg = 0xB800;
    else
        return 0;

    if (DosMapRealSeg(vid_seg, (long) 25*80*2, &sel) == 0)
        return sel;
    else
        return 0;
}
#endif
```

Notice that no other part of the program changes and that the changed function runs only once, during initialization. If DosMapRealSeg() will be used to create selectors that will only be used for part of the time that your program runs, it is important to free these selectors when finished with them, using the DosFreeSeg() function.

In a protected-mode environment that does not provide a handy "map" function, you must take care of the low-level details of mapping: allocating a selector and setting its corresponding descriptor's base address, limit, and access rights, perhaps by using DPMI INT 31h functions. The general idea is shown in the following pseudocode:

```
map(para, limit) :-
   sel = ALLOC_SELECTOR();   // e.g. INT 31h AX=0
   desc.base = para << 4;
   desc.limit = limit;
   desc.access = DATA;
   SET_DESC(sel, desc);      // e.g. INT 31h AX=0Ch
   return sel;
```

The same principles used with protected-mode direct screen writes apply to reading and writing of any other absolute memory locations in protected mode.

For example, to access the BIOS data area at address 400h, you would map in 1KB bytes of memory, starting at paragraph address 40h. In a number of cases (notably Windows), DOS extenders happen to provide protected-mode selector 40h as a "bimodal" selector to address 400h, but this is largely for "historical reasons" (i.e., pure chance) and should not be relied upon. With the strange exception of selector 40h, such "bimodal" selectors must be allocated out of the Global Descriptor Table (GDT) and are almost never available in DPMI-compatible environments.

Unsupported Interrupts and Functions

As noted earlier, not every interrupt or function available in real mode can possibly be supported in protected mode. The fact that an interrupt or function is not "supported" in protected mode merely means, however, that access to it won't be transparent. Since DOS extenders sit on top of DOS, and on top of any device drivers or memory-resident programs that a user may have, all real-mode functions and interrupts are still present—if you could only get to them from your protected-mode program.

For this reason, most DOS extenders provide functions that make it easy for protected-mode programs to generate real-mode interrupts. In the case of 286 | DOS-Extender, these functions are DosRealIntr(), DosRealFarCall(), and DosRealFarJump(). In Windows, you must use a low-level function such as DPMI INT 31h AX=0300h (Simulate Real Mode Interrupt).

The important point to note here is that, in protected-mode DOS, there are two types of interrupts: real-mode and protected-mode. When a protected-mode program contains an INT XXh instruction, it's issuing a protected-mode interrupt. When DOS itself generates interrupts, on the other hand, such as Ctrl-C (INT 23h) or Critical Error (INT 24h), they are coming from real mode. Furthermore, most protected-mode interrupts generated by programs are handled by the DOS extender and reissued (or "reflected," to use the lingo) in real mode (or in virtual-8086 mode, which looks like real mode). But, there are always some functions that any given DOS extender does not know how to handle.

For example, undocumented DOS functions are usually not supported in protected mode. The following short real-mode program, LASTDRV.C, is adapted from the book *Undocumented DOS* (edited by Andrew Schulman;

published by Addison-Wesley, 1990) and is a decent example of a program that usually requires modification for protected mode:

```
/* LASTDRV.C */

#include <stdlib.h>
#include <stdio.h>
#include <dos.h>

#ifndef MK_FP
#define MK_FP(seg,ofs) |
    ((void far *)(((unsigned long)(seg) << 16) | (ofs)))
#endif

typedef unsigned char BYTE;

void fail(char *s)  { puts(s); exit(1); }

main()
{
    union REGS r;
    struct SREGS s;
    BYTE far *doslist;

    segread(&s);
    r.x.ax = 0x5200;
    intdosx(&r, &r, &s);
    doslist = MK_FP(s.es, r.x.bx);

    if ((doslist == (BYTE far *) 0) ||
        (doslist == (BYTE far *) -1))
            fail("INT 21h AH=52h not supported");

    printf("LASTDRIVE=%c\n", 'A' - 1 +
        doslist[(_osmajor == 3 && _osminor == 0) ? 0x1b : 0x21]);

    return 0;
}
```

This program issues INT 21h AH=52h, which returns in ES:BX a far pointer to the undocumented DOS "List of Lists" (DOS internal variables table). The program then gets the LASTDRIVE byte from the List of Lists and displays it. Mere recompilation or relinking of this program for protected mode usually causes a

GP fault, because INT 21h AH=52h isn't supported by most DOS extenders. To get LASTDRV running in protected mode, we must do two things: issue a real-mode INT 21h AH=52h, and map in the *real-mode* pointer that it returns in ES:BX. This operation is shown in the following 286\DOS-Extender version of LASTDRV.C:

```
/* LASTDRV.C */

#include <stdlib.h>
#include <stdio.h>
#include <dos.h>
#include <phapi.h>

#ifndef MK_FP
#define MK_FP(seg,ofs) |
    ((void far *)(((unsigned long)(seg) << 16) | (ofs)))
#endif

void fail(char *s)  { puts(s); exit(1); }

main()
{
    REGS16 r;
    BYTE far *doslist;
    USHORT sel;

    /* do a real-mode INT 21h AH=52h */
    memset(&r, 0, sizeof(r));  /* important: clear to zero! */
    r.ax = 0x5200;
    if (DosRealIntr(0x21, &r, 0L, 0) != 0)
        fail("DosRealIntr call failed");
    doslist = MK_FP(r.es, r.bx);  /* real-mode pointer */

    if ((doslist == (BYTE far *) 0) ||
        (doslist == (BYTE far *) -1))
            fail("INT 21h AH=52h not supported");
    printf("Real-mode List of Lists = %Fp\n", doslist);

    /* convert the real-mode pointer to protected mode */
    if (DosMapRealSeg(FP_SEG(doslist),
                      FP_OFF(doslist) + 1024L, /* number of bytes */
                      &sel) != 0)
        fail("DosMapRealSeg failed");
    doslist = MK_FP(sel, FP_OFF(doslist));  /* prot-mode pointer now */
```

```
    printf("Protected-mode List Of Lists = %Fp\n", doslist);

    /* extract value of LASTDRIVE from protected-mode */
    printf("LASTDRIVE=%c\n", 'A' - 1 +
        doslist[(_osmajor == 3 && _osminor == 0) ? 0x1b : 0x21]);

    /* free selector */
    if (DosFreeSeg(FP_SEG(doslist)) != 0)
        fail("DosFreeSeg failed");

    return 0;
}
```

Whereas the real-mode version of LASTDRV.C uses the C intdosx() function, the protected-mode version uses DosRealIntr(). The problem isn't with intdosx(), but with the fact that, in a protected-mode program, naturally generates protected-mode interrupts. Here, we need to generate a real-mode interrupt. Like the intdosx() and int86x() functions, DosRealIntr() uses an image of the CPU registers. For C programs, it may be useful to package up a function such as DosRealIntr() so that it looks more like int86x(). For example:

```
/* RMINT86.C */

#include <stdlib.h>
#include <dos.h>
#include <phapi.h>

#define CLEAR(x)      memset((x), 0, sizeof(x))
#define IN(reg)       r.reg =in->x.reg
#define OUT(reg)      out->x.reg = r.reg

int rm_int86x(int intno, union REGS *in, union REGS *out,
    struct SREGS *sregs)
{
    REGS16 r;
    r.cs = sregs->cs; r.ds = sregs->ds; r.es = sregs->es;
    IN(ax); IN(bx); IN(cx); IN(dx); IN(si); IN(di);
    DosRealIntr(intno, &r, 0, 0);
    sregs->cs = r.cs; sregs->ds = r.ds; sregs->es = r.es;
    OUT(ax); OUT(bx); OUT(cx); OUT(dx); OUT(si); OUT(di);
    if ((out->x.cflag = (r.flags & 1)) != 0)
        _doserrno = r.ax;
    return r.ax;
}
```

With this function, protected-mode LASTDRV.C could now generate a real-mode INT 21h AH=52h with the following:

```
union REGS r;
struct SREGS s;
segread(&s);
r.h.ah = 0x52;
rm_int86x(0x21, &r, &r, &s);
doslist = MK_FP(s.es, r.x.bx);   /* real-mode pointer */
```

Note that, in addition to calling DosRealIntr(), this program also calls DosMapRealSeg(). With any real-mode interrupt or function that returns far pointers (i.e., that changes the value in a segment register), the pointer will naturally be a real-mode pointer, which must be mapped into your program's address space before it can be used. In this example, we happened to be reading a byte out of the List of Lists; if we were using one of the far pointers contained in the structure, that too would have to be mapped. (Following the DOS device chain is a good example.) Thus, even in an environment that happens to support undocumented DOS calls in protected mode (such as Phar Lap's 386 | DOS-Extender, Version 3.0 and higher), such embedded pointers would require mapping. This is another good example of what we've been calling "limits to transparency."

Many real-mode interrupts and functions expect you to pass in far pointers to buffers. Undocumented DOS function INT 21h AH=60h (Truename) is a good example. When calling such functions in real mode, you must, of course, pass in real-mode pointers. This, in turn, means that any buffers must be located *in conventional memory*, that is, below 1 megabyte. Most DOS extenders provide a function that allocates conventional memory. In Windows, this function is GlobalDOSAlloc(), and in 286 | DOS-Extender, it is DosAllocRealSeg(). These functions return a real-mode paragraph address, which you can pass to the real-mode code, plus a corresponding protected-mode selector, which your program can use to manipulate the conventional-memory buffer. Earlier, we asserted that in protected mode the difference between extended memory and conventional memory disappears. However, because of the occasional need to allocate conventional-memory buffers for use with real-mode code, we can now see that this assertion isn't entirely true.

Ctrl-C, Ctrl-Break, and Critical Error

Most commercial PC applications need to handle interrupts, the most important being Ctrl-C (INT 23h), Ctrl-Break (INT 1Bh), and Critical Error (INT 24h). If an application does not install a handler for at least Ctrl-C and Critical Error, it can be terminated by user action at any time. For most shrinkwrap software, this is unacceptable, so the ability to install handlers for these interrupts is essential.

For a protected-mode DOS-extended program, the problem is that interrupts such as Ctrl-C and Critical Error *come from real mode*. Of course, DOS extenders, as part of their INT 21h interface, provide the DOS Set Interrupt Vector function (INT 21h AH=25h), which is normally used to install interrupt handlers. However, it is important to consider what this function does in protected mode: it installs (not surprisingly) a protected-mode interrupt handler. But, we just said that Ctrl-C and Critical Error come from real mode! In a protected-mode program, therefore, INT 21h AX=2523h, for example, will install an INT 23h handler alright, but the handler will never see a Ctrl-C.

One solution is to use high-level language functions for handling these events. These functions, such as signal() and _harderr() in C, will already have been ported to protected mode. In fact, protected-mode code should, wherever possible, use functions such as these for handling breaks and critical errors. If a program merely needs to clean up before terminating, functions such as atexit() or onexit() in C can also be used.

However, there are still many situations in which a genuine interrupt handler must be written. Judging from technical support calls received by Phar Lap, interrupt handling is the most complicated aspect of DOS-extender programming.

PC compilers such as Microsoft C and Borland C++ provide an _interrupt keyword, which makes it relatively easy to write interrupt handlers without having to drop into assembly language. An image of the CPU registers is pushed on the stack of an interrupt handler, which allows the registers to be manipulated from C code. In a real mode program, such handlers are installed in the usual DOS way, with INT 21h AH=25h, although here too there are high-level wrappers in the form of the _dos_setvect() function in Microsoft C and setvect() in Borland C++. In a protected-mode program, too, handlers can be installed in this way, but such installation is inappropriate whenever (as is often the case) interrupts can originate in real mode instead of, or in addition to, originating in protected mode.

What we therefore need in a protected-mode DOS extender is an additional way to install an interrupt handler, such that both real-mode and protected-mode interrupts get sent to the protected-mode handler. In the DOS/16M DOS extender, these are called *passup* interrupts. In 286 | DOS-Extender, they are called PassToProt interrupts and are installed with a function whose long-winded but descriptive name is DosSetPassToProtVec(). In most situations, calls to INT 21h AH=25h (or to functions such as _dos_setvect()) should be replaced by calls to DosSetPassToProtVec().

An example is provided in the following program, CRITERR.C, which can be compiled either for real mode or protected mode (in either case, stack-checking should be turned off when compiling). This program installs a handler for critical errors, replacing the standard "Abort, Retry, Fail?" handler:

```
/* CRITERR.C */

#include <stdlib.h>
#include <stdio.h>
#include <string.h>
#include <ctype.h>
#include <process.h>
#include <conio.h>
#include <dos.h>
#include <phapi.h>

#ifdef DOSX286
PIHANDLER old_crit_err_prot;
REALPTR old_crit_err_real;
#else
void (interrupt far *old_crit_err)();
#endif

void put_str(char far *s)
{
    _asm push ds
    _asm mov ah, 9          // Display String
    _asm lds dx, s
    _asm int 21h
    _asm pop ds
}

int get_char(void)
{
```

```
    _asm mov ah, 1           // Character Input with Echo
    _asm int 21h
    _asm xor ah, ah
}

void interrupt far critical_error(REGS16 r)
{
    int c;
    unsigned _ah = r.ax & 0xFF00;
    unsigned _al;
    do {
        put_str("CRITICAL ERROR\r\n$");
#ifdef DOSX286
        put_str("HANDLED IN PROTECTED MODE\r\n$");
#endif
        put_str("Abort, Retry, Ignore, Fail? $");
        c = get_char();
        put_str("\r\n$");
    } while (! strchr("AaRrIiFf", c));

    switch (toupper(c))
    {
        enum { IGNORE, RETRY, ABORT, FAIL } criterr_ret;
        case 'A' : _al = ABORT; break;
        case 'R' : _al = RETRY; break;
        case 'I' : _al = IGNORE; break;
        case 'F' : _al = FAIL; break;
    }

    r.ax = _ah + _al;
}

main(int argc, char *argv[])
{
    if (argc < 2)
    {
        puts("usage: criterr [program [args...]]");
        puts("example: criterr \\bin\\ls.exe a:");
        return 1;
    }

#ifdef DOSX286
    DosSetPassToProtVec(0x24, critical_error,
        &old_crit_err_prot, &old_crit_err_real);

    /* can't do system() here: COMMAND.COM has its own INT 24 handler */
```

```
    spawnvp(P_WAIT, argv[1], &argv[1]);

    DosSetRealProtVec(0x24, old_crit_err_prot, old_crit_err_real,
        NULL, NULL);
#else
    old_crit_err = _dos_getvect(0x24);
    _dos_setvect(0x24, critical_error);
    /* can't do system() here: COMMAND.COM has its own INT 24 handler */
    spawnvp(P_WAIT, argv[1], &argv[1]);
    _dos_setvect(0x24, old_crit_err);
#endif
    puts("bye");
    return 0;
}
```

In addition to installing a new protected-mode handler for both protected-mode and real-mode interrupts, DosSetPassToProtVec() also returns the previous protected-mode and real-mode interrupt handlers. In CRITERR.C, these handlers are saved away in the variables old_crit_err_prot (a PIHANDLER, or pointer to interrupt handler) and old_crit_err_real (a REALPTR). If the new interrupt handler, critical_error(), needed to *chain* either to the old real-mode or protected-mode handler, it could do so, using either a function such as _chain_intr() in Microsoft C, or the PHAPI function DosChainToRealIntr(). A PassToProt handler can find which mode an interrupt "came from" by calling DosIsRealIntr().

It's worth underlining a point about the PassToProt handler shown in CRITERR.C: this is a protected-mode function, which also handles interrupts coming from real mode. This handler capability has an interesting implications; protected-mode programs can hook real-mode interrupts and thereby provide services, such as new APIs, to real-mode programs. We will examine this briefly later in this chapter.

There is one problem with PassToProt handlers: every time an interrupt occurs in real mode, the machine is switched into protected mode. This is fine for infrequently generated interrupts such as Ctrl-C or Critical Error, but the performance would be disastrous for time-critical hardware interrupts such as serial communications (for example, COM1 on INT 0Ch). Thus, many DOS extenders provide yet another interrupt-handling function that installs no-switch interrupt handlers; that is, separate interrupt handlers for real mode and protected mode. By installing separate handlers for each mode, you can then expect to deal with the interrupt without a mode switch.

A real-mode interrupt handler must, of course, be a piece of real-mode code. Where would such code live as part of a protected-mode program? As will be seen below, 286\DOS-Extender supports real-mode dynamic link libraries (DLLs); a key use for real-mode DLLs is holding real-mode interrupt handlers.

One final interrupt-handling consideration: protected-mode INT 21h AH=25h, which installs pure protected-mode interrupt handlers (that is, protected-mode code that handles interrupts originating in protected mode) is perfect for one situation: when you want to do the same thing the DOS extender itself does, and provide transparent access to real-mode services. For example, if a given DOS extender does not provide INT 13h in protected mode, you could install a protected-mode INT 13h handler that hides all the details of calling DosRealIntr(), DosAllocRealSeg(), and so on. In 286\DOS-Extender, such protected-mode handlers can be installed either with INT 21h AH=25h or with the DoSetProtVec() function.

New Features

In this lengthy discussion about porting real-mode code to a protected-mode DOS extender, we have only discussed the problems of making existing code work in the new environment. We have perhaps overemphasized the problems, because the fact is that 99 percent of your code will run as is, without change. Of course, the remaining 1 percent—which will involve rare situations such as interrupt handling, direct screen writes, calling unsupported interrupts, working with self-modifying code, and the like—will occupy 95 percent of your development time.

There's a whole additional facet of working with a DOS extender: taking advantage of any nifty new features it provides. It goes without saying that *more memory* is the primary new feature provided by a DOS extender. Taking full advantage of this newly enlarged address space may require anything from no work at all (your program simply no longer runs out of memory, and that's the end of the story), to a ruthless pruning of no-longer-needed code (expanded memory or overlay support, for example), to an involved reworking of your program's data structures so that they no longer assume that the world ends at 1 megabyte.

Some DOS extenders use protected mode to provide additional extensions to DOS. Windows, of course, provides a graphical, windowed, event-driven, multitasking, dynamic-linking environment on top of DOS. We examine how to take advantage of some of these non memory-related features in Chapter 6 of this book. Phar Lap's 286 | DOS-Extender, besides providing more memory, also provides dynamic linking under DOS, plus an emulation of several other key aspects of the OS/2 API, including sessions (screen groups), processes, threads, and various forms of interprocess communications.

Dynamic Linking Under DOS

It was noted earlier in this chapter that 286 | DOS-Extender can run certain OS/2 and Windows .EXE files under MS-DOS, with OS/2 and Windows nowhere in sight. Dynamic link libraries (DLLs) are what make this possible.

For example, the Microsoft C debugger used with 286 | DOS-Extender is protected-mode CodeView (CVP), an OS/2 program. CVP requires the following DLLs, normally found in OS/2:

```
DOSCALLS.DLL
KBDCALLS.DLL
MONCALLS.DLL
MOUCALLS.DLL
QUECALLS.DLL
VIOCALLS.DLL
SESMGR.DLL
NLS.DLL
MSG.DLL
```

To run CVP under DOS, 286\DOS-Extender provides versions of these DLLs, containing DOS versions of functions such as DosCreateThread(), DosPTrace(), DosStartSession(), KbdCharIn(), MouGetPtrPos(), and so on. These can also be used to run certain other character-mode OS/2 programs under DOS.

Likewise, the Borland C++ debugger, used with 286\DOS-Extender, is Turbo Debugger for Windows (TDW). TDW requires the following DLLs, normally found in Windows (though in some cases with an .EXE extension):

```
KERNEL.DLL
USER.DLL
KEYBOARD.DLL
WINDEBUG.DLL
WIN87EM.DLL
```

In other words, dynamic linking can provide emulation APIs that are robust enough to run unmodified *binaries*, out of the box. The same facilities that were used to create the Windows and OS/2 emulation libraries are available to any user of the DOS extender.

Besides "plug-in APIs," dynamic linking also provides a way to give applications user-extensible add-in capabilities. A set of functions for *run-time dynamic linking*, including DosLoadModule() and DosGetProcAddr(), allows programs to link to new routines and new DLLs while the program is running. This is the ideal way to let end users and third-party developers add their own extensions to your application.

The basic mechanics (though none of the usefulness) of run-time dynamic linking are illustrated by the short program below. In essence, this form of dynamic linking turns ASCIIZ strings (such as "DOSMKDIR") into callable function pointers:

```
/* CALLDLL.C */

#include <phapi.h>

main()
{
    unsigned doscalls;
    void (far pascal *dir_func)(char far *dir, unsigned long ul);

    DosLoadModule(NULL, 0, "DOSCALLS", &doscalls);
    DosGetProcAddr(doscalls, "DOSMKDIR", &dir_func);
    (*dir_func)("foobar", 0);
    DosGetProcAddr(doscalls, "DOSCHDIR", &dir_func);
    (*dir_func)("foobar", 0);
    (*dir_func)("..", 0);
    DosGetProcAddr(doscalls, "DOSRMDIR", &dir_func);
    (*dir_func)("foobar", 0);
    DosFreeModule(doscalls);
    return 0;
}
```

Run-time dynamic linking also allows the DOS extender itself to be extended or modified. The RUN286 DOS extender can load DLLs from the command line, using the -LOADDLL switch. This, together with the DosSetProcAddr() function provided as part of PHAPI, can be used to replace or extend (via chaining) any existing function in 9 DLL.

Finally, the run-time dynamic linking functions DosLoadModule() and DosFreeModule() can be used to implement protected-mode overlays.

Real-Mode DLLs

Another important function of DLLs is to provide an easy way to include real-mode code as part of a protected-mode application. Some programs, such as telecommunication packages, require that certain interrupt handlers be written as real-mode code; DLLs are the perfect place to put these. Furthermore, some code simply may be too difficult to port to protected mode; again, real-mode DLLs provide a solution.

Because real-mode code in 286 | DOS-Extender resides in DLLs, it has access to the same API mechanism as protected-mode code. In particular, just as protected-mode programs can call down into real mode, real-mode code can call up to protected mode, using the DosProtIntr(), DosProtFarCall(), or DosProtFarJump() routines. Realizing that, for better or for worse, real mode is not going to disappear any time soon, the designers of PHAPI sought to make it as symmetrical as possible between protected and real mode.

Benefits and Limitations

In the sections that follow, we will review the advantages and disadvantages of 16-bit protected-mode DOS extenders compared with: 640KB MS-DOS, with Windows, and with 32-bit DOS extenders.

MS-DOS

The advantages of 16-bit DOS extenders over "plain vanilla" MS-DOS seem fairly obvious: access to a maximum of 16 megabytes of memory versus access to up to 1 megabyte of memory; and hardware-assisted memory protection versus a complete absence of rules. Because of the larger real estate available in protected mode, large applications may also run faster in protected mode than in real mode. In addition, protected-mode DOS can also offer features such as dynamic linking and multitasking—in a far cleaner way than would be possible in real mode.

But 16-bit DOS extenders also have a few disadvantages to look out for. First, users must have an IBM AT (or better), to run a DOS-extended program. Second, most DOS-extended applications cannot be delivered to end users without obtaining a run-time license. Third, some programs run more slowly in protected mode than in real mode.

One other disadvantage of a DOS extender is that the vastly increased resources suddenly available (with very little work) may be a tempting license to write really bad code. Limitations aren't always such a bad thing; a lot of programs out there could benefit from having some stringent limitations placed on their size!

Windows

Microsoft Windows 3.0 (and higher), in Standard and Enhanced modes, is, of course, a DOS extender. However, as noted earlier in this chapter, it operates so differently from typical DOS extenders that we can deal with Windows almost as though it were an entirely different operating system rather than a DOS extender.

Both Windows and the more traditional form of DOS extender provide a large protected-mode address space while continuing to run under DOS. Windows, however, provides an entirely new API, whereas all other DOS extenders attempt to hide themselves as much as possible.

The benefits of a more traditional DOS extender over Windows, then, are that you can keep much more of your existing code, and while porting to a DOS extender may only take weeks, porting to Windows might take a year. Where DOS extenders attempt, as much as possible, to hide complexity, Windows seems to delight in exposing it. And, where DOS extenders provide extensive services for mixing real- and protected-mode code and data, Windows provides very poor functionality in this area, again requiring more change by the developer.

On the up side, Windows applications can take advantage of the Windows user interface—windows, menus, dialog boxes, fonts, graphics, scrolling, and so on—and this interface is not easily accessible from a non-Windows DOS application—even a protected-mode DOS application. There is also a perception, particularly among the all-important and ever-fickle computer magazines, that Windows programs are ipso facto sexier than non-Windows applications.

Weighing the time required to develop a Windows application and the enormous size of the non-Windows marketplace, against the growing importance of

Windows and its clear user-interface benefits, it probably makes sense to maintain work in parallel on both DOS and Windows versions of a commercial application. By providing DOS applications with the same, large protected-mode address space that Windows provides, a DOS extender can make it easier to maintain both non-Windows and Windows versions of a product.

32-bit DOS Extenders

One advantage of a 16-bit DOS extender (such as Phar Lap's 286 | DOS-Extender) over a 32-bit DOS-extender (such as Phar Lap's 386 | DOS-Extender) is that 16-bit DOS extended applications will run on 80286-based PCs, such as the IBM AT, whereas 32-bit DOS-extended applications require an 80386 or better.

But, the main advantage of a 16-bit DOS extender over a 32-bit DOS extender is that, with 16-bit protected mode, you can keep your existing development tools such as Microsoft C and Borland C++. In contrast, 32-bit protected mode requires entirely new tools: new compilers, linkers, libraries, debuggers, and so on. Whereas 16-bit protected-mode code is quite similar to real-mode code, 32-bit code is dramatically different. This requires more change from developers.

This code difference is also the primary benefit of 32-bit protected mode! The advantages of 32-bit code over 16-bit code are tremendous: anyone who has seen the code produced by 32-bit C compilers will never want to go back to 16-bit code. While 16-bit protected mode offers 16 megabytes of memory, an individual item cannot be larger than 64KB bytes, unless if you use huge pointers. In contrast, 32-bit protected mode, as Chapter 5 shows, allows single objects as large as 4 gigabytes. Segments essentially disappear in 32-bit code, replaced by a flat address space.

Most PC programmers would probably be happy if they never saw another segment in their lives. On the other hand, many of the same programmers are rightfully fearful of jumping to entirely different development tools, and many companies cannot yet require that all their customers have 80386 or 80486 machines. It's a tough decision.

Chapter 5

32-bit Protected-Mode DOS Extenders

M. Steven Baker

In 1991, over 50 percent of the PCs sold in the U.S. will use a 32-bit 386 or 486 CPU. By 1993, it is estimated that over 50 percent of the installed base of PCs will have 32-bit CPUs. This new hardware continues to outstrip the slower evolution of software development, and it is common to find 80386 and 80486 computers used merely as fast XT machines. The true power of these CPUs is unavailable in the real mode used by the venerable MS-DOS operating system. 386-based, protected-mode DOS extenders grew from the need to utilize the more powerful features of 80386 and now 80486 computers, without forgoing MS-DOS.

The 386 DOS extenders set up a bridge from the DOS environment to the protected mode so that both the 386 larger memory space and the full 386 instruction set are available. To an end user, an application built with a DOS extender can look like any other DOS program. When the user runs the program, control passes invisibly to the 386 DOS extender, which loads and runs the application in protected mode. Such a protected-mode application can transparently invoke real-mode DOS or BIOS services. 386 DOS extenders use essentially the same mechanism explained in detail in Chapter 4, although a 386 DOS extender has the option of running DOS and BIOS in Virtual 8086 mode rather than in real mode.

386 DOS extenders allow large applications to run under DOS until a true 386 operating system displaces DOS (if one ever does) . There is virtually no performance penalty when moving to 32-bit mode on 386/486 machines, and huge performance gains are available for large programs and applications with large data structures. As long as speed and power spur marketing, the developer can't neglect the 80386 and 80486 CPUs, even in the DOS marketplace. An application built with a DOS extender is likely to be much faster and have more features than a comparable DOS real-program, and it is often difficult or impossible to build a comparable real-mode DOS product.

This chapter will cover the 386 DOS extenders in some detail. To get our bearings, we'll start with a look at the history of 386 DOS extender development. Then, the benefits of using a 32-bit extender will be illustrated. For those of you who must know "how things work," we'll provide an overview of a typical DOS extender in action. We'll follow the overview with a survey of the available 386 DOS extenders and their capabilities, along with 32-bit programming tools.

We'll throw in a few small programming examples, mostly in C, to illustrate the development process. The examples will include a step-by-step outline of the construction of an application—from source code to testing/debugging to production. Along the way, we'll cover some of the stickier, more critical problems you might encounter porting existing applications to a 386 DOS extender: these include access to hardware, interrupt handlers, calling real-mode programs (device drivers, TSRs, etc.), and performance tuning. Finally, we'll illustrate the porting process with a more sizable programming project to tie things all together. Let's start by heading our time machine backwards.

Looking Back in Time

In late 1986, the skeptics who believed in DOS and its rich accumulation of user applications were the first to develop DOS extenders. Many industry watchers predicted their demise within two years. Even the software developers who were marketing DOS extenders thought they had only a narrow "window of opportunity," presuming that DOS would soon be supplanted by OS/2. Now after five years, 386 DOS extenders are solidly entrenched in the PC developer's market. MS-DOS, suitably extended, remains the operating system standard for the IBM microcomputer world, and the number of high-end commercial applications built with 386 DOS extenders continues to grow.

One surprise is that the four original players in this market—Phar Lap Software, Ergo Computing (formerly A.I. Architects), IGC, and Rational Systems—have remained the dominant marketers of 386 DOS extenders. Over time, only a handful of modest entries have joined the extended DOS ranks. For several years, Salford Software (Great Britain) has bundled its own DOS extender with 386/486 Fortran compilers marketed in the United States by OTG Systems. In 1990, Microsoft joined the club with the DOS extender and DPMI server built into Windows 3 Enhanced mode. In summer 1991, Zortech began to bundle their own 386 DOS extender with their C++ Developer's Edition. Although rumors have floated around for years that competing 386 DOS extenders were under development in the U.S. and abroad, so far none of these products has surfaced. In the interim, several of the existing 386 DOS extenders have been modified to run on special hardware—for example, the NEC 386 machines marketed in Japan and the Far East—thus opening up larger markets for 386 DOS applications.

Many features of the original DOS extenders have remained stable, but the producers have become much more complex and sophisticated with each successive version. The early 286 DOS extenders, discussed in the last chapter, could use the existing 16-bit compilers by supplying patches to their run time libraries for the protected mode. The 386 development tools were more limited and slow to develop. Some 386 DOS compilers were downright awkward to use compared with the DOS tools programmers had grown accustomed to. Source-code symbolic debuggers and execution profilers just weren't available. Nowadays you'll find an abundance of fine tools for 386 development, and the list keeps growing. As the market has matured, more and more programming tools continue to be ported from real-mode DOS and the minicomputer and workstation world to the extended DOS world. A wide choice of compiler languages and development environments is available, along with third-party libraries for every need, ranging from high-speed graphics to interrupt-driven serial communications.

DOS Extenders Today

With the introduction of Windows 3.0 in May 1990, a new set of problems and opportunities arose for the vendors of DOS extenders. Similar scenarios had occurred in the past. In 1987, Phar Lap Software and Quarterdeck Systems joined forces to develop the Virtual Control Program Interface (VCPI) discussed in Chapter 8. The VCPI headed off potential problems with DOS extenders and memory managers (such as Quarterdeck's QEMM, Qualitas's 386-Max, and Sourcer's Memory Commander), fighting for control of the 80386 in the protected mode. VCPI became an accepted standard in 1989, and VCPI support was swiftly added to almost all the DOS extenders and memory managers. The few exceptions were IGC's X-AM DOS extender and Microsoft's extended memory products.

After the development of VCPI, vendors of DOS extenders and memory managers responded to the XMS API, discussed in Chapter 3, for managing extended memory above 1MB. More recently, they have added support for Virtual DMA Services (VDS) specification needed for some hardware boards that incorporate their own DMA chips on the board (SCSI adapters and hard-disk controllers, for example). VDS ensures that programs (such as device drivers, tape backup software, etc.) can lock memory and retrieve an actual physical address that will be put on the system bus for DMA access. Without some sort of well-defined protocol, a memory manager, DOS extender, or multitasker might page out the target physical memory block during a transfer and substitute another logical chunk of memory.

Now Windows has introduced the DOS Protected-Mode Interface (DPMI) which we'll look at in detail in Chapter 9. DPMI was developed to manage memory access and virtualize PC hardware for DOS multitasking. But DPMI is general enough to allow DOS extended applications to run under any 386 operating system or control program that supports DPMI's specification. The first product to be released with support for DPMI, Windows 3.0, acts as a DPMI host. DPMI hosts have since been promised for IBM's OS/2 2.0 and from a number of 386/Unix vendors. For both 286 and 386 DOS extenders, the exciting changes are based on incorporating code to allow the extenders to operate as DPMI clients. Applications that incorporate these new DOS extender versions are able to run under Windows 3 in a DOS box and should run under future versions of OS/2 2.0 and Unix on 386/486 machines, as well as under plain old DOS.

The Windows 3 rollout in 1990 has been followed by a rash of new products and versions of 386 DOS extender products in 1991. Rational Systems, an early participant in the 286 DOS extender market, (discussed in the previous chapter) finally entered the 386 DOS extender market with several products in 1991. This year also saw a number of 386 compiler vendors adding products that allow their 386 DOS compilers to create stand alone 386 applications that run under Windows 3 without the use of a separate 386 DOS extender. Several of these products provide a true 32-bit Windows GUI API for programmers. If such a range of options sounds like a new lease on DOS life, that's because it is.

Products for Stretching DOS's Limits

Probably the best-known 32-bit DOS extender is Phar Lap Software's 386 | DOS-Extender. Applications built using the Phar Lap DOS extender include Interleaf Publisher (IBM), Mathematica (Wolfram Research), and AutoCAD 386 (Autodesk). Phar Lap defined the EASY OMF-386 format first used for 32-bit object files, and produces the basic development tools (a 386 assembler, linker, and librarian) traditionally used even with their competitors' DOS extenders.

This chapter focuses primarily on Phar Lap's 386 | DOS-Extender, but we'll look at a number of other 386 DOS extenders. Table 5-1 below describes these products, which include the following:

- OS/386 and EDU-32 from Ergo Computing
- IGC DOS extender, supplied with Intel and SVS compilers
- DBOS from Salford Software
- DOS/4G from Rational Systems
- DOSX extender, bundled with Zortech C++ Developer's Edition
- Windows 3 DOS extender and DPMI host

Table 5-1: 386 DOS Extenders at a Glance (Fall 1991).

Description				Memory Management			
Vendor	Product(s)	Current Version	First Introduced	VCPI Compatible	XMS Compatible	DPMI Compatible	Virtual Memory
Phar Lap	386 | DOS-Extender	4.0	1987	Y	Y	Y	Y
Ergo Computing	OS/386	2.1.05	1987	Y	Y	N	Y
	EDU-32	1.0	1991	Y	Y	Y	Y
Intel (IGC)	CodeBuilder	1.0c	1987	N	Y	Y	Y
Salford (OTG)	DBOS/WDB OS	2.44	1989	Y	Y	Y	Y
Rational	DOS/4G	1.0	1991	Y	Y	Y	Y
Zortech	DOSX	1.0	1991	Y	Y	N	N

Description				Memory Management			
Vendor	Product(s)	Current Version	First Introduced	VCPI Compatible	XMS Compatible	DPMI Compatible	Virtual Memory
Microsoft	Windows (DPMI)	3.0	1990	N	Y	—	Y

Ergo's new DPMI-compatible products—EDU-16 and EDU-32—are very similar to one another. OS/386 has been used in a number of important products, including Borland's Paradox/386 and Foxpro 2.0. The Ergo DOS extender is supplied with several 386 compilers (development systems) and has been attractive to commercial application developers because it is supplied with an unlimited run time license. This allows developers to create and market 386 extended applications without paying additional royalties or license fees for the DOS extender run time. The development software that bundles the Ergo DOS extender includes Lahey's Fortran F77L-EM/32; Microway's C, C++, Fortran, and Pascal compilers; and Meridien's OpenADA.

Rational Systems has recently introduced its 32-bit DOS/4G DOS extender—the 4G stands for 4 gigabytes. Again, this product is very similar to Rational Systems' DOS/16M. Lotus owns a substantial interest in Rational Systems, so we can presume that DOS/4G is likely to turn up in a future 386 version of Lotus 1-2-3. Although DOS/4G is a relative newcomer to the 386 DOS market, it is already shipped with several major 386 compilers. Microway bundles DOS/4G, with an unlimited run time license for the DOS extender, with its C, C++, Fortran, and Pascal compilers. Watcom also bundles DOS/4G, with an unlimited run time, with its C/8.5 386 and Fortran 77/386 development environments. These Watcom products also include the capability to create true 32-bit Windows GUI applications.

A 386 DOS extender from Intelligent Graphics Systems (IGC), based on its earlier X-AM product, is provided with the Intel 386/486 C Code Builder Kit and with new SVS C, Fortran, and Pascal 386 compilers. IGC markets its DOS extender as an OEM product, but compiler vendors like Intel and SVS bundle the extender with their development tools, including an unlimited run time license to the DOS extender. So, you can create and distribute extended DOS applications at no additional cost. And the Intel and SVS products are priced quite competitively, making them very attractive for small developers. The previous IGC DOS extender was also included in a number of important, older applications, including FoxBase+/386.

At least two other compiler vendors are bundling unlimited run time versions of 386 DOS extenders with their development environments: Alsys Ada (Phar Lap) and Zortech C++ (its own DOSX product).

We'll also briefly touch on the DBOS and WDBOS DOS extenders from Salford Software, which are more common in the European market.

Finally, we'll look at the DOS extender and the DPMI server provided with Windows 3, although we'll cover DPMI in greater detail in Chapter 9. A number of compiler vendors are providing products to create 386 applications that use Windows 3 instead of a separate 386 DOS extender. Some of these products are designed to create true 32-bit Windows GUI applications; others are designed to substitute the Windows 3 DOS extender for one of the separate DOS extender products.

386 DOS Extenders in the Marketplace

For several years now, the high-end CAD market on the PC has been dominated by the versions of CAD applications that incorporate 386 DOS extenders. These math-intensive, memory-hungry products benefit significantly from the 386 programming features made available by the DOS extenders, and the vendors in this market are virtually compelled to offer 386 versions to remain competitive.

386 DOS extenders are found in other graphics-and numerics-intensive applications, ranging from symbolic math packages such as Mathematica to high-end page layout programs such as Interleaf Publisher. Many of these products were ported from the Unix workstation world to the DOS environment. 386 DOS extenders have also appeared in database products—most notably Paradox/386, FoxBase+/386, and the newer FoxPro 2.0.

A number of program development environments employ 386 DOS extenders, including Smalltalk-80/386 (ParcPlace), Common Lisp CLOE-386 (Symbolics), Laboratory Microsystems UR/FORTH, APL-PLUS II (STSC), and Ada/386 (Alsys). Finally, it is now common to find DOS development tools incorporating 386 DOS extenders to free them from DOS memory constraints and code limitations. These tools range from Unix-style *lint* programs to PostScript interpreters.

Certainly, other schemes such as EMS and XMS can provide partial solutions to DOS memory limits. But 386 DOS extenders solve both memory and speed problems simply and directly. When your application outgrows memory space or needs a performance boost, it's time to consider 32-bit programming. Let's take a look at 32-bit benefits in more detail.

Onward to 32 Bits

How is a 386-based protected-mode DOS extender superior to the 286-based extenders we examined in Chapter 4? After all, these 286 extenders, while based on AT class machines, can also run on the 386 and 486. Since a purely 386-based extender has the obvious disadvantage of addressing a smaller share of the market, what advantages does it offer over a 286-based DOS extender?

Many of the advantages of using the 386's native mode can be summed up in the single phrase 32 bits. If you have heard this phrase in the trade press but have never seen a sample of 32-bit code, you are in for a treat. Once you've written 32-bit code, you're not likely to want to return to the 16-bit code you've been writing.

Let's take a realistic C function and examine the way it might be implemented, using 16-bit code first and then using 32-bit code:

```
void swap (char **p, char **q)
{
     char *temp;

     temp = *p;
     *p = *q;
     *q = temp;
}
```

This swap function would commonly be used by sorting functions to swap pointers to strings. If you were you to compile this code in small model (16-bit pointers) with a typical 16-bit MS-DOS compiler such as Microsoft's C 6.0, the resulting assembly output might look something like this:

```
push    bp                        ; setup stack frame pointer
mov     bp,sp
push    di                        ; preserve possible register variable
                                  ; register dx = temp
mov     di,word ptr [bp+4]        ; get pointer to p
mov     bx,word ptr [bp+6]        ; get pointer to temp

mov     dx,word ptr [di]          ; temp = *p
mov     ax,word ptr [bx]          ; *p = *q
mov     word ptr [di],ax
```

```
mov     word ptr [bx],dx          ; *q = temp

pop     di                        ; restore register variable
mov     sp,bp                     ; epilogue
pop     bp
ret
```

This assembly language implementation closely matches the higher-level C representation. It is hard to improve on this code.

If your application can live within the 64KB code and 64KB data limits of the 8086 small model, then 386 DOS extenders won't provide much benefit. Unfortunately, most commercial software (word processors, spreadsheets, database managers, telecommunications programs, etc.) require more code and data space than the 64KB maximum allowed by the small model. Thus, commercial PC software is more frequently compiled with the compact or large model, using 32-bit (4-byte) pointers in a 16-bit environment. Using, for example, another popular 16-bit DOS compiler (Borland C++), the large-model implementation of foo() looks like this:

```
push    bp                        ; setup stack frame pointer
mov     bp,sp
sub     sp,4                      ; allocate space for char *temp;
;           temp = *p
les     bx,dword ptr [bp+6]       ; get pointer to p
mov     ax,word ptr es:[bx+2]     ; move bottom half of p into AX
mov     dx,word ptr es:[bx]       ; move top half of p into DX
mov     word ptr [bp-2],ax        ; move AX into bottom half of temp
mov     word ptr [bp-4],dx        ; move DX into top half of temp
;         *p = *q
les     bx,dword ptr [bp+10]      ; get pointer to q
mov     ax,word ptr es:[bx+2]     ; move bottom half of q into AX
mov     dx,word ptr es:[bx]       ; move top half of q into DX
les     bx,dword ptr [bp+6]       ; get pointer to p
mov     word ptr es:[bx+2],ax     ; move AX into bottom half of p
mov     word ptr es:[bx],dx       ; move DX into top half of p
;         *q = temp;
les     bx,dword ptr [bp+10]      ; get pointer to q
mov     ax,word ptr [bp-2]        ; move bottom half of temp into AX
mov     dx,word ptr [bp-4]        ; move top half of temp into DX
mov     word ptr es:[bx+2],ax     ; move AX into bottom half of q
mov     word ptr es:[bx],dx       ; move DX into top half of q

mov     sp,bp
```

```
pop     bp
ret
```

What happened? Why did three simple C constructs swell into 21 assembly language statements? An inherent inefficiency of 16-bit code is revealed: 32-bit quantities such as longs (dwords) and far pointers are moved piecemeal, 16 bits (2 bytes) at a time. Remember that these 32-bit quantities are the rule rather than the exception in commercial software. Also remember that running this code on the fastest 386 or 486 CPU will not make it transfer more than 2 bytes at a time. To do that, you need 32-bit protected mode: not just protected mode, mind you, but *32-bit* protected mode, since a 286-based DOS extender, even running on a 386 machine, is still very much a 16-bit beast.

Now for a breath of fresh air. Here is how foo() is implemented in flat model (4-byte pointers) by one 32-bit C compiler, MetaWare High C v2.32, which produces code suitable for a 386 DOS extender:

```
push    ebx             : save possible frame pointer
mov     edx,8[esp]      ; get pointer to p
;        temp = *p
mov     ebx,[edx]       ; move p into temp (register EBX)
;         *p = *q
mov     eax,12[esp]     ; get pointer to q
mov     ecx,[eax]       ; move q into ECX
mov     [edx],ecx       ; move ECX into p
;         *q = temp
mov     [eax],ebx       ; move temp into q (EAX)
pop     ebx
ret
```

These nine lines of 32-bit code illustrate many of the advantages of using an 80386 machine as it was meant to be used—in protected mode, rather than as a fast 8088. First of all, we can see that once you decide to use the full 32-bit registers on the 386 (such as EAX instead of AX), 32-bit quantities can obviously be MOVed into the registers in one fell swoop. Second, having 32-bit registers opens the possibility of keeping 32-bit quantities in registers rather than on the stack or in memory. Third, the 386 allows indirectly referencing memory with almost any register, instead of with just the old base (BX and BP) and index registers (SI and DI). You can use a construct such as MOV EAX, [EAX] instead of having to write something like MOV BX, AX followed by MOV AX, [BX]. This more flexible use of registers helps with the notorious "too few registers" problem faced by compiler writers.

Fourth, note how the LES BX instruction disappeared when we switched to 32-bit protected mode. In fact, all mention of segmentation disappeared entirely. Again, this provides a sharp contrast with a 286-based protected-mode version, which not only requires the LES BX instruction, but which additionally exacts a stiff penalty for its use. Throughout this chapter, we will see that 32-bit protected mode allows you to largely forget about segmentation.

With the advantages exhibited in this tiny example, it is not surprising that 32-bit code can execute much faster than comparable 16-bit code on the same hardware. Table 5-2 below compares the execution time for a short test program that calls our *swap* function one million times on different 386/486 hardware. The waste involved in using 386s as "fast" XTs should now be clear.

Table 5-2: Execution time in seconds for calling swap() function.

Note: Execution times for 1 million iterations. Everex Step 386/25 and AMI 486/33 machines both have 128KB external static RAM caches. Microsoft C 6.0 produces slower large model code with the -G2 (80286) switch on 386/25 and 486/33 machines.

Compiler/model	Everex 386/25	AMI 486/33
Microsoft C 6.0a (small)	3.07	0.99
Microsoft C 6.0a (large)	6.70	3.07
DOS 16/M w C 6.0a (large)	9.83	4.06
MetaWare High C 386 v2.32	3.02	0.88

It should also be clear that, to reap the benefits of 32-bit protected mode, we cannot simply cannibalize the output of a 16-bit compiler as we did when using 286-based DOS extenders. Unless you are writing entirely in assembly language, using a 386 DOS extender requires that you switch to a 32-bit compiler, such as MetaWare High C-386, Watcom C/386, NDP Pascal-386, or Lahey Fortran F77-LEM/32.

Now, it is true that the full 32-bit registers can be used in real mode as well. Few MS-DOS compilers provide an option to generate 80386 instructions (Microsoft C, for example, has a -G2 switch to generate 286 instructions, but no equivalent -G3 switch). But, in parts of your program that will run only on a 386 or 486, you could include assembly language sequences such as the following (which read the 4-byte BIOS timer count into EAX):

```
xor ax,ax                    ; zero ax
mov es,ax                    ; mov 0 into ES
mov eax, es:[46Ch]           ; dereference dword ptr 0000:046C  into EAX
```

There are at least two limitations to this approach, however. First, when using 386 instructions in real mode, you are still stuck with the 640KB limit of MS-DOS—and the 64KB segments and the 1-megabyte limit of real mode itself. The benefit of 32-bit processing in 386 protected mode is not just greater speed, but a far larger space as well. Since 32-bit registers can be used as base and index registers, the near pointers loaded into these registers can use up to 32 bits for addressing memory. This, in turn, means that the maximum index within a memory segment is no longer FFFFH (64KB-1), but FFFFFFFFH (4GB-1).

Second, some multitasking software, such as the OS/2 1.0-1.2 DOS compatibility box, older versions of Windows/386, and even the 386 ROM BIOS code from several vendors, use only the bottom 16 bits of the registers to save a program's context. These problems can wreak havoc with real-mode programs that use 32-bit registers. Fortunately, newer BIOS software OS/2 1.3 and 2.0 and Windows 3.x do not have these shortcoming.

Benefits of Using 386 Protected-Mode DOS Extenders

We have seen that once a DOS extender opens up the power of the 80386/80486 CPU a number of key features are available to the programmer. Let's now look at the benefits systematically:

- large address spaces for code and data
- low overhead of the flat memory model
- powerful 32-bit instructions
- virtual memory options
- highly optimizing compilers
- faster numerics using Weitek and Cyrix memory-mapped math coprocessors.

Wide Open Spaces

While the 8088 microprocessor used in the original IBM PC could address only 1 megabyte of physical memory, the 80386 and 80486 CPUs can access much larger memory spaces—up to 4 gigabytes. Typical, older 80386 AT and PS/2-style machines support up to 16 megabytes of physical memory, but many of the new

ISA and EISA 80386 and 80486 computers (the Compaq SystemPro, for example) can support from 64 to 256 megabytes of physical memory. As memory chip prices have dropped and 4MBx9 SIMM modules (based on 4MBx1 dynamic RAM chips) have become available, it is now common to find 8 to 16 MBs of memory in many high-end 386 and 486 machines. Nowadays, a typical basic 486 machine would be outfitted with 8 megabytes.

In this context, the 640KB DOS memory limit is a barrier to developing large applications for the PC and to moving large applications to the PC. With the 640KB DOS limit, large PC programs that depend on overlays and swapping code or data to disk are prevented from taking advantage of the larger memory capacity of these 386/486 PCs. Furthermore, the segmented architecture of 80*x*86 real mode (and virtual-8086 mode, too) still limits code and data segments to 64KB, so 80386 instructions that would access memory without the inconvenience of 64K segment limits can't be used. These include the memory indirect and indexing instructions that use registers such as EBX with values greater than 64KB, the maximum 16-bit value of BX.

Reduced Overhead in the Flat Memory Model

Because 32-bit protected mode breaks the 64KB segment barrier in addition to the 640KB DOS barrier, the most common memory model is a flat one (analogous to real-mode "tiny" model used in .COM files) in which all segment registers (now selectors) point to the same block of memory—up to 4 gigabytes of 32-bit address space with no segments. In a high-level language such as C, a 32-bit near pointer is a 4-byte quantity. This in turn means that you almost never have to deal with segmented far pointers: once loaded, DS and CS can stay constant.

Using this model, 386 DOS extenders have much lower software overhead than their 286 extender cousins. Table 5-2 compared instruction times published by Intel for common 386 instructions operating in the flat model to those under a segmented model. While these instruction times will vary depending on various RAM caches and 386 memory system designs, they indicate the potential performance benefits of operating a 386 program in a flat model.

While no longer needed for an application's data and code, segmentation can still be used to implement sharing and to enforce protection. In a DOS extender, segments are sometimes used to access real-mode services. When you do need to specify a segment as well as an offset, the resulting far pointer is a 6-byte quantity (an fword).

On those rare occasions when you have to change a segment register, a penalty similar to the one we found in 286 protected mode applies to 386 instruction times. (See Table 5-2.)

32-bit Instructions

The 80386/486 microprocessors have full 32-bit wide internal data paths and registers. The low-end 80386SX chip has an external 16-bit data path designed to reduce hardware and motherboard costs. But the rest of the 386/486 chips in this family connect to the external world with a full 32-bit wide external path for memory access. On these chips, accessing a 32-bit-wide value in memory (a "long" in C) takes the same time as accessing a byte. And adding two 32-bit registers containing longs takes the same time as adding two bytes.

The 386/486 microprocessors feature instruction sets much closer in power to the CPUs used in minicomputers than to the instruction sets of older microprocessors like the 8086:

- Register and memory access is widened to 32 bits. 16-bit registers such as BX, BP, IP, and FLAGS have been extended to 32-bit registers such as EBX, EBP, EIP, and EFLAGS.
- All 32-bit registers, except ESP, can be used as either base or index registers for memory addressing.
- A scaling factor (2, 4, or 8) can be applied to an index register for memory addressing, providing faster array processing.
- Two additional segment registers (FS and GS) have been added for addressing memory.
- String instructions can now operate on double words (4 bytes).
- Instructions are available for converting an 8-bit or 16-bit operandi to 32 or 64 bits (CWDE, CDQ, MOVSX, MOVZX).
- Bit manipulation instructions are added for testing, setting, and scanning bits (BT, BTC, BTR, BTS, BSF, BSR) in registers or bit arrays in memory.
- The signed multiply (IMUL) instruction has a more general form that allows the use of any register for a destination.
- The LEA instruction is enhanced to perform fast integer multiplication.

- Instructions are added to set or clear bytes based on condition codes in the flags register (SETcc).
- Shift instructions support 8-bit, 16-bit, 32-bit, and 64-bit shifts (SHLD, SHRD).
- Additional system control registers (CR0, CR2, CR3), test registers (TR6, TR7), and debug registers (DR0, DR1, DR2, DR3, DR6, DR7) have been added.

With a few exceptions (some system control functions and memory addressing options), most of these instructions are available in 386 real mode as well as in protected mode. The 386 instruction set supports two instruction prefix override bytes:

- OPSIZ—operand size prefix (66h)
- ADRSIZ—address size prefix (67h)

Intel doesn't give these prefix bytes mnemonics, so I have used the acronyms used by Ross Nelson in Chapter 1. OPSIZ toggles the operandi word size of the next instruction. In protected mode, the normal word size is 32 bits. Prefixing an instruction with OPSIZ converts it to a 16-bit instruction. Similarly, when code is running in the real mode, the default word size is 16 bits, and applying the OPSIZ prefix converts a 16-bit instruction to a 32-bit instruction. So XOR AX,AX (zero the 16-bit AX register) in real mode becomes XOR EAX,EAX (zero the 32-bit EAX register) when the instruction is prefixed by OPSIZ. Similarly, the ADRSIZ prefix toggles between 16-bit addressing and 32-bit addressing.

But to use the features of the 80386 within real-mode DOS, a developer would have to provide two versions of an application—one for the 8086 and one for the 80386/486. The preferred scheme would be to have the program sense the presence of the 80386 at run time and use the faster 386 instructions available. To be most beneficial, the 80386 instructions need to be programmed as in-line code. Only a few 80386 instructions can justify such effort in real mode: MOVSD (double word move) and DIV and IDIV (long integer divide).

Many real-mode products already use MOVSD for moving blocks of data and for string routines when executing on the 386, because twice the amount of data is moved in the same amount of time. Examples include the PKZIP compression utility by PKWARE, FoxPro from Fox Software, as well as the standard C string and memory copying library functions provided with many DOS compilers such as Borland's C++ compiler.

The DIV and IDIV instructions were the slowest instructions on the 8086. In supporting the 4-byte data type such as the "long" in C and INTEGER in Fortran, subroutines for addition, subtraction, division, and multiplication needed to be called. On the 80386, these subroutines can be replaced with single in-line instructions. In terms of clock cycles, long division shows the greatest benefit in execution speed. A long divide library routine is one place where using these 386 instructions in real mode justifies the effort to detect the 80386.

The true benefits of the 386 instruction set can be realized only when a program is targeted directly for 32-bit protected mode. Instructions now operate on 32-bit wide registers and memory, as well as the 8-bit and 16-bit registers of earlier Intel chips.

In the earlier Intel CPUs, memory could be addressed using the BP and BX registers as base pointers, and SI and DI registers for indexing. The BX register defaulted to addressing the data segment (DS), and the BP register defaulted to the stack segment (SS) for local (dynamic) storage. The 80386 makes memory addressing more general: any 32-bit register can be used as a base register. And all eight 32-bit registers, except ESP, can be used for indexing. In addition, a scaling factor of 2, 4, or 8 can be applied to any register used for indexing, when referencing memory. This is a very attractive feature for indexing arrays of words (2-byte integers), double words (4-byte long integers and reals), quad words (8-byte double precision reals), and some multidimensional arrays. These addressing modes are well suited to the needs of high-level languages. In the following examples, note that the notation 12[edx] is equivalent to [edx+12]:

```
mov esi, [eax]            ; use EAX as a base register

mov eax, 12[edx]          ; use EDX as base with displacement

mov eax, [ecx + edx*4]    ; use ECX as base pointer and
                          ;  EDX as an index register with  scaling
mov eax, 256[esp + edx*8] ; use ESP as base, EDX as index  with
                          ;  a displacement (stack segment)
```

The 80386 string instructions support forms that operate on up to 32 bits at a time and can use the EAX register rather than AX. These instructions include LODSD, STOSD, MOVSD, CMPSD, and SCASD. The MOVSD instruction (move double from [ESI] to [EDI]) executes in the same time as the earlier MOVSW (move word from [SI] to [DI]). Since the ECX register is used for the loop counter, large blocks (up to 4 gigabytes) can be moved at one time:

```
cld                     ; set forward direction for block move
mov ecx, 28000h         ; count of double words to move
mov esi, source         ; point to source
mov edi, destination ;   and destination
rep movsd               ;   and move them
```

Several instructions are available for converting one operandi size to a larger one. CWDE (convert word to dword, extended) sign-extends AX into EAX. CDQ (convert dword to quadword) sign-extends EAX into EDX:EAX. MOVSX is a more general form that sign-extends a byte or a word into a 16-bit or 32-bit register. MOVZX is a similar instruction that zero-extends a byte or a word.

Six instructions are added to operate on bits in either registers or memory. BT (bit test) can be used to determine the setting of any arbitrary bit. For simple bit testing, the AND (logical) instruction can execute faster. But the BTC (bit test and complement), BTR (bit test and reset), and BTS (bit test and set) instructions combine bit testing with bit setting, clearing, and complementing, and are useful for implementing semaphores. BSF (bit scan forward) and BSR (bit scan reverse) find the first set bit (value of 1) in a bit stream. These instructions can be very useful when working on bit arrays, including graphics routines and allocation schemes for memory or disk space. A key feature is that these instructions can operate on bitmaps as large as 4 gigabits.

Several enhancements handle integer multiplication. IMUL (signed multiplication) is no longer limited to only the EAX register; any register can be the destination, providing greater flexibility. The fastest execution improvement is a new form of the LEA (Load Effective Address) instruction using scaled index addressing that performs fast integer multiplication in registers. This LEA form is limited to multiplications by small integers (2, 3, 4, 5, 8, and 9). However, this instruction executes in two clock cycles—far faster than either multiply or shift instructions—so a couple of LEA instructions can still execute faster than one multiply. The following example converts hours in the CH register to minutes in the EAX register:

```
; the traditional method
mov eax,60
mul ch

; using fast small integer multiplies
movzx eax,ch          ; start with hours
```

```
lea eax,[eax+eax*4] ; x 5 use some fast integer multiplies
lea eax,[eax*4]     ; x 20
lea eax,[eax+eax*2] ; x 60
```

A large group of SETcc (set byte on condition code) instructions are added to set or clear byte-sized booleans based on the CPU's status flags. All conditions supported by the JMP instructions are allowed. These instructions provide a way to avoid conditional JMPs that would empty the prefetch instruction queue:

```
; the traditional method
xor edx,edx             ; assume boolean variable is false
or eax,eax              ; test EAX for non-zero
jz next                 ; if zero, this JMP flushes the prefetch  queue
inc edx                 ; set EDX to true
next:

; using SETcc instruction
xor edx,edx             ; assume that boolean variable is false
or eax,eax              ;  and test for nonzero in EAX
setnz dl                ; set flag DL=true if EAX is non-zero
```

Paging and Virtual Memory

Along with the segmented memory management also found in 286-based protected mode, the 386 provides the ability to use paging, in which physical memory is tiled with 4KB pages to form a linear address space. The use of paging and segmentation combines the best of both memory management techniques. Such a combination is not unique to the 386 and is described in many standard textbooks on computer architecture.

Using the hardware paging capabilities of the 80386/486, Phar Lap Software has a virtual-memory option, 386|VMM (Virtual Memory Manager), to work with its 386|DOS-Extender. The other 386 DOS extenders also support paging and virtual memory. As in other, more powerful operating systems like Unix and VAX VMS, the amount of memory available for an application is limited by available disk space rather than by physical memory in the machine.

The virtual memory features provided by the 386 DOS extenders allow memory-hungry applications to run on 386 machines configured with relatively small amounts of physical memory (more common with 80386SX PCs). For example, in one high-end technical publishing program ported from a workstation environment (Interleaf Publisher), the original version for the 386 required a minimum of

5 megabytes of physical memory to run. The same program incorporating the Phar Lap Virtual Memory Manager needs only a 2-megabyte machine.

A large application ported from the minicomputer world may need to manipulate arrays of data several megabytes in size. This instantly becomes possible on PCs using 386 DOS extenders. Most 386 DOS compilers now support allocating arrays and memory structures up to 16 or 32 megabytes—larger than the physical memory size of most 386 machines. This is particularly attractive for sorting and indexing large database applications and manipulating large CAD and CAE graphics files.

Of course, you do incur a performance penalty when you virtualize memory. If the entire application will not fit in physical memory, some code or data is swapped to a disk file and automatically brought into memory as needed. The less swapping that takes place, the faster the program executes. A program targeted for operation under a virtual memory manager will benefit from some up-front planning and design to minimize swapping.

In addition, paging itself can also slow down memory access. Although the 80386 has a built-in, on-chip cache (the translation look aside buffer, TLB) of the 32 most recently used page table entries to speed memory access, it represents only 128KB of memory. Intel's simulations suggest that this should accommodate about 98 percent of normal memory access, but this depends on the code. If a page table entry is not in the cache, the 386 must read two double-word entries from the page translation table in memory before it can access the actual memory location of interest. But compared with code overlays and EMS, paging and virtual memory can provide much more flexible and superior performance.

If raw speed is of the utmost importance for your application, adding more physical memory will provide the fastest execution. This is seen in the many published benchmarks that compare programs run under 386 DOS extenders with those running Unix/386 on the same hardware. Since Unix provides virtual memory by default, the DOS extenders have a distinct advantage.

Optimizing Compilers

In addition to the language compilers moved up to the 386 from the DOS world, a number of highly optimizing compilers have been ported to the 386 from minicomputers and the Unix workstation world. These include the Numeric Data Processor (NDP) series from Microway (retargeting Green Hills compilers) and compilers from Silicon Valley Software (SVS), Liant Software (formerly LPI), and Alsys. Some of these compilers have a mainframe rather than a PC "feel," and are more likely to be used for porting an application "down" from the VAX to the 386 than for porting an application "up" from the PC.

Because these compilers run on the 386, both local and global optimizations which would be difficult or impossible within DOS memory limits, are possible. Special mainframe optimizations, like vectorizing and loop unrolling, that have previously been available only on the fastest machines are becoming available on the PC platform. The execution speed of the code generated from these optimizing compilers is most noticeable for math-intensive CAD and scientific applications.

However, not all 386 compilers are targeted for use with a DOS extender. A number of 386 compilers are designed to generate code for Unix or other operating systems. Many of the vendors that market 386 DOS extender development tools sell similar products for the Unix/386 or the embedded system marketplace. Although similar, these Unix compilers generate code for Unix or embedded applications, not for DOS extenders. This does allow a DOS or Unix/386 developer to more easily convert a product for these other platforms.

Faster Numerics with Memory-Mapped Coprocessors

Although PC software has supplanted many applications from the minicomputer and mainframe world (word processing, spreadsheets, and databases, for example), math-intensive applications have traditionally remained in the realm of the big machine. Historically, floating-point math has been much slower than similar integer-based arithmetic. As a result, chip designers have used separate math units as coprocessors.

The ability to run fast numeric applications was a design goal of the 386/486 chip family. The original 80386 supported three math chips:

- Intel 80287 coprocessor—I/O mapped
- Intel 80387 coprocessor—I/O mapped
- Weitek 1167 chip set—memory mapped

Today, the 386/486 family also supports the following chips:

- Intel 80387SX coprocessor—I/O mapped for 80386SX machines
- Intel 80487 coprocessor—I/O mapped and integrated with the 80486 CPU
- Cyrix EMC87—a faster, memory-mapped 80387

- Weitek 3167 coprocessor—a memory-mapped, single chip, 121-pin implementation of the 1167 for the 80386
- Weitek 4167 coprocessor—similar to the 3167, but for the 80486

In addition, pin-compatible replacement 80387 math coprocessors are now available from Cyrix, Integrated Information Technology (IIT), and Specialty Development Corporation (SDC). Chips and Technologies and AMD will soon enter this already crowded market.

Two physical approaches to attaching a coprocessor to the main CPU are available: I/O mapping and memory mapping. In I/O mapping, the math coprocessor is linked directly with the 386/486 by a direct connection over the I/O bus. Although this I/O connection is direct, the math chip and the CPU end up communicating over a high-speed synchronous interface that has significant handshaking and synchronization overhead.

Instead of communicating at I/O bus speeds, a memory-mapped coprocessor interfaces at much faster memory bus speeds. A memory-mapped coprocessor uses an address range in the 4-gigabyte memory space to communicate with the CPU chip. By convention, a Weitek or Cyrix memory-mapped coprocessor masquerades as a 64KB block of memory in the 80386's physical memory space at 0C0000000H; however, supporting software usually maps these addresses elsewhere.

Tables 5-3 and 5-4 compare the benchmark performance of these coprocessors in a 33MHz 80386 machine and a 33MHz 80486 machine (used with permission from "Divide and Conquer" by Mark Barrenchea in *Programmer's Journal*, v 9.5, September 1991). The benchmarks are based on separating the common Whetstone Program into scalar, matrix, and transcendental calculations. The memory-mapped coprocessors can deliver from 1.5 to 3 times the floating point speed of their I/O-mapped counterparts. In fact, it's interesting to observe that a 386 with a Cyrix EMC87 (memory-mapped) is, overall, slightly faster than the Intel 486/487 combination.

Table 5-3: Comparing coprocessors, single precision (KWhets/sec).

Coprocessor	WhetMat	WhetScal	WhetTrans	WhetStone
386:				
Cyrix 83D87	851	1445	2217	5075
Cyrix EMC87	1848	4050	3557	7934
Weitek 3167	2699	4332	1582	6719
Intel 387DX	849	1492	910	3800
486:				
Weitek 4167	5967	12995	4238	15148
Intel 487DX	2460	3876	1610	7934

Table 5-4: Comparing coprocessors, double precision (KWhets/sec).

Coprocessor	WhetMat	WhetScal	WhetTrans	WhetStone
386:				
Cyrix 83D87	711	1389	2890	4673
Cyrix EMC87	1186	3570	4427	6757
Weitek 3167	1120	3804	1570	5378
Intel 387DX	713	1339	1039	3509
486:				
Weitek 4167	2783	10756	3951	12995
Intel 487DX	2263	3651	1734	7577

While the I/O-mapped coprocessors are available in real mode, the faster memory-mapped math chips are generally supported by compilers and development tools only in protected mode. The two exceptions to this rule are the 16-bit DOS compilers from Lahey (F77L) and MetaWare (High C and Professional Pascal) that support the Weitek chips from real mode. (An EMS simulator that maps the Weitek chip to segment FFFEh must be installed.) If your application is math-intensive and requires blazing speed, the protected mode and the Cyrix EMC and Weitek coprocessors are for you.

The 386 DOS Extenders—How They Work

Before we explore your options for 386 DOS development, a brief explanation of how the whole DOS extender process works is in order. Although Windows 3.0 adds some new possibilities, the general scheme is the same for all 386 DOS extenders. In the process of building most 386 extended applications, you're actually combining two separate programs: your 386 application code is combined with the DOS extender run time code to create a single executable DOS file.

The DOS extender run time code is typically licensed from a vendor such as Phar Lap Software, Ergo Computing, or Rational Systems. However, some companies (Intel, SVS, MicroWay, Lahey, Zortech, Meridien, and Alsys, for example) now provide the run time code royalty-free with their compiler environments. In all cases, the DOS extender run time is bound to the beginning of your 386 program, using some tool supplied by the DOS extender vendor. Although the 386 application file may be very large, the *bind* tool builds the executable file so that only a small, initial part of it is considered the executable file that DOS will load.

From DOS's perspective, a bound 386 DOS application looks like any other program. DOS loads the program (in this case, it's most likely just the DOS extender run time part of the file) into conventional memory in real mode and passes control to the DOS extender. Then, the extender run time code swings into action. All the DOS extenders have several parts:

- Initialization code to set up and enter protected mode
- A protected mode initializer and loader for the 386 application to be executed
- Core DOS extender code that communicates between protected mode (your application) and real mode (DOS and BIOS services) and handles mode switching
- Clean up code to shut down from the protected mode and return to the real mode when the 386 application has terminated

The Initialization Process—What Kind of Machine Am I?

The DOS extender initialization code must complete a number of functions. First, it must test that the application is actually running on a 386 or 486 machine. If so, the initialization code continues by gathering a variety of other information, including the machine architecture IBM microchannel, EISA, or IBM-AT-compatible. Depending on the machine type, different code for mode switching may be used later on by the DOS extender.

Tests are made for the presence of various extended memory management APIs. To cope with all possible situations, DOS extenders must incorporate support for a number of different ways to allocate extended memory above 1 megabyte:

- Bottom-up extended memory allocation (first used by the VDISK.SYS RAM disk supplied with DOS)

- Hooking the INT 15h interrupt handler (function 88h) for top-down memory allocation
- Calling the VCPI provided by 386 memory managers (EMS and XMS simulators)
- Calling XMS drivers (the HIMEM.SYS device driver supplied with Windows and DOS 5)
- Using the DOS Protected Mode Interface (DPMI) supplied by Windows 3

Software interrupt vectors and the status of various hardware chips must be interrogated. All of this information is saved in data structures that are used later by the DOS extender run time.

Next, memory is allocated from the lower 640KB for system data structures used in the process: the Global Descriptor Table (GDT), Local Descriptor Table (LDT), Interrupt Descriptor Table (IDT), and page tables that will be used in the protected mode. We've discussed these data structures before in Chapter 1. These system data structures are built while the DOS extender is operating in real mode.

Finally, the DOS extender run time is ready to switch into the protected mode. In fact, to complete the initialization process, the DOS extender will commonly switch mode several times by calling entry points for protected mode routines.

The Protected Mode Loader

The extender usually does some parts of the initialization process in protected mode. It may allocate further memory for page tables and initialize these data structures. The DOS extender must also allocate extended memory for your 386 application and load the program. Under VCPI, the DOS extender must do a considerable amount of work to set up the proper data structures. To work around bugs in the Windows 3.0 DPMI implementation, the DOS extender run times may actually have to modify Windows 3 code on the fly.

The memory space needed to load and execute the 386 extended-DOS application is determined from a special 386 EXE-like header structure at the beginning of the 386 code. The 386 linker and binder will have created this header automatically. These 386 headers vary from one DOS extender to another.

The scheme used by the DOS extender to allocate extended memory will vary considerably depending on whether the DOS extender has detected VCPI, DPMI, XMS, or one of the other APIs. One method or combination of methods will be used to allocate extended memory for the application. The 386 executable code is then loaded from disk into extended memory. Any further data structures are created and initialized. The run time sets up the DOS environment for the application, including pointers (selectors) to the environment, to the program segment prefix (PSP), and to the default interrupt handlers for various DOS interrupts (for example, Control-Break and DOS terminate).

Once the initialization process is completed, much of this setup code can be jettisoned to reduce the amount of memory occupied by the DOS extender run time. Finally, the DOS extender transfers control to the 386 application.

The DOS Extender Core—Two Machines in One

One way to think of a DOS extender is as a communication system between two machines—a 386 protected-mode pseudoDOS computer and a real-mode DOS computer. The DOS extender run time has set up the IDT in such a way that any hardware, software, or exception interrupts will be vectored to itself, the DOS extender kernel. We need to distinguish among three types of interrupts:

- Hardware interrupts caused by an external event like a keypress, disk I/O completion, or the system clock tick every 52 milliseconds
- Software interrupts that are issued by a program generally to make DOS (INT 21h) or ROM BIOS calls
- Exceptions and traps built into the 386 chip that are triggered by some exceptional condition such as an invalid opcode, a general protection fault, or a divide by 0

The 386 application runs uninterrupted until it issues a software INT instruction, or a hardware interrupt or exception occurs. When an interrupt occurs in protected mode, several options are available for the DOS extender. Let's illustrate the process for a hardware interrupt first since it is simpler to understand.

Hardware Interrupt Processing

When a hardware interrupt occurs from the protected mode, it will be vectored to the protected-mode part of the DOS-extender kernel. Its default behavior will proceed as follows:

1. The DOS extender saves all the 32-bit registers and the interrupt number into a shared data structure (usually a stack) below 640KB and accessible from real mode.

2. The DOS extender switches to real mode and gives control to the real mode part of the DOS extenders.
3. The real-mode DOS extender reloads all of the general registers from the shared data structure. The segment registers are initialized with suitable values for real-mode.
4. The real-mode kernel reissues the interrupt.
5. After the hardware interrupt has finished executing, control returns to the real-mode DOS extender kernel.
6. The real-mode extender saves the returned registers (except the segment registers) into the shared system data structure.
7. The extender switches back to the protected mode and gives control to the protected-mode part of the DOS extender.
8. The protected-mode extender reloads all the general registers and the original segment registers and returns to the application.

The crucial part of this process is the two chunks of code that switch between real and protected mode. This code is written in assembly language to be as efficient and fast as possible. Depending on the machine architecture (IBM PS/2 microchannel, for example), different code will be used for mode switching.

Software Interrupt Processing

Handling of a software interrupt varies depending on whether the interrupt is a special one (DOS or BIOS) that the DOS extender supports and therefore watches for, or a non-special interrupt that is passed to real mode by default.

For a non special software interrupt, the process is virtually the same as for a hardware interrupt—the interrupt is reissued in the real mode. But for those special (DOS and BIOS) interrupts that we're most interested in, the DOS extender kernel may perform some further processing. For a DOS or ROM BIOS interrupt that uses only register values (none containing pointers), the process is much the same. But, for a software interrupt that passes pointers to data, the DOS extender adds another layer of processing to both the protected-and real-mode part. The parameters to the software interrupt must be passed between the protected-and real-mode machines.

Let's illustrate this with the DOS Open File call (INT 21h, function 3Dh). In 386 protected mode, the application supplies a pointer to an ASCIIZ string in registers DS:EDX. The DOS extender must copy this string from extended memory to a buffer below 640KB, and point DS:DX to this string before reissuing the DOS INT 21h call. In conventional memory during its initialization, the DOS-extender kernel typically sets aside a buffer for parameter passing. This default parameter buffer varies from 4KB to 64KB in size, depending on the DOS extender, and may be user configurable. If the software interrupt were for a file read or write, then the entire block of data to read/write would have to be copied between extended memory and conventional memory. A large read/write call issued from protected mode (larger than the parameter passing buffer) would have to be broken into smaller calls for the real-mode DOS kernel. This process is the same for all DOS and BIOS special interrupts that require processing by the DOS extender. Internally, the DOS extender maintains tables of functions for the interrupts of interest to simplify the actual work of parameter passing . A small subset of the DOS functions are handled completely by the protected-mode part of the DOS extender and are not reissued to real-mode DOS. These include memory management functions. To manage memory, the kernel mimics DOS behavior and manages the allocation and freeing of extended memory for the application.

In addition, all the DOS extenders support extended function calls unique to each extender for special services. The calling conventions to access these special services may vary from one vendor to another, but the general functions are similar. These services include interrupt handling, communication with real mode, and virtual memory swapping or paging control. For example, the DOS extenders all support calls to get and set both real-and protected mode interrupt vectors, and calls that control how interrupts are to be handled (for example, always pass a particular interrupt to the real-mode or protected-mode handler).

CPU Exception Processing

The final class of interrupts is CPU exceptions. Intel reserved the first 32 interrupts (INT 0 through 1Fh) for CPU exceptions and traps. Unfortunately, the original IBM PC hardware and ROM BIOS routines use some of these same interrupt vectors. The protected-mode extender kernel installs default handlers for exceptions such as divide by 0 trap and a general protection fault (memory access violation). For a general protection fault, the default behavior is to print out an offending instruction address (CS:EIP) and terminate the program. If a protected-mode debugger has been installed, such exceptions are taken over and fielded by the debugger. Because of the 386 protection mechanisms, the DOS extender may allow only limited access to these exception handlers from the application.

Closing Down Shop

When the protected mode application makes a DOS terminate call, or if a hardware event or CPU exception requiring termination occurs, the final chunk of DOS-extender code is executed. This cleanup code releases memory and shuts down the protected-mode machine before returning to DOS. Any extended memory that was allocated is released back to the provider, which may be a VCPI server, a DPMI host, or one of the other APIs. Various interrupt vectors are unhooked and restored to their original conditions. Hardware chips (the interrupt controller, for example) may be reprogrammed back to their original states. The tricky part of this process is restoring conditions in the proper order. Finally, control is returned to DOS in real mode, with an error code from the protected mode application in the AX register .

DOS Extenders Made Easy

Although this discussion may make DOS extender technology seem simple, don't be misled. Writing a professional DOS extender is no easy task. Here are the hardest parts of the DOS extender puzzle:

- Mode switching
- Nested interrupts
- General compatibility

Because of the various machine architectures (AT compatible, EISA bus, and MCA), different mode-switching code must be used depending on the machine type. Furthermore, a specific computer may require special code (a kludge) to handle mode switches appropriately for its particular design. Through trial and error, a DOS extender vendor may have added support for eight to 12 different mode-switch choices.

One of the most difficult tasks is handling nested interrupts. Let's illustrate nesting with a real example. Let's say that the application has taken over a COM port with its own interrupt handler. Your application issues a DOS or BIOS software interrupt, and the DOS extender switches the CPU to real mode (mode switch 1). A COM port interrupt occurs that requires switching to the protected mode for the application's handler (nested mode switch 2). While you're processing the serial port in the protected mode, another hardware interrupt occurs (say, the timer tick), requiring a switch to the real-mode handler (another nested mode switch—3). Nesting can be caused by a combination of hardware, exception, and software interrupts. It's not unusual to nest mode switches three or four deep and then run into trouble. Even Windows 3.0 doesn't always handle this nesting properly.

The other problem area we've mentioned is general compatibility. For example, the ROM BIOS code on many 386 machines may have bugs that the DOS extender must account for. The *block-move* code used in the INT 15h functions is a notorious example of untrustworthy code. These functions will often destroy the upper half of the 386 registers unless the functions are insulated by the DOS extender. Earlier versions of Microsoft's CodeView also hooked INT 15h and, under some circumstances, could destroy the ES register. The DPMI host code in Windows 3.0 contains a number of bugs for 32-bit applications for which a DOS extender must provide work arounds.

The various memory managers can also cause problems for the DOS extenders. DESQView's QEMM allocates both XMS and EMS from a single pool of memory, but many of the other products do not. Qualitas's 386MAX and Microsoft's EMM386.SYS and HIMEM.SYS allocate memory from separate pools. Some DOS extenders will allocate extended memory using only one of these methods at a time, limiting the available memory for the application. So, the knowledge built into the commercial DOS extenders is well worth the purchase price.

Hardware Choices

A variety of CPU chips are suitable for use with 386 DOS extenders. Introduced in late 1986, the 80386 is the original microprocessor Intel developed to follow its 80286. The original 80386 CPU was a 16 MHz part. Intel now calls these chips the 80386DX family, and parts are available in speeds of 16, 25, and 33 MHz. The 80386 has both an internal and an external 32-bit wide data bus. Memory can be read and written in 32-bit chunks. The 80386 CPU can address up to 4 gigabytes of physical memory although most PC motherboards limit this amount to 16 to 64MB.

Nowadays, most 80386 motherboards incorporate special circuitry to provide static RAM caches to speed external memory access. These RAM caches may range from 32 to 256KB of fast external cache memory. In 1991, Advanced Micro

Devices (AMD) introduced the AM386, an 80386 compatible chip that is built with static technology. This allows for lower power operation and dynamically reduces the clock speed for use in laptop and portable computers. The AMD chip is available in speeds of up to 40 MHz, making it faster than the comparable Intel part. Cyrix manufactures 387-compatible math chips rated at this 40 MHz speed.

In 1989, Intel began quantity shipments of the 80386SX CPU that supports the 80386 instruction set but has only a 24-bit external address bus and a 16-bit-wide external data bus. This chip allows less expensive circuit board design, but at a reduction in performance. Memory access is limited to 16-bit chunks, physical memory is limited to 16MB, and the available SX motherboards do not support use of the fast Weitek and Cyrix memory-mapped math coprocessors. Special 387SX math coprocessors are available from Intel, Cyrix, and IIT. The 386SX chip is widely available in 16 and 20MHz speeds, with 25MHz chips just starting to arrive. These chips were designed to be direct competitors for the faster 80286 CPUs manufactured by AMD, Harris, and others.

Many 386SX motherboards are of simple design without the external RAM caches of their 80386 siblings, although a few manufacturers have added these enhancements. Without external memory caches and limited by the 16-bit external bus, the performance of many 386SX machines is poor. In fact, at the same clock speed, an 80286 machine will often outperform a comparable 80386SX for DOS applications—the 286 motherboards often have better external memory designs.

Intel developed the 386SL chip, released in 1990, especially for laptop and portable computers. The 386SL is manufactured using static processes that allow a dynamic reduction in clock speed to decrease power consumption. A special *resume* instruction allows you to wake up the chip from its low-power mode. Although limited to 32 megabytes of physical memory, the 386SL has a full 32-bit external data bus.

The successor to these chips is the Intel 80486, which can be considered a fast 386 for most applications. A primary goal of the 80486 design was enhanced speed and complete software compatibility with the 80386. The 80486 CPU has an 8KB on-chip cache unit, and the numerics coprocessor (80387) has been incorporated within the CPU. The 80846 is available in 25 and 33 MHz speeds, but 50 MHz and 66 MHz units should soon be available. Intel has demonstrated chips with speeds of up to 100 MHz. Compared with the 386 family, only six new instructions were added to the 80486. Three of these instructions (INVD,

WBINVD, and INVLPG) are used for invalidating parts of the on-chip caching unit and do not affect application software development. The other new instructions are BSWAP (byte swap), XADD (atomic exchange and add), and CMPXCHG (atomic compare and exchange). The number of clock cycles required for executing many instructions was reduced in the 486, and the built-in 387 compatible math chip executes much faster (two to four times, typically) than the 80387. So, code optimized for speed on the 486 would not be the same as for the 386. For example, memory move instructions on the 80486 are now significantly faster than string operations. With the built-in 8KB RAM cache, the importance of external memory caches is reduced. However, 80486 motherboards can benefit from other external memory design features—the CPU supports a fast burst-mode for external memory access to fill its prefetch queue with 16 bytes at once.

Intel has since added the 80486SX and 80487SX chips to this line. From a hardware perspective, the 80486SX is not completely pin-compatible with the 80486, and the math coprocessor has been disabled internally. Available clock speeds are 20 MHz and 25 MHz. The 80487SX chip is merely a real 80486 with a different pin-out for compatibility with the 80486SX.

In 1992, AMD is expected to introduce 80486 compatible chips. Chips and Technologies (C&T) and NextGen are also expected to introduce 80386 compatible chips. Intel has already announced the 80586 CPU, an even faster microprocessor in the 80*x*86 family. So, choices for hardware to run 386 DOS applications keep expanding.

Choosing a Development Machine

To take advantage of the development possibilities provided by 386 DOS extenders, a PC must have an 80386 or 80486 CPU, along with some memory above the 640KB that DOS normally uses. Any of the above CPUs will suffice. A bare minimum configuration would be a 386 machine with 2 megabytes of physical memory. A machine equipped with 4 to 8 megabytes of physical memory, however, would be a more useful development platform, especially for debugging. The memory capacity of a development machine should be easily expandable for future enhancement.

The preferred development machine should also support both the Intel 80387 and the Weitek or Cyrix memory-mapped math coprocessor. The ideal arrangement for the 386 is separate sockets for each math chip. Daughter boards are available that plug into the extended math coprocessor 121-pin socket found on many 80386 PCs. These daughter boards provide separate sockets for both Intel and Weitek math chips. For the 80486 PCs with the Intel math coprocessor on-chip, a socket is needed only for the Weitek 4167 math chip. Either the 80386 with daughter board or the 80486 with a socket for the Weitek 4167 math chip will allow the development and testing of math-intensive applications for both the Intel and Weitek families of math chips.

Bugs in Early Chips

In developing with 386 DOS extenders, it's possible that users of early 386 machines may stumble across some hardware problems. The B-step 80386 chips contained a number of important bugs (Intel euphemistically calls these errata). The actual shipped number of these earlier chips is not available, but estimates have been as high as a million CPUs. The B-step chips are typically 16 and 20 MHz parts found in older machines, including Compaq 386/16s and IBM PS/2 Model 80s. The most common problem is Errata 21, caused by an interaction of 386 paging and the math coprocessor. On early machines, this errata is exhibited as a hardware lockup that occurs at somewhat unpredictable times when executing math-intensive programs with paging enabled. (All the 386 DOS extenders now use paging by default.) Many 80386 EMS emulators (such as Compaq's CEMM, Quarterdeck's QEMM, or Qualitas' 386Max) employ paging, so this problem can show up even in what seems like real mode (actually, virtual-8086 mode). The preferred fix is to replace the 80836 CPU with a newer 80386DX chip (D-step chip). Otherwise, paging might need to be turned off when executing math-intensive 386 applications. Phar Lap's DOS extender can be configured by end users to disable paging with the CFIG 386 utility.

Some older 386s may also exhibit the widely publicized multiply (MUL) bug, discovered in mid-1987. Phar Lap's DOS extender tests for this bug at startup and will exit back to DOS with an error message on machines with older 386 chips. MetaWare also supplies a small program to test for this bug. Again, the preferred solution is to upgrade the 386 chip; a temporary work around is to use Phar Lap's CFIG386 utility to force 386 | DOS-Extender to run anyway.

The early versions of the Intel 80486 CPU also exhibited a few bugs for 32-bit programs: the B-step 80486 CPUs do not handle the debug registers properly.

But, from a typical DOS user's standpoint, these early CPUs work just fine. Consequently, because demand was so high for early 80486 machines, these B6 chips were incorporated into a number of 80486 PCs. If you encounter problems with a 386 debugger on an older 486 machine, the B6 chip could be the culprit.

As you may already know, the 386 and 486 have a useful built-in software feature to identify the chip's type and revision level. For example, the current 386 identifier is 0308 which corresponds to the D1 step (an external name applied to revision levels). Different revision levels represent different internal workings, usually when anomalies are corrected, or the manufacturing process is changed.

Alas, this information is difficult to obtain. Like a mole unaccustomed to the daylight, it surfaces briefly in the DX register when the system is reset, and then disappears. There are actually two parts to the information: the component ID in DH (which is 03 for a 386, and 04 for a 486) and the revision level in DL (for example, 08 for the D1 step of the 386). User code has but a slim chance of latching onto this slippery value. The ROM BIOS code must save this value in memory. A new BIOS call was defined by Compaq, Intel, and others to return this information. If this call (AX=0C910h, INT 15h) is supported by the BIOS, it returns the component ID in CH and the revision level in CL. Unfortunately, many 386 BIOS ROMs still don't save the DX register on reset.

Phar Lap includes, with their 286 and 386 DOS extenders, a useful utility program (TELLME.EXE) that may also be distributed with any applications you create using the Phar Lap extender. Along with other useful system and memory information, TELLME will try to the determine the step level of 80386 chips by testing for other minor errata. TELLME can identify older B1-step 80836 chips that will likely require replacement, but unfortunately can't differentiate among 80846 chip steps.

For reference, Table 5-5 contains a list of several (but not all) component IDs, and the corresponding revision level for several 386s and 486s:

Table 5-5: 80386 and 80486 Component IDs.

NOTE: This material is based on personal correspondence with Bob Smith of Qualitas and author of 386Max and BlueMax.

Comp	Type	Step
0303	386	B1
0305	386	D0

Comp	Type	Step
0308	386	D1
0400	486	A0
0401	486	B2
0403	486	B3
0406	486	B6
0407	486	C1

Moving to 32-bit Programming—It's Easy

If you already have a PC background, then making the transition to 386 programming largely involves forgetting all the tricks you've learned to get around DOS and its real-mode limitations. Forget about dealing with objects in chunks smaller than 64K; forget about distinguishing between near and far pointers; forget about distinguishing between different memory models; pretty much forget about segmentation. With virtual memory, forget about available memory (but you had better be aware of disk space, and of the cost of using it!).

Most of your programming work is likely to depend on the high-level language that you feel most comfortable with. If the primary programming task is porting a large application from a workstation, minicomputer, or mainframe environment, it makes sense to choose the 386 compiler that most closely corresponds with the mainframe compiler. Note that most Fortran 386 compilers support some idiosyncratic mixture of VAX and IBM mainframe anachronisms. Several 386 compiler vendors are from the UNIX marketplace, so their products are likely to support UNIX nuances and anomalies. If an application is being moved from the DOS world, better DOS-compatible libraries are generally available from vendors moving up from the DOS marketplace, although this is changing. Those unusual programs to be written from scratch allow the most flexibility in choosing 386 development tools.

An important consideration when developing with C and C++ on the 80386 is that the widths of various data types are different from the widths of equivalent DOS counterparts. As noted earlier, on the 386/486, the int (integer) data type is now a full 32-bits wide, comparable to the long data type under 16-bit DOS C compilers. also, pointers (near) are now also 32-bits, the same size as an int. A side benefit is that code from the UNIX and minicomputer world, which assumed that an int was 32 bits wide and was the same width as a pointer type, will port quite easily to the 386. However, more care may be required when converting from DOS C code that may have inadvertently presumed that ints are 16 bits and are different in width from code and data pointers, depending on the memory model.

A Simple C Example

The short listing below is a simple C program that allocates memory and displays the results using ROM BIOS calls. We use both standard C *malloc()* calls for memory allocation and DOS specific *int86* calls to access ROM BIOS routines. To create 386 executable versions of this program, you can use the following command lines for compiling and linking:

```
icc malloc.c                [using the Intel C Code Builder Kit]
hc386 -fsoft malloc.c       [using MetWare High C 386 with no 80387]
wcl386 malloc.c             [using Watcom C/8.5 386] Kit]
mc386 malloc.c              [using Microway NDP C-386] Kit]
```

Using a real-mode C or C++ compiler this would be:

```
CL -AL malloc.c             [Microsoft C 6.0 large model]
BCC -ml malloc.c            [Borland C++ large model]
```

When run on 386/486 machine, this program will allocate available extended memory. For example, on my 80486/33 machine with 8 megabytes of physical memory, using the Phar Lap DOS extender, I can casually allocate about 7.3MB of memory. Figure 5-6 shows a screen snapshot of these results. Table 5-6 below compares memory allocation with several 386 DOS extender compilers and run times.

Table 5-6: Sample Memory Allocation Results with Standalone DOS Extenders.

NOTE: The results below obtained with AMI 486/33 with 8 megabytes of memory with no virtual memory configuration.

Ergo OS/386 v2.1.05		
MetaWare High C v2.32	6.87 MB	
Intel (IGC) DOS extender		
Intel 386/486 C v1.0c	6.87 MB	
Phar Lap RUN386:	-maxr 0ffffh	-maxr 0
MetaWare High C-386 v2.32	6.80 MB	7.27 MB
NDP C-386 v3.10	6.82 MB	7.27 MB

Table 5-6: Sample Memory Allocation Results with Standalone DOS Extenders.

Watcom C/8.5 386	6.80 MB	7.27 MB
Zortech DOSX		
Zortech C/C++ v3.0	----	7.40 MB

```
/*
 *    malloc - show allocation of ALL of memory using BIOS video
display.
 *
 *    used with Permission of Ergo Computing
 *    Copyright 1987, 1988 A.I. Architects, Inc.   ALL RIGHT RESERVED
 *
 *  This program demonstrates:
 *  (1) 386 DOS C compilers can be used with normal DOS C code.
 *      All the standard system facilities are supported.
 *  (2) Using standard memory allocation routines (MALLOC, CALLOC) a
 *      protected-mode program can allocate *MULTIPLE MEGABYTES* of
memory.
 *  (3) Direct calls to DOS and BIOS are supported exactly as in
real-mode.
 *
 */

#include <stdio.h>
#include <stdlib.h>
#include <string.h>

#include <dos.h>     /* 80x86 register union and int86x() prototype */

#define MAX_COL 80       /* Display parameters */
#define MAX_ROW 23
#define TEXT_PAGE 0      /* text page to use */
#define BOX_LENGTH (50+4)
#define BOX_HEIGHT (3)
#define scale(n) (((n)/(BOX_LENGTH-4)))

#define KB (1024)        /* a kilo byte */
#define MB (1024L * KB)      /* a mega byte */
#define MEGS   24        /* Max # of mega bytes to report */

short inc_kb = 10;       /* KBs to malloc between displays */
```

```
unsigned long total_bytes = 0L;       /* Total malloced */

union REGS inregs;

/* Function prototypes */
int get_a_meg(short row, short col);
void prchar(char c, short repeat);
void move_to (short row, short col);
void clear_screen();
void box(short row, short col);
void center(short row, short col, char *s);

int main() {
     short row, i;
     char b[80];

#ifdef __WATCOMC__
     setbuf(stdout,NULL);    /* make stdout unbuffered for Watcom C */
#endif
     clear_screen();
     move_to(3,25); printf(" A.I. Architects' Memory Allocator ");
     move_to(7,3); printf(" Mega Bytes ");
     move_to(11,3); printf(" Kilo Bytes ");
     box(6,14);
     move_to(10+BOX_HEIGHT+2,18); printf(" Bytes malloc'd = ");

/*   total_bytes = 0l; */
     for (row = 1, i = 0; i < MEGS; row += 4, ++i) {
          box(10,14);
          sprintf(b, " %d MB ", i);
          center(6, 14, b);
          if (!get_a_meg(10, 14))
               break;
          move_to(6+1, 14+2);
          prchar(0xb1, (i+1) * ((BOX_LENGTH-4) / MEGS));
     }
     move_to(MAX_ROW+1, 0);
     return(0);
}

/* MALLOC a megabyte of memory in inc_kb chunks and update display. */

int get_a_meg(short row, short col)
{
     char b[80];
     unsigned total_kb;
```

```
        for (total_kb = 0; total_kb < (MB/KB); ) {
            if (NULL == malloc(inc_kb * KB))    /* MALLOC a chunk */
                return (0);
            total_kb += inc_kb;
            total_bytes += inc_kb * KB;

            move_to(row+1, col+2+(total_kb / scale(1000)));
            prchar(0xb1,1);

            sprintf(b, "%d KB ", total_kb);
            center(row, col, b);
            move_to(row+BOX_HEIGHT+2,col+23);
            printf(" %ld ", total_bytes);
        }
        return (1);
}

/*    --- Display Facilities using ROM BIOS Video Calls ---- */

/* Put a char n times to the screen. */
void prchar(char c, short repeat)
{
        inregs.h.ah = 0x9;        /* write char & attribute */
        inregs.h.al = c;
        inregs.h.bh = TEXT_PAGE;     /* display page */
        inregs.h.bl = 0x70;       /* reverse video */
#ifdef __WATCOMC__
        inregs.x.ecx = repeat;        /* character count */
#else
        inregs.x.cx = repeat;         /* character count */
#endif
        int86(0x10,&inregs,&inregs);
}

/* Move cursor to a screen position. */
void move_to (short row, short col)
{
        inregs.h.ah = 2;              /* set cursor position */
        inregs.h.bh = TEXT_PAGE;      /* display page */
        inregs.h.dh = row-1;          /* row */
        inregs.h.dl = col-1;          /* column */
        int86(0x10,&inregs,&inregs);
}

/* Clear entire screen */
```

```
void clear_screen() {
     inregs.h.ah = 2;          /* set cursor position */
#ifdef __WATCOMC__
     inregs.x.edx = 0;         /* (0,0) */
#else
     inregs.x.dx = 0;          /* (0,0) */
#endif
     inregs.h.bh = TEXT_PAGE;    /* display page */
     int86(0x10,&inregs,&inregs);

     inregs.h.ah = 0x9;        /* write char w/attribute */
     inregs.h.al = ' ';
     inregs.h.bh = TEXT_PAGE;    /* display page */
     inregs.h.bl = 0x70;       /* reverse video */
#ifdef __WATCOMC__
     inregs.x.ecx = MAX_ROW * MAX_COL;
#else
     inregs.x.cx = MAX_ROW * MAX_COL;
#endif
     int86(0x10,&inregs,&inregs);
}

/* Make at box with (row,col) as the top lefthand corner. */
void box(short row, short col)
{
     short i;

     /* top line of the box */
     move_to(row, col); prchar(0xc9,1);
     move_to(row, col+1); prchar(0xcd, BOX_LENGTH-2);
     move_to(row, col+BOX_LENGTH-1); prchar(0xbb,1);

     /* body of the box */
     for (i = BOX_HEIGHT - 2, ++row; 0 < i; --i, ++row) {
         move_to(row, col); prchar(0xba,1);
         move_to(row, col+1); prchar(' ',BOX_LENGTH-2);
         move_to(row, col+BOX_LENGTH-1); prchar(0xba,1);
     }

     /* bottom line of the box */
     move_to(row, col); prchar(0xc8,1);
     move_to(row, col+1); prchar(0xcd, BOX_LENGTH-2);
     move_to(row, col+BOX_LENGTH-1); prchar(0xbc,1);
}

/* center a string in the bottom border of the box. */
```

```
void center(short row, short col, char *s)
{
     short n = strlen(s);

     row += BOX_HEIGHT - 1;          /* bottom line */
     col += (BOX_LENGTH / 2) - (n/2) - 1;
     move_to(row,col++); prchar(0xb5,1);
     while (*s) {
          move_to(row,col++);
          prchar(*s++,1);
     }
     move_to(row,col); prchar(0xc6,1);
}
```

You're likely to use a high-level language for the bulk of your development efforts. C and C++ are currently popular development tools. From the outset of 386 DOS extender development, 386 C compilers have been readily available. MetaWare High C-386 was the first available C compiler targeted for 386 DOS extenders. The High C 386 start-up code detects the major DOS extender run times and responds accordingly. Therefore, MetaWare High C-386 (now called MetaWare Extended-DOS High C) can be used for development, targeted to work with any of the DOS extenders. Many 386 compilers support working with several different DOS extenders.

Similarities and Differences Between 386 DOS Extenders

Although there are differences, for simple applications most 386 DOS extenders look surprisingly alike. All provide an interface from the protected mode that your application sees, which simulates DOS and ROM BIOS calls. This basic interface uses INT calls just like real-mode DOS. All the DOS extenders emulate DOS and the BIOS to a substantial degree. So, from most high-level languages, the basic underlying DOS extender appears the same. The compiler vendors hide any differences within their run time libraries. For example, the memory allocation and free routines in a 386 ANSI C run time library are standardized, but the underlying assembly language interface calls may differ depending on the target DOS extender.

For most low-level DOS INT 21h and ROM BIOS emulation functions, the DOS extender interface is identical for all of the run times. Compared with real-mode DOS calls, some registers are widened to use 32 bits. For example, all pointers use the full 32-bit registers, and counts, such as file read and write sizes, are 32 bits as well. These functions that don't vary between DOS extenders represent 80 to 90 percent of the standard DOS and BIOS calls. The places where you'll find differences between the DOS extender interfaces include:

- Memory allocation and free routines
- Interrupt-vector management
- Calls to *exec* other programs

In addition, each DOS extender supports a unique set of special functions that provide enhanced DOS extender control and programming access to some underlying data structures. Although many of these special functions may provide similar functions in each DOS extender, that's where the similarity ends. Each vendor has created its own unique set of interface routines to these special functions.

For most purposes, the Ergo and Phar Lap DOS extenders are similar enough to be used somewhat interchangeably. Both use the same memory model and identical hardwired selectors for access to the lower 1MB of memory and video RAM. Both run times will load and execute a Phar Lap EXP file. The Intel (IGC) and Rational DOS extenders use a differing flat memory model that allows transparent access to memory below 1MB, without segmentation, using near pointers. Intel and IGC use different executable file formats. The Ergo, Phar Lap, and Rational products come closest to emulating the real-mode DOS interface, while the Intel (IGC) DOS extender handles interrupt vectors and a few DOS functions with significant differences.

The DOS extenders differ in internal construction and their external impact under DOS. The memory footprint of the DOS extender below the 640KB mark varies along with the overall size of memory that the extender occupies. The overall memory size required by the extender is becoming less important with hardware prices plummeting and 4 to 8MB of physical memory becoming more common. However, if you anticipate that your application will be used on low-end 386SX machines with only 2MB of memory, or if your program requires real-mode memory for the execution of other DOS programs, then size may be more of a consideration.

The DOS extenders are packaged as development kits which include a debugger of some sort, utility programs used for development, and programming examples illustrating how to create and execute protected-mode 386 programs. Most extenders come with 32-bit linkers, but some may depend on your purchasing Phar Lap tools or on the linker being supplied with the 386 compiler. Several different executable file formats are supported (Phar Lap supports both an old and a new EXP executable, for example).

As noted above, these products do differ substantially in how they handle special extended functions. It would be preferable if the run times were closer together in their assortment of special functions and in the way they handle other hardware issues (the memory-mapped Weitek and Cyrix math chips, for example). But you're likely to choose a single DOS extender to use for most of your development work. And once you've made your selection, you can become familiar with the special features and functions offered by that particular DOS extender.

Choosing a 386 DOS Extender

Most programmers would prefer 80386 compilers and development tools on their own merits and be unaware of the underlying 386 DOS extender. Fortunately, this is becoming more feasible with the newer 386 development environments. It is now common for many 386 compilers to support two or more different DOS extenders. In this regard, MetaWare's Extended-DOS High C is the most flexible since it works with the four major DOS extenders from Phar Lap, Ergo, Rational, and Intel (IGC). But some 386 programming tools support only particular 386 DOS extenders, so flexibility is not always an option.

The current trend in 386 programming tools is for the compiler vendor to include a DOS extender for use with its compiler, linker, debugger, profiler, and other development tools. Most 386 compiler vendors are also including an unlimited license to the DOS-extender run time for bundling with any applications you may create. So, choosing a 386 compiler today is likely to also lock a programmer into the DOS extender supplied with it because of the attractive run time license (free) and other supplied tools, such as a symbolic debugger or profiler.

Let's take a typical application and divide the time spent on various tasks. You might spend 20 percent on planning and design, 40 percent on programming, and 40 percent on debugging. When you decide on a high-level language compiler, you are also likely choosing an associated symbolic debugger, execution profiler, and, without realizing it, the underlying DOS extender. Because of software differences, a debugger from one vendor is unlikely to work in another 386 environment.

Phar Lap 386|DOS Extender

Phar Lap markets 386 | DOS Extender SDK, which includes its DOS extender, 386 assembler, linker, librarian, and debugger package. Phar Lap also separately marketsspecial tools for embedded applications (LinkLoc). Phar Lap has been the traditional supplier of the 32-bit assembler and linker used for much of the 386 development under DOS (386 | ASM and 386 | LINK). Phar Lap defined the 386 object module (EASY-OMF) most commonly used under DOS. EASY-OMF is an extension of the Intel OMF-86 object module, in which some fields are extended to 32 bits for the 80386. An EASY-OMF object module is identified by a comment record at the start of the file containing the string *80386*. With a few exceptions (Lahey Fortran F77L-EM/32 and OTG Fortran FTN77/386, for example), all 386 DOS compilers can generate Phar Lap 386 object files and are supplied with Phar Lap-compatible libraries. The Lahey compiler uses the Microsoft 32-bit object module format, and requires the Lahey linker, L32.

Phar Lap's assembler and linker are provided in two forms under DOS: a real-mode version, and a protected-mode version that runs under DOS on an 80386 with extended memory. The protected-mode tools operate much faster but are otherwise equivalent to their real-mode counterparts. The protected-mode version of 386 | LINK can also link much larger programs. The Phar Lap debugger, 386 | DEBUG, is very similar to Microsoft's SYMDEB and supports symbolic debugging at the assembly language level.

RUN386, the Phar Lap DOS extender, supports a number of switches and options, and automatically senses the presence of other programs using extended memory (RAMdisks, EMS emulators, and so on). RUN386 supports the Virtual Control Program Interface (VCPI), XMS, and DPMI. In fact, Phar Lap and Quarterdeck Systems jointly drafted VCPI to allow multiple 386 programs to cooperate, averting the chaos that characterizes TSRs under DOS. RUN386 supports calls from protected mode to real mode. Phar Lap was the first vendor to support virtual memory for 386 applications, and, as noted earlier, a number of commercial products already incorporate the Phar Lap Virtual Memory Manager (386 | VMM). Another interesting aspect of 386 | DOS-Extender is its support for protected-mode TSRs: when a protected-mode program makes a TSR system call (e.g., Int 21H AH=31H), both the protected-mode program and RUN386 stay resident in memory.

Phar Lap developed and supports two different EXP file formats:

- The original Executable Protected mode (EXP)
- A P3 format EXP, which supports a packed mode that creates smaller executable file sizes.

RUN386 can also load a Relocatable Executable (REX) file used by the Intel Code Builder (IGC's XAM) DOS extender. The REX format is basically the original Phar Lap EXP file with relocation information. In general, however, RUN386 cannot execute these programs because of differences in the Phar Lap and Intel (IGC) run time environments.

The Phar Lap run time is a flat memory model with several hardwired segment selectors for memory mapping. For example, a program CS is set to 0CH, and DS and ES are set to 14H—all pointing to the same block of physical memory. There are also hardwired selectors for the video refresh buffer, the lower 1 megabyte of memory, and the program's environment block and program segment prefix (PSP). These are listed in Table 5-6 (Phar Lap and Ergo LDT hardwired selectors), later in this chapter.

Originally, both RUN386 and your application would run at ring 0 (most privileged), allowing your application complete control of the machine. However, with the latest version of RUN386, the default behavior is to run your application at ring 3, although this is configurable. In a DOS box under Windows 3.0, your application runs at ring 1, while Windows 3.1 is to run 386 DOS applications at ring 3.

Protected-mode DOS function calls are reasonably similar to real mode DOS calls, with a few exceptions. Of course, registers are 32-bits wide instead of 16 (EAX versus AX). Phar Lap defined an extension to the DOS GetVersion (AH=30H) that is used to return information about the run time. The other DOS extenders also partially support this call to facilitate determining dynamically which DOS extender is running. The DOS Get Vector (AH=35H) and Set Vector (AH=25H) calls are not supported, but are replaced with special DOS extender calls. FCB-type file I/O calls are not supported. Memory management and EXEC calls are slightly different from their DOS counterparts. The Weitek math chip is supported by mapping it into a 64KB block of memory pointed to by segment register FS upon startup.

Phar Lap provides a set of special system calls via Int 21 AH=25H. Since this MS-DOS function to set interrupt vectors was likely to be changed anyway for 32-bit protected mode, Phar Lap chose to use this as the interface to all special

Phar Lap system services. These services include support for protected-and real-mode interrupt handling, memory management, intermode communication (calling real-mode procedures from protected mode), and virtual memory. A service is chosen with a function number in the AL register. Phar Lap also provides a set of C-callable routines that encompass many of these functions. These special extender functions are similar for the other DOS extenders and cover:

- Interrupt control
- LDT descriptor management
- Extended memory management
- Conventional memory management (below 640 KB)
- Virtual memory management (386 | VMM)
- Debugging control
- Mixed real/protected mode programming and communication
- Debugging control
- Miscellaneous services

A number of these special functions are not available when running under Windows 3 (DPMI 0.9) and Phar Lap returns an error code. To debug 386 | DOS extender applications under Windows 3 Enhanced mode, you must install a special virtual device driver supplied by Phar Lap. This device driver provides access to the debug registers and simulates DPMI 1.0 debug services.

Upon request, Phar Lap provides developers with a debugging interface library (DIL) to RUN386 as a separate REX file. This REX file incorporates a standardized C-callable interface for debugging control which would be loaded dynamically by a debugger. By writing to this interface, a developer can painlessly update his or her debugger to a new version of the Phar Lap run time by replacing this REX file.

RUN386 is currently the only DOS extender that will allocate extended memory from several of the available services (EMS from VCPI and extended memory from XMS, for example) if these services coexist. This condition can occur if a separate XMS driver (like HIMEM.SYS) and an EMS emulator (such as EMM386.SYS from DOS 5) have both been used.

RUN386 can turn paging on or off. With paging enabled (the default) when running stand alone, RUN386 can also use memory below 640K for 386 applications. The Phar Lap DOS extender uses about 55KB of low memory aside from DOS, leaving about 500K of low memory, plus any extended memory above 1 megabyte available for protected-mode use. The default behavior of RUN386 is to allocate all memory below 640KB for use by the 386 DOS application, although this is easily configured. By default, this DOS extender makes the largest quantity of memory available for 386 programs. This can be a consideration for machines with relatively low memory (2 megabytes), like some 386SX PCs. By default, RUN386 allocates 16 KB buffers for parameter passing during mode switches.

Phar Lap supplies, by far, the best manuals for 386 DOS extender development. Included with the manuals and SDK are numerous examples illustrating how to use special extender features, including changes that may be required when running under DPMI. Phar Lap supplies a configuration program (CFIG386) and several utilities that may be distributed with your application to end users for tuning RUN386 parameters.

The run time must be licensed separately from the SDK for binding with your finished application. Virtual memory is supported as an extra-cost item that must also be separately licensed. The majority of 386 compilers generate code to operate using Phar Lap's DOS Extender. These include products from MetaWare, SVS, Microway, Alsys, and Watcom. Most of the shipping 386 DOS development products are probably based on the Phar Lap DOS extender. This may change with the recent trend toward 386 compiler vendors bundling other DOS extender run times. Phar Lap's licensing and accounting requirements have traditionally been more costly and restrictive than their competitors. This is reflected by the fact that an unlimited run time license for RUN386 is bundled with only the Alsys Ada development environment.

Ergo Computing's OS/386 and EDU-32

Similar to its competitors, Ergo Computing markets several DOS extenders: OS/386 (designed for 386 machines and the Ergo Hummingboard 80386/80387 coprocessor boards); the EDU-32 DOS extender (compatible with Windows); and OS/286 and EDU-16, 16-bit DOS extenders that were already mentioned in Chapter 4.

The OS/386 DOS extender supports VCPI and allows programs to run under Quarterdeck's DESQview 386, which provides multitasking capabilities. VCPI adherence also provides for compatibility with other conforming DOS extender applications. But OS/386 is not compatible with DPMI, therefore applications based on it will not run under Windows 3. EDU-32 is DPMI-compatible and is similar to EDU-16 DPMI, Ergo's Windows-compatible 286 DOS-extender product.

To function under Windows 3, a DOS extender must be able to act as DPMI client. EDU-16 and EDU-32 are currently the only DOS extenders aside from Windows 3 that also provide a DPMI host or server implementation. Since EDU-32 wasn't available for testing when this chapter was written, we'll focus the rest of our discussion on OS/386.

The OS/386 Developer's Kit includes the OS/386 kernel, a symbolic debugger, and several utility programs. Ergo's OS/286 supports a multiple segmented-memory model on the 286. The same memory map is supported on the OS/386 run time, along with the more common, flat, unsegmented memory model. For development purposes, the kernel is installed as a TSR (which can be removed from memory when not needed). This speeds the loading of protected-mode programs during both development and testing. The kernel runs at ring 0 (most privileged), while the protected-mode program runs at ring 3 (least privileged). The I/O privilege level (IOPL) for applications is set at 3 so that the application can input and output to hardware ports.

The resident OS/386 kernel can be configured to use only about 60K of the lower 640K DOS memory space, freeing more memory for other real-mode applications and TSRs. Memory management features include multiple heaps, automatic compaction, and control over where the protected-mode component of the kernel is loaded—below or above the 1-megabyte boundary. Memory management service functions allow access to page tables, selection of low or high memory heaps, and control over compaction. Interrupt handlers can be easily chained to real-mode handlers or shared between parent and child tasks. A supplied setup program tunes the OS/386 DOS extender run time for optimum performance on 386 machines.

Ergo's protected-mode programs use the file extension .EXP (Executable Protected mode) for both 16-bit and 32-bit programs. Unfortunately, this is the name Phar Lap used for its default executable files even though Ergo's and Phar Lap's files have different structures. Ergo can run the Phar Lap 32-bit files, using either the .PLX (Phar Lap Extended) or .EXP extension. A strength of the Ergo product is its similar support for both 80286 and 80386/486 protected-mode DOS.

Among the four DOS extender routines discussed in this chapter, OS/386 offers the closest emulation of DOS and BIOS. The OS/386 manual describes support for both compatible and slightly incompatible DOS calls. Primary variances from DOS are with FCB I/O calls (records are limited to 16K), DOS memory allocation, and EXEC calls. Otherwise, all DOS calls are fully supported, except that 32-bit registers are used.

A number of extended DOS calls are supported for calling real-mode procedures, setting arbitrary interrupt vectors, creating code and data segments, getting segment information, and doing block transfers to low memory. These services are invoked with Int 21H, with AH ranging from E0H to EDH, and are identical to those used by OS/286, an indication of the strong ties between OS/286 and OS/386. A set of C-callable routines are also provided for many of these functions. Ergo provides a demand-paged virtual-memory (VM) version of the OS/386 run time at no additional cost. This is similar to the Phar Lap virtual-memory manager discussed earlier.

The Ergo debugger, Command Processor (CP), is a command shell that can execute DOS-like built-in commands and batch files, as well as be used as an assembly language symbolic debugger. The shell includes a history command and a built-in command line editor using key bindings similar to the standard EMACS editor defaults. The shell has a macro processor which allows invoking a batch file of macros to make the debugger or shell look similar to SYMDEB, and other user interfaces are only a macro file away. A utility converts a link map or object file into a symbol file suitable for use with CP, providing symbolic debugging. During development, execution of a 386 program is preceded by UP (uniprocessor) or, if using Ergo's 386 coprocessor, by HB (HummingBoard), on the DOS command line. Ergo also provides a C-callable library for debugging, compatible with the Phar Lap DIL.

OS/386 supports an elegant mechanism that facilitates communication with real-mode routines, such as graphics and communications, located in low memory. Calling real-mode procedures from the protected mode allows 386 applications to use the extensive real-mode libraries until 386 versions of the libraries are available. This OS/386 mechanism provides an interface that may be written in either C or assembly language. It is discussed at length later in this chapter.

Currently, the 80386 compilers that support the OS/386 run time and produce 32-bit code are MetaWare High C-386 and Professional Pascal-386; Watcom C/386 and Fortan 77/386; Lahey FORTRAN F77L-EM/32; Meridien OpenADA; and Microway C, C++, Pascal, and Fortran-386. The Lahey 32-bit linker and librarian are supplied for development, along with several other utilities. An unlimited version of the Ergo DOS extender run time is bundled with Lahey

Fortran and Meridien OpenAda. A special version of the run time is also bundled with the Microway NDP compilers, but this arrangement requires an annual fee paid to Ergo for applications bound with the OS/386 run time.

Intel 386/486 C Code Builder Kit (IGC's X-AM)

Intelligent Graphics Corporation (IGC) has traditionally offered two families of 80386 system products—VM/386 (a multitasking control program similar to Microsoft Windows and Quarterdeck DESQview) and X-AM, IGC's 386 DOS extender. Although the IGC X-AM (Extended Address Mode) run time, also called VM/RUN, is now only offered as an OEM product, it is being shipped with several 386 development environments. Intel chose the IGC run time for bundling with its C Code Builder Kit.

The Intel 386/486 C Code Builder Kit represents the new trend in 386 DOS development tools. The kit consists of a 386 ANSI C compiler, linker, librarian, source-level symbolic debugger, make utility, and 386 DOS extender—all rolled into a single package. An unlimited license is provided for the DOS extender run time so you may distribute any 386 applications you create at no additional cost. The Intel kit does an excellent job of down playing the DOS extender for the developer and making 32-bit C development largely transparent. The C compiler, linker, librarian, and debugger were developed in-house by Intel. The make utility is a custom version of the Opus Make tool. The DOS extender is a new version of IGC's XAM that supports virtual memory, DPMI, and XMS.

The Intel kit is easy to use, and the run time C library is Microsoft-compatible. When you run the compiler driver (icc.exe), it automatically compiles and links your program, and binds in the DOS extender to produce a protected-mode executable. It comes with a 387 emulation library, so a math coprocessor is not required, yet fast 387 code is generated inline. An optional virtual mjemory manager may also be linked with the application. So, building a 386 application does not require the execution of separate DOS extender utilities or the post-processing of output files. The DOS extender is largely hidden from view, the way it should be.

The Intel DOS extender does not currently support VCPI. You can't run applications built with the DOS extender under QEMM, 386Max, or other VCPI-server memory managers. Intel and IGC are working to correct this deficiency and will no doubt provide an updated version with VCPI compatibility.

While by default, the Phar Lap and Ergo DOS extenders run DOS in real mode and 386 applications in protected mode, the Intel extender puts the entire system in protected mode and runs the DOS kernel below 640KB in virtual-8086 mode. The extender creates a completely flat memory model for the system, with applications loaded above the 1 megabyte address. No hardwired segments are used. Monochrome screen video memory is mapped at offset B0000H, and BIOS data at 400H—their actual physical addresses. All of this is done with paging. By default, parameter passing buffers for mode switches are up to 40KB, although this value can be configured with a supplied utility.

Although unsupported by the Intel C compiler, the IGC DOS extender provides access to the Weitek and Cyrix math chip, memory-mapped up high in the 386 address space, at the same location used by UNIX vendors on the 386.

Of the four major DOS extenders, the Intel (IGC) extender handles interrupts differently—the DOS extender always gets the control first and then *CALLs* any interrupt handlers supplied by the application. On startup, the extender passes a global data structure (GDA) with system information to the C startup routines and the application. (MetaWare High C-386 provides an include file, GDA.STR, for accessing this structure.)

The Intel Linker generates a REX (Relocatable Executable) file that is automatically bound with the DOS extender run time to produce a DOS executable file. The REX file format can also be generated by the Phar Lap 386 linker and includes relocation information. Under the IGC extender, the stack is completely protected and doesn't grow in size. A linker switch or a separate utility program sets the maximum stack size in executable programs. If the C programs exceeds the default stack limit, execution of the program may crash with a stack protection fault until the stack size is increased. The Intel symbolic debugger (db32.exe) is a solid source-level C debugging tool that eases finding and eliminating programming bugs.

Some of the items in the IGC Global Data Area (GDA) may be useful to the application program. The most important parameters are made available by the Intel C run time startup code to the application program. These include the PSP address, the data transfer address (DTA), and a pointer to the environment block. The GDA also contains the application start address, pointers to interrupt tables, the code and data selector for the application, available high and low memory, stack parameters, and pointers to other data structures. These other data structures, in turn, contain pointers to the GDT, IDT, page directory tables, an asynchronous terminal profile block for the COM ports, and a variety of internal data fields and working areas used by the DOS extender itself.

An entry in the GDA (GDA_SERV) points to a routine that provides a variety of special services to the IGC extender. Although documented in the earlier X-AM manuals and omitted from the Intel documentation, these extended functions can also be accessed from an application. Intel makes this information available on special request. The DOS extender does not use software interrupts for this interface. Instead, the AH register is loaded with A0H, AL is loaded with a subfunction number, and then EAX is loaded from the 386's CR2 register. (The older X-AM product used register CR0.) MOV EAX,CR2 is a privileged instruction in Ring 3 protected mode and in Virtual 8086 mode, and therefore causes an exception that allows the DOS extender to gain control. This technique only works when the IGC extender is run stand alone, not when run under a DPMI host like Windows 3. For example, to get the address of the GDA, an application running under the Intel extender would do the following:

```
gdaptr dd 0
;...
        mov eax, 0A007h        ; subfunction 7: get GDA  address
        mov eax, cr2           ; invoke extended function
        mov gdaptr, edx        ; the GDA pointer is returned  in EDX
```

These special functions are listed in Table 5-7.

Table 5-7: Intel (IGC) Special Extended Functions.

Interrupt Handling

AH=A0H AL=04H Issue a soft IRET from Virtual 8086 mode

Memory Management

AH=A0H AL=01H Move memory

AH=A0H AL=05H Load a real address from a virtual address

AH=A0H AL=06H Relocate a memory block

Real-mode Communications

AH=A0H AL=08H Call a 32-bit process from a Virtual 86 process

AH=A0H AL=09H Restart a 32-bit process from a Virtual 86 process

AH=A0H AL=0AH Call a Virtual 86 routine from a 32-bit process

Miscellaneous
AH=A0H AL=00H Initialize GDA from Virtual 86
AH=A0H AL=02H Transfer from Virtual 8086 to 32-bit protected mode
AH=A0H AL=03H Exit Virtual 86 mode and return to DOS extender in real mode
AH=A0H AL=07H Get GDA address

Silicon Valley Software (SVS) also bundles the Intel (IGC) DOS extender with their SVS C, Fortran, and Pascal 386 compilers, including an unlimited run time license. Other compilers that support the Intel (IGC) DOS extender include MetaWare Extended DOS High C and Professional Pascal compilers.

Rational's DOS/4G

Rational Systems has been a very strong contender in the 286 DOS extender market since 1987, but it didn't release a 386 DOS extender until Fall 1991. DOS/4G is a 386 DOS extender built on technology similar to the DOS/16M product. Like DOS/16M, DOS/4G is DPMI-compatible and comes with Rational's protected-mode linker (GLU32) and debugger (D32). The Rational DOS extender is compatible with all of the other extended memory APIs including VCPI, XMS, and VDISK. DOS/4G supports the familiar DOS INT 21h API and ROM BIOS routines.

The DOS/4G extender uses a flat memory model similar to the Intel (IGC) DOS extender, so no special selectors are required. This memory model allows near pointer access to the lower 1MB of address space, including video RAM. Virtual memory is supported. The DOS extender loads files that use the OS/2 2.0 Linear Executable (LE) file format. This file format is similar to the new Segmented Executable (NE) format used in OS/2 1.2 and was reverse engineered from the OS/2 2.0 executable files. The executable file contains a real-mode stub that provides the DOS/4G loader and run time, which then runs the application program. Supporting dynamic linking and attached resources, the executable file is geared for the protected mode. The OS/2 2.0 linker may also be used to generate these executable files.

A number of different 386 hardware platforms are supported, including Japanese 386 PCs from NEC, Fujitsu, Hitachi, and OKI. An environment variable (DOS16M) and a virtual memory configuration file (VMM.CFG) allow for custom configuration. Rational supplies utility programs that may be included with the extended DOS application for testing and setup.

The run time supports DOS INT 21H and BIOS calls, along with a library of C-callable routines for interfacing with special functions. These C routines are very similar to the corresponding DOS/16M functions. Your program may also make DPMI INT 31H calls into the DOS extender for special services. By default, DOS/4G uses an 8KB parameter passing buffer for mode switching.

The Rational extender currently works with compilers from MetaWare (C and Pascal), Watcom (C and Fortran), Microway (C, C++, Fortran, and Pascal), and the Microsoft/IBM OS/2 2.0 C compiler. Rational's extenders are usually priced as OEM products and not sold to casual end users. Although new on the 386 scene, a version of the Rational DOS extender is bundled with compilers from Watcom and Microway, including an unlimited run time license to the extender.

Salford's DBOS

Salford Software from Great Britain bundles the DBOS extender with their FTN77/386 and FTN77/486 development environments. OTG Software distributes these Salford products in the United States. These development environments include a 386 or 486 Fortran compiler, linker, librarian, source-level symbolic debugger, and the DBOS extender. Although DBOS may have limited use, some features of its design are interesting.

DBOS is installed as a TSR under DOS and can be removed from memory with a supplied utility program. The DOS extender uses the flat model, with the CS, DS, ES, and SS selectors pointing to the same memory. At the top of the address space is an area of virtual memory reserved for the system library. Part of this space is write-protected and contains code and data that is paged in from the DBOS.LIB system file. The application stack resides below this system library space, and the program starts at address 0. This model is closer to the way Unix is implemented on the 386 than to how the other DOS extenders work.

Programs communicate with DBOS through an INT 78h interface, which generates a General Protection exception into the kernel. An identification byte following the INT 78h instruction indicates the DBOS function request. For example, terminating a DBOS application would require:

```
Int     78h     ; DBOS interface call
db      0       ; terminate application function
```

About 50 calls are supported in all, and Salford provides Fortran-callable routines to ease their use. In addition, part of the Fortran run time library is actually included as part of the DBOS.LIB system file, supporting a form of dynamic linking. The Salford 32-bit linker (LINK77) plants calls to these routines containing a byte identifier—a byte length of the function followed by the string name (similar to Pascal). To make the call illegal, 8000000h (2 gigabytes) is added to the call address. At run time, the DBOS extender recognizes this construct, follows the pointer, looks up the routine in its map of the system library and executes it. With part of the library in the DOS extender, the 32-bit executable files can be quite small. Salford Fortran compilers support a form of in-line assembly language. The object files are non standard.

DBOS supports virtual memory using a DOS swap file or a separate hard disk partition (again similar to Unix). DBOS options are set with a supplied configuration utility that may be distributed with the application. The memory footprint for the DBOS extender below 640KB is less than 30KB. The new DPMI-compatible version of DBOS is called WDBOS.

Currently, DBOS is supported by the Salford Fortran compilers, however, 386 Pascal compilers are soon to be available. An unlimited run time license for DBOS for any applications created is available at a modest one-time cost from OTG.

Zortech's DOSX

Zortech's C++ 3.0 allows the creation of 32-bit executables and supports both the Phar Lap and the Zortech DOSX DOS extender. Zortech supplies DOSX with an unlimited run time license, while the Phar Lap SDK and a run time license to the Pha Lap DOS extender must be purchased separately. A command-line switch to the compiler driver will build either type of 32-bit executable (although the Phar Lap linker must be available to build a Phar Lap EXP file).

The DOSX interface is not well documented by Zortech. While designed to emulate the Phar Lap DOS extender API and special extended functions, DOSX is currently only partially compatible with Phar Lap. Support for some standard DOS calls is missing along with many of the Phar Lap special extended function calls. For example, DOSX currently does not support *spawn*, *exec*, or *system* calls. Other unsupported features include Weitek coprocessor support, and BIOS routines for raw disk I/O. Virtual memory is not available. In addition, the Zortech run time library code for *int86* and *int86x* does not currently work with versions 3.0 and 4.0 of Phar Lap's RUN386. Fortunately, these same *int86* run time library functions do work with Zortech's DOSX extender.

The Zortech tools support creating both Phar Lap EASY-OMF and Microsoft 32-bit object file formats. Since DOSX was designed to be Phar Lap-compatible, a single 32-bit run time library file will handle either target DOS extender. DOSX's support is unique to the Zortech environment.

The Windows 3 DOS Extender and DPMI

Before we look further at the DOS extender products, let's discuss the big incentive to the recent flurry of DOS extender updates and upgrades, namely, Windows 3. Although it may not be as friendly or consistent as the Mac OS, Windows 3 is the hot user interface in DOS town. And after all the years of bad-mouthing DOS extenders, Microsoft has gone ahead and incorporated one into their new Windows run time. The DOS extender in Windows even supports both 286 and 386 programs. You won't find much information about this in the Windows SDK manuals, so I'll point out a few places where you can find some. Although the manuals never directly mention DPMI services or DOS extenders, Windows 3 supplies a standard protected-mode INT 21h DOS-stretching interface to applications. We cover DPMI in detail in Chapter 9, so our discussion here will focus more on the Windows DOS extender.

The *Windows SDK Reference—Volume 1* briefly documents the calls DOS3Call (eventually issues an INT 21h to DOS) and NetBIOSCall (issues the NETBIOS interrupt 5Ch). Because only registers are used for entry and return values, both calls must be made from assembly language. These two routines are exported from KERNEL.EXE and are not defined in any Windows include files. The manual also states that using DOS3Call is faster than an INT 21h, presumably because you use a call gate instead of going through the interrupt descriptor table (IDT). Windows 3 can be run in either real, standard (286 protected), or enhanced (386 protected) mode. In the two protected modes, Windows acts as a DOS extender and transfers these DOS calls to the real-mode DOS system in the lower 640K of memory. Windows 3 in Enhanced mode actually runs DOS in the Virtual-8086 mode similar to the Intel (IGC) DOS extender.

Nowhere in the manuals will you find a list of the DOS function calls supported by this mechanism. Microsoft publishes a five-page technical note that describes the supported DOS calls and DPMI functions. The parameter transfer buffer is apparently limited to 4KB. Although undocumented, other DOS and ROM BIOS calls are also supported from protected mode. In general, most INT calls are passed to real mode by the Windows kernel. For example, do an INT 10h call from a Windows program, and you'll get garbage on your screen. The vendors of DOS extenders have the choice of using the Windows DOS extender or using DPMI to build a wrapper around Windows.

A number of other DOS-like file I/O functions are mentioned in the *Windows SDK Reference*. These include GetDriveType, GetTempDrive, GetTempFileName, _lclose, _lcreate, _lseek, _lopen, _lread, _lwrite, OpenFile, and SetHandleCount. The purposes of these functions all correspond reasonably well with their names, except for OpenFile, which can create, open, or delete a file.

Exploring the main Windows SDK library with a good librarian (such as SLR's OPTLIB) will turn up an assortment of undocumented selectors, data variables, and functions. A few of the more interesting ones are EnableDOS, DisableDOS, EnableKernel, DisableKernel, GlobalMasterHandle, OpenPathname, DeletePathname, GetLastDiskchange, NoHookDOSCall, KbdRst, FileCdr, DoSignal, and GetCurPid. You'll also find some undocumented exported functions that are related to selector handling. Some of these are GetTaskDS, PrestoChangoSelector, SelectorAccessRights, GetSelectorBase, SetSelectorBase, GetSelectorLimit, SetSelectorLimit, and AllocSelectortoArray. Undocumented data selectors include __ROMBIOS, __0000H, __0040H, __A000H, __C000H, __D000H, __E000, __F000H, and _FFFE_FARFRAME. A slew of undocumented exported functions deal with spooling printed output and network functions. But the most intriguing of all are the undocumented functions Death and Resurrection.

Volume 2 of the *Windows SDK Reference* briefly discusses (in Appendix E) the WINMEM32.DLL, which can be used by Windows apps for 32-bit memory management. This DLL supplies a standard method for implementing a 32-bit flat memory model. The SDK documentation states that use of these calls guarantees your application will run with future Windows versions. WINMEM32 contains eight functions that enable access to 32-bit memory segments from an application:

- **Global32Alloc** allocates a block of 32-bit memory.
- **GlobalRealloc** changes the size of a 32-bit memory object.
- **Global32Free** frees a 32-bit memory object.
- **Global16PointerAlloc** converts a 32-bit pointer to a 16-bit far pointer alias.
- **GlobalPointerFree** frees a 16-bit pointer alias.

- **Global32CodeAlias** creates a code alias for a 32-bit memory object.
- **Global32CodeAliasFree** frees a 32-bit code alias.
- **GetWinMem32Version** returns the version of the DLL.

The WINMEM32.DLL, shipped with Windows SDK, has a reputation for being buggy, and many developers have steered clear of it. For programmers, WINMEM32.DLL puts a pretty face on some DPMI calls. The original Windows 3 run time had several bugs related to DPMI and real-mode programming, so Microsoft updated it in late 1990. If you have an old version of Windows (files dated 05-01-90), you should update it to Version 3.0a.

DPMI is mentioned only in a short paragraph in a README file on one of the disks in the Windows Device Driver Kit, but it is part of Windows 3 in both Standard and Enhanced modes. One drawback to the Windows 3 implementation of DPMI is that it's available to both Windows and DOS applications in Enhanced mode, but available only to Windows applications in Standard (286) mode. In Standard mode, Windows doesn't support a call for DOS apps to find the entry point of the DPMI host.

Using the DOS extender supplied with Windows 3, it is now possible to write 286 and 386 apps that run under Windows and can access lots of memory. You may, however, need access to real-mode memory, interrupt vectors, or special services that are not openly provided by Windows; they may be there using DPMI, but it takes a good bit of work to make them function. Also, such applications will run *only* under Windows or some other DPMI host. If you want to ship a single executable that will run under DOS or Windows, a commercial DOS extender is a better solution.

Microway offers an interesting product based on the Windows 3 DOS extender for 386 developers. NDPWIN, designed for versions of its 386/486 compilers (C, C++, Pascal, and Fortran), runs under Windows 3 and allows you to develop applications that run under Windows 3 only. NDPWIN is a custom loader that runs as a Windows application. This in turn sets up a 386 flat model. The NDPWIN language libraries interface directly with both the WINMEM32 DLL supplied with the Windows SDK and the low-level Windows 3 I/O functions (OpenFile, _lread, etc.) Again, these are not true Windows applications; they're 386 character-based programs that run as Windows applications under Windows 3 Enhanced mode. No separate DOS extender is necessary for redistribution.

True 32-bit GUI Applications

We've talked about running 286 or 386 DOS-extender applications under Windows 3. This is a convenience to users who prefer Windows as their multitasker or menu interface to DOS. But the challenge is developing true 32-bit Windows GUI applications that support the full Windows API. Both Watcom and MetaWare offer products that accomplish that feat. Rational will also offer a similar product called BigWin, designed to link with several 386 C compilers.

The Microsoft Windows API is a large, 16-bit interface, and a number of functions issue call-backs to your code. Watcom and MetaWare have had to build a glue layer (they both call it a *supervisor)* that translates the Windows 16-bit API into a 32-bit clone of the Windows API for application programs. The challenge is making all this as transparent as possible for the developer. Some Windows calls may overload a passed parameter as either a **long** or a **far** pointer. The supervisor layer must translate a far pointer segment:offset (32 bits) from Windows to a far pointer (48 bits) for the 386. Parameters need to be passed from this supervisor layer that Windows sees to the 386 segments that your application runs in. The supervisor layer and the 386 application share a 64KB stack at the bottom of the 386 address space for parameter passing.

A separate DOS extender is not needed, because it is provided by Windows 3 and its DPMI services. Both MetaWare and Watcom have written a Windows virtual device driver so that their symbolic debuggers will run under Windows. Watcom bundles this 32-bit Windows supervisor with C/8.5 386 and FORTRAN 77/386. MetaWare calls its product the Windows Application Developer Kit, which must be purchased in addition to MetaWare's High C/386. Either of these products allows creating true 32-bit Windows extended-DOS applications without the purchase and licensing of any additional DOS extender.

How Windows 3.0 Bugs Affect DOS Extenders

In Table 5-6 we report the results of executing our simple memory allocation routine under several DOS extenders. When the above memory allocation program is run under Windows, your first result will likely be very disappointing. You must use the Windows PIF editor to change the default amount of XMS and EMS memory made available to this application. You can either modify these values for the _DEFAULT.PIF file or create specific PIF files for the various versions of this program. When running under the Phar Lap RUN386 loader, you need to create a RUN386.PIF. So, let's say we change the amount of XMS to 10240 KB (10MB) instead of the default of 1024 KB. Even after creating or modifying the PIF file, the memory that malloc.exp can allocate under RUN386 is still only 2 megabytes for RUN386. What's going on here?

Windows 3.0 has a major bug regarding 32-bit segments in its DPMI code. When virtual memory is being used, the DPMI code to grow a segment is broken. Part of an application that may be swapped out to disk can be lost by the Windows run time, resulting in a system crash. So for safety's sake, the 386 DOS extenders that don't use a completely flat model (Phar Lap and Ergo, for instance) must preallocate a segment that cannot grow. By default, Phar Lap's RUN86 will create a segment 2 MB bigger than the amount of memory needed to load a 386 application. A command-line option to RUN386 will change this value. The CFIG386 configuration utility can also be used to change this value. For example, invoking the Phar Lap extender with the following option will set the preallocated segment size to 4MB:

```
RUN386 -WIN3OLIMIT 4096 malloc
```

But the difficulty with this work around is that a 386 application might judiciously use a large amount of dynamic memory if it's available. Let's illustrate this with an example. Suppose you create an application built with the Phar Lap DOS extender with a segment limit under Windows of 6 MB more than your load image. If that much memory is unavailable from Windows when installed by your program's user, the Phar Lap DOS extender will just abort with an error message stating that there is inadequate memory to load the application. So, the end user of the application may need to reset this value for optimal performance. Although this Windows bug may be fixed in a subsequent update (Windows 3.1), five or six million copies of Windows 3.0 will already be in place.

Fortunately for Microsoft, this bug does not affect normal Windows applications, which are 16 bit—only 32-bit segments are affected.

This bug is not a problem for the DOS extenders based on a linear flat model like Intel (IGC) and Rational. This model has the lower 640KB at these same addresses and extended memory above 1 MB. Under this model, memory can be added to an application without growing the segment. Allocating memory from DPMI returns back an equivalent physical address in the flat memory space.

For other reasons, the DOS extender run time may want to limit the amount of memory available to the application. Under Windows 3.0, even though additional memory resources may be available using the virtual memory swap file, the 32-bit application should leave memory for other applications. The Intel compiler driver and linker has an *-xregion=size* option to restrict the application's "virtual resources." A configuration utility for the Intel tools can also change this value in the executable file.

Limitations and Trade-offs

Each 386 DOS extender has a certain amount of overhead associated with it. In terms of memory used by the DOS extender when running stand alone, the default differences are about 500K between the smallest memory needs (Phar Lap and DOSX) and the largest. This is primarily because, by default, Phar Lap allocates all memory below 640KB to the extended application. On 386SX machines with limited installed memory (2 megabytes, for example), this difference can represent a sizeable chunk of potential program and data space. If the Phar Lap DOS extender is not configured to automatically allocate real-mode memory, the amount of extended memory available to the application from the four major DOS extenders becomes very similar.

All the DOS extenders provide special functions to allocate memory below 640KB, but the C, Fortran, and other high-level language run time libraries don't normally include this memory in their heap management routines (malloc and free routines in C, for example). To use this memory below 640KB in the application, you must use the extender-specific functions. The convenience of using the ANSI C memory routines disappears. Also, under Windows 3 and DPMI, the real-mode DOS memory below 640KB cannot be allocated by the Phar Lap memory model for the application, so memory differences again disappear.

The DOS extenders are not ideal candidates for fast file I/O. Whenever a DOS call is made by a protected-mode application, the machine state is saved twice—once by the DOS extender and once by the underlying DOS system. Also, under normal circumstances, file I/O is handled by the real DOS and BIOS down low in physical memory, and copied by the DOS extender to the application's program's disk buffers in extended memory. These additional operations impose a performance penalty on file I/O. Therefore, it is best to minimize DOS file calls and perform file I/O in large chunks if possible. Each DOS extender allows some configuration of the default parameter passing buffer size used for transfers during mode switches. The maximum size limit of this transfer buffer is limited to a 64KB segment. For applications that are limited by file I/O, this buffer size should be increased to the maximum. You can profile and test the application with different buffer sizes to see any tradeoffs between file I/O speed and the need for memory below 640KB, used by DOS and other programs.

When programs operate in protected mode, memory protection has its benefits and costs. From a development standpoint, some programming errors that are often overlooked or missed when using DOS show themselves quite dramatically as memory protection violations. These include null pointer assignments, bad pointer values that exceed the limits of the data selector, and writing carelessly into code segments. Depending on the run time (if the application runs at ring 0), the DOS extender may actually crash and reboot as a result of the processor exception. This is particularly true of stack violations. In any case, a crashed DOS extender makes for difficult debugging.

Not long ago, the debuggers available for 386 DOS extender development were primitive by PC standards. Even now, three of the four debuggers supplied with the DOS extender toolkits are, at best, symbolic debuggers at the assembly language level. The Intel debugger is more representative of available tools from the compiler vendors. Intel, Watcom, SVS, Zortech, Lahey, Alsys, and Meridien bundle a source-level language debugger with their compiler environments. MetaWare and Microway make a similar debugger available as an optional product. Execution profilers are also available for use with Watcom, MetaWare, Microway, Alsys, and Meridien 386 compilers.

There is one disadvantage to the near absence of segmentation in 32-bit protected mode; it makes debugging more difficult. While page-level protection is still available when using the 386 as a linear address space, this protection is not nearly as powerful as segment-based protection in 16-bit protected mode.

High-Level Languages

A number of high-level languages are available for developing 386 DOS extender applications. Compilers targeted for the 386 include Ada, APL, BASIC, C, C++, Cobol, Forth, FORTRAN, Lisp, Pascal, PL/I, Prolog, and Smalltalk languages. C and Pascal compilers from MetaWare for the 386 DOS extender environment were the earliest products available, appearing in 1987. In fact, 386 DOS extender development depended on the availability of MetaWare High C-386. High C-386 was initially used for generating portions of the DOS-extender run times, utilities, assemblers, linkers, librarians, and debuggers.

MetaWare compilers were followed by the introduction of 386 compilers, which had been retargeted from the minicomputer and Unix workstation world. These products include compilers from Silicon Valley Software (SVS), MicroWay (retargeting Green Hills compilers), and Language Processors, Inc. (LPI). Several DOS language compilers, including Lahey and Watcom (with Zortech the most recent), have followed suit by porting their products to the 386 DOS-extender environment. For a lisitng of DOS Extender support by vendor, see Table 5-9.

A number of vendors now offer language compilers targeted for 386 DOS extenders. Table 5-8 shows a listing, by language, of the vendors that offer compilers.

Table 5-8: Languages Available for 386 DOS Extender Environments.

Language	Vendor	Products
ADA:	Alsys	Alsys Ada 386
		OpenAda
	Meridien Software Systems	
APL:	STSC, Inc.	APL-PLUS II
	dyadic	dyalog APL/386
BASIC:	Silicon Valley Software	SVS 386/BASIC PLUS
	TransEra Corp.	HTBasic
C:	Intel	Intel 386/486 C Code Builder
	Liant Software Corporation	LPI C
	MetaWare	Extended DOS High C
	Microway, Inc.	NDP C-386 and NDP C-486
	OASYS (Green Hills)	C-386
	Silicon Valley Software	SVS 386/C
	Watcom Systems, Inc.	Watcom C 8.5/386
C++:	INTEK	C++
	Microway, Inc.	NDP C++ 386 and NDP C++ 486
	Zortech	Zortech C++
COBOL:	Liant Software Corporation	LPI Cobol
FORTH:	Laboratory Microsystems (LMI)	UR/FORTH

Language	Vendor	Products
FORTRAN:	Lahey Computer Systems	F77L-EM/32
	Liant Software Corporation	LPI FORTRAN
	Microway, Inc.	NDP Fortran-386 and NDP Fortran-486
	OASYS (Green Hills)	FORTRAN-386
	OTG Systems, Inc.	FTN77/386 and FTN77/486
	Silicon Valley Software	SVS 386/FORTRAN
LISP:	Symbolics, Inc.	CLOE-386
PASCAL:	MetaWare	Professional Pascal-386
	Microway, Inc.	NDP Pascal-386 and NDP Pascal-486
	OASYS (Green Hills)	Pascal-386
	Silicon Valley Software	SVS 386/Pascal
PL/I:	Liant Software Corporation	LPI PL/I
PROLOG:	Epsilon	MProlog
	Expert Systems Int'l Inc.	Prolog-2
SMALLTALK:	ParcPlace Systems	Smalltalk-80/386
SPITBOL:	Catspaw	Spitbol-68K/386

Table 5-9: DOS Extender support by vendor.

		DOS Extenders Supported					Source-Level Tools	
Language	Vendor	PharLap	Ergo	Intel	Rational	Other	Debugger	Profiler
ADA	Alsys	Y					Y	Y
	Meridien		Y				Y	Y
APL:	STSC, Inc.			--interpreter--				
	dyadic			--interpreter--				
BASIC	SVS	Y		Y			Y	
	TransEra			--interpreter--				
C:	Intel			Y			Y	
	Liant (LPI)	Y						
	MetaWare	Y	Y	Y	Y		Y	Y
	Microway	Y	Y		Y		Y	Y
	SVS	Y		Y			Y	
	Watcom	Y	Y		Y		Y	Y
C++:	INTEK (1)	Y	Y	Y	Y			
	Microway	Y	Y		Y		Y	Y
	Zortech (2)	Y				Y	Y	
COBOL:	Liant (LPI)	Y						

		DOS Extenders Supported					Source-Level Tools	
Language	Vendor	PharLap	Ergo	Intel	Rational	Other	Debugger	Profiler
FORTH:	LMI	Y					Y	
FORTRAN:	Lahey		Y				Y	
	Liant (LPI)	Y						
	Microway	Y	Y		Y		Y	Y
	OTG						Y	
	SVS	Y		Y		Y	Y	
	Watcom	Y	Y		Y		Y	Y
LISP:	Symbolics	Y					Y	Y
PASCAL:	MetaWare	Y	Y	Y	Y		Y	Y
	Microway	Y	Y		Y		Y	Y
	SVS	Y		Y			Y	
PL/I:	LPI	Y						
PROLOG:	Epsilon			--interpreter--				
	Expert Systems			--interpreter--				
SMALLTALK:	ParcPlace	Y					Y	
SPITBOL:	Catspaw			--interpreter--				

(1) Intek C++ is a port of AT&T C++ translator, with enhancements that translates, C++ to C code. Libraries are supplied for MetaWare Extended DOS High C and Watcom C/386. So, the DOS extender that is supported is based on what these compilers support.

(2) Zortech C++ is bundled with its own DOSX extender and also supports the Phar Lap product. However, an unlimited run time license is provided for the Zortech DOSX run time, for bundling with any applications developed, while the Phar Lap DOS extender would have to be licensed separately.

Note: Oasys markets cross-compilers that run on Unix hosts and generate object files and executables that work with the Phar Lap 386 | DOS-Extender. These cross-tools (based on Green Hills products) include C, C++, Fortran, and Pascal compilers. These cross-compilers are available for Sun Workstations, 386/Unix, and SCO Xenix system V. The Oasys tools are not available with a source-level debugger or execution profiler. The Microway NDP compiler products are also based on Green Hills, execute under both 386 DOS and Unix/386 hosts, and include source-level debugging and profiling tools under DOS.

Interfacing with Assembly Language

If the major part of a programming project is in a high-level language (Ada, C, Pascal, or Fortran, for example), porting to the 386 DOS extenders can be a relatively painless task. High-level language compiler vendors have complied with protected-mode restrictions by writing appropriate run time libraries for protected mode, and can shield the programmer from much of the change wrought by memory and hardware protection. When problems arise, they are more likely to result from small sections of a large application that deal specifically with the underlying DOS environment. These problem areas include communicating directly with PC hardware, ROM BIOS routines, special DOS extender services, and interfacing with assembly language routines. Very often, small parts of an application have been hand-coded in assembly language for the express purpose of interfacing with hardware or the ROM BIOS. Assembly language may have been used for the following reasons:

- Faster execution speed
- Smaller memory space requirements
- Communication with video or other PC hardware
- Interface with existing real-mode libraries

Very often, small parts of an application have been hand-coded in assembly language for the express purpose of interfacing with hardware or the ROM BIOS. Fortunately, most of the 386 extended-DOS compilers have features to minimize the necessity for using assembly language. All of the C/C++ vendors support *int86()* routines that allow easy interfacing to DOS and BIOS services without resorting to assembly language. Many support an *interrupt* keyword, which marks a C routine as an interrupt handler along with *enable()* and *disable()* pseudo-functions that generate in-line STI and CLI instructions. And several support in-line assembly from within C and Fortran. See Table 5-9 for specific details on the various products.

Because many of the C and other language compilers for the 386/486 are highly optimizing, some of the benefits of assembly language may be moot. Although the instruction sets for the 80386 and 80486 are virtually the same (the 486 adds six new opcodes), there are distinct differences in execution times for various instructions. These variations are substantial enough that many compiler vendors have special versions or command-line options to generate different code targeted for the 386 and 486. On the 486, parameter passing conventions can even be changed to reap execution speed benefits. For math-intensive applications, the 486 can benefit from instruction scheduling to allow parallel execution of both floating-point and scalar instructions in the two separate on-chip execution units. Instruction scheduling is almost mandatory to reap the full benefits of the Weitek 4167 coprocessor on a 486.

To mask these differences, a reasonable strategy for most developers is to minimize the use of assembly language and focus on the best algorithms at the compiler language level. A parallel routine in C can always be replaced at a later phase with a faster hand-coded 80386 assembly language function.

No More Casual Programming Style

Although useful and sometimes necessary, interfacing with real-mode libraries will commonly create more problems than solve them. While the DOS extenders support special services to call real-mode code libraries and handle signal mechanisms from real mode (Ergo's OS/386 scheme is quite elegant), you must climb a steep learning curve to speed with these special DOS extender features. If source code for real-mode libraries is available (whether in assembly language or a high-level language), it is almost always preferable to revise and recompile or reassemble the source code expressly for the 386/486.

When programming in 386/486 protected mode, the developer must discipline the casual programming style typical of programming under DOS. Access to physical memory is no longer direct. Memory protection is enabled, and segment registers must be used with more care. Segment registers can no longer be used for arithmetic. Any value loaded into a segment register must now be a legitimate selector. As noted in Chapter 1, a selector represents an index to an entry in a Local (LDT) or Global Descriptor Table (GDT). These descriptors hold information about the segment type, length, privilege level, and base address. Without paging, the base address is the actual physical address in memory. With paging enabled, yet another level of logical-to-physical address translation takes place. In any event, actual addresses are no longer directly accessible to a program.

This opens the question of how to handle memory-mapped video and graphics under a 386 DOS extender. For speed, high-end applications often choose to write directly to video memory, bypassing the ROM and video ROM BIOS. Both text and graphics modes are often handled in this way. Because of memory protection issues in protected mode, video memory cannot be accessed at an absolute physical address, as it is under DOS. Under DOS extenders, a selector that points to the actual block of video or graphics memory must be used. All of the DOS extenders provide some built-in mechanism to readily address video memory. This mechanism is usually a predefined selector pointing to a chunk of video RAM. Also, special functions provided by the DOS extenders allow allocating a selector for any block of physical memory. These functions provide a scheme to handle most atypical video and graphic card options.

Assembly Language Tools

DOS assembly language tools for the 386 have traditionally been supplied by Phar Lap. Their 386 | ASM/LINK package includes an assembler, a linker, a librarian, and a mini-debugger. The Phar Lap assembly language tools generate EASY-OMF object modules, which are supported by most 386 compiler vendors. EASY-OMF extends various fields in the Intel 8086 object module to 32 bits to support the 386. EASY-OMF object modules are marked by a comment record at the beginning of the file containing the string "80386."

Microsoft MASM (version 5.0 or greater) and Borland's TASM can also be used to assemble 80386 code and generate a different (Microsoft extension) 386 object module format. Neither Microsoft nor Borland offers a linker or librarian to handle 386 object files. (The beta release of the OS/2 2.0 Software Development Kit contains a linker and librarian that run under both DOS and OS/2, which can handle these object files.) Ergo Computing bundles a 386 linker and librarian, written by Lahey Computer Systems, with their OS/386, which can handle both Microsoft and Phar Lap 386 object modules. The Lahey librarian can also convert Phar Lap libraries to its own 386 Lahey library format. These tools are the same language utilities supplied with Lahey F77L-EM/32, Ergo's 386 Fortran development system.

MetaWare bundles a very useful binary dump utility (BD.EXE) with High C 386 and Professional Pascal 386, which handles both Phar Lap and Microsoft 386 object modules. It will dump out both object module formats for inspection and allow patching an object module. BD's most valuable feature, however, is its ability to convert from one object module format to the other. The BD utility can be purchased separately if desired.

Accessing Hardware and Interrupt Vectors

Access to the interrupt vector tables and hardware can be more problematic than in simple DOS programming. The interrupt vector table is internal to the DOS extender. To install a replacement interrupt handler requires using a 386 DOS extender special function. There can be two interrupt handlers for each hardware interrupt:

- A real-mode handler that gains control when DOS is executing in lower memory
- A protected-mode handler that gains control when the program is operating in protected mode and the DOS extender is active.

Each DOS extender supports some way to pass a real-mode interrupt to a protected-mode interrupt handler, and some way to pass an interrupt from protected mode down to a real-mode handler. The DOS extender can also provide features to install dual interrupt handlers, which operate in both situations. Dual interrupt handlers provide the best interrupt response, because the DOS extender does not have to perform a mode switch from real to protected mode to process an event. The most common use for dual interrupt handlers would be with a serial device that generated many interrupts (graphics tablet, plotter, or high-speed modem). A dual interrupt handler would be set up to share a common data buffer in low memory to maximize response time. On fast 80386/486 machines, dual interrupt handlers are less necessary.

All the DOS extenders allow direct access to hardware devices through I/O ports, just like under real-mode DOS. This access accommodates any requirements for supporting unusual hardware in a 386 application. However, under multitasking programs like Windows 3, DESQView (Quarterdeck), and VM/386 (IGC), access to standard PC hardware may be virtualized. Under these conditions, although your application can read and write to I/O ports, the multitasker may actually be simulating the device (the EGA or VGA, for example) for your application so that the hardware may be shared among several applications. Windows 3.0 can virtualize the EGA when not running full screen, and Windows 3.1 will provide VGA virtualization, but at a very substantial performance degradation.

Special DOS Extender Features

A number of special features are provided by the various 386 DOS extenders, including the following:

- Writing directly to video memory
- Writing into code segments
- Installing interrupt handlers (real and protected mode)
- Mixing real-and protected-mode procedures
- Virtual memory and page-locking extensions

As noted above, these features or options are implemented differently depending on the DOS extender run time.

Writing Directly to Video Memory

All four major DOS extenders discussed in this chapter provide the capability to write directly to memory-mapped video for fast screen output. Both Phar Lap and the Ergo DOS extender provide hardwired selectors that point to the default video RAM (B000H or B800H are typical). Phar Lap and Ergo also support extended DOS function calls to map any physical address to a selector (segment). This mechanism is the most general one and will handle almost any memory-mapped device (standard video, high resolution TMS34010 graphics cards, network cards, and SCSI adapters). Phar Lap also provides special functions that allow mapping video memory into your data segment, making segment overrides unnecessary. Unfortunately, these special Phar Lap functions aren't available when running under Windows 3 (DPMI 0.9), so using a separate selector is a safer bet.

Intel (IGC) and Rational use the flat linear model so that video RAM is addressed at an offset corresponding to its physical address (B0000H or B8000H). Other memory-mapped devices can also be addressed at their physical addresses.

When a protected-mode program is loaded into memory, the Phar Lap and Ergo DOS extenders set up a number of hardwired segments (see Table 5-10). These selector values may differ, depending on whether the Phar Lap extender was configured to run your application at ring 0 or ring 3. The default behavior in RUN386 v4.0 is to run applications at ring 3, but this is configurable. Ergo's OS/386 always runs applications stand alone at ring 3. However, under Windows 3.0 and DPMI, your application is run at ring 1.

The lower 2 bits of the selector value indicate the protection level, so these selector values are the same after screening off the lower two bits. Fortunately, the 386/486 doesn't care about these lower two bits when reading or writing to data selectors. However, these must be set exactly for code and stack selectors or a protection violation will occur.

Table 5-10: Phar Lap and Ergo LDT Hardwired Selectors.

Phar Lap Segment Selector	Ergo Segment Selector	Description
0004H		A readable/writable data segment that points to the DOS program segment prefix (PSP) for the program.
000CH	000FH	Code selector pointing to the load image. A readable/executable code segment that points to the program. The initial selector value loaded in the CS register.
0014H	0017H	Data window on the load image. A readable/writable data segment that points to the program segment. This is the selector value initially loaded into the DS, SS, ES, FS, and GS registers (note FS exception later).
001CH	001FH	Screen. A readable/writable data segment that points to physical screen memory. This selector can be used by programs that write directly to screen memory for speed. The base address and limit of this selector are automatically updated by the DOS extender when BIOS system calls to change the video mode (Int 10H, Function 0) are made.
0024H	0027H	Program segment prefix. A readable/writable selector that is a duplicate of the descriptor that points to the program's PSP.
002CH	002FH	Pointer to environment. A readable/writable data selector that points to the DOS environment block for the program.
0034H	0037H	Base memory. A readable/writable data segment that maps the entire first megabyte of memory used by DOS.

Phar Lap Segment Selector	Ergo Segment Selector	Description
003CH	003FH	Weitek. A readable/writable selector that maps the memory space used by the Weitek 1167 (or 3167) numeric coprocessor. If the 1167 is present, this selector is initialized and the FS register is loaded with this selector value (003CH for Phar Lap). If the Weitek coprocessor is not present, the base and limit for this selector are both set to zero, and the FS register contains the same selector value as DS.
	00B0H	Monochrome video. A readable/writable data selector that maps onto the monochrome video refresh buffer at B000:0.
	00B8H	Color video. A readable/writable data selector that maps onto the color video refresh buffer at B800:0.

Writing Into Code Segments

Another capability that is sometimes needed is the ability to write into code segments. The Phar Lap and Ergo DOS extenders provide either system calls or a selector mechanism to alias a code segment with a data segment selector. Both the Phar Lap and the Ergo DOS extenders use hardwired overlapping segments for the initial code and data segments. The actual selectors would be identical, except that Phar Lap applications may run at ring 0, 1, or 3, while OS/386 applications run at ring 3. Ergo automatically creates an alias data selector for each code selector, using the code selector XOR 8. This same mechanism also works with the initial code and data segments set up by the Phar Lap DOS extender. The following code fragment outlines this scheme under both Phar Lap and Ergo DOS extenders:

```
push ds                 ; save the DS register
mov ax,cs               ; get our code selector
xor ax,8                ; and convert to data selector alias
mov ds,ax
.
.
                        ; now write into our code segment
.
.
pop ds                  ; and restore our data selector
```

Under the Intel (IGC) or Rational DOS extender all selectors are zero-based, so a 32-bit data offset is the same as the offset in the code selector. While convenient, this feature also allows a programmer to accidentally write over your application code. Although the 386 paging mechanism could be used to prevent this freedom, this would require substantial software overhead in the DOS extender and creating another mechanism to allow writing into code segments.

Installing Interrupt Handlers in Real and Protected Mode

Interrupts on the 80386/486 fall into three categories:

- Hardware interrupts generated by an external hardware event
- Software interrupts (commonly used for DOS and BIOS system services)
- Processor exceptions generated by the 386/486 chip when memory protection or other programming errors (divide by zero, for example) are detected

All three types of interrupts are handled in a similar manner by the DOS extenders. When an interrupt occurs in protected mode, the DOS extender always gains control unless the application has taken over an interrupt vector. Depending on the interrupt type, the DOS extender may switch the processor to the real mode (or virtual-8086 mode under the Intel DOS extender and Windows 3) and reissue the interrupt as a software interrupt. When the real-mode interrupt handler is finished, the DOS extender switches back to protected mode and returns to the protected-mode code that was executing when the interrupt occurred. The overhead required for a 386 DOS extender to switch from protected to real mode (and from real to protected mode) can range as high as 150 microseconds. Installation of a VCPI-compatible EMS emulator can also raise the switch time (for example, one EMS emulator raised the round-trip switch time on a 16 MHz Compaq 386 from 134 ms. to 552 ms.). Faster 80386 and 80486 machines have lower overhead.

On occasion, the application program may need control of one of the interrupt vectors. As a bare minimum, it may want to install a replacement for the DOS Control-Break and Critical Error handlers. When operating in protected mode, the interrupt table is not directly accessible. In general, a program cannot get interrupt addresses by reading them from the interrupt descriptor table (IDT), nor can the application take over interrupts by writing to the interrupt table. But all of the DOS extenders support installing custom interrupt handlers.

The actual function call mechanism varies from one implementation to another. Phar Lap, Ergo, and Rational extenders run DOS in the real mode. Therefore, these run times support installing both a protected-mode and a real-mode interrupt handler. If dual handlers are installed, a shared data and variable buffer must be used from low (below 640KB) memory. Writing interrupt code for both real-and protected-mode handlers accessing a shared data buffer can get a bit complicated.

Ergo, Rational, and Intel emulate DOS calls for handling protected-mode interrupt vectors using standard functions with 32-bit register conventions (set interrupt vector with AH=25H and get vector with AH=35H). Phar Lap uses extended function calls (set protected-mode vector with AH=2504H and get vector with AX=2502H). Both Phar Lap, Rational, and Ergo also provide extended functions to get and set an interrupt handler, which gains control in real mode, protected mode, or both. All three provide a family of C-callable functions for interrupt vector manipulation.

Under the Ergo DOS extender, an application runs at the least privileged ring 3 (386/486 protection level) and the Ergo run time operates at the most privileged level of ring 0. Processor exception interrupts can only be vectored to a ring 0 handler. Using this scheme, the Ergo run time handles all processor exception interrupts and passes only software and hardware interrupts to any user-installed interrupt handler.

In contrast, the Phar Lap DOS extender when executed stand alone can run both an application and the DOS extender at ring 0 (most privileged). Therefore, any user-installed interrupt handler must be prepared to handle processor exceptions if the Phar Lap handlers are replaced. Since hardware and processor exception interrupts overlap on the PC, this can pose additional programming difficulties. RUN386 can differentiate between hardware and exception interrupts, easing handling of exceptions for the programmer. The Phar Lap DOS extender can also relocate the hardware interrupts IRQ0-7 (10Int 08-0FH) to Int 78H-7FH, so hardware interrupts no longer conflict with processor exceptions. The hardware interrupts are remapped by reprogramming the Programmable Interrupt Controller (8259 PIC chip). By default, the BIOS PrintScreen handler (Int 05) is also relocated to Int 80H. This scheme improves compatibility, particularly for user-installed protected-mode handlers, since hardware interrupts can be handled separately from processor exceptions.

For most interrupt vectors of interest under Ergo, Phar Lap, and Rational run times, the address obtained by a GetVector function call is the address of a protected-mode surrogate for the current real-mode handler. The surrogate takes an interrupt received while the processor is in the protected mode and passes the interrupt down to a real-mode handler.

The Intel (IGC) extender handles interrupts differently from the other run times. Because IGC runs DOS in the virtual 8086 mode, all interrupts are received by IGC protected-mode handlers, which may pass them to a virtual-8086 DOS handler. The Intel (IGC) extender initially passes a global data structure (GDA) to a protected-mode application upon execution. The GDA contains pointers to two tables of interrupt vector intercepts—GDA_INTEL (the 32 lowest vectors reserved by Intel) and GDA_HINT (the remaining high interrupt vectors). GDA_HINT points to a table containing two word entries for each interrupt vector. The first entry is a flat address pointing to a routine to be executed before interrupt processing takes place, and the second entry is a a similar flat address pointing to a routine to be executed after interrupt processing completes. A non-zero value in either slot defines an active interrupt handler (really an intercept). GDA_INTEL points to a similar table for the 32 Intel-reserved interrupts, but only the first word entry can be active. Any intercept routines installed in these tables are actually CALLed by the IGC run time and must use a near return (RET) instruction. Both DOS interrupt functions (AH=25h and AH=35h) and special extended function calls are available to set values in these tables. Using the DOS functions makes for more portable code.

The Intel (IGC) DOS extender run time always gets control of any INT instruction and then passes control to the appropriate handler. The underlying IGC extender supports the standard DOS calls for manipulating interrupt vectors, but these are only the software vectors in the protected mode. Currently, if your application needs to take over a DOS virtual-8086 interrupt, this needs to be done using a TSR before the 386 application is loaded. The Intel C Code Builder Kit supports the *interrupt* keyword and a similar #pragma for C functions, and the standard DOS INT 25H and 35H routines for getting and setting protected-mode interrupt handlers. Intel provides Microsoft-compatible *intdos()* and *int86()* C functions to manipulate these interrupt handlers from a C program. The Intel 386/486 run-time library has two C routines callable only from within interrupt-handling functions:

- void _chain_intr (void(* *intr_func*)(void));
- void * _get_stk_frame (void);

These chain an interrupt handler to another handler and allow access and manipulation to the stack structure that an interrupt function receives. One of these fields in the stack frame is a *stk_opts* variable that controls the action taken by the extender once the interrupt function has terminated on return from the original interrupt handler or a chained interrupt handler. The default value of *stk_opts* is zero, indicating that this interrupt is to be reissued in virtual-86 (V86) mode. A V86 interrupt handler must be in place to receive any reissued interrupt. Other options prevent reissuing the interrupt in V86 mode, or terminating the application.

Exception Handling with ANSI C Signals

Although so far we have focused on the low-level aspects of interrupts, two schemes are available for handling some exceptions in C. Certain exceptions can be handled generically, using ANSI C standard run-time library routines independent of operating system. The user interrupt (Control-C) under DOS falls into this class and can be processed using the *signal* mechanism. The second category of interrupts are specific to the DOS environment and are not covered by the ANSI run-time standard. These idiosyncratic DOS interrupts (the DOS Critical Error interrupt, for example) are by far the most difficult to handle under the 386 DOS extenders. Before we discuss these more difficult problems, let's cover the simpler ones easily solved using ANSI C.

ANSI C supports a signal mechanism derived from event-driven systems and the Unix multitasking operating system. A signal is a real-time, asynchronous event that must be dealt with immediately. Signals are based on an interprocess communication model—a program or thread of execution in distress can send a signal that another process catches and immediately handles. Signals can result from a hardware event or from software. 386 DOS C run-time libraries include support for handling several exceptions with the signal mechanism by. By default, the C run-time startup code will take over several 80386 interrupt vectors and provide default actions for these signals. The signal.h include file may list several predefined signal types, but most DOS C run-times only support a handful:

- SIGINT, the user interrupt, is usually initiated by DOS as a result of typing Control-C or Control-Break. This is DOS INT 23h, not a hardware interrupt.
- SIGFPE, the floating point error signal, results from math errors. These are usually caused by CPU exceptions.
- SIGABRT, the abort signal, is generated by software typically with the C *abort* function. Signaling an abnormal program termination, it can be conveniently raised from many possible locations and can force execution to a single exception handler.
- SIGILL, execution of an illegal instruction, is generally not supported by DOS compilers.
- SIGSEGV, a segment violation, may be generated by the 80*x*86 BOUND instruction.
- SIGTERM, program termination, is typically software-generated and handled under DOS with SIGINT.

Although an application may raise these signals, DOS itself initiates only SIGINT and SIGFPE. (The Zortech C 386 run times seem to switch the behavior of SIGINT and SIGTERM from other DOS compilers.) The ANSI C library defines several predefined signal action codes:

- SIG_DFL installs a default action (the C run time library behavior) and is used mostly to reinstate default behavior after completion of a user-defined signal handler.
- SIG_IGN instructs the handler to ignore the signal.

Typically the DOS C run time library handles SIGINT and SIGFPE by terminating the program with exit(*n*), where *n* may be specific to the exception and the C compiler.

The short listing below uses the ANSI signal mechanism to install a signal handler for SIGINT (normally Control-C) to ignore the signal and set a global variable to true. This example also illustrates how to use the *intdos* function to get the DOS break flag status and restore it on exit. When break is turned on, DOS will check for Control-C during DOS file I/O calls. This allows the user the possibility of aborting a large file I/O request during the process.

```
#include <stdio.h>
#include <signal.h>
#include <dos.h>
```

```
unsigned char DOS_break = 0xff;   /* storage for old DOS break status */
int ControlC = 0;                               /* has a Control-C occurred */
void New_CtrlC_Handler (int signal)
{
    ControlC = 1;                                  /* set flag */
    /* Ignore further user interrupts */
    if (signal (SIGINT,SIG_IGN) == SIG_ERR)
        abort();

    printf("We received a Control-C interrupt\n");

    /* Restore our own handler back */
    if (signal ( SIGINT, New_Ctrlc_Handler) == SIG_ERR)
        abort();
}
int main()
{
    REGS inregs;
    void (*Old_CtrlC_Handler)( int signal);        /* declare variable */
    inregs.h.ah = 0x??;                     /* get DOS Break on/off status */
    intdos( &inregs, &outregs);
    DOS_break = inregs.dl;
    inregs.h.ah = 0x??;
    inregs.h.dl = 0x01;                                /* set break on */
Old_CtrlC_Handler = signal (SIGINT, New_CtrlC_Handler);/*install our handler*/
    if (Old_CtrlC_Handler == SIG_ERR)
        printf("Unable to install signal handler\n");
    else
    {
        inregs.h.ah = 0x33;
        inregs.h.al = 0;
        intdos( &inregs, &outregs);    /* get DOS Break on/off status */
        DOS_break = inregs.h.dl;                   /* and save it */
        inregs.h.ah = 0x33;
        inregs.h.al = 0x01;
        inregs.h.dl = 0x01;
        intdos( &inregs, &outregs);                    /* set break on */
    }
/* continue with rest of program */
    .
    .
/* possibly install default behavior on exit */
```

```
    if (signal( SIGINT, SIG_DFL) == SIG_ERR)
            printf("Unable to install default behavior\n");
    if (DOS_break != 0xff)                    /* restore DOS break status */
    {
        inregs.h.ah = 0x33;                   /* set break function */
        inregs.h.al = 0x01;
        inregs.h.dl = DOS_break;
        intdos( &inregs, &inregs);
    }
}
```

So far, we have treated Control-C and Control-Break as equivalent, which they appear to be from a signal handling perspective. But Control-C and Control-Break are two distinct events. Control-C is simply a key combination that DOS treats as special during file I/O and keyboard input functions. For Control-C, DOS issues an INT 23h, which by default will terminate the program. The 386 DOS extenders must install a default handler for INT 23h to do some cleanup operation, shutdown the protected-mode process, and free any allocated memory.

Control-Break is truly an asynchronous event recognized by the ROM BIOS keyboard interrupt that issues INT 1Bh immediately. The default DOS action is to flush the keyboard buffer and stuff a Control-C into it. DOS will see this keystroke on the next call for character I/O and also during file I/O if the break flag is on. The Control-C will then be considered a special event and an INT 23h will be issued. So, at the DOS level, where the *signal* function interfaces, Control-C and Control-Break are perceived as equivalent.

If the application must differentiate between the two, then much more work is required. Since the BIOS Control-Break interrupt (INT 1Bh) is an asynchronous event and DOS is not reentrant, DOS services are not available. Without an inordinate amount of work, about the only thing you can do is to set a flag and chain to the previous Control-Break handler or issue an interrupt return. If the application does not perform much I/O (say, a numerics-intensive program), you can use a Control-Break handler as possible method to notify the application of a user request for action without taking over some other hardware event like the keyboard interrupt.

Handling of the SIGFPE mechanism is less standardized in the DOS environment. Some run times may consider divide by zero as SIGFPE, while others may issue SIGFPE only on floating-point errors. Specific C and Fortran compilers may also differ in handling SIGFPE, depending on whether a Weitek or 80837 compatible coprocessor is being used. Also, most Fortran 386 run times allow floating-point underflow (which generates a number too small to be represented) to be replaced by zero without a floating-point exception being raised.

Critical Error Handling

Critical errors are, by their nature much more difficult to process from the protected mode. A critical error is typically issued by a device driver when unable to complete an operation due to a hardware problem, such as an open floppy drive door. DOS issues INT 24h, which, by default, offers the user the "Abort, Retry, Ignore, or Fail" message. Depending on the user response, the program may be terminated without any resources being cleaned up.

Again, two techniques are available for installing handlers for this interrupt. A DOS interrupt handler can be written for INT 24h and installed by your program's initialization module. Because of the way information is passed by this interrupt, the exception handler may need to be written in assembly language. Alternatively, some C compilers offer run-time functions for customizing critical error handling:

```
void _harderr(int (__far *__func)(unsigned __deverr,
                        unsigned __errcode,unsigned __far *__devhdr));
void _hardresume(int __result);
void _hardretn(int __error);
```

In addition, several equates are used with the *_hardresume* as defined below:

```
#define _HARDERR_IGNORE 0       /* Ignore the error */
#define _HARDERR_RETRY  1       /* Retry the operation */
#define _HARDERR_ABORT  2       /* Abort the program */
#define _HARDERR_FAIL   3       /* Fail the system call in progress */
```

Unfortunately, DOS C compilers often choose different parameter-passing orders, different function prototypes, and even different function names. The example functions above are from Watcom C/8.5 and are based on the Microsoft conventions. The Intel C Code Builder Kit also emulates these Microsoft functions. But the best advance is to look carefully at the run time library reference for the C/C++ compiler you are using. If these high-level functions are unavailable or not suitable for your needs, more work will be necessary.

For critical error handling, block and character devices are very different. DOS passes most error information for block devices in the Device Error word, including the failing device's logical name, the file system problem area, whether it's a read or write error, and possible user responses. For block devices, this information allows for reasonable handling of the exception. The handler can present the user with this information and with alternatives for action. After choosing an action, the handler can return control to DOS passing a code using the *hardresume* function.

Character devices are much more difficult because of their greater diversity. These devices more often require inspecting the device drive-header block, which is not as readily available from the protected mode. One possible strategy is to use *hardreturn* to accept the condition, bypass DOS and return directly to the application.

Since DOS is not reentrant, only DOS functions 1 though 0Ch and 59h can be used from within a critical error handler. If any C run time functions are used (*cputs* and *getch* for example), you have to ensure that low-level calls go only to these specific DOS routines. For generality, some 386 DOS C compilers may use higher level functions even for writing to the console. For example, Watcom internally buffers I/O even to stdout, which differs from most other C compilers.

Calling Real-Mode Code from the Protected Mode

Ergo, Rational, and Phar Lap support a mechanism to call real-mode code from the protected mode. These mechanisms are recommended only when source code to the real-mode procedures is not available. If source code is available, a better approach is to convert the real-mode code to run in the protected mode. These special functions are commonly used to incorporate real-mode libraries that are not yet available in the protected mode (graphics and serial communications, for example). This mixed-mode mechanism can also be used to access undocumented DOS functions and make system calls to another program, such as a network driver or SCSI device installed in memory at boot time.

In practice, a protected-mode stub copies passed parameters off the stack. These variables are passed through a data (transaction) buffer with an indication of what function to call (usually a table entry number) and block moved to the real-mode stub in low memory. The real-mode stub in low memory recreates the stack with suitable variables, loads the CPU registers with proper values, executes the call, and passes any results back up to the protected-mode stub. This feature can always be implemented by a programmer using the 386 DOS extender memory-block move functions, but the DOS extenders provide a simpler interface.

OS/386 has an elegant mechanism that also supports sending signals from real mode up to protected mode. The Ergo scheme uses a series of very sophisticated macros to simplify programmers, use of these functions. Two extended functions handle real-mode procedure calls. Under OS/386, a function call is made to first initialize a real-mode library to be called (Int 21H AH=0E0H) and then return a real-mode handle. This function takes the library name (pointed to by DS:EDX) which may be an executable file that will be loaded by the DOS extender in the real mode. Several different real-mode libraries can be initialized using this scheme, each given a unique handle. Calls to real-mode libraries use this handle for issuing the call to the proper procedure (Int 21H AH=0E1H). Macros provided by Ergo simplify the process of passing parameters of different types, doing what to parameter counts, and invoking the proper real-mode procedure from a library. For the developer, this design dramatically simplifies problems encountered when mixing real-mode code under OS/386. The transaction buffer for passing parameters to the real-mode libraries is limited to 4K, but this size should be ample for most real-mode procedures.

Ergo used inter-machine communication over a network as a model for its mechanism. As explained in the section in Chapter 4 on *OS/286 and the two-machine model*, the two modes of the 80x86 can be viewed as two machines residing on a very local area network: that is, real mode and protected mode can communicate, but do not share address space. Just as pointers cannot be passed between machines on a network, pointers cannot be passed between the two modes on an 80x86. For this reason, any pointer parameters used in RPCs must be converted to pass by value.

The Phar Lap DOS extender has several extended functions for use in calling real-mode procedures and issuing real-mode interrupts. A mechanism is also provided to call protected-mode procedures from the real mode in an application. The intermode call buffer can vary in size from 0 to 64K bytes and is allocated from conventional memory below 640K. In comparison with the OS/386 scheme, the Phar Lap mechanism is more bare bones, and requires the developer to handle the parameters more directly. Real-mode code must be copied from the protected-mode executable file to memory below 640KB. Phar Lap requires that any real-mode code be linked at the beginning of the EXP file and must be less than 64KB for code and data.

Several extended function calls support calling real-mode libraries. These functions differ only in the way that segment registers are set up for the real-mode procedure. One function sets the DS register to the same value as CS (Int 21H AX=250EH) and allows placing values in all of the general registers before invoking the real mode procedure. The second function (Int 21H AX=2510H) adds support for setting arbitrary values in all of the segment registers. The Phar Lap manuals contain a number of examples illustrating the procedures.

Virtual Memory and Page Locking Extensions

All four major DOS extenders support a demand-paged virtual memory. Phar Lap provides this as an added cost option, while the other run times often provide it with the base extender. Programs operating under a virtual memory manager (VMM) can access memory space for code and data that is larger than available physical memory in the computer. Unused sections of the applications code and data are paged to a disk swap file and automatically brought into memory when needed.

If virtual memory is used, certain chunks of code may need to be locked into memory. For example, interrupt handlers must be locked in memory along with any associated data and stack space that might be accessed from the handler. This prevents the interrupt handler from being swapped out to disk. To improve performance, you might also want to lock specific code modules used frequently within an application, into memory. All the DOS extenders support extended function calls to control the virtual memory manager, which allow locking and unlocking pages in memory, freeing physical memory pages, getting memory statistics, and controlling extended and conventional memory use. When a DOS extender is operating under Windows 3 and DPMI, the Windows run time provides the virtual memory to the application.

Memory allocation schemes may need to be handled differently by an application under a virtual memory manager. A program using VMM should allocate only the quantity of memory actually needed for the application. Allocating chunks of unnecessary memory only increases the size of the swap file used for paging. Ultimately, the available disk space for this swap file determines the available memory for the DOS extender application with VMM. When using a high-level language (C, Pascal, or Fortran, for example), memory allocation is generally handled by the run time library.

Most virtual memory schemes use a variation on the least recently used (LRU) algorithm for choosing memory to page to disk. The LRU design presumes that memory pages most recently used by an application are most likely to be referenced again soon. The least recently used chunks of memory are paged to disk when memory space is needed. Implementing a true LRU system on the 386 can be expensive in CPU time since each page reference would need to be timestamped. The most common approximation uses a count of how frequently a page is accessed by scanning the page tables at certain time intervals. The Phar Lap virtual memory manager supports two different page replacement algorithms—least frequently used and not used recently. The Phar Lap VMM also allows installing a custom page replacement handler written by the developer.

A Simple 386 DOS Extender Application

Many of the benefits of 386 DOS extenders, as well as some of the mechanics of compiling, linking, and running a 32-bit protected-mode DOS application, are illustrated in the following C program, which can produce a very large bitmap of prime numbers, using the Sieve of Eratosthenes. The Sieve has a bad name because it's been overused and misused in computer benchmarking, but this sieve is a little more interesting than most: it uses a bitmap rather than an array of integers, and the bitmap is dense in that multiples of the first two primes, 2 and 3, are neither computed nor stored.

The upshot is a program that, running under the Phar Lap 386|DOS-Extender on a 16 MHz Compaq Deskpro 386, takes seven seconds to find the 78,498 primes <= 1,000,000, using a 41KB bitmap. Since this sieve algorithm runs in linear time, and since the bitmap size also progresses linearly, you can extrapolate the time and space required to find p(*n*), the number of primes <= *n*, for any *n*. For instance, to find p(100,000,000) would take about 700 seconds and require a 4-megabyte bitmap. (The 80386/486 machines with static RAM caches will execute the sieve non linearly for smaller values of *n*.)

```
/*
SIEVE.C
Author: Andrew Schulman, February 1990
*/
```

```
#include <stdlib.h>
#include <stdio.h>
#include <malloc.h>
#include <math.h>
#include <limits.h>
#include <time.h>

#include "bitmap.h"

#define N(x)                ((x) / 3)  // exclude multiples  of 2 and 3

void fail(char *s)          { puts(s); exit(1); }

main(int argc, char *argv[])
{
    BITMAP map;
    FILE *f;
    double dsize;
    clock_t t1, t2;
     float run time;
    ULONG i, j, n, primes, size, sqrt_size, map_size;
    int incr, jincr;

    if (argc < 2)
        fail("syntax: [run386] sieve <x>");
    if ((dsize = strtod(argv[1], 0)) < 5)
        return 1;
    // estimate number of primes, using Legendre formula (1778)
    printf("Prime Number Theorem estimates: %.0f primes <=  %.0f\n",
        floor(dsize / (log(dsize) -1.08366)), dsize);

    if (dsize > ULONG_MAX)
        fail("number too large");
    size = (ULONG) dsize;
    map_size = N(size) + 1;
    if (! (map = make_bitmap(map_size)))
        fail("Insufficient memory");
    printf("bitmap: %lu bytes\n", bytes(SIZE(map)));

    // set composites
    sqrt_size = sqrt(dsize);
     t1=clock();
    for (i=5, incr=4, n=1; i<=sqrt_size; i+=(incr=6-incr),  n++)
        if (BIT_OFF(map, n))             // bit clear -> prime
            for (j=i, jincr=incr; j<=size/i; j+=(jincr=6-jincr))
                SET_TRUE(map, N(i*j));  // bit set -> composite
```

```
    // count primes
    // printf("2 3 ");
    for (i=5, incr=4, n=1, primes=2; i<=size; i+=(incr=6-incr),  n++)
        if (BIT_OFF(map, n))
        {
            primes++;
            // printf("%lu ", i);
        }
    run time=(t2=clock())-t1;

    printf("\n%lu primes <= %lu\n", primes, size);
    printf("%.2f seconds\n", run time/CLOCKS_PER_SEC);
    puts("Saving bitmap file PRIMES.DAT");
    f = fopen("primes.dat", "wb");
    fwrite(&size, sizeof(ULONG), 1, f);
    fwrite(map, 1, bytes(SIZE(map)), f);  // write out entire  bitmap
    fclose(f);
}
```

The file BITMAP.H provides a BITMAP data type and a set of operations to set and test bits:

```
/* BITMAP.H */

typedef unsigned long ULONG;
typedef unsigned char BYTE;
#ifdef HUGE_MAP
// only required for 16-bit code
#define ALLOC               halloc
#define FREE                hfree
typedef BYTE huge *BITMAP;
#else
#define ALLOC               calloc
#define FREE                free
typedef BYTE *BITMAP;
#define SIZE(map)           (*((ULONG *) map))
#define index(c)            (((c) >> 3) + sizeof(ULONG))
#define mask(c)             (1 << ((c) & 0x07))
#define BIT_ON(map,c)       (map[index(c)] & mask(c))
#define BIT_OFF(map,c)      (! BIT_ON(map,c))
#define SET_TRUE(map,c)     map[index(c)] |= mask(c)
#define SET_FALSE(map,c)    map[index(c)] &= mask(c)
#define free_bitmap(map)    FREE(map)
void set_true(BITMAP map, ULONG c) { SET_TRUE(map,c); }

ULONG bytes(ULONG size)
```

```
{
    return (size >> 3) + ((size & 0x07) ? 1 : 0) + sizeof(ULONG);
}

BITMAP make_bitmap(ULONG size)
{
    BITMAP map;
    if (map = (BITMAP) ALLOC(bytes(size), 1))
        SIZE(map) = size;
    return map;
}
```

To compile this program for a 386 DOS extender using Watcom C/8.5 386, use the following DOS command line:

```
wcl386 -3r -mf -Oaxt -fpc sieve.c
```

The WCL386 driver program will first run the Watcom C compiler, WCC386.EXE (and the back-end code generator 386WCG.EXE), and will then invoke the linker, WLINK.EXE. The resulting program, SIEVE.EXP, requires a 386 DOS extender. Phar Lap's DOS extender is contained in the loader program RUN386.EXE, and this can either be bound with SIEVE.EXP to form SIEVE.EXE (assuming you've bought a redistribution license from Phar Lap), or invoked from the DOS command line:

```
C:\XDOS>run386 sieve 30000000
Prime Number Theorem estimates: 1859537 primes <= 30000000
bitmap: 1250005 bytes
1857859 primes <= 30000000
Estimate off by 1678 (0.090319%)
233.000000 seconds
```

To compile the program using MetaWare High C 1.7 (locally optimizing) or v2.3 (globally optimizing), the command line is:

```
hc386 sieve.c
```

The HC386 driver first invokes the High C compiler, HCD386P.EXE, and then 386LINK. The Microsoft linker LINK.EXE cannot be used to produce 386 DOS extender applications. Note that, in contrast to the 286-based DOS extenders discussed in Chapter 4, no postprocessor (such as MAKEPM) is required.

Ergo's OS/386 can also run Phar Lap executables. To distinguish these EXP files from executables produced by another 32-bit linker, Lahey LINK-EM/32 (supplied with Lahey FORTRAN F77L-EM/32), Ergo recommends naming the executable file with a PLX extension. A program is supplied with OS/386 to bind the DOS extender run time with the protected-mode executable to form a stand alone DOS application.

The program can be compiled with any other DOS C compiler. For example, a real-mode, large-model Microsoft C 6.0 version can be compiled and linked using the following DOS command line:

```
cl -AL -Ox sieve.c
```

But the resulting program has a fundamental limitation in real-mode MS-DOS: the 64KB segment limit means that the bitmap must be less than 64KB; this, in turn, means that, at most, this real-mode SIEVE.EXE can be used to find p(1,600,000).

To work around this limitation in real-mode MS-DOS, the program can be recompiled to use a "huge" pointer for the bitmap:

```
cl -AL -DHUGE_MAP -Ox sieve.c
```

But this provides the program with only an amount of memory less than 640K. Furthermore, huge pointers, while largely transparent to the programmer, impose a penalty in execution time.

It is interesting to note that, to take advantage of the larger address space available under one of the 286-based protected-mode DOS extenders discussed in Chapter 4, the program still needs huge pointers. That is the only way to apply the benefits of a 16-bit DOS extender to this program. One key differences between 286-and 386-based DOS extenders is that, while both break the 640KB DOS barrier, only 386-based extenders also break the 64KB segment barrier.

Since SIEVE.C can be compiled and linked for so many other environments, what makes it a 386 DOS extender program? In addition to removing space limitations, compiling the program as a 32-bit application also produces an enormous jump in performance. Table 5-11 shows execution times for different versions of the SIEVE program running on a 16 MHz Compaq 386 with 2 megabytes of memory:

Table 5-11: Execution Times for a Bitmap Sieve.

			Seconds			
x	p(x)	Bitmap Size	MSC51 Large	MSC51 Huge	DOS/16M Huge	High C-386
100,000	9,592	4K	2	2	2	<1
1,000,000	78,498	41K	21	21	23	7
10,000,000	664,579	416K	N/A*	237	270	76
30,000,000	1,857,859	1.2M	N/A	N/A	827	236

*N/A—Insufficient memory

This comparison shows that, with identical source code and hardware, the 32-bit sieve runs more than three times faster than the 16-bit sieve. While this program is atypical in that it performs no I/O, its extensive manipulation of 4-byte pointers and large data arrays is typical of most programs you would consider porting to the 386.

Since all these programs were run on the same 386 machine, this test underlines the fact that running a program on a 386 does not make it a 386 program. To make good use of the 386 machine sitting on your desk, you need 32-bit software.

To remove as many restrictions as possible when running this code with 16-bit instructions, we've made all indices unsigned longs (ULONG) and have used the printf() "%lu" mask. In 32-bit code, a plain unsigned int works equally well, as does the printf() "%u" mask, since an int is the same as a long in 32-bit C. size of(int) and size of(unsigned) are each 4, not 2. Likewise, size of(void *) is 4. (Note that the DOS-specific construct size of(void near *) is also 4, and that size of(void far *) is 6.)

Likewise, the all-important ANSI C identifier, size_t—which is the unsigned type of the result of the size of() operator and the type used by function parameters that accept the size of an object—is a 4-byte quantity.

That has many ramifications for programming in 32-bit C. The C standard library functions such as malloc(), fwrite(), and strncpy() all take size_t parameters, and strlen() returns a size_t. These standard library functions deal in quantities between 0 and UINT_MAX. In the 16-bit code generated by MS-DOS compilers such as Microsoft C, UINT_MAX is 0xFFFF (65,535), yielding the familiar 64KB limit on PC array lengths, string lengths, and malloc() blocks. But in 32-bit code, UINT_MAX is 0xFFFFFFFF, or 4,294,967,295—the magical upper "limit" of 4 gigabytes. In the native mode of the 386, this is the upper bound on array lengths, string lengths, and malloc blocks: hardly a limit at all.

Using the SIEVE program to build a 1.2 megabyte bitmap to represent all prime numbers <= 30,000,000, we could save this entire bitmap to disk in one call to fwrite():

```
FILE *f = fopen("primes.dat", "wb");
fwrite(&size,  size of(ULONG), 1, f);
fwrite(map, 1, bytes(SIZE(map)), f);  // write out entire  bitmap
fclose(f);
```

This code would not work when using an MS-DOS compiler such as Microsoft C or Borland C++. The third parameter to fwrite() is a size_t num_items, yet we are passing in an unsigned long; in addition, huge pointers cannot be reliably passed to standard library functions. This is an example of how 16-bit mode forces the programmer to remember low-level aspects of the machine architecture. In contrast, 32-bit mode allows a far more "forgetful" style of programming, in which many more things work the way you wish they worked: passing a 1.2-megabyte buffer to fwrite() works just fine. "Normal" objects in 32-bit programming are true huge objects, without any of the limitations of what Microsoft calls huge objects.

How does this call to fwrite() actually work in a 32-bit DOS extender? Under MS-DOS, the C function fwrite() must eventually call Int 21H AH=40H (Write File or Device). A 32-bit DOS extender supports the Int 21H interface, even for objects that MS-DOS can't handle. We saw in Chapter 4 how a 16-bit DOS extender skillfully creates the illusion of an MS-DOS that can handle objects in extended memory. A 32-bit DOS extender must support not only this fiction, but also the fiction of an MS-DOS that can handle objects whose size is greater than 64KB. Standard references to the MS-DOS programmer's interface carry the following description for the DOS write function:

```
Int 21H Function 40H
Write File or Device
BX = handle
CX = number of bytes to write
DS:DX = segment:offset of buffer area
```

In a subtle but important difference, the manuals for Phar Lap's 386|DOS-Extender, Ergo's OS/386, Rational DOS/4G, and Intel's C Code Builder Kit (IGC's X-AM) show the following description:

```
Int 21H AH=40H
Write File or Device
BX = handle
ECX = number of bytes to write
DS:EDX = segment:offset of buffer area
```

The use of the 32-bit ECX and EDX registers, instead of the 16-bit CX and DX registers, is crucial. In the DOS extender's implementation, this function eventually calls the "real" Int 21H Function 40H, and so breaks up large requests into a series of smaller requests and moves data from extended memory to conventional memory. But this is all transparent to the programmer, particularly to the programmer using the standard library functions in a high-level language.

As noted later on, though, file I/O might be slower under a DOS extender than in real mode. To compensate for this, you might need to make sure that the DOS extender doesn't break up your large fwrite() call into many tiny DOS calls. The C function setvbuf() is useful here, as are the Phar Lap command-line switches -MINIBUF and -MAXIBUF, which control the size of the parameter data buffer used for DOS function calls. A program like SIEVE.EXP, which writes a large amount of data at one time, should allocate a large I/O buffer:

```
run386 -minibuf 32 -maxibuf 48 sieve 30000000
```

On occasion, you may have to be aware of small differences between the interface provided by a 32-bit DOS extender and that provided by MS-DOS, or between interfaces provided by the different DOS extenders. The best example is Int 21H AH=48H (Allocate Memory Block). Real-mode MS-DOS expects in BX the number of 16-byte paragraphs of memory needed. (Since BX can hold values up to 65,535, this means that Int 21H AH=48H can be used to allocate 16 * 65,535 bytes at once, which is the basis for real-mode huge pointers.) Ergo's OS/386 mimics the DOS interface, expecting in EBX the number of paragraphs needed, but Phar Lap's 386|DOS-Extender instead expects in EBX the number of 4K pages an application needs! Code generated by a compiler should detect which environment it is running under and pass the proper parameters.

Here, we used Watcom C 8.5/386 because it is convenient for this task. For large commercial applications, you may find that MetaWare High C 386 is an equally appropriate tool.

Adding Support for Virtual Memory

Another obvious 386 feature to use in our example program is virtual memory. If your machine has limited physical memory but a lot of free disk space, this might seem to be a perfect opportunity to try out the virtual memory option available with 386 DOS extenders. Unfortunately, though, a sieve is the worst possible test for virtual memory because the program runs through the entire bitmap for every prime number found. This implementation is fine if the entire bitmap is in memory, but it would cause serious thrashing if any part of the bitmap was located on disk.

The following program, PRIMES.C, is a better demonstration of using virtual memory under a 386 DOS extender. The program reads in the bitmap file PRIMES.DAT that was saved by the SIEVE program. The PRIMES example program can be run on a 386 computer with less memory than the machine that created the PRIMES.DAT file. The program allows the user to type a *?* to query the prime-number bitmap, a *V* to see virtual-memory statistics, or a *Q* to quit. The following example, run on a machine with only 2MB of physical memory, not only shows the difference a little virtual memory can make, but also shows the mechanics of using Phar Lap's 386 | VMM:

```
C:\BOOK>run386 primes
Insufficient memory

C:\BOOK>run386 -vm \pharlap\vmmdrv primes
;;; A LOT OF DISK ACTIVITY ;;;
> ? 99998000099
9998000099 is not prime
Prime factors: 99989 99991
> v
VM active for 36 seconds
Page faults: 248
Pages written to swap file: 245
Reclaimed pages: 105
Application physical pages: 175
Application VM pages: 316
Swap file pages: 146
> ? 1000000000061
1000000000061 is prime
> q
```

When we tried to run PRIMES without benefit of virtual memory, the program complained and exited back to DOS. But with the virtual-memory manager, the program's call to calloc() succeeds. 386 | VMM is enabled by using the

-vm flag on the DOS command line to RUN386. In the distribution version of an application, the VM driver would be bound with the DOS extender and the application itself into a single .EXE file, and so would be invisible to the user. Mathematica and UR/FORTH both have 386 | VMM built into their executables.

In this session, the PRIMES program allocated 316 4KB pages of memory, of which only 175 were located in physical memory. Thus, 141 pages of memory were located on disk in a swap file. The application must make a special system call to 386 | VMM to find these statistics, since in normal operation VM is invisible to the programmer. In the following source code for PRIMES.C, note that we allocate memory for the bitmap using the same make_bitmap() function used in SIEVE.C; this function in turn calls calloc(), which succeeds even though there isn't adequate physical memory to satisfy the request. A strong resemblance exists between VM and a government's ability to freely print paper money! Of course, here too, there is no such thing as a free lunch, and VM opens the possibility of slower execution time than that for code using only physical memory.

In the following code, note that Int 21H AX=2520H is used to get VM statistics. As we'll see later, the interface to Phar Lap's API replaces MS-DOS's Int 21H AH=25H. All the 386 C compilers support a 32-bit extended version of the Microsoft C intdos() and int86() functions for invoking software interrupts. The code below will compile using MetaWare C-386, Watcom C/8.5, SVS C-386, MicroWay NDP C-386, or Zortech C++ 3.0 for the Phar Lap DOS extender:

```
/*
PRIMES.C
Author: Andrew Schulman, February 1990
*/

#include <stdlib.h>
#include <stdio.h>
#include <float.h>
#include <math.h>
#include <limits.h>
#include <dos.h>

typedef enum { FALSE, TRUE } BOOL;

void fail(char *s) { puts(s); exit(1); }

#include "bitmap.h"
```

```
#define N(x)                ((x) / 3)  // exclude multiples  of 2 and 3

// don't test double for equality: DBL_EPSILON in <float.h>
#define EQ(x,y)             (((x) -(y)) < DBL_EPSILON)

BOOL is_prime(double x);
void prime_factors(double x);
void vm_stats(void);
void help(void);

BITMAP map;
ULONG size;


main()
{
    char buf[80], *s=buf;
    double d;
    FILE *f;
    ULONG map_size;

    if (! (f = fopen("primes.dat", "rb")))
        fail("requires PRIMES.DAT");
    fread(&size,  size of(ULONG), 1, f);
    fread(&map_size,  size of(ULONG), 1, f);
    if (! (map = make_bitmap(size)))
        fail("Insufficient memory");
    fseek(f, 4, SEEK_SET);
    fread(map, 1, bytes(map_size), f);
    for (;;)
    {
        printf("> ");
        gets(s);
        if (strlen(s+2) > DBL_DIG)
        {
            printf("Number too large\n");
            continue;
        }
        switch (toupper(*s))
        {
            case '?' :
                d = strtod(s+2,0);
                if (is_prime(d)) printf("%.0f is prime\n",  d);
                else
                {
```

```
                    printf("%.0f is not prime\n", d);
                    prime_factors(d);
                }
                break;
            case 'Q' : fclose(f); exit(1);
            case 'V' : vm_stats(); break;
            default  : help(); break;
        }
    }
}

void help(void)
{
    puts("? [x] --is x prime? if not, show prime factors");
    puts("Q --quit");
    puts("V --virtual memory stats");
}
BOOL is_prime(double x)
{
    ULONG i, n, lx, sqrt_x;
    int incr;

    if (x <= (double) size)
    {
        lx = x;
        if ((lx == 2) || (lx == 3)) return TRUE;
        if ((lx % 2) && (lx % 3) && BIT_OFF(map, N(lx))) return  TRUE;
        else return FALSE;
    }
    else
    {
        if (EQ(fmod(x,2),0) || EQ(fmod(x,3),0)) return FALSE;
        sqrt_x = sqrt(x);
        for (i=5, incr=4, n=1; i<=sqrt_x; i+=(incr=6-incr),  n++)
            if (BIT_OFF(map, n) && EQ(fmod(x,i),0)) return  FALSE;
        // still here -- primes are residue
        return TRUE;
    }
}
void prime_factors(double x)
{
    ULONG i, n;
    int incr;
    printf("Prime factors: ");
    while (! EQ(x,1))
    {
```

```
        if (is_prime(x))     { printf("%.0f\n", x); return;  }
        if (EQ(fmod(x,2),0)) { printf("2 "); x /= 2; continue;}
        if (EQ(fmod(x,3),0)) { printf("3 "); x /= 3; continue;}
        for (i=5, incr=4, n=1; i <= x; i+=(incr=6-incr), n++)
        if (BIT_OFF(map, n) && EQ(fmod(x,i),0))
            {
                printf("%lu ", i);
                x /= i;
            }
    }
    printf("\n");
}
void vm_stats(void)
{
    ULONG buf[25];
    union REGS r;
#ifdef __WATCOMC__
    r.x.edx = buf;
    r.x.ebx = 0;           // don't reset VM stats
    r.x.eax = 0x2520;
#else
    r.x.dx = (unsigned) (void *) buf;
    r.x.bx = 0;
    r.x.ax = 0x2520;
#endif
    intdos(&r, &r);
    if (buf[0])            // VM is present
    {
        printf("VM active for %lu seconds\n", buf[11]);
        printf("Page faults: %lu\n", buf[12]);
        printf("Pages written to swap file: %lu\n", buf[13]);
        printf("Reclaimed pages: %lu\n", buf[14]);
        printf("Application physical pages: %lu\n", buf[5]);
        printf("Application VM pages: %lu\n", buf[15]);
        printf("Swap file pages: %lu\n", buf[16]);
    }
    else
        puts("VM not present");
}
```

Summary

In this chapter, we showed that 32-bit protected mode is the key to tapping the power of 386/486 PC-compatible machines that would otherwise be used merely as "fast" 8088s. 386-based DOS extenders provide this key, without giving up MS-

DOS compatibility. Many commercial programs are already using 386-based DOS extenders. As the installed base of 386/486 computers grows, 32-bit code will be used more extensively since most software developers must remain committed to the still dominant DOS marketplace. These are exciting times for 386/486 development. Half the PCs sold today have either a 386 or 486 microprocessor. Hardware prices continue to decline. The prices of math chips (from Intel, Cyrix, and others) have dropped dramatically. The DOS-extender market appears healthy, with many promising new products for the developer.

Even with the many features of the 386 that were discussed in this chapter, two crucial features were barely mentioned: the 386's hardware support for multitasking, and its virtual-8086 mode. Because 386 DOS extenders exist to run one program at a time in 32-bit protected mode, these features of the 386 were not relevant here. In the next two chapters, we discuss two products, Microsoft's Windows and Quarterdeck's DESQview, which run particularly well on the 386 and 486, using its hardware support for multitasking and for multiple 8086 virtual DOS machines. Stay tuned for more ways to enhance this popular operating system.

Chapter 6

The Windows Operating Environment

Charles Petzold

The extensions to MS-DOS discussed in previous chapters were devised mainly to provide additional memory to DOS programs beyond the 640KB ceiling that results from the limitations of real mode and the memory architecture of the PC.

Microsoft Windows is different. Windows is first and foremost a graphical windowing environment that runs under DOS. While Windows provides extensive memory management (including the use of protected mode in Version 3.0), you don't want to write a Windows program solely to solve your memory problems. In fact, on a system with 640KB memory, a Windows program has access to less physical memory than ordinary DOS programs, due to the overhead of the Windows environment. And Windows 3.1 won't run on such a system at all.

You should write a Windows program if you want to make use of the consistent user interface that Windows provides; if you want to draw graphics and formatted text on video displays and printers, using a device-independent graphics interface; and if you want to integrate your program with other Windows applications through use of the Windows clipboard, Dynamic Data Exchange (DDE), and Object Linking and Embedding (OLE). The memory management in Windows must be viewed as icing on the Windows cake. It is necessary because of the large memory requirements and multitasking nature of Windows, but hardly a reason to program for the environment.

In the pages ahead, we will look at the major features of Windows and examine a sample Windows program. Windows is a big system, and this discussion is hardly exhaustive. However, it should help you decide if Windows is the right alternative for your application. Additional information on Windows programming can be found in the Microsoft Windows Software Development Kit (the primary source) and several books on the subject.

Windows: A GUI for MS-DOS

Microsoft Windows is a graphical user interface (GUI) for MS-DOS. It is designed to run programs specifically written for the Windows operating environment. Programs written for Windows share the video display and other resources of the personal computer.

Multiple programs running under Windows each occupy a rectangular window on the display. The programs are characterized by a consistent user interface containing visual objects such as menus, buttons, and scrollbars. Windows programs can make extensive use of graphics and formatted text in a device-independent manner. Windows provides multitasking (of the non-preemptive, cooperative sort) and allows data to be exchanged among Windows programs.

Windows can also run many programs written for MS-DOS, but these programs cannot take advantage of the Windows interface or graphics. In some cases particularly without a 386 processor, DOS programs must run in a full-screen mode under Windows and will not be windowed or multitasked.

A History of Windows

Windows was first announced by Microsoft in November, 1983 and released two years later, in November, 1985, as version 1.01. Almost no one uses Windows 1.01 anymore, but current Windows users might find it an interesting historical curiosity. Windows 1.01 used tiled windows rather than the more common overlapping windows, and could be run in 320KB of memory from two floppy disk drives.

In 1987, Microsoft extensively revised the "look and feel" of Windows, primarily to make it visually consistent with the forthcoming OS/2 Presentation Manager. In particular, overlapped windows replaced tiled windows, and an easier keyboard interface was added to menus and dialog boxes. Windows 2.0 was released in November, 1987, almost a year before the first version of the OS/2 Presentation Manager was ready.

In 1988, Windows 2.1 split into two products; the standard product became known as Windows/286. While it could still run on 8088 machines, Microsoft now recommended a 286. Windows/386 took advantage of the Virtual-86 mode of the 386 microprocessor to tame those DOS programs that wrote directly to the video display and hence could not be windowed or multitasked under previous versions of Windows. Windows/286 and Windows/386 merged into one Windows product when Microsoft released Windows 3.0 in May 1990. Windows 3.0 contained a number of enhancements to earlier versions.

In particular, Windows 3.0 can take advantage of 286-compatible protected mode when running on machines using the 286 or 386 microprocessors. This gives Windows and Windows applications access to up to 16 megabytes of memory. Windows 3.0 also includes enhancements to the application program interface (API), a revamped shell that makes increased use of color and icons, as well as an attractive three-dimensional visual design. Windows 3.0 can run in three distinct modes: real mode, standard mode, and 386 enhanced mode. Real mode requires 512KB of conventional memory. Standard mode requires a 286 microprocessor and at least 256KB of extended memory. Under standard mode, Windows 3.0 runs Windows applications in 286 protected mode. The 386 enhanced mode which allows Windows to take advantage of 386 paging requires a 386 microprocessor and at least 1 megabyte of extended memory. Since its release in May 1990, Windows 3.0 has become one of the most successful software packages in the personal computer industry. Several million copies and several tens of thousands of software development kits have been sold. Several thousand Windows applications are now available.

Windows 3.1 is expected to be released in late 1990 or early 1991. One big change is that Windows 3.1 will not run in real mode, and hence will require at least a 286 processor with 1 megabyte of total memory. Windows 3.1 also includes several enhancements, including TrueType (a scalable outline font technology originally developed by Apple for the Macintosh) and Object Linking and Embedding (OLE). In addition, Microsoft will release two significant extensions to Windows 3.x in 1990: The Multimedia Extensions support enhanced sound and music facilities, and the Pen-Windows Extensions support the use of small stylus-based PCs through the use of handwriting recognition.

Windows as a GUI

Windows is a graphical user interface, and is thus part of a tradition that began at Xerox Palo Alto Research Center (PARC) in the mid-1970s, entered the mass market with the ill-fated Apple Lisa (introduced in 1983) and the much more successful Macintosh (1984), and continues with the OS/2 Presentation Manager and UNIX-based systems such as X-Windows, Sun NeWS, OSF/Motif, and NeXT.

As the name implies, a graphical user interface provides facilities that assist programs in implementing a user interface and displaying graphics. The researchers at PARC considered the user interface to be a crucial part of a program because it is where man and machine meet. Programs that run under GUIs are often visually oriented and highly interactive.

The customary distinction between user input and program output is blurred in a GUI because graphical objects on the screen are used to obtain user input. That is, the screen itself serves as an input medium rather than simply echoing keyboard input back to the user. Manipulating objects on the screen requires the use of a pointing device such as a mouse. Windows, and many Windows applications, also have a keyboard interface that duplicates everything you can do with a mouse, but using a mouse is easier for many chores.

Because the windowing and user interface code is built into the system, programs written for a GUI can achieve a high degree of consistency in their use of common interface objects such as menus, scrollbars, and dialog boxes. This allows users to learn additional programs more easily after learning one.

Although a GUI-like windowing interface can be implemented in character mode, the support of graphics can extend the functionality of many programs considerably. For example, word processing programs can use WYSIWYG ("what you see is what you get") screen displays that mimic printer output. Database programs can allow graphics to be stored in database files along with text and numbers. Spreadsheet programs can use different fonts and display graphs.

While much of Windows is devoted to the support of the user interface and graphics, Windows also includes support for non-preemptive multitasking, memory management, RS-232 communications, and sound.

Windows and MS-DOS

Windows is referred to as an operating environment because it is not in itself a full operating system. However, when Windows runs on top of MS-DOS it assumes much of the application support usually associated with operating systems.

Windows handles multitasking, memory management, user input through the keyboard and mouse, graphics output to the screen and printer, RS-232 serial communications, and sound, all without any help from MS-DOS and with very little help from the system BIOS. When Windows is running, DOS is relegated to what it does best: file I/O, other disk operations (such as changing the current directory), and a few minor chores (like maintaining the current date and time).

For these DOS services, a Windows program uses either Int 21h or normal C library functions that translate into Int 21h calls. For everything else, a Windows program uses function calls provided by Windows. Windows can also run many programs written for MS-DOS. These are referred to in the Windows literature as standard applications but many Windows programmers call them old applications or old apps. Old applications are divided into two categories: good old apps can run in a window and be multitasked, while bad old apps cannot. (The word "bad" is not pejorative in this sense. Many of the best programs written for MS-DOS are bad apps when it comes to Windows.)

A good old application is a character-mode program that uses DOS and BIOS services rather than directly accessing hardware. Windows intercepts many of these DOS and BIOS calls and translates them into Windows functions. For example, when a DOS program makes BIOS video output calls to write text to the screen, Windows translates these calls into Windows functions that display a graphical rendering of the text in a window.

Bad applications are those that make use of graphics or directly access the machine's hardware. These programs must run in a full-screen mode. Windows suspends all programs currently running under Windows and removes most of itself from memory to give the DOS program as much memory space as possible.

When Windows is taking advantage of the 386 microprocessor, the distinction between good old apps and bad apps is blurred. By using the Virtual-86 mode of the 386 microprocessor, Windows can window and multitask many bad applications, even those that use graphics. However, performance of these programs is often necessarily degraded. If you want, you can write your DOS programs so they can run in a window under any version of Windows. The basic rules are: don't use a lot of memory, and do use DOS and BIOS services rather than directly accessing hardware. However, it is rare for DOS programmers to consider windowing compatibility. It's simply not an issue.

DOS programs that themselves take advantage of protected mode are a special case. Windows 3.0 has some support for these programs, based on the mode in which Windows is running (real mode, standard mode, and 386-enhanced mode, as discussed earlier). Table 6-1 shows the ways that a DOS program can use protected mode and extended memory and still run under Windows.

Table 6-1: Allowed use of protected mode and extended memory by DOS programs.

Windows 3.0 Mode	Interface Available to DOS Application
Real	XMS
Standard	XMS
386-Enhanced	XMS and DOS Protected Mode Interface

Windows does not itself have XMS support. This must be provided externally to Windows using the HIMEM.SYS driver included in the Windows retail package. The DOS Protected Mode Interface (DPMI) is provided by Windows when Windows is running in protected mode. DPMI is discussed in Chapter 9.

The Future of Windows

At the time of this writing (mid-1991), Windows forms the center of Microsoft's operating system strategy. Microsoft's slogan is "Windows everywhere," and they intend for Windows to be the standard GUI on everything from small stylus-based hand-held PCs to RISC-based workstations.

This is a significant change from Microsoft's earlier strategy. In April, 1987, IBM and Microsoft announced OS/2, a protected-mode replacement for DOS. Microsoft had developed the character-mode OS/2 kernel earlier, and the two companies began collaborating on OS/2's graphical interface, called the Presentation Manager (PM). Although PM was visually identical to Windows 2.0, it had a considerably different application program interface (API).

The existence of two different GUIs was confusing for both application developers and users. IBM and Microsoft attempted to clarify the OS/2 and Windows markets in November, 1989, by recommending that Windows be used on 286 processors with low memory. OS/2 was targetted for larger machines, particularly

386 boxes. Microsoft recommended that 16-bit code be written for Windows, while 32-bit applications should wait for the 32-bit version of OS/2 (called OS/2 2.0).

The enormous success of Windows 3.0—and the poor reception to OS/2 by users and programmers—caused Microsoft to reverse this strategy in late 1990. Windows will now become a 32-bit environment, currently dubbed "Win-32." This is basically the current Windows API ported to 32-bit with some enhancements, particularly in the area of preemptive multitasking and graphics.

In the retail market, Win-32 will exist in two forms: One will be a version of 32-bit Windows that runs under DOS, much like Windows currently runs today. The other is currently called NT-Windows. (NT stands for "new technology.") NT-Windows is a full replacement for DOS that is intended to be portable to RISC processors.

Programming Requirements

To program for Windows, you need a PC capable of running Windows with adequate performance. This is a 286- or 386-based personal computer with a hard disk and at least 640KB of memory (preferably a megabyte or two). An EGA is adequate; a VGA is better. Strictly speaking, a mouse is not required for running Windows and many Windows applications, but you'll need a mouse to test your programs. You should also have a printer or two if you intend to write programs that print.

You will need a copy of Windows, of course, and some special development software. Traditionally, Windows programs have been written in C. C offers the greatest flexibility in handling pointers and structures, both of which show up quite a bit in Windows programming. However, many C compilers do not provide the special support required for Windows programs. Today, the most common tools for Windows programming are the Microsoft C compiler 6.0 and the Microsoft Windows Software Development Kit (SDK). The SDK contains:

- a programmer's guide
- documentation of the Windows function calls
- the header files that declare all the Windows function calls
- import libraries necessary for linking Windows programs
- tools for creating icons, mouse pointers, dialog box templates, and fonts
- a version of the CodeView debugger suitable for debugging Windows programs.

Since the release of Windows 3.0, several alternatives to the SDK have become available. In particular, Borland C++ 2.0 includes everything you need to program for Windows. Borland has also released Turbo Pascal for Windows, and Microsoft has released Visual BASIC. Two companies (Digitalk and ParcPlace) have versions of Smalltalk for Windows, and Micro Focus sells tools that even let you program for Windows in COBOL. For this discussion, I'll be focusing on the use of C for Windows programming.

Commitments and Trade-offs

Learning how to program for Windows requires a big commitment of time and energy. If you have no prior experience programming for a graphical user interface, the learning curve can be steep. Most programmers cite a six-month period before they become adept at Windows programming.

Moreover, there is no middle ground between programming for MS-DOS and programming for Windows. There is no such thing as a program that makes use of some Windows functions but is not an all-out Windows program.

Much of what you may have learned when programming for DOS in not applicable in Windows. You can forget about using Int 10h to write to the video display; you can forget about using Int 16h to read keystrokes; you can forget about 25 lines of 80 columns each; you can forget about using C functions such as getch and printf; you can forget about directly accessing hardware; and you can forget about intercepting interrupts. Instead, you'll learn how to:

- make use of the Windows function calls
- structure your program to properly process messages from the Windows environment
- cooperate with the system and other Windows applications in your use of the processor, memory, and other resources
- write programs that run the same on a variety of hardware platforms
- use graphics in an attractive and meaningful manner
- design a program for the user's convenience rather than your own.

Like it or not, the graphical user interface has established itself as the standard computer interface for the 1990s. Continuing your programming career through this decade means that sooner or later you must come to grips with GUI programming and master it.

Architecture and Features

If your programming experience is limited to traditional environments such as MS-DOS or UNIX, a graphical user interface such as Windows may come as a big shock. Windows is so different from conventional environments that it influences the very structure of your programs. You will abandon a traditional top-down structure and adopt a more object-oriented structure. Indeed, Windows has often been characterized as an object-oriented environment with an event-driven or message-driven architecture.

The Object Called a "Window"

A Windows program creates one or more objects known as windows. Visually, a window is a rectangular area on the screen. The window receives user input from the keyboard and the mouse, and displays graphical program output. There are three general styles of windows: overlapped, pop-up, and child.

A Windows program generally uses an overlapped style for its main application window. An overlapped window usually has most or all of the window parts shown in Figure 6-1. A titlebar across the top of the window identifies the

Figure 6-1: The parts of an overlapped window.

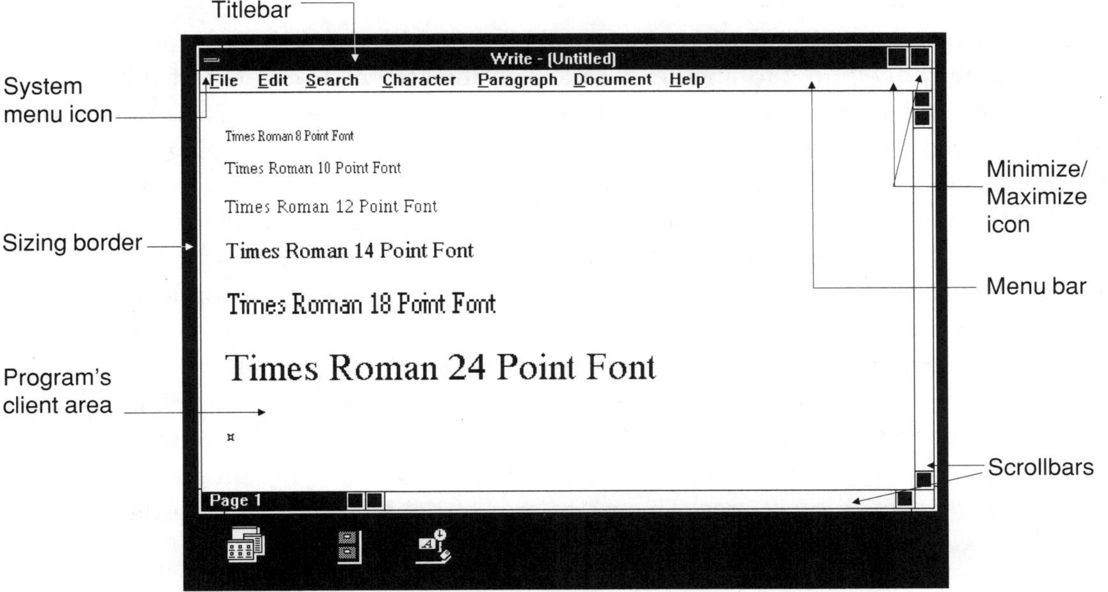

Figure 6-2: A pop-up window used as a dialog box.

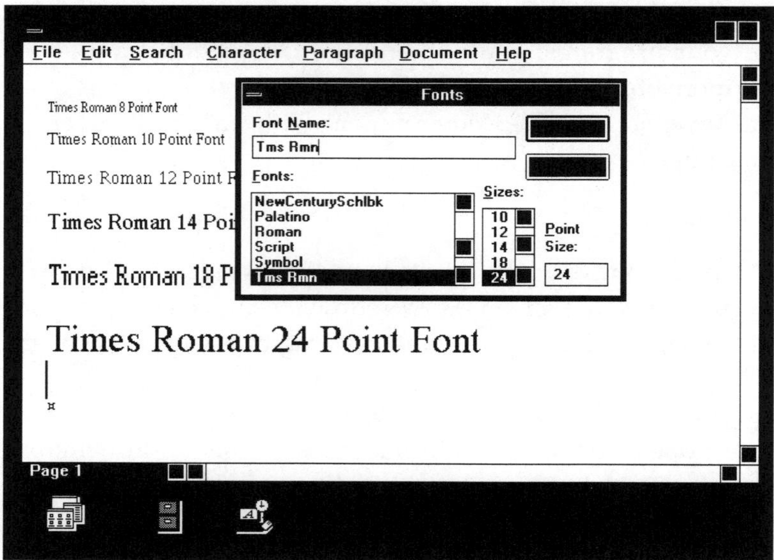

program. A user can move a window by grabbing the titlebar with the mouse and dragging the window to another location on the screen. To the left of the titlebar is the system menu icon. Clicking this icon with the mouse causes a menu to be displayed that lists several standard options, such as moving, sizing, or closing the window. To the right of the titlebar are minimize and maximize icons. Clicking the minimize icon causes the program to be displayed as a small icon on the bottom of the screen. Clicking the maximize icon causes the window to expand to fill the entire screen. Below the titlebar is the program's main top-level menu bar. Smaller pop-up menus are usually invoked from each item on the top-level menu. Surrounding the window is a sizing border. A user can change the size of a window by grabbing the sizing border with the mouse and dragging it. Scrollbars are often located within the sizing border on the right and bottom of the window. Within the sizing border and scrollbars and below the program's menu is the window's client area. This is the area of the window in which the program displays its output. All the other areas of the window are collectively referred to as non-client areas.

The second style of window is the pop-up window. Pop-up windows are generally used for short-lived windows that a program may create, such as the dialog box shown in Figure 6-2. A pop-up window usually has a fixed size. The window may or may not have a titlebar and system menu icon. Pop-up windows do not have minimize and maximize icons.

The third style of window is the child window. Child windows are generally used for small controls that take the form of buttons, text entry fields, list boxes, edit fields, and scrollbars. Most often, these appear on the surface of a dialog box, as shown in Figure 6-2. A Windows program can also place child window controls on the client area of an overlapped window.

The Window Procedure and Messages

Everything that appears on the Windows screen is a window. The user interacts with these windows. The architecture of a Windows program parallels this visual architecture.

Every window has an associated window procedure, which is a function that may be located either in the program that creates the window or somewhere in Windows itself. The window procedure is responsible for displaying the window on the screen and for processing keyboard and mouse input from the user.

Windows informs a window of interesting events that affect the window by sending the window messages. This may sound excessively abstract. What it really means is that Windows calls the window procedure, passing information about the message as parameters. Think about it for a moment: you are undoubtedly accustomed to writing programs that make calls to the operating system to perform various services. In the case of Windows, the operating environment makes calls to functions (window procedures) that are located in your program.

What are these interesting events that take the form of messages? User input certainly qualifies as an interesting event and; indeed, keyboard and mouse input messages are among the most important in Windows.

What if you grab an overlapped window's sizing border with the mouse and change the size of a window? Is that important to the window? You bet it is, and Windows has a message to tell an overlapped window when its size has been changed. Of course, when a window's size is changed, it's a good idea for the window to redraw itself, so another message indicates when a window needs repainting.

The various messages that a window procedure receives are identified by numbers, but the Windows header file defines handy identifiers that allow a program to refer to them by name. These identifiers have a prefix of WM, which stands for window message.

For example, WM_KEYUP, WM_KEYDOWN, and WM_CHAR are keyboard messages. WM_LBUTTONDOWN (the "L" stands for "left") and WM_MOUSEMOVE are mouse messages. The WM_SIZE message indicates a window's size has changed, WM_PAINT indicates that the surface of the window needs repainting, and WM_COMMAND indicates that the user has selected something from the program's menu. WM_CREATE is the first message a window procedure receives when the window is created; WM_DESTROY is the last message received when the window is destroyed.

When a Windows program begins execution, Windows creates a message queue for the program. This message queue is used to store messages to all the windows that the program creates. The program retrieves messages from this message queue and dispatches them to the appropriate window procedure. Most of the messages stored in the message queue are for keyboard or mouse input. These messages are said to be posted to the message queue. Other messages are sent directly to the window procedure from Windows.

Window procedures can also communicate among themselves, using messages. For example, dialog boxes very often contain a pushbutton or two. The pushbutton receives WM_LBUTTONDOWN and WM_LBUTTONUP messages when the user clicks the button with the mouse. The pushbutton responds by sending the window procedure for the dialog box window a WM_COMMAND message, indicating that the button has been pressed. This organization of code into window procedures lends itself well to a high degree of modularity and encapsulation. A window that has a distinct appearance and performs a very specific function (such as a pushbutton) can be completely defined by a window procedure. Such window procedures are located in Windows rather than application code.

We said earlier that every window is associated with a window procedure. More precisely, every window that a program creates is based on a window class. The window class identifies the window procedure that processes messages to the window. This concept allows many different windows to be created, based on the same window class. For example, the pushbuttons in all Windows programs are based on the same window class and hence use the same window procedure.

The non-preemptive form of multitasking that Windows supports is also based on messages. If a Windows program attempts to retrieve a message from its message queue and the message queue is empty, Windows switches control to a program that has unprocessed messages in its queue.

The Application Program Interface

The application program interface (API) of Windows 3.0 consists of about 550 functions that Windows programs may call. These functions have descriptive names using mixed upper- and lowercase, such as CreateWindow and CheckMenuItem. All the Windows functions are declared in a large header file named WINDOWS.H, which is included in the Windows Software Development Kit. Near the top of every Windows program is the statement:

```
#include windows.h
```

This includes the WINDOWS.H header file in the compilation.

Generally, a program uses these Windows functions the same way it uses C library functions in a normal C program. There are some important differences, however. First, all the Windows functions are defined with the keywords far and pascal. Second, with one rather oddball exception, all pointers that are passed as parameters to Windows functions must be far pointers. The function templates in WINDOWS.H defines all the Windows functions in this way; the C compiler performs any pointer conversion for you, so you usually don't have to worry about it.

The WINDOWS.H header file also defines over 70 data structures used in Windows function calls and messages, and about 1,500 defined identifiers of numeric constants. For example, the message identifiers discussed above are all defined in WINDOWS.H.

One important part of the API is the concept of the handle. A handle is a number that refers to an object. For example, in MS-DOS programming, a file handle is a number that refers to an open file. In Windows programming, many other objects are identified by handles. Generally, you create (or obtain access to) an object by calling a Windows function. The function returns a handle to the object. You then use the handle to refer to the object in other function calls. When you're finished using the object, you destroy (or release) it, at which time the handle becomes invalid. For example, when a program creates a window by calling CreateWindow, the function returns a handle to the window. This is the most important handle in Windows. You use this handle to refer to the window when calling functions that affect the window.

Another important handle is the handle to a device context. The device context is the drawing surface of a window or other output device such as a printer. You need a device context to use graphics on an output device. In the sample program described later in this chapter, you'll also encounter an instance handle (a handle that refers to the program itself), a handle to a menu, a handle to an icon, a handle to a mouse cursor, and a handle to a brush (which is a pattern used to fill an enclosed graphical area).

Although it is not strictly part of the API, Windows programmers often use a variable naming convention that involves prefacing a variable name with a lowercase abbreviation of the data type, such as lpsz for a long pointer to a string terminated with a zero byte. Many of the structures defined in WINDOWS.H have field names that use this variable naming convention.

The software interface between a Windows program and the Windows operating environment is unusual for MS-DOS: first, unlike some other DOS windowing libraries, a Windows executable does not contain any code for implementing the Windows function calls. All these functions are in Windows itself. Second, unlike the case of MS-DOS and the ROM BIOS, a Windows program does not call a Windows function through a software interrupt provided in a binding library. Instead, when you compile and link a Windows program, the calls to the Windows functions remain unresolved far calls. Windows resolves these calls to the Windows functions when the program is loaded into memory to run. This process is known as dynamic linking.

Dynamic Linking

Dynamic linking is an important architectural component of Windows. It is the process of resolving a function call from a program to the actual function located in a dynamic link library (DLL). Windows itself is mostly composed of several dynamic link libraries. A dynamic link library is a file that contains functions that programs or other dynamic libraries may use. Like program files, a Windows dynamic link library file has a filename extension of .EXE.

Each function in a dynamic link library that can be called from outside the module is said to be exported. The dynamic link library's .EXE file contains a table that lists all the exported functions. Functions can be exported either by name (that is, the name of the function) or by ordinal, a positive number that uniquely identifies the function within the module.

When a program contains a call to a function in a dynamic link library, that function is said to be imported to the program. The program's .EXE file contains a table of all imported functions. The functions are identified by a module name (which is the filename of the dynamic link library without the .EXE extension) and either the function name or its ordinal. Dynamic link libraries also often make use of imported functions.

When you run a Windows program, Windows examines the list of imported functions in the program's .EXE file. It then locates the dynamic link libraries that have exported these functions, and resolves the far calls by linking the program code with the DLL code. One of the big advantages of dynamic linking is that it allows Windows to make more efficient use of memory. If two Windows programs require the same function in the same dynamic link library, the DLL code can be shared between the two programs. It is not necessary for all the DLL code that a program requires to be loaded into memory at once. Parts of the dynamic link library can remain on disk until needed.

When you run LINK to create an executable Windows program, you make use of an import library included in the Windows Software Development Kit. For each Windows function a program can call, the import library identifies the module containing that function and its name or, more commonly, its ordinal number. (The ordinal numbers are preferred because they require less space in the .EXE file.) LINK uses this information to create the imported functions table in the program's .EXE file. The three major dynamic link libraries included in Windows are: KERNEL, USER, and GDI. KERNEL contains the tasking and memory management functions, USER contains the windowing and user interface functions, and GDI contains the Windows Graphics Device Interface functions.

You can create your own Windows dynamic link libraries. This is a convenient way to share code that may be required by several different programs. Dynamic link libraries can also be products in themselves, to provide extensions to the Windows interface. Dynamic linking is one of several architectural features developed for Windows that later found their way into OS/2.

The New EXE format

We have mentioned tables in the .EXE file. If you're familiar with the format of the MS-DOS .EXE file, you may be wondering where these tables are located.

Although Windows executables and dynamic link libraries retain the filename extension of .EXE, the files are actually a different format, called the "New Executable" format. The New Executable format is an extension of the MS-DOS .EXE format, because the New Executable file begins with the MS-DOS .EXE header and (optionally) a non-Windows MS-DOS program. Commonly, a Windows .EXE file contains an MS-DOS program that simply displays the message This program requires Microsoft Windows and then terminates. This is why you see this message when you attempt to execute a Windows program on the DOS command line.

The New Executable format also has a second header section, which contains an extensive amount of information that Windows uses for dynamic linking and memory management. For example, an MS-DOS .EXE file simply contains a binary image of an entire program. In the New Executable format, each code and data segment in the program is separate, and identified in a table in the second header section. A detailed explanation of the New Executable file format can be found in Microsoft Systems Journal, September 1991, page 43. Like dynamic linking, the New Executable format is also used in OS/2, OS/2 version 1.0 through 1.3, although in a slightly different format.

Real-Mode Memory Management

Memory management has always been one of the strong points of Windows, even prior to the use of protected mode in Windows 3.0. Memory can be tight in a graphical user interface, particularly when multitasking is also supported. As programs are started up and terminated, memory can become fragmented. It is therefore necessary for Windows to move blocks of memory in order to consolidate free space.

We will first examine how Windows handles memory in real mode, which is still an option when running Windows 3.0. Even under real mode, Windows implements many features that are more common to protected mode. Specifically, Windows can do the following:

- share program (and dynamic link library) code and read-only data between multiple copies of the same program (multiple copies of the same program are called instances)
- move code and data segments in memory to consolidate free memory space
- discard code and read-only data segments from memory (based on a least-recently-used algorithm), and later reload them from the .EXE file when necessary

While these features are expected in protected mode, they are not easy to implement in real mode. It requires a lot of tricky code in Windows, cooperation from the programmer, some special C compiler switches, more cooperation from the programmer, the new .EXE file format, and still more cooperation from the programmer.

All memory management in Windows is based on segments, which (as in 16-bit protected mode) are blocks of memory that can range in size from 1 byte to 64K. A segment can be classified as fixed (cannot be moved in memory), moveable (movement is allowed to consolidate free memory space), or discardable (can be discarded from memory if necessary). Discardable segments are always also moveable. The global heap (which is all the memory that Windows commands) is organized as shown in Figure 6-3. Fixed segments are allocated from the bottom up. Discardable segments are allocated

Figure 6-3: The organization of global memory in Windows.

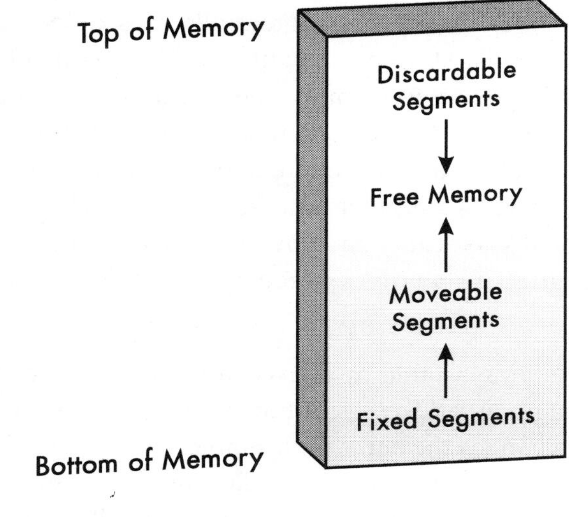

from the top down. Moveable segments are allocated above the fixed segments. If a new fixed segment must be allocated, and no space is available at the bottom of memory, then Windows will move the moveable segments up in memory to consolidate free space.

It is highly recommended that Windows programs be compiled for either small model (one code and one data segment) or medium model (multiple code segments and one data segment). Because the program has only one data segment in both these models, only near (16-bit offset) pointers are required by the program to access data in that segment. These near pointers can be stored in the data segment, and they remain valid if the data segment is moved. This allows the program's data segment to be moveable.

If a program is compiled for compact or large model, the data segments must be fixed in memory. This is not recommended because it doesn't fully cooperate with Windows' memory management. You must be careful not to store any far (32-bit segment and offset) pointers to other moveable segments, because the pointers can become invalid if the other segment is moved.

Of course, if programs were allowed only one data segment, they could not use more than 64KB of data. For this reason, Windows supports the allocation of additional data segments outside the program's own data segment. That these allocated data segments can also be moveable does not, at first, seem possible under real mode. For example, if a program allocates a block of memory outside its data segment, it must store a far pointer to that segment. If Windows then moves the allocated segment in memory, the pointer is no longer valid.

To avoid this problem, Windows defines its own memory management functions. The memory allocation function does not return a pointer. Instead, it returns a handle, which is simply a number that uniquely refers to the allocated segment. The GlobalAlloc function shown below allocates a block of moveable memory 1K in length. The handle is stored in the variable Memory:

```
hMemory = GlobalAlloc (GMEM_MOVEABLE, 1024) ;
```

Windows maintains a table in a fixed area of memory that contains these handles and the segment addresses of the memory blocks. When the segment is moved, Windows changes the entry in this table.

If the program wishes to access the allocated segment, it must call GlobalLock to lock the segment in memory. The function call returns a long pointer to the segment:

```
lpMemory = GlobalLock (Memory) ;
```

When a program calls GlobalLock, the memory block is temporarily fixed in memory, and Windows cannot move it. When the program is finished accessing the memory, it calls the GlobalUnlock function:

```
GlobalUnlock (Memory) ;
```

Following this function call, Windows is free to move the block of memory again. The next time the program calls GlobalLock, the pointer returned may well be different.

When the program is entirely finished using the segment, and no longer needs it, the segment can be freed:

```
GlobalFree (Memory) ;
```

It is recommended that a Windows program call GlobalLock only when accessing a block of memory, and GlobalUnlock when it is finished accessing the memory. This should be done in the course of processing a single message. For example, a word processing program might allocate a block of memory to store the document. It would only need to lock the block when changes are being made to the document (usually on receipt of WM_CHAR messages from the keyboard or WM_COMMAND messages from the menu) or when accessing the document for other reasons (such as updating the screen during a WM_PAINT message or when printing).

Several other functions (most notably GlobalRealloc and GlobalSize) are available to change and obtain the size of an allocated segment. Windows does not require you to allocate only moveable segments using GlobalAlloc. You can use the GMEM_FIXED flag to allocate a segment that is always fixed in memory. In this case, GlobalAlloc returns the segment address of the allocated segment.

A GMEM_DISCARDABLE flag also exists for allocating a discardable segment. Windows is free to discard this segment from memory when it is unlocked. A segment that has been discarded by Windows is indicated by a NULL return value from GlobalLock. Usually a program does not use discardable segments unless the data in the segment can be regenerated easily. However, it is possible for a program to implement its own swapping with discardable segments. If you pass the address of a function in your program to the GlobalNotify function, Windows calls the function whenever it is about to discard a discardable segment. You can then save the contents of the memory block to disk.

Windows also includes an analogous collection of memory allocation functions named LocalAlloc, LocalLock, LocalUnlock, LocalReAlloc, LocalSize, LocalFree, and LocalNotify. These functions do for the local heap (the memory that can be allocated from the program's data segment) what the other functions do for the global heap. The organization of memory in the local heap is the same as the organization of the global heap, except that we're speaking now of memory blocks, and not segments. If necessary, Windows can expand the program's data segment up to 64KB to accommodate a larger local heap.

Making use of these local memory allocation functions is much less important than using the global memory allocation functions, but they exist if you want to make efficient use of local memory. You can still use C memory allocation functions like malloc if you wish. The special Windows libraries cause malloc to behave like LocalAlloc called with the LMEM_FIXED parameter.

So far, we've seen how Windows is able to move data segments in memory. If you use small or medium model, do not save any long pointers in static memory, and use the global memory allocation functions, as recommended, then you are cooperating with Windows' memory management.

Code segments in Windows are generally moveable and discardable. If a code segment is discarded, Windows can reload it from the .EXE file when needed. (Windows always maintains an area in memory equal in size to the largest code segment of all the programs running under Windows. Thus, reloading the code segment never fails for space reasons.) Obviously, storing variables in a discardable code segment or writing self-modifying code leads to problems and is not recommended.

A medium model program contains multiple code segments. Functions in one code segment must make far calls to functions in the other code segments. All intersegment calls in a program are listed in a table in the .EXE file. Intersegment calls between two moveable code segments are handled by a small piece of intermediate code that Windows creates. This piece of code is called a thunk.

Thunks are located in a fixed area of memory. Any intersegment calls from one code segment are resolved to call a thunk. The thunk then branches to the actual function in the target code segment. When Windows moves the target code segment in memory, it adjusts the thunks accordingly. The thunk code also sets a flag whenever the thunk is called. This indicates that a particular code segment has been used. Windows uses these flags for implementing its least-recently-used algorithm to determine what code segments are candidates for discarding when memory gets low.

These thunks also take care of code segments that may be discarded from memory, or that haven't yet been loaded. When Windows discards a code segment from memory, it alters the thunk to call a function that reloads the segment from the disk file into memory. Windows then restores the thunk to its normal state and branches through the thunk again to jump to the function.

Calls from a program to a dynamic link library (DLL) are also handled through thunks. In addition, DLL entry points contain code to save the program's data segment (DS) address, load DS with the segment address of the DLL's own data segment, and restore the program's DS on exit from the function. When Windows moves a DLL data segment in memory, it must adjust the function prologues of its exported functions accordingly.

A Windows dynamic link library can call a function in a program. This occurs whenever Windows sends a message to a program's window procedure. The window procedure cannot directly load the program's DS, because multiple instances of the program may be running, and they will have different data segments. This little problem is handled by another type of thunk, which is unique to each instance of the program. The thunk loads DS with the instance's data segment address and then branches to the window procedure.

It is possible that a program may call a function in a Windows DLL, which then calls another function in another Windows DLL, which then allocates some memory that requires that the code segment in the previous DLL be moved or discarded. In this case, when the second DLL returns control to the first DLL, the code segment is gone. To compensate for this, Windows performs a trick called "walking the stack." When moving or discarding a code segment, it checks the stack to see if the code segment has been called. Windows can then adjust return addresses to the new location of the code segment, or to code that reloads the code segment in memory when it's required.

All of this may sound to you like either an extraordinary feat of software engineering or a horrible kludge. It is both. Windows memory management is ugly, confusing, and the primary source of bugs in Windows applications. Yet, it works, and nothing else in the MS-DOS world comes close to Windows in the sophistication of its real-mode memory management.

Expanded and Extended Memory Support

Beginning with version 2.0, Windows began directly supporting the Lotus/Intel/Microsoft Expanded Memory Specification version 4.0 (LIM EMS 4.0), which is discussed in detail in Chapter 2. EMS 4.0 establishes a "bank line" in memory, above which memory is paged. With a full hardware implementation of EMS 4.0, this bank line is at the 256KB mark in MS-DOS memory, which usually falls somewhere in the global heap of Windows.

EMS support is mostly transparent to Windows applications. Each Windows application (including its code segments, data segment, and additional memory allocated using the GlobalAlloc function) is allocated from EMS 4.0 pages, if possible. When Windows switches from one Windows application to another, it makes EMS 4.0 calls to page out the first application's pages, and page in the second application's pages.

Windows locates dynamic link library data and resources below the bank line. This allows the DLL data to be shared among all Windows applications. Additional shared data segments that a dynamic link library may need must be allocated with a special GlobalAlloc flag: GMEM_NOT_BANKED. Thunks and other data structures that must be present in a fixed area of memory at all times are also located below the bank line. Dynamic link library code, however, can be located above the bank line. In this case, multiple copies of the code can exist in several applications' EMS pages.

Windows programs can transfer data among themselves using the clipboard or dynamic data exchange (DDE). In these cases, Windows copies the data from one application's EMS pages to another. Programs that share memory in other ways, however, should use the GMEM_NOT_BANKED flag to allocate memory below the bank line. In many ways, the support of protected mode in Windows 3.0 simplifies memory management. The various techniques used in previous versions of Windows to emulate protected-mode features are not required. The code to implement these techniques must still be present in Windows, however, because Windows 3.0 can be run in real mode.

When running in protected-mode, Windows itself and all Windows applications share the same Local Descriptor Table (LDT). This does not offer adequate inter-process protection, of course, but makes the implementation of shared memory (necessary for the Windows clipboard and DDE) easier to implement.

In addition, Windows does not make significant use of protected-mode privilege levels.

When a program calls GlobalAlloc under protected-mode, the handle is simply a protected-mode selector. The GlobalLock call basically turns the selector into an virtual 32-bit address by taking a 0 offset to it. The memory block is always movable. Contrary to popular belief, Windows does not normally swap data segments to disk. The disk activity that occurs under Windows is due to the loading and reloading of code segments and read-only resources (such as fonts). When running in the 386 enhanced mode, however, Windows 3.0 uses the 386 paging mechanism to swap data areas.

Keyboard and Mouse Input

All user input in Windows comes through the keyboard and the mouse. A Windows program obtains this input through messages that are posted to the application's message queue. Keyboard and mouse messages are always directed to a particular window, and only one window procedure receives each message.

The window that receives keyboard input messages is the focus window, also called the window with input focus. Only one window can have the focus at any time. The user can shift focus from one application window to another, using the mouse or the Alt-Escape or Alt-Tab keys. In a dialog box, the user can shift the focus among control windows using the mouse, the Tab key, or arrow keys.

A window is responsible for indicating to the user that it has the input focus. For example, a word processing program will indicate that it has the input focus by displaying a small caret. (In other environments, the caret would be called a cursor, but that word is reserved in Windows for the bitmapped image representing the mouse.) Child window controls in a dialog box indicate they have the input focus in various ways. For example, a pushbutton displays a dotted outline around the text when it has the input focus.

Windows defines several keyboard messages, the most important of which are WM_KEYDOWN, WM_KEYUP, and WM_CHAR. The WM_KEYDOWN and WM_KEYUP messages occur whenever a key is pressed and released. The key is identified by a virtual key code. A virtual key code is defined in WINDOWS.H for every key on the keyboard. The WM_CHAR message is generated whenever a key (first indicated by a WM_KEYDOWN message) and the state of the shift keys generate an ASCII character code. The message identifies the ASCII code.

A window procedure receives mouse messages whenever the mouse cursor is positioned over the window. Pressing and releasing the left mouse button generates WM_LBUTTONDOWN and WM_LBUTTONUP messages. Similarly, the right mouse button generates WM_RBUTTONDOWN and WM_RBUTTONUP messages. Moving the mouse results in a WM_MOUSEMOVE message.

A Windows program can "capture the mouse" to continue receiving mouse input even when the mouse cursor leaves the window. For example, if you press a mouse button with the cursor positioned over a pushbutton, the pushbutton changes appearance to indicate that it has been pressed. If you keep the mouse button down and move the mouse cursor outside the pushbutton window, the window returns to normal. The pushbutton knows when the mouse cursor has left its window, because it captured the mouse.

Child Window Controls

We mentioned earlier that the architecture of a Windows program often parallels the user's visual perception of the screen. For example, a dialog box usually contains a number of input devices such as text entry fields, list boxes, scrollbars, and buttons of various sorts. The dialog box is a window, and each of these input devices is also a window. These are called child window controls, or control windows, or simply controls. Although controls most often appear in dialog boxes, they may also appear on the client area of a window.

Windows includes several predefined controls. These controls are predefined because Windows registers window classes for them. The window procedures are located in a Windows dynamic link library. Placing one of these controls on the client area of your window involves calling CreateWindow to create a window based on one of these preregistered classes. (It's even easier when you use controls on a dialog box. You need only define the size and placement of the controls in a dialog box template.) The window procedure then receives messages from the controls when the user interacts with them. The window procedure can also send messages to the controls.

The Static window class is very simple because windows based on this class ignore user input and send no messages. This window class displays windows that consist of text strings, frames, and filled rectangles.

The Button window class supports a variety of buttons, including radio buttons, check boxes, and pushbuttons. Each of these buttons has a distinctive appearance and contains some text.

Radio buttons are used to indicate one of several possible options, much like the buttons on car radios. The button displays a small circle and some text. Several radio buttons are grouped together. Clicking one radio button with the mouse selects that button (indicated by a filled-in circle) and deselects all the others.

Check boxes indicate program options. They consist of a square and some text. Clicking the check box with the mouse puts an X in the square. Clicking again removes it.

A pushbutton is a rectangle with text inside. Clicking the button usually indicates that the program should respond in some way. Pushbuttons are often used to dismiss dialog boxes.

You can also "press" a button using the Space Bar on the keyboard if the button currently has the input focus. Whenever a button is pressed, it sends a message to its parent window (usually the window that created the control) indicating this.

The Scrollbar window class supports vertical and horizontal scrollbars often used by applications (such as word processing programs) that display a part of a larger document in the window. By clicking various parts of the scrollbar, you can move the document within the window.

Windows based on the Edit window class are editable text-entry fields, both in single line or multiline formats. A multiline edit control actually has much of the functionality of a rudimentary editor. The Windows NOTEPAD program is little more than a multiline edit control occupying the program's client area.

The Listbox window class supports a scrollable list of text strings. The user can select one (or, in some cases, more than one) text string using the mouse. Listboxes are commonly used for selecting a file to load into memory.

The Combobox window class is one of the enhancements to Windows 3.0. A combobox is a combination of an edit control and a listbox. The listbox is normally hidden until the user presses a little button to the right of the edit field.

In addition, you can create your own controls. If the window procedure for a custom control is located in a dynamic link library, it can be shared among multiple applications.

Graphics Device Interface (GDI)

The API of any graphical environment must include a graphics programming language. In Windows, this is known as the Graphics Device Interface, or GDI. GDI is a device-independent graphics programming language. What this means is that you use the same function calls for any graphics output device (including video displays and printers) for which a Windows device driver is present. You do not need to know the particulars of the output device; the device driver does all the translation for you. Conceptually, a program draws graphics on device context, which is a drawing surface associated with a graphics output device. For drawing on the video display, a window procedure can obtain a device context for the window by calling BeginPaint (during the WM_PAINT message) or GetDC (during other messages). These functions return a handle to the device, which is passed as a first parameter to the GDI functions.

For printer or plotter graphics, a program obtains a device context by calling CreateDC. This same function can be used for creating device contexts not directly associated with an actual output device. These are the memory device context (useful for working with bitmaps) and the metafile device context (for creating a metafile). The device context stores attributes that determine how the GDI drawing functions operate on the device. For example, one attribute is the color and style of the "pen" used to draw lines.

By default, all coordinates passed to GDI drawing functions are in units of pixels relative to the upper left-hand corner of the output device. However, a program can set an alternative mapping mode to draw in units of inches, millimeters, or arbitrary coordinates. The program can also set the coordinate origin anywhere relative to the surface of the output device. GDI supports five basic graphics primitives:

- lines
- filled areas
- text
- bitmaps
- regions

Use the MoveTo and LineTo functions to draw a straight line. The MoveTo function sets the beginning of the line, and LineTo sets the end of the line. The PolyLine function draws a series of connected straight lines, and the Arc function draws a curved line defined by the circumference of an ellipse. All lines are drawn using an object called a pen. The pen defines the color of the line, its width, and its style (whether it is solid, or composed of various dashes or dots).

Windows also has several functions for filling enclosed areas. The Rectangle function draws a rectangle, RoundRect draws a rectangle with rounded corners, Ellipse draws an ellipse, Chord and Pie draw sections of an ellipse, and Polygon fills the area enclosed by a polyline. GDI fills the area using an object called a brush. A brush is defined by a color and a style (such as solid or consisting of several variations of hatch marks).

The standard text output function is called TextOut. The text begins at a specified location on the output device. By default, a program that draws text uses the Windows system font, which is a variable-pitch font in Windows 3.0 and a fixed-pitch font in earlier versions. A program can select a different font for the output device (depending on what the output device supports) and obtain text metrics for that font. These metrics provide information about the dimensions of the font.

Bitmaps are rectangular arrays of pixels used for storing complex images. The BitBlt and StretchBlt functions can copy a bitmap from one device context to another. The StretchBlt function can stretch or compress a bitmap to change its size. These functions actually perform much more than simple copies: they can render a source (the bitmap) on a destination surface combined with a brush in any of 256 possible bit-wise combinations.

A region is a combination of rectangles, polygons, and ellipses. Regions can be filled, outlined, inverted, or used for clipping. Graphics attribute and drawing functions may be saved in metafiles. These are binary coded representations of GDI functions. Metafiles can be stored in memory or on disk.

Resources

A .EXE file (either a program or a dynamic link library) almost always contains code and data segments, but it may also contain another type of segment known as a resource segment. Resources are read-only data that are stored in the .EXE file and loaded into memory when required. Resources are shared among multiple instances of a program.

For example, a program's icon (which is actually a small bitmap) is stored as a resource. So are any customized mouse cursors you may create. Resources also include menu templates (used to define a program's menu), dialog box templates (used to define the layout of a program's dialog boxes), keyboard accelerators (which translate certain keystrokes into menu commands), and fonts.

Interprocess Communication

To allow users to transfer data from one program to another, Windows supports a form of shared memory known as the clipboard.

Generally, Windows programs that work with documents have an item on the top-level menu called Edit. The Edit submenu usually has several options, including Cut, Copy, and Paste. The Cut option removes a selected area of a document and copies it to the clipboard. The Copy option copies the selected area to the clipboard without removing it from the document. Paste copies data from the clipboard to the document.

Windows defines several clipboard data formats. The three most common are ASCII text, bitmaps, and metafiles. In addition, programs can define their own clipboard formats for storing data during cut-and-paste operations. This allows a user to copy a selection from one instance of a particular word processing program to another instance without losing formatting.

An increasingly popular form of inter-process communication under Windows is Dynamic Data Exchange or DDE. DDE is a protocol rather than a specific feature of Windows. It is based on the Windows messaging system and hence requires very little in the way of additional support from Windows.

Two programs are involved in a DDE transaction. A program called the client wants data that may be available from another program. The program that has the data is known as the server. A DDE transaction begins when the client broadcasts a message to all windows running under Windows asking if they can supply data identified by some keywords. A program responding affirmatively with a message to the client becomes a server. The server can either give the client the data and end the transaction, or keep the client informed when the data changes.

Any software manufacturer who writes a program that can perform DDE server functions would tell buyers of that program the keywords required to access its data. The user can then use these keywords in any Windows application that supports DDE, perhaps in a macro language or directly in a spreadsheet or word processing field.

One popular demonstration of DDE involves a Windows server application that receives broadcast stock quotations via special radio hardware. A spreadsheet program can establish a DDE link and keep a spreadsheet and bar graph updated with the latest stock quotes.

More recently, Microsoft has developed a new protocol called Object Linking and Embedding (OLE). OLE allows a Windows program to work with a document that contain multiple forms of data, some of which are understood only by other applications.

A Sample Program

The best way to understand what Windows programming is all about is to examine in gory detail a complete, working Windows program. The CLOCK7 program, shown running under Windows in Figure 6-4, shows the current time, using a simulated seven-segment LCD display. The time is updated every second. (For purposes of the non-color illustration, the program shows white numbers on a black background; the program actually displays red numbers on a black background.)

The menu bar has two items: Set and Format. When you select the Set option, CLOCK7 displays a drop-down menu with three options: Set Alarm, Exit, and About Clock7. The Set Alarm option displays the dialog box shown in Figure 6-5. You can enter a time, and when that time occurs, CLOCK7 displays a message box with the words "Wake up! Wake up! Wake up!" The Exit option exits the program. The About Clock7 option displays a dialog box with some information about the program.

Figure 6-4: The CLOCK7 program running under Windows.

Figure 6-5: The CLOCK7 dialog box for setting the alarm.

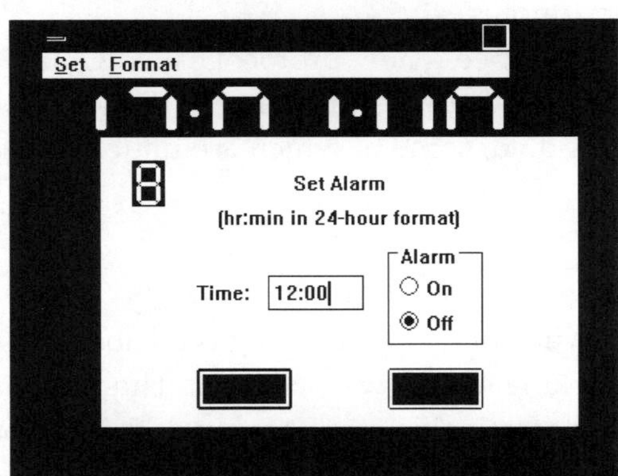

When you select the Format item, CLOCK7 displays a drop-down menu that lets you switch between a 12-hour format and a 24-hour format. The current selection is indicated by a check mark.

CLOCK7 illustrates many of the concepts discussed above, including window creation, message handling, resources, and graphics. If you don't understand all the workings of this program at first encounter, don't worry about it. That's normal. Windows programming is not something that can be picked up in an hour or two.

The Source Files

Programs for Windows are generally constructed from several different files. The six files required for CLOCK7 are fairly standard. You'll have similar files for almost every Windows program you write.

You first need a make-file that automates compilation and linking of the program. If you're using the Microsoft C Compiler 6.0 and the Microsoft Windows Software Development Kit, the CLOCK7 make-file looks like this:

```
#-------------------------------------------
# CLOCK7.MSC make file for Microsoft C 6.0
#-------------------------------------------
clock7.exe : clock7.obj clock7.def clock7.res
     link clock7, /align:16, NUL, /nod slibcew libw, clock7
     rc clock7.res
clock7.obj : clock7.c clock7.h
     cl -c -Gsw -Ow -W3 -Zp clock7.c
```

```
clock7.res : clock7.rc clock7.h clock7.ico
     rc -r clock7.rc
```

You can create the CLOCK7.EXE file from the DOS command line by executing:

```
NMAKE CLOCK7.MSC
```

If you're using the Borland C++ 2.0 compiler, the CLOCK7 make-file looks like this:

```
#-----------------------------------------
# CLOCK7.BCP make file for Borland C++ 2.0
#-----------------------------------------

clock7.exe : clock7.obj clock7.def clock7.res
     tlink /c /n /Tw /L\borlandc\lib c0ws clock7, clock7, NUL, \
           /nod cwins cs import, clock7
     rc clock7.res
clock7.obj : clock7.c clock7.h
     bcc -c -w-par -W clock7.c
clock7.res : clock7.rc clock7.h clock7.ico
     rc -r -i\borlandc\include clock7.rc
```

You can create CLOCK7.EXE by executing:

```
MAKE -fCLOCK7.BCP
```

The make-file is not only a convenient way to create the executable; it also shows how the other five files contribute to the program.

A make-file consists of several sections (in the case of CLOCK7, three) that begin with a left-justified line showing a target file, a colon, and one or more dependent files. If any of the dependent files has been modified more recently than the target files, NMAKE or MAKE runs the indented commands that follow.

The first section of CLOCK7 indicates that CLOCK7.OBJ is created from CLOCK7.C, shown below:

```
/*-------------------------------------------------------------
   CLOCK7.C -- Seven-Segment Clock Program for Microsoft Windows
            Programmed by Charles Petzold
  -------------------------------------------------------------*/

#include <windows.h>
#include <stdlib.h>
#include <string.h>
#include <time.h>
#include "clock7.h"
#define ID_TIMER 1
long FAR PASCAL WndProc (HWND, WORD, WORD, LONG) ;
BOOL FAR PASCAL AlarmDlgProc (HWND, WORD, WORD, LONG) ;
BOOL FAR PASCAL AboutDlgProc (HWND, WORD, WORD, LONG) ;
```

```
void DisplayTime (HDC, struct tm *, BOOL) ;
void DisplayDots (HDC) ;
void DrawDigit (HDC, int, int, int) ;
BOOL bAlarmOn = FALSE ;
int  iHour, iMin ;
int PASCAL WinMain (HANDLE hInstance, HANDLE hPrevInstance,
                    LPSTR lpszCmdParam, int nCmdShow)
     {
     static char szAppName [] = "Clock7" ;
     HWND        hwnd ;
     MSG         msg ;
     WNDCLASS    wndclass ;
     if (!hPrevInstance)
          {
          wndclass.style              = 0 ;
          wndclass.lpfnWndProc        = WndProc ;
          wndclass.cbClsExtra         = 0 ;
          wndclass.cbWndExtra         = 0 ;
          wndclass.hInstance          = hInstance ;
          wndclass.hIcon              = LoadIcon (hInstance, szAppName) ;
          wndclass.hCursor            = LoadCursor (NULL, IDC_ARROW) ;
          wndclass.hbrBackground      = GetStockObject (BLACK_BRUSH) ;
          wndclass.lpszMenuName       = szAppName ;
          wndclass.lpszClassName      = szAppName ;
          RegisterClass (&wndclass) ;
          }
     hwnd = CreateWindow (szAppName,                // window class name
                    "Seven-Segment Clock ",         // window caption
                    WS_OVERLAPPEDWINDOW &           // window style
                    ~WS_THICKFRAME & ~WS_MAXIMIZEBOX,
               CW_USEDEFAULT,                       // initial x position
                    CW_USEDEFAULT,                  // initial y position
                    CW_USEDEFAULT,                  // initial x size
                    CW_USEDEFAULT,                  // initial y size
                    NULL,                           // parent window handle
               NULL,                                // window menu handle
                    hInstance,                      // program instance handle
                    NULL) ;                         // creation parameters
     ShowWindow (hwnd, nCmdShow) ;
     UpdateWindow (hwnd) ;
     while (GetMessage (&msg, NULL, 0, 0))
          {
          TranslateMessage (&msg) ;
          DispatchMessage (&msg) ;
          }
     return msg.wParam ;
     }

long FAR PASCAL WndProc (HWND hwnd, WORD message, WORD wParam, LONG lParam)
     {
```

```
     static BOOL        b24Hour = FALSE ;
     static FARPROC     lpfnAlarmDlgProc, lpfnAboutDlgProc ;
     static HANDLE      hInstance ;
     static HMENU       hMenu ;
     LPCREATESTRUCT     lpcrst ;
     HDC                hdc ;
     long               lTime ;
     PAINTSTRUCT        ps ;
     POINT        pt ;
     RECT               rect ;
     struct tm          *datetime ;

     switch (message)
          {
          case WM_CREATE:
               lpcrst = (LPCREATESTRUCT) lParam ;
               hInstance = lpcrst->hInstance ;

               lpfnAlarmDlgProc = MakeProcInstance (AlarmDlgProc, hInstance) ;
               lpfnAboutDlgProc = MakeProcInstance (AboutDlgProc, hInstance) ;

               hdc = GetDC (hwnd) ;
               SetMapMode (hdc, MM_HIENGLISH) ;
               pt.x =  4000 ;
               pt.y = -1000 ;
               LPtoDP (hdc, &pt, 1) ;
               ReleaseDC (hwnd, hdc) ;

               rect.left   = 0 ;
               rect.top    = 0 ;
               rect.right  = pt.x ;
               rect.bottom = pt.y ;
               AdjustWindowRect (&rect, WS_OVERLAPPEDWINDOW & ~WS_THICKFRAME,
                                   TRUE) ;

               MoveWindow (hwnd, lpcrst->x, lpcrst->y, rect.right - rect.left,
                              rect.bottom - rect.top, FALSE) ;

               hMenu = GetMenu (hwnd) ;
               SetTimer (hwnd, ID_TIMER, 1000, NULL) ;
               return 0 ;

          case WM_COMMAND:
               switch (wParam)
                    {
                    case IDM_HOUR12:
                         CheckMenuItem (hMenu, IDM_HOUR12, MF_CHECKED) ;
                         CheckMenuItem (hMenu, IDM_HOUR24, MF_UNCHECKED) ;
                         b24Hour = FALSE ;
                         return 0 ;

                    case IDM_HOUR24:
                         CheckMenuItem (hMenu, IDM_HOUR12, MF_UNCHECKED) ;
                         CheckMenuItem (hMenu, IDM_HOUR24, MF_CHECKED) ;
                         b24Hour = TRUE ;
                         return 0 ;
```

```
                    case IDM_ALARM:
                         DialogBox (hInstance, "AlarmBox", hwnd,
                                   lpfnAlarmDlgProc) ;
                         return 0 ;
                    case IDM_ABOUT:
                         DialogBox (hInstance, "AboutBox", hwnd,
                                   lpfnAboutDlgProc) ;
                         return 0 ;
                    case IDM_EXIT:
                         SendMessage (hwnd, WM_CLOSE, 0, 0L) ;
                         return 0 ;
                    }
               break ;
          case WM_TIMER:
               time (&lTime) ;
               datetime = localtime (&lTime) ;
               if (datetime->tm_hour == iHour && datetime->tm_min == iMin
                         && bAlarmOn == TRUE)
                    {
                    bAlarmOn = FALSE ;
                    MessageBox (hwnd, "Wake Up! Wake Up! Wake Up!",
                              "Alarm", MB_OK | MB_ICONASTERISK) ;
                    }
               hdc = GetDC (hwnd) ;
               DisplayTime (hdc, datetime, b24Hour) ;
               ReleaseDC (hwnd, hdc) ;
               return 0 ;
          case WM_PAINT:
               time (&lTime) ;
               datetime = localtime (&lTime) ;

               hdc = BeginPaint (hwnd, &ps) ;
               DisplayTime (hdc, datetime, b24Hour) ;
               DisplayDots (hdc) ;
               EndPaint (hwnd, &ps) ;
          return 0 ;
          case WM_DESTROY:
               KillTimer (hwnd, ID_TIMER) ;
               PostQuitMessage (0) ;
          return 0 ;
          }
     return DefWindowProc (hwnd, message, wParam, lParam) ;
     }
BOOL FAR PASCAL AlarmDlgProc (HWND hwnd, WORD message, WORD wParam, LONG lParam)
     {
     static BOOL bLocalAlarmOn ;
     static char szAlarmTime[10] = "12:00" ;
     char        szParseTime[10] ;
     switch (message)
```

```
          {
          case WM_INITDIALOG:
               SendDlgItemMessage (hwnd, IDD_ALARMTIME, EM_LIMITTEXT, 6, 0L) ;
               SetDlgItemText (hwnd, IDD_ALARMTIME, szAlarmTime) ;
               CheckRadioButton (hwnd, IDD_ALARMON, IDD_ALARMOFF,
                                 bAlarmOn ? IDD_ALARMON : IDD_ALARMOFF) ;
               bLocalAlarmOn = bAlarmOn ;
               return TRUE ;
          case WM_COMMAND:
               switch (wParam)
                    {
                    case IDD_ALARMON:
                    case IDD_ALARMOFF:
                         bLocalAlarmOn = (wParam == IDD_ALARMON) ;
                         CheckRadioButton (hwnd, IDD_ALARMON, IDD_ALARMOFF,
                                           wParam) ;
                         return TRUE ;

                    case IDOK:
                         GetDlgItemText (hwnd, IDD_ALARMTIME, szAlarmTime, 10) ;
                         strcpy (szParseTime, szAlarmTime) ;
                         iHour = atoi (strtok (szParseTime, ":")) ;
                         iMin  = atoi (strtok (NULL, " :")) ;

                         if (iHour < 0 || iHour > 23 || iMin < 0 || iMin > 59)
                              {
                              MessageBox (hwnd, "Time is not valid!", NULL,
                                          MB_OK | MB_ICONEXCLAMATION) ;
                              SetFocus (GetDlgItem (hwnd, IDD_ALARMTIME)) ;
                              return TRUE ;
                              }

                         bAlarmOn = bLocalAlarmOn ;
                         EndDialog (hwnd, TRUE) ;
                         return TRUE ;

                    case IDCANCEL:
                         EndDialog (hwnd, FALSE) ;
                         return TRUE ;
                    }
               break ;
          }
     return FALSE ;
     }
BOOL FAR PASCAL AboutDlgProc (HWND hwnd, WORD message, WORD wParam, LONG lParam)
     {
     switch (message)
          {
          case WM_INITDIALOG:
               return TRUE ;

          case WM_COMMAND:
```

```
                switch (wParam) ;
                     {
                     case IDOK:
                     case IDCANCEL:
                          EndDialog (hwnd, 0) ;
                          return TRUE ;
                     }
          }
     return FALSE ;
     }

void DisplayTime (HDC hdc, struct tm *datetime, BOOL b24Hour)
     {
     SetMapMode (hdc, MM_HIENGLISH) ;
     SetWindowOrg (hdc, 0, 1000) ;

     if (!b24Hour)
          if ((datetime->tm_hour %= 12) == 0)
               datetime->tm_hour = 12 ;

     DrawDigit (hdc, 100, 100,  datetime->tm_hour / 10 != 0 ?
                                   datetime->tm_hour / 10 : 10) ;
     DrawDigit (hdc,  700, 100, datetime->tm_hour % 10) ;
     DrawDigit (hdc, 1500, 100, datetime->tm_min / 10) ;
     DrawDigit (hdc, 2100, 100, datetime->tm_min % 10) ;
     DrawDigit (hdc, 2900, 100, datetime->tm_sec / 10) ;
     DrawDigit (hdc, 3500, 100, datetime->tm_sec % 10) ;
     }

void DrawDigit (HDC hdc, int x, int y, int iDigit)
     {
     static BOOL bSegmentOn[11][7] = {     1, 0, 1, 1, 1, 1, 1,    // 0
                                           0, 0, 0, 0, 1, 0, 1,    // 1
                                           1, 1, 1, 0, 1, 1, 0,    // 2
                                           1, 1, 1, 0, 1, 0, 1,    // 3
                                           0, 1, 0, 1, 1, 0, 1,    // 4
                                           1, 1, 1, 1, 0, 0, 1,    // 5
                                           1, 1, 1, 1, 0, 1, 1,    // 6
                                           1, 0, 0, 0, 1, 0, 1,    // 7
                                           1, 1, 1, 1, 1, 1, 1,    // 8
                                           1, 1, 0, 1, 1, 0, 1,    // 9
                                           0, 0, 0, 0, 0, 0, 0 } ; // blank
     static int    iSegmentType[7]    = {  0, 0, 0, 1, 1, 1, 1 } ;
     static LOGBRUSH logbrBlack       = {  BS_SOLID, RGB(0,0,0),   0 } ;
     static LOGBRUSH logbrRed         = {  BS_SOLID, RGB(255,0,0), 0 } ;
     static POINT ptSegOrigin[7]      = {    0, 800, 0, 400,    0, 0, 0, 400,
                                           400, 400, 0,    0, 400, 0 } ;
     static POINT ptSegment[2][6]     = {   25,    0,   75,   50,  325,   50,
                                           375,    0,  325,  -50,   75,  -50,
                                             0,   25,   50,   75,   50,  325,
                                             0,  375,  -50,  325,  -50,   75 } ;
     HBRUSH          hbrBlack, hbrRed ;
```

```
     int              iSeg ;

     hbrBlack = CreateBrushIndirect (&logbrBlack) ;
     hbrRed   = CreateBrushIndirect (&logbrRed) ;
     SaveDC (hdc) ;
     OffsetWindowOrg (hdc, -x, -y) ;

     for (iSeg = 0 ; iSeg < 7 ; iSeg++)
          {
          SaveDC (hdc) ;
          OffsetWindowOrg (hdc, -ptSegOrigin[iSeg].x, -ptSegOrigin[iSeg].y) ;
          SelectObject (hdc, bSegmentOn[iDigit][iSeg] ? hbrRed : hbrBlack) ;
          Polygon (hdc, ptSegment[iSegmentType[iSeg]], 6) ;
          RestoreDC (hdc, -1) ;
          }

     SelectObject (hdc, GetStockObject (BLACK_BRUSH)) ;
     RestoreDC (hdc, -1) ;
     DeleteObject (hbrBlack) ;
     DeleteObject (hbrRed) ;
     }

void DisplayDots (HDC hdc)
     {
     static LOGBRUSH logbrRed = { BS_SOLID, RGB(255,0,0), 0 } ;
     HBRUSH              hbrRed ;

     hbrRed = CreateBrushIndirect (&logbrRed) ;
     SelectObject (hdc, hbrRed) ;
     Ellipse (hdc, 1250, 350, 1350, 250) ;
     Ellipse (hdc, 1250, 750, 1350, 650) ;
     Ellipse (hdc, 2650, 350, 2750, 250) ;
     Ellipse (hdc, 2650, 750, 2750, 650) ;
     SelectObject (hdc, GetStockObject (BLACK_BRUSH)) ;
     DeleteObject (hbrRed) ;
     }
```

CLOCK7.C requires the CLOCK7.H file shown below:

```
/*----------------------
   CLOCK7.H header file
  ----------------------*/

#define IDM_HOUR12          1
#define IDM_HOUR24          2
#define IDM_ALARM           3
#define IDM_EXIT            4
#define IDM_ABOUT           5

#define IDD_ALARMTIME       10
#define IDD_ALARMON         11
#define IDD_ALARMOFF        12
```

The compiler flags shown in the CLOCK.MSC and CLOCK7.BCP are normal for compiling a Windows program. In particular, the -Gsw switch (which is actually two switches, -Gs and -Gw) inhibits stack checks and causes the compiler to create a special prologue on far functions necessary for loading the program's data segment on entry to a window procedure.

The third section of the CLOCK7 make file shows that CLOCK7.RES (a compiled resource file) is created from CLOCK7.RC (the resource script shown below), CLOCK7.H, and CLOCK7.ICO by running the RC.EXE resource compiler included with the Windows Software Development Kit.

```
/*---------------------------
   CLOCK7.RC resource script
  ---------------------------*/

#include <windows.h>
#include "clock7.h"

Clock7 ICON clock7.ico

Clock7 MENU
      {
      POPUP "&Set"
            {
            MENUITEM "&Set Alarm...",   IDM_ALARM
            MENUITEM SEPARATOR
            MENUITEM "E&xit",                 IDM_EXIT
            MENUITEM SEPARATOR
            MENUITEM "A&bout Clock7...",      IDM_ABOUT
            }
      POPUP "&Format"
            {
            MENUITEM "&12 Hour",        IDM_HOUR12, CHECKED
            MENUITEM "&24 Hour",        IDM_HOUR24
            }
      }

AlarmBox DIALOG 20, 20, 160, 100
   STYLE WS_POPUP | WS_DLGFRAME
      {
      CTEXT "Set Alarm"                          -1,     0,  12  160,    8
      CTEXT "(hr:min in 24-hour format) "        -1,     0,  24, 160,    8
      ICON  "Clock7"                             -1,     8,   8,   0,    0
      LTEXT "Time:"                              -1,     3,  50,  20,    8
      EDITTEXT                       IDD_ALARMTIME,     56,  48,  32,   12,  ES_AUTOHSCROLL
      GROUPBOX "Alarm"                           -1,    96,  36,  32,   36,
      RADIOBUTTON "On"                 IDD_ALARMON,    100,  46,  24,   12,  WS_GROUP
      RADIOBUTTON "Off"               IDD_ALARMOFF,    100,  58,  24,   12
      DEFPUSHBUTTON "OK"                      IDOK,     32,  80,  32,   14,  WS_GROUP
```

```
    PUSHBUTTON "Cancel"           IDCANCEL,     96, 80,  32,  14,   WS_GROUP
    }

AboutBox DIALOG 20, 20, 160, 80
  STYLE WS_POPUP | WS_DLGFRAME
    {
    CTEXT "Clock7"                               -1,  0, 12, 160,  8
    ICON  "Clock7"                               -1,  8,  8,   0,  0
    CTEXT "Seven-Segment Clock"                  -1,  0, 36, 160,  8
    CTEXT "Programmed by Charles Petzold"        -1,  0, 48, 160,  8
    DEFPUSHBUTTON "OK"                         IDOK, 64, 60,  32, 14, WS_GROUP
    }
```

CLOCK7.ICO is a binary file containing an image of the program's icon. Figure 6-6 shows CLOCK7.ICO as it appears in the SDKPAINT program supplied with the Windows Software Development Kit. The icon is simply a "figure 8."

The third section of the CLOCK7 make file shows that CLOCK7.EXE is created from CLOCK7.OBJ, CLOCK7.RES, and CLOCK7.DEF (the module definition file shown below). This involves running the LINK.EXE linker with the special C libraries. The last parameter indicates the CLOCK7.DEF file. The RC.EXE resource compiler is then run again to add the compiled resources to CLOCK7.EXE.

```
;------------------------------------
; CLOCK7.DEF module definition file
;------------------------------------
NAME            CLOCK7

DESCRIPTION     'Seven-Segment Clock Program for Microsoft Windows'
EXETYPE         WINDOWS
STUB            'WINSTUB.EXE'
CODE            PRELOAD MOVEABLE DISCARDABLE
DATA            PRELOAD MOVEABLE MULTIPLE
HEAPSIZE        1024
STACKSIZE       4096
EXPORTS         WndProc
                AlarmDlgProc
                AboutDlgProc
```

The CLOCK7.C File

CLOCK7.C contains all the source code for the program. It begins by including the WINDOWS.H header file:

```
    #include windows.h
```

Also included are a few normal C header files and CLOCK7.H. CLOCK7.C has three global variables defined near the top of the file: bAlarmOn, iHour, and iMin. These indicate the time for the alarm. CLOCK7 calls some 40 different Windows functions, and much of this discussion will concentrate on what these function calls do.

Figure 6-6: The CLock.ICO file shown in SDKPAINT.

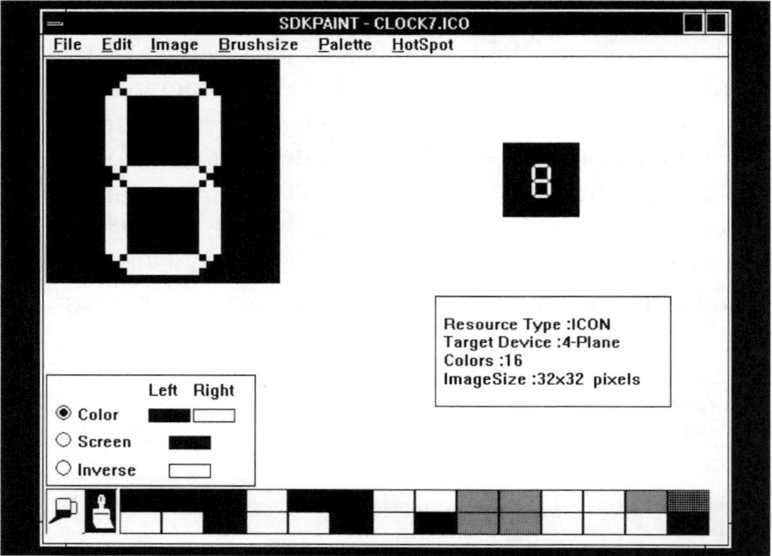

The WinMain Function

Just as main() is the entry point to a conventional C program, a function called WinMain is the entry point to a Windows program. CLOCK7's WinMain function is fairly standard. Similar code appears in almost every Windows program.

WinMain has four parameters: the first (hInstance) is called an instance handle. This is a number that uniquely identifies the program in Windows. It is equivalent to a "task ID" or "process ID" in other operating systems. The second parameter is hPrevInstance, the instance handle of the most previously executed instance of the program still running under Windows. If no other copy of the program is running under Windows, hPrevInstance equals NULL (0).

The lpszCmdParam parameter to WinMain is not used in CLOCK7. This is a zero-terminated string that contains any parameters passed to the program on a command line. The last parameter (nCmdShow) is a number that indicates whether CLOCK7 is to be displayed initially as a normal window or as an icon.

The first job for WinMain is registering a window class for the program's window. This requires setting the fields of a structure of type WNDCLASS (a structure defined in WINDOWS.H) and passing a pointer to the structure to the RegisterClass function. Because all instances of the same program can share the same window class, this need only be done if hPrevInstance is not equal to NULL.

The two most important fields of the WNDCLASS structure are the second and the last. The second field is lpfnWndProc, which is set to the function WndProc, the window procedure to be used for all windows based on this window class. The last field is lpszClassName, the name of the window class. This is set to the string "Clock7" (stored in szAppName).

The WNDCLASS structure also defines the icon, cursor, background color, and menu to be used for all windows based on this window class. The LoadIcon function loads the icon from the resource segment of the CLOCK7.EXE file and returns a handle to the icon. CLOCK7's icon is defined by the name "Clock7" in the CLOCK7.RC resource script.

The LoadCursor function loads one of the standard Windows mouse cursors (the arrow cursor) and returns a handle to the cursor. This cursor appears when the mouse is positioned over CLOCK7's window. The GetStockObject function returns a handle to a solid black brush pattern. The lpszMenuName field is set to the name of the program's menu (in this case, "Clock7") as defined in the CLOCK7.RC resource script.

After CLOCK7 registers the window class, it can create a window by calling CreateWindow. The first parameter indicates the window class, the second parameter is the text that will appear in the window's titlebar, and the third parameter defines the style of the window, using identifiers from WINDOWS.H, beginning with the WS ("window style") prefix. The most common window style is WS_OVERLAPPEDWINDOW. This identifier is actually a combination of several other WS identifiers, each of which is a bit flag indicating one of the components of the application's window. CLOCK7 doesn't have a sizing border or maximize box, so these bit flags are eliminated by a bitwise AND operation with the inverses of WS_THICKFRAME and WS_MAXIMIZEBOX.

CreateWindow returns a handle to the window. CLOCK7 uses this handle in the next two function calls:

The ShowWindow call displays the window on the screen. The first parameter is hwnd, and the second is nCmdShow, the last parameter to WinMain. The value of nCmdShow depends on whether the program was run normally, or loaded to be displayed initially as an icon. The call to UpdateWindow instructs the window to paint itself.

WinMain then enters the standard Windows message loop. The message loop consists of calls to GetMessage, TranslateMessage, and DispatchMessage in a while loop. GetMessage retrieves the next message from the program's message queue and stores the message in a structure of type MSG. TranslateMessage performs some keyboard translation, and DispatchMessage sends the message to a window procedure for processing.

GetMessage returns a non-zero value for every message except one: a special message named WM_QUIT. WM_QUIT indicates that the program is terminating. The program drops out of the message loop and WinMain ends, ending the program. (We'll discuss how the WM_QUIT message gets into the message queue later.)

The WndProc Window Procedure

It is unusual for a C program to contain a function that is not directly called from the program. Yet this is the case with the function named WndProc. WndProc is the window procedure for CLOCK7's application window. The function is called from Windows when sending messages to that window.

A window procedure has four parameters. These parameters are the first four fields of the MSG structure used in WinMain to retrieve messages from the message queue and dispatch them to a window procedure.

The first parameter, hwnd, is the handle to the window that is to receive the message. In CLOCK7, this is the same value returned from CreateWindow. When multiple windows are based on the same window class (and hence use the same window procedure) this parameter allows the window procedure to identify the particular window receiving the message.

The second parameter to WndProc is named message. This is a number that identifies the message. All the messages have constant identifiers defined in WINDOWS.H, beginning with the prefix WM ("window message"). The last two parameters (wParam and lParam) are called message parameters. These parameters provide more information about particular messages. Their values, and how they are interpreted, depend on the message they accompany.

Programmers who write for Windows often use a switch and case construction to process messages sent to the window procedure. CLOCK7 processes five messages: WM_CREATE, WM_COMMAND, WM_TIMER, WM_PAINT, and WM_DESTROY (each of which is described below). Generally, after processing a message, the window procedure returns zero.

WndProc receives many more messages besides these five, but it doesn't process any of them. Any message that a window procedure chooses to ignore must be passed to DefWindowProc for default processing. This occurs near the bottom of WndProc in CLOCK7.C.

Calling DefWindowProc for all unprocessed messages is important. In particular, this function processes all messages involving non-client areas of the window. For example, the WM_NCPAINT message instructs the window procedure to paint the non-client areas of the window, such as the titlebar and the sizing border. WndProc doesn't want to bother with this job, so it passes the message on to DefWindowProc. DefWindowProc also processes keyboard and mouse input to the non-client areas. This is how a program's menu can be functional without requiring any code to handle keyboard and mouse input to the menu.

Local variables defined in the window procedure can be either static or automatic. The static variables are those that must retain their values between messages. You can use automatic variables for anything that is required only during the course of a single message.

The WM_CREATE Message

The WM_CREATE message is the first message the window procedure receives. This is usually a good time to perform window initialization.

The WM_CREATE message is sent to the window procedure when the program calls CreateWindow in WinMain to create the window: control passes from WinMain to the CreateWindow function in Windows, to WndProc in CLOCK7 to process WM_CREATE, back to Windows to finish the CreateWindow call, and then back to WinMain. By the time CreateWindow returns, WndProc has already processed the WM_CREATE message.

During the WM_CREATE message, the lParam parameter to the window procedure is a long pointer to a structure of type CREATESTRUCT. This structure contains all the data passed as parameters to the CreateWindow function. WndProc casts lParam to an LPCREATESTRUCT type (defined in WINDOWS.H as a long pointer to a structure of type CREATESTRUCT) and stores it in a variable named lpcrst. WndProc then obtains the hInstance handle from this structure. The next two lines of code in WndProc require a little background:

We discussed earlier how Windows is able to move a code segment in memory even if the segment contains a function that is called from outside the segment with a far call. There are three such functions in CLOCK7. The first is WndProc, which is called from Windows whenever Windows sends it a message. The other two are AlarmDlgProc and AboutDlgProc, which are dialog box procedures (very similar to window procedures) for the two dialog boxes.

Windows must create a thunk for the window procedures and dialog box procedures. This thunk is located in a fixed area of memory. The thunk sets the correct data segment address for the instance of the program and branches to the actual function in the moveable segment.

The calls to MakeProcInstance during the WM_CREATE message create the thunks for the dialog box procedures. The addresses of the two dialog box procedures are passed as parameters to the MakeProcInstance function. The function returns the address of the thunk. WndProc saves these addresses in static memory for later use when invoking the dialog boxes.

The next job for WM_CREATE is somewhat messy. Usually, an application window has a sizing border that the user can drag to change the size of the window. CLOCK7, however, has a window with a fixed size, with a client area four inches wide by one inch high.

When CLOCK7 creates the window in WinMain by calling CreateWindow, the CW_USEDEFAULT identifier is used to specify that Windows is responsible for initially positioning and sizing the window. This default size and position can be overridden by a call to MoveWindow.

The size of the window, however, must be specified in units of pixels, so the four inch by one inch size must be converted to pixels. The size in pixels will be different, depending on the type of video adapter, so the conversion must be done in a device-independent manner. To do this, WndProc first obtains a device context for the window by calling GetDC. This is the normal way to obtain a device context when processing a message other than WM_PAINT. WndProc then sets the mapping mode of the device context to MM_HIENGLISH using the SetMapMode function. This causes the device context to have logical coordinates of 0.001 inches.

WndProc sets the two fields of a POINT structure named pt to the desired size of the client window in units of 0.001 inches. The x field is set to 4000 and the y field is set to -1000. (The minus sign is required because of a different vertical orientation between MM_HIENGLISH units and pixels.) This POINT structure is passed to LPtoDP, which converts logical points (in units of MM_HIENGLISH) to device points (pixels). The device context is then released by calling ReleaseDC.

Now we have the size of the client area in units of pixels, and we're almost there. What the MoveWindow function requires is the size and position of the whole window, not just the client area. This is the job of AdjustWindowRect, which can convert a client area position and size specified in a RECT (rectangle) structure to a full window position and size. The MoveWindow function then positions and sizes the window.

There are two more much smaller jobs left for the WM_CREATE message. GetMenu obtains a handle to the window's menu. This is stored in a static variable and later used when processing WM_COMMAND messages. The SetTimer function sets the Windows timer. The third parameter, of 1000, indicates that Windows should post a WM_TIMER message to the window procedure once every 1,000 milliseconds, or one second.

The WM_COMMAND Message

A window procedure receives a WM_COMMAND message when the user selects an option from the program's menu. What really happens is that DefWindowProc handles all keyboard and mouse input to the menu, and then sends the window a WM_COMMAND message when the user selects an option.

The menu is defined as a template in CLOCK7.RC, the resource script file. The template begins with the name of the menu (in this case "Clock7") and the MENU keyword. This name was assigned to the lpszMenuName field of the

WNDCLASS structure prior to calling RegisterClass in main(). That's how the menu becomes part of the CLOCK7 window.

The menu template is fairly self-explanatory. The POPUP keyword is for an item on the main menu bar that invokes a pop-up menu. The pop-up menu is defined by a series of MENUITEM statements that list the options on the pop-up menu. An ampersand (&) in the text string of each item specifies which letter is to be underlined and used for the menu's keyboard interface.

All the items a user can select for a program command are associated with an identifier beginning with the prefix IDM, which stands for "ID for a Menu item." These identifiers are defined in CLOCK7.H. When the user selects one of these items, the window procedure receives a WM_COMMAND message with the wParam parameter set to the value of the identifier. Generally, a window procedure uses another switch and case construction to process menu selections, based on the value of wParam.

The first two menu items processed in the WM_COMMAND section of WndProc are IDM_HOUR12 and IDM_HOUR24, which indicate the user has selected the "12 Hour" or "24 Hour" time format, respectively. The program must place a check mark next to the selected option and remove the check mark from the other option. WndProc does this by calls to CheckMenuItem. It then sets the static variable b24Hour to FALSE or TRUE, depending on which option the user selected.

A wParam value of IDM_ALARM indicates that the user has selected the "Set Alarm" option. The program must respond by displaying a dialog box. This is the job of the DialogBox function. The "AlarmBox" parameter refers to the name of the dialog box template defined in the CLOCK7.RC resource script. The lpfnAlarmDlgProc is the address returned from the MakeProcInstance call in WM_CREATE. This is the address of the thunk for the AlarmDlgProc function in CLOCK7.C. The DialogBox function does not return until the dialog box has been dismissed.

Similarly, a wParam value of IDM_ABOUT means that the user wants to see the program's "About" dialog box. The call to DialogBox specifies the "AboutBox" template and the thunk for the AboutDlgProc dialog procedure.

Finally, a wParam value of IDM_EXIT indicates that the user has selected the "Exit" option. WndProc does something very strange in response to this message: it calls SendMessage to send itself a WM_CLOSE message. This means that

WndProc is called recursively. But it doesn't process the WM_CLOSE message! DefWindowProc, however, does, and it responds to the WM_CLOSE message by calling DestroyWindow to destroy the window. The DestroyWindow call sends WndProc a WM_DESTROY message, which WndProc processes.

The Dialog Box Procedures

Now is a good time to take a brief break from WndProc and examine the two dialog box procedures in CLOCK7.C. These are AlarmDlgProc, for the user to set the alarm, and AboutDlgProc, to display the program's About box.

The appearance of the dialog boxes is defined in dialog box templates in CLOCK7.RC. Each control in the dialog box is defined by a keyword, such as CTEXT for centered text and EDITTEXT for an edit control. The dialog box and each control have four numbers associated with them that indicate the placement of the upper left-hand corner of the window and the size of the window. These special dialog box units are based on the height and width of the default system font. Using these coordinates allows the dialog box to be approximately the same shape and size regardless of the resolution of the video display. A dialog procedure is structured similarly to a window procedure, but with an important difference: whenever the dialog procedure processes a message, it returns TRUE. Otherwise, it returns FALSE. The dialog procedure does not call DefWindowProc.

AboutDlgProc is the simplest of the two dialog procedures. The dialog box contains some text and a pushbutton labeled "OK." When the user presses the pushbutton, it generates a WM_COMMAND message (just like a menu). The value of wParam is a number associated with the button in the dialog box template defined in the resource script. In this case, the button generates a wParam value of IDOK, an identifier defined in WINDOWS.H as 1. The dialog box also generates a WM_COMMAND message with wParam equal to IDCANCEL (the value 2) if the user presses the Escape key. In either case, AboutDlgProc calls EndDialog to dismiss the dialog box.

AlarmDlgProc is more complex. Besides some text, it contains five controls: a text entry field (for entering an alarm time), two radio buttons (labeled "On" and "Off"), and two pushbuttons ("OK" and "Cancel"). AlarmDlgProc performs some initialization during the WM_INITDIALOG message: the edit control is limited to six characters, and is initialized with a time stored in the szAlarmTime variable. One of the two radio buttons is set, depending on the value of bAlarmOn.

The WM_COMMAND message indicates that one of the two radio buttons or two pushbuttons has been pressed. For the two radio buttons, AlarmDlgProc stores the new state of the button. For the "OK" pushbutton, AlarmDlgProc obtains the time the user entered, parses it to obtain the hour and minute, and possibly displays a message box if the time is not valid. It ends the dialog box by calling EndDialog. For the "Cancel" button, AlarmDlgProc only ends the dialog box.

The WM_TIMER Message

Now let's return to WndProc to continue examining the messages.

The third message that WndProc processes is WM_TIMER. The WM_TIMER messages in CLOCK7 are initiated by a call to SetTimer during the WM_CREATE message. Windows posts a WM_TIMER message to CLOCK7's message queue once per second.

WM_TIMER processing begins with calls to the C time() and localtime() functions. If the bAlarmOn variable is set, and the time matches the time set by the user in the dialog box, CLOCK7 calls the MessageBox function to display a message box with the text "Wake Up! Wake Up! Wake Up!".

It then obtains a device context handle by calling GetDC, calls the DisplayTime function (described shortly) in CLOCK7.C, and releases the device context handle with a call to ReleaseDC.

The WM_PAINT Message

The first WM_PAINT message occurs during the UpdateWindow call in WinMain. This instructs the window procedure to paint its client area. Thereafter, a WM_PAINT message occurs whenever part of the window has become invalid and must be repainted. This could occur when the program is minimized and then redisplayed, or if part of the window has been obscured by another window and is then moved into full view.

CLOCK7 processes the WM_PAINT message similarly to the WM_TIMER message. It obtains the time by calling time() and localtime(), obtains a device context handle by a call to BeginPaint, updates the display with calls to Display

Time and DisplayDots, and then ends WM_PAINT processing with a call to EndPaint.

The Drawing Functions

Toward the end of CLOCK7.C are the three functions the program uses to draw the clock: DisplayTime, DrawDigit, and DisplayDots.

WndProc calls the DisplayTime function while processing the WM_TIMER and WM_PAINT messages. The DisplayTime function calls SetMapMode to set the mapping mode for the device context, using the MM_HIENGLISH constant so that all coordinates passed to GDI functions are in units of 0.001 inch. Coordinates on the horizontal x axis increase to the right, and coordinates on the vertical y axis increase going up.

By default, however, the origin of the device context–the point (0,0)–is positioned at the upper right corner of the window. This is a little clumsy because all the coordinates within the window have negative y values. It is preferable to have the origin at the lower left corner of the window so that the window can be treated as if it were an upper right quadrant of a Cartesian coordinate system. The SetWindowOrg call in DisplayTime does this.

DisplayTime then calls DrawDigit six times, once for each of the six digits. The second and third parameters are the x and y coordinates of the lower left corner of the digit relative to the lower left corner of the window. For example, the lower left corner of the first digit is 100 units (1/10 inch) from the left side and bottom of the window. The last parameter is the digit to display. DisplayTime obtains these from the C tm structure containing the current time. If the first digit is zero, DisplayTime sets the parameter to 10, indicating a blank.

DrawDigit draws one digit on the window. Like a seven-segment LED display, each digit is composed of seven segments–three horizontal segments and four vertical segments. A number of variables are defined in DrawDigit to make the job a bit easier. The bSegmentOn array contains seven zeroes and ones for each of the digits 0 through 9 that indicate whether a particular segment should be illuminated or not (and 10, indicating the digit should be blank). The order of the seven segments is: the three horizontal segments from top to bottom, then the four vertical segment–stop left, top right, bottom left, and bottom right.

The iSegmentType array contains seven ones and zeroes for the seven segments. A zero means that the segment is horizontal, and a one means the segment is vertical. The ptSegOrigin variable is an array of seven POINT structures that indicate the lower left corner of each segment, relative to the lower left corner of the digit. The ptSegment array contains the six points that define the outline of a horizontal segment, and the six points that define the outline of a vertical segment, all relative to the lower left corner of the segment.

DrawDigit begins by creating two brushes, a black brush and a red brush. These brushes are used to fill the segment. A segment that is illuminated must be colored red; a segment that is not illuminated must be colored black, the same color as the background of the window. (DrawDigit draws the black segments as well as the red segments to effectively erase the previous digit.)

The SaveDC function saves all the attributes of the device context. When all the drawing is complete, the RestoreDC call restores the saved attributes. This is necessary because DrawDigit alters the window origin attribute and must return it to normal in preparation for the next DrawDigit call.

When DisplayTime calls DrawDigit, the origin of the device context is at the lower left corner of the window. The OffsetWindowOrg function moves the origin to the lower left corner of the digit to be displayed, based on the second and third parameters to DrawDigit.

DrawDigit then loops through the seven segments. Once again, a call to SaveDC saves the attributes of the device context. The origin is then adjusted again for the particular segment that is based on the POINT structure in the ptSegOrigin array. Now the origin is at the lower left corner of the segment in the digit. Based on the value of bSegmentOn, the SelectObject function selects either the red brush or the black brush in the device context. The Polygon function uses the six points in ptSegment to draw the segment and fill it with the brush. RestoreDC then restores the saved attributes of the device context (in particular, the device context origin) in preparation for the next segment.

The function cleans up by calling SelectObject to select the default black brush in the device context, RestoreDC to restore the device context to its default attributes, and DeleteObject to delete the two brushes.

The final drawing function in CLOCK7.C is DisplayDots, which displays the colon between the hour and minutes, and between the minutes and seconds. The function is called by WndProc only during processing of the WM_PAINT message. (It could be called from the WM_TIMER message, but it's not necessary because the dots never change position.)

DisplayDots creates a solid red brush and selects it into the device context. Four Ellipse functions draw the four dots. The second and third parameters to Ellipse are the x and y coordinates of the upper left corner of the dot; the fourth and fifth parameters are the x and y coordinates of the lower right corner. DisplayDots cleans up by selecting the default black brush back into the device context, and deleting the red brush.

The WM_DESTROY Message

We have examined all the messages except WM_DESTROY. The WM_DESTROY message is the last message the window procedure receives. A window procedure usually takes this opportunity to do some clean-up work.

Examining in a little detail where the WM_DESTROY message comes from can be helpful in understanding how messages work, and also the importance of DefWindowProc.

When you use the keyboard or mouse to select the Close option from the system menu, all keyboard and mouse activity takes place outside the area. Window procedures usually ignore this activity because it involves messages that the window procedure can pass on to DefWindowProc for default processing.

When DefWindowProc determines that the user has selected Close from the system menu, it sends the window a WM_SYSCOMMAND message with wParam set to SC_CLOSE. WndProc ignores this message and passes it on to DefWindowProc. DefWindowProc responds by sending the window a WM_CLOSE message. WndProc ignores this message also and passes it on to DefWindowProc. DefWindowProc responds to the WM_CLOSE message by calling DestroyWindow. DestroyWindow destroys the window after sending it a WM_DESTROY message.

Why all this activity if WndProc is ignoring these messages? The window procedure doesn't have to ignore the messages. If it wants, it can intercept the WM_SYSCOMMAND or WM_CLOSE message in WndProc and prevent the program from terminating when the user selects Close from the system menu. The window procedure is being kept informed of what is going on even if it chooses to let DefWindowProc handle the messages.

The user can also exit the program by selecting the Exit option from CLOCK7's Set menu. As we saw earlier, this generates a WM_COMMAND message with wParam equal to IDM_EXIT, and WndProc responds by sending itself a WM_CLOSE message, just as DefWindowProc does when it receives a WM_SYSCOMMAND message with wParam set to SC_CLOSE.

WndProc responds to the WM_DESTROY message by cleaning up. The only clean-up required in CLOCK7 is to stop the timer by calling KillTimer. WndProc then calls PostQuitMessage. This function places a WM_QUIT message in the program's message queue.

When the GetMessage call in WinMain retrieves WM_QUIT from the message queue, GetMessage returns zero. This causes WinMain to drop out of the while loop and exit, terminating the program.

The CLOCK7.DEF Module Definition File

The only file we haven't discussed yet is CLOCK7.DEF, the module definition file. The module definition file contains information that LINK uses to create the CLOCK7.EXE executable. Most of the uppercase words in the CLOCK7.DEF file are keywords recognized by LINK.

The NAME line gives the program a module name, which is the same name as the program. The DESCRIPTION line is embedded in the CLOCK7.EXE file; this is generally a copyright notice. The EXETYPE is given as WINDOWS. (Module definition files are also used in OS/2 programming.)

The STUB line indicates a file of WINSTUB.EXE, a small DOS program included in the Windows Software Development Kit. The WINSTUB.EXE program simply displays the message This program requires Microsoft Windows and terminates. As mentioned earlier, the new executable format used for Windows programs begins with a header section that is the same as the MS-DOS .EXE format. The header could be followed by a non-Windows DOS program, which is specified in the WINSTUB statement.

The CODE statement in the CLOCK7.DEF file indicates that the program's code segment is MOVEABLE. This is normal. The DATA statement indicates that the program's data segment is also MOVEABLE. The MULTIPLE keyword means that each instance of the program gets its own data segment.

The HEAPSIZE statement specifies the size of the area in the program's data segment allocated for a local heap. This is really a minimum size, because Windows can expand the data segment if necessary. The STACKSIZE statement specifies the size of the stack, and 4KB is normal for Windows programs.

Finally, the EXPORTS statement lists all the window procedures and dialog procedures in the CLOCK7 program. This is a requirement of Windows memory management. LINK stores the addresses of these functions in CLOCK7.EXE so that Windows can adjust the thunks to load the program's data segment address in the DS register when Windows calls the window procedure.

The 32-Bit Future

Although Windows is currently a 16-bit environment, version 3.0 includes some support for 32-bit Windows applications when running on a 386 processor. This support takes the form of a dynamic link library named WINMEM32 that exports 32-bit memory allocation functions.

Basically, a Windows program that uses WINMEM32 must be divided into two sections: One 16-bit section contains all the Windows-dependent code including the window procedures and all calls to Windows functions. The 32-bit section consists of lower-level functions that make use of 32-bit registers and memory blocks. Calling these 32-bit routines from the 16-bit code is rather messy because it involves switching stacks (among other things), but some tools are expected that may make this fairly transparent. Of course, WINMEM32 is only an interim solution to writing 32-bit code for Windows. The real solution is the 32-bit version of Windows that I discussed earlier. This will make use of a flat 32-bit memory model and will eliminate the need for dealing with segments.

It is expected that porting applications from 16-bit Windows to 32-bit Windows will be as smooth as possible—or at least much smoother than porting to the OS/2 Presentation Manager. Where necessary, some parameters to existing function calls will be expanded from 16-bit values to 32-bit values.

In a longer time frame, you will be able to write single-source graphical programs that can be compiled for multiple platforms, such as Windows, Presentation Manager, and the Apple Macintosh. This will involve the use of an object-oriented language such as C++, and class libraries that provide a platform-independent interface to the particular graphical environment. At that time, programming directly to the Windows or Presentation Manager API will probably become as unusual as assembly language programming has become in recent years.

Chapter 7

DESQview

Stephen R. Davis

The DESQview environment consists of two separate parts that are independent enough to operate alone, but that are designed to combine into a single, powerful whole: QEMM, Quarterdeck's memory manager, and DESQview itself.

Quarterdeck Expanded Memory Manager

QEMM is actually a generic name for a series of memory managers, each one designed for a different hardware platform—for example, QEMM 50/60 for the IBM PS/2 Models 50 and 60. However, the most popular of the series is QEMM-386, designed to operate with all 80386 PCs. QEMM-386 performs two related functions.

First, QEMM-386 uses the hardware paging unit of the 80386 CPU to emulate EMS 4.0 memory, using simple extended memory. In Virtual 86 mode, the 80386 CPU, can map 4 kbyte blocks of physical memory to different logical addresses by simply changing a value in a page table. QEMM-386 intercepts requests to map EMS memory into and out of the EMS page frame and fulfills these requests using this 80386 mapping feature. With QEMM-386 loaded on an 80386 or 80486 based machine, application software is provided with very fast, quite capable EMS 4.0 memory. (See Chapter 2 for further details.)

With all of the talk about the famous 640KB barrier, one might think that 640KB was somehow designed into the 8086 processor. In fact, as we saw in Chapter 1, this is not the case. In the 8086-emulating Real Mode, an 80x86 process can address 1024KB. However, within this one megabyte, the blocks of address space claimed by the BIOS ROM, the hard disk ROM, and other plug-in cards, sit like islands surrounded by unused address regions. The famous 640KB boundary stems from the location of the first of these islands at address A0000H.

QEMM-386 can map memory into these regions to make more physical memory available to the CPU while running in Real Mode. Microsoft calls these memory blocks between 640KB and 1024KB, Upper Memory Blocks (UMBs). (QEMM50/60 can do the same thing for IBM PS/2s and QRAM for 80286 based machines if sufficiently capable EEMS or EMS4.0 is available.)

Since DOS programs must be in contiguous memory, DOS cannot use any of the UMBs for programs. However, this space can be used for small programs, such as device drivers and Terminate and Stay Residents utilities (TSRs), which would otherwise be loaded into the conventional memory area below 640KB. In this way, although DOS programs cannot make direct use of the area, they can benefit.

Device drivers are loaded into high memory using the LOADHI.SYS device driver, while TSRs use the executable LOADHI.COM. Thus, a mouse driver might be loaded from the CONFIG.SYS file as

```
DEVICE=LOADHI.SYS MOUSE.SYS
```

A TSR style mouse driver, of the form MOUSE.COM, would be loaded from the AUTOEXEC.BAT file or from the command line via the following:

```
LOADHI MOUSE.COM
```

QEMM-386 also allows the user to load several of the DOS buffers in high memory to further reduce the amount of memory DOS requires below 640KB. For example, the majority of the buffers specified in the CONFIG.SYS BUFFERS= command, as well as the File Control Blocks specified in the FILES= command, may be loaded high. These regions are represented graphically in Figure 7-1.

QEMM-386 provides one final feature known as "Shadow RAM". RAM hardware responds faster than ROM; thus, ROM cards must often insert multiple wait state on every access to give the ROM chips sufficient time to react. In addition, ROM chips are often found on plug-in cards (in particular, the video ROM is often located on plug video cards). This memory is only accessible over the relatively slow card bus. To avoid these bottlenecks, QEMM-386 first copies the contents of any ROM it finds into a RAM area of the same size. It then maps that RAM block into the address space previously occupied by the ROM. The result can be significantly faster execution.

Installing QEMM-386 is handled automatically by the installation program. The program first searches the address range between 640KB and 1024KB, looking for areas that are not otherwise occupied by RAM or ROM memory. The areas it finds are immediately occupied with extended memory. The program then examines the CONFIG.SYS and AUTOEXEC.BAT file for device drivers and TSRs, which can be loaded into this region to free up conventional application memory. The install program examines the memory requirements of the various device drivers and TSRs and compares them with the sizes of the available UMB areas to determine the optimum configuration.

Figure 7-1: The first megabyte of memory, showing areas where QEMM can load TSRs and device drivers.

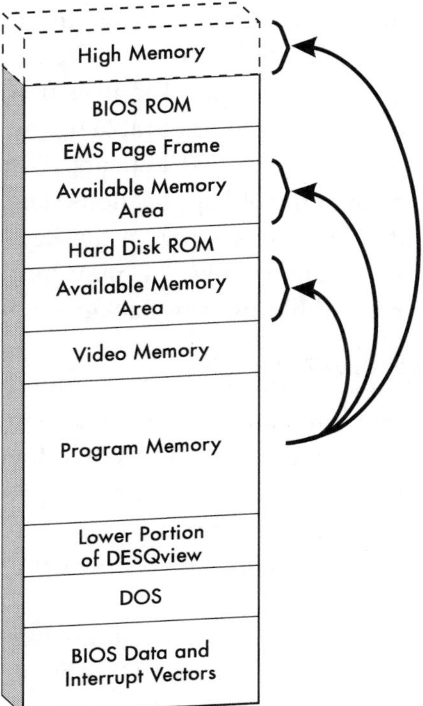

If the user is not satisfied with the arrangement QEMM-386 has chosen or if certain TSRs must be loaded in a particular order (something which QEMM-386 does not understand), the user can change the load order manually by editing the CONFIG.SYS and AUTOEXEC.BAT files. This is best handled by allowing QEMM-386 to take its best shot and then tweak the results. Command line options are available to control almost every aspect of QEMM: exclude certain upper memory areas, include other areas, specify number of EMS page frames, etc. (Quarterdeck offers a separate product, Manifest, which displays lower memory pictorial to simplify this process considerably.)

Although Quarterdeck was significantly ahead of the pack when QEMM-386 was introduced, Microsoft eventually offered most of these features with DOS 5.0. DOS 5's EMM386 maps extended memory into Upper Memory Blocks and allowed the user to load device drivers (via DEVICEHIGH) and TSRs (via LOADHIGH) into this area. Of course, QEMM-386 still offers a few advantages, such as automatically deciding the optimum configuration for these devices, while DOS 5 leaves it to the user.

DESQview

Like Windows, DESQview, from Quarterdeck Office Systems, is a DOS-compatible operating environment capable of executing one or several DOS programs simultaneously in a windowed environment. DESQview can operate like a switcher, by allowing the user to pop up a new DOS program at any time. The user first taps the "DESQ key" (usually defined as the Alt key, but user-configurable to any key desired) and then selects the application from the menu that appears. The new application appears immediately in a window over the old applications. The user may move or resize the window, either with the mouse or from the keyboard, to allow windows in the background to remain visible. He may also "zoom" the window out to fill the screen, completely hiding any background windows.

As with Windows in its 386 Enhanced mode, applications in the background continue to execute. A user may start a compilation, for example, and then pop up an editor to begin work on another source file in the foreground while the compilation completes. This is the famous "compiling in the background" capability. DESQview runs as a shell over DOS. In this way, programs continue to "see" the familiar DOS interface as much as possible. This keeps DESQview compatible with the vast majority of DOS applications.

In fact, the DESQview-DOS combination looks enough like DOS that the user can bring up Windows 3.0 in either Real or Standard mode within a DESQview window. (It is a very satisfying feeling playing solitaire from within Windows and then tapping the DESQ key to see the DESQview menu instantly appear.) DESQview will remain compatible with each new version of DOS. DESQview currently supports DOS 2.0 through 5.0, and Quarterdeck is committed to supporting future versions as they are released.

DESQview adds capabilities to DOS beyond multitasking for programs that care to use them. DESQview defines a series of service calls known as the Applications Program Interface (API). The API does not hide the basic DOS services, but serves as an extension of these capabilities. The API provides support for:

- character-based windowing
- multitasking
- pointers (such as the mouse)
- timers (both time duration and time of day)
- panels
- interprocess communication

DESQview must have these capabilities for its own use. Through the API, DESQview makes these abilities available to application programs as well. DESQview even allows programs to control or limit capabilities normally provided through DESQview's pop-up menus. For example, a program can prevent the user from closing it prematurely from DESQview.

As we will see in this chapter, the DESQview API provides a powerful means for reducing the amount of memory required by an application. The program can divide its problem up into several, independently executing but communicating programs, each of which responsible for solving some part of the overall problem. While each of these programs is individually subject to the limitations of DOS, the overall group of programs is not limited. In machines equipped with QEMM-386 and an 80386 or better processor, or QRAM and a powerful EMS card, the 640KB barrier is broken for dedicated applications.

DESQview, as shipped from Quarterdeck, arrives on a single floppy disk with a manual. The standard offering includes DESQview itself, installation and setup programs, and installation files for most common applications. Quarterdeck's memory products—QRAM, QEMM50/60, and QEMM-386—are available separately; however, DESQview may be ordered together with QEMM-386 in a single package called DESQview 386.

For the programmer interested in writing programs to access the DESQview API, Quarterdeck offers an assortment of tools. There are API Libraries for C,

Pascal, BASIC and Clipper, as well as the API Debugger. There is also the Panel Design Tool, which allows the programmer to design windows the same way one might draw a picture with PC Paint; once complete, these windows are then incorporated directly into the user application.

The DESQview API

Broadly speaking, three types of programs execute under DESQview:

- DESQview-oblivious programs, which are totally unaware of DESQview's presence
- DESQview-aware programs, which are aware of DESQview's presence, but do not rely on it
- DESQview-specific programs, which make use of DESQview's features through its API

DESQview-Oblivious Programs

DESQview-oblivious programs are programs originally written for DOS. Since they know nothing of DESQview and multitasking, they do not expect other programs to be executing in the same machine simultaneously. Such programs expect to have total control of the computer, including all of its memory. As long as they are well behaved, DESQview has little trouble compelling them to coexist with their neighbors. If, however, they are "antisocial," there may be limitations.

The most common example of antisocial behavior occurs in the area of display output. To force the output of a normally full-screened program into a window, DESQview intercepts DOS and BIOS calls. Requests for video output are filtered and cropped into the appropriate window. However, to enhance video display speed, the majority of DOS programs do not output via DOS or the BIOS, preferring instead to write directly to screen memory. Being unaware of the physical boundaries of its window, such a program tends to write all over the display, including on top of the windows of other programs. DESQview provides special programs called loaders for many of these offenders. These loaders are automatically executed when the user starts the program from the Open menu. The loader is given control after the program is loaded into memory but before it is allowed to start. The loader can then "reach into" the application and patch the output section so that its output may be windowed. Of course, to do this, the loader must have specific knowledge about the application. Each application must have its own unique loader.

On an 80386-based processor, DESQview can window screen-writing applications, whether a loader exists or not. On these machines, DESQview uses the page-mapping capabilities of the chip to allocate a different virtual display to each ill-behaved application. The application unknowingly writes to this virtual memory instead of to the real video adapter. Periodically, a DESQview daemon collects these virtual displays and paints them into the windows of the real video memory. This process is known as virtualizing the application's display.

However, if a loader does not exist for the program, and if the base processor is not an 80386 or better, it is not possible for DESQview to window its output. Such programs can only execute in the foreground and only in full-screen mode. Zooming such an application into a window or switching it into the background suspends it.

A further problem with programs built to execute under DOS is that the .EXE file does not contain enough information for a multitasking environment. For example, DOS normally hands over all available memory to each new program as it begins. This is fine if you assume that no new program will start until this program has completed, which is true under DOS. But in a multiprogram environment, this assumption is not valid. In addition, if the program requires a loader, or must be virtualized to be windowed properly, this information must also be recorded.

To adapt DOS .EXE files to its own use, DESQview can use the same .PIF file used by Windows. Over the years, however, DESQview has added to the basic .PIF file, extending it into what Quarterdeck calls the .DVP (DesqView Pif) file. DESQview supplies .DVP files for the most common applications. These .DVP files can be created in the event one does not exist for a particular program, or edited to match the user's tastes at any time, from the DESQview menu.

DESQview-Aware Programs

The second category of software, DESQview-aware programs, includes such best-sellers as Paradox, dBASE, and WordPerfect. These programs acknowledge that they may not be the only task executing on the machine, and that they should refrain from dangerous or unfriendly tricks. For example, they use the BIOS clock instead of CPU timer loops to mark time, and they use the BIOS services rather than providing their own, as much as possible. However, such programs must still be able to write directly to screen memory. To allow these programs to execute within a DESQview window, DESQview provides shadowing capability.

The api_shadow() API call is built so that if DESQview is not present, DOS returns the call with no ill effect. If, however, DESQview is loaded, the system call returns the segment address of a logical display area to which the application can write. This allows displays to be virtualized on any CPU type.

DESQview-Specific Programs

The final category of programs, DESQview-specific programs, makes direct use of DESQview via the API. A DESQview specific program must first check that DESQview is present and, if not, must terminate. The program can be set up so that DESQview is not apparent or accessible to the user (except for the copyright notice, which must appear when DESQview is initiated).

The DESQview API interfaces to user written programs through the separately available API Library packages. For example, the API C Library consists of two .OBJ files, which the user must bind with his program at link time. The libraries do nothing more than provide a native language interface between the user's program and DESQview.

The API C Library defines some 200 functions. To make the purpose of each function easier to remember, the functions are grouped into 12 categories, depending on what type of object the function accesses. The first three letters of a function's name indicate what category it belongs to. For example, functions beginning with "win_" act on windows; those beginning with "key_" effect the keyboard; and those beginning with "ptr_" access the pointing device (mouse).

The programming model used in coding for DESQview use is somewhere between that used for DOS and that for Windows (often called the Model-View-Controller approach). In DOS, the application is always in firm control—DOS acts strictly in response to the application's request and only performs the minimum steps necessary to carry it out. Under Windows, however, the relationship is much more symbiotic. The application must be built to carry out commands for Windows as well as the reverse.

The DESQview API retains the flavor of DOS. The applications program is never forced to field DESQview messages. If it does not, DESQview will assume some default action. In this mode, programming for DESQview is much like programming for DOS. On the other hand, the user program may inform DESQview that it would like to be informed if certain things happen. For example, a program can tell DESQview to send it a message every time its window is moved by the user. Applications programs do not receive Repaint requests, however, as DESQview maintains copies of all windows and handles all window overlaying itself.

To better see how a programmer goes about writing a DESQview specific application, we can examine the same simple clock program that appeared in the discussion of Windows in Chapter 6, rewritten DESQview-style. Although a simple application, CLOCK is written in such a way as to make best use of the DESQview API. That is, CLOCK is constructed the way a much larger DESQview application would be. An examination of its features should teach the reader much about the DESQview API.

The Clock Example

Figure 7-2 shows a screen image of the CLOCK program executing. Since DESQview is not graphically oriented, it is difficult to generate displays such as analog clocks with sweeping second hands or the large "LED mimicking" windows typical of Windows. CLOCK's display is a single character-mode line encased within a window carrying the title "Clock."

Figure 7-2: The Clock window.

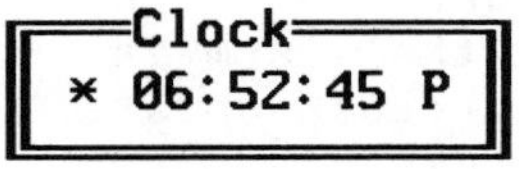

```
╔═Clock══════╗
║ * 06:52:45 P ║
╚════════════╝
```

In the middle of the window is the time, which updates every second. Immediately to the right of the time is the AM/PM indicator. Selecting this field toggles the display between 12-hour and 24-hour mode. Since DESQview supports but does not assume the presence of a mouse, a field may be selected by either a) clicking on it, b) using the cursor keys to move the cursor over to it and pressing Enter, or c) pressing the "select key" for that field (in this case S for "switch").

Just to the left of the time appears an asterisk. Selecting this field (either by clicking on it or by pressing the * key) opens the "Set Alarm" window shown in Figure 7-3. Although this window appears virtually identical to the first, the time (initially 00:00:00) does not update automatically. Instead, this window waits for

Figure 7-3: The Set Alarm window.

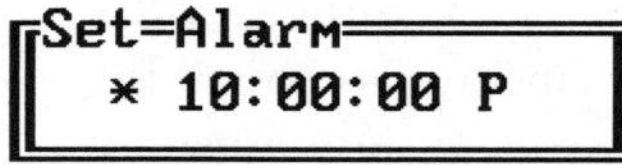

Figure 7-4: The Alarm window.

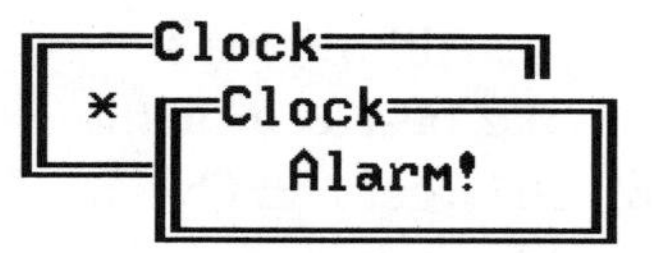

the user to enter an alarm time. Selecting the asterisk in this window closes the window, sets the alarm, and returns the user to the clock window.

When the prescribed alarm time arrives, CLOCK opens a brightly colored Alarm window and beeps the speaker repeatedly at 2-second intervals (shown in Figure 7-4). Since CLOCK is designed to execute in the background, the Alarm window must automatically bring CLOCK to the foreground to ensure it is visible. Pressing Escape or clicking on the Alarm window removes the window and restores CLOCK to the background. The alarm may be disabled before it expires by reselecting the asterisk in the CLOCK window.

The source code for the DESQview specific CLOCK.C program appears below.

```
/*CLOCK - this program displays a small clock on the screen.
         The user can position the clock anywhere on the screen
         desired using the DESQview menu. Display is in 12-hour
         format. Selecting the A/P indicator switches the
         clock to 24 hour format and back. Selecting the '*'
         button opens a new window to allow the user to set an
         alarm. The clock continues to run while the alarm is
         being set and when alarm window appears (clock update
         runs as its own task). The alarm may be disabled by
         deselecting the '*' button.*/

#include <stdio.h>
#include <stdlib.h>
#include <dos.h>
#include <string.h>
#include "dvapi.h"                    /*DESQview include file*/

/*prototypes for locally declared procedures*/
void main (void);
void program_body (void);
void alarmonoff (ulong panhan, ulong panelwin,
```

```
                  ulong timalarm, ulong panelkey);
void definealarm (ulong panhan);
void setalarm (ulong timalarm, struct timstruct *alarmtime);
void declarealarm (ulong panelwin);
int beep (void);
int ticktock (void);
void ourtime (struct timstruct *asciitime);
void bcd2asc (char *string, char bcdnum);
void updatetime (ulong panelwin, struct timstruct *asciitime);

/*minimum API version required is DESQview 2.00*/
#define required 0x200

/*panels containing the alarm and clock windows - built with
  the Panel Design Tool*/
extern char clockwin[];          /*this is the clock panel which
                                   contains the description of our
                                   clock windows*/
extern int lclockwin;            /*the length of the panel*/

                                 /*the clockwin panel defines the
                                   following fields*/
#define FLD_ALARM   01                /*the alarm select field*/
#define FLD_HOURS   02                /*hours*/
#define FLD_MINUTES 03                /*minutes*/
#define FLD_SECONDS 04                /*seconds*/
#define FLD_AMPM    05                /*AM/PM indicator*/
/*global flags and structures*/
struct timstruct {               /*structure to hold current time*/
     char hour[3];
     char min[3];
     char sec[3];
     char afternoon;             /*'A' -> AM, 'P' - > PM*/
     };                          /*'*' -> 24 hour mode*/

struct timstruct currenttime;    /*currently displayed time*/
struct timstruct alarmtime =     /*last alarm time*/
          {"00", "00", "00", 'A'};   /*initial alarm time*/

struct panelmsg {                /*message from the panel*/
      char fldid;                /*field number*/
      int  length;               /*length of data*/
      char data;
      };

struct windowmsg {               /*message to ticktock subtask*/
```

```
      ulong windowhandle;         /*handle of window to write to*/
      };

int mode24;                       /*1 -> we are in 24 hour mode;
                                    0 -> we are in 12 hour mode*/

/*main - standard pattern for all DESQview programs -
         check to make sure that DESQview is present; if
         not generate error message; otherwise, proceed*/
void main (void)
{
  int  version;

  version = api_init();
  if (version < required)
       printf ("This program requires DESQview %d.%02d or later.\n",
                required >> 8, required & 0xff);
  else {
       /*tell DESQview what extensions to enable
         and then start real application*/
       api_level (required);
       program_body();
  }
  /*if DESQview present (even if wrong version), shut it down*/
  if (version)
       api_exit();
}

/*program body - open up the clock panel built with the Panel
                 Design Tool. Define the necessary objects
                 and then sit in a loop waiting on messages*/

void program_body (void)
{
    ulong panhan;                 /*the handle for the CLOCKWIN panel*/
    ulong panelwin;               /*window handle for the clock*/
    ulong panelkey;               /*keyboard handle for clock panel -
                                    used to read select fields*/
    ulong timalarm;               /*timer handle used for alarm*/
    ulong tskhan;                 /*handle of clock update subtask*/
    ulong malhan;                 /*mailbox handle of subtask*/
    ulong obqhan;                 /*handle returned from object queue*/

#define STACKSIZE 1000
    char taskstack [STACKSIZE]; /*stack for the update time task -
                                    notice that this MUST be declared
```

```
                                        on a stack that is permanent*/
    struct windowmsg message;    /*message to send to subtask*/

    /*first order of battle is to open the panel file and display the
      clock panel - this will put a clock on the screen*/
    panhan = pan_new();
    if (!pan_open (panhan, clockwin, lclockwin))
        if (!pan_apply (panhan, win_me(), "CLOCK", 5,
                       &panelwin, &panelkey)) {

            /*start the ticktock task and send it a message with the
              window handle to start the clock ticking*/
            tskhan = tsk_new (ticktock, taskstack, STACKSIZE,
                              "", 0, 0, 0);
            malhan = mal_of (tskhan);
            message.windowhandle = panelwin;
            mal_write (malhan, (char *)&message, sizeof message);

            /*define the alarm clock timer*/
            timalarm = tim_new();

            /*now wait in an infinite loop for input from:
              - keyboard : user clicked a field; execute command
              - alarm    : alarm has gone off; put up alarm message*/
            for (;;) {
                 /*now wait for an event to occur*/
                 obqhan = obq_read();
                 if (obqhan == panelkey)    /*keyboard input*/
                     alarmonoff (panhan, panelwin,
                                 timalarm, panelkey);

                 if (obqhan == timalarm)    /*alarm timer*/
                     declarealarm (panelwin);
            }
        }
}

/*alarmonoff - interpret the clock window's select field input*/
void alarmonoff (ulong panhan, ulong panelwin,
                 ulong timalarm, ulong panelkey)
{
     struct panelmsg *panelinput;
     int              inputlength;

     /*read the message from the clock's panel manager*/
     key_read (panelkey, &(char *)panelinput, &inputlength);
```

```
     /*field number 5 switches between 12 and 24 hour mode*/
     if (panelinput -> fldid == FLD_AMPM) {
          mode24 = (panelinput -> data == 'Y');

          /*update the clock in this task for instant response*/
          ourtime (&currenttime);
          updatetime (panelwin, &currenttime);
     }

     /*field number 1 sets/clears the alarm;
       N -> clear the alarm, Y -> set the alarm*/
     if (panelinput -> fldid == FLD_ALARM)
          if (panelinput -> data == 'N')
               tim_close (timalarm); /*stop the timer*/
          else {
               definealarm (panhan); /*set the alarm*/
               setalarm (timalarm, &alarmtime);
          }
}

/*definealarm - put up the alarm set panel where the user
               may enter the alarm time*/
void definealarm (ulong panhan)
{
     ulong alarmwin, alarmkey;
     struct panelmsg *alarminput;
     int             inputlength;

     /*first, open the ALARM panel to display Alarm Set window*/
     if (!pan_apply (panhan, win_me(), "ALARM", 5,
                           &alarmwin, &alarmkey)) {

          /*update the window to the previous alarm time...*/
          updatetime (alarmwin, &alarmtime);

          /*...and position the cursor for time entry*/
          fld_cursor (alarmwin, FLD_HOURS);

          /*now wait for the user to update the time fields*/
          for (;;) {
               key_read (alarmkey, &(char *)alarminput, &inputlength);
               switch (alarminput -> fldid) {

               /*selecting fields 2 thru 5 just
                 fills values into the alarm time*/
```

```
            case FLD_HOURS:
                strncpy (alarmtime.hour, &alarminput -> data, 2);
                break;
            case FLD_MINUTES:
                strncpy (alarmtime.min,  &alarminput -> data, 2);
                break;
            case FLD_SECONDS:
                strncpy (alarmtime.sec,  &alarminput -> data, 2);
                break;
            case FLD_AMPM:
                alarmtime.afternoon = alarminput -> data;
                break;

            /*selecting field 1 removes the alarm window and
              returns control to the main program*/
            case FLD_ALARM:
                win_free (alarmwin);
                return;
            }
        }
    }
}

/*setalarm - start the alarm timer*/
void setalarm (ulong timalarm, struct timstruct *alarmtime)
{
    ulong settime;
    int hours, mins, secs;

    /*convert the hours, minutes, and seconds into time since
      midnight*/
    hours = atoi (alarmtime -> hour);
    mins  = atoi (alarmtime -> min);
    secs  = atoi (alarmtime -> sec);

    /*if PM, add 12 to the hour (don't make result > 24)*/
    if (alarmtime -> afternoon == 'P')
        hours += 12;
    hours %= 24;

    /*convert the entire thing into 1/100ths of seconds since
      midnight and set the alarm to go off at that time*/
    settime = ((((hours * 60L) + mins) * 60L) + secs) * 100L;
    tim_write (timalarm, settime);
}
```

```
/*declarealarm - alarm has gone off; open an alarm window and
                 display alarm message*/
void declarealarm (ulong panelwin)
{
    ulong beeptaskhan;
    char  stack [400];

    char *msg = "    Alarm!    ";
    int  length;

    /*push ourselves into the foreground so user can see us*/
    app_gofore (win_me ());

    /*start a subtask beeping every 2 seconds*/
    beeptaskhan = tsk_new (beep, stack, sizeof stack, "", 0, 0, 0);

    /*display a simple alarm message - user acknowledges with Escape
      or by clicking on it with the mouse*/
    length = strlen (msg) - 1;
    win_disperor (panelwin, msg, length, 1, length, 0, 0);

    /*stop that infernal racket - kill the beeping task and
      unqueue any sound*/
    tsk_free (beeptaskhan);
    api_sound (0, 0);

    /*now push ourselves back into the background...*/
    app_goback (win_me ());

    /*...and deselect the alarm set button to show no alarm pending*/
    fld_type (panelwin, FLD_ALARM, FLT_DESELECT);
}

/*beep - a subtask to beep every two seconds when alarm goes off*/
int beep (void)
{
    for (;;) {
         api_sound (1000,  9);  /*1000 Hz for  .5 (9/18.2) sec*/
         api_sound (    0, 27);  /*silence for 1.5 secs*/
    }
}


/*ticktock - small subtask used to constantly update the clock*/
int ticktock (void)
{
```

```
    ulong winhandle;            /*handle of window to update*/
    ulong timpause;             /*handle of timer to delay with*/
    struct windowmsg *winmessage;
    int              messagelength;

    /*first read the message sent to us with the handle of the
      window to which we should write the time*/
    mal_read (mal_me(), &(char *)winmessage, &messagelength);

    /*save the clock window handle locally*/
    winhandle = winmessage -> windowhandle;

    /*now define an update timer*/
    timpause = tim_new();

    /*sit in a loop - */
    for (;;) {
        /* - start the timer for 1 second and wait for it to expire*/
        tim_addto (timpause, 100);
        tim_read (timpause);

        /* - when it does, (re)display the time*/
        ourtime (&currenttime);
        updatetime (winhandle, &currenttime);
    }
}

/*ourtime - get the current time into an ASCII structure*/
void ourtime (struct timstruct *asciitime)
{
     union REGS regs;

     /*use the BIOS Get-Time-of-Day call to quickly get the time*/
     regs.h.ah = 0x02;
     int86 (0x1A, &regs, &regs);

     /*set afternoon flag and round the hour off if in 12 hour mode
       (notice that arithmetic on BCD is slightly strange)*/
     asciitime -> afternoon = '*';
     if (!mode24) {
         asciitime -> afternoon = 'A';
         if (regs.h.ch > 0x12) {
              asciitime -> afternoon = 'P';
             if (((regs.h.ch -= 0x12) & 0xf) > 0x09)
                 regs.h.ch -= 6;
         }
```

```
      }

      /*convert the BCD to ASCII strings*/
      bcd2asc (asciitime -> hour, regs.h.ch);
      bcd2asc (asciitime -> min , regs.h.cl);
      bcd2asc (asciitime -> sec , regs.h.dh);
}

/*bcd2asc - convert a BCD number into an ASCII string*/
void bcd2asc (char *string, char bcdnum)
{
      *string++ = (bcdnum >> 4)   + '0'; /*upper digit*/
      *string++ = (bcdnum & 0x0f) + '0'; /*now the lower digit*/
      *string   = '\0';
}

/*updatetime - update the time display by writing the time to
               the hours, minutes, second and AM/PM fields of
               the specified panel window*/
void updatetime (ulong panelwin, struct timstruct *asciitime)
{
     /*write the time into fields 2 thru 4*/
     fld_write (panelwin, FLD_HOURS,   asciitime -> hour, 2);
     fld_write (panelwin, FLD_MINUTES, asciitime -> min,  2);
     fld_write (panelwin, FLD_SECONDS, asciitime -> sec,  2);

     /*and put up the AM/PM indicator into field 5*/
     fld_write (panelwin, FLD_AMPM,   &asciitime -> afternoon, 1);
}
```

The first attribute that distinguishes this from a non-DESQview-specific program is the appearance of: #include "dvapi.h". This include file defines the constants commonly used in API calls. It also contains the prototype definitions for the API functions. Two versions of the file are supplied with the API C Library: one that supports the Kernighan and Ritchie standards, and another that supports the more stringent ANSI C typing standards (available in versions 1.1 and later of the C Library).

The API interface functions are contained in two object files also supplied with the API C Library—API1.OBJ—and API2.OBJ, which must be linked with the user's object files. Versions for the major C compilers are included, but adapting to other C compilers should be simple, because the source code to both object files is provided. Linking these object files can be handled either specifically, as with this Microsoft C example:

```
LINK USER.OBJ+API1.OBJ+API2.OBJ,,/ST:32768
```

or, in languages that support MAKE or Project files, as in this Turbo C project file:

```
API1.OBJ API2.OBJ
USER.C
LIB\CL.LIB
```

These object files are quite small, since they only provide the interface between the user's high level language and the API, which is a permanent part of DESQview and always present. The API itself remains a part of the operating system and not the application.

All pointers in the DESQview API are far pointers (32 bit). It would be possible to carefully define all pointers to be of a far type; however, the functions provided in the API libraries carry far addresses as well. Therefore, Quarterdeck strongly advises all developers programming for the API to compile only under the large memory model. Most C compilers allow compiling under the large memory model. Under Turbo C, select Large under the Options/Compiler/Model menu and specify the Large C library in the project file, as in the example. Under Microsoft C, use the /AL switch.

In addition, structures under DESQview are assumed to be packed on byte boundaries. Any module that exchanges a structure with the API should specify the byte alignment. Under Turbo C, select Byte alignment from the Options/Compiler/Code Generation menu. Under Microsoft, specify /Zp on the compile line. (If your compiler does not support byte alignment, you can get around this by declaring all structure members to be integers, and packing the bytes yourself.)

The main() for CLOCK follows the pattern for all DESQview-specific programs:

```
#include "dvapi.h"

/*main - standard pattern for all DESQview programs -
         check to make sure that DESQview is present; if
         not, generate error message; otherwise, proceed*/
void main (void)
{
  int  version;

  version = api_init();
  if (version < required)
```

```
            printf ("This program requires DESQview %d.%02d or later.\n",
                    required >> 8, required & 0xff);
       else {
            /*tell DESQview what extensions to enable
              and then start real application*/
            api_level (required);
            program_body();
       }
       /*if DESQview present (even if wrong version), shut it down*/
       if (version)
            api_exit();
}

/*program body - do the actual work here*/
void program_body (void)
{
     ...
}
```

Since DESQview does not have an .EXE format that distinguishes DESQview specific programs from others, CLOCK must first check to make sure that DESQview is present before continuing. Even if DESQview is present, CLOCK should make sure that it is a current enough version to support the functions used within the program. CLOCK requires version 2.00 or better, and so tests for this. The api_init() service call is designed to return the version number if the program is executing under DESQview, and return a 0 if it is not.

Windowing

Generally, the first thing a program wants to do upon starting is open a window on the screen. Sometimes this is not necessary, since DESQview automatically opens the first window when the program begins. But even then, the application cannot be sure how large the window is, where it is placed, or what the default color scheme might be (these things are specified in the .DVP file, which is subject to change by the user). Therefore, even if the application uses the default window, it will probably want to place size and color the window itself.

Thus, a typical program begins as follows:

```
ulong windowhandle;
char windowname[] = {"Main Process"};
```

```
/*Open initial window, then position, size and draw it*/
windowhandle = win_new(windowname, sizeof windowname - 1, 10, 10);
win_move (windowhandle, 1, 1);
win_attr (windowhandle, 1);
win_unhide (windowhandle);
win_redraw (windowhandle);
```

The first call, to win_new(), creates a window bearing the name "Main Process" in the upper left corner of the border. This window has a border (the default) and is 10 columns wide by 10 rows high. Since the DESQview API is not C-based and does not subscribe to the "null terminates strings" rule, it is necessary to give the length of the window's name (minus the null on the end) as well as the name itself (this is true of all strings passed to the API).

DESQview is designed around character mode. This is why the window size information is based on columns and rows and not on pixels. The box that outlines a window is constructed using the special block graphics characters. A window may contain graphics information, requiring the video adapter to be in a graphics mode; however, even in graphics mode, DESQview draws and positions its character-based windows.

Notice that what is returned from the win_new() call is a long int (ulong is defined in DVAPI.H as an unsigned long int). This identifier is not unlike the file handles with which C manipulates files. The long int returned from win_new() will be used by the remainder of the program to identify that window. Since a program may have several windows open at a time, these identifiers serve to keep them straight. In DESQview nomenclature, the new window is an object, and the identifier is the handle of that object (hence the variable name windowhandle).

As we will see, handles exist for other types of objects. For example, keyboard input is handled through a keyboard object. Each type of object is manipulated by its own type of API function. To distinguish the various types of API calls, the first three letters of the function name refer to the type of object the function manipulates. Thus, win_ calls are for window objects and key_ calls for keyboard objects. We will see several other types of objects as we proceed. An object handle may be a pointer to a structure DESQview uses to describe the object, but the programmer should simply think of it as a tag or identifier. A program should never try to access the object directly by using the handle as an address.

The next window call, to win_move(), positions our new window at row 1, column 1; that is, the upper left-hand corner of the display. The win_attr() call selects the color scheme. Up to 16 different color schemes may be defined, and these may be defined differently for CGA, monochrome, and EGA/VGA adapters, to best utilize the colors and shades available for each screen.

The final two calls, win_unhide() and win_redraw(), are interesting. All windows are created "hidden" (the default window created when the application was first started is unhidden by DESQview before the application is given control). A hidden window is invisible. Even making it unhidden, however, is not sufficient to make it appear on the display. Calls to win_ functions change the window object in memory, but not on the screen. It is not until the win_redraw() API call that the screen is actually "redrawn" onto the display. Although this may seem odd, there are several good reasons for this.

First, just as an architect does not generally want the public to see the frame holding up a building, the programmer does not want the user to see all the window manipulations going on behind the scenes to make the final display. If the window were visible as soon as it was created in our example, the user would first see the window created in some unknown location, then redrawn in the upper left-hand corner, but with the wrong color pattern, and finally redrawn yet again with the correct color scheme. It is better that these window manipulations go on behind the scenes so that the user only sees the window appear once, after it is ready.

Another reason concerns execution speed. Video memory is generally very slow, since the CPU must compete with the video adapter for access. Redrawing the window each time before it is actually ready wastes time. It is faster to make all the adjustments before writing the window to display memory a single time.

A third reason is related to response times. Consider, for a moment, a program with three different drop-down menus used for different command types. Each of these menus would normally be implemented as a separate window. The program could wait until the user clicked onto a menu bar option before creating the menu window and unhiding it. If we assume that the user will click on each menu bar option at least once, a more attractive option presents itself. The application can create all of the menu windows when it is first started. When the user decides to select a menu bar option, all the application must do to make it visible is to unhide and redraw it. When the user is finished with a menu, the program hides it again, where it remains ready for the next time it is needed. Although building all menus at once slows down program initialization a bit, it makes the program respond very rapidly to user input. Users expect programs to take a certain amount of time to start, but they like to see commands executed quickly.

The only major win_ API calls that do not require win_redraw() are the printf-type functions, such as win_printf().

The window that is automatically opened for the application, sometimes called the default window, is initially sized and positioned by information in the .DVP used to open the application. This window may be manipulated the same as any other window. Its handle is returned from the win_me() API call. For example, to resize its initial window, an application might do the following:

```
ulong defaultwindow;

defaultwindow = win_me();
win_resize (defaultwindow, num_rows, num_cols);
win_redraw (defaultwindow);
```

We should note at this point that windows opened by DESQview are different from those opened by add-on windowing libraries. As we have already seen, the code to manipulate DESQview windows is part of the environment, and not part of the application. Although this makes the application dependent on DESQview, it also means that the application can be considerably smaller.

Even more important, applications can do much more with DESQview windows. For example, a window opened with a win_new() call can be manipulated by the user using the normal Resize and Move menu commands or by grabbing them with the mouse. (The application may prevent this from happening with the win_disallow() API call.) Further, an application may push a window in front of, or behind, other windows, even if they belong to other applications. In our sample program, since CLOCK does not specifically forbid it, the user can put the clock window anywhere on the screen.

The concept of handles associated with objects is an important one in DESQview. DESQview relies heavily on them. For example, all input and output under DESQview is through object handles. This is why both a window object and a keyboard object must be opened automatically at program initiation: DESQview converts calls to BIOS screen and keyboard routines into win_ calls to the default window object, and key_ calls to the default keyboard object. In this way, a DESQview oblivious program that performs a printf() actually performs a win_printf(win_me()) in a roundabout way.

Panels

A DESQview application tends to have many windows: a window for each different menu, a window for different types of data, and so on. It is possible for the application to create and manipulate each of these windows using discrete win_ API calls. However, this might result in a confusingly large number of win_ calls to set things up properly, and changing a menu or output window might prove difficult. Quarterdeck has made window generation much easier by providing a separate utility known as the Panel Design Tool.

The Panel Design Tool allows the programmer to "draw" windows using a MacDraw or PC Paint type of interface. The programmer draws out a box, sets such properties as border type and color from menu bars across the top, and types in any text that should appear within the window. DESQview calls a window generated in this way a panel. Each panel is given an eight-character name so that it may be identified easily. Once they are completed, the Panel Design Tool combines up to 255 panels into what is known as a panel file.

Panel files may have either of two formats: they may be a separate binary file that the program reads at execution time, or they may take the form of a .OBJ file, which the programmer simply links in with the application at link time. The latter method is usually more convenient.

Both the Clock and Set Alarm windows within CLOCK are implemented as panels within a Panel File known as CLOCKWIN. The CLOCKWIN.OBJ generated by the Panel Design Tool must be linked together with CLOCK.OBJ, just like the API1.OBJ and API2.OBJ files. CLOCKWIN.OBJ defines two global labels that CLOCK needs: clockwin and lclockwin. The label clockwin is the address of the panel file in memory, and lclockwin is its length.

To make a panel window appear on the screen, the program must first acquire the handle of an empty panel object using the pan_new() call. Opening the panel file using the pan_open() API call makes the individual panels available for display. Applying the panel using the pan_apply() API call displays the window. In CLOCK it looks like:

```
extern char clockwin[];          /*this is the clock panel that
                                   contains the description of our
                                   clock windows*/
extern int lclockwin;            /*the length of the panel*/
```

```
ulong panhan;                        /*the handle for the CLOCKWIN panel*/
ulong panelwin;                      /*window handle for the clock*/
ulong panelkey;                      /*keyboard handle for clock panel -
                                       used to read select fields*/

panhan = pan_new();
if (!pan_open (panhan, clockwin, lclockwin))
   if (!pan_apply (panhan, win_me(), "CLOCK", 5,
                   &panelwin, &panelkey))
```

Notice that if either the pan_open() or the pan_apply() function returns a non zero value, the function was not successful, and the program should terminate (the value returned is indicative of the problem encountered). Also, notice that pan_apply() returns the handle of a window object. The window opened by a panel may be further manipulated just like any other window, using this handle. In addition, pan_apply() returns the handle of the keyboard object that the application should read to receive input from the window.

Figure 7-5: Field definitions for Clock and Alarm Set panels.

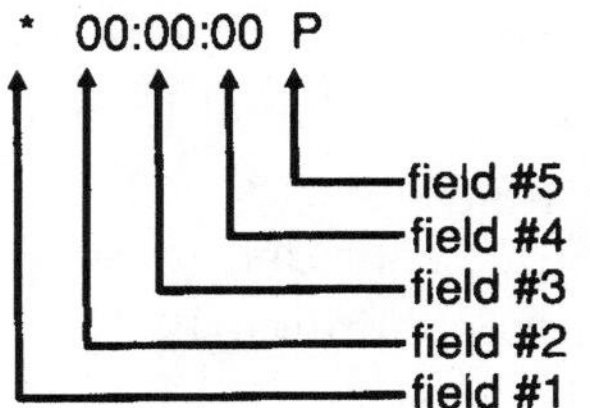

Not only can you paint fixed text into windows using the Panel Design Tool, you can also define variable text areas known as fields. Each field within a panel window carries a number. You can output to these fields via their field numbers. This is the way CLOCK handles output. In both the Clock and Alarm Set windows, the fields are numbered as in Figure 7-5. Output to these fields is via the fld_write() API call. #defines can be used to make the meaning of the different fields clearer. In the case of CLOCK, these defines look like this:

```
                                  /*the clockwin panel defines the
                                        following fields*/
#define FLD_ALARM    01             /*the alarm select field*/
#define FLD_HOURS    02             /*hours*/
#define FLD_MINUTES  03             /*minutes*/
#define FLD_SECONDS  04             /*seconds*/
#define FLD_AMPM     05             /*AM/PM indicator*/
```

For example, when it is time to display the current time from the structure asciitime into a window, CLOCK uses the following function:

```
/*updatetime - update the time display by writing the time to
               the hours, minutes, seconds and AM/PM fields of
              the specified panel window*/
 void updatetime (ulong panelwin, struct timstruct *asciitime)
 {
    /*write the time into fields 2 thru 4*/
    fld_write (panelwin, FLD_HOURS,   asciitime - hour, 2);
    fld_write (panelwin, FLD_MINUTES, asciitime - min,  2);
    fld_write (panelwin, FLD_SECONDS, asciitime - sec,  2);
   /*and put up the AM/PM indicator in field 5*/
    fld_write (panelwin, FLD_AMPM, &asciitime - afternoon, 1);
 }
```

The final argument to fld_write() is simply the length of the string supplied in the third argument.

Fields give panels their true power. Panels are more than just a method to define windows quickly without coding many series of boring win_ calls. Panels allow you to separate the form of an application from its function. When CLOCK outputs the time to fields 2 through 5, it does not know or care where they are in the window. If you wanted to move (or remove) fields within the Clock or Set Alarm windows, you would simply redraw the screen using the Panel Design Tool, and relink. It would not be necessary to change the C program at all.

The CLOCK program is probably too simple to seriously consider going to the trouble; however, large, real-world applications change continuously. New windows may be added, requiring existing windows to be redesigned to make room. Changing existing source code to accommodate such format changes requires programmer time plus expensive retesting, and invites errors. Panels allow you to restructure the output of a program, using the Panel Design Tool without the need to change the application code, resulting in considerable savings in cost and time.

Another problem addressed by panels is that of multiple versions. Some companies offer several versions of the same program. This may be to support different human languages, different price tags, or different levels of user sophistication. (For example, while the instructor version of some test administering software might have a "Show Correct Answer" menu option, the student version most certainly would not.)

While generating modified versions of software from the original is not conceptually difficult, it is a process full of pitfalls. Adding conditional compilation statements or commenting out sections of code invites programming problems. The Panel Design Tool allows you to code an application once. You can then create different versions of the application by changing the panel file. Reduced versions use panels with fields missing or replaced. Thus, in our example above, the student can't "Show Correct Answer," not because the code won't allow it, but because the panel does not display the option to do so. Of course, the entire panel may be rearranged so that it is not obvious to the student that the missing field was ever present.

DESQview Tasks

Of course, the DESQview API also supports multitasking. Before discussing multitasking, we need to define two very important terms: task and process. A task in DESQview is a single-execution thread; that is, a path the CPU takes through the program. A related concept is that of process. A process is the total of all memory areas unique to a program. Thus, a single-tasked application consists of a single task (one execution thread) within a single process (the application's code, data, and window memory).

A simple analogy is a wood with several trails. The process corresponds to the wood itself: the trees and the area they cover. There are multiple trails that people may take through the woods, just as there are many logical paths through an application. A task corresponds to a hiker strolling along one of these trails.

It is not always clear when multitasking is useful. CLOCK could be implemented in a single task; however, it would be difficult to accept user input, including setting the alarm time, and still update the time reliably every second. Therefore, CLOCK consists of two tasks: one to accept user input, and a second independent task that simply puts up the time every second. Even when the first task is blocked, awaiting input, the second task ticks reliably on.

Starting a new task in DESQview is handled with the tsk_new() API call shown below. The parent task must supply the address of the function where the subtask is to begin, the location of its stack, and the name and size of its initial window. In this example, the subtask begins with the function ticktock(). It is allocated STACKSIZE bytes of stack, and given a window of size NUMBER_ROWS by NUMBER_COLS, bearing the label "Subtask." The value returned from tsk_new() is the task handle that is used to identify the task in future API calls.

```
ulong taskhandle;
int ticktock (void);
char stack [STACKSIZE];
char windowname[] = {"Subtask"};

taskhandle = tsk_new (ticktock, stack, STACKSIZE,
                      windowname, sizeof windowname - 1,
                      NUMBER_ROWS, NUMBER_COLS);
```

Notice that a task's stack must be a section of memory that will remain untouched by any other task. It may be returned from a malloc() call or defined as a fixed global array; however, any stack checking code that may be inserted by the compiler may have difficulty with a stack segment that is different from the main task's stack segment.. Most notably, Microsoft C has a problem in this area. This can be addressed by defining the subtask's stack within the main task's stack (as CLOCK does). In this case, it must be declared in a function that does not return as long as the subtask is executing, because returning would surrender the memory space for other uses.

If a task is to operate silently in the background, it may not need a window. This is also true if the task intends to operate on a window that has already been opened by another task. In either case, you may specify a window size of zero rows by zero columns, and no window will be opened on the screen when the task is started. This is the case with the ticktock() function in CLOCK.

Invoking a subtask via tsk_new() is very similar to calling a function, except that control returns to the caller before the subtask completes. If we look at our "hiker in the woods" model, calling a normal function is similar to a hiker taking a side path off the main trail. This side path winds around, perhaps taking side paths of its own, before eventually returning to the main trail via the function return. No matter what happens in the side path, progress down the main trail is suspended until the hiker returns from the side path. Spawning a subtask is as if the hiker splits in two. The original hiker is allowed to continue down the main trail while the clone simultaneously sets off along the side path.

Tasks can terminate in one of three ways. If the program aborts for any reason, all of its tasks are automatically terminated. Alternatively, if a subtask attempts to return from its highest level function (the one named in the tsk_new()

call), DESQview terminates it. Conceptually, this is identical to a single-tasked program returning from main() to the operating system. Finally, a task may be aborted at any time via the tsk_free() call. The tsk_free() call requires the task handle returned from the tsk_new() call that created it. Freeing a task's object kills the task. (A task may acquire its own handle using the tsk_me() API call if it needs to kill itself.)

Of course, there is only one CPU, so the two tasks don't actually make progress simultaneously. One task proceeds a few steps along the program trail, or until the next time it must wait for input, and then the second task gets a turn to proceed. Still, it is easier for the programmer to train several hikers individually, each in a single job, than to train one hiker task to do it all.

DESQview uses a preemptive tasking algorithm to decide which task gets control of the CPU at any given time. That is, scheduling is based on the hardware clock. Each task is allowed to execute for a certain number of clock ticks—the task's time slice before control is wrestled from it and given to the next task in line.

A task normally executes for a complete time slice, but it may give up the remainder of its time slice if it runs out of things to do. For example, a program suspends itself any time it reads the keyboard. Suspended tasks do not receive any CPU time. A task may also have its time slice taken away from it if it polls the keyboard more than a given number of times in a single time slice (this time is specified in the .DVP file). A DESQview-specific program can pass control on without suspending itself using the api_pause() API call.

DESQview recognizes three types of tasks: the foreground task, the background tasks, and interrupt handlers. All background tasks are given the same time slice. The foreground task is given a different size time slice. The defaults are nine-clock ticks for the foreground task, and three for each background task, but the user can change these, both at Setup and from the DESQview menu. Giving the foreground task more time results in livelier keyboard response at the expense of background tasks. Foreground and background tasks are scheduled in a "round-robin" fashion. DESQview may suspend a foreground or background task to schedule an interrupt task immediately to service a hardware interrupt.

As we noted already, tasks within the same process share the same code and data space. Such tasks appear as functions within a single executable file and are bound together at link time. This must be so, since the argument to tsk_new() is the address of the function that is to begin the subtask. Thus, tasks "know" about each other. They have access to all the same functions and all the same global variables. Both of these facts present their own problems.

Access to common global variables brings with it certain problems in a multitasking environment. Since the programmer cannot be sure when the hardware alarm will strike and when the task will lose control, a task cannot write to a location that another task may write to and expect the value to stay unchanged. This is true whether the location is in RAM or on disk.

To illustrate, suppose your bank uses an accounting program with two tasks—task A and task B—both of which use a global variable customer_balance. Suppose also that task A decides it is time to credit the daily interest to your savings account. Task A dutifully loads your balance into the global variable and calculates your new balance. Before it can write this balance back out to disk, however, task A's time slice is up, and control is passed to task B. As luck would have it, task B's job is to credit a deposit that has just arrived. Task B reads some other person's account into customer_balance, adds the deposit, and writes the result back out to disk. When task A eventually gets control back, it continues with its write operation, writing the contents of customer_balance into your savings account. Unfortunately for you and the bank, the content of customer_balance now has nothing to do with the real balance in the savings account.

The problem here is that task A and task B use the same fixed memory location, customer_balance. Solving the problem in this case is quite simple. There is no reason to locate customer_balance in global memory. If both task A and task B are modified to declare customer_balance locally, the conflict does not occur. While both tasks might continue to refer to a variable customer_balance, since it is now declared locally, it no longer refers to the same location in memory.

A similar problem arises with functions shared by subtasks. Suppose, for example, that the global variable in the above example is only accessed from a single function, say, update_balance(). We might think that no conflict is possible; that is not the case, however, because update_balance() might be executed by both task A and task B at the same time. To return to our hiker analogy briefly, update_balance() is simply a stretch of trail that two hikers might walk along at the same time. In this case, we say that the function update_balance() is not reentrant; that is, it cannot be reentered while another task is in the function.

It is interesting to note that DOS itself is not reentrant; two different tasks may not execute DOS service calls at the same time. DESQview must be careful to control tasks entering and exiting DOS to preclude this from happening. (It is widely known that DOS actually consists of two parts: calls with numbers below 0BH, and those above. These two sections are mutually reentrant, in that one program may be executing one of the lower DOS calls, while another is executing a call from the upper range.)

If a task attempts to make a DOS call and DESQview detects that a second task is already in the middle of such a call, the calling task must be suspended. When the second task is subsequently given control, it will eventually complete its DOS call. As it exits DOS, DESQview unsuspends the first task, allowing it to continue into DOS the next time it is scheduled.

The ANSI.SYS device driver provided with DOS is not reentrant either. In this case the solution is much simpler, however: DESQview comes with a reentrant version of ANSI.SYS called ANSI.COM, which can be installed within an application window. As an aside, tasks that are part of the same executable file share a single process and, therefore, share the same .DVP file. It is not possible to specify that one such task writes directly to screen memory and should be virtualized, while another task does not.

In addition, the user controls multiple tasks of the same program together. Selecting a window of one task brings the windows of all tasks that are part of the same program to the foreground together. It is not possible for the user to suspend one task without affecting the rest. If, for example, a program opens a menu controlled by another task, the user should not be able to select the menu separately from the program that created it. As far as the user is concerned, all task windows are part of the same program.

DESQview does allow a type of parent task that can be handled individually. DESQview calls it an application. A normal task belongs to the parent task that created it. Acting on the parent task (by selecting it or closing it, for example) affects all of its subtasks. A newly spawned application task doesn't belong to a parent task. It becomes its own parent and can be operated on independently.

Take the example of a spreadsheet program. All the drop-down menus are handled by normal subtasks, as they are part of the application. Suppose, however, that the program allowed multiple spreadsheets to be worked on at one time. This would best be handled by spawning the same code as separate applications, one for each spreadsheet. This would allow the user to manipulate the spreadsheets separately. The user could bring one spreadsheet to the foreground, leaving another in the background; zoom a spreadsheet on top of the other windows in the background; even close a spreadsheet from the DESQview menu.

A new application is spawned using the app_new() API call, whose arguments are identical to those of tsk_new(). The app_new() call returns a task handle just like that returned from tsk_new(). The user has the illusion that the applications are completely independent programs, even though they share the same code and data space. The only exception to this rule is that if DESQview must write an application to disk, it must write all applications within the same process to disk. It is the process the applications share that actually gets written.

DESQview Processes

Just as a task can spawn a subtask in the same process, so can a task spawn a subtask in a different process. This is analogous to the DOS or UNIX exec call, in which one program can execute another program. DESQview handles this using the app_start() API call. Unlike the DOS exec() command, the argument to app_start() is the address of the .DVP structure for the process.

```
ulong taskhandle;
struct DVP processDVP;

taskhandle = app_start (&processDVP,
                        sizeof processDVP);
```

A task created by the app_start() call is completely independent from the task that started it. The two tasks share neither code nor data. Their windows are independent, one may be brought to the foreground and the other left in the background. The two tasks may be swapped out to disk or terminated independently. Because they occupy different processes, the two tasks are like completely separate programs.

The ticktock() function could be written as a separate process. To do so, we would create a separate TIKTOK.C file containing a main() that first checked for the presence of DESQview and then called ticktock(). Any functions that ticktock() shared with the rest of CLOCK would be repeated in TIKTOK. We would then compile CLOCK, generating a CLOCK.EXE without ticktock() and a TIKTOK.EXE with only ticktock(). When CLOCK performed the app_start() call, DESQview would load TIKTOK.EXE into a separate memory area and start it.

The .DVP structure provided to app_start() may be initialized by reading a .DVP file into a buffer from the disk. Alternatively, the necessary data may be hard-coded in the source program, using the C structure that appears in the example below. It is not necessary to supply a .DVP structure when starting a new task, since each subtask remains in the same process. With app_start(), however, we are not only creating a new hiker, we are building a whole new wood. Notice that it is not necessary to specify the name of the executable file to app_start() since this is contained in the .DVP structure along with the rest of the information.

```
struct DVP {
  unsigned reserved1;         /*set to 0x0097*/
  char     title [30];        /*program title - pad with blanks*/
  unsigned maxmem;            /*maximum memory required [kbytes]*/
  unsigned minmem;            /*minimum memory required [kbytes]*/
  char     command [64];      /*start command [ASCIIZ]*/
  char     drive;             /*default drive in ASCII
                                (blank for none)*/
  char     directory [64];    /*default directory [ASCIIZ]*/
  char     params    [64];    /*parameters to command [ASCIIZ]*/
  char     screenmode;        /*initial screen mode (0 - 7)*/
  char     numpages;          /*number of video pages*/
  char     firstvect;         /*first interrupt vector to be saved*/
  char     lastvect;          /*last interrupt vector to be saved*/
  char     rows;              /*no. rows in logical window*/
  char     cols;              /*no. columns in logical window*/
  char     yloc;              /*initial row position*/
  char     xloc;              /*initial column position*/
  unsigned reserved2;         /*system memory - overridden later*/
  char     sharedprog [64];   /*name of shared program [ASCIIZ]*/
  char     shareddata  [64];  /*name of shared data*/
  char     controlbyte1;      /*control byte 1 -
                                0x80 - writes directly to screen
                                0x40 - foreground only
                                0x20 - uses 8087
                                0x10 - accesses keyboard buffer
                                0x01 - swappable*/
  char     controlbyte2;      /*control byte 2 -
                                0x40 - uses command line params
                                0x20 - swaps interrupt vectors*/

                              /*DESQview 1.00 extensions*/
  char     startkeys [2];     /*starting keys from menu*/
  char     scriptsize [2];    /*size of script file [bytes]*/
```

```
    unsigned autopause;         /*pause after this many keyboard
                                  requests in one clock tick*/
    char     disablecolormap;   /*1 -> disable color mapping*/
    char     swappable;         /*1 -> application is swappable*/
    char     reserved3 [3];
    char     closeonexit;       /*1 -> close on exit*/
    char     keyfloppy;         /*1 -> key floppy required*/

                                /*DESQview 2.00 extensions*/
    char     DVPformat;         /*00 -> DV 1.2  and later,
                                  01 -> DV 2.00 and later,
                                  02 -> DV 2.20 and later*/
    char     sharesmem;         /*1 -> uses shared system memory*/
    char     physrows;          /*no. rows in initial physical window*/
    char     physcols;          /*no. cols in initial physical window*/
    unsigned expandedmem;       /*amount of avail EMS [kbytes]*/
    char     controlbyte3;      /*control byte 3 -
                                   0x80 - automatically assign pos
                                   0x20 - honor max memory value
                                   0x10 - disallow close command
                                   0x08 - foreground only when graphics
                                   0x04 - don't virtualize*/
    char     kbdconflict;       /*keyboard conflict (normally 0)*/
    char     graphicspages;     /*no. of graphics pages*/
    unsigned systemmem;         /*system memory size*/
    char     initmode;          /*initial video mode - default 0xff*/

                                /*DESQview 2.20 extensions*/
    char     serialports;       /*serial port usage -
                                  -1 -> use all serial ports,
                                   0 -> uses no serial ports,
                                   1 -> uses port 1,
                                   2 -> uses port 2*/
    char     controlbyte4;      /*control byte 4 -
                                   0x80 - automatically close on exit,
                                   0x40 - swappable if not using ports,
                                   0x08 - virtualize text,
                                   0x04 - virtualize graphics,
                                   0x02 - share CPU in foreground,
                                   0x01 - share EGA when zoomed*/
    char     protectlevel;      /*degree of protection*/
    char     reserved4[19];
  };
```

Reading a .DVP file in from disk is straightforward. The .DVP files are most easily created using the Add a Program option under the DESQview Open menu option. All .DVP files are created in the \DV directory, but once there, they can be copied anywhere you desire. Of course, it is also possible to read the default .DVP file in the above structure and then change some value, such as the initial directory, before executing the app_start() call.

The fact that the processes share neither code nor data space grants them a level of independence that is not possible with simple tasks. In the interest of saving memory, however, it is sometimes desirable that two processes share some code. This is possible using shared programs.

Shared programs are executable files specified in the .DVP file. Normally, a shared program is a loader used to make a DESQview-oblivious program adaptable to a multitasking environment; however, shared programs have a unique property: before a shared program is loaded, DESQview checks to see if a copy is already resident in memory. If so, the already resident version is used again. The shared program stays in memory as long as at least one program that uses it is still executing. When the last program that loaded the shared program terminates, the shared image is unloaded from memory.

Although this is a long way from Dynamic Link Libraries (DLLs), a form of DLL can be implemented using shared libraries. For example, you might put common library routines into a shared program where they can be accessed from several processes, reducing the size of each process.

Memory Under DESQview

As we have seen, DOS loads itself as low as possible in memory. The first several hundred bytes are consumed by the interrupt table and BIOS data areas, then come DOS, its buffers, and any device drivers. Finally, any terminate-and-stay-resident (TSR) programs that the user has loaded appear. Any memory between the last TSR and the end of conventional memory is available for the application program's use under simple DOS.

When the user executes DESQview, DOS loads it into this memory area, as it would any other program. On a system with 640KB or less of conventional memory, and without any expanded or extended memory, DESQview consumes roughly 150KB (depending on configuration) of conventional memory; however, when either extended or EMS 4.0 memory is available, DESQview repays this memory penalty in several ways.

First, DESQview can increase the size of conventional DOS memory by noting that this area ends at 640KB only because this is where the memory space reserved for video adapters begins. On machines equipped with either CGA or monochrome display adapters, actual video RAM does not begin until some 64 to 96KB later. On PCs equipped with capable EMS 4.0 memory (or an 80386 or 80486 with QEMM-386), DESQview can map memory into the region between 640KB and the beginning of video memory to increase the space available to user programs. (Some EMS 4.0 cards do not support mapping memory into these lower ranges.)

In addition, DESQview comes with a special loader, XDV, which can load the vast majority of DESQview into memory above video RAM, the so-called UMB region, made available by QEMM-386. With sufficient HMA and UMB memory, XDV can reduce the overhead of DESQview in conventional memory to a mere 10k.

Once loaded into memory, DESQview consists of more than just DV.EXE. DESQview also builds a series of tables in an area called common memory. Common memory is located immediately above the low portion of DESQview, in the lower 640KB. In addition to internal tables, DESQview stores objects and interprocess messages here. This memory area, like DESQview itself, is never remapped, and so is available to all programs. The user may adjust the size of this area at setup time, but it is fixed once DESQview is loaded.

Every time a process is started, DESQview assigns it its own region of memory known as process memory. Process memory includes the program's code and data areas: the script buffers used to hold any scripts defined for the program: the context save area, where the CPU's registers are stored when the task is not executing: and the process's system memory. System memory is used to hold window buffers, panels, and messages between tasks in the same process.

One process may wish to share its system memory with another process. This is the case, for example, when one program wants to write into another program's window. To do this, you may include a "*" in the "Shared Program Pathname" field of the .DVP file menu. This causes DESQview to allocate system memory from an area called shared system memory. This area is kept immediately above common memory and is available to all programs. (Any program that has a shared program also uses shared system memory.) Shared system memory starts out zero length and grows as processes require it.

When a program is executed, its .DVP file indicates how much memory it requires. DESQview could load the program low in memory and then set the end of memory value kept in the BIOS area to the end of the memory range dedicated to that program. This approach has two problems, however. First, few DOS programs ever check to see where this upper boundary is. If insufficient memory is available when you execute under DOS, you either simply do not load or else you crash. Second, most EMS 4.0 cards map the upper range of conventional memory, and not the lower range. Since DESQview wants as much of the application within EMS's mappable area, as we shall see, it is better to load the program as high as possible.

Figure 7-6: DESQview memory areas.

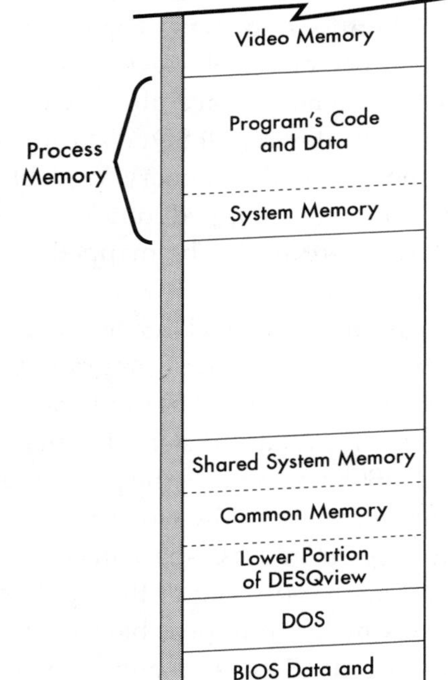

Figure 7-6 represents a single DOS application as it appears in memory.

Therefore, when the user starts a program, DESQview allocates its process memory as high as it can in the lower 640KB. The first program loads immediately below the video adapter memory at the end of conventional memory. The second application is generally loaded below the first, and so on. All of the programs loaded into conventional memory continue to execute.

When the user attempts to load a program and DESQview determines that not enough conventional memory is left, DESQview attempts to free up memory by swapping out applications. Starting with the oldest application, and continuing with successively newer applications, DESQview continues to write the process memory of each application out until enough memory exists to load the new application. The user has some control over swap devices, but DESQview generally goes of decreasing speed. EMS 3.2 memory is the preferred swap device. If EMS 3.2 memory is not available, DESQview then begins swapping applications to a swap file on the disk. Applications that have been swapped out are "frozen" and do not continue to execute in the background; however, the user may switch them back into the foreground and, thus, back into conventional memory, at any time.

DESQview has much more flexibility with the loading of programs when EMS 4.0 memory can replace conventional memory in the lower 640KB range. With today's machines, this generally involves disabling memory above some limit, via a switch on the motherboard.

DESQview uses the ability of EMS 4.0 boards to define multiple page frames of differing size and locations to map memory into any memory areas left unpopulated, up to the beginning of video memory (this is the same process used to fill gaps in the memory space above video RAM). Rather than swap applications out to a swap device, DESQview can simply remap new memory pages into lower memory to make memory available for each new application. Since EMS memory can be remapped quickly, applications that have been mapped out of the lower 640KB may be mapped back in to execute. Figure 7-7 represents this process graphically.

This slightly changes the approach DESQview takes in loading programs into memory. When it is time to load the first program, DESQview reserves as much EMS memory as indicated by the .DVP file and maps it immediately below video RAM. The program is then loaded and started in this area. When it is time to load the second program, DESQview repeats the process, again mapping the required amount of memory immediately below video RAM. Thus, each application occupies roughly the same logical address space in conventional memory. Of course, the first program must be mapped out of this space so that the second program can be mapped in. This makes it impossible for the two applications to access each other's memory directly. Expressed another way, a task in one process cannot access memory in a different process. Processes do share the lower memory areas, including DOS and DESQview (including command memory and any shared system memory).

Figure 7-7: Multitasking with EMS 4.0 memory.

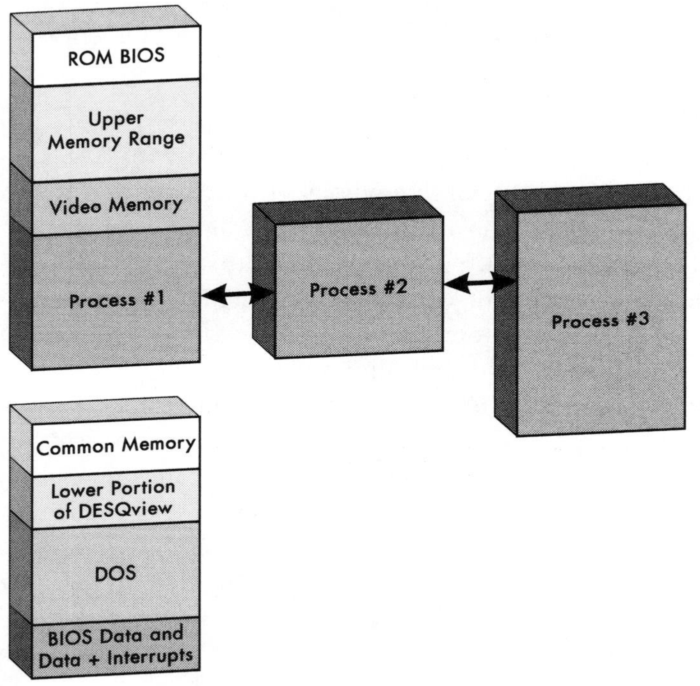

When an EMS 4.0 emulator is installed in an 80386- or 80486-based machine, all of available memory becomes swappable. This, in part, is why Quarterdeck bundles QEMM-386 together with DESQview in the DESQview386 package. With DESQview386, it is not necessary to disable motherboard memory. In addition, since there is no limit to the size of the EMS page frame, it is not possible for an application to be larger than the page frame and, therefore, unmappable. (An application may be too large to fit into the remaining 640KB at all, of course.)

With DESQview386, the user may load as many applications as can be held in available memory. A 2-megabyte machine can execute four or five normal-sized applications simultaneously, before memory is exhausted. Once available memory is depleted, applications are swapped to disk as needed.

DESQview386 can use some of the protection features of the 80386 processor as well. For example, if the user desires, DESQview386 can trap any attempt by

DESQview386 can use some of the protection features of the 80386 processor as well. For example, if the user desires, DESQview386 can trap any attempt by an application to write memory outside of its own process. Except for these protection features, DESQview386 treats 80386 memory as EMS 4.0 memory.

Intertask Communication

When we started as programmers, especially if we started with BASIC, our programs tended to be one large monolithic whole with little or no internal structure. Eventually, we came to see the advantage in dividing our programs up into functions. This allowed us to break a problem down into a series of smaller problems, each of which could be dealt with separately, with a resulting savings in time. As soon as we broke our programs into functions, however, the problem arose of how these functions should communicate.

The first solution was simply to use the same techniques for communicating that had worked between blocks of code before. One function simply leaves some value in a global variable so that the other function can conveniently find it there when it is called. Soon, we discovered that this was not the ideal means of communication. While global variables are fast, it is generally far better to forgo the speed for the increased control and safety of passing data to and from functions via arguments. This is the primary means of communication between functions in a single-tasked environment.

In some multitasking environments, it is possible to pass arguments to tasks in exactly the same way as they are passed to simple functions. Unfortunately, this is not the case in DESQview. The tsk_new() API call accepts the address of a function that takes no arguments and returns nothing (the fact that in the prototype this function is of type Int is a throwback to K&R—in fact, the function should have been declared to be of type void).

In the absence of function arguments, the question arises of how we should communicate between tasks within a single process. Our first response might be to drop back to past experience and simply use global variables again. The parent task can store a value into a global variable before starting the subtask. Once the subtask is started, it examines the location to find the data. This works for data that is set once and does not change thereafter, but what about changing data?

If more than a single value is to be communicated, the two tasks must agree on some sort of protocol. They may agree on what constitutes "no data," which can then be stored into the location once data has been read out, as an indication that it is now available to hold new data. If this is not possible, a second location may be used as an access flag. For example, a flag value of zero might correspond to "no data," while a nonzero flag indicates data is waiting to be accessed.

If the communication is two-way, in that both tasks can write into the location, data may get overwritten and lost in the following way: the parent task reads the location and checks that it is currently set to "no data." Before it can write its data into the location, however, its time slice comes to an end. When the other task starts its time slice, it reads the same location and also sees that it contains the "no data" value. This second task then writes its data. Now, when the first task gets control back, it continues with the write operation that was suspended before, overwriting the second task's data. (This is very similar to the customer_balance problem discussed earlier.)

The loss of data due to its being overwritten by another task is known as a data collision. In some applications, the occasional loss of a data word is insignificant, but for the majority of programs this is a serious problem. For these programs, a section of code where such a data collision might occur is known as a critical region. The specific operation in this example the reading and writing of a variable in memory, is called the critical operation.

There are several ways to avoid data collisions. If you notice that the problem only arises when two or more tasks write to the same location, you can try to avoid this situation. Often, we can split communications into two separate paths. In this case, the parent task might use the location data to send information to the subtask, while the subtask might use the next location, data from, to send information in the opposite direction. If each task reads both locations but only writes to one of them, the collision is avoided.

Often it is not possible to agree on a protocol or divide the global data up in such a way so as to guarantee that a collision will not occur. This is usually the case when more than two tasks are potentially involved, or when critical regions arise around objects other than memory locations.

Suppose, for instance, that one application decides it needs to send output to the printer. While it is printing, another task detects an alarm condition and decides to print the warning message. If access to the printer is not controlled, what appears on the printer will be a mix of the output of the two tasks, and the alarm warning may be illegible. Thus, the print operation represents a critical region between these two tasks. These types of critical regions cannot be protected with "no data" type protocols, since they do not represent memory locations and cannot be read.

It is clear from our examples that collisions occur because one task is so unfortunate as to get rescheduled during a critical operation. The most obvious solution then is for a task to disable rescheduling before beginning a critical operation, and only reenable it after it has completed the operation.

In DESQview, the api_beginc() API call ("beginc" stands for "begin critical operation") disables rescheduling. Once rescheduling has been disabled, a task is assured that it will retain control until it either reenables scheduling via an api_endc() API call, or performs a system call that suspends the task. (If DESQview left scheduling disabled when the task suspended itself, the system would hang forever, since no one would be allowed to run.)

Wrapping a critical region in api_beginc() and api_endc() calls is a common ploy. It appears to be fairly straightforward and so is very popular with programmers new to multitasking. What they quickly realize, however, is that it is often a very unsatisfactory solution. One problem is that leaving rescheduling off for long periods adversely affects the performance of the system. Imagine, for instance, if rescheduling were disabled for the entire time it took to print a letter, just so another print operation could not start. If the critical operation takes very long to perform, the user notices the system halt and lurch as rescheduling is turned on and off.

A worse problem with this approach is that it is voluntary. A task might come along and access the controlled memory location or device without disabling rescheduling first. Such a violation is not easily detected. Suppose, for example, the print warning message module in the above example printed without disabling rescheduling. Module testing is not likely to reveal the problem. It is not until another task decides to begin printing just after an alarm starts printing that the user begins complaining of lost warning messages on the system. Rare collisions around data variables resulting in incorrect bank balances or a crashing system are even worse and even more difficult to find.

A task may violate this protocol unintentionally as well. A function called while scheduling is disabled may inadvertently reenable it by performing a seemingly innocuous system call. Any DOS call can result in the task being suspended and scheduling reenabled, for instance. While the programmer may have the best of intentions, it is difficult to make absolutely sure that rescheduling remains disabled over a large segment of code.

Still, reading data out of a global variable or flag, checking it, setting it, and storing it right back does not take very long, and it should not require very many instructions. Therefore, protecting access to such common memory locations by disabling rescheduling temporarily is an acceptable practice.

Larger critical areas may be protected by a flag, often called a lock. The idea is to assign a flag to each critical operation. Before entering the critical section of code, the program checks the flag. If the flag is clear, it is safe to proceed into the critical section. The task then sets the lock to ward off other tasks that may attempt to enter and continue on. Once the task is finished, it clears the flag and proceeds. Obviously, the checking and setting of the flag is itself a critical operation and must be protected with an api_beginc() call. In DESQview, such an operation is as follows:

```
int latchvar;
void latch (void)
 {
      for (;;) {
          api_beginc ();          /*disable scheduler*/
          if (latchvar == 0)      /*if latch clear...*/
             break;              /*...continue; else...*/
         api_endc ();            /*...reenable scheduler...*/
         api_pause ();           /*...and give up control*/
      }
      latchvar = 1;               /*set latch and return*/
      api_endc ();
 }

void unlatch (void)
 {
      latchvar = 0;
 }
```

This approach to collision avoidance is much better than the simple disable rescheduling approach. Here, tasks not attempting to enter the critical region are not affected. While a task that is attempting to print might be suspended for a long time waiting for another to finish, all of the tasks that are not trying to print are not affected. The system continues to execute smoothly. However, a new problem arises with this approach. Requesters are not granted access in the order in which they request it.

Suppose, for example, that three tasks all attempt access to the printer. Task A requests the latch and is granted it. Task B and then task C request the latch but must wait. When task A completes printing and clears the latch, there is no guarantee that task B will get control next, even though its request preceded that of task C. The order in which tasks B and C are granted access is completely random. In fact, if task A restored the latch but then decided to print again before its time slice was completed, it would be granted clearance by the cleared flag before either task B or task C could "wake up" and grab it.

An even worse problem is common to all of these solutions. They all rely upon the fact that the several tasks involved all have access to some global variable. With tasks that share the same process memory this is true, but for tasks in different processes, this cannot be the case. Processes do not share code or data segments. For these types of tasks, DESQview offers a different communications path: intertask messages.

Intertask Messages

The principle behind intertask messages is simple. The sending task simply bundles up the information to be transmitted in a locally defined structure and mails it to the other task using a mal_write() DESQview API call. The message is copied into a mailbox maintained for the other task in system memory (messages between tasks in separate processes are saved in common memory). These mailboxes can hold a number of messages in a first-in-first-out queue. The receiving task may read these messages out of its mailbox at any time by executing a mal_read() API call. Each subsequent mal_read() call returns the next message. If the mailbox queue is empty, mal_read() suspends the caller until a message appears. If a task does not wish to be suspended, it may poll the mailbox first, using the mal_sizeof() call. This call returns the number of messages in the queue. If the count is nonzero, the task can mal_read() the mailbox without being suspended.

Intertask messages avoid most of the intertask communication problems inherent in other communications paths. First, all access to common locations is controlled by the operating system, making data collisions impossible. When a task sends a message, it is copied out of its space. Like a variable passed to a function by value, any subsequent changes it makes to the message buffer are not copied to the sender. Second, tasks do not have to wait to send messages. A task may send a message and continue, even if other messages are already queued up for the task to work off. Third, the order of requests is retained. If task A sends a message before task B, then task A's message gets processed first, despite the randomness of task scheduling.

Finally, intertask messages, like function calls, represent a "point to point" communication path. That is, when task A sends a message to task B, it is clear where the message is going and who will receive it. It is not possible that some task C might come along and intentionally or unintentionally interfere with this communication path. Not only is this important to the programmer writing the program, it is equally important to the person who must come along years later and maintain the program. This can make a very large difference in the ability to maintain large programs.

When a task is started, along with the default window and keyboard objects that DESQview opens, a default mailbox object is also opened. The handle of the default mailbox associated with any task can be returned from the mal_of() API call. A task may know its own mailbox handle by executing the mal_me() call.

In our CLOCK program, the function program_body() starts the subtask ticktock() to update the time in the Clock window. For ticktock() to write to this window, however, it must have the window's handle. Program_body() could have simply stored the Clock window handle in a global variable, which ticktock() could then have accessed. Instead, program_body() stores the handle into the structure "message" and sends it to ticktock()'s mailbox, as in the following code segment:

```
ulong panelwin;                 /*window handle for the clock*/
ulong malhan;                   /*mailbox handle of subtask*/
struct windowmsg message;       /*message to send to subtask*/

tskhan = tsk_new (ticktock, taskstack, STACKSIZE,
                  "", 0, 0, 0);
malhan = mal_of (tskhan);
message.windowhandle = panelwin;
mal_write (malhan, (char *)&message, sizeof message);
```

For its part, ticktock() reads the message immediately upon starting, as in the following:

```
ulong winhandle;
struct windowmsg *winmessage;
int               messagelength;

/*read the message with the window handle*/
mal_read (mal_me(), &(char *)winmessage, &messagelength);
winhandle = winmessage -> windowhandle;
```

Notice that the message is copied out of the sender's memory area and into system memory when it is sent. The caller is free to reuse that space as soon as control is returned from the mal_write() call. It is not copied into the receiver's memory area, however. Instead the receiver is given a pointer to the message in DESQview's memory. This is why the second argument to mal_read() is not the address of a message buffer but "a pointer to a pointer" to a message (the cast (char *) is only so the call matches the prototype declaration). The data in the message stays valid until the next time the task performs a mailbox read. Therefore, ticktock() copies the data out of the message and into local, safe storage.

(Incidentally, CLOCK also uses a global variable communication path when ticktock() stores the current time in the current time structure, which is subsequently used within the parent task. It is valid here since the parent task never writes this structure, thus precluding any chance of collision.)

This point-to-point message scheme means that both the sender and receiver must know the mailbox's handle. A task can always find its own handle, using mal_me(). A parent task can always find the default mailbox of any of its subtasks by using the mal_of() API call on the task's handle.

However, a task may open up additional mailboxes using a mal_new() call, and these are not associated with the task handle. To solve this problem, a task may assign any mailbox a name using mal_name(). Any other task can then find the handle of this mailbox by looking up its name via the mal_find() call. This can considerably enhance the readability of the resulting code. For example, ticktock() could name its mailbox "Update Clock Display." Then,x any task that wanted its display updated on a regular basis could send a message to the Update Clock Display mailbox.

This is very common in applications fraught with collision problems, such as a database. If every task in the program can access the database, controlling all the locks necessary to avoid database contention can become a real problem. It is easier to name one task as the database engine and allow it to perform all reads and writes, acting as a form of traffic cop to avoid data collisions. This database engine may even be in a separate process. In fact, this process may not even be on the same machine! Assigning a name like "Data base" to the mailbox for this task allows each of the other tasks to find its handle to make requests. The intent is clear to even the most casual reader what a task sending requests to a mailbox named Database is trying to do.

Of course, the database must be able to answer the requests. The requesting task can simply store the mailbox handle where it expects its answer in the request message, but this is not necessary. If a task receives a message, calling the mal_addr() API function returns the mailbox handle of the task that sent the message, so it is possible to reply to messages even if you do not otherwise know where they came from.

The overhead of copying large messages into system (or common) memory during the mal_write() may become objectionable. DESQview does allow messages to be passed by reference with the mal_subfrom() call. That is, when the receiving task receives a message address, it is, in fact, pointing directly at the message in the calling task.

This can be very dangerous, however. First, the calling task may not reuse the message space until the receiving task is through with it. For this reason, some protocol must be established for returning the buffer to the originating task.

Second, the receiving task must have access to this memory. This is no problem for tasks within the same process; however, for tasks in other processes, this is a real problem. Such a task would receive a logical address to a region that may not be mapped into memory when the task is. Because how the processes are mapped is a function of the hardware type and configuration, this is the type of problem that might not appear during development, and would only show up on user's equipment.

This problem can be avoided by using shared system memory; that is, specifying a "*" in the .DVP for each process, and then allocating memory from this area to build the message via the api_getmem() API call. Since shared system memory comes out of the lower 640KB, however, there is not enough room for truly large messages. In systems with EMS memory, it is just as simple to allocate a block of expanded storage in which to build the message. The handle for this EMS storage can then be inserted into a normal message and sent to the other process. This process then maps the EMS memory into its page frame and accesses the message directly. This allows messages to be built up to the size of available EMS memory.

Notice that either way, the sending task may continue to access the memory area—even as the receiving task is using it—as long as a protocol is established to avoid collisions. In fact, this is exactly the same collision problem as that presented by global variables between tasks. Passing EMS handles or pointers to shared system memory allows processes to establish the same common memory communication path available to tasks, but brings with it identical problems.

Avoiding access by multiple tasks to global variables only eliminates the data collisions. The intertask messages we have seen so far cannot solve non data collisions such as those that might arise around devices. We have already seen how we can use a lock variable to control access between tasks within the same process. The same method could be applied to tasks in different processes if we first allocate a small section of shared system memory and pass its address to all of the tasks requiring access via messages. Mailboxes provide a better solution, however.

In some message-based operating systems, control to such a critical region can be controlled in the following way. The parent task first creates a "lock mailbox" and sends it a single dummy message known as a semaphore. Any task that desires entry into the critical region must first read the semaphore from the mailbox. Once the task has read the message, it may continue. Once it has left the critical section, it must then send a dummy message back to the mailbox to restore the semaphore. If a second task reads the mailbox while the first task is in the critical region, the semaphore message is not there (having been read by the first task) and the second task is suspended. When the first task returns the semaphore, the second task is unsuspended and allowed to proceed.

Similar in concept to simple locks, semaphore mailboxes have the same advantages that normal intertask messages have over global variables: tasks are not rescheduled needlessly, requests are processed, tasks need not be in the same process, and so on. Under DESQview, however, two tasks may not actually read the same mailbox. Therefore, DESQview defines two special API calls to allow mailbox semaphores to be established: mal_lock() and mal_unlock(). The first task to perform a mal_lock() API call on a mailbox is allowed to pass. Subsequent tasks that attempt to mal_lock() the mailbox are suspended until the first task performs a mal_unlock(). (Actually, the first task may mal_lock() a mailbox multiple times; the lock is not cleared until the same number of mal_unlock()s have been performed.) The same mailbox may not be used as a normal message mailbox and a semaphore mailbox; once a task has locked a mailbox, it may no longer read it or send it a message.

How DESQview Uses Messages

In our discussion of messages, it may have struck you that reading a mailbox object is a lot like reading the keyboard under DOS using BIOS calls. Performing a BIOS read command of the keyboard suspends the calling program until a key arrives. A program can simply poll the keyboard to see if a key is present to avoid being suspended. And finally, keystrokes arriving from the keyboard are queued up into the keyboard input buffer. This is not very surprising since the keyboard queue is designed to handle exactly the same problem as message mailboxes: communication between two independent entities. In this case, however, the two entities are the single DOS task and the user.

DESQview encounters the same problem as DOS with almost all of its Input/Output paths. It is not very surprising, then, that DESQview uses intertask messages for the majority of its communication with application software. A task that performs a key_read() of the keyboard object is merely reading a message from the keyboard mailbox. Every time the user strikes a key, DESQview places the key into a message and sends it to a keyboard object.

DESQview generally uses the position of a task's windows to decide which keyboard object gets the message. DESQview sends keyboard messages to the task that has the window nearest the foreground. Usually, this is the foreground window (the window marked with a double border). Thus, the foreground task "hears" the keyboard and the others do not.

Just as DESQview can send keystroke messages to a keyboard object, an application task can mal_write() a message to another task's keyboard object just as it might to the task's mailbox object. The mechanism is exactly the same. The effect on the receiving task is as if the user had typed in whatever the sending task sent.

In fact, DESQview itself sometimes sends messages other than simple keystrokes to a keyboard object. The reader may have noticed that the pan_apply() API call used to display a panel in CLOCK returned not only the window handle used to manipulate the panel's window but also the handle of a keyboard object.

This keyboard handle allows a task to input from a panel as well as output to it. DESQview handles the actual user input, the manipulation of the mouse, cursor keys, and so on. There are several modes of operation for panels, but in the most common mode, the application task receives a message containing simply the field number followed by what the user entered in that field.

Panel Messages

There are three types of fields under DESQview: output fields, input fields, and select fields. The user may not enter data into output fields. The user may enter free text into an input field. When the user presses the Enter key, DESQview sends a message containing the field number along with the contents of the entire field, and moves the cursor to the next input field. Special flags allow the message to be sent as soon as the user exits the field (even without pressing Enter), to automatically convert everything to uppercase, to right justify input, and so on. DESQview does not support a flag to allow only numerical input to a field.

Users may select a select field by clicking on it with the mouse, by placing the cursor on the field and pressing Enter, or by entering the special "select" character defined for the field. No other form of input is possible. To inform the user when a select field is properly pointed at, DESQview changes its color to the "pointed at" color. When the field is selected, it changes again to the "selected" color. Reselecting an already selected field, causes it to deselect, reverting back to the "normal" color. When a select field is selected, DESQview sends a message containing the field number and a "Y"; when the field is deselected, DESQview sends the same message with an "N".

Referring back to our CLOCK program, the definealarm() function, which reads the alarm clock input, appears as follows:

```
/*definealarm - put up the alarm set panel where the user
                may enter the alarm time*/
void definealarm (ulong panhan)
{
     ulong alarmwin, alarmkey;
     struct panelmsg *alarminput;
     int              inputlength;

    /*first, open the ALARM panel to display Alarm Set window*/
    if (!pan_apply (panhan, win_me(), "ALARM", 5,
                               &alarmwin, &alarmkey)) {
```

```
            /*update the window to the previous alarm time...*/
            updatetime (alarmwin, &alarmtime);

            /*...and position the cursor for time entry*/
           fld_cursor (alarmwin, FLD_HOURS);

           /*now wait for the user to update the time fields*/
            for (;;) {
                 key_read (alarmkey, &(char *)alarminput, &inputlength);
                 switch (alarminput -> fldid) {

                /*selecting fields 2 thru 5 just
                   fills values into the alarm time*/
                 case FLD_HOURS:
                       strncpy (alarmtime.hour, &alarminput -> data, 2);
                       break;
                 case FLD_MINUTES:
                       strncpy (alarmtime.min,  &alarminput -> data, 2);
                       break;
                 case FLD_SECONDS:
                       strncpy (alarmtime.sec,  &alarminput -> data, 2);
                       break;
                 case FLD_AMPM:
                       alarmtime.afternoon = alarminput -> data;
                       break;

                 /*selecting field 1 removes the alarm window and
                   returns control to the main program*/
                 case FLD_ALARM:
                       win_free (alarmwin);
                       return;
                 }
            }
      }
}
```

Applying the Set Alarm panel returns the keyboard object handle alarm key. The next two calls simply update the time display in the Set Alarm window to the previously entered alarm time, and position the cursor at the beginning of the time field to simplify entering the time. The function then begins reading messages from the panel. When the user enters data into any of the input fields, DESQview generates a message containing the one or two ASCII characters entered. These are dutifully copied into the structure alarm time. Define alarm() responds to a message from field 1, the asterisk, by removing the panel from display with win_free() and returning to the caller.

Input fields are a powerful part of panels. The application program is spared the difficulty of writing code to handle arrow keys, mouse movement, deletes, overstrikes, and the rest. The resulting program is smaller and easier to write, but there is a further advantage. All programs written using panels for input have the same "look and feel." In a given situation, pressing the Tab key, for example, has a predictable result, no matter what the application. If you wonder what that look and feel is, try popping up the DESQview manual of the DESQview windows are panels.

Notification Messages

DESQview can sometimes send messages to a task's mailbox object as well. When a task displays a window on the screen, normally, the user is allowed to move it, resize it, and scroll it at will. For some applications, this is unacceptable. In this case, the task may disable these functions for the particular window. In other cases, it is enough that DESQview informs the application task that its windows are being manipulated. This is called turning on notification for a particular window and is handled via the win_notify() call. The notification flags are defined in Table 7-1 below.

Table 7-1: Notification types available for DESQview windows.

Type	Notify On
NTF_HMOVE	The window is moved horizontally
NTF_VMOVE	The window is moved vertically
NTF_HSIZE	The window is resized horizontally
NTF_VSIZE	The window is resized vertically
NTF_HSCROLL	The window is scrolled horizontally
NTF_VSCROLL	The window is scrolled vertically
NTF_CLOSE *	The window is closed
NTF_HIDE *	The window is hidden
NTF_HELP	Help is selected from the DESQview menu
NTF_POINTER	A message is sent to an application
NTF_FORE *	The window is brought to the foreground
NTF_BACK *	The window is brought to the background
NTF_VIDEO *	Video adapter changes mode

Type	Notify On
NTF_CUT	Cut is requested
NTF_PASTE	Paste is requested
NTF_DVKEY *	DESQview key is entered
NTF_DVDONE *	DESQview menu is closed

* indicates notification sent no matter where mouse points

Once a notification event is enabled with win_notify(), DESQview sends a message to the default mailbox object of the task that opened the window if: a) the notification event occurs, and b) the mouse pointer is pointing to the window. (For those notification events marked with an asterisk, the second requirement is not necessary.)

This is sometimes a very useful capability. For example, a DESQview-specific word processor might want to be informed if the user attempts to close it from the DESQview menu. When the close message arrives, the editor can then ask the user whether it should save the file being edited before the application is terminated and the edits lost. (In addition, the word processor might disable notification of the Close Window command when the file has not been changed, such as immediately after a save. Closing the program at this point will not lose data. The program might then reenable notification of the Close command when the buffer has been changed and data could be lost.)

An even more interesting notification event is the Help event. With notification of this event enabled, the application receives a message whenever the user enters the Help command on the DESQview menu. This knowledge lets a user application add its own Help capability to that of DESQview.

Messages to Other Object Types

Besides using the keyboard and mailbox objects, DESQview uses two other object types to communicate with the user application: the pointer object and the timer object.

The pointer object is the interface between the program and the "pointing device." The location of the mouse pointer is indicated by a white diamond on the screen. The pointing device might be a mouse, but DESQview also supports something known as a "keyboard mouse." When using the keyboard mouse, pressing the "mouse key" causes the diamond to appear on the screen. It can then be moved about with the arrow keys. Pressing the mouse key once more returns the arrow keys to their normal use.

After creating a pointer object using the ptr_new() API function, an application must associate that pointer with a window, using the ptr_open() call. Doing so informs DESQview that pointer messages should be sent to that object whenever the pointer is within that window. DESQview normally generates a message whenever the mouse moves enough to cause the mouse pointer to change rows or columns. An application cannot determine mouse resolution finer than a row or a column. The message received contains the row and column of the mouse, plus the status of both the left and right mouse buttons.

The ptr_addto() API call can set flags associated with the pointer object. For example, one flag tells DESQview that the application is not interested in mouse movement, but only in mouse clicks. In this case, DESQview only sends a message when the user clicks either or both mouse buttons. Other flags control whether a message is sent both when the mouse buttons are pressed and released or simply when they are pressed, whether the screen location should be screen relative or window relative, and whether the mouse diamond should be visible or invisible. These flags are outlined in Table 7-2.

Table 7-2: Pointer flags.

Flags	Description
PTF_CLICKS	Only report pointer clicks (default is to report mouse movements as well)
PTF_UPDOWN	Generate message both on press and release (default is press only)
PTF_RELSCR	Row and column are screen-relative (default is window-relative)
PTF_MULTI	Multiclick messages (accumulate rapid clicks and report them together instead of individually)
PTF_BACK	Generate messages even when app is in background
PTF_NOTTOP	Generate messages even when window is not top-most in application
PTF_HIDE	Hide pointer diamond when in window

Normally, only the top window of the top-most application receives pointer messages. This prevents the user from selecting a menu option when a submenu has been opened on top of it. An application can specify, however, that a task wants to receive pointer messages, even if it is not the top-most window. In fact, a window can indicate that it wants to receive pointer messages, even if its application is not top-most; that is, it is executing in the background. Of course, no matter what is selected, the application only receives messages when the pointer is within a visible portion of its associated window.

Notice that although our CLOCK program accepts mouse input, because it performs all input through the panel, it can allow DESQview to handle the mouse. CLOCK, therefore, does not open a pointer object itself.

The final object type is the timer object. As the name implies, user applications use this object type to measure or delay specific lengths of time. A timer object is first created with a tim_new() API call. It may then be set to go off either for a specific time of day, using the tim_write() function, or after a given duration, using the tim_addto() call. Once a timer object is set, a task may then read the object using tim_read().

Just as with any other object, reading an empty timer object results in the calling task being suspended. When the timer expires, DESQview sends a message to the object, and the task is unsuspended. The task does not continue execution until the next time it is scheduled. A task may "peek" into a timer object to see how much time is left with a separate API call.

CLOCK uses both forms of timer object. The ticktock() function delays for one second at a time between updates of the clock window, while setalarm() sets a timer object to expire at the user-selected alarm time. A portion of ticktock() appears below:

```
ulong timpause;

timpause = tim_new();
for (;;) {
    /*start a 1 second timer and wait for it to expire*/
    tim_addto (timpause, 100);
     tim_read (timpause);
              .
              .
              .
 }
```

With so many different types of objects about, servicing them all could get quite confusing. Consider, for example, a program that poses a question to the user and awaits input. Suppose that, just to be user-friendly, this program puts up a help screen if the user selects Help or if there is no input for 10 seconds. To do this, the task must read three different objects: the keyboard object from where input is to come; a timer object, which will go off after 10 seconds; and the default message object, where DESQview will send a message if the user selects Help.

The task cannot simply read any of these objects, since doing so suspends the task until a message appears in the object read, irrespective of what might happen to the others. The task could poll each of the objects using the _sizeof() calls in a loop, rescheduling after each pass via an api_pause() call to allow other tasks a chance to execute. As soon as _sizeof() returns a nonzero count for any of the objects, the task can then read it out without fear of being suspended.

This isn't a very clean solution, and it wastes CPU time. The task must repeatedly be scheduled to run even though all that is likely to happen is that it will check three empty queues and then give up control again. It would be better if the task could suspend itself until a message appeared in any of its objects.

For this, DESQview defines a special object known as the object queue. The object queue is simply a queue of object handles. Unlike other object types, a task has only one object queue. (It is created automatically when the task is started, and may not be deleted with an obq_free(), nor can new ones be added with an obq_new() call.) Every time a task creates a new object (or has one created for it; for example, when it applies a panel), the object is added to the object queue's list. Whenever a message is sent to any of these objects, the handle of that object is placed in the object queue.

Reading the object queue via an obq_read() suspends the calling task. When a message appears in any of the task's objects, the handle of the object is returned from the obq_read() call. This handle is then compared with the handles returned from the previous _new() calls to determine which object has received the message. Objects may be prioritized under DESQview 2.20 and later, so that certain objects go to the front of the list to be serviced even when other handles are already queued up.

CLOCK reads the object queue when waiting for either keyboard input from the Clock panel or for the alarm timer when the alarm clock expires. The code to do that appears below:

```
for (;;) {
     /*now wait for an event to occur*/
      obqhan = obq_read();
```

```
        if (obqhan == panelkey)    /*keyboard input*/
            alarmonoff (panhan, panelwin,
                        timalarm, panelkey);

         if (obqhan == timalarm)    /*alarm timer*/
             declarealarm (panelwin);
    }
```

This is the normal structure of a DESQview-specific task with multiple inputs.

Why use DESQview?

As a DOS-based multitasking environment, DESQview has its limitations. It does allow the user to run DOS extender programs that are compatible with the Virtual Control Program Interface (VCPI), but otherwise provides no support for single programs larger than 640KB comparable to the memory management in Microsoft Windows. It does not run in protected mode on 286 CPUs, so it cannot take advantage of extended memory on 286-based machines. And its character mode-based windows and panels are not as attractive as the graphics-mode displays of Windows.

But weighed against these drawbacks, DESQview provides an elegant object-oriented model of communication, both between application tasks and between applications and the multitasking environment. The DESQview API is straightforward and easy to learn (it has a much shorter learning curve than Windows, for example). The DESQview Panel Design Tool allows rapid development of uniform but highly adaptable windows for information display and data entry. Most important, DESQView's overhead is low, and its hardware requirements are small. Applications run under DESQview retain 90 percent of their performance on plain, non multitasking DOS. DESQview occupies a scant 200KB of RAM (including DOS). And DESQview can (unlike Windows) be used effectively on 8086/88 machines.

It is interesting to anticipate what the future might hold for DESQview. As of this writing, Quarterdeck's next generation product, DESQview X is still in final test, due for release in the latter half of 1991. DESQview X is a full implementation of X-Windows Ver. 11, Release 4; however, unlike most X-Windows implementations, DESQview X has at its core not Unix but DESQview.

X-Windows is a full featured, windowing environment that has become the standard for workstations, irrespective of manufacturer. In addition, X-Windows supports execution over LANed environments, including remote task activation and file sharing. X-Windows has not historically been available to the PC world due to the amount of equipment necessary to run it properly (a minimum X-Windows configuration would typically be 8 megabytes of RAM and 200 megabytes of disk on a 4 MIP machine.)

Much of these hardware requirements stem from Unix, however. By replacing Unix with the much smaller DESQview kernel, Quarterdeck has demonstrated X-Windows applications executing satisfactorily on a 20 MHz 80386 with 2 Megabytes of RAM. Since X-Windows applications tend not to access Unix, making their requests for services through X-Windows instead, many X-Windows applications will become immediately portable to DESQview X as soon as it becomes available.

In short, DESQview is an environment capable of ushering programmers into the next generation of application software, without giving up support for the last generation of DOS-based software and the huge existing base of 8086/88-based PCs.

Chapter 8

VCPI for EMS/DOS Extender Compatibility

Robert Moote

VCPI (Virtual Control Program Interface) is a program interface that allows EMS emulators and DOS extenders to coexist on an 80386- or 80486-based PC. The interface is defined as an extension to EMS 4.0; it consists of a set of calls provided by the EMS emulator (the VCPI server) and used by the DOS extender (the VCPI client). Without the cooperation made possible by the VCPI interface, a user could not run an extended DOS application on a machine with an EMS emulator installed.

Conceptually, VCPI is quite simple. The principal services provided by a VCPI server are mode switching and memory management. The mode switching services allow the VCPI client to switch from V86 mode to protected mode and back, and the memory management calls offer access to the memory pool managed by the EMS emulator. The VCPI server and client have a "peer" relationship; they each administer separate, privileged, protected mode program environments. This design was chosen because it made VCPI support relatively easy to implement in existing EMS emulators and DOS extenders. It is also the fundamental difference between VCPI and DPMI; a DPMI client runs as an unprivileged program in the environment provided by the DPMI server.

VCPI was originally designed and implemented (in 386 | DOS-Extender and QEMM-386) in late 1987 by Phar Lap Software and Quarterdeck Office Systems. A VCPI Developer's Conference held in April 1989 resulted in some fleshing out of the specification, but no changes to the interface. Participants in the 1989 conference included Ergo Computing, Lotus Development Corp., Phar Lap Software, Quadram, Qualitas, Quarterdeck Office Systems, and Rational Systems. Today, all widely used EMS emulator and DOS extender products support the VCPI standard.

The primary goal of VCPI is interoperability between EMS emulators and extended DOS applications, with no need for intervention by the end user. Because EMS emulators can be configured in a number of ways to solve a variety of problems, that goal is not always achieved. We'll start off this chapter with a look at what kind of EMS emulator configurations can result in puzzling error messages like "Can't run in V86 mode" from extended DOS applications, and how to eliminate such problems.

The bulk of the chapter is concerned with describing the contention that arises between EMS emulators and DOS extenders, and how VCPI works to resolve the conflicts. Because most programmers will never write code that makes VCPI calls (very few people other than writers of EMS emulators or DOS extenders have occasion to use VCPI directly), this chapter does not provide guidelines or programming examples for using VCPI. Instead, to illustrate the use of VCPI, we'll see an example of a DOS extender making VCPI calls to run a simple protected mode program, and take a close look at a code fragment that switches between the EMS emulator and DOS extender environments, one of the trickier operations in a VCPI server implementation.

End-User Encounters with VCPI

It's extremely frustrating to install an EMS emulator, or switch to using Microsoft's EMM386 emulator when installing DOS 5.0, and suddenly have one or more extended DOS applications, such as 1-2-3 or AutoCAD 386, stop working. You may get a cryptic error message to the effect that the program can't run in V86 mode. Or the program may complain of lack of memory, or run much more slowly than it used to. What's going on?

One clue is that EMS emulators aren't marketed as EMS emulators any more; they're called memory managers. In addition to expanded memory, most EMS emulators now also provide XMS services, backfilling unused memory locations between 640KB and 1 MB with RAM, and a "loadhigh" feature for loading device drivers and TSRs into the backfilled memory above 640KB. The loadhigh capability is a particularly popular solution to the RAM cram problem below 640KB. With these added features come more complex configuration options for the EMS emulators, and some configurations can cause difficulties for extended DOS applications.

The NOEMS Option

If you're using an EMS emulator primarily to load device drivers high, you want as much backfilled memory above 640KB as possible. Turning off the EMS interface frees up a 64KB memory region that is normally used for the EMS page frame. In fact, this option (typically called *noems*) is explicitly recommended by Microsoft's documentation for DOS 5.0.

Unfortunately, turning off EMS also turns off VCPI, because VCPI is an extension to the EMS interface. Without VCPI, extended DOS applications cannot run, because the EMS emulator is using V86 mode to backfill memory, so the DOS extender can't switch to protected mode. This is the source of those "Can't run in V86 mode" error messages; don't use the *noems* option if you want to run extended DOS applications.

The FRAME=NONE Option

A better way to obtain more backfilled memory is disabling the EMS page frame without turning off the EMS interface. This option, typically called *frame=none*, is explicitly permitted by the EMS interface spec, and is supported by most EMS emulators (including Microsoft's EMM386, though it isn't mentioned in the DOS 5.0 documentation). With the EMS interface active, VCPI is available so extended DOS applications can run.

With the EMS page frame disabled, real mode programs can allocate EMS memory, but can't map it into the first megabyte to access it. However, DOS extenders are able to use EMS memory via VCPI calls, so extended DOS applications can still use all available memory.

There are some extended DOS applications that can't run with the *frame=none* option selected. While most DOS extenders now make no use of the EMS page frame (precisely so they can work with frame=none), older versions of some extenders required a page frame. If you use an application built with one of these older DOS extenders, you'll have to give up on using the 64BK EMS page frame region for backfilled memory.

Whether or not disabling the EMS page frame is possible, DOS 5.0 users can usually load more device drivers and TSRs high by switching from EMM386 to a more sophisticated memory manager such as QEMM-386 or 386-to-the-MAX. These products do a better job of finding unused locations between 640KB and 1 MB to use for backfilled memory, and also offer considerably more flexibility in locating individual drivers in backfilled memory to minimize fragmentation and wasted memory.

Memory Partitioning and Insufficient Memory Problems

You may notice that your extended DOS application runs more slowly with an EMS emulator installed. This is usually the result of less memory being available to the application, so that it has to keep more data on disk, or (if it uses virtual memory) it is paging more heavily. Usually reduced memory availability is a result of partitioning of the computer's extended memory into part EMS memory and part XMS memory, or into part EMS memory and part extended memory. Most extended DOS applications will only allocate the EMS memory, and memory available from other sources will go unused. While currently only Phar Lap's 286 | DOS-Extender and 386 | DOS-Extender are capable of simultaneously allocating all available EMS, XMS, and extended memory, other DOS extender vendors will likely follow suit because partitioning of extended memory is much more common since the advent of DOS 5.0. However, end users will have to deal with extended DOS applications that don't "see" XMS or extended memory when an EMS emulator is installed for some time to come, because of the time lag between the introduction of new features in DOS extenders and the release of new application versions that incorporate the new extenders.

If you suspect memory partitioning is causing an application to run slowly, use a memory utility program to see how much EMS, XMS, and extended memory is available. (Most EMS emulators include a utility that can display available memory, or under DOS 5.0 use the MEM program).

If extended memory is partitioned into some EMS and some extended memory, the solution is simple: just give all the memory to the EMS emulator. Extremely few programs other than disk caches and RAM disks (and extended

DOS applications) use extended memory directly, and even those are usually capable of using EMS memory instead. If necessary, leave just enough extended memory free for the disk cache or RAM disk driver.

If extended memory is partitioned into some EMS and some XMS memory, if possible use the same solution: give all the memory to the EMS emulator. However, that may not be feasible; for example, if you sometimes run Windows you need XMS memory to be available. This is a very common situation with DOS 5.0, because you want XMS memory to load DOS high (in the XMS HMA) and also to run Windows, and you want EMM386 to load device drivers high.

The best solution to EMS/XMS partitioning is to replace the HIMEM.SYS and EMM386.SYS combination in DOS 5.0 with a single memory manager such as QEMM-386. QEMM supports both XMS and EMS in a single driver, and allocates both XMS and EMS memory out of the same memory pool—so there is no need to partition memory. (You can tell if EMS and XMS memory is partitioned or is allocated from the same memory pool by running the DOS 5.0 MEM program and examining the total amount and available amount of both EMS and XMS memory). Getting rid of the need to fiddle with memory sizes and partitioning will make life much easier.

Why VCPI: Incompatibilities Between EMS Emulators and DOS Extenders

VCPI was designed to solve compatibility problems between EMS emulators and DOS extenders. To see how conflicts arise, let's review how these products work.

DOS extenders allow large applications to run under DOS by making it possible for them to run in protected mode. A DOS extender provides a protected-mode environment on top of the standard DOS environment, and also directly allocates extended memory for use by the application program. While implementation details differ, this process is fundamentally the same on a 286 machine as on a 386 or 486.

EMS emulators are software-only products that turn extended memory into expanded memory. An EMS emulator directly allocates a chunk of extended memory and makes it look like expanded memory to programs making EMS calls. On 286 PCs, this is done by using the BIOS Block Move Int 15h Function 87h call to physically copy memory contents as EMS pages are mapped in. On 386/486 machines, the emulator uses the protected mode of processor operation to take advantage of the hardware paging capabilities of the chip, thereby avoiding costly memory copying operations.

On any 286 or later machine there is contention for extended memory. Without VCPI, a user who runs both extended DOS applications and EMS-sensitive applications is forced to either reboot the machine between applications in order to install and deinstall the EMS emulator, or partition extended memory by configuring the EMS emulator to allocate some extended memory and leave some free. Neither approach is desirable, since both are inconvenient for the user.

On 386 and 486 PCs, additional conflicts arise out of the need of both the EMS emulator and the DOS extender to use protected mode. The only way to run an extended DOS application is to turn off the EMS emulator or deinstall it. If the emulator is turned off, the memory in the EMS memory pool cannot be used, and the computer must be rebooted to remove the emulator.

VCPI is designed to solve both the extended memory contention problems and the protected-mode conflicts. Since VCPI is 386/486-specific, we cannot use it for compatibility on 286 PCs. The reasons for this choice are: 1) protected-mode conflicts do not exist on 286s, and 2) EMS emulators are not popular on the 286, due to the overhead required for memory copying; most 286 EMS users install add-in hardware EMS boards instead.

Protected-Mode Conflicts

EMS emulators for 386- or 486-based PCs operate in protected mode and use V86 mode to run DOS and DOS-based applications. Using V86 mode allows the EMS emulator to utilize the paging capability of the processor, while still permitting standard 8086 DOS programs to execute. When an EMS emulator is installed, the processor runs primarily in V86 mode. When an interrupt occurs, the EMS emulator control software gains control in protected mode; it then chooses whether to service the interrupt in protected mode (for EMS system calls), or "reflect" the interrupt back to V86 mode for normal processing by the DOS or BIOS interrupt handler.

When the processor runs in V86 mode, it always operates at privilege level 3, the least privileged level. Software executing above privilege level 0 cannot execute certain instructions, including instructions to access the system registers (control registers, debug registers, and so on). Thus, when an EMS emulator switches the processor to V86 mode, a DOS extender cannot subsequently gain control of the machine and switch to protected mode for its own purposes. Any attempt to switch to protected mode results in a processor exception, which passes control to the EMS emulator's protected-mode exception handler.

Since an unaided switch to protected mode is not possible, extended DOS applications cannot run on a 386 or 486 PC with an EMS emulator installed. Recall that 286-specific DOS extenders can also run on 386/486 systems; they still run in protected mode, but differ from 386/486 DOS extenders by supporting 16-bit rather than 32-bit execution. While the protected mode compatibility problem is restricted to operation on 386/486 PCs, all DOS extenders, including 286-specific products, are affected.

The most important service that VCPI provides is, therefore, a means for a DOS extender to switch between V86 mode and protected mode. This service actually involves more than just switching processor modes. Since both the EMS emulator and the DOS extender provide protected-mode environments, the mode switch must also be accompanied by a switch to the appropriate environment. The DOS extender uses several VCPI calls to initialize its own protected-mode environment, making this mode and environment switching possible.

Extended Memory Allocation

Before we examine the problem of memory contention between DOS extenders and EMS emulators, let's see how DOS programs allocate extended memory.

MS-DOS is an 8086 program, and can only address memory below 1 megabyte. For this reason, no DOS services exist to allocate extended memory. Extended memory is an important resource used not only by EMS emulators and DOS extenders, but also by popular products such as RAM disk drivers, disk cache programs, and XMS drivers. Programs must mark their usage of extended memory to prevent corruption by another program attempting to use the same memory. Two common techniques exist for allocating extended memory: top-down and bottom-up.

Top-down memory allocation obtains memory from the end of extended memory, down. The program allocating extended memory hooks the BIOS Get Extended Memory Size call Int 15H Function 88H and reduces the apparent extended memory size accordingly. Suppose that a program needs 1 megabyte of extended memory, and is executing on a machine with 3 megabytes of extended memory (4 megabytes of total memory): it installs an Int 15H handler that returns 2 megabytes (rather than 3) when the BIOS Get Extended Memory Size call is made. The program has effectively allocated extended memory between 3 and 4 megabytes.

Bottom-up memory allocation takes extended memory, starting at 1 megabyte, and grows up. The bottom-up technique is an older, more complicated method first used by the IBM VDISK driver. The extended memory usage is marked in two locations. A program using bottom-up allocation must hook Int 19H, the reboot interrupt. At a specific offset in the segment at which the Int 19H interrupt vector points, the program places an ASCII signature identifying the owner of the interrupt as a VDISK driver. At a second offset in the same segment is a value specifying the amount of extended memory the program uses.

The second location at which a program using bottom-up allocation marks its memory usage is a data structure called a *boot block* (remember, this method was first used by a RAM disk product). The boot block data structure is always placed in memory at 1 megabyte. Among other information, it contains a signature identifying it as a VDISK, and a value indicating its usage of extended memory.

Regardless of which technique a program uses, it must respect allocations already made by other programs. The top of extended memory must be obtained by calling the BIOS Get Extended Memory Size function. The bottom of extended memory is calculated by checking for a VDISK signature and extended memory usage in both the Int 19H handler and the boot block at 1 megabyte. Cautious programs print a warning message and use the larger of the two bottom-up values if they differ, or if a VDISK signature is found in one location but not in the other.

Most or all currently available EMS emulators, DOS extenders, disk cache programs, and XMS drivers use top-down extended memory allocation. Older RAM disk drivers use the bottom-up allocation technique.

Both top-down and bottom-up allocation permit multiple programs to allocate extended memory. However, both techniques suffer from the same restriction: for each technique, only the last program to allocate extended memory can dynamically modify the amount of memory allocated. For example, if program A uses top-down allocation to take memory from 3 megabytes to 4 megabytes, and program B later uses top-down allocation to obtain memory from 2 megabytes to 3 megabytes, program A cannot increase (or decrease) its usage of extended memory, because it is no longer first in the Int 15H handler chain.

Figure 8-1 shows an example of memory allocation on a machine with 8 megabytes of memory and four active programs using extended memory. One program, a RAM disk, uses bottom-up allocation to obtain memory from 1 to 1.5 megabytes. Three programs have allocated extended memory with the top-down method: first (and therefore last in the Int 15H handler chain), a disk cache using memory from 7 to 8 megabytes; next, an EMS emulator with an EMS memory pool from 4 to 7 megabytes; and last, a DOS extender. In addition to making calls to the EMS emulator to obtain memory from the EMS memory pool, the DOS extender directly allocates extended memory between 2 and 4 megabytes. Extended memory from 1.5 to 2 megabytes, which is still unused, could be allocated by a fifth program using either top-down or bottom-up allocation. Alternatively, either the DOS extender or the RAM disk could choose to increase its memory allocation, since they are the last programs installed using their respective allocation methods. In practice, a RAM disk doesn't change its memory allocation dynamically, but a DOS extender is quite likely to do so.

Figure 8-1: Extended memory allocation.

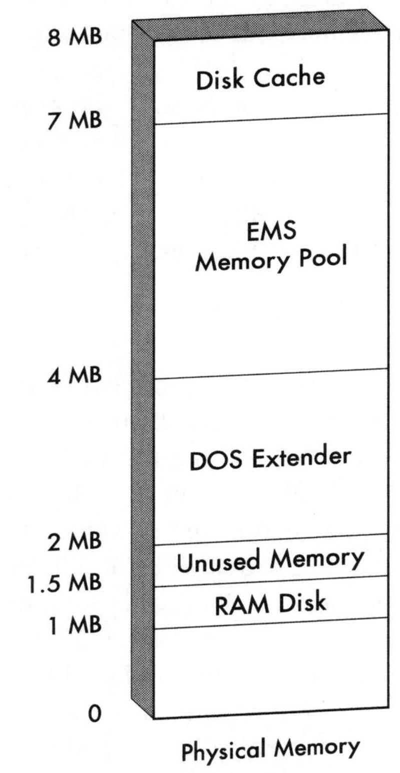

With these techniques for allocating extended memory in mind, we can consider contention problems between EMS emulators and DOS extenders. Since the available allocation methods are not dynamic, an EMS emulator grabs all of its memory when it is installed. If the user configures the emulator to take all available extended memory (the default for most products), none is then available for a subsequent extended DOS application. A DOS extender can, of course, allocate EMS memory; but there is no service in the EMS interface to get the physical address of allocated memory—information that is needed by the DOS extender.

VCPI, therefore, includes services both to allocate EMS memory and obtain its physical address directly, and to obtain physical addresses for memory allocated through the standard EMS interface. Since a user can configure an EMS emulator to take all, some, or none of the available extended memory, a DOS extender should be capable of both allocating extended memory directly and using EMS memory (and, of course, other sources of memory such as conventional DOS memory and XMS memory). The DOS extender can then obtain the maximum amount of available memory regardless of how the user configures the EMS emulator.

The VCPI Interface

VCPI consists of a set of services provided by the EMS emulator (the *server*) and used by the DOS extender (the *client*). Technically, a VCPI server is any program that provides both the EMS 4.0 and the VCPI interface, and a VCPI client is any program that makes VCPI calls. In this chapter, we use the term *server* interchangeably with EMS emulator, and *client* with DOS extender.

Table 8-1 lists the calls provided by a VCPI server (a more complete reference can be found in Appendix C). Some calls are provided in V86 mode only, some in both V86 and protected modes, and one (a mode switch) only in protected mode. V86-mode calls are made via the standard EMS Int 67H interface, with an EMS function number of DEH in register AH, and a VCPI function number in register AL. The client makes VCPI calls in protected mode with a far procedure call to an entry point in the server. The server's protected-mode entry point is obtained during the interface initialization process. As with V86-mode calls, protected-mode VCPI calls set register AH to DEH and pass a VCPI function number in AL.

Table 8-1: VCPI call summary.

Function Number	Modes Available	Function Name	Description
Initialization			
00h	V86	VCPI Presence Detection	Used to detect the presence of an EMS emulator that provides the VCPI interface.

Function Number	Modes Available	Function Name	Description
01h	V86	Get Protected Mode Interface	Allows the server to initialize portions of the client's system tables to facilitate communication between client and server in protected mode.
02h	V86	Get Maximum Physical Memory Address	Returns the physical address of the highest 4K memory page the server will ever allocate.
Memory Allocation			
03h	V86, Prot	Get Number of Free 4K Pages	Determines how much memory is available.
04h	V86, Prot	Allocate a 4K Page	Allocates a page of memory.
05h	V86, Prot	Free a 4K Page	Frees a previously allocated page of memory.
06h	V86	Get Physical Address of 4K Page in First Megabyte	Translates a linear address in the server's memory space to a physical address.
System Register Access			
07h	V86	Read CR0	Obtains value in the CR0 register.
08h	V86	Read Debug Registers	Obtains values in the six debug registers.
09h	V86	Load Debug Registers	Loads specified values into the debug registers.
Interrupt Controller Management			
0Ah	V86	Get 8259A Interrupt Vector Mappings	Obtains the interrupt vectors used to signal hardware interrupts.
0Bh	V86	Set 8259A Interrupt Vector Mappings	Notifies the server that the client has reprogrammed the interrupt controllers to use different interrupt vectors.
Mode Switching			
0Ch	V86	Switch From V86 Mode to Protected Mode	Allows the client to switch to protected mode and set up its own environment.
0Ch	Prot	Switch From Protected Mode to V86 Mode	Allows the client to switch back to execution in V86 mode in the server's environment.

The calls are grouped into five distinct categories. Only the memory allocation calls, and the call to switch from protected mode to V86 mode, are available when the client is executing in protected mode. The same VCPI function number, 0CH, is used for the mode switch call in both directions.

Interface Initialization

When a DOS extender begins execution, it detects the presence of a VCPI server by: 1) checking for the presence of an EMS driver, 2) allocating an EMS page to turn the EMS emulator on if it is off, thus causing it to switch the processor to V86 mode, and 3) making the VCPI presence detection call Function 00H). The EMS emulator must be turned on to enable the VCPI interface.

During initialization, the client makes the Get Protected Mode Interface call Function 01H). This call sets up the conditions that make it possible for the server to switch between its own environment and that of the client, and for the client to make calls to the server from protected mode. The Get Interface call also returns the server's protected-mode entry point for VCPI calls. We will examine this call in more detail in the section *Inside VCPI,* later in this chapter.

The client may optionally choose to use Get Maximum Physical Memory Address Function 02H during initialization. This call is provided for clients who need to know in advance the physical address of the highest memory page that will ever be allocated, so they can initialize their memory management data structures.

Memory Allocation

Memory is allocated in units of 4KB pages under VCPI. Notice this is the page size used by the 386/486 hardware paging unit, not the 16KB page size used by the EMS interface. The EMS memory pool is a contiguous chunk of extended memory allocated by the emulator when it is installed. The memory pool can be thought of as an array of 16KB EMS pages (see Figure 8-2). Each 16KB page is further subdivided into four 4KB pages (which are aligned on 4KB physical address boundaries, a requirement of the processor's paging unit). Memory can be allocated in the EMS memory pool in two ways: 1) by making EMS calls to allocate memory in 16KB units, or 2) by making VCPI calls to allocate memory in 4KB units.

A VCPI client can choose to use either or both of the above allocation methods to obtain memory from the EMS emulator. The VCPI allocation calls are provided for clients who prefer the page size units used by the hardware, or who want to allocate memory in protected mode without the overhead of mode switching. Memory allocated with VCPI calls is required to be in the processor's memory address space (excluding, for example, hardware expanded memory boards).

Figure 8-2: The EMS memory pool.

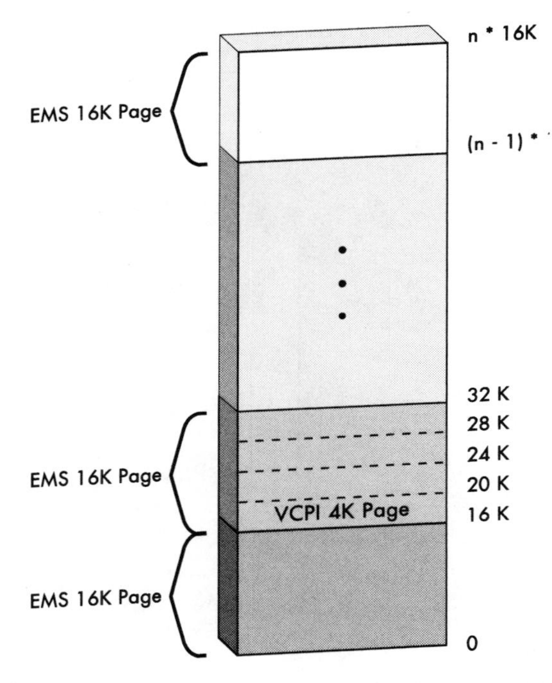

VCPI includes calls to allocate Function 04H and free Function 05H a single 4KB page of physical memory. The number of free 4KB pages available can be obtained via Function 03H. These calls can be made in both V86 and protected mode. Allocated pages are identified by their physical address rather than an arbitrary "handle"; clients must deal in physical memory addresses since they set up their own protected-mode environment, including page tables mapping allocated memory.

The Get Physical Address of 4KB Page in First Megabyte call Function 06H is provided for clients using the EMS interface to allocate memory. The client allocates an EMS page and maps it into the EMS page frame in the usual way. It then calls Function 06H to obtain the physical address of each of the four 4KB pages that make up the EMS page. This call gives the client the ability to allocate EMS memory with standard EMS calls. Unlike the VCPI allocation calls, both the EMS calls and the Get Physical Address VCPI call can be made only in V86 mode, since, of course, the server's environment must be in effect for the server to translate a linear address to a physical address.

Figure 8-3 compares the two methods for allocating physical pages. It shows a physical address space, in which all extended memory is used for the EMS memory pool. On the left side of the diagram, the VCPI Allocate 4KB Page call allocates a single 4KB memory page and obtains its physical address. On the right side, EMS calls allocate a 16KB EMS page and map it into the EMS page frame in the DOS memory space. Then the VCPI Get Physical Address function obtains the physical address of one of the 4K pages in the 16K EMS page.

Figure 8-3: Allocating EMS memory.

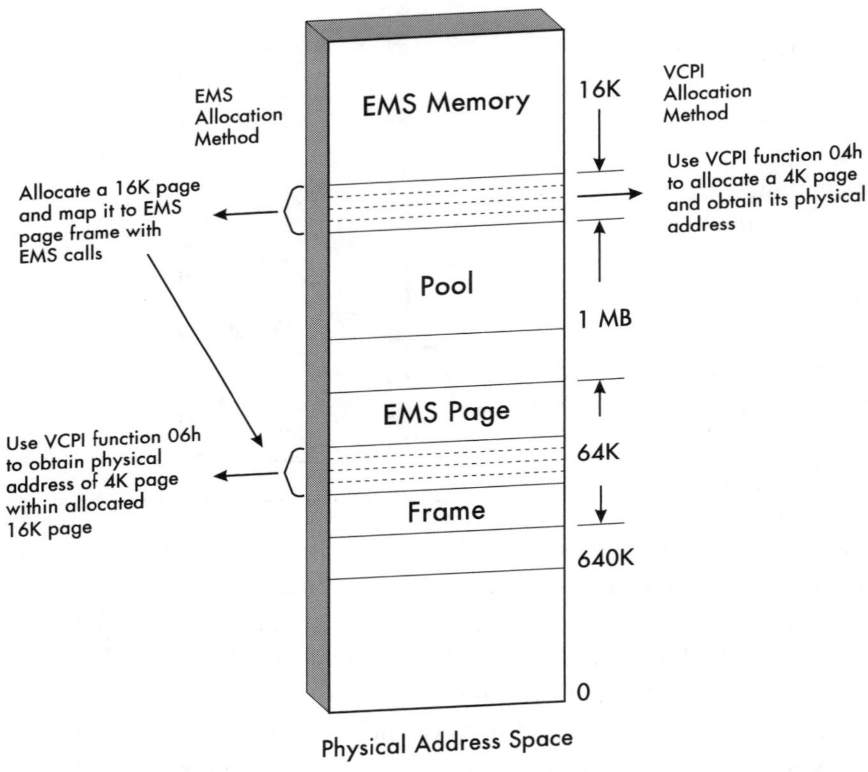

System Register Access

The system registers of the 386/486 processors (CR0, CR2, CR3, GDTR, LDTR, IDTR, TR, the test registers, and the debug registers) cannot be directly stored or loaded in V86 mode; any attempt to do so results in a processor exception. VCPI clients do not need access to most of these registers in V86 mode; several of them are useful only in protected mode, and are loaded as part of the environment switch that is performed when a mode switch is requested. The interface does support V86 mode access to some of the system registers.

Read CR0 Function 07H is provided to give the client the ability to examine the CR0 register, which is not normally accessible in V86 mode. This call exists primarily for historical reasons; many clients do not use it, and the low 16 bits of CR0 can, in any case, be read directly in V86 mode with the SMSW instruction.

The Read Debug Registers and Load Debug Registers calls Functions 08H and 09h allow the client to read and write the processor debug registers in V86 mode. The debug registers are used to set up to four code breakpoints and/or data watchpoints in application programs, and to determine the source of a debug exception. Most 386-specific debuggers use these debug registers.

Since DOS extenders support application programs that run partially in protected mode and partially in real mode, debuggers for extended DOS applications must be capable of setting breakpoints and watchpoints in real-mode code as well as protected-mode code. While a client could always access the debug registers directly by first switching to protected mode, it is often more convenient to read and write debug registers in V86 mode when debugging real-mode code.

Interrupt Controller Management

DOS extenders must handle all interrupts that occur when their protected-mode environment is in effect. Hardware interrupts are often processed slightly differently than software interrupts, so the DOS extender typically needs to know which interrupt vectors are used for hardware interrupts. If the standard DOS hardware interrupt vectors are still in effect, some DOS extenders relocate IRQ0-IRQ7 to make it easier to distinguish between hardware interrupts and processor exceptions.

The Get and Set 8259A Interrupt Vector Mappings calls (Functions 0AH and 0Bh) give the client the ability to determine which interrupt vectors are used for hardware interrupts. In real mode, vectors 08h-0FH are used for IRQ0-IRQ7, and vectors 70h-77H are used for IRQ8-IRQ15. Because interrupts 08H-0FH are also used for processor exceptions, some protected-mode control programs reprogram the interrupt controllers to use different interrupt vectors for hardware interrupts. The Get 8259A Mappings call allows the client to determine which vectors are used for hardware interrupts.

If the standard vector mappings are still in effect, the client is permitted to reprogram the interrupt controllers and make the Set 8259A Mappings call to inform the server of the new vector mappings. If the interrupt controllers have already been reprogrammed, the client is not permitted to modify the mappings.

Mode Switching

A DOS extender must perform mode switches to V86 mode and back again every time an interrupt occurs, whether it is a hardware interrupt, a processor exception, or a software interrupt such as a DOS or BIOS system call. Mode switches are made with the VCPI calls Switch From V86 Mode to Protected Mode and Switch From Protected Mode to V86 Mode. These calls use the same function number (you can think of Function 0CH as the *mode switch* function).

The mode switch calls do more than just switch processor modes; they also switch between the server's and the client's environments. This switching of environments is what really makes VCPI work; it allows both server and client to behave as if they "own" the machine.

Scenario of VCPI Use

As an example of how a DOS extender uses the VCPI interface, let's take a look at some of the actions performed to execute the simple protected-mode assembly language program shown below. The program just makes two DOS calls: one to print the message "Hello world!" and the second to terminate.

```
;
; This is a complete protected mode program. It is built with the
; Phar Lap assembler and linker commands:
;       386asm hello.asm
;       386link hello.obj
;
; It is "bound" with Phar Lap's 386|DOS-Extender as follows:
;       bind386 run386b.exe hello.exp
;
; This creates a HELLO.EXE file, which is run in the standard DOS fashion:
;       hello
;
        assume  cs:cseg,ds:dseg
cseg    segment byte public use32 'code'
```

```
start   proc     near
        mov      ah,09h                    ; Print hello world
        lea      edx,hellomsg
        int      21h

        mov      ax,4C00h                  ; exit to DOS
        int      21h
start   endp
cseg    ends

dseg    segment dword public use32 'data'
hellomsg db      'Hello world!',0Dh,0Ah,'$'
dseg    ends

sseg    segment dword stack use32 'stack'
        db       8192 dup (?)
sseg    ends

        end start
```

Figure 8-4a shows the initialization phase of the DOS extender. The client determines that the VCPI interface is present by using Function 00H as part of the detection sequence described earlier. It then calls Function 0AH Get 8259A Interrupt Vector Mappings to obtain the interrupt vectors used to signal hardware interrupts, so it can set up appropriate protected-mode interrupt handlers for each of the 256 interrupts.

Next, Get Protected Mode Interface Function 01H is called to initialize the page table mappings for up to the first 4 megabytes of the client's linear address space, and to get the protected-mode entry point in the EMS emulator. The DOS extender then completes the setup of the page table mappings for the rest of its protected-mode linear address space, and initializes its system data structures (GDT, LDT, IDT, and so on). In this example, the memory for the system tables is allocated from the EMS memory pool, to minimize use of conventional DOS memory. This is done by allocating and mapping in EMS pages, and using VCPI Function 06H to obtain physical addresses for the 4KB pages within each allocated EMS page. (The DOS extender is unlikely to allocate memory with the Allocate 4KB Page call during initialization because it is not yet prepared to switch to protected mode, so it has no way to initialize memory for which it has only a physical address.)

Figure 8-4a: DOS extender initialization phase.

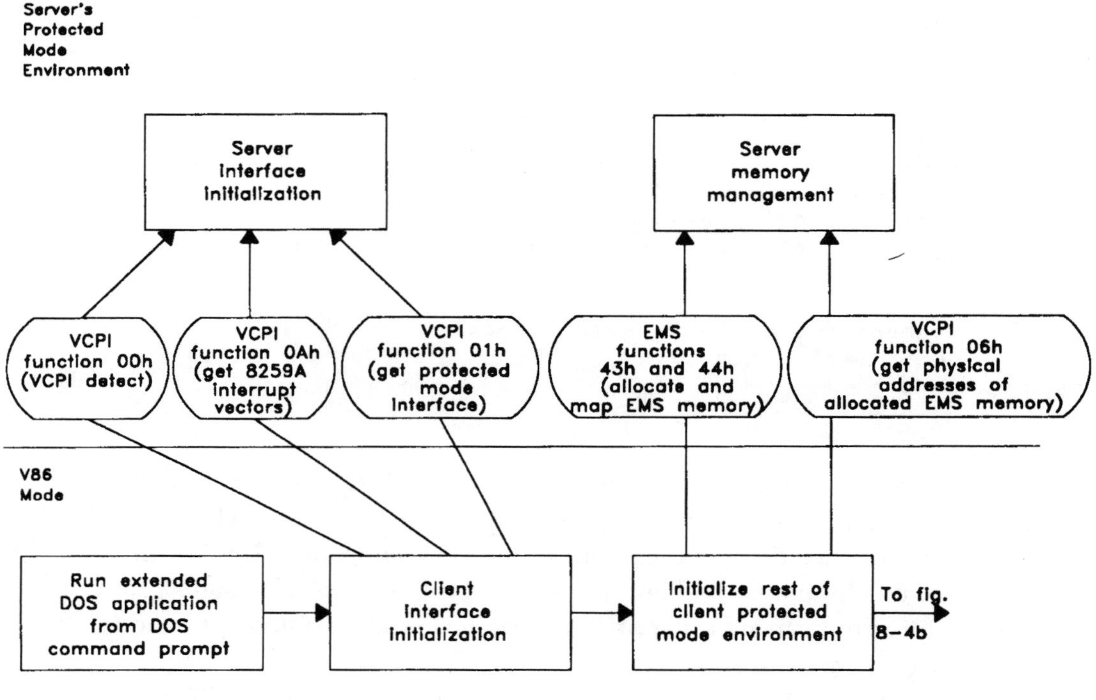

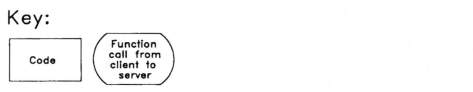

With the above processing completed, the DOS extender is now prepared to switch to protected mode and load the application program. Figure 8-4b shows the program loading phase. First, the DOS extender uses VCPI Function 0CH to switch to protected mode. It then allocates memory in which to load the program by making repeated calls to Allocate 4K Page Function 04H).

Figure 8-4b: Program loading phase.

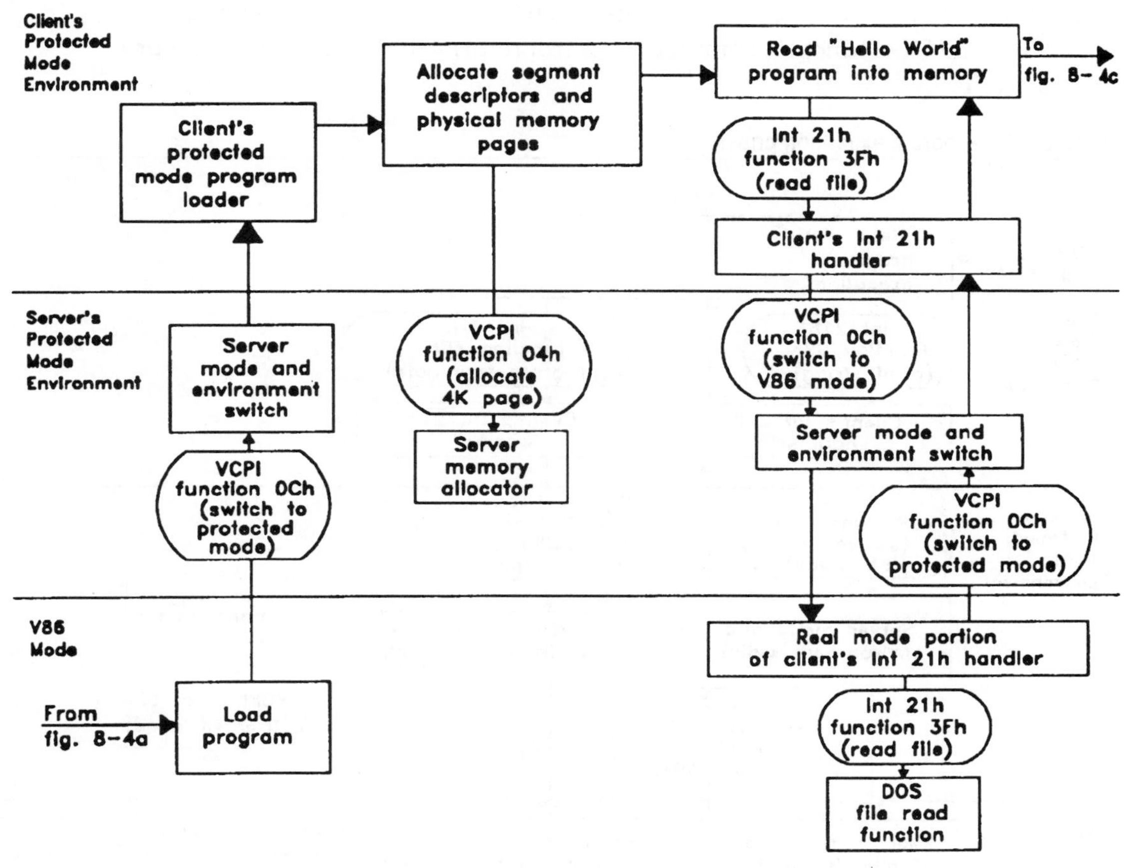

The application program is then loaded into the allocated memory. The file I/O to read the program in from disk is done with DOS Int 21H function calls. The software interrupt causes control to pass to the DOS extender's protected-mode Int 21H handler. This handler switches to V86 mode and reissues the interrupt to DOS, taking care of buffering data appropriately.

Figure 8-4c shows the application program execution phase. The DOS extender passes control to the application's entry point in protected mode. The application issues an Int 21H to print the "Hello world!" string. This invokes the DOS extender protected-mode Int 21H handler, which copies the string to a buffer located in the first 640KB, where it can be addressed by DOS. The handler then switches back to V86 mode and reissues the Int 21H so DOS can process the call. After the DOS function completes, control returns to the application, in protected mode.

Figure 8-4c: Program execution phase.

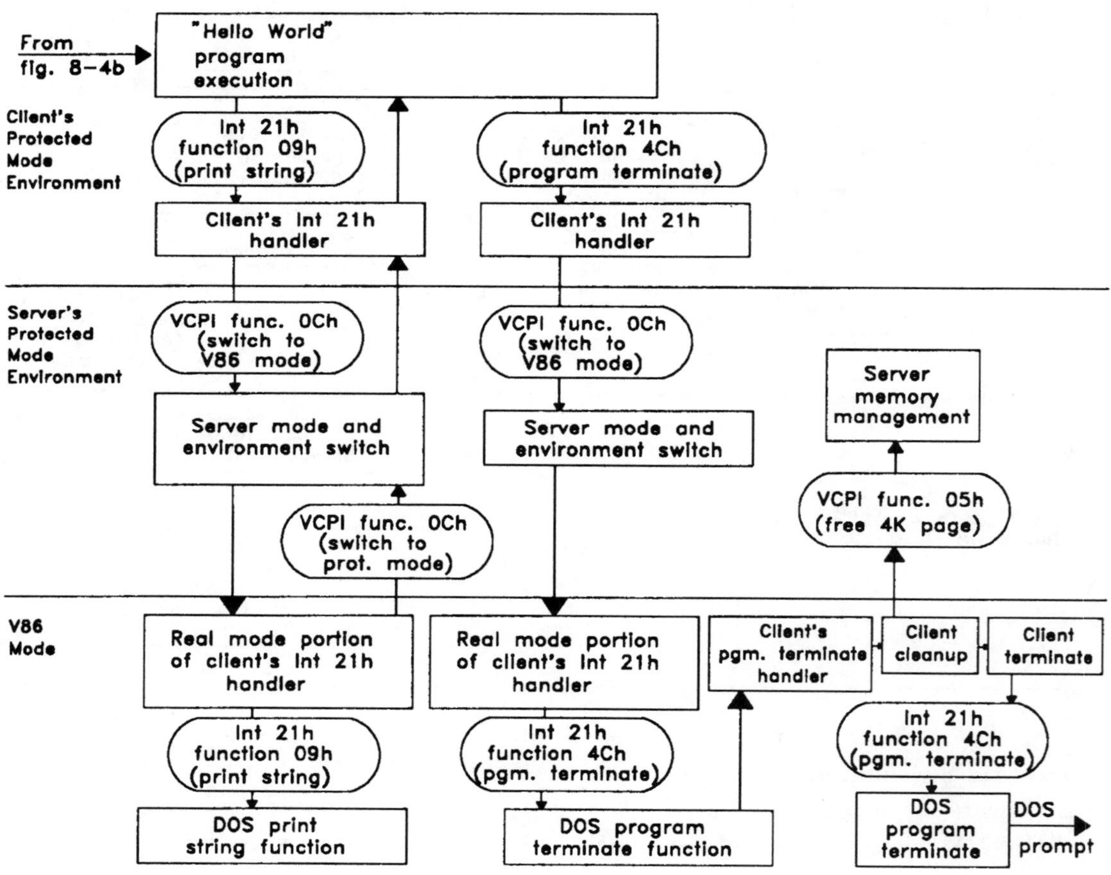

Finally, the application makes the DOS program terminate call, which is handled in the same fashion as the earlier print string call. The DOS extender gets control from DOS in V86 mode after the application program terminates. The client then frees physical memory that was allocated to the application program. VCPI memory is returned to the server with VCPI Function 05H, conventional memory is freed by calling DOS, and so on. After completing its cleanup, the DOS extender calls the DOS terminate function to exit back to the DOS command prompt.

Inside VCPI

Both EMS emulators and DOS extenders, when run independently, "own" the machine; that is, they control the system tables (GDT, LDT, IDT, TSS, and page tables) required for operation when the processor is in protected mode. Each program expects to see its own protected-mode environment (*environment* refers to the set of system tables listed above) when it is active.

Under VCPI, the server always has control while the processor is executing in V86 mode. When the client calls the server to switch from V86 to protected mode, the server must give control to the client in the client's protected-mode environment. Conversely, when the client requests a switch back to V86 mode, the server must switch back to its own protected-mode environment before passing control to the client in V86 mode.

Environment Correspondence

Switching between two protected-mode environments is a tricky operation. Some correspondence between the two environments is required for the switch to be possible. The Get Protected Mode Interface call Function 01H allows the server to initialize two key aspects of the client's environment: the page table mappings for up to the first 4 megabytes of the client's linear address space, and descriptor table entries for up to three segments in the client's GDT.

The server initializes some or all of the client's 0th page table (linear addresses from 0 to 4 megabytes). The interface requires the server to duplicate the first megabyte of its own address space in the client's page table. This linear address space duplication provides the basis for communication between the server and client in protected mode. It also gives the client the ability to access the V86 one-megabyte address space from protected mode when the client's environment is active.

The three segments the server creates in the client's GDT are used for communication between client and server when the client's environment is active. The first segment must be used as a code segment. The second and third may be used in any way the server desires; typically, at least one is used as a data segment. The server locates all three segments in the linear address region shared by the server and the client, since the server has no knowledge of the rest of the client's linear address space.

Address Space Organization

Figure 8-5 demonstrates one possible memory configuration in a VCPI environment. Keep in mind that this example is a simplified diagram and does not accurately depict memory organization under actual EMS emulators or DOS extenders; it leaves out information that does not relate directly to operation under VCPI. This diagram can help us understand how the relationships between the server's and client's environments make VCPI work.

The physical address space in the example is 4 megabytes in size. The first megabyte has the usual DOS configuration: 640KB of RAM memory, with the BIOS ROM and video memory located above 640KB. The entire 3 megabytes of extended memory is allocated by the EMS emulator (with the top-down allocation method) as a memory pool for EMS memory.

At any given moment, either the server's or the client's address space is in effect. As we saw in Chapter 1, the page tables are used to map the linear address space into the physical address space. Since the CR3 register contains the physical address of the page directory, modifying CR3 selects a linear address space by switching to a different set of page tables.

The linear address space set up by the EMS emulator is shown in the left half of the diagram. The first megabyte is given the identity mapping: linear addresses equal physical addresses. Linear addresses up to 2 megabytes are used to map the server's code and data segments. Addresses from 2 to 5 megabytes are used for additional data, such as a memory management area and the system tables (GDT, IDT, and TSS). In this example, the server does not use an LDT. In addition to a system segment for the TSS, the GDT contains the server's code and data segments. The GDT itself is, of course, located in the linear address space; it is shown as a separate structure in the figure to minimize the tangle of arrows.

All of the linear region containing the server's code and data, including system tables, is mapped to physical memory in the EMS memory pool. The server's page tables, mapped by CR3 directly in physical memory rather than in the linear address space, are also placed in the EMS memory pool.

Figure 8-5: Example of environment relationships.

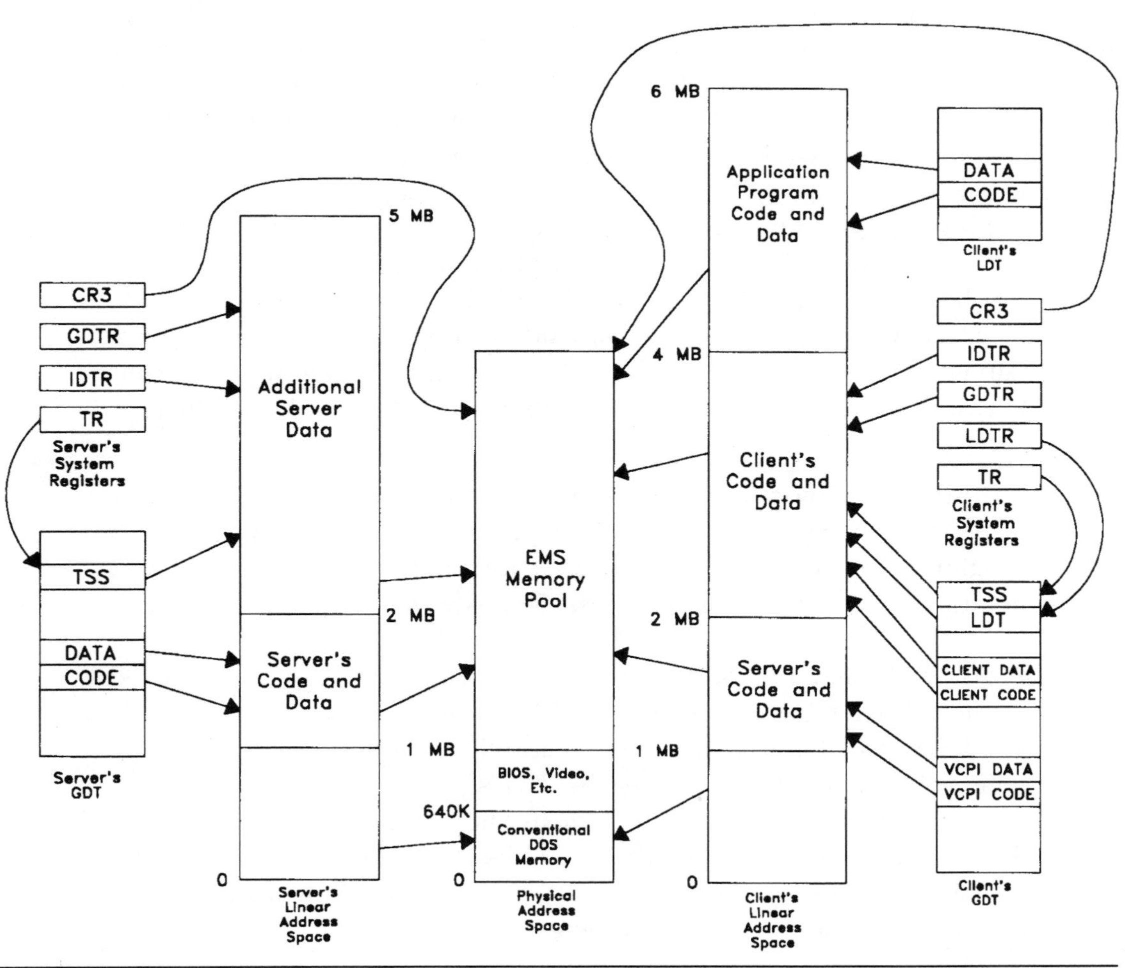

The client's linear address space is on the right side of the diagram. As required by the interface, the client maps linear addresses from 0 to 1 megabytes exactly as they are mapped in the server's address space. In this example, the server has initialized the client's page table such that the two linear address spaces are identical up to 2 megabytes. The server's code and data segments are located above 1 megabyte in the server's address space, and are mapped identically in both environments.

In this example, the DOS extender uses linear addresses from 2 megabytes to 4 megabytes to map its own code and data segments, including its GDT, LDT, IDT, and TSS. Linear addresses from 4 megabytes to 6 megabytes contain the protected-mode application's code and data. The GDT contains six segments: the system segments for the client's LDT and TSS, the client's code and data segments, and the VCPI code and data segments. The server initializes the VCPI segments in the client's GDT when the client makes the Get Protected Mode Interface call.

The linear region containing the client's code, data, and system tables, and the application's code and data, is mapped to physical memory in the EMS memory pool. The client's page tables are likewise allocated in the EMS memory pool.

It is instructive to consider how a real-world configuration might complicate the situation shown in the example. As you read the following (by no means comprehensive) list of likely differences, try to visualize how each item changes Figure 8-5.

- The 64KB of memory directly above 1 megabyte is mapped by the server to physical memory from 0 to 64KB; this is for compatibility with DOS programs, which rely on the address space wrapping at 1 megabyte that occurs when address line 20 is disabled, as is normally the case under DOS.
- A disk cache and a RAM disk are installed; they each use some extended memory, leaving less available for the EMS memory pool.
- The EMS emulator is configured to "backfill" unused address space in the region between 640KB and 1 megabyte. This extra memory is used to load TSRs and device drivers, keeping them out of the 640KB DOS memory. Some linear regions in the server's address space between 640KB and 1 megabyte are now mapped to physical memory in the EMS memory pool, rather than given the identity mapping.

- The EMS page frame, also located between 640KB and 1 megabyte, points to some allocated and mapped EMS pages in the memory pool.
- The client's GDT contains several code and data segments, at least two of which map V86 code and data located in the first 640KB of the linear address space.
- The client's LDT has segments to map the application program's PSP and DOS environment variables in the first 640KB of the linear address space.
- The physical memory allocated for the application's code and data segments (client linear addresses from 4 to 6 megabytes) comes partially from the EMS memory pool, and partially from physical memory below 640KB.
- The DESQview386 multitasker is installed. The first 150KB of the linear address space has the identity mapping, but linear addresses between 150KB and 640KB are mapped to physical memory in the EMS memory pool because more than one virtual machine is active.

Switching Between Environments

Switching from the server's environment to the client's (or back again) requires the following operations:

- Reloading CR3, the page directory base register, which switches from the server's linear address space to the client's.
- Reloading GDTR, the register containing the GDT linear base address and limit.
- Reloading LDTR, the register containing the LDT segment selector. This selector references an LDT system segment descriptor in the client's GDT.
- Reloading TR, the register containing the segment selector for the TSS system segment descriptor in the GDT. Before loading TR, the "task busy" bit in the TSS segment descriptor must be cleared, since the instruction that loads TR sets the task busy bit, and generates a processor exception if the busy bit was previously set.
- Reloading IDTR, the register containing the IDT linear base address and limit.

The server has limited flexibility in its choice of the order in which to perform these operations. CR3 must be loaded first, since all the other register values have relevance only in the context of the client's linear address space. LDTR and TR must be loaded after loading GDTR, since they reference segment descriptors in the GDT. IDTR may be loaded at any point after loading CR3. Note, however, that interrupts must remain disabled for the duration of this operation, since the segment registers all contain selectors referencing the server's GDT—so interrupt handlers (which save and restore the contents of segment registers) must not be permitted to execute.

The VCPI call to switch from V86 mode to protected mode passes to the server the linear address of a data structure containing the client's system register values, and the protected-mode entry point in the client (see the VCPI call descriptions). This VCPI call is implemented in the example below. The environment switch is accomplished with just a few instructions, but the logic is complex enough to be worth a close look.

```
;
; This protected-mode code fragment switches from the server's environment
; to the client's environment and transfers control to the client. This is
; part of the processing performed when the client makes the VCPI call
; Switch From V86 Mode to Protected Mode.
; The code can be assembled with the Phar Lap assembler as follows:
;       386asm switch.asm
;
; The following requirements must be met by the server before calling this
; routine to transfer control to the client:
;  1. This routine and the current stack must both be located within the
;     linear address region that is mapped identically by both server
;     and client.
;  2. DS must be loaded with a selector for a writable data segment whose
;     base address is zero and whose limit is 4 GB.
;  3. Interrupts must be disabled. This routine is required to transfer
;     control to the client with interrupts still disabled.
;  4. On entry to this routine, all general registers contain the values
;     they had when the client issued the Switch to Protected Mode call.
;     This routine can modify only EAX, ESI, and the segment registers.
;

        .prot           ; enable assembly of privileged instructions
        assume  cs:cseg
cseg  segment byte public use32 'code'
switch      proc    far

;
; Format of the data structure to which ESI points on entry to this routine
;
SWSTR   struc
        SW_CR3          dd      ?       ; client's CR3 value
        SW_GDTOFFS      dd      ?       ; offset of client's GDTR value
        SW_IDTOFFS      dd      ?       ; offset of client's IDTR value
        SW_LDTR         dw      ?       ; client's LDTR value
```

```
        SW_TR           dw      ?       ; client's TR value
        SW_EIP          dd      ?       ; entry point in client
        SW_CS           dw      ?
SWSTR   ends

        mov     eax,[esi].SW_CR3        ; load CR3 to switch to client's linear
        mov     cr3,eax                 ; address space
        mov     eax,[esi].SW_GDTOFFS    ; set up client's GDT
        lgdte   pword ptr [eax]
        mov     eax,[esi].SW_IDTOFFS    ; set up client's IDT
        lidte   pword ptr [eax]
        lldt    [esi].SW_LDTR           ; set up client's LDT
        mov     eax,[esi].SW_GDTOFFS    ; set EAX = linear base address of
        mov     eax,2[eax]              ; client's GDT
        push    ebx                     ; index to client's TSS descriptor
        mov     bx,[esi].SW_TR
        and     ebx,0FFF8h
        add     eax,ebx
        pop     ebx
        andbyte ptr 5[eax],not 2    ; clear task busy bit in TSS descr.
        ltr     [esi].SW_TR             ; set up client's TSS
        jmp     pword ptr [esi].SW_EIP  ; jump to client's entry point

switch  endp
cseg    ends
        end
```

The first operation the code performs is reloading CR3, which sets up the client's page tables, thus switching to the client's linear address space (the right-hand side of Figure 8-5). Since an entry requirement of the routine is a DS segment with a base address of zero and a limit of 4 gigabytes, the linear address in ESI is used as a direct offset in the (assumed) DS data segment. For this operation to succeed, the code and any data it references (including its stack) must be located in the linear region (0 - 2 megabytes in our example) mapped identically in the server's and client's address spaces. Recall that the VCPI call Switch to Protected Mode requires the data structure passed in by the client to reside in the first megabyte; this guarantees it can be accessed in either address space.

After switching to the client's address space, and before setting up the rest of the client's environment, we must be careful to avoid any operation that references a linear address above the linear region shared by the server and client. This includes loading segment registers; the GDTR still contains the address of the server's GDT, which is no longer accessible because it is not in the shared linear region. Likewise, interrupts cannot be permitted, since the IDT is also no longer mapped.

You may be wondering how the processor can execute code or access data if the GDT is unavailable. The answer lies in the way the processor addresses segments in protected mode. The segment descriptor in the GDT or LDT is only read when a segment register is loaded with a selector; the processor keeps the segment's linear base address, limit, and access rights in an internal cache register, so it doesn't have to constantly reference the GDT or LDT. Thus, if we don't attempt to reload a segment register, we can continue to use existing server segments, provided they are located in the shared linear address region.

The second and third operations load the GDTR and IDTR registers. These registers contain the linear base address and limit of the client's GDT and IDT. It may seem reasonable to enable interrupts at this point, since the client's page tables, GDT, and IDT are all in effect, but in fact, this isn't possible. To see why, consider how a typical interrupt handler operates. It saves registers it plans to modify—including segment registers—on the stack, processes the interrupt, restores the saved register values, and returns. The trouble arises when the handler reloads segment registers with saved values: the saved values are selectors that reference descriptors in the server's GDT, but the current GDT is the client's GDT.

Next, the LDTR register is loaded. Since the LDTR register contains a segment selector that references a system segment descriptor in the client's GDT, it must be loaded after loading GDTR.

Next, the TR register is loaded. This register contains a segment selector referencing a TSS descriptor in the GDT. The LTR instruction sets the task busy bit in the TSS descriptor, and requires that the busy bit be clear before the instruction is executed. The server must therefore clear the busy bit in the descriptor before loading TR. The tricky part of this operation arises because the client's GDT is not located in the shared linear space. The server, however, has the linear base address of the client's GDT available—it is part of the 6-byte value loaded into GDTR. This requirement to clear the task busy bit is the reason the code needs a DS segment with a limit of 4 gigabytes—the server has no control over where the client locates its GDT in the linear address space.

Finally, the code transfers control by jumping to the client's protected-mode entry point. For reasons noted above, the client must reload all segment registers, including setting up its own stack, before re-enabling interrupts.

Memory Allocation in Protected Mode

Apart from the call to switch back to V86 mode, the only VCPI calls the client can make from protected mode are memory allocation calls (see Table 8-3). These calls are provided in protected mode for program performance. In fact, performance and the convenience of 4KB page size units are the only reasons the Allocate 4KB Page and Free 4KB Page calls are provided at all, since the client can also obtain memory by making an EMS allocate call, mapping EMS 16KB pages into the EMS page frame, and using VCPI Function 06h to obtain physical addresses of the allocated memory.

When the client makes a VCPI call in protected mode, the server gets control with the client's environment in effect (see Table 8-2). The only knowledge the server has of the environment is the portion of the linear address space the server initialized when the client made the Get Interface call, and the three segment descriptors the server set up in the client's GDT. Depending on the architecture of the server program, this may be sufficient to service the VCPI request. If not, the server must switch to its own protected-mode environment, service the call, and then switch back to the client's environment to return the result to the client.

Table 8-2: Data structure for switch to protected mode.

Offset	Description
00H	(DWORD) client's CR3 value
04H	(DWORD) linear address below 1 megabyte of 6-byte variable containing client's GDTR value
08H	(DWORD) linear address below 1 megabyte of 6-byte variable containing client's IDTR value
0CH	(WORD) client's LDTR value
0EH	(WORD) client's TR value
10H	(PWORD) protected-mode entry point in client

Table 8-3: Data structure for switch to V86 mode.

Offset	Description
00H	(QWORD) FAR return address from procedure call (not used)
08H	(DWORD) client's V86-mode EIP value
0CH	(DWORD) client's V86-mode CS value
10H	(DWORD) reserved for EFLAGS value

Offset	Description
14H	(DWORD) client's V86-mode ESP value
18H	(DWORD) client's V86-mode SS value
1CH	(DWORD) client's V86-mode ES value
20H	(DWORD) client's V86-mode DS value
24H	(DWORD) client's V86-mode FS value
28H	(DWORD) client's V86-mode GS value

Summary

When programs use resources not managed by the operating system under which they run, potential conflicts arise. In the case of DOS extenders and EMS emulators, the non-DOS resources used by both are extended memory and the protected mode of processor execution. The VCPI interface is designed to resolve the contention for these two resources.

VCPI can be thought of as an extension of EMS 4.0 for the 386/486, and consists of a set of services used by a DOS extender. The EMS emulator, which is installed first (usually as a device driver at boot time), is the provider of the VCPI interface. When an extended DOS application is run, the VCPI-aware DOS extender detects the presence of the interface and uses VCPI calls to allow it to switch to protected mode and allocate memory owned by the EMS emulator. Most popular EMS emulators, and most DOS extenders used to create protected-mode DOS applications, now support VCPI. PC users can install EMS emulators on their 386 and 486 machines and run extended DOS applications without worrying about conflicts—in fact, without even being aware of any potential resource contention problems or of the existence of VCPI. While VCPI solves only one specific compatibility problem, it is a valuable technology because of the large (and growing) popularity of both EMS emulators and extended DOS application programs.

Chapter 9

The DOS Protected-Mode Interface (DPMI)

Ray Duncan

I will never forget how startled I was when I encountered the DOS Protected-Mode Interface (DPMI) in its primordial form for the first time. I was sitting in a Microsoft OS/2 2.0 ISV seminar in the Fall of 1989, with my mind only about half-engaged during an uninspiring session about OS/2 2.0's Multiple Virtual DOS Machines (MVDMs), when the speaker mentioned in passing that OS/2 2.0 would support a new interface for the execution of DOS Extender applications. This casual remark focused my mind remarkably, because I was at that time up to my ears in the production of the first edition of this very book. The last thing I wanted to hear was that there was an important new protected-mode DOS programming interface which our as-yet-unpublished book was going to totally neglect.

After the speaker finished, I went up to him and asked for more information, explaining that his mystery interface was about to have a severe impact on a book project near and dear to my heart. In a couple of hours, the Microsoftie returned with a thick document entitled "DOS Protected Mode Interface Specification, Revision Pre-release 0.04" still warm from the Xerox machine and generously garnished with "CONFIDENTIAL" warning messages. I suspect I made a most amusing spectacle, as I flipped through the pages with my eyes bugging out and my jaw dropping to the floor. The document I had been handed was nothing less than the functional specification of a protected-mode version of DOS!

In retrospect, the fact that Microsoft was cooking up something like DPMI should have been obvious. Every computer journalist in America, not to mention thousands of beta testers, was well aware that the as-yet-unannounced Windows 3.0 was somehow able to take advantage of extended memory by executing applications in protected mode, even though it ran on top of DOS and used the DOS file system. It was even widely known that you could use a utility program to "mark" the EXE file headers of "old" (i.e. Windows 2.03) applications, and that many such programs would then run (at least for a while) in protected mode although they had not been recompiled or relinked. But I never saw a word of speculation in print on how this was accomplished, and I must confess that for my own part, I never gave it a second thought. I was much too preoccupied with the shifting sands of OS/2 at that point to spend any time puzzling over the internals of a forthcoming version of Windows.

How does Windows 3.0 work its magic? The answer is simple: Windows 3.0 has a built-in DOS Extender, and this DOS Extender is functionally almost identical to the DOS Extenders we've already discussed in Chapters 4 and 5 of this book! When an application is running in protected mode, Windows traps the application's requests for DOS and ROM BIOS services by intercepting its execution of software interrupts (INT instructions). Windows then performs any virtual to physical address conversions that may be required, copies data from extended memory into conventional memory if necessary, switches the CPU into real mode, and re-issues the function call. When control returns from DOS or the ROM BIOS, Windows switches the CPU back into protected mode, converts addresses from physical to virtual and/or copies data from conventional memory to extended memory as appropriate, and finally hands the machine back to the application.

It is ironic that by releasing Windows 3.0, Microsoft legitimized the very DOS Extender technology OS/2 was supposed to replace.

The Politics of Protected Mode

Although the DPMI had its primal origins in the Windows 3 development project, and Windows 3.0 is the only commercially available DPMI server as this chapter is being rewritten for the 2nd edition of this book, the industry DPMI standard as we know it today only vaguely resembles that original internal Microsoft specification I saw so long ago. Microsoft originally defined the DPMI in two layers: a set of low-level functions for interrupt management, mode switching, and extended memory management; and a higher-level interface that provided access to MS-DOS, ROM BIOS, and mouse driver functionality via protected-mode execution of Int 21H, Int 10H, Int 33H, and so on. The higher-level DPMI functions were implemented, of course, in terms of the low-level DPMI functions and the extant real-mode DOS and ROM BIOS interface.

When details of Microsoft's DPMI began to leak out to the general community of MS-DOS developers, the rumors provoked more than a few hard feelings and harsh words for two very good reasons. First, the vendors of other DOS Extenders suspected that Microsoft, having realized that OS/2 was not going to replace DOS any time soon, had decided to barge into the market niche they had established so painfully and elbow them out through the sheer weight of its development resources and marketing power. Second, Microsoft had designed the DPMI with total disregard for compatibility with the existing industry standard for DOS-based protected-mode software—the Virtual Control Program Interface (VCPI).

The VCPI was developed in 1987 by Phar Lap Software and Quarterdeck Office Systems with a fairly narrow objective: to allow 80386 protected-mode DOS Extender applications to coexist with 80386-specific memory managers and expanded memory (EMS) emulators such as Qualitas's 386-to-the-Max and Quarterdeck's QEMM-386. In spite of (or perhaps because of) its limited goals, the VCPI was quite successful. It became an accepted industry standard in April, 1989, and by the beginning of 1990 virtually every 80386-specific software product on the market supported or was capable of using the VCPI interface—except for products of Microsoft.

As we saw in Chapter 8, the VCPI assumes a "client-server" model where the DOS Extender application is the client and the EMS emulator is the server. The client invokes the server via an extension of the Lotus/Intel/Microsoft Expanded Memory Specification (EMS) Int 67H interface to switch between real mode and protected mode, allocate memory, program the interrupt controller(s), and inspect or set the 80386 debug registers. If a VCPI-compliant DOS Extender application is loaded and a VCPI server is not present, the DOS Extender must either abort its execution or (more realistically) assume complete control of the machine and carry out these hardware-dependent manipulations directly.

In the context of the problems it was designed to solve, the VCPI works extremely well, but it is an inadequate platform for *multitasking* of DOS Extender applications. The VCPI allows client programs to run at the highest privilege level (Ring 0). This makes it impossible for a VCPI server to enforce device virtualization (for example, to run graphical applications in a window), provide centralized virtual memory management services, or shield one DOS Extender application from interference by another. Another, somewhat less important drawback of the VPCI interface is that it is fundamentally based on the concept of 80386 hardware paging, and therefore it cannot be implemented on 80286 machines.

The creators of the VCPI were well aware of its limitations, and were already hard at work on a 2nd-generation specification called Extended VCPI (XVCPI) when Microsoft arrived on the scene with the beta-test versions of Windows 3 and its DPMI. For a few months, it appeared that the fledgling DOS Extender market was going to fragment in two mutually-exclusive directions, resulting in additional headaches for software developers, hassles for end-users, and juicy fees for lawyers. Luckily, cooler heads prevailed. Microsoft turned control of the DPMI specification over to an industry committee with open membership, and the previous backers of the XVCPI effort decided to join forces behind the DPMI. Intel, with its understandable enthusiasm for *anything* which might sell more 80386 chips, was instrumental in bringing about this reconciliation, and also took on the responsibility of publishing and distributing the DPMI Specification.

As part of this process of accommodation, Microsoft agreed to the deletion of the portions of the DPMI which cross into DOS Extender territory, specifically, direct support of the DOS and ROM BIOS interrupts in protected mode. Consequently, DPMI version 0.9, the first public version of the specification which was released by the DPMI Committee in May 1990, defines only the "low-level" or "building block" functions that I mentioned earlier. The additional functions in the DPMI version 1.0 specification, which was announced in November 1990 and finally published in March 1991, are also relatively low-level and are directed at specific issues of 386 paged memory management and memory sharing (see Table 9-1). Naturally, the higher-level or DOS Extender interface of Windows 3 still exists, but it has receded back into the twilight zone of semi-support and semi-documentation. The only official Microsoft documentation on the Windows 3 DOS Extender is a five-page technical note, entitled "Windows Int 21H and NetBIOS Support for DPMI," that is mainly remarkable for what it *doesn't* say.

Although the circumstances of DPMI's birth were somewhat stormy, I think it's fair to say that everyone involved now agrees that the DPMI is a sizable improvement over the VCPI. In many respects, a DPMI "host" program is similar to a VCPI server, in that it provides mode-switching and extended memory management services to client programs. But unlike a VCPI server, a DPMI host runs (or can run) at a higher privilege level than its clients using the hardware to enforce a "kernel/user" protection model. This allows a DPMI host to support demand-paged virtual memory and maintain full control over client programs' address spaces and access to the hardware. Furthermore, the DPMI's functions for memory and interrupt management are much more general than those in the VCPI, so the DPMI can be implemented on 80286 machines as well as 80386/486 machines. DPMI version 1.0 also has provisions to support protected-mode TSRs and interprocess communications via shared memory that are not present in VCPI, although these functions are so elaborate that it may be years before DPMI 1.0 servers are widely available.

In the long run, existence of the DPMI *may* simplify life significantly for vendors of DOS Extenders, multitasking environments, expanded memory emulators, and protected-mode programming tools. During the transition period, however, the developers of DOS Extenders in particular are finding their jobs more complicated than ever. Not only must each DOS Extender have to be capable of performing all hardware-dependent management functions on its own, but it must be able to coexist peacefully with primitive bottom-up extended memory allocators like VDISK.SYS, top-down or Int 15H allocators such as the older Compaq disk cache programs, XMS-compatible memory managers such as Microsoft's HIMEM.SYS, VCPI servers such as QEMM or 386-to-the-Max, and DPMI hosts such as Windows version 3.0 and 3.1. This is a goal akin to writing a single graphical application that could execute equally well under Digital Research GEM, Microsoft Windows, OS/2 Presentation Manager, or in the absence of any operating system at all! The recent battles between Microsoft and IBM concerning Windows and OS/2 have also muddied the waters. Microsoft originally stated that Windows 3.1 would be able to run as a DPMI client, but has recently reneged on this commitment—making life more difficult for IBM's OS/2 developers in their quest for Windows compatibility.

The DPMI Programming Interface

DPMI host programs make their services available to client programs via software interrupts 2FH and 31H. The Int 2FH functions are:

- Function 1680H Release Current Virtual Machine's Time Slice
- Function 1686H Get CPU Mode
- Function 1687H Return Real-to-Protected Mode Switch Entry Point
- Function 168AH Get Vendor-Specific API Entry Point

Remember that Int 2FH is the so-called DOS Multiplex Interrupt, used by many different drivers and resident utilities. Most of the DPMI functions supported on Int 2FH can be called in either real or protected mode, and furthermore some of the Int 2FH functions listed above may also be supported by other types of 80386 control programs or multitasking operating systems.

The Int 31H DPMI services are the heart of the DPMI programming interface and are summarized in Table 9-1. They can be grouped into eight general categories:

- The *LDT Management* functions allow a program to manipulate its Local Descriptor Table (LDT). It can allocate and free descriptors (and their associated selectors), inspect or modify the descriptors, map real-mode addresses onto protected-mode selectors, change the access rights of a segment (for example, from read-write to read-only), and obtain a read/write data selector ("alias") for an executable selector.
- The *Extended Memory Management* functions are used to allocate, resize, and release blocks of physical memory above the 1-megabyte boundary. The functions are low-level in that they do not allocate selectors or build descriptors for the extended memory blocks; the program must allocate selectors and map the memory onto the selectors with additional DPMI calls. On an 80386 or 80486 with paging enabled, the allocated blocks are always a multiple of 4 KB. Named shared memory blocks with serialized access are also supported.
- The *Page Management* functions allow memory to be locked or unlocked for swapping on a page-by-page basis, in terms of the memory's linear

address. There are also functions to query the page size supported by the host CPU, and to tune the system's behavior by marking pages for discard or immediate replacement. These functions are only relevant when the host machine is an 80386 or 80486.

- The *DOS Memory Management* functions provide a protected-mode interface to the real-mode MS-DOS Int 21H Functions 48H (Allocate Memory Block), 49H (Free Memory Block), and 4AH (Resize Memory Block). Using these functions, a protected-mode program can obtain memory below the 640 KB limit that it can use to exchange data with MS-DOS itself, TSRs, ROM BIOS device drivers, and other real-mode programs.
- The *Interrupt Management* functions support interception of software or hardware interrupts that occur in real or protected mode, installation of handlers for processor exceptions and faults (such as general protection faults, divide by zero, and overflow), and maintenance of a separate "virtual interrupt flag" for each active process.
- The *Translation Services* provide a mechanism for cross-mode procedure calling. They allow a protected-mode program to transfer control to a real-mode routine by either a simulated far call or a simulated interrupt, and pass parameters by value or by reference. A protected-mode program can also declare an entry point (known as a Real-Mode Call-Back), which can be invoked by a real-mode program with an implied mode switch.
- The *Debugging Services* are used to inspect and modify the 80386/486 debugging registers for execution and data breakpoints. DPMI clients are not allowed to manipulate these registers directly because many DPMI hosts support multitasking and thus must maintain these registers on a per-process basis.
- The *Miscellaneous Services* include coprocessor management, protected-mode TSR support, and functions to get the DPMI version number and DPMI host capabilities.

Table 9-1: DPMI Int 31H Functions Listed by Functional Group.

Function Number	Function Name	DPMI 0.9	DPMI 1.0
LDT Management Services			
0000H	Allocate LDT Descriptor	●	●
0001H	Free LDT Descriptor	●	●
0002H	Map Real-Mode Segment to Descriptor	●	●
0003H	Get Selector Increment Value	●	●
0006H	Get Segment Base Address	●	●
0007H	Set Segment Base Address	●	●
0008H	Set Segment Limit	●	●
0009H	Set Descriptor Access Rights	●	●
000AH	Create Alias Descriptor	●	●
000BH	Get Descriptor	●	●
000CH	Set Descriptor	●	●
000DH	Allocate Specific LDT Descriptor	●	●
000EH	Get Multiple Descriptors		●
000FH	Set Multiple Descriptors		●
Extended Memory Management Services			
0500H	Get Free Memory Information	●	●
0501H	Allocate Memory Block	●	●
0502H	Free Memory Block	●	●
0503H	Resize Memory Block	●	●
0504H	Allocate Linear Memory Block		●
0505H	Resize Linear Memory Block		●
0506H	Get Page Attributes		●
0507H	Set Page Attributes		●
0508H	Map Device in Memory Block		●
0509H	Map Conventional Memory in Memory Block		●
050AH	Get Memory Block Size and Base		●
050BH	Get Memory Information		●
0800H	Physical Address Mapping	●	●

Function Number	Function Name	DPMI 0.9	DPMI 1.0
0801H	Free Physical Address Mapping		●
0D00H	Allocate Shared Memory		●
0D01H	Free Shared Memory		●
0D02H	Serialize on Shared Memory		●
0D03H	Free Serialization on Shared Memory		●
Page Management Services			
0600H	Lock Linear Region	●	●
0601H	Unlock Linear Region	●	●
0602H	Mark Real-Mode Region as Pageable	●	●
0603H	Relock Real-Mode Region	●	●
0604H	Get Page Size	●	●
0702H	Mark Page as Demand Paging Candidate	●	●
0703H	Discard Page Contents	●	●
DOS Memory Management Services			
0100H	Allocate DOS Memory Block	●	●
0101H	Free DOS Memory Block	●	●
0102H	Resize DOS Memory Block	●	●
Interrupt Management Services			
0200H	Get Real-Mode Interrupt Vector	●	●
0201H	Set Real-Mode Interrupt Vector	●	●
0202H	Get Processor Exception Handler Vector	●	●
0203H	Set Processor Exception Handler Vector	●	●
0204H	Get Protected-Mode Interrupt Vector	●	●
0205H	Set Protected-Mode Interrupt Vector	●	●
0210H	Get Extended Processor Exception Handler Vector in Protected Mode		●
0211H	Get Extended Processor Exception Handler Vector in Real Mode		●
0212H	Set Extended Processor Exception Handler Vector in Protected Mode		●
0213H	Set Extended Processor Exception Handler Vector in Real Mode		●
0900H	Get and Disable Virtual Interrupt State	●	●

Function Number	Function Name	DPMI 0.9	DPMI 1.0
0901H	Get and Enable Virtual Interrupt State	●	●
0902H	Get Virtual Interrupt State	●	●
Translation Services			
0300H	Simulate Real-Mode Interrupt	●	●
0301H	Call Real-Mode Procedure with Far Return Frame	●	●
0302H	Call Real-Mode Procedure with Interrupt Return Frame	●	●
0303H	Allocate Real-Mode Callback Address	●	●
0304H	Free Real-Mode Callback Address	●	●
0305H	Get State Save Addresses	●	●
0306H	Get Raw CPU Mode Switch Addresses	●	●
Debug Support Services			
0B00H	Set Debug Watchpoint	●	●
0B01H	Clear Debug Watchpoint	●	●
0B02H	Get State of Debug Watchpoint	●	●
0B03H	Reset Debug Watchpoint	●	●
Miscellaneous Services			
0400H	Get DPMI Version	●	●
0401H	Get DPMI Capabilities		●
0A00H	Get Vendor-Specific API Entry Point	●	●
0C00H	Install Resident Service Provider Callback		●
0C01H	Terminate and Stay Resident		●
0E00H	Get Coprocessor Status		●
0E01H	Set Coprocessor Emulation		●

The DPMI Int 31H functions are only available to programs which are executing in protected mode. A client invokes one of these functions by placing a function number in AX, passing other parameters in registers or by reference, and executing a software interrupt 31H. For example:

```
mov   ax,function_number     ; select DPMI function
.                            ; load other registers with
.                            ; function specific parameters
int   31h                    ; transfer to DPMI host
jc    error                  ; jump if function failed
```

If the function succeeds, it returns the Carry flag clear and (most commonly) other results in registers or in data structures in the client's address space. If the function fails, it returns with the Carry flag set and (in the case of DPMI 1.0) an error code in AX. A list of these error codes can be found in Table 9-2

More detailed information on the DPMI Int 2FH and Int 31H functions can be found in Appendix D.

Using DPMI Functions

Nearly all of the DPMI functions are intended for use by DOS Extenders, which in turn use the DPMI capabilities to implement a "DOS-like" and "ROM BIOS-like" function call interface for use by protected-mode application programs. It's highly unlikely that you will ever need to call DPMI functions directly in a program of your own, unless your program is controlling a memory-mapped device or coprocessor directly or has similar special requirements. But it will help us make more sense of the large and complex DPMI repertoire of function calls if we associate them with what we already learned about how DOS Extenders work in Chapters 4 and 5. Let's put ourselves in the shoes of the author of a typical DOS Extender, and see how we would exploit the DPMI functions to put the burden of hardware management on the DPMI host and make our DOS Extender more portable.

A stand-alone DOS Extender must include a great deal of code to manage mode switching on the various PC architectures, keep all the special CPU registers updated properly, handle all of the possible interrupts and faults that might occur, and maintain the various descriptor tables and page tables that support protected-mode addressing. A DPMI-based DOS Extender is relieved of nearly all of these chores, because they are responsibilities assumed by the DPMI host. In order to make the initial switch into protected mode, instead of building a GDT, LDT, IDT, task state segment, page tables, and the rest, then setting the PE bit in the CPU's machine status word, a DPMI-based DOS Extender first calls Int 2FH Function 1687H to test for the presence of the DPMI host and obtain the mode-switch entry point:

```
mov   ax,1687h     ; get address of DPMI host's
int   2fh          ; mode switch entry point
or    ax,ax        ; exit if no DPMI host
jnz      error
```

If no DPM host is present, register AX is returned non-zero. Otherwise, the registers contain the following values:

- AX = 0
- BX = Flags (bit 0 = 1 if 32-bit programs supported)
- CL = Processor type (02H=80286, 03H=80386, 04H=80486, 05H=80586)
- DH = DPMI major version number
- DL = DPMI minor version number
- SI = number of paragraphs required for DPMI host private data (may be 0)
- ES:DI = DPMI mode switch entry point

The DPMI-based DOS Extender then stores the address of the mode switch entry point into a double-word variable, allocates memory for the DPMI host's private data area if any is needed, puts the paragraph address of that area in register ES, and performs an indirect far call to put the CPU into protected mode:

```
modesw     dd    0                        ; far pointer to DPMI host's
                                          ; mode switch entry point
       .
       .
       .
       mov     word ptr modesw,di         ; save address of
       mov   word ptr modesw+2,es         ; mode switch routine
       or    si,si ; any private data area?
       jz    @@1   ; no, jump

       mov     bx,si                      ; allocate DPMI private data
       mov   ah,48h                       ; area below 1 MB boundary
       int   21h                          ; transfer to DOS
       jc    error                        ; jump, allocation failed
       mov   es,ax                        ; let ES=segment of data area

@@1:   mov   ax,0  ; bit 0=0 for 16-bit app
       call  modesw                       ; switch to protected mode
       jc    error                        ; jump if mode switch failed
       .
       .
       .
```

If the Carry flag is set upon return, the mode switch was unsuccessful, the client is still running in real mode, and register AX contains an error code. If the Carry flag is clear, the CPU has been switched to protected mode, and the following conditions apply:

- CS = 16-bit selector with base of real-mode CS and a 64 KB limit
- SS = selector with base of real-mode SS and a 64 KB limit
- DS = selector with base of real-mode DS and a 64 KB limit
- ES = selector to program's PSP with a 100H byte limit

- FS = 0 (if running on an 80386 or later)
- GS = 0 (if running on an 80386 or later)

Our hypothetical DOS Extender is now in fat city. It can use the DPMI "Allocate DOS Memory Block" function (0100H) to allocate buffers below 640 KB (and selectors that map to those buffers) that it will use to communicate with DOS and the ROM BIOS. It can use the "Allocate Extended Memory Block" function (0501H), "Allocate LDT Descriptor" function (0000H), and "Set Descriptor Contents" function (000CH) to create one or more extended memory blocks to hold the protected-mode application program, and to provide itself (and the application) with executable and data read/write selectors for that memory. It can use the "Map Real-Mode Segment to Descriptor" function (0002H) to create special descriptors for the video refresh buffers, the ROM BIOS data area, the PSP and environment block, and other in-memory structures that applications like to manipulate directly. It can use the "Set Processor Exception Handler" function (0203H) to install its own exception handlers for GP faults and the like. And it can use the "Set Protected Mode Interrupt Vector" function (0205H) to install its own protected-mode handler for MS-DOS Int 21H function calls, as well as for any ROM BIOS, NetBIOS, or other software interrupts it may care to trap and support in protected mode.

Once it reaches this point, the DOS Extender can begin to lean on its own routines, and run like a DOS extended application for a little while to complete the initialization of the actual application. In other words, the DOS Extender can now call Int 21H functions, which of course are intercepted and processed by its own Int 21H handler, to open the file containing the protected-mode application and read the application into memory. It can then perform any necessary relocations on the application's executable code and transfer control to the application's entry point. Once the application is running, the DOS Extender carries out its vital role as an interface between the protected-mode application and real-mode DOS via its interrupt handlers. Any interrupts that the DOS Extender has not specifically installed a handler for will be disposed of appropriately by the DPMI host, usually (unless the interrupt is a fatal CPU exception of some kind) by temporarily switching the CPU into real mode and "reflecting" the interrupt to the real-mode owner of the corresponding interrupt vector.

Let's look a little more closely at how our DPMI-based DOS Extender's protected-mode Int 21H handler might work. There are basically four classes of functions that the DOS Extender must be concerned with:

- Functions which require little more than a mode switch;
- Functions which address application buffers and therefore require data movement and address translation;
- Functions which must be completely replaced to make them meaningful in protected mode; and
- Function calls that are unique to the DOS Extender itself and provide special services that have no equivalent in MS-DOS or the ROM BIOS.

In the first class of functions, all parameters are passed in registers, and the parameters do not include any addresses. The MS-DOS character I/O functions for the console, serial port, and printer are good examples. Handling of these function calls is straightforward. After it has intercepted the Int 21H in protected mode, the DOS Extender stores the registers into a DPMI-defined array called a "real mode register data structure" and then requests the DPMI "Simulate Real Mode Interrupt" function (0300H). The DPMI host saves the protected-mode registers, switches the CPU into real mode, loads up the real-mode CPU registers from the data structure, and issues the software interrupt in real mode—thus passing control to DOS. When DOS returns from the function call, the DPMI host stores the real mode registers into the same data structure, switches the CPU back into protected-mode, restores the original contents of the protected mode registers, and returns control to the DOS Extender's Int 21H handler. The DOS Extender's handler then performs any additional processing it might need, retrieves the results of the function call from the real-mode register data structure, and executes an IRET to return control to the protected-mode application.

The next, somewhat more complex class is composed of functions whose parameters include the address of a buffer or other data structure. In their original form, these addresses are meaningless to MS-DOS or the ROM BIOS for two reasons: the address is in the form of a selector and offset rather than a segment and offset, and the buffer or data almost always lies above the 1 MB boundary. The DOS Extender handles this problem by using buffers below the 640 KB boundary, which it allocated during its initialization, as intermediary storage. For example, in the case of a file write request (Int 21H Function 40H), the DOS Extender intercepts the protected-mode Int 21H, copies the data from the application's buffers in extended memory to a buffer in conventional memory, substitutes the conventional memory buffer address for the original buffer address, and then calls the DPMI "Simulate Real Mode Interrupt" function (0300H) to pass the I/O request to DOS in the manner already described.

The third class of functions, where the DOS Extender must replace MS-DOS or ROM BIOS services with new ones appropriate to protected mode, are mainly related to memory management. For example, the MS-DOS "Allocate Memory Block" function (Int 21H Function 48H) is typically superseded by a DOS Extender function that calls the DPMI "Allocate Extended Memory Block" (0501H), "Allocate LDT Descriptor" (0000H), and "Set Descriptor Contents" (000CH) functions to allocate a block of the appropriate size in extended memory and map a selector to the memory, then returns the selector to the application. The DOS Extender must also maintain internal structures of its own to track the selectors and associated memory blocks, since the DPMI host treats these as independent pools of resources. As another example, the DOS Extender might want to intercept MS-DOS "Set Interrupt Vector" (Int 21H Function 25H) function calls by the protected mode application, and then disallow them completely, or interpose its own handlers, or translate the function calls into DPMI "Set Real Mode Interrupt Vector" (0201H), "Set Processor Exception Handler Vector" (0203H), or "Set Protected Mode Interrupt Vector" (0205H) function calls as needed.

The last class of functions —services that are made available uniquely by the DOS Extender—cover a broad spectrum. For example, there are usually DOS Extender function calls to translate between real-mode and protected-mode addresses, alter various fields of descriptors, manipulate the interrupt descriptor table, allow a direct call on a real mode subroutine from a protected mode application, allocate chunks of conventional memory, and so on. Most of these function calls are for highly specialized or demanding situations and are not used in typical application programs, and nearly all of them can be implemented in a hardware-independent fashion by a DPMI-based DOS Extender using the DPMI interface.

What happens when the application program executes the DOS "Terminate with Return Code" function (Int 21H Function 4CH)? Since the DOS Extender has installed its own protected-mode handler for Int 21H, it is going to "see" this function request first. It can go ahead and perform any necessary clean-up activities of its own, and then "chain" to the original protected-mode owner of the Int

21H vector—which is typically the DPMI host itself. The host then frees up all extended memory and protected-mode interrupt vectors that have been allocated to the DOS Extender and its application, and destroys the supporting data structures such as the LDT and IDT. Finally, the DPMI host puts the CPU back into real mode and "passes down" the Int 21H Function 4CH request to DOS, which is responsible for flushing file buffers, closing any remaining file and device handles, and releasing the conventional memory that belonged to the DOS Extender and its application.

Programming Example: TheTINYDOSX.ASM DOS Extender

I always find source code much more enlightening than windy explanations, so I've decided to illustrate this chapter's discussion of DPMI with an actual (if somewhat skeletal) DOS Extender called TINYDOSX.ASM that you can use in your own programs. TINYDOSX relies only on the existence of a DPMI 0.9 host, such as the one found in Windows 3.0. It can be linked into any small model C program and will cause that program to execute in protected mode provided that the C program doesn't call any runtime library functions that include self-modifying code, use segment registers for scratch storage, perform segment register arithmetic, or in general execute any instruction that will result in a general protection fault. Although Windows 3.0 includes a DOS Extender of its own, TINYDOSX doesn't use it and will run equally well in other DPMI version 0.9 environments (at least theoretically; no such other environments were available to me for testing when this chapter was written).

The initialization portion of TINYDOSX, embodied in the routine INITDOSX, is straightforward. To keep things simple, we allow the C application to get control first in real mode, and require it to explicitly call the DOS Extender, rather than the other way around. INITDOSX first calls Int 2FH Function 1687H to find out if a DPMI host is present, and if so, the address of the mode switch entry point. If a DPMI host is not found, INITDOSX bails out with an error message; otherwise, it proceeds to allocate the private data area required by the DPMI host and then requests the switch into protected mode. Once running in protected mode, INITDOSX installs protected mode handlers for general protection faults (so that Windows won't blow our little programming blunders out of the water with its uninformative "Application has violated system integrity" dialog box) and for MS-DOS Int 21H. INITDOSX also allocates a 64 KB area of conventional memory that the Int 21H handler can later use to pass data back and forth to MS-DOS. Finally, INITDOSX returns control to the C application, which continues its execution in protected mode.

When the C application requests an MS-DOS service, the protected-mode Int 21H handler, named DOSCALL, receives control. DOSCALL saves the flags and registers, then branches through the table DISPATCH to the appropriate subroutine. As you'll notice, I've stubbed out most of the less common DOS functions to either return an error or abort the application. The functions that TINYDOSX supports, however, are relayed to DOS using the DPMI translation function "Simulate Real Mode Interrupt." Use of this translation function, rather than the more speedy DPMI "raw mode switch" function, eliminates all sorts of messy problems that are best left to the imagination and experiments of adventurous readers. Naturally, DOSCALL monitors for the fateful Int 21H Function 4CH and cleans up after itself accordingly.

Assuming DPMI 0.9 as our platform and linking TINYDOSX directly into the protected-mode application allows us to take some shortcuts that would never suffice in a commercial-grade DOS Extender. First, we don't have to build our own loader for the protected-mode application; since TINYDOSX is linked right into the application, DOS loads TINYDOSX and the application as a single unit. Second, we don't have to allocate any memory for the application or build any descriptors; we get these services "for free" when DPMI creates code and data selectors during the initial switch to protected mode. Third, we only need to support those DOS services in our DOS Extender that we know our application is actually going to use; we don't have the obligation to translate every known (and unknown) DOS function for protected mode the way a "real" DOS Extender does.

```
        title   TINYDOSX DPMI-Based Tiny DOS Extender

; TINYDOSX.ASM  Tiny DPMI-Based DOS Extender
; Copyright (C) 1991 Ray Duncan

stdin   equ     0                       ; standard input handle
stdout  equ     1                       ; standard output handle
stderr  equ     2                       ; standard error handle
cr      equ     0dh                     ; ASCII carriage return
lf      equ     0ah                     ; ASCII line feed

DGROUP  group   _DATA

_DATA   segment word public 'DATA'
```

```
modesw  dd      0                       ; far pointer to DPMI mode
                                        ;   switch entry point
int0dv  dd      0                       ; address of previous
                                        ;   GP fault handler
int21v  dd      0                       ; address of previous
                                        ;   Int 21H handler
realseg dw      0                       ; segment of real mode buffer
realsel dw      0                       ; selector for real mode buffer

gpfmsg  db      cr,lf,lf
        db      'TINYDOSX: general protection fault!'
        db      cr,lf
gpfmsg_len equ  $-gpfmsg

abmsg   db      cr,lf,lf
        db      'TINYDOSX: unsupported DOS function!'
        db      cr,lf
abmsg_len equ   $-abmsg

regs    label   word                    ; real mode register structure
                                        ; for DPMI translation services
regDI   label   word                    ; 00H DI or EDI
regEDI  dd      0
regSI   label   word                    ; 04H SI or ESI
regESI  dd      0
regBP   label   word                    ; 08H BP or EBP
regEBP  dd      0
        dd      0                       ; 0CH (reserved)
regBX   label   word                    ; 10H BX or EBX
regEBX  dd      0
regDX   label   word                    ; 14H DX or EDX
regEDX  dd      0
regCX   label   word                    ; 18H CX or ECX
regECX  dd      0
regAX   label   word                    ; 1CH AX or EAX
regEAX  dd      0
cpuFLAGS dw     0                       ; 20H cpu status flags
regES   dw      0                       ; 22H ES
regDS   dw      0                       ; 24H DS
regFS   dw      0                       ; 26H FS
regGS   dw      0                       ; 28H GS
regIP   dw      0                       ; 2AH IP (CS:IP ignored by
regCS   dw      0                       ; 2CH CS  DPMI function 0300H)
regSP   dw      0                       ; 2EH SP (SS:SP=0 to have DPMI
regSS   dw      0                       ; 30H SS  host supply a stack)

protDX  dw      0                       ; save protected mode DX
protSI  dw      0                       ; save protected mode SI
protES  dw      0                       ; save protected mode ES

dispatch label  word                    ; Int 21H dispatch table
        dw      offset _TEXT:fxn00h     ; fxn 00H terminate
```

```
        dw      offset _TEXT:fxn01h     ; fxn 01H char input+echo
        dw      offset _TEXT:fxn02h     ; fxn 02H char output
        dw      offset _TEXT:fxn03h     ; fxn 03H aux input
        dw      offset _TEXT:fxn04h     ; fxn 04H aux output
        dw      offset _TEXT:fxn05h     ; fxn 05H printer output
        dw      offset _TEXT:fxn06h     ; fxn 06H raw console I/O
        dw      offset _TEXT:fxn07h     ; fxn 07H raw input no echo
        dw      offset _TEXT:fxn08h     ; fxn 08H char input no echo
        dw      offset _TEXT:abort      ; fxn 09H
        dw      offset _TEXT:abort      ; fxn 0AH
        dw      offset _TEXT:fxn0bh     ; fxn 0BH input status
        dw      offset _TEXT:abort      ; fxn 0CH
        dw      offset _TEXT:fxn0dh     ; fxn 0DH disk reset
        dw      offset _TEXT:fxn0eh     ; fxn 0EH select disk
        dw      offset _TEXT:abort      ; fxn 0FH
        dw      offset _TEXT:abort      ; fxn 10H
        dw      offset _TEXT:abort      ; fxn 11H
        dw      offset _TEXT:abort      ; fxn 12H
        dw      offset _TEXT:abort      ; fxn 13H
        dw      offset _TEXT:abort      ; fxn 14H
        dw      offset _TEXT:abort      ; fxn 15H
        dw      offset _TEXT:abort      ; fxn 16H
        dw      offset _TEXT:abort      ; fxn 17H
        dw      offset _TEXT:abort      ; fxn 18H
        dw      offset _TEXT:fxn19h     ; fxn 19H get current drive
        dw      offset _TEXT:abort      ; fxn 1AH
        dw      offset _TEXT:fxn1bh     ; fxn 1BH get cur. drive data
        dw      offset _TEXT:fxn1ch     ; fxn 1CH get drive data
        dw      offset _TEXT:abort      ; fxn 1DH
        dw      offset _TEXT:abort      ; fxn 1EH
        dw      offset _TEXT:abort      ; fxn 1FH
        dw      offset _TEXT:abort      ; fxn 20H
        dw      offset _TEXT:abort      ; fxn 21H
        dw      offset _TEXT:abort      ; fxn 22H
        dw      offset _TEXT:abort      ; fxn 23H
        dw      offset _TEXT:abort      ; fxn 24H
        dw      offset _TEXT:abort      ; fxn 25H
        dw      offset _TEXT:abort      ; fxn 26H
        dw      offset _TEXT:abort      ; fxn 27H
        dw      offset _TEXT:abort      ; fxn 28H
        dw      offset _TEXT:abort      ; fxn 29H
        dw      offset _TEXT:fxn2ah     ; fxn 2AH get date
        dw      offset _TEXT:fxn2bh     ; fxn 2BH set date
        dw      offset _TEXT:fxn2ch     ; fxn 2CH get time
        dw      offset _TEXT:fxn2dh     ; fxn 2DH set time
        dw      offset _TEXT:fxn2eh     ; fxn 2EH set verify flag
        dw      offset _TEXT:abort      ; fxn 2FH
        dw      offset _TEXT:fxn30h     ; fxn 30H get DOS version
        dw      offset _TEXT:abort      ; fxn 31H
        dw      offset _TEXT:abort      ; fxn 32H
        dw      offset _TEXT:fxn33h     ; fxn 33H get/set break flag
        dw      offset _TEXT:abort      ; fxn 34H
```

```
dw      offset _TEXT:abort      ; fxn 35H
dw      offset _TEXT:fxn36h     ; fxn 36H get drive info
dw      offset _TEXT:abort      ; fxn 37H
dw      offset _TEXT:error      ; fxn 38H
dw      offset _TEXT:fxn39h     ; fxn 39H create directory
dw      offset _TEXT:fxn3ah     ; fxn 3AH delete directory
dw      offset _TEXT:fxn3bh     ; fxn 3BH select directory
dw      offset _TEXT:fxn3ch     ; fxn 3CH create file
dw      offset _TEXT:fxn3dh     ; fxn 3DH open file
dw      offset _TEXT:fxn3eh     ; fxn 3EH close file
dw      offset _TEXT:fxn3fh     ; fxn 3FH read file
dw      offset _TEXT:fxn40h     ; fxn 40H write file
dw      offset _TEXT:fxn41h     ; fxn 41H delete file
dw      offset _TEXT:fxn42h     ; fxn 42H seek
dw      offset _TEXT:fxn43h     ; fxn 43H get/set attributes
dw      offset _TEXT:error      ; fxn 44H
dw      offset _TEXT:fxn45h     ; fxn 45H dup handle
dw      offset _TEXT:fxn46h     ; fxn 46H redirect handle
dw      offset _TEXT:fxn47h     ; fxn 47H get cur. directory
dw      offset _TEXT:error      ; fxn 48H
dw      offset _TEXT:error      ; fxn 49H
dw      offset _TEXT:error      ; fxn 4AH
dw      offset _TEXT:error      ; fxn 4BH
dw      offset _TEXT:fxn4ch     ; fxn 4CH terminate
dw      offset _TEXT:abort      ; fxn 4DH
dw      offset _TEXT:error      ; fxn 4EH
dw      offset _TEXT:error      ; fxn 4FH
dw      offset _TEXT:abort      ; fxn 50H
dw      offset _TEXT:abort      ; fxn 51H
dw      offset _TEXT:abort      ; fxn 52H
dw      offset _TEXT:abort      ; fxn 53H
dw      offset _TEXT:fxn54h     ; fxn 54H get verify flag
dw      offset _TEXT:abort      ; fxn 55H
dw      offset _TEXT:error      ; fxn 56H
dw      offset _TEXT:fxn57h     ; fxn 57H get/set file date
dw      offset _TEXT:error      ; fxn 58H
dw      offset _TEXT:abort      ; fxn 59H
dw      offset _TEXT:fxn5ah     ; fxn 5AH create temp file
dw      offset _TEXT:fxn5bh     ; fxn 5BH create unique file
dw      offset _TEXT:fxn5ch     ; fxn 5CH lock/unlock
dw      offset _TEXT:abort      ; fxn 5DH
dw      offset _TEXT:error      ; fxn 5EH
dw      offset _TEXT:error      ; fxn 5FH
dw      offset _TEXT:abort      ; fxn 60H
dw      offset _TEXT:abort      ; fxn 61H
dw      offset _TEXT:abort      ; fxn 62H
dw      offset _TEXT:error      ; fxn 63H
dw      offset _TEXT:abort      ; fxn 64H
dw      offset _TEXT:error      ; fxn 65H
dw      offset _TEXT:error      ; fxn 66H
dw      offset _TEXT:error      ; fxn 67H
dw      offset _TEXT:fxn68h     ; fxn 68H commit file
```

```
        dw      offset _TEXT:abort          ; fxn 69H
        dw      offset _TEXT:abort          ; fxn 6AH
        dw      offset _TEXT:abort          ; fxn 6BH
        dw      offset _TEXT:error          ; fxn 6CH
        dw      offset _TEXT:abort          ; fxn 6DH
        dw      offset _TEXT:abort          ; fxn 6EH
        dw      offset _TEXT:abort          ; fxn 6FH

_DATA   ends

_TEXT   segment byte public 'CODE'

        assume  cs:_TEXT,ds:DGROUP
;
; Initialization routine for the Tiny DOS Extender.  First we test for
; the presence of a DPMI host, get the address of the mode switch entry
; point, and request the switch to protected mode.  Then we install
; a handler for GP faults to circumvent the Win 3 brain-damaged dialog
; box, and allocate some memory below 1 MB to use as a buffer for
; communication with DOS.  Finally we install our own Int 21H handler
; so we can service DOS calls from the protected mode application.
;
        public  initdosx
initdosx proc   near

        mov     ax,1687h                    ; get address of DPMI
        int     2fh                         ;   mode switch entry point
        or      ax,ax                       ; bail out if no DPMI
        jnz     init9
        mov     word ptr modesw,di          ; save far pointer to
        mov     word ptr modesw+2,es        ;   DPMI entry point

        mov     bx,si                       ; allocate DPMI private data
        mov     ah,48h                      ; area below 1 MB boundary
        int     21h
        jc      init9                       ; jump, allocation failed

        mov     es,ax                       ; pass segment of data area
        mov     ax,0                        ; bit 0=0 indicates 16-bit app
        call    modesw                      ; switch to protected mode

        mov     ax,0202h                    ; get address of previous
        mov     bl,0dh                      ; owner of GP fault vector
        int     31h
        mov     word ptr int0dv,dx          ; save as far pointer
        mov     word ptr int0dv+2,cx

        mov     ax,0203h                    ; install our GP fault handler
        mov     bl,0dh
        mov     cx,cs                       ; CX:DX = handler address
        mov     dx,offset _TEXT:gpfisr
        int     31h
```

```
        jc      init9                   ; jump, couldn't install

        mov     ax,0100h                ; allocate 64 KB buffer in
        mov     bx,1000h                ; conventional memory for
        int     31h                     ; communication with DOS
        jc      init9                   ; jump, allocation failed
        mov     realseg,ax              ; save segment of block
        mov     realsel,dx              ; save selector for block

        mov     ax,0204h                ; get address of previous
        mov     bl,21h                  ; owner of Int 21H vector
        int     31h
        mov     word ptr int21v,dx      ; save as far pointer
        mov     word ptr int21v+2,cx

        mov     ax,0205h                ; install our Int 21H handler
        mov     bl,21h
        mov     cx,cs                   ; CX:DX = handler address
        mov     dx,offset _TEXT:doscall
        int     31h

        xor     ax,ax                   ; return in protected mode
        ret                             ; AX = 0 to signal success

init9:  mov     ax,-1                   ; return with AX <> 0 to
        ret                             ; signal initialization failure

initdosx endp
;
; Interrupt service routine for GP faults. Entered by a far call
; from DPMI host with CS:IP, flags, CPU error code on stack.
; We force transfer to our error message routine by changing
; return address in the stack frame.
;
gpfisr  proc    far

        push    bp                      ; point CS:IP in stack frame to
        mov     bp,sp                   ; GP fault error message routine
        mov     word ptr [bp+8],offset _TEXT:gpferr
        pop     bp
        ret

gpfisr  endp
;
; This routine gains control after the GPFISR returns to the DPMI host.
; It simply displays an error message and terminates cleanly, subverting
; Win 3's "Application has violated system integrity" dialog box.
;
gpferr  proc    near

        mov     dx,offset DGROUP:gpfmsg ; display GP fault message
        mov     cx,gpfmsg_len           ; on standard output
```

```
        mov     bx,stdout
        mov     ah,40h
        int     21h
        mov     ax,4c01h                ; and terminate with
        int     21h                     ; nonzero return code

gpferr  endp
;
; The DOSCALL routine is the runtime portion of the Tiny DOS Extender.
; It traps Int 21H requests in protected mode and performs any necessary
; mode switching, data movement, and address translation on a
; function-by-function basis.  Anything DOSCALL doesn't want to handle,
; it either fails by setting the Carry flag and returning, or
; it aborts the current program.  In particular, all FCB-related
; functions are aborted.  When a termination function is detected,
; the interrupt handlers are unhooked and the function call is
; passed down to the DPMI host so that all other protected mode
; resources will be deallocated.
;
doscall proc    far

        push    bx                      ; save register BX
        mov     bl,ah                   ; function number * 2
        xor     bh,bh
        cmp     bx,6fh                  ; function no. too big?
        ja      abort                   ; yes, bail out
        add     bx,bx                   ; no, branch through table
        jmp     [dispatch+bx]           ; to function handler

abort:                                  ; unsupported DOS function
        mov     dx,offset DGROUP:abmsg  ; display error message
        mov     cx,abmsg_len
        mov     bx,stdout
        mov     ah,40h
        int     21h
        mov     ax,4c01h                ; and exit to DOS
        int     21h

error:                                  ; unsupported DOS function
        pop     bx
        push    bp                      ; set Carry flag in stack
        mov     bp,sp                   ;   frame to indicate
        or      word ptr [bp+6],1       ;   function failed
        pop     bp                      ; load AX = error code for
        mov     ax,1                    ;   "invalid function number"
        iret                            ; return to application

                                        ; common handling for entirely
                                        ;   register-based functions
fxn01h:                                 ; function 01H: char input+echo
fxn02h:                                 ; function 02H: char output
fxn03h:                                 ; function 03H: aux input
```

```
fxn04h:                               ; function 04H: aux output
fxn05h:                               ; function 05H: printer output
fxn06h:                               ; function 06H: raw console I/O
fxn07h:                               ; function 07H: raw input no echo
fxn08h:                               ; function 08H: char input no echo
fxn0bh:                               ; function 0BH: input status
fxn0dh:                               ; function 0DH: disk reset
fxn0eh:                               ; function 0EH: select disk
fxn19h:                               ; function 19H: get current drive
fxn1bh:                               ; function 1BH: get cur. drive data
fxn1ch:                               ; function 1CH: get drive data
fxn2ah:                               ; function 2AH: get date
fxn2bh:                               ; function 2BH: set date
fxn2ch:                               ; function 2CH: get time
fxn2dh:                               ; function 2DH: set time
fxn2eh:                               ; function 2EH: set verify flag
fxn30h:                               ; function 30H: get DOS version
fxn33h:                               ; function 33H: get/set break flag
fxn36h:                               ; function 36H: get drive info
fxn3eh:                               ; function 3EH: close file
fxn42h:                               ; function 42H: seek
fxn45h:                               ; function 45H: dup handle
fxn46h:                               ; function 46H: redirect handle
fxn54h:                               ; function 54H: get verify flag
fxn57h:                               ; function 57H: get/set filedate
fxn5ch:                               ; function 5CH: lock/unlock
fxn68h:                               ; function 68H: commit file
        pop     bx                    ; restore BX
        call    saveregs              ; unload general registers
        call    realdos               ; transfer to DOS
        call    loadregs              ; load general registers & flags
        iret                          ; return to application

                                      ; common handling for functions
                                      ;   passing ASCIIZ addr in DS:DX
fxn39h:                               ; function 39H: create directory
fxn3ah:                               ; function 3AH: delete directory
fxn3bh:                               ; function 3BH: select directory
fxn3ch:                               ; function 3CH: create file
fxn3dh:                               ; function 3DH: open
fxn41h:                               ; function 41H: delete file
fxn43h:                               ; function 43H: get/set attributes
fxn5ah:                               ; function 5AH: create temp file
fxn5bh:                               ; function 5BH: create unique file
        pop     bx                    ; restore BX
        call    saveregs              ; unload general registers
        mov     es,realsel            ; ES:DI = virtual address of
        xor     di,di                 ;         real mode buffer
        mov     si,dx                 ; DS:SI = virtual address of
        cld                           ;         protected mode buffer
@@1:    lodsb                         ; copy ASCIIZ string to
        stosb                         ; real mode buffer
```

```
        or      al,al                   ; reached null yet?
        jnz     @@1                     ; no, copy another character
        mov     ax,realseg              ; set address of real mode buffer
        mov     regDS,ax                ; into register data structure
        mov     regDX,0
        call    realdos                 ; transfer to MS-DOS
        call    loadregs                ; load general registers & flags
        mov     dx,protDX               ; restore protected mode DX, ES
        mov     es,protES
        iret                            ; return to application

fxn3fh:                                 ; function 3FH: read file
        pop     bx                      ; restore BX
        call    saveregs                ; unload general registers
        mov     ax,realseg              ; set address of real mode buffer
        mov     regDS,ax                ; into register data structure
        mov     regDX,0
        call    realdos                 ; transfer to MS-DOS
        mov     cx,regCX                ; CX = actual length of data
        push    ds                      ; ES:DI = virtual address of
        pop     es                      ;         protected mode buffer
        mov     di,protDX
        mov     ds,realsel              ; DS:SI = virtual address of
        xor     si,si                   ;         real mode buffer
        cld                             ; copy data from real mode
        rep movsb                       ; buffer to protected mode buffer
        push    es                      ; restore DS = our DGROUP
        pop     ds
        call    loadregs                ; load general registers
        mov     dx,protDX               ; restore protected mode DX, ES
        mov     es,protES
        iret                            ; return to application

fxn40h:                                 ; function 40H: write file
        pop     bx                      ; restore BX
        call    saveregs                ; unload general registers
        mov     es,realsel              ; ES:DI = virtual address of
        xor     di,di                   ;         real mode buffer
        mov     si,dx                   ; DS:SI = virtual address of
        cld                             ;         protected mode buffer
        rep movsb                       ; copy data to real mode buffer
        mov     ax,realseg              ; set address of real mode buffer
        mov     regDS,ax                ; into register data structure
        mov     regDX,0
        call    realdos                 ; transfer to MS-DOS
        call    loadregs                ; load general registers & flags
        mov     dx,protDX               ; restore protected mode DX, ES
        mov     es,protES
        iret                            ; return to application

fxn47h:                                 ; function 47H: get directory
        pop     bx                      ; restore BX
```

```
        call    saveregs                ; unload general registers
        mov     ax,realseg              ; set address of real mode buffer
        mov     regDS,ax                ; into register data structure
        mov     regSI,0
        call    realdos                 ; transfer to MS-DOS
        push    ds                      ; ES:DI = virtual address of
        pop     es                      ;         protected mode buffer
        mov     di,protSI
        mov     ds,realsel              ; DS:SI = virtual address of
        xor     si,si                   ;         real mode buffer
        cld
@@2:    lodsb                           ; copy ASCIIZ string from real
        stosb                           ; mode buffer to prot mode buffer
        or      al,al                   ; found null character yet?
        jnz     @@2                     ; no, copy another character
        push    es                      ; restore DS = our DGROUP
        pop     ds
        call    loadregs                ; load general registers
        mov     si,protSI               ; restore protected mode SI, ES
        mov     es,protES
        iret                            ; return to application

fxn00h:                                 ; function 00H: terminate
fxn4ch: pop     bx                      ; function 4CH: terminate
        push    ax                      ; save return code
        mov     ax,0203h                ; restore old GP fault handler
        mov     bl,0dh
        mov     cx,word ptr int0dv+2
        mov     dx,word ptr int0dv
        int     31h
        mov     ax,0205h                ; restore old Int 21H handler
        mov     bl,21h
        mov     cx,word ptr int21v+2
        mov     dx,word ptr int21v
        int     31h
        mov     ax,0101h                ; release real mode buffer
        mov     dx,realsel
        int     31h
        pop     ax                      ; chain to DPMI Int 21H handler
        int     21h                     ; for cleanup and termination

chain:                                  ; general fallthrough point
                                        ; (useful during debugging)
        pop     bx                      ; restore register BX
        jmp     int21v                  ; chain to prev Int 21H owner

doscall endp
;
; Save general registers into real mode data structure for a call to
; real mode routine via DPMI translation services.  Note that segment
; registers are NOT unloaded into structure because they are not valid
; for real mode anyway.
```

```
;
saveregs proc   near

        mov     regAX,ax                ; save general registers
        mov     regBX,bx
        mov     regCX,cx
        mov     regDX,dx
        mov     regSI,si
        mov     regDI,di
        mov     regBP,bp
        mov     protDX,dx               ; extra copies for non-
        mov     protSI,si               ; register-based functions
        mov     protES,es
        ret

saveregs endp
;
; Load general registers from real mode data structure.  Note that
; segment registers are NOT loaded because their real mode values
; would cause a GP fault in protected mode.
;
loadregs proc   near

        mov     bp,sp                   ; update CPU flags in
        push    cpuFLAGS                ; stack frame to return
        pop     [bp+6]                  ; DOS function status
        mov     ax,regAX                ; load general registers
        mov     bx,regBX
        mov     cx,regCX
        mov     dx,regDX
        mov     si,regSI
        mov     di,regDI
        mov     bp,regBP
        ret

loadregs endp
;
; Call the DPMI translation function 0300H to simulate a real mode
; software interrupt 21H, transferring control to MS-DOS, passing
; the values stored into the real mode register structure 'regs'.
;
realdos proc    near

        push    es
        mov     ax,0300h                ; DPMI Function 0300H
        mov     bl,21h                  ; software interrupt 21H
        mov     bh,0                    ; flags (bit 0 must be 0)
        mov     cx,0                    ; no. of stack words to copy
        push    ds                      ; ES:DI = address of real
        pop     es                      ; mode register structure
        mov     di,offset DGROUP:regs
        int     31h                     ; to DOS via DPMI host
```

```
        pop     es
        ret

realdos endp

_TEXT   ends

        end
```

TESTDOSX,C contains the source code fora simple protected-mode C application that you can link with TINYDOSX.ASM for experimental purposes. To create the executable version of TESTDOSX, you need Microsoft MASM 5.1 or a compatible assembler and Microsoft C 6.0 or a compatible compiler. Enter the following commands:

```
MASM /Mx TINYDOSX;
CL TESTDOSX.C TINYDOSX
```

Make sure that you are compiling and linking for the small memory model. The resulting application, TESTDOSX.EXE, must be run in one of the "DOS boxes" of Windows 3.0 in 386 Enhanced mode so that it has access to DPMI services.

```
/*
    TESTDOSX.C --- illustrates use of the DPMI-based
    DOS Extender TINYDOSX to display a message in protected mode.

    Copyright (C) 1991 Ray Duncan

    Build with Microsoft C 6.0 SMALL MODEL as follows:

          MASM TINYDOSX;
          CL TESTDOSX.C TINYDOSX

    Execute under Windows 3.0 in the DOS Box only!
*/

#include <stdio.h>

unsigned extern pascal InitDosX(void);

main()
{
    unsigned saveCS, saveDS;

    _asm mov saveCS,cs          ; store real mode CS
    _asm mov saveDS,ds          ; and DS for display

    printf("\nHello, real mode world! \tCS=%04xh DS=%04xh",
```

```
        saveCS, saveDS);

    if(InitDosX())              // attempt mode switch
    {
        puts("\nDPMI initialization failed.");
        exit(1);
    }

    _asm mov saveCS,cs          ; store protected mode CS
    _asm mov saveDS,ds          ; and DS for display

    printf("\nHello, protected mode world! \tCS=%04xh DS=%04xh\n",
        saveCS, saveDS);

    _asm mov ah,4ch             ; exit directly to DOS to avoid
    _asm int 21h                ; GP fault in RTL cleanup code
}
```

Suppose we wanted to turn TINYDOSX into a not so tiny, more robust DOS Extender—where would we start? We'd have to enlarge the support for Int 21H functions to include (at minimum) all the documented MS-DOS services. We'd need to support the immense battery of ROM BIOS services (most of which, luckily, are register-based anyway) and probably, in addition, the Microsoft Mouse Int 33H and the NetBIOS interfaces. We'd want to add more sophisticated facilities for installation of interrupt handlers by the application. My first impression of the way to do this would be to incorporate a loader for "segmented EXE" (also called "New EXE") files into our DOS Extender, build the application with the Microsoft Segmented Linker, and bind our DOS Extender into the EXE file as the "real-mode stub." This would be, in fact, very similar to the approach that was used by Phar Lap Software in their 286 DOS | Extender product.

Table 9-2: DPMI Error Codes.

Error Code	Name	Explanation
8001H	Unsupported function	Returned in response to any function call which is not implemented by this host, because the requested function is either undefined or optional.
8002H	Invalid state	Some object is in the wrong state for the requested operation.
8003H	System integrity	The requested operation would endanger system integrity, e.g., a request to map linear addresses onto system code or data.

Error Code	Name	Explanation
8004H	Deadlock	Host detected a deadlock situation.
8005H	Request cancelled	A pending serialization request was cancelled.
8010H	Resource Unavailable	The DPMI host cannot allocate internal resources to complete an operation.
8011H	Descriptor unavailable	Host is unable to allocate a descriptor.
8012H	Linear memory unavailable	Host is unable to allocate the required linear memory.
8013H	Physical memory unavailable	Host is unable to allocate the required physical memory.
8014H	Backing store unavailable	Host is unable to allocate the required backing store.
8015H	Callback unavailable	Host is unable to allocate the required callback address.
8016H	Handle unavailable	Host is unable to allocate the required handle.
8017H	Lock count exceeded	A locking operation exceeds the maximum count maintained by the host.
8018H	Resource owned exclusively	A request for serialization of a shared memory block could not be satisfied because it is already serialized exclusively by another client.
8019H	Resource owned shared	A request for exclusive serialization of a shared memory block could not be satisfied because it is already serialized shared by another client.
8021H	Invalid value	A numeric or flag parameter has an invalid value.
8022H	Invalid selector	A selector does not correspond to a valid descriptor.
8023H	Invalid handle	A handle parameter is invalid.
8024H	Invalid callback	A callback parameter is invalid.
8025H	Invalid linear address	A linear address range (either supplied as a parameter or implied by the call) is invalid.
8026H	Invalid request	The request is not supported by the underlying hardware.

Note: DPMI 0.9 hosts indicate an error by returning from an Int 31H function call with the Carry bit set. DPMI 1.0 hosts indicate an error by returning from the function with the Carry bit set but, in addition, return an error code in AX that provides more information about the cause of the error. If the Carry flag is set and bit 15 of AX is clear (0), the error code is being passed through from DOS. If the Carry flag is set and bit 15 of AX is set (1), the error code is generated by the DPMI host and the meaning of these codes is found in the table above.

Chapter 10

Multitasking and DOS Extenders

Robert Moote

PC multitaskers capable of running DOS programs fall into two broad categories. One is multitasking environments, such as Windows and DESQview, that run on top of DOS. The other is multitasking operating systems, such as OS/2 and Unix, that replace DOS but provide emulation of the DOS environment. Either kind of multitasker can run extended DOS applications by providing either the DPMI or VCPI interface. Currently only DESQview (with VCPI support) and Windows (with DPMI 0.9 support) are compatible with extended DOS applications. However, IBM has stated publicly that OS/2 2.0 will include DPMI 0.9 support.

Quarterdeck first supported VCPI in QEMM and DESQview to gain compatibility with extended DOS applications in early 1988. Since VCPI has been around long enough that most extended DOS applications support it, DESQview is compatible with almost all currently shipping extended DOS products. The design of VCPI was partially driven by the need to make it relatively easy to implement in existing products; as we saw in Chapter 8, one result is that VCPI clients run at privilege level zero. This means that DESQview cannot virtualize the hardware for extended DOS applications. While this results in some restrictions, DESQview customers have been successfully multitasking extended DOS applications for over three years.

By the time Microsoft was finalizing the design of Windows 3.0 in 1989, there were enough popular extended DOS applications (such as Lotus 1-2-3 and AutoCAD 386) in the marketplace that Microsoft could no longer ignore them. Windows engineers had strong objections to VCPI because it doesn't support hardware virtualization. Instead, they designed a new interface, DPMI, that does support virtualization, and included that in the 1990 release of Windows 3.0. All the major DOS extender vendors except Ergo have now released products that support DPMI in addition to VCPI. Many current extended DOS applications are still built with older DOS extenders and can't run under Windows enhanced mode, but over time new releases of these applications will include DPMI support. Windows standard mode can run most extended DOS applications, since in standard mode no special interfaces are needed for a DOS extender to run.

It's interesting to note that Windows 3.1 can run as a VCPI *client* in standard mode. This means you can run Windows 3.1 under DESQview. (Windows 3.0 also runs under DESQview, but only because DESQview patches Windows at load time.) Despite rumors that Windows 3.1 would run as a DPMI client, it does not; you won't be able to run Windows under OS/2 2.0.

In this chapter we'll take a closer look at multitasking extended DOS applications under Windows and DESQview. We'll also compare the differences between using DPMI 0.9 and VCPI. Because there are no DPMI 1.0 hosts either currently available or announced, this chapter concentrates on DPMI 0.9 rather than 1.0.

Windows Standard Mode

Standard mode is the 286-compatible mode of Windows. Because there is no V86 mode on a 286 processor, DOS programs are run in real mode. Hardware virtualization for DOS applications is not possible, because real-mode programs run at privilege level 0, the most privileged level of the processor. Windows does not provide virtual memory support in standard mode.

Windows standard mode does not support DPMI for DOS applications (though it does for native Windows applications). It turns out DPMI is not needed; since the standard mode DOS box runs in real mode, DOS extenders loaded under Windows are free to take control of the machine and run in protected mode. If the DOS extender provides virtual memory support, it can continue to do so. In fact, from the point of view of an extended DOS application running under Windows standard mode is no different from running under DOS.

Contention for extended memory is handled by installing HIMEM.SYS (the Microsoft XMS driver) and using the PIF editor to make XMS memory available in the DOS box. Both Windows and the extended DOS application obtain memory by making XMS calls. You can control the maximum amount of XMS memory consumed by the application by changing the XMS limit for the DOS box.

If you run Windows in standard mode, you have to run the DOS box full screen, and you can't multitask DOS applications. But extended DOS applications often perform better because they can provide their own virtual memory instead of relying on Windows. All extended DOS programs, rather than only DPMI-compatible applications, are supported. Also, since standard mode Windows 3.1 is a VCPI client, you can run it under memory managers such as QEMM or 386-to-the-Max. If you're having compatibility or performance problems running DOS applications under Windows, consider using standard mode instead of enhanced mode.

Windows Enhanced Mode and DPMI

Windows enhanced mode is the preferred mode on 386 or later CPUs, because it offers virtual memory, multitasking of DOS applications, and hardware virtualization. Enhanced mode includes DPMI suppport, to allow DOS extenders to run in the Windows protected mode environment.

Windows can virtualize the hardware for extended DOS applications, because the DOS extender runs as an unprivileged program. Since the DOS extender can no longer perform privileged operations directly, but instead must operate within the restrictions imposed by the DPMI interface, the DOS extender may be forced to limit the features provided to application programs. In the short term, this may delay the migration of applications to DPMI compatibility, as both DOS extender vendors and developers adjust to these limitations.

Hardware Virtualization under Windows

Windows uses the processor's I/O permission bit map to virtualize the hardware when running standard real-mode DOS programs in V86 mode, or when running extended DOS applications in protected mode. Because real mode programs running in V86 mode always run at the least privileged level of the processor, and because DPMI clients run unprivileged in protected mode, Windows can arrange to get control when any program executes an I/O instruction, attempts to access a system register, or attempts to read from or write to a portion of the memory space (such as the video memory) which Windows wants to protect. Windows can let each program think it has direct control of the hardware, but still prevent simultaneously executing programs from interfering with each other.

In theory, the hardware virtualization made possible by DPMI means you can run extended DOS applications in a window rather than full screen. Unfortunately, Windows 3.0 provides only EGA virtualization, and the VGA virtualization in Windows 3.1 is painfully slow. Under Windows, you sometimes pay for this hardware virtualization regardless of whether it's necessary; for example, the performance of the communications port is severely degraded in a DOS window, even if only one program is using the port.

Of course, hardware virtualization means all devices (not just the video) can be virtualized. Practically speaking, there isn't much contention for devices other than the screen, because most of them are interactive so background programs don't use them. Under Windows, you sometimes pay for this hardware virtualization regardless of whether it's necessary; try opening a single full screen DOS window and running any DOS program that sends output at 9600 baud over a serial port to a dumb terminal. Under Windows 3.0, only a few characters a second are sent. For some reason, running in a window rather than full screen improves performance; very fast rates approximating 300 baud are then possible.

Virtual Memory under Windows

DOS extenders that provide virtual memory support must disable that functionality when running under Windows enhanced mode, because DPMI provides no calls to support it. Since Windows provides virtual memory, the application still runs in a virtualized environment. Unfortunately, the Windows virtual memory implementation performs less well than that provided by most DOS extender vendors, so extended DOS applications often run more sluggishly under Windows than under DOS or DESQview.

Kernel Protection

Because the DOS extender runs unprivileged in the host's environment under DPMI, it is then possible for the host to prevent either the DOS extender or the protected-mode application from writing to memory locations owned by the host, thereby crashing the entire system. This kernel protection is one of the theoretical advantages of DPMI over VCPI. However, in the Windows DPMI implementation, no kernel protection measures are implemented, so any application can modify the GDT, LDT, or any part of the Windows kernel. This is actually fortunate, since it simplifies the job of providing workarounds for the bugs in Windows' DPMI implementation.

The extended DOS application below uses DPMI calls to print out GDT segment descriptors, and the contents of the GDT segments. Since DPMI is available to native Windows applications as well as DOS applications, you could write equivalent code in a Windows program.

```
/*
 * WINGDT.C --- Extended DOS application that uses DPMI calls
 *         to print out Windows GDT segment descriptors
 *         and segment contents. Note this program ASSUMES
 *         it is running under a DPMI host.
 * Copyright (C) 1991 Robert Moote
 *
 * To build program with MetaWare High C, Phar Lap 386|ASM
 * and 386|LINK:
 *   hc386 wingdt.c -c
 *   386asm wingdta.asm
 *   386link wingdt wingdta -lib \hc386\small\hce
 *
 * To run program under Windows extended mode with Phar Lap
 * 386|DOS-Extender:
 *   run386 wingdt
 */

#include <stdio.h>
#include <ctype.h>

/* Useful data types and constants */
#define TRUE 1
#define FALSE 0
typedef unsigned long ULONG;
typedef unsigned short USHORT;
typedef unsigned char UCHAR;

/* macro to initialize a FAR pointer */
#define FP_SET(fp, off, sel) ((*(ULONG *)&fp=(ULONG)(off)),\
(*(((USHORT *)&fp) + sizeof(ULONG)/sizeof(USHORT))=sel))

/* Format of a segment selector */
#define SEL_IDX 0xFFF8          /* offset into GDT or LDT */
#define SEL_LDT 0x0004          /* LDT (not GDT) selector */
#define SEL_RPL 0x0003          /* requested privilege level */
```

```
/* Descriptor format for code, data, and some system segments */
/* System gate descriptors have a different structure */
typedef struct
{
     USHORT limit0_15;     /* Bits 0-15 of segment limit */
     USHORT base0_15;      /* Bits 0-15 of segment base */
     UCHAR base16_23;      /* Bits 16-23 of base */
     UCHAR arights;        /* Access rights */
     UCHAR limit16_19;     /* Bits 16-19 of limit, and flags */
     UCHAR base24_31;      /* Bits 24-31 of base */
} SegDes;
/* Flag bits in limit16_19 byte */
#define L16_PGRAN    0x80 /* segment limit is page granular */
#define L16_USE32    0x40 /* USE32 code or stack segment */
#define L16_HLIM     0x0F /* mask for bits 16-19 of limit */

/* Access rights byte fields */
#define AR_PRESENT   0x80 /* Segment is present */
#define AR_DPLM      0x60 /* DPL mask */
#define AR_DPLSC     5    /* DPL shift count */
#define AR_USER      0x10 /* Code or data (not system) segment */
#define AR_TYPEM     0x0F /* Segment type mask */
/* Segment type field for code or data segments */
#define AR_CSEG      0x08 /* Code (not data) segment */
#define AR_CCONF     0x04 /* Code segment; conforming */
#define AR_CREAD     0x02 /* Code segment; readable */
#define AR_EDOWN     0x04 /* Data segment; Expand down */
#define AR_DWRITE    0x02 /* Data segment; Read/write */
#define AR_ACCESSED  0x01 /* segment has been accessed */
#define AR_CODE (AR_PRESENT | AR_USER | AR_CSEG | AR_CREAD)
#define AR_DATA (AR_PRESENT | AR_USER | AR_DWRITE)
/* Segment type field for system segments */
#define SYS_A286TSS  0x01 /* Available 286 TSS */
#define   SYS_LDT         0x02 /* LDT */
#define SYS_B286TSS  0x03 /* Busy 286 TSS */
#define   SYS_CG286  0x04 /* 286 call gate */
#define SYS_TG       0x05 /* Task gate */
#define SYS_IG286    0x06 /* 286 interrupt gate */
#define SYS_XG286    0x07 /* 286 trap gate */
#define SYS_A386TSS  0x09 /* Available 386 TSS */
#define SYS_B386TSS  0x0B /* Busy 386 TSS */
#define   SYS_CG386  0x0C /* 386 call gate */
#define SYS_IG386    0x0E /* 386 interrupt gate */
#define SYS_XG386    0x0F /* 386 trap gate */
/* Prototypes for assembly language routines */
extern int SysRegs(ULONG *gdtbasep, USHORT *gdtlimp, ULONG *idtbasep,
          USHORT *idtlimp, USHORT *ldtrp, USHORT *trp, USHORT *csp);
extern int AllocDesc(USHORT *selectorp);
extern int WriteDesc(USHORT selector, SegDes *bufp);
main()
```

```
{
	ULONG	gdtbase;	/* GDT linear base address */
	USHORT	gdtlim;		/* GDT byte limit */
	ULONG	idtbase;	/* IDT linear base address */
	USHORT	idtlim;		/* IDT byte limit */
	USHORT	ldtr;		/* LDTR register value */
	USHORT	tr;		/* TR register value */
	USHORT	cs;		/* CS for this program */
	UCHAR	dpl;		/* descriptor privilege level */
	SegDes	desc;		/* buffers a seg descriptor */
	USHORT	gdtsel;		/* LDT data seg mapping GDT */
	SegDes _far *gdtp;	/* FAR pointer to Windows GDT */
	ULONG	selector;	/* selector to display */
	SegDes _far *descp;	/* FAR ptr to descriptor in GDT */
	ULONG	base;		/* segment linear base address */
	ULONG	limit;		/* segment limit, in bytes */
	UCHAR	type;		/* segment type from access rights */
	USHORT	aliassel;	/* data alias for a GDT segment */
	ULONG	offset;		/* offset in seg of data to display */
	ULONG _far *datap;	/* FAR ptr to data in GDT segment */

	/* print out system register values, and get our */
	/* privilege level and shift it to proper position */
	/* for descriptor access rights byte */
	SysRegs(&gdtbase, &gdtlim, &idtbase, &idtlim, &ldtr, &tr, &cs);
	printf("GDT base = %08Xh, limit = %04Xh\n", gdtbase, gdtlim);
	printf("IDT base = %08Xh, IDT limit = %04Xh\n", idtbase, idtlim);
	printf("LDTR = %04Xh, TR = %04Xh\n", ldtr, tr);
	dpl = (UCHAR) ((cs & SEL_RPL) << AR_DPLSC);
	/* Allocate some LDT descriptors */
	if (AllocDesc(&gdtsel))
		goto ALLOCERR;
	if (AllocDesc(&aliassel))
		goto ALLOCERR;
	/* set up data segment to map GDT */
	desc.base0_15 = (USHORT) gdtbase;
	desc.base16_23 = (UCHAR) (gdtbase >> 16);
	desc.base24_31 = (UCHAR) (gdtbase >> 24);
	desc.limit0_15 = gdtlim;
	desc.limit16_19 = 0;
	desc.arights = AR_DATA | dpl;
	if (WriteDesc(gdtsel, &desc))
		goto WRDESCERR;
	FP_SET(gdtp, 0, gdtsel);

	/* loop until user requests exit */
	while (TRUE)
	{
		/* print out GDT descriptor contents */
		if (GetHexVal("\nEnter hex GDT selector, 0 to exit: ",
						&selector))
```

```
            break;
        if (selector == 0)
            break;
        if (selector >= gdtlim || selector & SEL_LDT)
        {
            printf("Invalid selector: %04Xh\n",
                                    selector);
            continue;
        }
        descp = gdtp + ((selector & SEL_IDX) >> 3);
        if (!(descp->arights & AR_PRESENT))
        {
            printf("Selector: %04Xh not present\n",
                                    selector);
            continue;
        }
        type = descp->arights & AR_TYPEM;
        if (!(descp->arights & AR_USER) &&
            type != SYS_A286TSS && type != SYS_LDT &&
            type != SYS_B286TSS && type != SYS_A386TSS &&
            type != SYS_B386TSS)
        {
            printf("Gate segment %04Xh: %08Xh %08Xh\n",
                selector, *((ULONG _far *)descp),
                *(((ULONG _far *)descp) + 1));
            continue;
        }
        base = (ULONG) descp->base0_15;
        base += ((ULONG) descp->base16_23) << 16;
        base += ((ULONG) descp->base24_31) << 24;
        limit = (ULONG) descp->limit0_15;
        limit += ((ULONG) (descp->limit16_19 & L16_HLIM)) << 16;
        if (descp->limit16_19 & L16_PGRAN)
            limit = (limit << 12) + 0xFFF;
        if (!(descp->arights & AR_USER))
            printf("System");
        else
        {
            if (!(descp->arights & AR_CSEG))
                printf("Data");
            else if (descp->limit16_19 & L16_USE32)
                printf("USE32 Code");
            else
                printf("USE16 Code");
        }
        printf(" segment %04Xh: access rights = %02Xh\n",
                        selector, descp->arights);
        printf("\tbase = %08Xh, limit = %08Xh\n",
                                base, limit);
        /* print out 4 doublewords of data from GDT seg */
        if (GetHexVal("Enter hex offset to display data: ",
                                    &offset))
```

```
                break;
            if (offset + 15 < offset || offset + 15 > limit)
            {
                printf("Offset %08Xh is past segment \
                limit %08Xh\n", offset, limit);
                continue;
            }
            *((ULONG *)(&desc)) = *((ULONG _far *)descp);
            *(((ULONG *)(&desc)) + 1) = *(((ULONG _far *)descp) + 1);
            desc.arights = AR_DATA | dpl;
            if (WriteDesc(aliassel, &desc))
                goto WRDESCERR;
            FP_SET(datap, offset, aliassel);
            printf("%04Xh:%08Xh: %08Xh %08Xh %08Xh %08Xh\n",
                selector, offset, *datap, *(datap + 1),
                *(datap + 2), *(datap + 3));
        }
        return FALSE;
ALLOCERR:
        printf("Unable to allocate LDT descriptors\n");
        return TRUE;
WRDESCERR:
        printf("Unable to write to LDT descriptors\n");
        return TRUE;
}
/*
 * GetHexVal - print prompt and read a hexadecimal value
 *
 * Returns:     TRUE, if end-of-file
 *          FALSE, if success
 */
GetHexVal(promptp, valp)
UCHAR*promptp;  /* pointer to prompt string */
ULONG*valp;           /* returned; value entered */
{
        char buf[128]; /* buffers line of input */
        char *p;          /* scan ptr thru buffer */
RESTART:
        /* get line of input */
        printf("%s", promptp);
        if (gets(buf) == NULL)
            return TRUE;

        /* convert ascii hexadecimal to binary */
        for (p = buf; *p != 0 && !isprint(*p); ++ p)
            ;
        if (*p == 0)
            goto BADVAL;
        for (*valp = 0; *p != 0; ++ p)
        {
            if (!isxdigit(*p))
```

```
                goto BADVAL;
            if (*valp & 0xF0000000)
                goto BADVAL;
            *valp <<= 4;
            if (isdigit(*p))
                *valp += (ULONG)(*p - '0');
            else
                *valp += 10 + (ULONG)(toupper(*p) - 'A');
        }
        return FALSE;
BADVAL:
        printf("Invalid value\n");
        goto RESTART;
}

;
; WINGDTA.ASM -- Utility routines for WINGDT.C program
;
.386p
TRUE equ   1
FALSE equ  0
        assume    cs:cseg
cseg segment    use32 public 'code'
;
; SysRegs(ULONG *gdtbasep, USHORT *gdtlimp, ULONG *idtbasep,
;       USHORT *idtlimp, USHORT *ldtrp, USHORT *trp, USHORT *csp)
;
; Reads values of system registers
;
; Returns: none
;
        public    SysRegs
SysRegs proc    near
#csp equ   (dword ptr 32[ebp])
#trp equ   (dword ptr 28[ebp])
#ldtrp equ (dword ptr 24[ebp])
#idtlimp equ    (dword ptr 20[ebp])
#idtbasep equ   (dword ptr 16[ebp])
#gdtlimp equ    (dword ptr 12[ebp])
#gdtbasep equ   (dword ptr 8[ebp])
#reg48     equ  (pword ptr -8[ebp])
        push ebp        ; set up stack frame
        mov  ebp,esp             ;
        sub  esp,8      ; allocate local variables
        sgdte #reg48            ; return GDTR to caller
        mov  ecx,#gdtbasep
        mov  eax,dword ptr (#reg48 + 2)
        mov  [ecx],eax
        mov  ecx,#gdtlimp
        mov  ax,word ptr #reg48
        mov  [ecx],ax
        sidte #reg48            ; return IDTR values to caller
```

```
        mov    ecx,#idtbasep
        mov    eax,dword ptr (#reg48 + 2)
        mov    [ecx],eax
        mov    ecx,#idtlimp
        mov    ax,word ptr #reg48
        mov    [ecx],ax
        sldt   ax           ; return LDTR value to caller
        mov    ecx,#ldtrp
        mov    [ecx],ax
        str    ax           ; return TR value to caller
        mov    ecx,#trp
        mov    [ecx],ax
        mov    ax,cs        ; return CS value to caller
        mov    ecx,#csp
        mov    [ecx],ax
        mov    esp,ebp          ; restore stack frame & exit
        pop    ebp
        ret
SysRegs endp

;
; AllocDesc(USHORT *selectorp)
;
; Makes a DPMI call to allocate an LDT segment descriptor
;
; Returns: TRUE, if error
;          FALSE, if success
;
        public     AllocDesc
AllocDesc proc  near
#selectorp equ  (dword ptr 8[ebp])
        push ebp          ; set up stack frame
        mov    ebp,esp
        mov    cx,1        ; allocate 1 LDT descriptor
        mov    ax,0
        int    31h
        jc     short #err ; branch if error
        mov    ecx,#selectorp ; return selector to caller
        mov    [ecx],ax
        mov    eax,FALSE  ; return success
#exit:
        mov    esp,ebp          ; restore stack frame & exit
        pop    ebp
        ret
#err:
        mov    eax,TRUE   ; return error
        jmp    #exit
AllocDesc endp

;
; WriteDesc(USHORT selector, SegDes *bufp)
;
; Makes a DPMI call to write to an LDT segment descriptor
```

```
;
; Returns: TRUE, if error
;       FALSE, if success
;
     public    WriteDesc
WriteDesc proc  near
#bufp equ (dword ptr 12[ebp])
#selector equu  (word ptr 8[ebp])
     push ebp         ; set up stack frame
     mov  ebp,esp
     push ebx         ; save regs
     push es
     mov  edi,#bufp  ; write descriptor
     mov  ax,ds
     mov  es,ax
     mov  bx,#selector
     mov  ax,000Ch
     int  31h
     jc   short #err ; branch if error
     mov  eax,FALSE  ; return success
#exit:
     pop  es          ; restore regs
     pop  ebx
     mov  esp,ebp          ; restore stack frame & exit
     pop  ebp
     ret
#err:
     mov  eax,TRUE   ; return error
     jmp  #exit
WriteDesc endp
cseg ends
end
```

The program uses unprivileged instructions to obtain the contents of the GDTR, IDTR, LDTR, and TR registers. It then takes advantage of the fact that Windows' DPMI implementation permits creation of LDT segments that map any part of the linear address space, including the Windows kernel. It creates one LDT data segment that maps the GDT, and uses that to print out GDT descriptors. To print the contents of an individual GDT segment, the program creates a data segment alias in the LDT and uses that to examine the segment contents. The sample program printout below shows Windows' TSS segment descriptor and the first 16 bytes of the TSS contents; the second and third doublewords in the TSS are the ring 0 stack address, so Windows' ring 0 stack is located at 30:804F2FCCH.

```
GDT base = 8010011Ch, limit = 010Fh
IDT base = 8069C000h, IDT limit = 02FFh
LDTR = 0078h, TR = 0018h
```

```
Enter hex GDT selector, 0 to exit: 18
System segment 0018h: access rights = 8Bh
     base = 80010390h, limit = 00002069h
Enter hex offset to display data: 0
0018h:00000000h: 00000000h 804F2FCCh 00000030h 00000000h
```

Of course, Windows provides an approved method, virtual device drivers, for obtaining access to kernel information; in fact, you must write a device driver to examine or modify certain data structures, such as page tables. But for simple tasks, you may find it easier to use DPMI calls than to write a VxD. Also, if Windows spelunking is required by your application, using DPMI calls instead of a VxD means you don't have to tell users to install a device driver.

DPMI Functionality Limitations

One problem with DPMI 0.9 is that access to chip features is limited to the functionality selected by Microsoft. In particular, there is no access in DPMI 0.9 to paging capabilities of 80386 or later processors. This means existing DOS extender products, which previously could take advantage of any chip capability, must restrict the features provided to extended DOS applications when running under Windows or another DPMI host. For applications that take advantage of these DOS extender features, obtaining Windows compatibility is not simply a matter of rebuilding with a newer, DPMI-compatible, version of the DOS extender; changes must also be made to the application itself. This will slow the migration of extended DOS applications to Windows compatibility.

A particular restriction of the Windows DPMI implementation is that only one DPMI client can run in each virtual machine. It's actually quite common to run two DOS applications simultaneously; program A has an "escape to DOS" feature, and the user then runs program B from the DOS command prompt. Under Windows, this won't work if both programs A and B are extended DOS applications. Some products, such as Phar Lap's 286 | DOS-Extender and 386 | DOS-Extender, provide workarounds for this Windows limitation, as long as both applications are built with the same DOS extender. But even then, it's not possible, for example, to run one application built with 286 | DOS-Extender and another built with DOS/16M.

There are also some important capabilities missing in both DPMI 0.9 and DPMI 1.0. The most obvious of these is that a hardware interrupt handler in a DPMI client is unable either to find out where the client was most recently executing, or to change the return address in the client's code when the interrupt handler terminates. Among other implications, there are two quite common operations this restriction prevents. It's impossible to write a code profiler that hooks the timer tick and looks to see where the application is executing. It's also impossible to write a useful floating point coprocessor exception handler (the 80287/387 coprocessor exception is signalled through a hardware interrupt on the PC). The handler can query the coprocessor to determine the address of the coprocessor instruction causing the exception, but the main line of program execution is usually several instructions further on by the time the exception occurs, and may even be megabytes away if a jump or call was executed. Since a DPMI hardware interrupt handler can't (a) terminate the program, (b) see where the program was executing so it can patch in a jump or a breakpoint, or (c) change the return address when it terminates to retain control after the host cleans up from the interrupt, it can't do either of the operations typically performed by a coprocessor exception handler: clean up and kill the program, or display an error message and restart the application at some higher level. Despite these caveats, the advantages of DPMI far outweigh its disadvantages.

DESQview and VCPI

DESQview 386 is capable of multitasking extended DOS applications because it cooperates with the VCPI interface. The QEMM-386 EMS emulator distributed with DESQview provides VCPI, and DESQview uses VCPI to cooperate with DOS extender clients. Because VCPI clients run at privilege level 0, DESQview is unable to provide hardware virtualization for extended DOS applications. This results in some restrictions on how the programs can run. Since almost all extended DOS applications are VCPI compatible, DESQview can run most available products.

Hardware Virtualization Under DESQview

Because DOS extenders run at privilege level 0 and provide an independent protected mode environment under VCPI, DESQview is unable to prevent an extended DOS application from directly accessing hardware devices. The most commonly used hardware resource is the display; many programs write directly to the video memory, or to VGA registers, for performance reasons. (Program access to the display, or to any hardware device, via DOS or BIOS calls can be virtualized, since the DOS or BIOS call is serviced in V86 mode and can be intercepted by DESQview). Protected-mode programs that write directly to the display must be run in full-screen mode. Other tasks can be run simultaneously, but they must run in the background and not in a window on the display.

Interestingly, *DESQview-aware* extended DOS applications can be run in a window. This is accomplished using the old Topview INT 21h functions FEh and FFh calls to access a screen buffer provided by DESQview, rather than the physical screen memory. Unlike hardware virtualization, there is no loss of program performance with this technique. This is of more interest to the programmer writing DESQview applications than to end users, however, since the majority of popular extended DOS applications are not DESQview-aware.

Resolving contention for the keyboard and mouse is usually not a problem—almost all extended DOS application programs use the real-mode mouse driver and the BIOS to perform I/O to those devices, and these are accessed through software interrupts that can be monitored by DESQview. Likewise, disk I/O is nearly always performed with DOS system calls, which are handled in V86 mode where they can be virtualized.

A significant percentage of extended DOS applications perform I/O directly to the serial communication ports. This can cause conflicts—but even in V86 mode where I/O can be virtualized it's hard to envision a situation where two programs can productively perform I/O over the same comm port. The same is true of most special-purpose hardware that can be added to a PC—it usually only makes sense for one program to use it at a time.

It is possible to imagine pathological cases that could not be run in protected mode under DESQview. For example, if a protected-mode application programs the keyboard controller chip to turn off the keyboard, you probably would not want to run it in a DESQview window. But such socially unacceptable behavior is the exception rather than the rule—practically speaking, the only restriction on multitasking protected-mode programs under DESQview is that they must be run in full-screen mode if they write directly to the display.

Virtual Memory under DESQview

DESQview does not provide virtual memory services to DOS applications. DOS extenders can provide virtual memory to applications under DESQview, because the VCPI interface allows the DOS extender to run at privilege level 0. Extended DOS applications often run better under DESQview than Windows, because the

DOS extender virtual memory implementation performs better than the Windows implementation.

When DESQview multitasks two extended DOS applications, they each independently provide their own virtual memory services. One potential problem with this arrangement is fairness—if one application gets more physical memory than the other, the "starved" application may thrash badly. DESQview simultaneously runs multiple memory-hungry programs by limiting the amount of physical memory available to each program. It does this by intercepting DOS and EMS memory allocation calls to make it appear to the application as if less memory exists than is actually the case. Users of DESQview can set specific physical memory consumption limits on a window or an application to enforce fairness.

Protected-mode VCPI calls to allocate and free memory cannot be filtered by DESQview since they do not require a transition through V86 mode where the DESQview environment is active. An extended DOS application could potentially bypass the memory restrictions placed by a user on a DESQview window and allocate all available EMS memory, thereby preventing applications in other windows from obtaining enough memory to run.

There are two solutions to this problem. The first is for the DOS extender to allocate all EMS memory via EMS calls in V86 mode rather than with VCPI calls in protected mode. Since memory allocation is now performed in V86 mode, DESQview is able to intercept the calls and limit memory consumption.

The second solution requires the voluntary cooperation of the DOS extender. During initialization, the DOS extender makes the EMS Get Number of Pages call (Int 67H Function 42H). If DESQview is not present, this call returns the total amount of free memory in the EMS memory pool. If the program is running under DESQview, the returned value reflects the user-imposed memory limitations for that window. The DOS extender then deliberately limits its allocation of VCPI memory to the amount returned by the EMS call.

Both methods for limiting physical memory consumption work, and all DOS extender products that support VCPI implement one of these two solutions. While neither approach is elegant, either achieves the practical goal of solving the memory contention problem.

Multitasking Two Protected-Mode Programs

When DESQview multitasks two extended DOS applications, the VCPI interface is used to switch between three different protected mode environments!

DESQview/QEMM set up one protected mode environment, and each DOS extender sets up another, separate, environment. Let's examine how the programs use VCPI to make this work.

Figure 10-1: Multitasking extended DOS applications with VCPI.

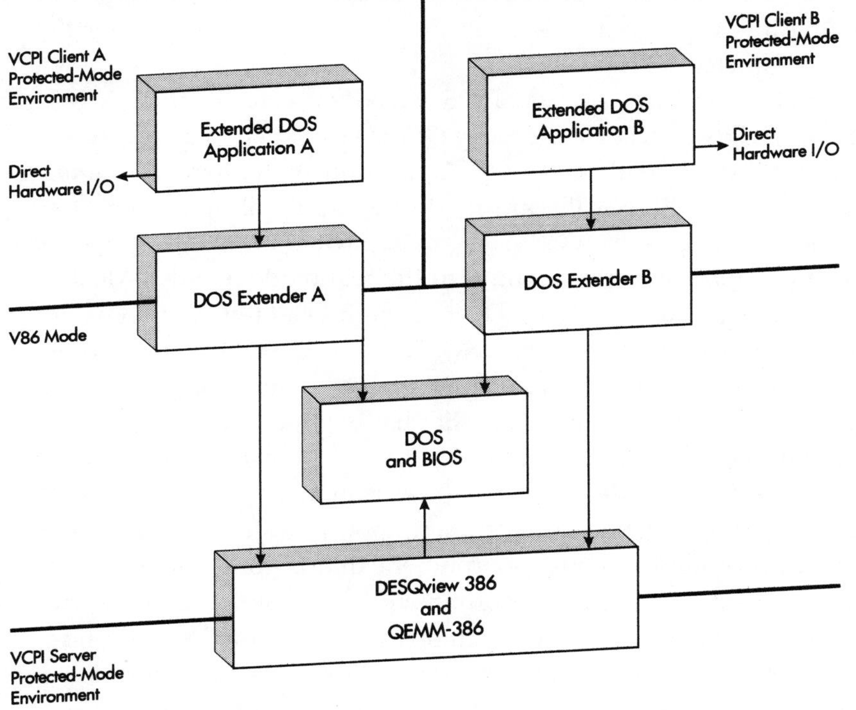

Suppose the user opens window A and window B, and wants to run an extended DOS application simultaneously in each window. Figure 10-1 shows how control passes between DESQview and the two applications. DESQview and QEMM set up a V86 mode environment in which DOS and other real-mode code can run, and a protected-mode environment which is used by DESQview and QEMM for performing system-level activities. Each DOS extender has real-mode code that runs in the V86 environment, and protected-mode code that runs in the protected-mode environment set up by the DOS extender. VCPI calls are used by the DOS extender to switch between V86 mode and its own protected-mode environment.

All communication between the programs is performed in V86 mode, which is the environment they all have in common. The control flow between programs, shown as arrows in Figure 10-1, is accomplished primarily with interrupts—either hardware interrupts, or software interrupts such as DOS and BIOS system calls. The direction of the arrows shows the flow of control when the interrupt occurs; as with any interrupt, control is returned along the same path after the interrupt handler completes.

Suppose application A is fired up first. DOS extender A starts running in V86 mode, then uses the VCPI services provided by QEMM to switch to its protected-mode environment, where it loads and runs application A. As hardware interrupts occur, or as DOS or BIOS calls are made by the application, the DOS extender fields them and uses the VCPI services to switch back to V86 mode, where it reissues the interrupt to pass control to the real-mode handler. Most of these interrupts are processed directly by DOS or the BIOS. However, some are handled entirely, or at least filtered, by DESQview and QEMM. For example, DESQview filters the timer tick hardware interrupt so it can monitor elapsed time and switch tasks when a program's time slice has expired.

Eventually the user presses the DESQview hot key and instructs DESQview to start up application B. DOS extender B runs application B in protected mode exactly as described for application A, with the important difference that DOS extender B provides a protected-mode environment that is completely disjoint from DOS extender A's protected-mode environment. After application B has run for a while, its time slice expires. A timer tick interrupt occurs, and DOS extender B switches to V86 mode and reissues the interrupt. DESQview gets control and decides to switch control back to application A. It "returns" to DOS extender A from the keyboard interrupt for the hot key, which was the last event seen by DOS extender A before the user started application B running.

Thus, each application runs until it terminates, gives up control implicitly by execution of a software interrupt for a DOS or BIOS service, its time slice expires, or some other hardware interrupt (including those caused by keyboard entries) occurs. Any of these events can result in DESQview transferring control of the machine from one application to the other. At any given moment, code is running in one of four environments: the V86 mode environment controlled by DESQview/QEMM, DOS extender A's protected-mode environment, DOS extender B's protected-mode environment, or DESQview/QEMM's protected-mode environment.

This seems complex on the surface, but an underlying simplicity is actually present. At any moment, only one protected-mode environment is active. The program controlling that environment—either DESQview/QEMM, DOS extender A, or DOS extender B—can act as if it controls the machine, and as if no other protected mode environment exists. The VCPI interface is used to switch between environments as necessary. Each DOS extender has no knowledge of the other DOS extender, or of DESQview; as far as it's concerned, it's just using the VCPI interface to switch between V86 mode and its own protected-mode environment.

DESQview doesn't need to treat the extended DOS applications any differently from normal DOS applications; it simply passes control to each program in V86 mode, and the fact that the program later uses the VCPI interface to switch to its own protected-mode environment has no relevance to the multitasking aspect of DESQview. All this environment switching activity can occur without noticeable overhead because the switching is accomplished with a very small piece of code, as was demonstrated in Chapter 8.

As noted previously, the primary restriction of VCPI is the inability of the DESQview to virtualize hardware access. This is depicted in Figure 10-1 by the arrows at the top of the diagram showing the extended DOS applications performing direct hardware I/O. Since that I/O is performed in the context of a protected-mode environment controlled by a DOS extender, DESQview cannot make any provision to trap the I/O and virtualize it.

Windows/DPMI vs. DESQview/VCPI

Table 10-1 summarizes the differences between using DPMI and VCPI to multitask extended DOS applications. The implementations in Windows and DESQview are used to make the comparison.

Table 10-1: Comparison of Extended DOS Under DPMI and VCPI.

Feature	Windows/DPMI 0.9	DESQview/VCPI
multitasking	no limitations	no limitations
compatibility	only a few extended DOS applications are currently DPMI compatible.	almost all extended DOS applications are VCPI compatible.

Feature	Windows/DPMI 0.9	DESQview/VCPI
hardware virtualization	yes, but impractically slow	no
virtual memory	provided by Windows	provided by DOS extender
memory allocation	DPMI calls directly to Windows kernel 20 EMS/VCPI calls to QEMM.	DESQview can limit physical memory consumption by intercepting the EMS "size of free memory" call.
multiple extended DOS apps in one virtual machine	no	yes

Both systems can multitask compatible extended DOS applications. Currently, DESQview is compatible with more applications than Windows. Extended DOS applications also tend to perform better under DESQview, because the DOS extender is able to provide virtual memory services. Unlike DESQview, Windows is able to virtualize hardware devices such as the screen, though performance is often disappointing. DESQview has no restrictions on multiple extended DOS application in a single virtual machine, while Windows requires separate virtual machines for each application.

Summary

Both DPMI (as implemented in Windows) and VCPI (as implemented in DESQview) can be used by multitasking hosts to run extended DOS applications. DPMI allows full hardware virtualization by the host, but VCPI is less restrictive and permits compatibility with a larger installed base of applications. Over time, most extended DOS applications will become DPMI compatible, since all major DOS extender vendors now provide DPMI compatibility.

With Windows and DESQview already providing compatibility with extended DOS applications, and the upcoming 2.0 release of OS/2 about to include DPMI support, users of multitaskers face fewer problems with existing applications. Within a couple of years, the need to upgrade or discard your favorite applications when you switch to a multitasker may almost disappear.

Developers also have more choices; they are no longer faced with choosing between releasing a memory-bound real mode DOS program that can run anywhere, or a Windows- or OS/2-specific version that only sells to a limited market. It's now possible to release a powerful, multi-megabyte extended DOS application that runs under DOS, Windows, DESQview, and soon OS/2.

Appendix A

Table A-1: The EMS Programming Interface.

Function	EMS Version	Parameters	Results if Successful*
EMS Function 40H Get Status	3.0	AH = 40H	AH = 00H
Note: This function should only be used after an application has established that the expanded memory manager is in fact present.			
EMS Function 41H Get Page Frame Address	3.0	AH = 41H	AH = 00H BX = segment base of page frame
Note: The page frame is divided into four 16K pages. In EMS 4.0, pages may be mapped to other locations than the page frame.			
EMS Function 42H Get Number of Pages	3.0	AH = 42H	AH = 00H BX = unallocated pages DX = total pages
EMS Function 43H Allocate Handle and Pages	3.0	AH = 43H BX = pages to allocate (must be nonzero)	AH = 00H DX = EMM handle
Note: The pages allocated by this function are always 16K. Zero pages may not be allocated.			
EMS Function 44H Map Expanded Memory Page	3.0	AH = 44H AL = physical page BX = logical page DX = EMM handle	AH = 00H
Note: In EMS 4.0, if this function is called with BX = -1, the specified physical page is unmapped.			
EMS Function 45H Release Handle and Expanded Memory Pages	3.0	AH = 45H DX = EMM handle	AH = 00H
EMS Function 46H Get EMS Version	3.0	AH = 46H	AH = 00H AL = EMS version
Note: The version number is returned in binary coded decimal (BCD) format, with the integer portion in the upper 4 bits of AL and the fractional portion in the lower 4 bits.			
EMS Function 47H Save Page Map	3.0	AH = 47H DX = EMM handle	AH = 00H
Note: This function saves the mapping state only for the 64K page frame defined in EMS 3.x.			
EMS Function 48H Restore Page Map	3.0	AH = 48H DX = EMM handle	AH = 00H
Note: This function restores the mapping state only for the 64K page frame defined in EMS 3.x.			

*Failure of an EMS Function is indicated by return of a nonzero error code in register AH. A list of these error codes may be found in Table 2-4.

Function	EMS Version	Parameters	Results if Successful*
EMS Function 49H Reserved	3.0		
EMS Function 4AH Reserved	3.0		
EMS Function 4BH Get Number of Active Handles	3.0	AH = 4BH	AH = 00H BX = number of active handles
Note: The maximum number of active handles is 255.			
EMS Function 4CH Get Number of Pages for Handle	3.0	AH = 4CH DX = EMM handle	AH = 00H BX = number of pages
Note: The maximum number of pages which may be allocated to a handle is 512 in EMS 3.x and 2,048 in EMS 4.0.			
EMS Function 4DH Get Pages for All Handles	3.0	AH = 4DH ES:DI = buffer address	AH = 00H BX = number of active handles *and* page information in buffer
Note: The buffer is filled in with a series of dword (32-bit) entries, one per active EMM handle. The first word of an entry contains the handle, and the second word contains the number of pages allocated to that handle.			
EMS Function 4EH Subfunction 00H Save Page Map	3.2	AH = 4EH AL = 00H ES:DI = buffer address	AH = 00H *and* mapping information in buffer
Note: The size of the buffer required by this function can be obtained with EMS Function 4EH Subfunction 03H.			
EMS Function 4EH Subfunction 01H Restore Page Map	3.2	AH = 4EH AL = 01H DS:SI = buffer address	AH = 00H
Note: The mapping information in the buffer must be prepared by a previous call to EMS Function 4EH Subfunction 00H or 02H.			
EMS Function 4EH Subfunction 02H Save and Restore Page Map	3.2	AH = 4EH AL = 02H DS:SI = buffer containing mapping information ES:DI = buffer to receive mapping information	AH = 00H *and* mapping information in buffer pointed to by ES:DI
Note: The mapping information in the buffer pointed to by DS:SI must be prepared by a previous call to EMS Function 4EH Subfunction 00H or 02H. The size of the buffers required by this function can be obtained with EMS Function 4EH Subfunction 03H.			
EMS Function 4EH Subfunction 03H Get Size of Page Map Information	3.2	AH = 4EH AL = 03H	AH = 00H AL = buffer size (bytes)

*Failure of an EMS Function is indicated by return of a nonzero error code in register AH. A list of these error codes may be found in Table 2-4.

Function	EMS Version	Parameters	Results if Successful*
EMS Function 4FH Subfunction 00H Save Partial Page Map	4.0	AH = 4FH AL = 00H DS:SI = map list ES:DI = buffer to receive mapping state	AH = 00H *and* buffer pointed to by ES:DI filled in with mapping information
Note: The map list contains the number of mappable segments in the first word, followed by the segment addresses of the mappable memory regions (one segment per word). EMS Function 4FH Subfunction 02H can be called to obtain the size of the buffer to receive the mapping information.			
EMS Function 4FH Subfunction 01H Restore Partial Page Map	4.0	AH = 4FH AL = 01H DS:SI = address of buffer containing mapping information	AH = 00H
Note: The buffer containing the mapping information must be prepared by a previous call to EMS Function 4FH Subfunction 00H.			
EMS Function 4FH Subfunction 02H Get Size of Partial Page Map Information	4.0	AH = 4FH AL = 02H BX = number of pages	AH = 00H AL = buffer size (bytes)
EMS Function 50H Subfunction 00H Map Multiple Pages by Number	4.0	AH = 50H AL = 00H CX = number of pages DX = EMM handle DS:SI = address of buffer containing mapping information	AH = 00H
Note: The buffer contains a series of dword entries which control the pages to be mapped. The first word of each entry contains the logical page number, and the second word contains the physical page number. If the logical page is -1 the physical page is unmapped.			
EMS Function 50H Subfunction 01H Map Multiple Pages by Address	4.0	AH = 50H AL = 01H CX = number of pages DX = EMM handle DS:SI = address of buffer containing mapping information	AH = 00H
Note: The buffer contains a series of *dword* entries which control the pages to be mapped. The first word of each entry contains the logical page number, and the second word contains the physical segment address. If the logical page is -1, the physical page is unmapped.			
EMS Function 51H Reallocate Pages for Handle	4.0	AH = 51H BX = new number of pages DX = EMM handle	AH = 00H BX = pages owned by handle
Note: If the requested number of pages is zero, the handle is still active and its allocation can be changed again at a later time.			

*Failure of an EMS Function is indicated by return of a nonzero error code in register AH. A list of these error codes may be found in Table 2-4.

Function	EMS Version	Parameters	Results if Successful*
EMS Function 52H Subfunction 00H Get Handle Attribute	4.0	AH = 52H AL = 00H DX = EMM handle	AH = 00H AL = attribute *0 = volatile* *1 = nonvolatile*
Note: A non-volatile memory handle and the contents of the expanded memory pages which are allocated to it are maintained across a system restart using Ctrl-Alt-Del.			
EMS Function 52H Subfunction 01H Set Handle Attribute	4.0	AH = 52H AL = 01H BL = attribute *0 = volatile* *1 = nonvolatile* DX = EMM handle	AH = 00H
Note: If the system does not support non-volatile handles, an error is returned.			
EMS Function 52H Subfunction 02H Get Attribute Capability	4.0	AH = 52H AL = 02H	AH = 00H AL = handle attribute capability *0 = volatile only* *1 = volatile and non-volatile*
EMS Function 53H Subfunction 00H Get Handle Name	4.0	AH = 53H AL = 00H DX = EMM handle ES:DI = buffer address	AH = 00H *and* buffer contains 8-byte handle name
Note: A handle's name is initialized to 8 zero bytes when it is allocated or deallocated.			
EMS Function 53H Subfunction 01H Set Handle Name	4.0	AH = 53H AL = 01H DX = EMM handle DS:SI = address of 8-byte handle name	AH = 00H
Note: The bytes in a handle name need not be ASCII characters. The default name for a handle is 8 zero bytes. The name of a non-volatile handle will be preserved across a warm boot.			
EMS Function 54H Subfunction 00H Get All Handle Names	4.0	AH = 54H AL = 00H ES:DI = buffer address	AH = 00H AL = number of active handles *and* handle name information in buffer
Note: The buffer is filled with a series of 10-byte entries. The first two bytes of an entry contain an EMM handle, and the next eight bytes contain the handle's name. The maximum size of the returned information is 2,550 bytes.			
EMS Function 54H Subfunction 01H Search for Handle Name	4.0	AH = 54H AL = 01H DS:SI = address of 8-byte handle name	AH = 00H DX = EMM handle
EMS Function 54H Subfunction 02H Get Total Handles	4.0	AH = 54H AL = 02H	AH = 00H BX = number of handles

*Failure of an EMS Function is indicated by return of a nonzero error code in register AH. A list of these error codes may be found in Table 2-4.

Function	EMS Version	Parameters	Results if Successful*
EMS Function 55H Subfunctions 00H and 01H Map Pages and Jump	4.0	AH = 55H AL = 0 *to map by physical page numbers,* 1 *to map by physical page segments* DX = EMM handle DS:SI = buffer address	AH = 00H
Note: The buffer pointed to by DS:SI is formatted as: *dword* far pointer to jump target *byte* number of pages to map before jump *dword* far pointer to map list The map list consists of *dword* entries; one per page to be mapped. The first word of an entry contains the logical page number, and the second word contains a physical page number or segment (depending on the value in AL).			
EMS Function 56H Subfunctions 00H and 01H Map Pages and Call	4.0	AH = 56H AL = 0 *to map by physical page numbers,* 1 *to map by physical page segments* DX = EMM handle DS:SI = buffer address	AH = 00H
Note: The buffer pointed to by DS:SI is formatted as: *dword* far pointer to call target *byte* number of pages to map before call *dword* far pointer to call map list *byte* number of pages to map before return *dword* far pointer to return map list *8 bytes* reserved Both map lists consist of *dword* entries; one per page to be mapped. The first word of an entry contains the logical page number, and the second word contains a physical page number or segment (depending on the value in AL).			
EMS Function 56H Subfunction 02H Get Stack Space Required for Map Page and Call	4.0	AH = 56H AL = 02H	AH = 00H BX = stack space required (bytes)
EMS Function 57H Subfunction 00H Move Memory Region	4.0	AH = 57H AL = 00H DS:SI = buffer address	AH = 00H
Note: The buffer pointed to by DS:SI controls the move operation and is formatted as: *dword* region length in bytes *byte* source memory type (0 = conventional, 1 = expanded) *word* source memory handle *word* source memory offset *word* source memory segment or logical page number *byte* destination memory type (0 = conventional, 1 = expanded) *word* destination memory handle *word* destination memory offset *word* destination memory segment or logical page number The maximum length of a move is 1 megabyte. If the length exceeds a single page, consecutive pages supply or receive the data. Overlapping addresses are handled correctly.			

*Failure of an EMS Function is indicated by return of a nonzero error code in register AH. A list of these error codes may be found in Table 2-4.

Function	EMS Version	Parameters	Results if Successful*
EMS Function 57H Subfunction 01H Exchange Memory Regions	4.0	AH = 57H AL = 01H DS:SI = buffer address	AH = 00H
Note: The format of the buffer controlling the exchange operation is the same as for EMS Function 57H Subfunction 00H. The maximum length of an exchange is 1 megabyte. Consecutive pages are used as required. Source and destination addresses may not overlap.			
EMS Function 58H Subfunction 00H Get Addresses of Mappable Pages	4.0	AH = 58H AL = 00H ES:DI = buffer address	AH = 00H CX = number of entries in buffer *and* address information placed in buffer
Note: The returned information in the buffer consists of *dword* entries, one per mappable page. The first word of an entry contains the page's segment base address, and the second contains its physical page number. The entries are sorted in order of ascending segment addresses.			
EMS Function 58H Subfunction 01H Get Number of Mappable Pages	4.0	AH = 58H AL = 01H	AH = 00H CX = number of mappable pages
EMS Function 59H Subfunction 00H Get Hardware Configuration	4.0	AH = 59H AL = 00H ES:DI = buffer address	AH = 00H *and* hardware configuration information in buffer
Note: The format of the information returned in the buffer is: *word* size of raw expanded memory pages (paragraphs) *word* number of alternate register sets *word* size of context save area (bytes) *word* number of register sets assignable to DMA channels *word* DMA operation type (0 = DMA can be used with alternate register sets, 1 = only one DMA register set available)			
EMS Function 59H Subfunction 01H Get Number of Raw Pages	4.0	AH = 59H AL = 01H	AH = 00H BX = number of free raw pages DX = total raw pages
Note: Raw memory pages may have a size other than 16K.			
EMS Function 5AH Subfunction 00H Allocate Handle and Standard Pages	4.0	AH = 5AH AL = 00H BX = number of 16K pages	AH = 00H DX = EMM handle
Note: Allocation of zero pages with this function is not an error.			
EMS Function 5AH Subfunction 01H Allocate Handle and Raw Pages	4.0	AH = 5AH AL = 01H BX = number of raw pages	AH = 00H DX = EMM handle
Note: Raw memory pages may have a size other than 16K. Allocation of zero pages is not an error.			

*Failure of an EMS Function is indicated by return of a nonzero error code in register AH. A list of these error codes may be found in Table 2-4.

Function	EMS Version	Parameters	Results if Successful*
EMS Function 5BH Subfunction 00H Get Alternate Map Registers	4.0	AH = 5BH AL = 00H	AH = 00H BL = current alternate register set, or zero if alternate set not active ES:DI = address of alternate map register set save area (if BL = 0)
Note: The address of the save area must be specified in a previous call to EMS Function 5BH Subfunction 01H, and the save area initialized with a previous call to EMS Function 4EH Subfunction 00H.			
EMS Function 5BH Subfunction 01H Set Alternate Map Registers	4.0	AH = 5BH AL = 01H BL = alternate map register set number, or zero ES:DI = address of map register context save area (if BL = 0)	AH = 00H
Note: The buffer address specified in this call is returned by subsequent calls to EMS Function 5BH Subfunction 00H. The save area must be initialized by a previous call to EMS Function 4EH Subfunction 00H.			
EMS Function 5BH Subfunction 02H Get Size of Alternate Map Register Save Area	4.0	AH = 5BH AL = 02H	AH = 00H DX = size of buffer required (bytes)
EMS Function 5BH Subfunction 03H Allocate Alternate Map Register Set	4.0	AH = 5BH AL = 03H	AH = 00H BL = alternate map register set number, or zero if no alternates available
Note: The contents of the currently active map registers are copied into the newly allocated alternate map registers.			
EMS Function 5BH Subfunction 04H Deallocate Alternate Map Register Set	4.0	AH = 5BH AL = 04H BL = alternate map register set number	AH = 00H
Note: The current alternate map register set cannot be deallocated.			
EMS Function 5BH Subfunction 05H Allocate DMA Register Set	4.0	AH = 5BH AL = 05H	AH = 00H BL = DMA register set number, or 0 if none available
EMS Function 5BH Subfunction 06H Enable DMA on Alternate Map Register Set	4.0	AH = 5BH AL = 06H BL = alternate map register set number DL = DMA channel number	AH = 00H
Note: If a DMA channel is not assigned to a specific register set, DMA for that channel will be mapped through the current register set.			

*Failure of an EMS Function is indicated by return of a nonzero error code in register AH. A list of these error codes may be found in Table 2-4.

Function	EMS Version	Parameters	Results if Successful*
EMS Function 5BH Subfunction 07H Disable DMA on Alternate Map Register Set	4.0	AH = 5BH AL = 07H BL = alternate map register set number	AH = 00H
EMS Function 5BH Subfunction 08H Deallocate DMA Register Set	4.0	AH = 5BH AL = 08H BL = DMA register set number	AH = 00H
EMS Function 5CH Prepare Expanded Memory Manager for Warm Boot	4.0	AH = 5CH	AH = 00H
Note: This function affects the current mapping context, the alternate register set in use, and any other hardware dependencies that would ordinarily be initialized when the system is reset.			
EMS Function 5DH Subfunction 00H Enable EMM Operating System Functions	4.0	AH = 5DH AL = 00H BX:CX = access key (if not first call)	AH = 00H BX:CX = access key (if first call)
Note: Enables EMS Functions 59H, 5BH, and 5DH (this is the default condition). An access key is returned on the first call to either Subfunction 00H or 01H of EMS Function 5DH. This key must be used in subsequent calls to either subfunction.			
EMS Function 5DH Subfunction 01H Disable EMM Operating System Functions	4.0	AH = 5DH AL = 01H BX:CX = access key (if not first call)	AH = 00H BX:CX = access key (if first call)
Note: Disables EMS Functions 59H, 5BH, and 5DH.			
EMS Function 5DH Subfunction 02H Release Access Key	4.0	AH = 5DH AL = 02H BX:CX = access key	AH = 00H
Note: A new access key will be returned by the next call to EMS Function 5DH Subfunction 00H or 01H.			

*Failure of an EMS Function is indicated by return of a nonzero error code in register AH. A list of these error codes may be found in Table 2-4.

Appendix B

Table B-1: The XMS Programming Interface.

Function	Parameters	Results if Successful	Results if Unsuccessful
XMS Function 00H Get XMS Version	AH = 00H	AX = XMS version BX = XMM (driver) version DX = HMA indicator 0000H if no HMA 0001H if HMA exists	AX = 0000H BL = error code
Note: Version numbers are binary coded decimal (BCD). The value returned in DX is not affected by any previous allocation of the HMA by another program.			
XMS Function 01H Allocate High Memory Area (HMA)	AH = 01H DX = HMA bytes needed (driver or TSR) or 0FFFFH (application program)	AX = 0001H	AX = 0000H BL = error code
Note: The maximum HMA allocation is 65,520 bytes. The base address of the HMA is 0FFFF:0010H. If an application fails to release the HMA before it terminates, the HMA becomes unavailable to other programs until the system is restarted.			
XMS Function 02H Free High Memory Area (HMA)	AH = 02H	AX = 0001H	AX = 0000H BL = error code
XMS Function 03H Global Enable A20 Line	AH = 03H	AX = 0001H	AX = 0000H BL = error code
Note: This function should only be used by programs that have successfully allocated the HMA. The A20 line should be disabled before the program releases control of the system.			
XMS Function 04H Global Disable A20 Line	AH = 04H	AX = 0001H	AX = 0000H BL = error code
Note: This function should only be used by programs that have successfully allocated the HMA.			
XMS Function 05H Local Enable A20 Line	AH = 05H	AX = 0001H	AX = 0000H BL = error code
Note: This function should be used by programs that do not own the HMA. The A20 line should be disabled before the program releases control of the system.			
XMS Function 06H Local Disable A20 Line	AH = 06H	AX = 0001H	AX = 0000H BL = error code
Note: This function should be used by programs that do not own the HMA.			

Function	Parameters	Results if Successful	Results if Unsuccessful
XMS Function 07H Query A20 Address Line Status	AH = 07H	*If A20 line is enabled* AX = 0001H *If A20 line is disabled* AX = 0000H BL = 00H	AX = 0000H BL = error code
XMS Function 08H Query Free Extended Memory	AH = 08H	AX = largest free extended memory block (KB) DX = total free extended memory (KB)	AX = 0000H BL = error code
Note: The size of the HMA is not included in the returned values, even if it is not in use.			
XMS Function 09H Allocate Extended Memory Block (EMB)	AH = 09H DX = requested block size (KB)	AX = 0001H DX = EMB handle	AX = 0000H BL = error code
Note: An EMB block length of zero is explicitly allowed.			
XMS Function 0AH Free Extended Memory Block (EMB)	AH = 0AH DX = EMB handle	AX = 0001H	AX = 0000H BL = error code
Note: If an application fails to release its extended memory before it terminates, the memory becomes unavailable for use by other programs until the system is restarted.			
XMS Function 0BH Move Extended Memory Block (EMB)	AH = 0BH DS:SI = segment:offset of parameter block	AX = 0001H	AX = 0000H BL = error code
Note: Parameter block format: *dword* length of block (bytes) *word* source EMB handle *dword* source offset *word* destination EMB handle *dword* destination offset. If source and/or destination handle is zero, the corresponding offset is assumed to be a normal far pointer. The EMB need not be locked. The state of the A20 line is preserved.			
XMS Function 0CH Lock Extended Memory Block (EMB)	AH = 0CH DX = EMB handle	AX = 0001H DX:BX = 32-bit linear address of locked block	AX = 0000H BL = error code
Note: This function is intended for use by programs which enable the A20 line and then access extended memory directly. Lock calls may be nested.			
XMS Function 0DH Unlock Extended Memory Block (EMB)	AH = 0DH DX = EMB handle	AX = 0001H	AX = 0000H BL = error code
Note: After an EMB is unlocked, the 32-bit linear address returned by any previous lock call becomes invalid and should not be used.			

Function	Parameters	Results if Successful	Results if Unsuccessful
XMS Function 0EH Get EMB Handle Information	AH = 0EH DX = EMB handle	AX = 0001H BH = lock count (0 if block not locked) BL = number of handles still available DX = block size (KB)	AX = 0000H BL = error code
XMS Function 0FH Resize Extended Memory Block (EMB)	AH = 0FH BX = new block size (KB) DX = EMB handle	AX = 0001H	AX = 0000H BL = error code
Note: Blocks may not be resized while they are locked.			
XMS Function 10H Allocate Upper Memory Block (UMB)	AH = 10H DX = requested block size (paragraphs)	AX = 0001H BX = segment base of allocated block DX = actual block size (paragraphs)	AX = 0000H BL = error code DX = size of largest available block (paragraphs)
Note: Upper memory blocks are always paragraph aligned. The A20 line need not be enabled to access an UMB.			
XMS Function 11H Free Upper Memory Block (UMB)	AH = 11H DX = segment base of block	AX = 0001H	AX = 0000H BL = error code

Appendix C

Table C-1: VCPI Calls.

Function	Input Parameter	Output Parameter
VCPI Presence Detection	AX = DE00h	If VCPI present: AH = 0 BL = VCPI minor version number, in binary BH = VCPI major version number, in binary If VCPI not present: AH = nonzero
Note: The presence detection call is made after checking for the presence of an EMS emulator and allocating one EMS page to make sure the EMS driver is turned on and has switched the processor to V86 mode.		
Get Protected Mode Interface	AX = DE01h ES:DI = pointer to client's 0th page table DS:SI = pointer to three descriptor table entries in the client's GDT	AH = 0 DI = advanced to first uninitialized page table entry in client's page table EBX = offset of server's entry point in protected mode code segment
Note: When the client makes the Get Interface call, the server initializes a portion of the client's 0th page table, which maps linear addresses from 0 to 4 megabytes in the client's address space. The server is required to map linear addresses from 0 to 1 megabyte exactly as they are mapped in the server's address space. The server also initializes up to three descriptor table entries in the client's GDT. The first of these three descriptors is required to be a code segment; the server returns its entry point in this code segment, to be used for making VCPI calls from protected mode. This segment and address space initialization lays the groundwork that makes switching between server and client environments, and communication in protected mode, possible.		
Get Maximum Physical Memory Address	AX = DE02h	AH = 0 EDX = physical address of highest 4K page server will allocate
Note: The client uses this call during initialization to determine the largest physical page address the server can allocate. Some clients use the information for memory management; it is convenient to set up a segment mapping the entire physical address space, so physical pages can be read and written directly.		
Get Number of Free 4K Pages	AX = DE03h	AH = 0 EDX = number of free 4K pages
Note: The Get Number of Free Pages call returns the current number of unallocated 4K pages in the server's memory pool. This call can be made in both protected mode and V86 mode.		
Allocate a 4K Page	AX = DE04h	If success: AH = 0 EDX = physical address of 4K page If failure: AH = nonzero EDX = unspecified
Note: The client makes this call to allocate a page of memory. This call can be made in both protected mode and V86 mode.		

Function	Input Parameter	Output Parameter
Free a 4K Page	AX = DE05h EDX = physical address of previously allocated 4K page	If success: AH = 0 If failure: AH = nonzero
Note: The Free Page call is used to free a page of memory allocated via Function 04H. The client is required to free all allocated memory before exiting. This call must not be used to free memory allocated through the EMS interface. The Free Page call can be made in both protected mode and V86 mode.		
Get Physical Address of 4K Page in First Megabyte	AX = DE06h CX = page number (linear address of page shifted right 12 bits)	If success: AH = 0 EDX = physical address of 4K page If invalid page number: AH = nonzero
Note: The client uses this call primarily to obtain the physical addresses of memory allocated through the EMS interface and mapped into the EMS page frame. If the allocated memory is to be used in protected mode, the client needs the physical address so it can map the page in its own page tables.		
Read CR0	AX = DE07H	AH = 0 EBX = CR0 value
Note: The Read CR0 call returns the current value in the CR0 register.		
Read Debug Registers	AX = DE08h ES:DI = pointer to array of 8 DWORDs, DR0 first in array, DR4 and DR5 not used	AH = 0
Note: The client makes this call to obtain the current debug register values.		
Load Debug Registers	AX = DE09h ES:DI = pointer to array of 8 DWORDs, DR0 first in array, DR4 and DR5 not used	AH = 0
Note: The client uses this call to load the debug registers with the specified values.		
Get 8259A Interrupt Vector Mappings	AX = DE0Ah	AH = 0 BX = interrupt vector for IRQ0 CX = interrupt vector for IRQ8
Note: This call returns the interrupt vectors generated by the 8259A interrupt controllers when a hardware interrupt occurs.		
Set 8259A Interrupt Vector Mappings	AX = DE0Bh BX = interrupt vector for IRQ0 CX = interrupt vector for IRQ8 Interrupts disabled	AH = 0
Note: The client uses this call to inform the server that it has reprogrammed the interrupt controllers to use different interrupt vectors. The client is required to disable interrupts before reprogramming the interrupt controllers, and to make this call before re-enabling interrupts. The client is permitted to perform this operation only if the standard DOS hardware interrupt vectors (08h - 0FH for IRQ0 - IRQ7, 70H - 77H for IRQ8 - IRQ15) are in effect before the client reprograms the interrupt controller. If the client reprograms the interrupt controllers, it is required to restore the original vector mappings and inform the server with this call before terminating.		

Function	Input Parameter	Output Parameter
Switch From V86 Mode to Protected Mode	AX = DE0Ch ESI = linear address below 1 megabyte of data structure specified below Interrupts disabled	GDTR, IDTR, LDTR, TR loaded with client's values Interrupts disabled Control transferred to specified FAR entry point in client EAX, ESI, DS, ES, FS, GS unspecified
Note: The data structure at which ESI points on input to this call is organized as shown in Table 8-2. The server switches to the client's environment by loading the processor's system registers with the client's values, and then transfers control to the specified entry point in the client. Care is required when switching environments; the section *Inside VCPI,* early in this chapter, contains an example implementation of this call.		
Switch From Protected Mode to V86 Mode	AX = DE0Ch Interrupts disabled DS = segment with a base address of 0 and a limit at least as large as the address space initialized by the server when the Get Protected Mode Interface call was made. SS:ESP must be in linear memory below 1 megabyte, and points to the data structure described in Table 8-3.	GDTR, IDTR, LDTR, TR loaded with server's values Interrupts disabled SS:ESP, DS, ES, FS, GS loaded with specified values Control transferred to specified FAR entry point in client EAX unspecified
Note: The data structure on the top of the stack is organized as shown in Table 8-3. The server switches to its own protected-mode environment by loading the processor's system registers with its own values, and then passes control to the client in V86 mode with the segment registers loaded with the values in the data structure on the stack. The data structure is organized so that the server can switch to V86 mode and load the client's registers with a single IRETD instruction. The server must initialize the EFLAGS value, since it controls the IOPL setting in V86 mode. This call can be made only from protected mode.		

Appendix D

Table D-1: DPMI Programming Reference .

Function	DPMI Version	Parameters	Results if Successful*
Int 2FH Function 1680H Release Current Virtual Machine's Time Slice	1.0	AX = 1680H	AL = 0
Int 2FH Function 1686H Get CPU Mode	0.9	AX = 1686H	AX = 0 if in protected mode, nonzero if in real mode
Int 2FH Function 1687H Obtain Real-to-Protected Mode Switch Entry Point	0.9	AX = 1687H	AX = 0 BX = flags (bit 0=0 if 16-bit programs only supported, bit 0=1 if 32-bit programs supported CL = processor type (02H=286, 03H=386, 04H=486) DH = DPMI major version number DL = DPMI minor version number SI = paragraphs of memory needed for DPMI private data area ES:DI = segment:offset of mode switch entry point
Int 2FH Function 168AH Get Vendor-Specific API Entry Point	1.0	AX = 168AH DS:(E)SI = selector:offset of ASCIIZ DPMI host vendor name	AL = 0 ES:(E)DI = selector:offset of extended API entry point
Int 31H Function 0000H Allocate LDT Descriptors	0.9	AX = 0000H CX = number of descriptors to allocate	Carry = clear AX = base selector
Int 31H Function 0001H Free LDT Descriptor	0.9	AX = 0001H BX = selector	Carry = clear
Int 31H Function 0002H Segment to Descriptor	0.9	AX = 0002H BX = real mode segment	Carry = clear AX = selector

* If the function fails, the Carry flag is returned set. Under DPMI 1.0 hosts, an error code is also returned in AX (a list of these error codes can be found in Chapter 9 in Table 9-2).

Function	DPMI Version	Parameters	Results if Successful*
Int 31H Function 0003H Get Selector Increment Value	0.9	AX = 0003H	Carry = clear AX = selector increment value
Int 31H Function 0006H Get Segment Base Address	0.9	AX = 0006H BX = selector	Carry = clear CX:DX = 32-bit base address
Int 31H Function 0007H Set Segment Base Address	0.9	AX = 0007H BX = selector CX:DX = segment base address	Carry = clear
Int 31H Function 0008H Set Segment Limit	0.9	AX = 0008H BX = selector CX:DX = segment limit	Carry = clear
Int 31H Function 0009H Set Descriptor Access Rights	0.9	AX = 0009H BX = selector CL = access rights/type byte Ch = 80386 extended access rights/type byte	Carry = clear
Int 31H Function 000AH Create Alias Descriptor	0.9	AX = 000AH BX = selector	Carry = clear AX = data selector (alias)
Int 31H Function 000BH Get Descriptor	0.9	AX = 000BH BX = selector ES:(E)DI = address of 8-byte buffer	Carry = clear and descriptor placed in buffer
Int 31H Function 000CH Set Descriptor	0.9	AX = 000CH BX = selector ES:(E)DI = address of 8-byte descriptor	Carry = clear
Int 31H Function 000DH Allocate Specific LDT Descriptor	0.9	AX = 000DH BX = selector	Carry = clear
Int 31H Function 000EH Get Multiple Descriptors	1.0	AX = 000EH CX = number of descriptors ES:(E)DI = address of buffer containing alternating selectors (set by client) and associated descriptors (returned by host)	Carry = clear and descriptors placed in buffer
Int 31H Function 000FH Set Multiple Descriptors	1.0	AX = 000FH CX = number of descriptors ES:(E)DI = address of buffer containing alternating selectors and associated descriptors	Carry = clear
Int 31H Function 0100H Allocate DOS Memory Block	0.9	AX = 0100H BX = number of paragraphs	Carry = clear AX = real mode segment address of block DX = selector for block
Int 31H Function 0101H Free DOS Memory Block	0.9	AX = 0101H DX = selector	Carry = clear

* If the function fails, the Carry flag is returned set. Under DPMI 1.0 hosts, an error code is also returned in AX (a list of these error codes can be found in Chapter 9 in Table 9-2).

Function	DPMI Version	Parameters	Results if Successful*
Int 31H Function 0102H Resize DOS Memory Block	0.9	AX = 0102H BX = new block size in paragraphs DX = selector of block	Carry = clear
Int 31H Function 0200H Get Real Mode Interrupt Vector	0.9	AX = 0200H BL = interrupt number	Carry = clear CX:DX = segment:offset of interrupt handler
Int 31H Function 0201H Set Real lMode Interrupt Vector	0.9	AX = 0201H BL = interrupt number CX:DX = segment:offset of interrupt handler	Carry = clear
Int 31H Function 0202H Get Processor Exception Interrupt Vector	0.9	AX = 0202H Bl = exception number	Carry = clear CX:(E)DX = selector:offset of exception handler
Int 31H Function 0203H Set Processor Exception Interrupt Handler	0.9	AX = 0203H Bl = exception number CX:(E)DX = selector:offset of exception handler	Carry = clear
Int 31H Function 0204H Get Protected Mode Interrupt Handler	0.9	AX = 0204H Bl = interrupt number	Carry = clear CX:(E)DX = selector:offset of interrupt handler
Int 31H Function 0205H Set Protected Mode Interrupt Handler	0.9	AX = 0205H Bl = interrupt number CX:(E)DX = selector:offset of interrupt handler	Carry = clear
Int 31H Function 0210H Get Extended Processor Exception Handler Vector (Protected Mode)	1.0	AX = 0210H BL = exception number	Carry = clear CX:(E)DX = selector:offset of exception handler
Int 31H Function 0211H Get Extended Processor Exception Handler Vector (Real Mode)	1.0	AX = 0211H BL = exception number	Carry = clear CX:(E)DX = selector:offset of exception handler
Int 31H Function 0212H Set Extended Processor Exception Handler Vector (Protected Mode)	1.0	AX = 0212H BL = exception number CX:(E)DX = selector:offset of exception handler	Carry = clear
Int 31H Function 0213H Set Extended Processor Exception Handler Vector (Real Mode)	1.0	AX = 0213H BL = exception number CX:(E)DX = selector:offset of exception handler	Carry = clear

* If the function fails, the Carry flag is returned set. Under DPMI 1.0 hosts, an error code is also returned in AX (a list of these error codes can be found in Chapter 9 in Table 9-2).

Function	DPMI Version	Parameters	Results if Successful*
Int 31H Function 0300H Simulate Real Mode Interrupt	0.9	AX = 0300H Bl = interrupt number BH = flags (must be zero) CX = number of stack words to copy ES:(E)DI = selector:offset of real mode register data structure (see Note)	Carry = clear ES:(E)DI = selector:offset of modified real mode register data structure

Note: The format of the real mode register data structure used by the various DPMI translation functions is as follows:

Offset	Length	Contents
00H	4	DI or EDI
04H	4	SI or ESI
08H	4	BP or EBP
0CH	4	reserved, should be zero
10H	4	BX or EBX
14H	4	DX or EDX
18H	4	CX or ECX
1CH	4	AX or EAX
20H	2	CPU status flags
22H	2	ES
24H	2	DS
26H	2	FS
28H	2	GS
2AH	2	IP (reserved, ignored)
2CH	2	CS (reserved, ignored)
2EH	2	SP
30H	2	SS

Function	DPMI Version	Parameters	Results if Successful*
Int 31H Function 0301H Call Real Mode Procedure with Far Return Frame	0.9	AX = 0301H BH = flags (must be zero) CX = number of stack words to copy ES:(E)DI = selector:offset of real mode register data structure	Carry = clear ES:(E)DI = selector:offset of modified real mode register data structure
Int 31H Function 0302H Call Real Mode Procedure with IRET Frame	0.9	AX = 0302H BH = flags (must be zero) CX = number of stack words to copy ES:(E)DI = selector:offset of real mode register data structure	Carry = clear ES:(E)DI = selector:offset of modified real mode register data structure
Int 31H Function 0303H Allocate Real Mode Callback Address	0.9	AX = 0303H DS:(E)DI = selector:offset of protected mode procedure ES:(E)DI = selector:offset of buffer to receive real mode register data structure	Carry = clear CX:DX = segment:offset of real mode callback

* If the function fails, the Carry flag is returned set. Under DPMI 1.0 hosts, an error code is also returned in AX (a list of these error codes can be found in Chapter 9 in Table 9-2).

Function	DPMI Version	Parameters	Results if Successful*
Int 31H Function 0304H Free Real Mode Callback Address	0.9	AX = 0304H CX:DX = segment:offset of real mode callback	Carry = clear
Int 31H Function 0305H Get State Save/Restore Addresses	0.9	AX = 0305H	Carry = clear AX = state buffer size (bytes) BX:CX = segment:offset of real mode save/restore state routine SI:(E)DI = selector:offset of protected mode save/restore state routine
Int 31H Function 0306H Get Raw Mode Switch Addresses	0.9	AX = 0306H	Carry = clear BX:CX = segment:offset of real to protected mode switch address SI:(E)DI = selector:offset of protected to real mode switch address
Int 31H Function 0400H Get DPMI Version	0.9	AX = 0400H	Carry = clear AH = DPMI major version AL = DPMI minor version BX= flags (see Note) CL = processor type (02H=286, 03H=386, 04H=486) DH = current value of PIC master base interrupt DL = current value of PIC slave base interrupt

Note: the flags returned by this function are as follows:

Bits	Significance
0	0 = host is 16-bit DPMI implementation 1 = host is 32-bit (80386) DPMI implementation
1	0 = CPU returned to Virtual 86 mode for reflected interrupts 1 = CPU returned to real mode for reflected interrupts
2	0 = virtual memory not supported 1 = virtual memory supported
3	reserved, for historical reasons
4-15	reserved for later use

*If the function fails, the Carry flag is returned set. Under DPMI 1.0 hosts, an error code is also returned in AX (a list of these error codes can be found in Chapter 9 in Table 9-2).

Function	DPMI Version	Parameters	Results if Successful*
Int 31H Function 0401H Get DPMI Capabilities	1.0	AX = 0401H ES:(E)DI = selector:offset of 128-byte buffer	Carry = clear AX = flags (see Note) CX = 0 DX = 0 ES:(E)DI = selector offset of capability information in caller's 128-byte buffer (see Note)

Note: The flags returned by this function in register AX are as follows:

Bits	Significance
0	0 = PAGED ACCESSED/DIRTY capability *not* supported 1 = PAGED ACCESSED/DIRTY capability supported
1	0 = EXCEPTIONS RESTARTABILITY capability *not* supported 1 = EXCEPTIONS RESTARTABILITY capability supported
2	0 = DEVICE MAPPING capability *not* supported 1 = DEVICE MAPPING capability supported
3	0 = CONVENTIONAL MEMORY MAPPING capability *not* supported 1 = CONVENTIONAL MEMORY MAPPING capability supported
4	0 = DEMAND ZERO-FILL capability *not* supported 1 = DEMAND ZERO-FILL capability supported
5	0 = WRITE-PROTECT CLIENT capability not supported 1 = WRITE-PROTECT CLIENT capability supported
6	0 = WRITE-PROTECT HOST capability not supported 1 = WRITE-PROTECT HOST capability supported
7-15	reserved

Note: The format of the information placed in the 128-buffer is:

Offset	Length	Contents
0	1	Host major version number as a binary number
1	1	Host minor version number as a binary number
2	1-126	ASCIIZ (null-terminated) string identifying the DPMI host vendor

Function	DPMI Version	Parameters	Results if Successful*
Int 31H Function 0500H Get Free Memory Information	0.9	AX = 0500H ES:(E)DI = selector:offset of 48-byte buffer	Carry = clear ES:(E)DI = selector:offset of information in caller's buffer (see Note)

Note: the format of the information returned by this function is as follows:

Offset	Length	Contents
00H	4	Largest available free block in bytes
04H	4	Maximum unlocked page allocation in pages
08H	4	Maximum locked page allocation in pages
0CH	4	Linear address space size in pages
10H	4	Total number of unlocked pages
14H	4	Total number of free pages
18H	4	Total number of physical pages
1CH	4	Free linear address space in pages
20H	4	Size of paging file/partition in pages
24H	0CH	Reserved, all bytes set to 0FFH

*If the function fails, the Carry flag is returned set. Under DPMI 1.0 hosts, an error code is also returned in AX (a list of these error codes can be found in Chapter 9 in Table 9-2).

Function	DPMI Version	Parameters	Rsults if Successful*
Int 31H Function 0501H Allocate Memory Block	0.9	AX = 0501H BX:CX = block size (bytes)	Carry = clear BX:CX = linear address of block SI:DI = block handle
Int 31H Function 0502H Free Memory Block	0.9	AX = 0502H SI:DI = block handle	Carry = clear
Int 31H Function 0503H Resize Memory Block	0.9	AX = 0503H BX:CX = new size (bytes) SI:DI = block handle	Carry = clear BX:CX = new linear address of block SI:DI = new block handle
Int 31H Function 0504H Allocate Linear Memory Block	1.0	AX = 0504H EBX = desired linear address of block, or zero ECX = block size (bytes) EDX = flags (bit 0=0 create uncommitted pages, bit 0=1 create committed pages, other bits always zero)	Carry = clear EBX = linear address of block ESI = block handle
Int 31H Function 0505H Resize Linear Memory Block	1.0	AX = 0505H ESI = block handle ECX = new block size (bytes) EDX = flags (bit 0=0 create uncommitted pages, bit 0=1 create committed pages, bit 1=0 if no segment descriptor update, bit 1=1 if descriptor update desired, other bits always zero) and, if bit 1 of EDX is set: ES:EBX = selector:offset of array of selectors EDI = number of selectors in array	Carry = clear EBX = new linear address of block ESI = new block handle
Int 31H Function 0506H Get Page Attributes	1.0	AX = 0506H ESI = block handle EBX = base offset of page(s) ECX = number of pages ES:EDX = selector:offset of buffer	Carry = clear ES:EDX = selector:offset of page attributes in buffer (see Note)

Bits	Significance
0-2	page type (0-7)

Value	Meaning
0	uncommitted page
1	committed page
2	mapped page

*If the function fails, the Carry flag is returned set. Under DPMI 1.0 hosts, an error code is also returned in AX (a list of these error codes can be found in Chapter 9 in Table 9-2).

Bits	Significance	
	Value	Meaning
	3-7	currently unused
3	0 = page is read-only 1 = page is read/write	
4	0 = accessed/dirty bits not available for this page 1 = accessed/dirty bits are supplied for this page in bits 5-6	
5	0 = page has not been accessed (if bit 4=1) 1 = page has been accessed (if bit 4=1)	
6	0 = page has not been modified (if bit 4=1) 1 = page has been modified (if bit 4=1)	
7-15	reserved, currently zero	

Function	DPMI Version	Parameters	Results if Successful*
Int 31H Function 0507H Set Page Attributes	1.0	AX = 0507H ESI = block handle EBX = base offset of page(s) ECX = number of pages ES:EDX = selector:offset of buffer containing page attributes (see Note)	Carry = clear

Note: the format of the page attributes used by this function is as follows:

Bits	Significance	
0-2	page type (0-7)	
	Value	Meaning
	0	create page uncommitted
	1	create page committed
	2	not allowed
	3	modify attributes without changing page type
	4-7	not allowed
3	0 = page is read-only 1 = page is read/write	
4	0 = don't modify accessed/dirty bits for page 1 = set accessed/dirty bits as specified in bits 5-6	
5	0 = mark page as not accessed (if bit 4=1) 1 = mark page as accessed (if bit 4=1)	
6	0 = mark page as not dirty (if bit 4=1) 1 = mark page as dirty (if bit 4=1)	
7-15	reserved, should be zero	

Function	DPMI Version	Parameters	Results if Successful*
Int 31H Function 0508H Map Device in Memory Block	1.0	AX = 0508H ESI = memory block handle EBX = base offset of page(s) ECX = number of pages EDX = physical address	Carry = clear

*If the function fails, the Carry flag is returned set. Under DPMI 1.0 hosts, an error code is also returned in AX (a list of these error codes can be found in Chapter 9 in Table 9-2).

Function	DPMI Version	Parameters	Results if Successful*
Int 31H Function 0509H Map Conventional Memory in Memory Block	1.0	AX = 0509H ESI = memory block handle EBX = base offset of page(s) ECX = number of pages EDX = linear address of conventional memory	Carry = clear
Int 31H Function 050AH Get Memory Block Size and Base	1.0	AX = 050AH SI:DI = block handle	Cary = clear SI:DI = block size BX:CX = block base address
Int 31H Function 050BH Get Memory Information	1.0	AX = 050BH ES:(E)DI = selector:offset of 128-byte buffer	Carry = clear ES:(E)DI = selector:offset of information in caller's buffer (see Note)

Note: the format of the information returned by this function is as follows:

Offset	Length	Contents
00H	4	Total allocated bytes of physical memory controlled by DPMI host
04H	4	Total allocated bytes of virtual memory controlled by DPMI host
08H	4	Total available bytes of virtual memory controlled by DPMI host
0CH	4	Total allocated bytes of virtual memory for this virtual machine
10H	4	Total available bytes of virtual memory for this virtual machine
14H	4	Total allocated bytes of virtual memory for this client
18H	4	Total available bytes of memory for this client
1CH	4	Total locked bytes of memory for this client
20H	4	Maximum locked bytes of memory for this client
24H	4	Highest linear address available to this client
28H	4	Size in bytes of largest available free memory block
2CH	4	Size of minimum allocation unit in bytes
30G	4	Size of the allocation alignment unit in bytes
34H	4CH	Reserved, currently zero

Function	DPMI Version	Parameters	Results if Successful*
Int 31H Function 0600H Lock Linear Region	0.9	AX = 0600H BX:CX = base linear address SI:DI = size of region (bytes)	Carry = clear
Int 31H Function 0601H Unlock Linear Region	0.9	AX = 0601H BX:CX = base linear address SI:DI = size of region (bytes)	Carry = clear
Int 31H Function 0602H Mark Real Mode Region as Pageable	0.9	AX = 0602H BX:CX = base linear address SI:DI = size of region (bytes)	Carry = clear
Int 31H Function 0603H Relock Real Mode Region	0.9	AX = 0603H BX:CX = base linear address SI:DI = size of region (bytes)	Carry = clear
Int 31H Function 0604H Get Page Size	0.9	AX = 0604H	Carry = clear BX:CX = page size in bytes

*If the function fails, the Carry flag is returned set. Under DPMI 1.0 hosts, an error code is also returned in AX (a list of these error codes can be found in Chapter 9 in Table 9-2).

Function	PMI Version	Parameters	Results if Successful*
Int 31H Function 0702H Mark Page(s) as Demand Paging Candidate	0.9	AX = 0702H BX:CX = base address of page(s) SI:DI = size of region (bytes)	Carry = clear
Int 31H Function 0703H Discard Contents of Page(s)	0.9	AX = 0703H BX:CX = base address of page(s) SI:DI = size of region (bytes)	Carry = clear
Int 31H Function 0800H Physical Address Mapping	0.9	AX = 0800H BX:CX = physical address SI:DI = size of region (bytes)	Carry = clear BX:CX = linear address
Int 31H Function 0801H Free Physical Address Mapping	1.0	AX = 0801H BX:CX = linear address	Carry = clear
Int 31H Function 0900H Get and Disable Virtual Interrupt State	0.9	AX = 0900H	Carry = clear Al = 0 if interrupts were previously disabled, =1 if interrupts previously enabled
Int 31H Function 0901H Get and Enable Virtual Interrupt State	0.9	AX = 0901H	Carry = clear Al = 0 if interrupts were previously disabled, =1 if interrupts previously enabled
Int 31H Function 0902H Get Virtual Interrupt State	0.9	AX = 0902H	Carry = clear Al = 0 if interrupts are disabled, =1 if interrupts are enabled
Int 31H Function 0A00H Get Vendor-Specific Entry Point	0.9	AX = 0A00H DS:(E)SI = selector:offset of ASCIIZ string to identify DPMI host vendor	Carry =clear ES:(E)DI = selector:offset of entry pointer
Int 31H Function 0B00H Set Debug Watchpoint	0.9	AX = 0B00H BX:CX = linear address of watchpoint DL = size of watchpoint (1, 2, or 4 bytes) DH = watchpoint type (0=execute, 1=write, 2=read/write)	Carry = clear BX = watchpoint handle
Int 31H Function 0B01H Clear Debug Watchpoint	0.9	AX = 0B01H BX = watchpoint handle	Carry = clear
Int 31H Function 0B02H Get State of Debug Watchpoint	0.9	AX = 0B02H BX = watchpoint handle	Carry = clear AX = watchpoint status (bit 0=0 if watchpoint has not been encountered, bit 0=1 if watchpoint has been encountered)
Int 31H Function 0B03H Reset Debug Watchpoint	0.9	AX = 0B03H BX = watchpoint handle	Carry = clear

*If the function fails, the Carry flag is returned set. Under DPMI 1.0 hosts, an error code is also returned in AX (a list of these error codes can be found in Chapter 9 in Table 9-2).

Function	DPMI Version	Parameters	Results if Successful*
Int 31H Function 0C00H Install Resident Service Provider Callback	1.0	AX = 0C00H ES:(E)DI = selector:offset of 40-byte buffer (see Note)	Carry = clear

Note: the buffer passed to this function must contain information in the following format:

Offset	*Length*	*Contents*
00H	8	Descriptor for 16-bit data segment
08H	8	Descriptor for 16-bit code segment
10H	2	Offset of 16-bit callback procedure
12H	2	Reserved
14H	8	Descriptor for 32-bit data segment
1CH	8	Descriptor for 32-bit code segment
24H	4	Offset of 32-bit callback procedure

Function	DPMI Version	Parameters	Results if Successful*
Int 31H Function 0C01H Terminate and Stay Resident	1.0	AX = 0C01H BL = return code DX = number of paragraphs of DOS memory to reserve	Not applicable
Int 31H Function 0D00H Allocate Shared Memory	1.0	AX = 0D00H ES:(E)DI = selector:offset of shared memory allocation structure (see Note)	Carry = clear and structure fields at offsets 04H, 08H, and 0CH updated

Note: the buffer passed to this function must have the following format:

Offset	Length	Contents
00H	4	Requested length of shared memory block (set by client, may be zero)
04H	4	Length actually allocated (set by host)
08H	4	Shared memory handle (set by host)
0CH	4	Linear address of shared memory block (set by host)
10H	6	Offset32:selector of ASCIIZ (null-terminated ASCII) name for shared memory block (set by client)
16H	2	Reserved
18H	4	Reserved, must be zero

Function	DPMI Version	Parameters	Results if Successful*
Int 31H Function 0D01H Free Shared Memory	1.0	AX = 0D01H SI:DI = block handle	Carry = clear
Int 31H Function 0D02H Serialize on Shared Memory	1.0	AX = 0D02H SI:DI = block handle DX = option flags (see Note)	Carry = clear

Note: the option flags passed to this function having the following significance:

Bit	Significance
0	0 = suspend client until serialization available 1 = return immediately with error if serialization not available
1	0 = exclusive serialization requested 1 = shared serialization requested
2-15	reserved, must be zero

*If the function fails, the Carry flag is returned set. Under DPMI 1.0 hosts, an error code is also returned in AX (a list of these error codes can be found in Chapter 9 in Table 9-2).

Function	DPMI Version	Parameters	Results if Successful*
Int 31H Function 0D03H Free Serialization on Shared Memory	1.0	AX = 0D03H SI:DI = block handle DX = option flags (see Note)	Carry = clear

Note: the option flags passed to this function having the following significance:

Bit	Significance
0	0 = release exclusive serialization 1 = release shared serialization
1	0 = don't free pending serialization 1 = free pending serialization (see Note)
2-15	reserved, must be zero

Function	DPMI Version	Parameters	Results if Successful*
Int 31H Function 0E00H Get Coprocessor Status	1.0	AX = 0E00H	Carry = clear AX = status (see Note)

Note: the status returned by this function is interpreted as follows:

Bit	Significance
0	MPv (MP bit in the virtual MSW/CR0) 0 = numeric coprocessor is enabled for this VM 1 = numeric coprocessor is disabled for this VM
1	EMv (EM bit in the virtual MSW/CR0) 0 = client is not emulating coprocessor instructions 1 = client is emulating coprocessor instructions
2	MPr (MP bit from the actual MSW/CR0) 0 = numeric coprocessor is not present 1 = numeric coprocessor is present
3	EMr (EM bit from the actual MSW/CR0) 0 = host is not emulating coprocessor instructions 1 = host is emulating coprocessor instructions
4-7	coprocessor type 00H = no coprocessor 02H = 80287 03H = 80387 04H = 80486 with numeric coprocessor 05H-0FH reserved for future numeric processors
8-15	not applicable

Function	DPMI Version	Parameters	Results if Successful*
Int 31H Function 0E01H Set Coprocessor Emulation	1.0	AX = 0E01H BX = coprocessor flags (see Note)	Carry = clear

Note: the flags passed to this function have the following significance:

Bit	Significance
0	new value of MPv bit for client's virtual CR0 0 = enable numeric coprocessor for this VM 1 = disable numeric coprocessor for this VM
1	new value of EMv bit for client's virtual CR0 0 = client will not supply coprocessor emulation 1 = client will supply coprocessor emulation
2-15	not applicable

*If the function fails, the Carry flag is returned set. Under DPMI 1.0 hosts, an error code is also returned in AX (a list of these error codes can be found in Chapter 9 in Table 9-2).

Appendix E

Exploring Protected Mode with Instant-C

Rational Systems' Instant-C, an interactive protected-mode C compiler and integrated development environment is based on DOS/16M, Rational's DOS extender for 286- and 386-based PC compatibles. Instant-C (IC) provides interactive execution, linking, editing, and debugging of C code. In addition to loading .C files, C expressions can be typed in at IC's # prompt for immediate evaluation, at global scope, outside any function. Figure B-1 offers a look at Instant-C.

The following example uses the Microsoft C _dos_allocmem() function and the DOS/16M D16MemStrategy() function, first to allocate extended memory, and then to allocate low memory. Note how C statements, declarations, and preprocessor statements can be freely mixed at the # prompt, somewhat like mixing statements and declarations in C++. Note also that leaving the semicolon off a statement tells IC to print its value; this is one way that interactive C differs from "normal" C:

```
# #include "dos16.h"
DOS16.H included.
# unsigned seg, seg2;
# D16MemStrategy(MForceExt);
# #include <dos.h>
DOS.H included.
# _dos_allocmem(1000, &seg);
# seg
   3080 (0xC08)
# D16AbsAddress(MK_FP(seg,0))
   1910176 (0x1D25A0)
# D16MemStrategy(MForceLow);
# _dos_allocmem(1000, &seg2);
# seg2
   3088 (0xC10)
# D16AbsAddress(MK_FP(seg2,0))
   236064 (0x39A20)
```

IC can be used as a test bed in which functions are tried out, variables are declared, expressions are evaluated, and so on, without actually writing a program. At the same time, the product manages to maintain fairly high compatibility with ANSI C, including full support for function prototypes.

Aside from running in protected mode and consequently having the ability to handle much larger programs, its "immediate mode" is what most sets IC apart from other integrated development environments like Borland's Turbo C or Microsoft's Quick C. There is a fundamental difference between fully interactive C on the one hand and a merely fast C like Turbo C or Quick C on the other (though Turbo C and Quick C do produce *much* faster code than IC).

In many ways, IC represents the interactive style of languages like Forth and Lisp, made available for the C programming language. But, contrary to the stereotype of an interpreter, IC uses native object code. In fact, IC can dynamically load and link .OBJ and .LIB files, and can write out stand-alone .EXE files. Such stand-alone executables include a built-in protected-mode DOS extender.

The two major benefits of protected mode—memory protection and a large address space—mesh with the needs of a C development environment. The large address space (up to 16 megabytes of memory) means that even very large C programs can be developed interactively. Hardware-based memory protection helps insulate IC from bugs in user code, and assists IC in finding bugs. An interpreter running in protected mode can off-load some of its type-checking onto the CPU.

Figure B-1: Instant-C: a protected-mode C develpment environment.

```
Instant-C/PM 4.0L  2,700K unused Level 1,  Memory File: GDT.C
 ## 474: Step in sel, line    8
void sel(void far *fp)
    {
    unsigned seg = FP_SEG(fp);
    unsigned index = seg >> 3;  // same as SELECTOR bitfield
    DESCRIPTOR far *dt = MK_FP((seg&4)?0x68:0x8, 0);
  // in DOS/16M, selector 0x08 is GDT; selector 0x68 is LDT
    ACCESS_RIGHTS *pacc = (ACCESS_RIGHTS *) &dt[index].access;
▶   printf("SEL=%04X ADDR=%02X%04X LIMIT=%04X ACCESS=%d%c%c%c%c%c%c\n",
        seg, dt[index].addr_hi, dt[index].addr_lo,
        dt[index].limit,
        pacc->dpl,
        pacc->accessed ? 'a' : '-',

     access = 'ô' (0x93);
     reserved = 0;}
# dt[seg >> 3]
   struct  at 0008:0028 {
     limit = 255 (0xFF);
     addr_lo = 10240 (0x2800);
     addr_hi = '\002';
     access = 'ô' (0x93);
     reserved = 0;}
#
```

IC also illustrates an important trend in DOS extender technology: moving DOS extenders into language compilers. Other examples of this trend are the inclusion of Eclipse Computer Solutions' OS/286 in Lahey Fortran F77L-EM/16 and in Gold Hill Lisp, and its forthcoming inclusion in Lattice C. IC is an unusual and striking example of this trend.

IC is not only a product built using a DOS extender, it is also an example of why "Extended DOS" is necessary in the first place. IC has been in existence since 1984. As features were added to the product, it began to strain against the artificial 640K "Berlin Wall" of real-mode MS-DOS. Rational Systems in fact developed DOS/16M for IC, to cope with its expanding features and resulting expanding memory consumption. Thus, DOS/16M is based on IC, as much as IC is based on DOS/16M.

For a short time, Rational Systems marketed a separate protected-mode IC/16M alongside its real-mode IC. For an even shorter time, the name was changed to IC/PM but unfortunately this sounded like a reference either to OS/2's Presentation Manager or to the CP/M operating system! In October 1989, with IC version 4.0, Rational Systems discontinued the real-mode version.

There's one more reason to use IC as a tool for exploring protected mode: price. At $795, IC is not cheap, but it is more affordable than the $5,000 that Rational Systems charges for DOS/16M. It should be noted that IC and DOS/16M are totally different products. IC is not a scaled-down version of DOS/16M, nor is it intended to be used by itself as a DOS extender. But because it is both interactive and based on a DOS extender, IC does provide an excellent base to explore protected-mode programming.

Running LLIBCE.LIB in Protected Mode

Out of the box, IC runs in medium model; its data pointers are 2-byte quantities that hold only an offset. IC supports the Microsoft near and far keywords, but rather than explicitly specify void far * when we need more than 64K of data or require 4-byte data pointers, a large-model version of IC is useful.

Right away we encounter an unusual feature of IC: its ability to create new versions of itself. IC's #savemod command writes out a new version of IC.EXE, built-in DOS extender and all. Such a feature seems unusual in a C compiler, but IC is almost a full-blown protected-mode linker, and its ability to clone new versions of itself is a subset of this larger capability.

Working with a "quick" environment always raises the issue of compatibility with production compilers. IC has a standard library, but if you would rather, say, use the Microsoft C library, IC has scripts to: load in Microsoft C's real-mode, large-model LLIBCE.LIB; load in some IC-supplied .LIB modules to replace the few Microsoft functions that don't work in protected mode; load the Microsoft #include files into IC; and then write out a new, large-model MSC-compatible IC. The new executable not only runs your C programs in protected mode under MS-DOS, it executes the Microsoft C library in protected mode too.

It seems like quite an accomplishment to load real-mode object code and execute it in protected mode, but, as we've seen, this is standard procedure for 16-bit DOS extenders such as DOS/16M and OS/286.

Having built a large-model MSC-compatible version of IC with #savemod, it is also useful to add the DOS/16M library to IC.EXE, using the #load command. The names #load and #savemod show how IC provides a command language in the form of C preprocessor statements. The # can be left off most of these commands, but it indicates how these commands behave like preprocessor statements. In addition to the DOS/16M library, we also add the macros FP_SEG, FP_OFF, and MK_FP:

```
# #load dos16lib.c
// ...
# #defineg MK_FP(seg,ofs)    \
#    ((void far *) (((unsigned long) (seg) << 16) | (ofs)))
# #defineg FP_OFF(fp) ((unsigned short) (fp))
# #defineg FP_SEG(fp)    \
#    ((unsigned short) (((unsigned long) (fp)) >> 16))
# #savemod ic.exe
IC.EXE: 615K bytes in file.
# D16ExtAvail() + D16LowAvail()
    776240 (0xBD830)
# #quit
```

The #defineg command is like the C preprocessor #define statement, but defines a preprocessor symbol *globally*, across all .C files. This is another example of how a compiler-oriented language like C changes in an interactive environment.

Evaluating the expression D16ExtAvail() + D16LowAvail(), we see that on a 2-megabyte machine with several TSRs loaded, there is still 776K free, even with the inclusion of the Microsoft library, the DOS/16M library, and the IC environment itself. Because DOS/16M has an extremely small low-memory footprint and its default strategy is to allocate first out of extended memory, most of the lower 640K is free. On my computer there is 572K free low memory before entering IC; how much is free inside IC?

```
# D16LowAvail()
    525168 (0x80370)
```

It is practical to execute a text editor from within IC (though IC does come with a decent text editor built in), and even run another compiler or an assembler to produce an .OBJ file that IC can then load. This material was written from within IC:

```
# void e(char *s) {
>    char cmd[80];
>    sprintf(cmd, "epsilon %s", s);
>    system(cmd);                     // pass cmd to MS-DOS
>    if (strstr(s, ".c")) {           // after editing a C file...
>        sprintf(cmd, "#load %s", s); // #load it
>        _interpret(cmd);             // pass cmd to IC
>        }
>    }
e defined.
# void book() { e("\\extdos\\chap04.doc"); }
book defined.
# book()
```

In this interactive environment, the C programming language also becomes a powerful "macro" command language. Since the programming language and command language are one and the same, there isn't the usual debugger problem of having to learn a new command language.

GP Faults and the Protected-Mode Interpreter

The interactive style of Instant-C is useful when you want to test whether a C expression is legal in protected mode and, in particular, in DOS/16M. For example, even if you don't have DOS/16M itself, you could use IC to try out the TICKS() macro given earlier. You don't need a program, and you don't need main():

```
# #define TICKS()    *((unsigned long far *) 0x46c)
# #define SECONDS() (TICKS() / 18)       // since midnight
# SECONDS()
 ## 534: Reference through null far pointer in command line
# #reset
# #define TICKS()    *((unsigned long far *) 0x0040006c)
# SECONDS()
    70957 (0x1152D)
```

Here, IC saw that the first version of TICKS() dereferenced the null pointer. The more interesting case is when protection violations are detected, not by IC, but by the CPU itself. For these, IC displays a different message. Take the example of the program BAD.C, which caused a GP fault when the user neglected to supply a command-line argument:

```
# load bad.c
STDIO.H included.
main defined.
BAD.C loaded.
# run 100
100
# run
 ## 492: Invalid address 0A80:4552 at __CATOX+000E
```

When the CPU detects a protection violation, it doesn't shut down the offending application. In fact, it wouldn't know how to: terminating applications is an operating system's business! All the processor does is issue an Int 0DH (GP fault). This is an interrupt like any other, and someone has to install a handler for it. Protected-mode operating systems like OS/2, and DOS extenders like DOS/16M, install Int 0DH handlers that respond to GP faults by shutting down the offending application. We saw an example of this earlier, when a version of the LIST program was shut down by DOS/16M for trying to use the bad version of the TICKS() macro.

This presents a problem for a protected-mode interpreter. The operating environment's GP fault handler just knows that an application caused a GP fault. The DOS/16M GP fault handler doesn't know that IC is an interpreter, and that its GP faults are actually caused by user input, not by the interpreter itself. If this default INT 0DH handler were in effect, IC itself would get shut down every time we typed in a protection violation!

But IC doesn't shut down when we commit a GP fault. Instead, *our* code is squelched, while the interpreter stays in control. This is exactly the behavior one wants in a protected-mode interpreter. That we can freely type protection violations in at the # prompt is due to the fact that IC installs its own Int 0DH handler. Instead of DOS/16M's default GP fault handler, IC's handler catches the signals that the CPU sends. (For a lengthy discussion of this issue, see "Stalking GP Faults," *Dr. Dobb's Journal*, January 1990 [Part 1] and February 1990 [Part 2].)

IC indicated that a GP fault occurred at _CATOX+000E. Unfortunately, IC currently doesn't have an object-code disassembler (it really needs to be more like the DOS/16M debugger), but it seems pretty obvious that _CATOX() was called from atoi(). If in doubt, we could use the IC #backtrace:

```
# back
Level 1 condition:  492: Invalid address 0A80:4552 at __CATOX+000E
  occurred in function ##unknown##
  called from function  atoi" line 0:
=>      393: source code unavailable
  called from function  main" line 3:
        {
=>          printf("%d\n", atoi(argv[1]));
        }
  called from function in object code
```

Anyway, the protection violation alerts us to the fact that our code needs fixing. We can use the editor built into IC, rerun the test, and save the source code back out to a file:

```
# #ed main
// use IC editor to add test: if (argc > 1)
# #run
// no GP fault now
# #save good.c
GOOD.C: 180 chars; 11 lines
```

The #save command will reformat your source code, according to formatting options set by assigning to variables such as _braceundent, _KRbrace, and so on.

Using Protection

In addition to helping find bugs during development, the hardware-based memory protection of the Intel processors can be put to work in the deliverable version of a product as well.

For example, functions often perform range checking. Each time the function is called, it checks its parameters against the size of the target object. The size may have been stored in the object header.

Since the hardware does range and type checking in protected mode anyway, and since we pay a performance penalty for this checking, we should get the hardware to do *our* checking as well. You've already paid for protection; you might as well get the most out of it.

This requires devoting a separate selector to each object for which you want hardware-assisted checking. To see why, let's overstep the bounds of an array and see whether the Intel processor detects an off-by-one fencepost error:

```
# char *p;
# p = malloc(2013)
    address 03B8:01A6: ""
# p[2013] = 'x'
    'x' (0x78)
```

The pointer p points to a block of 2,013 bytes, numbered 0 through 2012, so p[2013] clearly oversteps its bounds. If protected mode is all it's cracked up to be, the CPU should have complained. Why didn't it?

The reason is that malloc() and other high-level-language memory allocators suballocate out of pools of storage. They do not ask the operating system for memory each time you ask them for memory, nor would you want them to. Out of one segment, malloc() may allocate several different objects. While we think of the object p as containing 2,013 bytes, the processor sees a considerably larger object: the block of memory malloc() received the last time it asked DOS for memory. What is the object size the CPU sees?

```
# D16SegLimit(p)
    24575 (0x5FFF)
```

If this explanation is correct, trying to poke p[0x5FFF] had better cause a GP fault:

```
# p[0x5fff] = 'x'
 ## 492: Invalid address 0BF8:002A in command line
```

Now, we need a way to make the CPU see things *our* way. Since 80286 memory protection is based on segmentation, we must devote a separate selector to each object for which we want hardware-assisted checking. Notice I said *selector* and not *segment*. We can continue to use malloc() to allocate objects, but when we want the CPU to know how big we think the object is, we provide an *alias* in the form of another selector which points at the same physical memory, but whose limit is smaller. The segment limit indicates the highest legal offset within a block of memory and is checked by the CPU for each memory access.

To create an alias q for the pointer p, where q's limit is equivalent to the array bounds, we can use two other DOS/16M functions:

```
# char *q;
# q = D16SegAbsolute(D16AbsAddress(p), 2013);
    0C08:0000
```

This takes the physical address returned by D16AbsAddress(), together with the limit we're imposing for access to this memory, and passes them to D16SegAbsolute(), which constructs a protected-mode selector for the same absolute physical address but with a different limit. Did it work?

```
# D16AbsAddress(p) == D16AbsAddress(q)
    1
# D16SegLimit(p) == D16SegLimit(q)
    0
# D16SegLimit(p)
    24575 (0x5FFF)
# D16SegLimit(q)
    2012 (0x7DC)
```

```
# q[2013]
## 492: Invalid address 0BF8:002A in command line
```

Notice that attempting even to *read* from this invalid array index now causes a GP fault. We can dispense with explicit bounds checking; the CPU will check for us. To control the error message displayed when a GP fault occurs, we could write our own INT 0DH handler and install it using the DOS set-vector function (INT 21H AH=25H). Thus, instead of littering error checking throughout our code, protected mode allows us to centralize it in an interrupt handler. Errors can be handled after the fact, rather than up-front. In a way, this resembles ON ERROR, one of the more powerful concepts in BASIC (which got it from PL/I).

This meshes with the advice given by advocates of object-oriented programming: "If you are expecting a sermon telling you to improve your software's reliability by adding a lot of consistency checks, you are in for a few surprises. I suggest that one should usually check less. . . . defensive programming is a dangerous practice that defeats the very purpose it tries to achieve" (Bertrand Meyer, "Writing Correct Software," *Dr. Dobb's Journal*, December 1989).

By using protection, you may be able to make an application run faster in protected mode than under real mode, since a lot of error-checking and "paranoia" code can be made unnecessary in protected mode.

When finished with the pointer p, it is important not only to free(p), but also to release the alias in q. Don't use free() to release this selector, though. The C malloc() manager doesn't know anything about q and, in any case, q is just an alias, a slot in a protected-mode descriptor table. We need to free up this slot because, as noted earlier, the number of selectors available in protected mode is quite limited:

```
# free(p)
# D16SegCancel(q)
```

In moving from real to protected mode, programmers may regret that segment arithmetic is so restricted. However, the ability to create aliases, different "views" of the same block of physical memory, means that protected-mode selector manipulation is actually far *more* versatile than real-mode segment arithmetic.

The Intel 286 Protected-Mode Instructions

While transparency is a major goal of "Extended DOS," sometimes it is useful to not be so transparent. For example, DOS extender diagnostic programs and DOS extender utilities will generally be non-portable, hyper-aware that they are running in protected mode. Also DPMI programming requires familiarity with the Intel data structures.

The 80286, and also the 286-compatible 386 and 486 chips, have a number of instructions that Intel provides primarily for use by protected-mode operating systems, but which are also useful for utilities and diagnostic programs:

- LSL (load segment limit)—size of a segment
- LAR (load access rights)—access rights of segment
- VERR (verify read)—can segment be peeked?
- VERW (verify write)—can segment be poked?
- SGDT (store GDT)—base address and size of GDT
- SIDT (store IDT)—base address and size of IDT
- SLDT (store LDT)—selector to LDT.

For example, in the last section we called D16SegLimit() to find the size of the segments pointed to by p and q. In operation (though not in implementation), D16SegLimit() corresponds to the LSL instruction, which takes a selector in the source operand and, if the selector is valid, returns its limit (size - 1) in the destination operand. For example:

```
lsl ax, [bp+6]
```

Similarly, the LAR instruction will load the destination operand with the *access rights* of the selector in the source operand, if it contains a valid selector:

```
lar ax, [bp+6]
```

The instructions LSL, LAR, VERR, and VERW are special because, even if the selector in the source operand is *not* valid, the instructions don't GP fault; instead, the zero flag is cleared. This means that, if these instructions were available in a high-level language, we could construct protected-mode memory browsers and other utilities simply by looping over all *possible* selectors. This is an odd form of segment arithmetic:

```
for (unsigned i=0; i<0xFFFF; i++)
    if (lar(i) is valid)
        print_selector(i)
```

It is easy to make the Intel protected-mode instructions available to C and other high-level languages, and they can be used interactively in IC. PROT- MODE.ASM is a small library of functions, including lsl() and lar(), that can be assembled into PROTMODE.OBJ using either the Microsoft Assembler (version 5.0 and higher) or Turbo Assembler:

```
;       protmode.asm -- 286 protected-mode instructions
;       requires MASM 5.0 or higher or TASM
;       masm -ml protmode;
;       or, tasm -ml protmode;

        dosseg
        .286p
        .model large
        .code

        public  _lsl, _lar, _verr, _verw, _sgdt, _sidt, _sldt

;       extern unsigned far lsl(unsigned short sel);
;       input:   selector
;       output:  if valid and visible at current protection level,
;                   return segment limit (which is 0 for 1-byte seg!)
;                else
;                   return 0
;
_lsl    proc
        enter   0, 0
        sub     ax, ax
        lsl     ax, [bp+6]
        leave
        ret
_lsl    endp

;
;       extern unsigned short far lar(unsigned short sel);
;       input:   selector
;       output:  if valid and visible at current protection level,
;                   return access rights (which will never be 0)
;                else
;                   return 0
;
```

```
_lar    proc
        enter   0, 0
        sub     ax, ax
        lar     ax, [bp+6]
        shr     ax, 8
        leave
        ret
_lar    endp

;
;       extern BOOL far verr(unsigned short sel);
;       input:   selector
;       output:  valid for reading ? 1 : 0
;
_verr   proc
        enter   0, 0
        mov     ax, 1
        verr    word ptr [bp+6]
        je      short verr_okay
        dec     ax
verr_okay:
        leave
        ret
_verr   endp

;
;       extern BOOL far verw(unsigned short sel);
;       input:   selector
;       output:  valid for writing ? 1 : 0
;
_verw   proc
        enter   0, 0
        mov     ax, 1
        verw    word ptr [bp+6]
        je      short verw_okay
        dec     ax
verw_okay:
        leave
        ret
_verw   endp

;
;       extern void far sgdt(void far *gdt);
;       input:   far ptr to 6-byte structure
;       output:  fills structure with GDTR
;
_sgdt   proc
        enter 0, 0
        les   bx, dword ptr [bp+6]
        sgdt  fword ptr es:[bx]
        leave
        ret
_sgdt   endp

;
;       extern void far sidt(void far *idt);
;       input:   far ptr to 6-byte structure
;       output:  fills structure with IDTR
;
_sidt   proc
```

```
        enter 0, 0
        les   bx, dword ptr [bp+6]
        sidt  fword ptr es:[bx]
        leave
        ret
_sidt   endp

;
;       extern unsigned short sldt(void);
;       input:   none
;       output:  Local Descriptor Table register (LDTR)
;
_sldt   proc
        sldt  ax
        ret
_sldt   endp

        end
```

Note that PROTMODE.ASM uses the DOSSEG directive, which simplifies writing assembly-language subroutines, and uses the ENTER and LEAVE instructions, provided on the 80286 and higher for working with high-level-language stack frames. These execute a little slower than the corresponding PUSH BP / MOV BP, SP prolog and POP BP epilog, but provide more compact source code.

If your C compiler has an in-line assembler facility, rather than use PROTMODE.ASM, you can instead place these functions inside a .C file. For example, using Microsoft C 6.0, lsl() can be defined as follows (compile with -G2):

```
unsigned lsl(unsigned sel)
{
    _asm sub ax, ax
    _asm lsl ax, sel
}
```

PROTMODE.ASM provides nothing more than a functional interface to the Intel protected-mode instructions. While completely non-portable with real mode, this module is highly portable among 16-bit protected-mode systems (it would require some modification for use with a 32-bit DOS extender). Once assembled into PROTMODE.OBJ, it can be linked into any 16-bit protected-mode program (including an OS/2 program). It can be loaded into IC with the following command:

```
#loadobj "protmode.obj"
```

IC can also load .LIB modules, using the #loadlib command (this is how an MSC-compatible version of IC is produced). The object code can be produced by an assembler (as in the example of PROTMODE.OBJ), or by another C compiler. One unfortunate limitation is that IC attaches no meaning to the pascal keyword, so object code that uses the Pascal calling convention cannot be successfully called from within IC.

You need to supply stub definitions for the individual routines in an object module loaded into IC. These look almost like declarations or function prototypes, except that they are followed by the construct {extern;}. For example, after loading PROTMODE.OBJ, lsl() would be defined to IC as:

```
unsigned lsl(unsigned short sel) {extern;}
```

PROTMODE.H is a C #include file that contains function prototypes for use with IC (#ifdef InstantC) or any other 16-bit protected-mode environment:

```
/* PROTMODE.H */
typedef enum { FALSE, TRUE } BOOL;
```

```
#ifdef InstantC
unsigned far lsl(unsigned short sel)        {extern;}
unsigned short far lar(unsigned short sel)  {extern;}
BOOL far verr(unsigned short sel)           {extern;}
BOOL far verw(unsigned short sel)           {extern;}
void far sgdt(void far *gdt)                {extern;}
void far sidt(void far *idt)                {extern;}
unsigned short sldt(void)                   {extern;}
#else
extern unsigned far lsl(unsigned short sel);
extern unsigned short far lar(unsigned short sel);
extern BOOL far verr(unsigned short sel);
extern BOOL far verw(unsigned short sel);
extern void far sgdt(void far *gdt);
extern void far sidt(void far *idt);
extern unsigned short sldt(void);
#endif
```

Now it's time to test the functions. Let's allocate a 10K segment, and see what limit lsl() returns:

```
# char *p;
# p = D16MemAlloc(10240)
    address 0C08:0000
# lsl(FP_SEG(p))
    10239 (0x27FF)
```

Clearly, 10,239 is the last legal offset within a 10K segment, so lsl() seems to work. (Actually, there is an obscure bug in lsl(). Can you spot it? Hint: what is the LSL for a one-byte segment? For an invalid segment?)

The verw() function, like the VERW instruction, returns TRUE if a selector can be written to, or FALSE if the selector is read-only:

```
# verw(FP_SEG(p))
    1
```

We can use a DOS/16M function to mark this segment as read-only, and then see if verw() has picked up on the change in the selector attributes:

```
# D16SegProtect(p, 1)
    0
# verw(FP_SEG(p))
    0
```

As the IC manual explains, D16SegProtect() can be used if you have some data that is being clobbered, or if you wish to ensure that only certain functions can update some data structure. It is important to note that the read-only attribute, like other aspects of the protected-mode access rights, applies to a *selector*, not to the underlying block of memory. One selector can be read-only and another read/write, while both correspond to the same physical memory.

Having tested the PROTMODE.OBJ routines we can, as promised, write a simple loop to display all valid selectors within our program. In IC, of course, we can just type this in at the # prompt:

```
unsigned i;
for (i=0; i<0xFFFF; i++)        // for all possible selectors
    if (lar(i))                 // if a valid selector
        printf("%04X\n", i);    // print selector
```

This will display all valid selectors within a protected-mode program (not just a DOS/16M program). But to be genuinely useful we need to print out some additional information about the selectors:

```
/* BROWSE.C */

#ifdef InstantC
#loadobj "protmode.obj"
#endif
#include "protmode.h"

void browse()
{
    unsigned long addr;
    unsigned i, acc;
    for (i=0; i<0xFFFF; i++)        // for all possible selectors
        if (acc = lar(i))           // if a valid selector
        {
            addr = D16AbsAddress(MK_FP(i,0));
            printf("%04X %06lX LAR=%02X LSL=%04X PL=%02X %s %s %s %s\n",
                i,                              // selector
                addr,                           // physical base addr
                acc,                            // access-rights byte
                lsl(i),                         // segment limit
                i & 3,                          // protection level
                verr(i) ? "VERR" : "    ",      // readable?
                verw(i) ? "VERW" : "    ",      // writable?
                i & 4 ? "LDT" : "GDT",          // which table?
                i == addr >> 4 ? "TRANS" : ""); // transparent?
        }
}
```

In addition to using several of the functions in PROTMODE.ASM, the code in BROWSE.C also performs some manipulations on the selector number itself: the bottom two bits are extracted with the expression *i & 3, and the third bit is extracted with the expression i & 4.*

It was noted earlier that a protected-mode selector is almost, but not exactly, a "magic cookie," in that the number itself actually has semantic meaning. Now all can be told: a selector is comprised of three fields. The bottom two bits contain a protection level, zero (most privileged) through three (least privileged). The third bit from the right contains a *table indicator*—zero means the selector belongs to the GDT, and one means it belongs to the LDT—and the remaining 13 bits form an index into this table.

Running under IC, a small part of the output from BROWSE.C looks like this:

```
0038 000000 LAR=93 LSL=FFFF PL=00 VERR VERW GDT
003C 000000 LAR=93 LSL=FFFF PL=00 VERR VERW LDT
0040 000400 LAR=93 LSL=0FFF PL=00 VERR VERW GDT TRANS
0044 000400 LAR=93 LSL=0FFF PL=00 VERR VERW LDT
0048 034FE0 LAR=93 LSL=FFFF PL=00 VERR VERW GDT
004C 034FE0 LAR=93 LSL=FFFF PL=00 VERR VERW LDT
0050 110010 LAR=93 LSL=200F PL=00 VERR VERW GDT
0054 110010 LAR=93 LSL=200F PL=00 VERR VERW LDT
0058 032050 LAR=81 LSL=0067 PL=00           GDT
005C 032050 LAR=81 LSL=0067 PL=00           LDT
0060 FA0000 LAR=93 LSL=FFFF PL=00 VERR VERW GDT
0064 FA0000 LAR=93 LSL=FFFF PL=00 VERR VERW LDT
0068 100010 LAR=82 LSL=FFF8 PL=00           GDT
```

The list runs on for quite a while.

What is the value of this? In contrast to real mode where every address you can form points *somewhere*, protected-mode memory is a sparse matrix. At any given time, most segment:offset combinations are not valid addresses—dereferencing them causes a protection violation. Producing a list like this gives us an idea of the memory organization of a DOS extender program.

From this list, we can see that while protected-mode memory is a sparse matrix, under DOS/16M it's not as sparse as under OS/2. From the vast number of valid selectors displayed by this program, it is obvious that IC is compiled with the full 64K GDT available under DOS/16M (the size of the GDT can be controlled with the MAKEPM utility).

We can also see that all the entries are marked PL=00, indicating that everything is running at Ring 0. To double check that this is so, the following code represents the query, *Are any segments not at Ring 0?*:

```
for (i=0; i<0xFFFF; i++)
    if (lar(i) && (i & 3))
        printf("%04X PL=%02X\n", i, i & 3);
```

Under IC, this produces no output. Everything is running at the most privileged protection level. This is one of the differences between DOS/16M and a full-blown protected-mode operating system like OS/2. Because DOS/16M is just a shell to support one program at a time in protected mode, Rational Systems chose not to establish different protection levels.

Along the same lines, the selectors you'll use in IC or in DOS/16M actually refer, not to your program's LDT, but instead to the GDT. Since there is only one program running, the distinction between GDT and LDT, while crucial in a multitasking operating system like OS/2, is fairly artificial in the "one program at a time" world of DOS/16M.

On the other hand, Eclipse's OS/286, while sharing many of the same goals as DOS/16M, makes a sharper distinction between the kernel (the OS/286 DOS extender itself) and the program supported by the DOS extender. OS/286 programs run at Ring 3, while OS/286 itself runs at Ring 0. This just shows that there are few fixed rules about how a DOS extender *must* be organized; protected mode allows for a wide variety of styles in operating environments.

In a version of DOS/16M that complies with Microsoft's planned DOS Protected Mode Interface (DPMI), DOS/16M programs more closely resemble OS/286 in that they have to use the LDT, and have to run at Ring 3. This, in turn, means that the only available *transparent* selector may be 40H. Rational Systems expects only about one-half of its clients to switch to this DPMI-compliant version.

IC requires a large GDT partially to support a large number of transparent selectors. In the example above, selector 40H has a physical base address of 400H, corresponding to the BIOS data area. Using the same code from PROT- MODE.ASM, it is trivial to form the query, *Which selectors are transparent?*:

```
for (i=0; i<0xFFFF; i++)
    if (lar(i) && (i == D16AbsAddress(MK_FP(i,0)) >> 4))
        printf("%04X ", i);
```

The preceding discussion of the three fields that make up a protected-mode selector, along with the discussion of transparent selectors, indicates that transparent selectors will generally come out of the GDT. Since the physical base address dictates the number of a transparent selector, since this number is merely a representation of the three fields, and since a zero in bit 3 indicates the GDT, it follows that whenever we want a transparent selector to a real-mode segment such as 40H or B800H, it *must* belong to the GDT. This also applies to OS/2 bimodal pointers.

Examining the Protected-Mode Descriptor Tables

We have already used an indirect method to examine the DOS/16M memory map: loop over all possible selectors and see if they're legal. We can also directly examine the GDT, IDT, and LDT.

PROTMODE.ASM contains a functional interface to the SGDT instruction, which returns the physical base address of the GDT. SGDT expects a pointer to 6 bytes of storage (an FWORD PTR), into which it copies the contents of the CPU's GDT register (GDTR). The GDTR holds the 24-bit physical base address and 16-bit limit of the GDT, and corresponds to the following C structure (most of the structures that follow must be byte-aligned; in IC, set _struct_alignment=1, in batch compilers like Microsoft C, use #pragma pack(1)):

```
typedef struct {
    unsigned      limit, lo;
    unsigned char hi, reserved;
    } GDTR;
```

(Note that this structure is not accurate when running under a 32-bit DPMI host such as Windows Enhanced mode.) This structure can be used in IC, along with sgdt():

```
# GDTR g;
# sgdt(&g)
# g
   struct  at 2F1C {
      limit = 65528 (0xFFF8);
      lo = 16 (0x10);
      hi = '\020' (0x10);
      reserved = '\0';}
```

Now that we have the physical base address (100010H) and limit (FFF8H) of the GDT, we need to map this into our address space. A protected-mode descriptor table is an array of 8-byte segment descriptors. Each descriptor contains the 24-bit physical base address and 16-bit limit for the segment, as well as an access-rights byte. There is also a 2-byte field used in 32-bit protected mode on the 386. All this can be expressed in C (again, the following is not accurate when running under a 32-bit DPMI host):

```
typedef struct {
    unsigned      limit;     // size minus 1
    unsigned      addr_lo;   // physical base addr - paragraph.byte
    unsigned char addr_hi;   // physical base addr - megabyte
    unsigned char access;    // see ACCESS_RIGHTS below
    unsigned      reserved;  // for 386 (32-bit)
    } DESCRIPTOR;
```

After typing or loading this structure definition into IC, we can create a pointer to the GDT:

```
# DESCRIPTOR *gdt;       // GDT is array of DESCRIPTOR
# gdt = D16SegAbsolute((long) MK_FP(g.hi, g.lo), g.limit + 1)
    address 0C08:0000
```

Now we have a pointer to the GDT, let's make it read-only to make sure we don't mess anything up (though if you were working in a protected-mode environment that didn't have convenient functions for changing selector attributes, you might actually *want* to write to the GDT!):

```
# D16SegProtect(gdt, 1);
```

If bit 3 of a selector indicates that it belongs to the GDT, then the top 13 bits of the selector can be used as an index into the GDT. Take the example of the GDT pointer itself:

```
# gdt[FP_SEG(gdt) >> 3]
   struct  at 0C08:0C08 {
      limit = 65527 (0xFFF7);
      addr_lo = 16 (0x10);
```

```
            addr_hi = '\020' (0x10);
            access = 'Q' (0x91);
            reserved = 0;}
```

This confirms what we already know about the GDT: that its physical base address is 100010H and that its limit is FFF7H.

Now that we have a pointer to the GDT, we could dispense with such functions as D16SegAbsolute() and D16SegLimit(), and write portable protected-mode code. Data structures such as the GDT are a feature of protected mode itself, not of any environment in particular. Thus, while we're using DOS/16M and IC as examples here, almost all of this discussion really pertains to protected mode as a whole.

Since we can write portable protected-mode code once we have a pointer to the GDT, the question arises of whether there is a *portable* way to get this pointer. Unfortunately, there isn't. Getting its physical base address *is* portable, since this requires the Intel SGDT instruction, but this physical base address must then be mapped into an application's address space, and that will require some special facility within your protected-mode environment. Here, we used D16SegAbsolute(), which obviously won't work outside DOS/16M. But an equivalent function can always be found. For example, in OS/2 you would use the PhysToUVirt device driver helper function (DevHlp).

Returning to the GDT, let's examine the access-rights value which the CPU in protected mode uses to ensure proper use of a selector such as 0C08H. We can use a C bitfield to display the individual fields that make up an access-rights value like 91H. As noted when presenting a similar structure in Chapter 1, though, the ordering of bit fields is compiler-dependent; in addition, the following access-rights structure must be *byte*-aligned:

```
typedef struct access {
    unsigned accessed   : 1;  // has segment been accessed? &1
    unsigned read_write : 1;  // if data 1=write; if code 1=read &2
    unsigned conf_exp   : 1;  // expansion direction &4
    unsigned code_data  : 1;  // 0 = data, 1 = code &8
    unsigned xsystem    : 1;  // 0 = system descriptor &16
    unsigned dpl        : 2;  // protection level: 0..3 & (32/14)
    unsigned present    : 1;  // is segment in memory? &128
    } ACCESS_RIGHTS;

# *((ACCESS_RIGHTS *) &gdt[FP_SEG(gdt) >> 3].access)
   struct access at 0C08:0C0D {
      accessed : 1 = 1;         // it's been used
      read_write : 1 = 0;       // it's read-only
      conf_exp : 1 = 0;         // it's not a stack
      code_data : 1 = 0;        // it's data
      xsystem : 1 = 1;          // it's not a system descriptor
      dpl : 2 = 0;              // protection level 0
      present : 1 = 1;}         // it's present in memory
```

All these data structures are described in the Intel literature on 286 and 386 protected mode. Seeing them come to life in IC, though, is a great aid to understanding protected mode.

One of the tricks of protected-mode programming is to acquire an in-depth knowledge of these data structures and then, when programming, to forget about them. The operating environment takes care of maintaining the GDT, and the descriptors within the GDT, and the access-rights bytes within the descriptors. The CPU will take care of using these data structures to maintain the integrity of the system. You're better off not thinking too closely about them, but it does help to have been familiar with them at some point or other.

While DOS/16M (and consequently IC) doesn't make much use of the LDT, this table is crucial in other protected-mode environments. To get a selector to your LDT, simply call sldt(). Though this is the LDT for your process, it may not be valid within your address space. It is simple to test if it is:

```
DESCRIPTOR far *ldt;
if (verr(sldt()))
    ldt = MK_FP(sldt(), 0);
```

If the LDT selector is not valid within your address space, then you can instead look up its descriptor within the GDT:

```
DESCRIPTOR ldt_desc; ldt_desc = gdt[sldt() >> 3];
```

and then get a pointer to the absolute address you find there, using whatever function is equivalent to D16SegAbsolute:

```
ldt = D16SegAbsolute((long) MK_FP(ldt_desc.addr_hi, ldt_desc.addr_lo),
    ldt_desc.limit + 1);
```

Now that we have these structures and have tested them, we can write a function to display selector attributes:

```
void sel(void far *fp)
{
    extern DESCRIPTOR far *gdt;
    extern DESCRIPTOR far *ldt;
    unsigned seg = FP_SEG(fp);
    unsigned index = seg >> 3;
    DESCRIPTOR far *dt = (seg & 4) ? gdt : ldt; // table indicator
    ACCESS_RIGHTS *pacc = (ACCESS_RIGHTS *) &dt[index].access;
    printf("SEL=%04X ADDR=%02X%04X LIMIT=%04X ACCESS=%d%c%c%c%c%c%c\n",
        seg, dt[index].addr_hi, dt[index].addr_lo, dt[index].limit,
        // display access rights as if they were file attributes:
        pacc->dpl,
        pacc->accessed ? 'a' : '-',
        pacc->read_write ? ((pacc->code_data) ? 'r' : 'w') : '-',
        pacc->conf_exp ? ((pacc->code_data) ? 'f' : 'e') : '-',
        pacc->code_data ? 'c' : 'd',
        pacc->xsystem ? '-' : 's',
        pacc->present ? 'p' : '-');
}
```

This code contains no references to DOS/16M. Once you have a pointer to the GDT and LDT, this function will work in any 16-bit protected-mode system.

We can test this function using some selectors hard-wired into DOS/16M:

- 00H—Null descriptor
- 08H—Global Descriptor Table (GDT)
- 10H—Interrupt Descriptor Table (IDT)
- 28H—Program Segment Prefix (PSP)
- 30H—DOS environment
- 38H—Descriptor for physical address 0
- 40H—Transparent descriptor for BIOS data area (paragraph 40)
- 68H—Local Descriptor Table (LDT).

For instance, selector 40H should point to physical address 400H, should be 4K (its limit should be 4,095 or FFFH), and it should be writable data:

```
# sel(MK_FP(0x40,0))
SEL=0040 ADDR=000400 LIMIT=0FFF ACCESS=0aw-d-p
```

In addition, we see that the selector has been accessed, is present in memory (IC currently does not include VM), and can be accessed only from Ring 0.

How about the GDT itself?

```
# sel(MK_FP(0x08,0))
SEL=0008 ADDR=100010 LIMIT=FFF8 ACCESS=0aw-d-p
```

The GDT is located at physical address 100010H; its limit is FFF8H. This is the maximum size for a GDT in 16-bit protected mode—there are 8,192 selectors.

Sel() can be used to examine the selector for any pointer, such as sel()'s own function pointer. The attributes display indicates this is readable code running at protection level zero:

```
# sel(sel)
SEL=0A68 ADDR=472BB0 LIMIT=43FF ACCESS=0ar-c-p
```

Finally, we can save all our structure and function definitions out to a file, using the IC #save command. The results can be read back in using the #load command.

IC as Protected-Mode Linker

A final feature of IC is the #make command, which creates stand-alone protected-mode executables. The resulting executables are rather large (the minimum size is 169K), and IC-compiled code is extremely slow (for compiled code; for interpreted code, it is very fast!), but since IC can load object code compiled by Microsoft C, including object code containing the function main(), IC could be used as a protected-mode linker. You have to produce an {extern;} declaration for each function. Here is an example, in which a tiny program is typed in IC, written out to a file with #save, compiled with Microsoft C, the compiled code loaded back into IC with #loadobj, and a protected-mode executable written out with #make:

```
C:\IC>ic
# void main(void) {
>   extern long D16LowAvail(), D16ExtAvail();
>   printf("Low memory: %lu\n", D16LowAvail());
>   printf("Extended memory: %lu\n", D16ExtAvail());
>   }
main defined.
# #save mem.c
MEM.C: 121 chars; 5 lines
# system("cl -AL -Ox -c mem.c");
Microsoft (R) C Optimizing Compiler Version 5.10
Copyright (c) Microsoft Corp 1984, 1985, 1986, 1987, 1988. All rights
reserved

mem.c
# #delete main
# #loadobj mem
# void main(void) {extern;}
main defined.
# #make mem.exe
MEM.EXE: 186K bytes in file.
# #qquit
C:\IC>mem
DOS/16M Protected Mode Run-Time     Version 3.62
```

```
Copyright (C) 1987,1988,1989 by Rational Systems, Inc.
Low memory: 420384
Extended memory: 1023088
```

This is slightly cumbersome, but if IC were improved any more along these lines, it would start to compete with Rational Systems' other product, DOS/16M!

Appendix F

Documents and Specifications

The VCPI Interface Specification is available from Phar Lap Software, Inc., 60 Aberdeen Avenue, Cambridge, MA 02138, (617) 661-1510 or from Quarterdeck Office Systems, 150 Pico Boulevard, Santa Monica, CA 90405, (213) 392-9851.

The eXtended Memory Specification (XMS) version 2.0 is available from Microsoft Corporation, Box 97017, Redmond, WA 98073, (206) 882-8080.

The Lotus/Intel/Microsoft Expanded Memory Specification (EMS) version 4.0 is available from Intel Corporation, 5200 N.E. Elam Young Parkway, Hillsboro, OR, 97124.

The DESQView API Toolkit is available from Quarterdeck Office Systems, 150 Pico Boulevard, Santa Monica, CA 90405, (213) 392-9851.

The DOS Protected Mode Interface (DPMI) Specification version 1.0 is available as part number 240977 from Intel Literature JP-26, 3065 Bowers Ave., P. O. Box 58065, Santa Clara, CA 95051.

INDEX